MyEducationKit is an online solution designed to connect your textbook to real teaching situations and provide you with opportunities to practice the technology integration skills necessary to support learning. It is fully integrated with your textbook; wherever you see the **MyEducationKit** logo in the margins or elsewhere in the text, follow the simple instructions to access the multimedia assignments and other resources in the **MyEducationKit** site that correspond with the chapter content.

prepare

WITH THE POWER

of classroom practice

PEARSON
myeducationkit™

Register for **MyEducationKit** today at **www.myeducationkit.com**.

■ **Practice integrating technology for meaningful learning. •** The Transformation Lesson Plan module on **MyEducationKit** allows you to practice transforming a traditional lesson into one infused with technology to enhance student learning. An extension of the Technology Transformation Lesson Plan feature in the text, this module will help you learn how to choose the appropriate technology to meet your learning goals and transform the student learning experience.

■ **Build your technology skills. •** Twenty new Camtasia video tutorials include step-by-step guidance to help you develop proficiency with a variety of current educational technology tools for teaching and learning purposes. Tutorials include Microsoft applications, Inspiration, Kidspiration, Dreamweaver, iMovie, MovieMaker, blogs and wikis, and more.

■ **Test your mastery of chapter concepts. •** Explore **MyEducationKit** to find multiple-choice assessments tied to chapter objectives. You will also receive feedback explaining why particular items are correct or incorrect, as well as links to the appropriate chapter excerpts to review content you have not mastered.

■ **Use actual classroom situations to strengthen your lesson development skills and demonstrate ways to integrate technology. •** The Growing and Leading with Technology module on **MyEducationKit** is an extension of the text feature of the same name. It provides you the opportunity to create an initial plan for infusing technology using the chapter's learning goals and one or more of the technologies featured in the chapter, to compare your ideas and strategies for infusing technology with a follow-up from the actual classroom to see what the classroom teacher did with his/her class, and to assess the two plans and consider what can be improved.

■ **Analyze video of technology integration in real classrooms. •** Look for marginal notes throughout this text that send you to Assignments and Activities on **MyEducationKit**. This module provides you with authentic classroom videos that illustrate technology integration in real classrooms, as well as interviews with experts, teachers, and administrators. These video activities align with chapter objectives and provide you with questions to guide your observation, analysis, and discussions about effective technology integration.

To start using **MyEducationKit**, activate the access code packaged with your book. If your instructor did not make **MyEducationKit** a required part of your course, or if you have purchased a used book without an access code, **go to www.myeducationkit.com to purchase access to this wonderful resource!**

Transforming Learning with New Technologies

Robert W. Maloy
University of Massachusetts Amherst

Ruth-Ellen Verock-O'Loughlin
University of Massachusetts Amherst

Sharon A. Edwards
University of Massachusetts Amherst

Beverly Park Woolf
University of Massachusetts Amherst

PEARSON

Boston   Columbus   Indianapolis   New York   San Francisco   Upper Saddle River
Amsterdam   Cape Town   Dubai   London   Madrid   Milan   Munich   Paris   Montreal   Toronto
Delhi   Mexico City   Sao Paulo   Sydney   Hong Kong   Seoul   Singapore   Taipei   Tokyo

Acquisitions Editor: Kelly Villella Canton
Senior Development Editor: Mary Kriener
Development Editor: Amy Nelson
Editorial Assistant: Annalea Manalili
Vice President, Director of Marketing: Quinn Perkson
Senior Marketing Manager: Darcy Betts
Production Administrator: Gregory Erb
Editorial Production Service: Omegatype Typography, Inc.
Manufacturing Buyer: Megan Cochran
Electronic Composition: Omegatype Typography, Inc.
Interior Design: Omegatype Typography, Inc.
Photo Researcher: Annie Pickert
Cover Designer: Linda Knowles

For related titles and support materials, visit our online catalog at www.pearsonhighered.com.

Between the time website information is gathered and then published, it is not unusual for some sites to have closed. Also, the transcription of URLs can result in typographical errors. The publisher would appreciate notification where these errors occur so that they may be corrected in subsequent editions.

Library of Congress Cataloging-in-Publication Data

Transforming learning with new technologies / Robert Maloy . . . [et al.].
     p. cm.
  Includes bibliographical references and index.
  ISBN-13: 978-0-13-159611-5 (pbk.)
  ISBN-10: 0-13-159611-X (pbk.)
 1. Internet in education.   2. Computer-assisted instruction.   I. Maloy, Robert W.
  LB1044.87.T73 2011
  371.33'44678—dc22

              2009041539

Printed in the United States of America.

10 9 8 7 6 5 4 3 2 1 CIN 14 13 12 11 10

Credits appear on page 356, which constitutes an extension of the copyright page.

www.pearsonhighered.com

ISBN-10: 0-13-159611-X
ISBN-13: 978-0-13-159611-5

To our students and their students,
the teachers of today and tomorrow.

About the Authors

Robert W. Maloy

Robert W. Maloy is a senior lecturer in the Department of Teacher Education and Curriculum Studies in the School of Education at the University of Massachusetts Amherst, where he coordinates the history and political science teacher education programs. He codirects the TEAMS Tutoring Project, a community outreach initiative where university students provide academic tutoring to culturally and linguistically diverse students in public schools throughout the Connecticut River Valley region of western Massachusetts. His research focuses on technology and educational change, teacher education, and student writing and learning. He is coauthor of five books, including *Ways of Writing with Young Kids: Teaching Creativity and Conventions Unconventionally; Kids Have All the Write Stuff: Inspiring Your Child to Put Pencil to Paper; The Essential Career Guide to Becoming a Middle and High School Teacher; Schools for an Information Age;* and *Partnerships for Improving Schools.* In 2004, Robert received the University of Massachusetts President's Award for Public Service as well as the School of Education's Outstanding Teacher Award. He was awarded the Chancellor's Certificate of Appreciation for Outstanding Community Service in 1998 and 1993.

Ruth-Ellen Verock-O'Loughlin

Ruth-Ellen Verock-O'Loughlin is a lecturer in the Department of Teacher Education and Curriculum Studies in the School of Education at the University of Massachusetts Amherst. She coordinates Bridges to the Future, a year-long master's degree and teacher license program serving rural school systems in Franklin County, Massachusetts. Prior to joining the School of Education, Ruth was an elementary school classroom and reading teacher in Virginia and Massachusetts. Her academic research focuses on new teacher education, technology in teaching, and community service learning in K–12 schools. She is coauthor with Robert W. Maloy and Sharon A. Edwards of *Ways of Writing with Young Kids: Teaching Creativity and Conventions Unconventionally.* She received the School of Education's Outstanding Teacher Award in 2007. She has also served as coordinator of the 2003 University of Massachusetts/WGBY National Teacher Training Institute (NTTI) and was an educational researcher for the 1999–2000 Harvard University Evidence Project.

Sharon A. Edwards

Sharon A. Edwards is a clinical faculty member in the Department of Teacher Education and Curriculum Studies at the University of Massachusetts Amherst. Recently retired from public school teaching, she taught primary grades for 32 years at the Mark's Meadow Demonstration Laboratory School, a public laboratory school in Amherst, Massachusetts. As a clinical faculty member she mentors undergraduate students and graduate student interns in the early childhood teacher education, constructivist teacher education, and secondary teacher education programs. Her course and workshop presentations focus on children's writing, reading, and math learning; curriculum development; instructional methods; and diversity in education. She also codirects the University's TEAMS Tutoring Project. In 1989, Sharon was the inaugural recipient of the national Good Neighbor Award for Innovation and Excellence in Education given by the State Farm Insurance Companies and the National Council of Teachers of English for her work with young children's writing. She received her doctor of education degree from the University of Massachusetts Amherst in 1996. She is coauthor with Robert W. Maloy of two books: *Ways of Writing with Young Kids* and *Kids Have All the Write Stuff.*

Beverly Park Woolf

Beverly Park Woolf is a research professor in the Department of Computer Science at the University of Massachusetts Amherst. She holds two doctoral degrees, one in computer science and one in education. Her research focuses on building intelligent tutoring systems to effectively train, explain, and advise users. Extended multimedia capabilities are integrated with knowledge about the user, domain and dialogue to produce real-time performance support, and on-demand advisory and tutoring systems. The tutoring systems use intelligent interfaces, inferencing mechanisms, cognitive models, and modifiable software to improve a computer's communicative abilities. She is the author of *Building Intelligent Interactive Tutors: Student-Centered Strategies for Revolutionizing e-Learning.*

Brief Contents

Contents

3

Developing Lessons with Technology   58

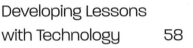
4

Integrating Technology and Creating Change   82

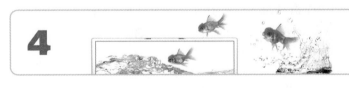

PART TWO: ENGAGING LEARNERS WITH DIGITAL TOOLS

5

Researching and Evaluating Internet Information   112

8

Communicating and Networking with Websites, Blogs, Wikis, and More   206

Features of the Book

New and Emerging Technologies

Chapter Title	Learning Goal	New Technologies
1 Becoming an e-Teacher	**Readiness to Be a Technology-Using Educator:** Examining your personal attitudes and goals while reviewing key issues in the field of educational technology	• Ultraportable computers • Online technology information resources
2 Transforming Learning with Unique, Powerful Technology	**Teaching and Learning Using Technology:** Exploring ways technology can transform teaching and learning in schools	• Visual learning resources • Information resources • Engagement and collaboration resources • Feedback resources • Creativity resources
3 Developing Lessons with Technology	**Technology-Based Lesson Planning and Assessment:** Using technology tools to support how teachers develop and evaluate learning experiences for students	• Web-based lesson development resources • Electronic grading software • Web-based K–12 testing policy information • Online rubrics and quizzes
4 Integrating Technology and Creating Change	**Technology Integration and Educational Change:** Using technology effectively as a teacher to create change in schools	• One-to-one computing • Digital pens and digital notebooks • Tablet computers • Web-based technology integration resources
5 Researching and Evaluating Internet Information	**Internet-Based Research:** Using the Internet to teach students how to access and assess online information	• Internet search engines • Web evaluation tools • Photo- and audio-sharing websites • Electronic note-takers • Wikipedia • Web browser customizing tools • Plagiarism checking software
6 Teaching with Educational Websites and Other Online Resources	**Digital Content and Educational Websites:** Using Web-based educational materials and digital content in your teaching	• Bookmarking tools • Social bookmarking tools • Information alerts • WebQuests • Virtual field trips • Interactive maps • Interactive videoconferencing • Lesson plan websites • Student-to-expert communication websites • Real-time and recorded data websites • Archival and primary source websites • Skills/practice websites • Exploration and discovery websites

7 Problem Solving and Inquiry Learning with Software and Web Tools	**Inquiry Learning and Problem Solving:** Using educational software and Web-based tools to promote problem solving and inquiry learning	• Open source software • Composing and calculating software • Building, inventing, and creating software • Visual thinking and concept mapping software • Discovery learning software • Computer-based and Web-based educational games • Virtual worlds • Digital games for learning • Intelligent tutoring systems
8 Communicating and Networking with Websites, Blogs, Wikis, and More	**Information Communication:** Using communication technologies to enhance learning through interactive information exchanges and networking	• Email and instant messaging • Teacher-/student-authored websites • Teacher-/student-authored blogs • Digital image scanners • Wikis and wikitexts
9 Creating and Sharing Information with Multimedia Technologies	**Multimedia Presentations:** Using presentation tools and multimedia technologies with students	• PowerPoint presentation software • Multimedia projectors • Interactive whiteboards • Videos and DVDs • Video sharing websites • Webcasts • Digital storytelling and digital art making • Digital cameras • Digital video recorders • Digital video editing software • iPods • Podcasts and vodcasts
10 Promoting Success for All Students through Technology	**Differentiated Instruction for All Students:** Using assistive technologies to differentiate instruction and promote learning success for all students	• UDL resources for teachers • Assistive technologies • Electronic spellers and dictionaries • Handheld and online calculators • Text reading software • Speech recognition software • Interactive digital storybooks
11 Engaging Teachers and Students in Learning and Self-Reflection	**Teacher and Student Self-Reflection about Learning:** Using digital portfolios and other performance assessment technologies to evaluate one's own learning	• Digital portfolios • Technology tools in democratic classrooms • Online survey software • Student participation systems and clickers

TECHNOLOGY TRANSFORMATION LESSON PLAN

5	Think Globally. Act Locally! Conducting Social Studies Research on the Internet
6	Weather Station WebQuest: Investigating Science Using Interactive Web Resources
7	Making and Reading Graphs: Exploring Math Using Educational Software
8	Blogging the News from Room 145: Reading and Writing Using Web Communication Tools
9	The Shortest Motion Picture You Can Make in Words: Writing Poetry Using Digital Cameras
10	Measuring Shadows: Differentiating Science Learning Using Technology
11	Encyclo-ME-dia: Documenting Student Learning Using Digital Portfolios

CONNECTIONS and POSSIBILITIES

TECH TOOL

t ·· F O G W

Welcome to *Transforming Learning with New Technologies*. We have written this book to demonstrate the limitless ways to create highly interactive learning opportunities for elementary and secondary school students using computers, the Internet, interactive educational websites and software, and a full range of existing technologies and emerging Web 2.0 tools. The technologies presented here are effective for promoting student engagement in learning through interactive, inquiry-based teaching and learning experiences for students.

Our goal is to help you transform your classrooms into technology-infused places of learning where you and your students are active educational partners, working together to use and understand technology. Focusing on the day-to-day realities of elementary and secondary schools, each chapter addresses the needs of educators who are new to teaching or technology. Instructional examples and lesson ideas from across the curriculum at all grade levels give teachers starting points from which they can develop their own technology-infused lessons.

Written to be interactive, thought provoking, and practical for teachers, we designed *Transforming Learning with New Technologies* to provide information and also raise issues and open discussions about the role of computers and other new and emerging technologies in schools. We address what teachers need to know about the methods, strategies, and complexities of technology so that they can use all electronic tools to improve teaching and learning.

The book reflects exciting new developments in the fields of education and technology, specifically, the movement for 21st century skills and the NETS (National Educational Technology Standards) revised frameworks for teaching and learning with technology from ISTE (International Society for Technology in Education). The 21st century skills movement and the NETS revisions mark a fundamental shift in how you need to learn about technology and education. Because computers are transforming every aspect of our society, from science and business to family and education, everyone must rethink the roles of technology in K–12 schools.

Our technological, knowledge-based society demands that teachers and students possess new and expanded skills to be successful in work and life—what the Partnership for 21st Century Skills calls 21st century student outcomes of three types: learning and innovation skills; information, media, and technology skills; and life and career skills. Gaining these skills requires changes in the way we think about and use technology in schools. Knowing how to use computer hardware and software (often called *educational technology*) is only a beginning step in this process. Teachers and students need a *21st century learning mindset* where they become active users and evaluators of technology. Moving from "ed tech" to "21st century learning" means teachers prepare, deliver, and assess lessons differently while students think critically and creatively about the learning they do and the technologies they use.

Throughout this book, we've incorporated numerous Web 2.0 tools that reflect the changing nature of technology in schools and society in general. As you think about these technologies, imagine a symphony orchestra on a stage. The musicians are sitting in a fan-like arrangement with a conductor in front. String instruments are placed on either side of the conductor, while wood-wind, brass, and percussion instruments are located in the center, positioned from front to back. To perform any musical composition, the parts of the orchestra must work together effectively; each instrument and musician playing a role as directed by the conductor.

The technologies in this book are the instruments and musicians of your teaching orchestra. You are center stage, at the conductor's stand. Instead of a baton, you have an Internet-accessible computer (laptop or desktop), a printer, and a collection of professional productivity tools in-cluding word processing, spreadsheet, database, and email software. Moving outward from your centrally placed computer are the technologies of your orchestra—a collection of handheld and desktop tools that perform specialized functions. There are computer programs, educational games, programs that can be downloaded from the Internet, Web-based sources of educational information, and a variety of electronic devices you can use educationally. As a teacher, your re-sponsibility is to understand what each instrument/technology can do and how you can use it to create engaging learning experiences for students. In this context, orchestrating technology means knowing when and how to blend these tools instructionally and professionally, using technology to transform learning, in and out of the classroom.

Each of us—young and old, novice or experienced with technology—is in the midst of a revolution as technologies remake virtually every aspect of our daily lives in work, play, and learn-ing. How computer-based technologies change K–12 schools will continue to evolve throughout your career, affected and directed by the creative influences that teachers bring to classrooms. In that spirit, we join you to examine how teachers can use *new technologies* to create *new opportunities* for teaching and learning in elementary, middle, and high schools.

How This Book Is Organized

Every chapter in *Transforming Learning with New Technologies* is organized around specific learn-ing goals for teachers and students that focus directly on the ideas and information you need to know about technology in order to create successful learning environments. As teachers ac-quire and increase their knowledge of technology and learning, they are able to support their students in doing the same. Therefore, every chapter incorporates practical teaching strategies and instructional methods for integrating computers, the Internet, and other interactive tech-nologies across the K–12 curriculum—in math, science, English/language arts, and social studies.

In Part I, Chapter 1 clarifies personal motivations in becoming a technology-using educator while identifying key issues in the field of educational technology today. Chapter 2 analyzes learn-ing theories and ways that technology can transform educational experiences for students both inside the classroom and outside the school. Chapter 3 looks at how teachers use technology to develop lessons, including incorporating technology into learning activities, lesson planning, and student assessment. Chapter 4 discusses the issues and dynamics of integrating technology into teaching while creating educational change in schools.

In Part II, Chapter 5 examines the topic of Internet research and the information literacy skills needed to critically evaluate online information. Chapter 6 focuses on using educational websites and other online sources of digital content in teaching. Chapter 7 shows how teachers can develop the inquiry learning and problem solving skills of their students using educational software and Web tools. Chapter 8 explains how teachers and students can use communication technologies to promote collaboration, information-sharing, and new learning. Chapter 9 explores multime-dia technologies and their roles in creating and presenting information in schools. Chapter 10 emphasizes the multiple ways that technology promotes learning success for all students through differentiated instruction and universal design for learning. Finally, Chapter 11 demonstrates how teachers and students can become active participants in evaluating and assessing their own growth as learners using technology.

Issued by the Partnership for 21st Century Skills and endorsed by the departments of education in more than a dozen states, their standards emphasize skills that every individual will need in the world of today and tomorrow. Accordingly, our book specifically addresses 21st century skills in the following chapters:

- Chapter 1 introduces 21st century learning as part of the key learning goals of the book.
- Chapter 2 looks at how technology fosters the 21st century skills of *creativity* and *innovation* as well as other forms of unique, powerful, and transforming learning.
- Chapters 5 and 6 focus directly on *information literacy* and *information, communications, and technology literacy* (ICT) while Chapter 9 addresses *media literacy*—each of which are essential elements of 21st century skills.
- Chapter 7 explores *critical thinking and problem solving* while Chapter 8 addresses *communication and collaboration,* key learning and innovation skills within the 21st century learning framework.
- Technology Transformation Lesson Plans, both in the text and online in MyEducationKit, emphasize student use of the 21st century skills of *initiative and self-direction, working effectively with others,* and *leadership.*

Features of This Edition

Transforming Learning with New Technologies includes a number of features that enhance technology learning and understanding.

NETS for Teachers and Students. Issued by the International Society for Technology in Education (ISTE), the 2008 National Educational Technology Standards for Teachers (NETS-T) and the 2007 National Educational Technology Standards for Students (NETS-S) reflect a fundamental shift in the field of educational technology from how to use technology technically to what can be done with technology educationally. These standards shift teachers' attention from a focus on technology skills and toward an emphasis on student learning goals and outcomes. Accordingly, this book correlates closely with the new NETS and considers ways to use computers and other information and communication technologies to create new patterns of teaching and learning in schools.

- Each chapter provides specific correlations to the NETS standards and explains their relation to the content of the book.
- Technology Transformation Lesson Plans are correlated to NETS-S.
- Each Tech Tool feature offers ways to meet the Technology Operations and Concepts Standard in NETS for Students 2007.

Existing Technologies and Emerging Web 2.0 Tools. More than 70 existing and emerging computer-based educational technologies and Web 2.0 tools are highlighted throughout the book, connected to each chapter's learning goal. Every technology is presented in terms of how it directly advances the work of teachers and the learning of students. The inclusion of Web 2.0 tools reflects the changing nature of technology from singular tools used by individuals to interactive and collaborative tools used by groups and communities.

Chapter Opening Pedagogy. Each chapter opens with a graphic organizer outlining the chapter learning goal, emerging technologies to

be discussed, and connections to the NETS-S and NETS-T standards addressed in the chapter. A set of focus questions guide your reading of key concepts within the chapters, and a brief vignette sets the stage for the discussion in the chapter.

VOICES
from the classroom

A high school teacher noted how technology enables her to teach her students to think critically using online material:

It was interesting to watch students as they found information about their topics. Two students found Web pages that contradicted each other. I was able to use this example to talk to these students and the ones around them about why you should find multiple sources. I was able to tell my students the story of a former student who found a website that claimed Abraham Lincoln was an alien. The students better understood why they should double-check their facts when they are confronted with this situation. They better understood why you have to be careful about where you get your information. Having them discover that misinformation is also on the Internet and that it can be difficult to tell was really important.

Voices from the Classroom. Each chapter includes short, first-person comments from teachers who offer classroom-based perspectives about the impact of technology on instructional practices and student learning.

CONNECTIONS
and
POSSIBILITIES

Connections and Possibilities. This feature provides a description of projects around the country that are using computer technology in innovative ways. These projects offer future-focused snapshots of how teachers, administrators, higher education faculty, business leaders, and others can collaborate to use technology to promote learning and improve schools.

Emerging Technologies

Do you remember when you first heard the term *Web 2.0* and began to understand its importance for technology-using teachers? The term is new, first appearing in the media as recently as 2004. It refers to interactive technologies that promote new forms of information creation and collaboration among computer users. You probably have heard about such Web 2.0 tools as blogs, wikis, social networking, folksonomies, and podcasts, but you may be far less familiar with how to integrate these emerging technologies into teaching and learning in schools.

As an educator learning about integrating technology into teaching, there are two key ideas to keep in mind about Web 2.0. First, Web 2.0 is more than just various new technological tools; it is a group of new practices among computer users. At the heart of Web 2.0 is the idea of using technology to promote greater communication and interaction among people. Such exchanges allow people to produce knowledge for themselves as opposed to having that information created solely by experts and authorities.

For example, sports fans used to get information about their favorite teams and players by reading newspapers, listening to the radio, and watching TV. Today, using blogs and wikis, those same sports fans can communicate with one another technologically by sharing information collaboratively and extending what they have learned from various media sources. They can add value to their enjoyment of sports by both reading traditional

Emerging Technologies Database

Launched in 2008, the Emerging Technologies Database is an initiative of ISTE (International Society of Technology in Education), one of the nation's leading technology education organizations. ISTE's technology education standards for teachers and students have been widely adopted by K–12 schools as well as colleges and universities that prepare teachers, and we are using them as one of the organizing features of this book.

As created by technology educators Ferdi Serim, Kathy Schrock, and the other members of ISTE's Emerging Technologies Task Force, the Emerging Technologies Database is designed to be an online collection of the best examples of teachers and students using new technologies to positively affect learning in schools. All information is being collected and distributed online. Teachers will not only be able to consult but also contribute to this database.

ISTE is drawing on Web 2.0 tools to document how educators are using Web 2.0 tools in schools. The database focuses on emerging technologies so teachers will have an ongoing and evolving collection of best practices to draw on as they integrate Web 2.0 tools in their classrooms. You can learn more about the project by visiting the ISTE website, watching a video on YouTube, and seeing emerging technology in action at the ISTE section of the virtual world, Second Life.

TECH TOOL 9.3
DIGITAL STORYTELLING AND DIGITAL ART MAKING

Digital Storytelling

The Center for Digital Storytelling in Berkeley, California, is devoted to supporting individuals and organizations using digital media to tell personal stories. Its slogan is "Listen Deeply/Tell Stories." "Digital storytelling" refers to ways that written text, audio, and video imagery can be combined to make unique story presentations (Alexander & Levine, 2008, November/December; EDUCAUSE Learning Initiative, 2007, January). Digital storytelling connects directly to the history/social studies and language arts curriculum. In history, students can assemble oral histories, personal memories, and life stories from people throughout the school and the community. In language arts, digital storytelling offers ways to teach about personal narrative, biography, and autobiography, as well as fiction writing.

You can locate more storytelling resources at the Educational Uses of Digital Storytelling site maintained by the College of Education at the University of Houston. The site features a useful introduction, examples, tools, evaluation criteria, and links to many resources.

Digital Art Making

The National Gallery of Art has an amazing interactive site for young artists entitled NGA Kids: The Art Zone.

Tech Tools. Appearing in every chapter, this boxed feature offers a guide to high quality, easy-to-use and easy-to-obtain digital tools and Web-based resources that will enhance your work both instructionally and professionally. Each of the Tech Tool resources has been class-tested by the authors. Many of the Tech Tools discussed also link to online Web activities on the MyEducation-Kit for this book; these activities encourage you to learn more about the technology and experiment with its uses.

Your Judgment Matters. Throughout each chapter, this feature promotes interpretation, consideration, and decision-making by asking you to stop and reflect about how you would respond to an issue or question under discussion. The surrounding text includes survey data, classroom examples, or online materials offering background information about the questions being posed. Keep in mind the following three points as you encounter each feature:

YOUR JUDGMENT
MATTERS

Based on these suggestions, consider the following questions:

- What examples would you add under critical and creative thinking?
- What examples would you add under memorization and practice?
- What technologies can be used to support both creative thinking and skills practice?

1. How do you see the ideas of different researchers, commentators, or policy-makers affecting your teaching?
2. What new research have you found that might offer further insights about a topic?
3. What does your own practice tell you about the best ways to use technology in teaching and learning?

TECHNOLOGY TRANSFORMATION LESSON PLAN

The Shortest Motion Picture You Can Make in Words
Writing Poetry Using Digital Cameras

Grade(s)	Grades 2 to 8
Subject(s)	Language Arts and Science
Key Goal/Enduring Understanding	Just as a microscope in a laboratory enables scientists to see small things in great detail, short poems let poets describe common moments in imaginative, expressive language.
Essential Question	How can written words and video film combine to create short poems about occurrences in everyday life?
Learning Standards	**National Council of Teachers of English/International Reading Association—** *Standards for the English Language Arts* **Standard 4:** Students adjust their use of spoken, written and visual language (e.g., conventions, style, vocabulary) to communicate effectively with a variety of audiences and for different purposes. **Standard 12:** Students use spoken, written and visual language to accomplish their own purposes (e.g., for learning, enjoyment, persuasion, and the exchange of information). **International Society for Technology in Education (ISTE)—***NETS-S* **Standard 1:** *Creativity and Innovation.* Students demonstrate creative thinking, construct knowledge, and develop innovative products and processes using technology.

Technology Transformation Lesson Plans. Found at the ends of Chapters 5–11, this feature shows teachers how to infuse technology in a substantive and meaningful way using a standard lesson plan template with objectives, methods, assessment strategies, national subject area curriculum standards, and National Education Technology Standards for Students (NETS-S). Relating directly to the learning goals and new technologies that are featured in the chapter, each lesson plan offers "before-and-after" insights via a table that includes a column called "Minimal Technology" (the "before" mode), which describes how teachers might conduct a lesson without a significant role for technology, and an "Infusion of Technology" column ("after" mode), which shows how well-chosen technology fundamentally enhances a lesson and transforms the learning experience for students and teachers. A follow-up exercise on MyEducationKit allows students to *practice* transforming a traditional lesson into one infused with technology.

End of Chapter Activities. These activities provide a thorough review and extend student thinking further. Elements included in each chapter are:

- **Chapter Summaries** of the major ideas in each chapter correspond to the focus questions found at the beginning of the chapter.
- **Key Terms** serve as a review of new and important terminology found in the chapter. Terms are found in bold within the chapter text.
- **Activities for Your Teacher Portfolio** offer a collection of questions and exercises

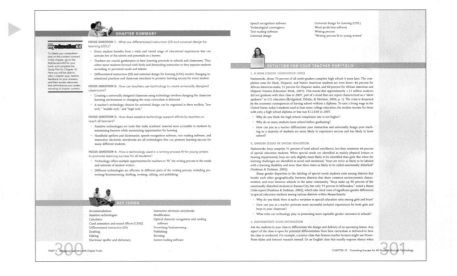

including individual reflection, group dialogue, personal writing, as well as activities to use with elementary or secondary school students that reinforce chapter content and its learning goals. Teacher candidates can add these activities to their ongoing professional portfolios.

- **Growing and Leading with Technology** features in Chapters 5–11 include classroom scenarios drawn from actual classroom situations. Each scenario is designed to strengthen lesson development skills while demonstrating ways to integrate technology into teaching and learning. The Growing and Leading with Technology activities follow a five-step interactive model. Steps 1 (chapter review) and 2 (classroom scenario) appear in the text to set the stage. Steps 3 to 5 appear on MyEducationKit and ask you to create an initial plan for infusing technology using the chapter's learning goal and one or more of the technologies featured in the chapter, to compare ideas and strategies for infusing technology with a follow-up from the actual classroom to see what the classroom teacher did with his or her class, and to assess the two plans and consider what can be improved.

My Education Kit

PEARSON myeducationkit

Dynamic Resources Meeting Your Needs

MyEducationKit is a dynamic website that connects the concepts addressed in the text with effective teaching practice. Plus, it's easy to use and integrate into assignments and courses. Whenever the MyEducationKit logo appears in the text, follow the simple instructions to access a variety of multimedia resources geared to meet the diverse teaching and learning needs of instructors and students. Here are just a few of the features that are available.

Study Plan

A MyEducationKit Study Plan is a multiple-choice assessment with feedback tied to chapter objectives. A well-designed Study Plan offers multiple opportunities to fully master required course content as identified by the objectives in each chapter:

- **Chapter Objectives** identify the learning outcomes for the chapter and give students targets to shoot for as they read and study.
- **Multiple-Choice Assessments** assess mastery of the content. These assessments are mapped to chapter objectives, and students can take the multiple choice quiz as many times as they want. Not only do these quizzes provide overall scores for each objective, but they also explain why responses to particular items are correct or incorrect.
- **Study Material: Review and Enrichment** gives students a deeper understanding of what they do and do not know related to chapter content with text excerpts connected to chapter objectives.

Assignments and Activities

Designed to save instructors preparation time and enhance student understanding, these assignable exercises show concepts in action (through video, cases, and/or student and teacher artifacts). They help students synthesize and apply concepts and strategies they read about in the book.

- **Videos.** The authentic classroom videos in MyEducationKit show how real teachers handle actual classroom situations. Discussing and analyzing these videos not only deepens understanding of concepts presented in the text, but also builds skill in observing children and classrooms.
- **Web Links.** On MyEducationKit you don't need to search for the sites that connect to the topics covered in your chapter. Here, you can explore web sites that are important in the field and that give you perspective on the concepts covered in your text.

Video Tutorials

Twenty new Camtasia tutorials have been added to this text's MyEducationKit. These tutorials include step-by-step, hands-on exercises that develop proficiency with a variety of current educational technology tools. Tutorials include hardware and software products.

Technology Transformation Lesson Plans

A follow-up exercise to the text feature of the same name, this MyEducationKit module allows students to practice transforming a traditional lesson into one infused with technology, based on the learning goals and new technologies that are featured in each chapter.

Growing and Leading with Technology

An extension of the text feature of the same name, this MyEducationKit module provides the opportunity to create an initial plan for infusing technology using the chapter's learning goal and one or more of the technologies featured in the chapter, compare your ideas and strategies for infusing technology with a follow-up from the actual classroom to see what the classroom teacher did with his or her class, and assess the two plans and consider what can be improved.

General Resources on MyEducationKit

The Resources section on MyEducationKit is designed to help students pass their licensure exams, put together effective portfolios and lesson plans, prepare for and navigate the first year of their teaching careers, and understand key educational standards, policies, and laws. This section includes:

- **Licensure Exams.** Contains guidelines for passing the Praxis exam. The Practice Test Exam includes practice multiple-choice questions, case study questions, and video case studies with sample questions..
- **Lesson Plan Builder.** Helps students create and share lesson plans.
- **Licensure and Standards.** Provides links to state licensure standards and national standards.
- **Beginning Your Career.** Offers tips, advice, and valuable information on:
  - *Resume Writing and Interviewing.* Expert advice on how to write impressive resumes and prepare for job interviews.
  - *Your First Year of Teaching.* Practical tips on setting up a classroom, managing student behavior, and planning for instruction and assessment.
  - *Law and Public Policies.* Includes specific directives and requirements educators need to understand under the No Child Left Behind Act and the Individuals with Disabilities Education Improvement Act of 2004.

Visit www.myeducationkit.com for a demonstration of this exciting new online teaching resource.

Instructor Supplements

This text has the following ancillary materials to assist instructors in maximizing learning for their students. These instructor supplements may be downloaded from Pearson's password-protected Instructor Resource Center at www.pearsonhighered.com/irc.

The **Instructor's Resource Manual** provides concrete suggestions to promote interactive teaching and actively involve students in learning. Each chapter contains chapter objectives, a discussion of key concepts, helpful instructional tips, and additional activities for using assets available on MyEducationKit.

Pearson MyTest is a powerful assessment generation program that helps instructors easily create and print quizzes and exams. Questions and tests are authored online, allowing ultimate flexibility and the ability to efficiently create and print assessments anytime, anywhere! Instructors can access Pearson MyTest and their test bank files by going to www.pearsonmytest.com to log in, register, or request access. Features of Pearson MyTest include:

Premium Assessment Content

- Draw from a rich library of assessments that complement your Pearson textbook and your course's learning objectives.
- Edit questions or tests to fit your specific teaching needs.

Instructor-Friendly Resources

- Easily create and store your own questions, including images, diagrams, and charts using simple drag-and-drop controls similar to Microsoft Word.
- Use additional information provided by Pearson, such as the question's difficulty level or learning objective, to help you quickly build your test.

Time-Saving Enhancements

- Add headers or footers and easily scramble questions and answer choices—all from one simple toolbar.
- Quickly create multiple versions of your test or answer key, and when ready, simply save to Word or PDF format and print!
- Export your exams for import to Blackboard 6.0, CE (WebCT), or Vista (WebCT).

Acknowledgments

We have been inspired to write *Transforming Learning with New Technologies* by the many hundreds of teachers and students with whom we have worked in the past 25 years at the University of Massachusetts Amherst, motivating us to envision technology-infused schools where every student can realize her or his fullest potentials.

We would like to specifically thank the following individuals whose ideas and insights have improved this book immeasurably: Irene LaRoche, Elizabeth Rockett, Heather Batchelor, Adam Waters, Kelley Brown, Lawrence O'Brien, Leah Mermelstein, Lois Cohen, Sue Hunt Apteker, Matt Ganas, Dinah Mack, Val Babson, Erica Winter, Treacy Nichols, Lily Richards, Michelle Poirier, Therese Roberts, Hilary Smith, Tracy Creek, Ashley Winn, Randy Phillis, and Shawn Sheehan.

We want to express our gratitude to friends and colleagues for their support: David Hart, Gordon Anderson, Irving Seidman, Richard J. Clark, Tony Sindelar, Fred Zinn, Kate Strub-Richards, Kathleen Gagne, Martha Ryan, Amy Ryan, Richard Rogers, Tim Sheehan, Julianne Eagan, Andy Hamilton, Mei-Yau Shih, Autumn McGuffey, Dwight Allen, John Fischetti, Byrd L. Jones, and Huihong Bao.

As in any project, realizing this point would not have been possible without the assistance of numerous individuals who helped sharpen the focus of this edition—the reviewers for this edition: Agnes Helen Bellel, Alabama State University; David Bullock, Portland State University; Craig Cunningham, National-Louis University; Carrie Dale, Eastern Illinois University; Jane Eberle, Emporia State University; Loretta Enlow, Indiana Wesleyan University; Sonja Heeter, Clarion University of Pennsylvania; Barbara Jones, Golden West College; Bernadette Kelley, Florida A&M University; Valerie Larsen, University of Virginia; Ashley Navarro, Seminole Community College; Robert Perkins, College of Charleston; Andrew B. Polly, University of North Carolina–Charlotte; Ken Rushlow, Middle Tennessee State University; Diana Santiago, Central New Mexico Community College; Shannon Scanlon, Henry Ford Community College; and Patricia Weaver, Fayetteville Technical Community College

A book project requires great patience and support from family members. We especially want to thank Dennis O'Loughlin, Robert and Ruth O'Loughlin, Roy and Flo Edwards, Peg Maloy, Michael and Mary Verock, Jared and Justin Cormier, Zoe Lehtomaki, Joey Lehtomaki, Brian Edwards, Sam Edwards, Emily Cutting, Kyle Cutting, Ryan Cutting, Alexander Trostle, and Sarah Trostle.

Finally, we want to thank our editors: Acquisitions Editor, Kelly Villella Canton; Senior Development Editor, Mary Kriener; Development Editor, Amy Nelson; Editorial Assistant, Annalea Manalili; Production Editor, Gregory Erb; and Senior Marketing Manager, Darcy Betts. Their wonderful guidance and thoughtful suggestions have made this book so much better.

Transforming Learning with New Technologies

1

Becoming an e-Teacher

We are talking about a personal and malleable technology that you can shape . . . in ways that are limited only by your imagination and the effort you are willing to make.

—Seymour Papert, *The Connected Family: Bridging the Digital Generation Gap* (1996, p. 20)

CHAPTER LEARNING GOAL	CONNECTING to the NETS	NEW TECHNOLOGIES
Readiness to Be a Technology-Using Educator	**NETS-T**	• Ultraportable computers
Examining your personal attitudes and goals while reviewing key issues in the field of educational technology	**1** Facilitate and Inspire Student Learning and Creativity	• Online technology information resources
	5 Engage in Professional Growth and Leadership	
	NETS-S	
	1 Creativity and Innovation	

CHAPTER OVERVIEW

Chapter 1 explores your personal motivations for becoming a technology-using educator through survey questions about key issues in the field of educational technology. As you consider your answers to these questions, you will envision ways to use technology to inspire learning and creativity for students, a specific goal of Standard 1 in NETS-T and NETS-S.

Each question is followed by a short review of important issues facing technology-using educators in schools today. These commentaries connect to NETS-T Standard 5, Part c, which expects teachers to "evaluate and reflect on current research and professional practice on a regular basis." As you review your own motivations for using technology in light of key issues in the field, you determine ways to support students in developing creativity and innovativeness, the central theme of NETS-S Standard 1. When students answer the questions posed in the chapter, they meet NETS-S Standard 1, Part d.

The chapter concludes by introducing the concept of learning goals for teachers and students as an organizing theme for the rest of the book. Every chapter, including this one, is organized around an essential set of understandings that computer-using educators need to know to help students and teachers succeed in schools today.

FOCUS QUESTIONS

1. How do new technologies create new opportunities for teaching and learning?

2. What six key issues should a teacher consider when looking to integrate technology?

3. What constitutes a highly interactive, inquiry-based learning environment?

Donasha, Max, and Ava, all college students preparing to become teachers, were sitting in the library, working on an assignment for their technology in teaching course. They viewed a DVD clip of two teachers—a veteran and a beginner—utilizing handheld electronic spellers and dictionaries with second-graders. They consulted the library's electronic databases to research information about educational theorists for an upcoming in-class PowerPoint presentation. As they walked to the café in the lobby for a break, Donasha scanned emails on her iPhone, Max checked his cell phone's text and voice messages, and Ava listened to the latest free podcast download on her iPod. Over food, the three continued discussing how they planned to use technology as first-year teachers.

Donasha, an early adopter of technology in her own learning (with a computer of her own since elementary school and a laptop and a desktop in college), avidly tracks technological developments in the medical and educational fields. Infusing technology into the curriculum, she declared, is unquestionably where teaching needs to be going in the future.

Computers and other tools, said Donasha, create many exciting new opportunities for teaching and learning: "Kids are able to control many parts of their learning environment. I am able to make learning more interesting for more children. Technology is a bigger force for kids wanting to learn than I ever anticipated it would be when I started to use it." Looking ahead, Donasha concluded: "There is so much more that I can teach with technology than I can teach without it that I must use it with students."

"I am skeptical about technology in classrooms," Max said, noting that the equipment at the school where he is planning to student teach is out of date and often not working properly. "But my skepticism is not solely because of equipment problems," he explained. "I think students should have limited use of computers, DVDs, and videos because they need to be able to figure things out for themselves and not become reliant on machines for all their knowledge."

Ava admitted that although she is interested in technology as a way to promote student learning, she feels uncertain about how to use computers or the Internet or any of the other "new" technologies now appearing on the educational scene. "Technology is changing so rapidly," she observed, "and the children appear to know more about it than I do. I realize that there are some wonderful opportunities for learning using computers, but when do I learn about them first so I can teach them with confidence instead of apprehension?" Ava saw integrating technology as a full-time job in itself: "I just do not see how I will have the time to add technology to my teaching," she declared, "unless I can learn more about it first."

Donasha, Max, and Ava, like you, are determining how to best use computers and other technology resources as they begin their teaching careers. They, and you, are encountering two overarching questions:

- What kind of technology-using student are you?
- What kind of technology-using educator do you plan to become?

Technology's Influence

Technology plays an enormously influential role in the lives of the children and adolescents who will be your students. Infants, toddlers, and preschoolers are "immersed in media," interacting regularly with a variety of technologies and creating a new category of experience that sociologists call an **electronic childhood.** According to one national report, "Nearly all children (99%) live in a home with a TV set, half (50%) have a TV set in their bedroom, nearly three out of four (73%) have a computer at home, and about half (49%) have a video game player. . . . Nearly all of them (97%) have products—clothes, toys and the like—based on characters from TV shows or movies" (Rideout, Vandewater, & Wartella, 2003, p. 4).

Computers are a major component of students' media experience; 85 percent of 5- to 17-year-olds use computers at school and 68 percent use them at home (U.S. Department of Commerce, 2008). Nearly four in five of those computer-using youngsters go online (Figure 1.1), and one-third do so on a daily basis (Scholastic, 2008).

Adolescents live media-saturated lives, spending an average of nearly 6½ hours a day with media (Rideout, Roberts, & Foehr, 2005, p. 6). Across the seven days of the week, this amounts to the equivalent of a full-time job, with a few extra hours thrown in for overtime (see Figure 1.2). Some educators now refer to today's technology-using youngsters as **Generation M,** or children who have grown up using computers, the Internet, and other media.

FIGURE 1.1 Percentage of Youngsters Online

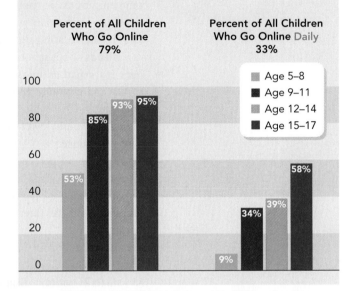

Many Children Are Introduced to the Internet Early

- After age 11, nearly all children use the Internet.
- Even 85% of 9–11 year olds and just over half of 5–8 year olds go online.
- Daily Internet use grows dramatically from childhood, to adolescence, to the teen years.

Source: Scholastic. (2008). *2008 Kids and Family Reading Report: Reading in the 21st Century/Turning the Page with Technology.* © 2008 Scholastic Inc. Reprinted with permission.

FIGURE 1.2 Time Spent with Media among 8- to 18-Year-Olds

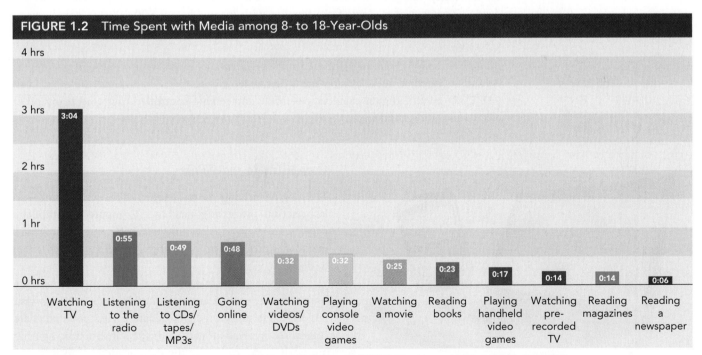

Source: "Generation M: Media in the Lives of 8–18 Year-Olds" (Report #7251), The Henry J. Kaiser Family Foundation, March 2005. This information was reprinted with permission from the Henry J. Kaiser Family Foundation. The Henry J. Kaiser Family Foundation, based in Menlo Park, California, is a nonprofit, private operating foundation focusing on the major health care issues facing the nation and is not associated with Kaiser Permanente or Kaiser Industries.

Data from the National Center for Education Statistics show how extensively computer technologies are woven into the fabric of everyday life for students and their families (DeBell & Chapman, 2006; Project Tomorrow, 2008):

- *Computer use begins with the youngest learners and continues from there.* Nationally, 91 percent of all children from nursery school to grade 12 use computers. At the youngest age, about two-thirds of nursery school children and 80 percent of kindergartners use computers; by high school (grades 9–12), that figure rises to 97 percent of students.
- *Gender differences are not pronounced.* Overall use of computers and the Internet by boys and girls is now about the same. Gaming, music downloading, social networking, and electronic communications are the most prominent ways students use technology outside of school. In school, students mainly use technology for writing assignments; online research; checking assignments; creating slideshows, videos, and Web pages; or emailing and instant messaging with friends about schoolwork.
- *There is a digital divide.* Use of computers and other new technologies varies dramatically by race and ethnicity. More white students use computers and the Internet than do African American and Hispanic students. Indeed, computer use for African American students is 7 percentage points lower than their white peers, and the difference in Internet use is even more pronounced at 21 percentage points. Similar numbers exist for Hispanic students. In homes, while 54 percent of white students use computers, the figures for African American (27 percent) and Hispanic (26 percent) students are much lower.
- *Parental education is a factor in technology use.* Students whose parents are highly educated use computers and the Internet more than students whose parents have fewer years of formal education.
- *Computer use is different for different groups.* Students with disabilities, students from single-parent households, and students living in urban centers use computers and the Internet less than students without disabilities, students from two-parent households, and students living outside urban centers.
- *Family income affects technology use dramatically.* Students living in higher-income households use computers and the Internet more than students living in lower-income households. Indeed, 37 percent of students from families with income below $20,000 use computers at home, compared with 88 percent of students living in families with annual incomes of $75,000.
- *Multiple technologies are in use.* Children and adolescents are extensive users not just of computers and the Internet, but television and VCRs, video games, cell phones, handheld calculators, CD/DVD players, digital cameras, electronic and remote-controlled toys, and many other electronic and digital devices.

Computers are no longer stand-alone devices that sit on desks or in labs. Lightweight, ultraportable laptops and powerful smartphones provide teachers and students with anywhere, anytime learning opportunities.

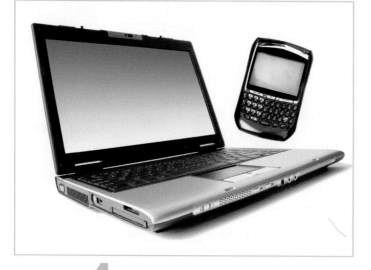

Computer Technologies

The engine driving these changes is the **computer**—an information processing machine. Computers manipulate data by following instructions given by human programmers. In other words, computers do what we tell them to do.

Computers, in Lawrence Snyder's succinct phrase, are "instruction execution engines" (2003, p. 157). Using what Snyder refers to as a "fetch/execute cycle," computers are constantly involved in "getting the next instruction, figuring out what to do, gathering the data needed to do it, doing it, saving the result, and repeating" the process again and again. All this is done millions of times a second, far exceeding human capacity to do the same tasks. For this reason, computers provide people the ability to process information in ways never before possible.

Like any technology, one way to understand the role of computers as information processors is to imagine what people would do if the technology did not exist. Computers are a recent invention; ask parents and other family members to recall how people did things before there was word processing software, email, online banking and shopping, cell phones, digital cameras, or other electronic devices that have revolutionized our lives.

Interestingly, as use of computers and other information technologies becomes more common, they tend to "disappear" from our view. All of us tend to take widely used technologies for granted, hardly noticing their technological power or the changes they bring to the way we conduct our daily lives. As two sociologists noted: "We move from looking at the technology as an addition to life to looking at life through that technology. The embedding of the technology in the matrix of our lives makes it invisible" (Bruce & Hogan, 1998, p. 270).

It is easy to forget that humans created computer technologies and defined their initial uses, and, if they choose, humans can recreate these technologies and redefine their uses in other, more productive ways. As teachers, you possess exciting choices about how to use computers and other technologies to engage students and transform learning in your classes.

Technology in the Classroom

Teaching, a career that matters, is filled with powerful complexities and wonderful rewards. As a teacher you are expected to

- Convey essential academic material in ways that students will understand and remember. Doing so produces an immense sense of personal and professional accomplishment.
- Teach and reach all your students, each a unique individual with varied learning needs and interests, in large- and small-group settings. Doing so builds your identity as a creative educator who can create success from challenges.
- Maintain learning for all students while balancing outside-of-school factors (social class, family income, race, gender, language, and exceptionalities) with inside-the-classroom dynamics (type of academic content, teaching methods, assessment practices, interpersonal dynamics, classroom management activities, tone of voice, and daily routines). Doing so establishes you as a force for positive change in the lives of students, families, and communities.

As Philip Jackson (1968) suggested more than 4 decades ago, these teaching responsibilities must be managed at the rate of some 200 separate and important interpersonal interactions every hour, 6 hours a day, for 180 school days each year.

The complexities of teaching influence teachers to teach as they were taught, using whole-group instruction in which desks are arranged in rows and students are mostly listening, taking notes, or completing worksheets, with grades determined by test scores—all familiar educational activities. These practices often fail to engage at least half of the students who are experiencing active, engaging learning environments in other parts of their lives. Suggesting that you should create more lively and inspiring teaching situations is much easier than making this reality in a classroom with students of many backgrounds, possessing different levels of interest in the curriculum and divergent learning styles.

Technology lets you change teaching and learning in enriching and productive ways: by differentiating instruction to offer students many learning experiences, by motivating disengaged individuals, by creating group and cooperative learning situations, by allowing access to academic information

VOICES
from the classroom

Recalling her own experiences with computers as a student, a teacher shared her view of technology as a positive force for learning.

I can remember in the ninth grade when we were introduced to a basic programming class using primitive Apple computers. Of course, it was a real novelty back then, and it's amazing to see how far the technology has come in just 20 years or so. My students today have grown up with computers and in some ways take for granted what the technology offers. By the end of high school, I was using a word processor and a computer for typing papers. In my first year at Stonehill College, a new computer center was built where most students were required to take a writing class that used computers. Having to use the lab to draft and print our papers really helped me see the benefits of using computers for drafting and revising writing. That appreciation is something that I've tried to convey to my students today.

from multiple sources, and by letting students visit places to see what cannot be seen without electronic systems. The list of creative possibilities is endless. Technology is an essential tool for expanding your skills and talents whether you are a novice practitioner or an experienced teacher.

Technology has been defined as an innovation designed to "solve problems and extend human capabilities" (International Technology Education Association, 2000). It is a "practice, a technique, or a device for altering the experience of the world" (Solnit, 2003). In short, technologies make accomplishing important goals easier for people to do.

Information and communication technologies (ICTs), or *new technologies,* are tools that encompass "virtually everything we encounter when sitting down to a personal computer" (Snyder, 2003, p. 4), including the following:

- What is on a computer (software and other applications)
- What can be accessed by a computer (Internet websites and Web-based technology tools)
- What can be connected to a computer (printers, scanners, digital cameras, iPods, and other tools for learning)

Computers are transforming every aspect of our society. "Information technology changes everything," contends George Washington University scientist William E. Halal (2008). Describing the enormous impact of e-commerce, online entertainment, and wireless technologies, Halal notes: "Even more powerful systems lie just ahead. As broadband and wireless provide ever larger bandwidth, computer power continues to rise exponentially, and artificial intelligence (AI) becomes human-like, all this capability will soon allow almost any social function to be performed online."

The transforming power of information and communication technologies makes it possible, indeed necessary, to rethink the way technology is used in K–12 schools. Our knowledge-based society demands that teachers and students possess new and expanded technology "life skills." Learning how to use computer hardware and software is only a beginning step in this process. Teachers and students need an "Information Learning" mindset in which they transform from passive users into active designers, creators, and assessors of technology. Teachers prepare, deliver, and assess lessons differently while students think critically and creatively about the learning they do and the technologies they use.

Computer-based ICTs differ dramatically from the noncomputer-based technologies that have been previously used in K–12 schools (e.g., overhead projectors, audiotapes, reel-to-reel movies, and 35mm slides). Those older technologies lack the technological power to create interactive teaching and learning experiences for students and teachers. Tech Tool 1.1 describes a new ICT—ultraportable computers.

Many of today's new technologies are often referred to as **Web 2.0** tools—a term denoting how the Internet is evolving into a more open medium capable of promoting interaction and collaboration among teachers and students. While the early Internet featured content developed by experts, "Web 2.0 is characterized by frequently updated sites, publicly constructed and shared information, and easy-to-use online applications, most of them free" (Rozema, 2007).

Web 2.0 technologies include blogs, wikis, podcasts, social bookmarking and social networking tools, inquiry-based educational websites, photo-sharing websites, virtual worlds, and other highly interactive tools and services that are just now becoming resources for teaching and learning in schools (Dolan, 2008; Solomon & Schram, 2007; Waldrop, 2008). Web 2.0 tools give rise to what Harvard University Professor Christopher Dede calls "Web 2.0 knowledge"—bottom-up, democratically derived, consensus-driven ideas and information that differ dramatically from the theoretical knowledge created by experts and elites. One of the challenges for schools is to find ways to incorporate Web 2.0 knowledge in the curriculum so students develop the skills to critically analyze information that comes from multiple sources (Dede, 2008, June).

Key Issues for Technology-Using Teachers

This section explores your thinking about technology and teaching using six important questions. The survey items are adapted from technology surveys conducted at the University of Massachu-

ULTRAPORTABLE LAPTOP COMPUTERS

College students who are becoming teachers quickly find that every part of the teaching job is tied to computers and the information they manage. Also, they need that information in at least three places: the school classroom, college classes, and a home office study area. Carrying files in a zip disk from home to the library and back is insufficient. As teachers, you will likely need a whole new approach to using computers as information collection and management resources.

First and foremost teachers need day-to-day access to the Internet. Transporting information from place to place is another story, however. There is so much work that needs to get done that hardly anyone manages it all within the confines of the school day. Perhaps you have heard the story of the high school teacher who after teaching five classes a day with 30 students in each class calculated that a 140-hour work week would be needed in order to leave none of his students behind (Gleibermann, 2007). Facing the multiple demands of being both a student teacher and college student, you will likely be working at home, in local coffee shops and libraries, or any other place where you can turn on a computer and access the information needed.

Because teachers do not so much carry their lessons in their heads as they carry their entire job in their computers, ultraportable laptop machines that weigh between two and eight pounds are a professional resource worth your consideration. While lightness is a significant feature, the computing power of these machines is what makes them vitally useful for teachers. You need a machine with substantial battery life, an easy-to-read screen display in all kinds of light, sufficient memory to run multiple applications, and enough processing speed to handle downloading information and processing files. Although these machines are called notebook computers, they have enough storage to be filing cabinets and enough powerful help to be virtual libraries.

Battery life, weight, and memory are three features you will want to consider before choosing a laptop. Ask yourself, "What role will the laptop play in my life?" and "What kind of laptop user will I be?" If you are a frequent note taker, you may want to consider battery life. If you are traveler, weight may be your number one concern. If you store lots of data, hard disk size may be your shopping focus.

Popular ultraportable computer options include the following:

- Apple MacBook Air: memory: 1 GB; processor: 2.1 GHz Intel processor; weight: 5.0 lbs.; WiFi battery: 3+ hours
- Dell Inspiron 1318: memory: 2 GB; processor: 1.86 GHz Intel processor; weight: 4.9 lbs.; WiFi battery: 2.25 hours
- ThinkPad X200: memory: 4 GB 1066 MHz DDR3; processor: Intel Core 2 Duo P8400; weight: 2.95 lbs.; WiFi battery: 9.8 hours

Totals may vary depending on how much memory is used. All specs are available online at www.lenovo.com.

---

setts Amherst (Office of the Provost, 2004, 2007). Each question addresses important issues with regard to educational technology in K–12 schools:

- What is your readiness to integrate technology into teaching and learning in schools?
- What are your reasons for wanting to use technology in your teaching?
- What are your views of the barriers that block teachers from using technology in their classes?
- What are your plans for the types of technologies you will use in your classroom?
- What are your goals for the kinds of teaching methods you plan to use in your classroom?
- What is your knowledge of the technologies your students are using both inside and outside of school?

In asking these questions, we make a distinction between **computer-based technologies** and **noncomputer-based technologies** in teaching. Computer technologies are the "new technologies" such as the Internet, educational software, blogs and wikis, assistive technologies, digital portfolios, and a host of other educational and instructional tools and applications. Noncomputer technologies are those that are no longer driving forces for change, including overhead projectors, 35mm slides, audio and VHS tapes, movies, television, and other resources that do not use computer technology as their basis of operation. There are no right or wrong answers to the questions. Your answers are intended to open your thinking as you may find that your ideas will change over time.

Issue 1: Using Technology in Teaching

The first question (see Figure 1.3) asks you to examine your level of interest in using computer technology for teaching. Choose one category that most closely describes you at the present time.

FIGURE 1.3 How Would You Classify Yourself with Regard to Your Interest in and Use of Technology in Teaching?

Select one:

Frontier Developer/Innovator	Skeptical Observer
Early Adopter	Pay Little Attention
Quick to Follow Proven Success	See Very Little Promise
Cautious Observer	

FIGURE 1.4 Rogers Innovation Adoption Care

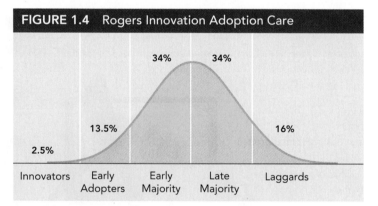

Source: Reprinted with permission of Value Based Management.net (www.valuebasedmanagement.net).

Responding to Innovation and Change. Your response to this first question establishes where you are in relation to other teachers on a technology innovation use scale. In every organization, including schools, certain individuals seek innovation and change more than others do; they are eager to try new ideas and approaches in their professional practice. Some are quick to follow once others take the lead while still others wait for change and remain behind the pace of new developments.

Figure 1.4 depicts how individuals in business and management respond to change (Rogers, 1962; Value Based Management.net, 2004). Rogers's model, the **Rogers innovation curve,** proposes that with every new idea, there is always a small percentage of innovators and early adopters followed by a sizable majority of followers who will sooner or later adopt new practices. Other research models have percentages for groups of adopters consistent with those of Rogers—innovators typically comprise about 2.5 percent of organizational members, followed by 13.5 percent early adopters, 34 percent early majority users, 34 percent late majority users, and 16 percent who lag behind the process of change (Gillard, Bailey, & Nolan, 2008).

A "frontier developer" corresponds to an "innovator," who is followed by an "early adopter." A person who is in the early majority is someone who is "quick to follow proven success" while late majority individuals are "cautious" and "skeptical observers." The group Rogers defines as "laggards" corresponds to those who choose to "pay little attention" or "see very little promise" on the survey.

Applying Rogers's model to K–12 education, teachers and teacher candidates divide themselves this way:

- Small group of technology innovators eager to integrate computers into their teaching
- Somewhat larger group of skeptical and cautious adopters who worry about the problems of system crashes and inadequate equipment before they appreciate technology's potential to engage learners
- Majority of undecided observers who would welcome technology if they felt more confident about how to use it

8

Groups of Technology Users.   The Pew Internet & American Life Project has also character-ized how people use computers and other information technologies, dividing Americans into three major groups, each with several subgroups (Horrigan, 2007):

Elite tech users (31 percent of the U.S. population) are the leaders in using computers, the Internet, cell phones, and other devices that allow people to connect and interact electronically. Among the elite are

- "Omnivores," who have the most tools and services
- "Connectors," who use the Internet and cell phones extensively
- "Lackluster veterans," who use the Internet but are less likely to use cell phones
- "Productivity enhancers," who possess strongly positive attitudes about the value of technology

Middle-of-the-road tech users (20 percent of the U.S. population) are work-oriented users of technology who are not, however, always happy with the results. These users include

- "Mobile centrics," who use cell phones frequently but are not on the Web as regularly
- "Connected but hassled," who use technology, but often find it is an intrusion in their lives

Few technology assets (49 percent of the U.S. population) are only loosely connected to comput-ers and other new technologies. Those in this category include

- "Inexperienced experimenters," who are occasional users of the Web and cell phones
- "Light but satisfied" users, who are content using technology only when they need it
- "Indifferents," who are sporadic users of technology and do not find the experience pleasant or helpful
- "Off the network" individuals, who do not use computers, the Web, or cell phones

You can take a Pew Internet & American Life Project "What Kind of Tech User Are You?" quiz based on the categories listed above by going online to www.pewinternet.org/Participate/What-Kind-Of-Tech-User-Are-You.aspx.

As new, more sophisticated, increasingly interactive technologies arrive, every teacher faces crucial decisions about leading, following, or staying behind the technological innovation curve. Some of you will be constant innovators, others of you will wait to see if change makes sense, and still others may be a change leader in one area (creating a class wiki or blog to post assignments and showcase student work) while taking a wait-and-see approach to change in another area (us-ing handheld devices or student participation systems as instructional tools). Before entering the classroom, each of you must begin to make these choices, drawing on information from the courses you take, the skills you learn, and the perspectives you adopt related to technology and teaching.

Issue 2: Motivating Factors

Question 2 explores possible motivating factors behind your technology use (Figure 1.5). Rate each motivating factor in the question as a "major reason," "minor reason," or "not a reason."

Developing Lessons and Engaging Students.   Perhaps you have indicated that you intend to use technology as a lesson planning and development tool. Many other teachers agree, as found by Project Tomorrow—a technology information organization that collects the views of teachers, students, and parents through its "Net Day Speak Up" studies. In 2006, Net Day's national survey of some 21,000 educators (80 percent of whom were classroom teachers) found that more than half said technology affected their teaching and instructional support activities by making lesson plans more accurate, timely, and interesting (Project Tomorrow, 2006, October).

However, technology is also a powerful way to motivate and engage students. Many of the participants in the Net Day 2006 study came to this conclusion as well. Not surprisingly student engagement is a deep and perplexing problem in American education today. Many students, at every grade level, report feeling detached and alienated from school (Quaglia Institute for Student

FIGURE 1.5 What Motivates You to Use or to Consider Using Computer-Based Technologies in Your Teaching?

Motivating Factor	Major Reason	Minor Reason	Not a Reason
Enhances my ability to teach academic material			
Lets me use my time more efficiently			
Helps me manage large class enrollments			
Promotes sound pedagogy-based best teaching practices			
Exposes my students to computers and other technologies			
Responds to my students who are encouraging me to use it			
There is technical support in my school to assist me			
Engages students in learning in new and exciting ways			
Elicits offers of motivation and support from other teachers			
Improves my annual evaluation as a teacher			
Other			

Aspirations, 2007; Yazzie-Mintz, 2007). Teachers see this disengagement in blank and bored faces, in defiant and resentful behavior, and in let-me-get-this-done-quick responses to classroom activities or homework assignments.

Broad national statistics reported by Indiana University's yearly "High School Survey of Student Engagement" (HSSSE) show a persistent pattern of student boredom and alienation:

- Two-thirds of high school students report feeling bored in one or more classes every day.
- Half of all high school students spend 4 hours a week or less doing homework or otherwise preparing for their classes; 20 percent spend 1 hour or less a week.
- More than half of high school students said they never discuss academic material from their classes or readings with teachers outside of class.
- Half said they never receive prompt feedback from teachers on assignments.
- Just over half of high school students (57 percent) said they participate frequently in class discussions or ask questions (52 percent) of their teachers.
- Just over half of high school students indicated putting "a great deal of effort" into their schoolwork. (Center for Evaluation & Education Policy, 2005, pp. 5, 6, 12; Yazzie-Mintz, 2007)

Disaffection with school is one of the factors leading to the high number of students who leave education before high school graduation (Hammond, Smink, & Drew, 2007). Nationwide, 30 percent of all students do not graduate high school with a regular diploma; the percentage is 15 percentage points or more higher among African Americans, Hispanics, Native Americans, and students attending urban schools (Pinkus, 2006; Swanson, 2008).

The top reason for dropping out, cited by 47 percent of survey respondents (see Figure 1.6), was that school is simply not engaging or stimulating enough to stay (Bridgeland, DiIulio, & Morison, 2006). Classes featured repetitive modes of instruction and teachers failed to connect academic material from the textbook to real-world issues and problems in the lives of students. As

PEARSON

Go to the Assignments and Activities section of Chapter 1 in MyEducationKit and complete the video activity "Authentic Learning with Technology."

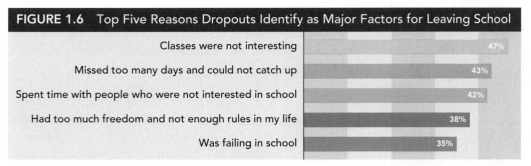

FIGURE 1.6 Top Five Reasons Dropouts Identify as Major Factors for Leaving School

Classes were not interesting	47%
Missed too many days and could not catch up	43%
Spent time with people who were not interested in school	42%
Had too much freedom and not enough rules in my life	38%
Was failing in school	35%

Source: Civic Enterprises. (2006). *The Silent Epidemic: Perspectives of High School Dropouts.* Reprinted with permission of Civic Enterprises.

a result, absence from school became more frequent, propelling a downward spiral of frustration and failure. To stay in school, these youngsters wanted better teachers, smaller classes, individualized assistance, a school climate that fosters achievement, and a strong relationship with at least one adult in the school who believes in them and their potential for educational success.

As a teacher—someone who wants students to succeed with learning—you can use computers and other information technologies to create different designs for learning, as suggested below:

Technology fosters critical and creative thinking as well as inquiry and problem-based learning through	**Technology supports memorization of information and basic skill building through**
Writing and design programs	Electronic worksheets
Online information research and retrieval	Drill-and-practice software
Web or computer-based games and simulations	Online tutoring programs

Using Technology to Improve Teaching. Computers and other technological tools affect the two central aspects of the work of teachers—instructional practices and administrative/professional activities.

- **Instructional practices** refers to working directly with your students as an integral part of teaching and learning activities. Using a theatrical analogy, instructional practices are the "front of the stage" times when a teacher is interacting directly with students. Examples of applying technology to these activities include accessing the Web for class discussion, utilizing computers to show presentations or simulations, having students use handheld and wireless devices as part of group projects, and integrating different technologies into various in-class academic assignments or activities.

- **Administrative/professional activities** refers to the planning, organizing, and recordkeeping needed to support the direct instruction of students. Continuing the theatrical analogy, administrative/professional activities are the "backstage" tasks that make a theatrical performance succeed. Examples include keeping academic records with grading software, maintaining correspondence through email, conducting research using Web resources, and writing reports with word processing software.

Many technological tools support both instructional practice and administrative/professional activities. Email, for example, provides students with feedback about their writing and research projects (instructional practice) while also communicating with families about school (administrative/professional activities). Similarly, a teacher-created website could display notes from class, provide homework assignments, and

YOUR JUDGMENT
MATTERS

Based on these suggestions, consider the following questions:

- What examples would you add under critical and creative thinking?
- What examples would you add under memorization and practice?
- What technologies can be used to support both creative thinking and skills practice?

School classrooms are becoming technology-infused settings where teachers and students use different tools to create hands-on, minds-on learning experiences in every subject.

present project grading rubrics (instructional practices) while providing a publishing format for students' work, visual records of class field trips, or a calendar of upcoming events (administrative/professional activities).

Teachers have tended to use computers and the Internet for preparation and support activities more than for instructional practice. Many teachers, especially recent college graduates, are skilled at writing on computers, corresponding by email, and keeping records on spreadsheets and databases. These experiences naturally transfer to their use of technology in handling the preparation and support tasks that make up such a large part of a teacher's workday.

At the same time, most teachers have had far less experience integrating technology easily and seamlessly into the day-to-day fabric of the classroom. They ignore the potential of technology as an instructional tool because of their lack of familiarity with its options and opportunities. Part of the challenge and excitement of being a teacher today lies in developing ways to make new technologies truly part of classroom teaching and student learning. In doing so, you will create new patterns, build new models, and set new standards of technology-based learning in schools.

Another way to consider how technology supports teachers is to consider what you believe happens when someone is teaching well. When we asked students this question, they placed the following items at or near the top of their lists:

Go to the Assignments and Activities section of Chapter 1 in MyEducationKit and complete the video activity "Teaching with Computers."

- Challenging students to think
- Giving clear and organized presentations
- Using student-centered teaching methods
- Motivating students to learn
- Giving feedback to students
- Showing enthusiasm for teaching and learning
- Teaching to multiple learning styles
- Teaching to different ways of thinking
- Asking provocative, thought-provoking questions
- Providing students with needed skills
- Slowing the flow of information to make sure everyone understands the material
- Having positive interactions with students

Based on this list, consider the following question: How can technologies support or enable teachers to achieve the goals of good teaching?

Issue 3: Barriers to Technology Use

Question 3 examines the barriers to using technology as a teacher. Figure 1.7 asks you to rate each of a series of factors as a "major reason," "minor reason," or "not a reason."

Obstacles Facing Teachers.   Perhaps you cited lack of access as one of the greatest barriers to using technology regularly with students. Other teachers certainly have (National Education Association, 2008). The reality is that K–12 schools have less technology than is the norm in higher education or corporate America, and the educational technology that is available gets replaced or updated less often.

At the same time, the growth of technology in schools has been extensive, as evidenced by 2006 data from the National Center for Education Statistics:

- Nearly 100 percent of public schools had Internet access, compared to 35 percent in 1994.
- 94 percent of instructional classrooms had Internet access, compared with 3 percent in 1994.

FIGURE 1.7 What Impedes Your Use of Computer-Based Information Technologies in Your Teaching?

Impeding Factor	Major Reason	Minor Reason	Not a Reason
Lack of classroom computer equipment			
Lack of home computer equipment			
Lack of time			
Lack of support services to assist me			
Lack of incentives and rewards			
Lack of technical skills			
Technology does not fit my teaching style			
Technologies change too quickly			
Technology fails to include the pedagogy needed to teach my subject			
I am intimidated by technology			
Other			

- 97 percent of Internet-connected schools had broadband access; 45 percent used wireless connections.
- The ratio of students to instructional computers with Internet access was 3.8 to 1 compared with 12.1 to 1 in 1998.
- 19 percent of schools provided handheld computers to teachers and students; 10 percent of schools lent laptops to students. (Editorial Projects in Education Research Center, 2008; Wells & Lewis, 2006, pp. 4–8)

While technological access has dramatically increased, a constant squeeze between expanding technological capabilities and declining operational budgets has forced schools to curtail their technology goals. Technology spending dropped by more than 24 percent from 2001–2002 to 2002–2003 and has not rebounded since. While there are some schools with multiple computers in every classroom—along with a large screen television, VCR with cable access, and a teacher workstation computer from which an instructor can control what is happening on the machines in the room—in many schools the technology infrastructure remains locked in the past. Computers are out of date and in poor condition, software is limited, and software and hardware are often incompatible due to differences in computer memory and operating system requirements.

In the late 1990s, Henry Becker and his colleagues (Becker, 2000; Becker & Ravitz, 1999, 2001) identified a combination of factors preventing teachers from integrating computers more fully into classroom teaching—factors still present today.

- *Access.* Teachers with multiple computers in their classroom (five to eight machines) are more likely to use technology as an integral part of classroom learning. Multiple machines in a classroom make it easier for a teacher to divide a class into smaller groups, with some students using computers while others do other activities. Still, more than half the teachers surveyed in 2007 indicated that the number of computers in their classroom (usually one or two) was not adequate for technology-infused learning (National Education Association, 2008).

- *Teaching schedules.* Teachers with long block teaching schedules (class periods that last for 90 to 120 minutes) were slightly more likely to use computers. Longer class periods mean teachers have more time into which to integrate computer use. Many schools, however, feature class periods of less than an hour, and the time needed to get students from the classroom to a computer lab or library and back again makes it difficult to create computer-infused activities.

- *Curriculum coverage.* Facing pressure to teach and review large amounts of curricular material, teachers felt they did not have the time to integrate technology into their classes. Teachers responsible for fewer topics were twice as likely to have students using computers in class on a regular basis (although this situation applied to only 1 out of every 13 teachers in the Becker study).

- *Technology skills.* More-technologically-skilled teachers integrate technology into their classes more frequently than do less-technologically-skilled teachers, although teachers in general feel they do not get sufficient technical assistance and support for using equipment and software for teaching (National Education Association, 2008). Interestingly, knowledge of Web browsing or word processing were not the key skills possessed by technology-using teachers. Instead, across subject areas, "multimedia-authoring-capable teachers have students use computers more and with greater variety of software than do other teachers teaching the same subject" (Becker, 2001). Moreover, teachers who are "able to produce slide shows using presentation software are among the most active computer-assigning teachers" in their subject area. Math teachers whose students used computers regularly were an exception. These teachers were no more knowledgeable about technology than were the math teachers who did not ask students to use computers often.

To Becker's list, we would add the following factors:

- *Organizational support.* Teachers in schools where there is not strong leadership for technology integration among principals and other teachers, nor a schoolwide emphasis on technology use, find it more difficult to make technology part of their teaching. Administrators generally set the tone and style in a school, and teachers find it easier to integrate technology when they know their principal supports them.

- *Personal attitudes.* A teacher's personal attitude is also a decisive factor in how often that teacher uses technology in teaching. "Unless a teacher holds a positive attitude toward technology," noted two educational researchers, "it is not likely that he or she will use it in teaching" (Zhao & Frank, 2003, p. 808). Without a commitment to using technology, many teachers are reluctant to spend the time needed to learn all the ins and outs of different technologies.

- *Digital divide.* Access to and use of technology is not distributed throughout society or schools, creating what educators and social scientists call a **digital divide** (Cooper & Weaver, 2003; Monroe, 2004; O'Hara & Stevens, 2007). The digital divide affects mainly low-income, nonwhite, and rural communities. Presently, 30 million households do not have a computer. Lacking home technology, 45 percent of African American and 39 percent of Latino students can only access computers at school or in libraries, compared to 11 percent of Asian and 15 percent of white youngsters (Long, 2008).

- *Digital continuum.* Recent research suggests that home access to technologies such as cable television, DVD players, mobile phones, computers, and Internet access has increased across all income levels, but more expensive and emerging technologies (such as handheld and wireless devices) are much less commonly found among families making less than $25,000 a year (Cohen et al., 2007). These findings have led some educators to adopt the term **digital continuum** because it suggests that technology access exists along a wide spectrum of experiences. Virtually every household has access to some technologies—television or cell phones, for example. However, far fewer low-income households have the latest computer technologies or high-speed Internet. Students from low-income households do not have the same media and computer literacy learning experiences at home as their more affluent peers.

As teachers, you will face some or perhaps all of these obstacles to technology use. While there are no instant solutions, finding ways to solve barriers and obstacles is central to the job of a teacher. Most educators work in organizations that are underfunded and underresourced. For years, teachers have compensated for systemic shortages by putting in enormously long hours, spending their own money on materials and supplies, working together in informal networks, taking extra courses and workshops, writing grants, and lobbying policymakers for change. Responding to technology's barriers will require all of the above and continuous evaluation of its potential for helping students to learn.

Issue 4: Ideas for Technology Use

Question 4 explores your ideas for using technology in teaching, with an emphasis on different roles that technology might play for you and your students. Some of the potential uses of technology in this survey question have been suggested by the USEiT (Use, Support, and Effect of Instructional Technology) study done by researchers at Boston College (DeBell & Russell, 2006). Using Figure 1.8 to choose one answer for each of the potential roles listed will help you clarify your own ideas on this topic.

Patterns of Technology Use by Teachers. Your answers to this question raise a fascinating and complex issue in educational technology today. Most schools "still use technology sparingly, rather than as a critical component of all education operations," noted the authors of a report on preparing today's students for the world of the 21st century (State Educational Technology Directors et al., 2007). Education, a federal government study concluded, is the "*least* technology-intensive" part of the American economic system (U.S. Department of Commerce, 2002).

At the classroom level, while 80 percent of teachers use computers for email, word processing, and recordkeeping and data management functions, only slightly more than half use them

FIGURE 1.8 How Often Do You Use or Plan to Use the Following Computer-Based Information Technologies in Your Teaching?				
Technology Use	**All the Time**	**Regularly**	**Occasionally**	**Hardly Ever**
Computer at school for your professional work (communicating with teachers, parents, administrators)				
Computer for classroom presentations and demonstrations (Internet sites, PowerPoint)				
Computer for creating and maintaining a class website or blog				
Internet resources for WebQuest or other Web-based activity				
Internet to research academic content and lesson plans				
Videos or video clips as teaching tools to show concepts and processes in action				
Publishing tools for student projects (digital cameras, Photoshop, PageMaker)				
Computer software and learning games (Sammy's Science House, Math Blaster, Zoombinis)				
Handheld or wireless devices for student use in research and projects				
Internet as an information management tool				
Word processing tools for student writing				
Computers for creating a test, quiz, or other assignment or activity to assess students				
Computers for adapting an activity to students' individual needs				
Other				

in classroom teaching (Rother, 2005). In Maryland, a state with one of the nation's best student-to-computer ratios (4 students to every 1 computer), "only 30% of public school students use technology to perform measurements and collect data and 39% use technology to manipulate, analyze or interpret information" (Maryland Business Roundtable for Education, 2007). These numbers also include a stark digital divide between low-poverty and high-poverty schools; in high-poverty schools students are far less likely to use technology for tasks that require "higher level thinking and meaningful application of knowledge and skills" (Maryland Business Roundtable for Education, 2005).

In Massachusetts, researchers from the USEiT study at Boston College found computer use by students greatly exceeded computer use by teachers. Teachers, in general, reported technology as "being valuable to their teaching," mostly using computers to "make handouts for students"; "create a test, quiz, or assignment"; or "perform research or lesson planning on the Internet" (Higgins & Russell, 2003, p. 67). Teachers said they were fairly regular email users (several times a month), communicating mainly with colleagues and less frequently with school administrators or parents. Much less frequently, however, did teachers create Web-based activities for students, build technology into a lesson, or maintain their own class Web page.

Eighth- and eleventh-graders told the USEiT study researchers that over 50 percent of their teachers "never use computers when teaching" (Russell, O'Brien, Bebell, & O'Dwyer, 2003, p. 60). Fifth-graders reported more frequent use of computers in their classrooms while eighth- and eleventh-graders were more likely to use computers in labs or in the library. Older students were given more computer-based assignments than younger students, but with the exception of eighth-grade science and eleventh-grade English, students did not use computers in academic classes a majority of the time. Rarely, the students said, did they participate in creating a Hyperstudio or

CONNECTIONS and POSSIBILITIES

Technology Fairs: TED (Technology, Entertainment, Design) and the Canada Wide Virtual Science Fair

Imagine you and your students are joining the world's top thinkers and researchers to share ideas about new inventions, powerful products, and scientific ingenuity via the Internet. You can do this online with TED (Technology, Entertainment, Design), an annual conference event where 1,000 experts gather in New York City to share ideas for the future. The list of TED speakers ranges from brain scientist Jill Bolte Taylor; music artist Peter Gabriel; ocean explorer David Gallo; and other notables from the fields of technology, business, entertainment, science, design, global studies, culture, and the arts. During every TED convention, speakers take 18 minutes to introduce project ideas, poetry and music performances, sustainability projects, and innovative new products that pose solutions to worldwide challenges. These short talks are then posted online for everyone to see and hear.

Memorable sessions from recent TED conferences include Nicholas Negroponte demonstrating the XO computer, the "$100 Laptop"; global health professor Hans Rosling presenting data tools that exhibit complicated statistics in easy-to-read and eye-catching graphics; and Jeff Han drawing with his

hands on the multiuse "touch screen" made famous by the iPhone.

K–12 educators may access this site as a way to show students how scientists think, act, and communicate. Many classrooms and schools around the world hold similar virtual thinking and learning conferences by creating audio and video broadcasts for the Internet.

The Canada Wide Virtual Science Fair is a K–12 version of TED where students participate in a Web-based science and technology fair. The goal of the project is twofold—first, to encourage students to think and act like scientists in a public forum with peers and, second, to encourage and highlight a diverse learning and teaching experience in a modern technological format.

You can visit the Canada Wide Virtual Science Fair at www.virtualsciencefair.com and explore how students have published their research findings in a worldwide forum. Or stop by the TED website and tour over 200 video archives shared under a creative commons license whereby you can use and share videos in their original form for educational purposes.

PowerPoint presentation or work with spreadsheets and databases (Russell, O' Brien, Bebell, & O'Dwyer, 2003).

Limited use of technology by teachers has been a consistent finding of researchers going back to the 1998 Teaching, Learning and Computing (TLC) survey of more than 4,000 teachers in over 1,100 schools across the United States. That study found "significant use" of technology by teachers (20 or more times a year) occurred mainly in four instructional situations: separate computer classes (80 percent); prevocational classes in business and other occupational fields (70 percent); self-contained elementary school classes (42 percent); and English/language arts classes where students were using word processing as a way to present their work to teachers. TLC survey researcher Henry J. Becker (2001) noted:

> The one area where one might imagine learning to be most impacted by technology—students acquiring information, analyzing ideas, and demonstrating and communicating content understanding in secondary school science, social studies, mathematics and other academic work—involves computers significantly in only a small minority of secondary school academic classes.

Critics of Technology in Schools. Technology's slow integration into classroom instruction has led some educators to conclude that computers and other information technologies have not and will not produce substantive changes in how teaching and learning take place in K–12 schools. Stanford University historian Larry Cuban (2003) has argued that computers and related technological innovations have been "oversold and underused." In Cuban's view, the use of computers in schools has mainly featured

- Drill-and-practice worksheets but not exploratory learning software
- Student use of word processing for publishing but not for writing or other creative self-expression
- Use of the Internet as an encyclopedia of information but not a place for learning about how to do research and analysis
- Scant consideration of digital cameras, scanners, and handheld or wireless devices as potential tools for learning

YOUR JUDGMENT
MATTERS

Based on your own experiences, consider the following questions:

- Do you agree with Cuban's view that technology has not changed traditional patterns of classroom instruction?
- Do you see as yet unrealized potentials for using technology to change how teaching and learning happen in schools?
- If so, what are some specific steps you plan to take in your own classroom?

Other commentators regard technology as a negative force, distracting students from academic learning. A report on reading from the National Endowment for the Arts (2007) concludes that reading habits and reading skills are in decline among U.S. teenagers and young adults, and electronic media is largely to blame. Young people aged 15 to 24 read books or other print materials on average only 10 minutes a day, far less time than they spend watching television, listening to music, or engaging with computers.

Some educators believe that computers negatively affect children's intellectual development. As evidence, they cite intense online commercial marketing messages, encouraging children and families to buy items from the consumer culture (Seiter, 2005). Then there are the negative impacts of many computer software programs on the children who use them. Psychologist Jane Healy (1999, 2004), a long-term critic of technology, argues that parents and teachers should severely restrict computer use by children younger than 7 years old. In her view, most children's software features right-and-wrong answer games that "empty their minds of the attributes that make people imaginative, creative and thoughtful" (quoted in Westreich, 2000, p. 22).

You will be faced with competing perspectives about the value of technology for learning. You need to be aware of such debates and your role in them. Your use of technology in the classroom for instruction and outside the classroom for planning, administration, and communication will be trendsetting in many schools. The Rogers innovation curve, discussed earlier, suggests that the leading actions of some individuals will bring others along with them as changes take hold within an organization's culture. Your actions as a technology-using educator, therefore, will stretch beyond your classroom, affecting the larger school and district where you are teaching.

Go to the Assignments and Activities section of Chapter 1 in MyEducationKit and complete the video activity "Using Technology to Increase Student Achievement."

Type of Teaching Method	Always	Regularly	Occasionally	Rarely	Never
Large-group teacher-led discussions and lectures					
Cooperative learning					
Small-group activities					
Student presentations and performances					
Independent research by students					
Computer-based activities					
Differentiated instruction (tailoring curriculum to learning styles)					
Portfolios, exhibitions, performances, and other alternative assessments					
Other (please describe) _____ _____					

Issue 5: Teaching Methods

The next question (see Figure 1.9) asks you to consider the different types of teaching methods you plan to use in your classroom. Take the survey and provide an answer for each type of teaching method listed.

Your Teaching Philosophy.   Your answers to this question, however tentative and still in formulation, reflect the reality that every teacher acts on a vision or plan for how her or his classroom will function. Called a **teaching philosophy,** it includes ideas and assumptions about what and how to teach so students will learn. Broadly speaking, there are two primary types of teaching philosophies:

- *Teacher-centered teaching.* Some teachers regard teaching as the formal conveyance of information from a knowledgeable instructor to novice students. They regard "teaching as telling" and use student scores from tests and other quantitative measures to determine who has learned and who has not. Such approaches to teaching are commonly called **teacher-centered teaching.** Those most firmly committed to this definition of teaching occupy one end of a teaching philosophy continuum.
- *Student-centered teaching.* At the other end of the teaching philosophy continuum are those who view teaching as orchestrating different experiences for students. The role of the teacher is to create puzzles, ask questions, and engage in conversations with students, who learn key information and essential skills through exploration and discovery. **Student-centered** teaching is also called "constructivist," "progressive," or "project or problem-based teaching."

Using data from the TLC survey, Becker and Ravitz (1999) sought to characterize teaching philosophies among U.S. teachers. They created a series of continuums that put more inquiry and discovery-based approaches on one end of a scale and more teacher-centered methods on the other. They paid particular attention to four key aspects of how teachers delivered academic content and organized their classrooms:

- *Teacher's role.* A scale that went from teachers' facilitation of learning to teachers' presentation and explanation of academic material
- *Goal of learning.* A scale that went from students' understanding of ideas and concepts to students' learning of specific curriculum content

- *Student motivation.* A scale that went from students' showing of interest and effort to students' knowledge of the material in the textbooks and the curriculum
- *Classroom organization.* A scale that went from students' engagement in multiple small-group activities to students' engagement in mostly whole-group activities

Teachers in any given school may be more or less student-centered or teacher-centered in their approaches. Beliefs about teaching may vary considerably among educators, even those who are members of the same high school department, middle school instructional team, or elementary school grade level. In Becker's survey, the majority of teachers reported they were somewhere in the middle of each continuum in terms of their philosophy (see Figure 1.10).

YOUR JUDGMENT MATTERS

Reviewing the four continuums in Figure 1.10, consider the following questions:

- Where would you place yourself on the teacher philosophy continuums and why would you do so?
- What other scale(s) might you construct to measure additional aspects of your teaching philosophy?

National Educational Technology Standards and Technology-Supported Learning. Your teaching philosophy can be examined in relation to a broad vision of schooling featuring technology-supported learning environments for every student that has been set forth by the International Society for Technology in Education (ISTE) in its National Educational Technology Standards (NETS) for teachers and students (2002, 2007, 2008). NCATE (the National Council for Accreditation of Teacher Education), many states, and hundreds of teacher education programs in colleges and universities throughout the nation support these standards. We connect each chapter of this book to the standards for teachers and each of our Technology Transformation Lesson Plans to the standards for students.

At the core of the NETS is the view that technology makes possible new learning experiences that teach academic content, promote innovative and creative thinking, and prepare students for citizenship in a digital world—while also addressing the needs of all learners in equitable ways. Table 1.1 contrasts these new learning environments with traditional learning environments.

NETS for Students (NETS-S) and NETS for Teachers (NETS-T) were significantly updated in 2007 and 2008. In the language of the revised standards, teachers are expected to inspire student learning and creativity while designing digital-age learning experiences, modeling digital-age work, promoting digital citizenship, and engaging in professional development and leadership in schools. Students are asked to think creatively, communicate and work collaboratively, learn the skills of information research and fluency, think critically while solving problems and making decisions, and practice digital citizenship, all while expanding their knowledge of technology operations and concepts.

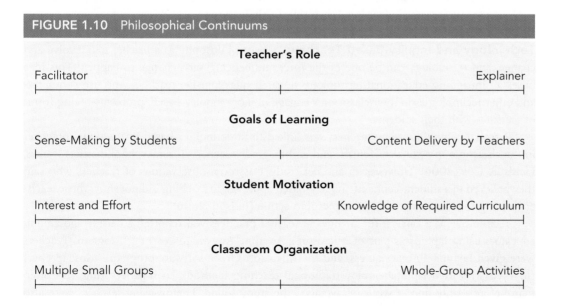

FIGURE 1.10 Philosophical Continuums

Teacher's Role

Facilitator   Explainer

Goals of Learning

Sense-Making by Students   Content Delivery by Teachers

Student Motivation

Interest and Effort   Knowledge of Required Curriculum

Classroom Organization

Multiple Small Groups   Whole-Group Activities

TABLE 1.1 Transforming Learning Environments with Technology

Traditional Environments	Emerging Learning Landscape
Teacher-directed, memory-focused instruction	Student-centered, performance-focused learning
Limited media, single-sense stimulation	Media-rich, multisensory stimulation
Lockstep, prescribed-path progression	Flexible progression with multipath options
Knowledge from limited, authoritative sources	Learner-constructed knowledge from multiple information sources and experiences
Isolated work on invented exercises	Collaborative work on authentic real-world projects
Mastery of fixed content and specified processes	Student engagement in definition, design, and management of projects
Factual, literal thinking for competence	Creative thinking for innovation and original solutions
Traditional literacy and communication skills	Digital literacies and communication skills
Isolated assessment of learning	Integrated assessment of learning

Source: NETS for Students. Reprinted with permission from *National Educational Standards for Students, Second Edition,* 2007, ISTE (International Society for Technology in Education) www.iste.org. All rights reserved.

In ISTE's view, as a matter of policy and of day-to-day practice, teachers and schools should decrease the traditional practices on the left-hand side of Table 1.1 while increasing the emerging styles on the right-hand side. ISTE's call for new learning environments echoes what many progressive education reformers have urged for decades, namely that schools become places where students are directly involved in learning at every grade level, as shown in the following recommendations:

- Less teacher talk and more adult and student interaction and discussion
- Less individual work by students at their desks and more groupwork and collaborative projects by students in and out of the classroom
- Less emphasis on tests that measure factual recall of information and more time using assessments that measure student inquiry, problem solving and critical thinking

Technology and Inquiry-Based Teaching.   Your philosophy as a teacher may evolve and change, and technology can be one of the forces influencing such change to happen. This idea raises an intriguing educational technology research question: Do teachers who use computers and other technologies in their classrooms engage in more inquiry-based, problem-solving forms of teaching with their students?

Personal computer use by teachers was linked to more inquiry-based instructional practices in the classroom in a study of fourth- and eighth-grade teachers in rural school districts (Rakes, Fields, & Cox, 2006). However, in another study, classroom observations of teachers who said they believed in a student-centered, inquiry-based approach to teaching did not show those teachers putting those constructivist principles into action (Judson, 2006).

Technology as a catalyst for changes in teacher practices was reported a decade ago among educators using laptops as part of Microsoft's Anytime Anywhere Learning Program. Teachers were given laptops, Internet access, and the Microsoft Office software program. "Most teachers surveyed who used laptops employ traditional teaching methods, such as lecturing, less often than before—only once a week on average," the study found. Laptop-using teachers were also "increasing the frequency at which they assign projects where students teach other students (90 percent of teachers who use laptops vs. 46 percent of teachers who do not)" (Microsoft Press Pass, 2000, September).

These studies build on results from the 1998 TLC survey that showed that as teachers adopt more inquiry-based approaches, they make other changes in their teaching practices, such as

(a) being more willing to discuss a subject about which they lack expertise and allowing themselves to be taught by students,

(b) orchestrating multiple simultaneous activities occurring during class time,

(c) assigning long and complex projects for students to undertake, and

(d) giving students greater choice in their tasks and the materials and resources they can use to complete them. (Becker & Ravitz, 1999, p. 381)

As a technology-using teacher, you may experience changes in your teaching methods and styles by engaging in more inquiry-based, problem-solving forms of teaching with your students. After developing a class website with his tenth-graders as part of a study of the novel *To Kill a Mockingbird,* a veteran English teacher told us that the lessons he developed as part of the website project were the best he had ever taught. He was doing less lecturing and the students were taking more responsibility for their own learning. In less than half a year, his teaching approach had shifted—both in terms of his technology skills and his vision for how to motivate and engage students in literature study. Like that English teacher, you too may be changed as a teacher through your use of technology, often in ways that you will not fully anticipate or expect.

Issue 6: Students and Technologies

The final question explores how students are using technology, in and out of school. Use Figure 1.11 to rate each of the listed technologies as to whether you think student use is "decreasing," "staying the same," or "increasing."

Differing Paths to Literacy with Technology.   Your answers to this question will likely highlight that children and adolescents today tend to develop literacy with technology differently from older adults. Author Marc Prensky (2001, October) distinguishes the two as **digital natives** and **digital immigrants.** Young people (those born since 1980) who have grown up using instant and interactive computer and wireless technologies are digital natives. According to Prensky, an average college graduate has spent some 10,000 hours playing video games and 20,000 hours watching television as compared to 5,000 hours engaged in reading. Many teachers, by contrast, might be considered digital immigrants who are still learning how to interact with computer technologies. When it comes to technology, non-technology-using teachers do not share the same frame of reference as their students.

There are key differences between the learning experiences of digital natives and digital immigrants. Using in-depth interviews, Selfe and Hawisher profiled the technology experiences of people in the United States during the past 30 years (2004, p. 9) and found the following:

- People in their 50s and 60s, including many older teachers, "who came to computers in the 1970s and early 1980s were likely to have considerable exposure to programming languages (e.g., Cobol, Fortran, Pascal, Basic)." Learning to use a computer began with a focus on the machines themselves (hardware) and included learning computer programming and sometimes authoring one's own programs in a programming language.

- Those individuals a few years to a decade younger, including many relatively new teachers, "defined computer literacy by their knowledge of various software applications (e.g., WordPerfect, PageMaker, HyperCard)." Learning to use a computer began with a focus on applications and functions (software), and included gaining expertise in the multiple ways to use word processing, spreadsheets, databases, and other general software programs.

- These two sets of experiences stand in marked contrast to today's elementary and secondary school students who are more likely to learn about technology through video games,

Technology	Decreasing	Staying the Same	Increasing
Television			
Web surfing			
Desktop computer			
Laptop computer			
Online games			
Video games (home)			
Video games (handheld)			
Email			
Instant messaging			
Videos			
DVD players			
MP3 players			
Cell phones			
Radio			
Music CDs			
Calculators			
PDAs			
Digital cameras			
Digital video recorders			
Blogs (weblogs)			
Social networking websites			
Other technologies			

FIGURE 1.11 How Are Your Students Using Technology In and Out of School?

electronic communication systems, and multimedia. For them, computer use begins with game playing and Internet explorations, and includes a view of technology as omnipresent tools that can be manipulated for fun or serious purposes.

In Selfe and Hawisher's interviews, it was clear that a person's early or initial experiences with technology provide a lens or filter through which their current technology experiences are understood. A telling example of this point occurred early in the writing of this book. We ordered a tablet PC. The machine arrived, was unpacked, logged in, and set up by two young undergraduate student technicians from our department's business office. The technicians then delivered the machine to our office and pronounced it ready to run. "Where is the instruction manual?" we asked. Perplexed, the students replied they had left it behind. They assumed that no one reads about computers or other technologies; they turn them on and figure them out through trial-and-error explorations. We, on the other hand, could hardly imagine operating these tools without a user's guide nearby. Personal histories with computers meant that we and our students saw the same situation in very different terms.

Selfe and Hawisher's research on how people learn about technology has at least two fascinating implications for teachers.

- *Student perspectives.* Students are likely "to consider the reading and composing skills they acquired in electronic environments—literacies marked by the kinesthetic, the visual, the navigational, the intercultural; by a robust combination of code, image, sound, animation, and words—to be more compelling, far more germane to their future success than the more traditional literacy instruction they have received in school" (Selfe & Hawisher, 2004, p. 204).
- *Teacher actions.* Teachers may need to make changes to accommodate the different technological experiences of their students. Traditional writing instruction, for example, with its focus on informational and expository text, may not prepare "young people for a world that will depend on visual literacy, web literacy, gaming/simulation literacy; in short, multimodal literacies" (Selfe & Hawisher, 2004, p. 208).

YOUR JUDGMENT MATTERS

Think about Selfe and Hawisher's research and consider the following questions:

- What are implications of this research from your point of view as a teacher who will also be a computer-using educator?
- How will you teach your students in ways that respond to their interest in and experiences with technology?

Overcoming a Digital Disconnect

Schools are filled with youngsters who are comfortable using technology and teachers who are much less confident technologically (Prensky, 2007). The **digital disconnect** refers to the differences that many students perceive between themselves—Internet-savvy computers users able to streamline all types of educational tasks, inside and outside of school—and their teachers, whose integration of technology into classroom content seems to them to be painfully slow by comparison (Levin & Arafeh, 2002; Project Tomorrow, 2008).

Computer and online experiences have greatly influenced student attitudes about using technology for learning. Five metaphors describe how they think about the Internet when they are not at school and not under the direction of their teachers:

- Internet as virtual textbook and reference library
- Internet as virtual tutor and study shortcut
- Internet as virtual study group
- Internet as virtual guidance counselor
- Internet as virtual locker, backpack, and notebook

In each case, youngsters tend to be more comfortable finding information online than they do locating it in books and other print sources or asking adults directly.

One key aspect of the digital disconnect is how rapidly technology changes and how quickly today's students become engaged with new practices such as iPods, social networking sites (like MySpace and Facebook), digital storytelling, and online video games. When asked in a national survey what technologies they wished they could use for learning, students replied:

- A small wireless, voice-activated computer for every student
- Student-friendly, easily accessible Internet sites for educational learning
- Online classes at school and at home
- Computer-based math learning games and interactive e-textbooks
- Intelligent digital tutoring systems and 3-D virtual reality simulations (Project Tomorrow, 2008, p. 6)

It is not easy to stay in touch with changing student attitudes about technology. Tech Tool 1.2 lists online resources for staying up to date in the continually evolving world of computer and educational technology.

Another way the digital disconnect manifests itself is in how the Internet is used by students and teachers. Students

Technology enables teachers to create new patterns of learning at every grade level.

TECH TOOL 1.2

ONLINE RESOURCES FOR LEARNING ABOUT TECHNOLOGY

New tools and new approaches are constantly changing the field of educational and instructional technology. For example, the idea of teachers maintaining their own blogs was hardly mentioned even a few years ago. Now, blogs are a growing trend as educators seek new ways to connect to their technology-interested students.

As a teacher, you have a constant need for reliable resources that will keep you informed about emerging educational technologies. Happily, using technology to learn about technology is an effective way for teachers to stay current about the latest materials and trends.

Encyclopedia of Educational Technology

The Encyclopedia of Educational Technology is a collection of short multimedia essays written specifically for teachers and students by graduate students and faculty members in the Department of Educational Technology at San Diego State University under the editorship of Professor Bob Hoffman. The site functions like a dictionary or similar reference tool with topics arranged alphabetically. You can look up most key terms and concepts related to both computer hardware and computer use in educational, business, and social settings.

7 Things You Should Know About . . . (EDUCAUSE)

"7 Things You Should Know About . . . " is a series of short, practical briefs on new and emerging technologies written by the EDUCAUSE Learning Initiative, a nonprofit organization of more than 2,200 colleges, universities, and other educational and corporate groups.

Each "7 Things" brief follows a similar format with answers to questions about a technology:

What is it?
Who's doing it?
How does it work?
Why is it significant?
What are the downsides?
Where is it going?
What are the implications for teaching and learning?

enjoy multitasking, so they use the Internet for schoolwork while listening to music, maintaining friendships, eating meals, and spending time in their room engaging in self-directed learning (Ito et al., 2008). The experience is free flowing, flexible, social, and unscripted. At school, Internet use is tightly managed within the confines of traditional classroom schedules while school firewalls and filters block online access. Students resent these restrictions, preferring to be able to use laptops, cell phones, or other mobile devices for learning (Project Tomorrow, 2008).

A further illustration of the digital disconnect comes from a study done by the BellSouth Foundation of Atlanta, Georgia. After spending 10 million dollars in 10 southern states on new technology expenditures and teacher professional development, the foundation found it had indeed dramatically increased the number of teachers who were interested in integrating technology into the classroom. Teachers in the school districts served by the project reported that they

While the briefs mainly focus on the use of information technologies in higher education settings, the material is relevant to all K–12 teachers. You will get a basic overview of a new technology and you can see ways that what is happening in higher education can also take place in elementary and secondary schools.

There are "7 Things" briefs about many of the technologies discussed in this book, including data visualization, digital storytelling, Google Earth, virtual worlds, blogs, wikis, Wikipedia, instant messaging, and clickers.

How Stuff Works: Computer Channel

How Stuff Works is an extensive information portal designed to answer all kinds of questions about everything from automobiles, business, and money to health science and travel. The site includes a separate section dealing with computers and technology called How Stuff Works: Computer Channel. Teachers and students will find far-reaching question-answering resources at this site, complete with written text, live hyperlinks with the paragraphs, video material, image galleries, and connections to additional Internet resources beyond those included within the site.

Initially founded by a professor at North Carolina State University, How Stuff Works is now owned by Discovery Communications, the parent company for television's Discovery Channel. The site's goal is to become a fully multimedia encyclopedia on every topic imaginable. In technology, material is organized into five major areas related to computers: hardware, peripherals, security, software, and Internet.

The search function is easy to use and the descriptions are clearly written. Students will find the site easy to navigate. One drawback is that product ads tend to clutter every page.

CONTACT INFORMATION

Encyclopedia of Educational Technology   http://coe.sdsu.edu/eet

"7 Things" briefs   www.educause.edu/content.asp?page_id=7495&bhcp=1

How Stuff Works: Computer Channel   http://computer.howstuffworks.com

intended to use computers and other electronic resources to create more engaging, interdisciplinary, student-centered instruction.

However, the students saw little change in their school experience, reporting that technology is "still an 'add-on,'" "rarely plays a role in classroom assignments," and "is seldom integral to the outcome of those assignments" (BellSouth Foundation, 2003, p. 8). Students did not want to be restricted to using only teacher-selected technologies for specific assignments, and they especially objected to teachers using technology as a punishment/reward device. The study authors concluded: "Overall, students themselves are not being given the opportunity to use appropriate technological tools independently."

To begin bridging the gap between teacher and student views about technology, the Bell-South study concluded that teachers do not need to be technological "experts." Rather, teachers needed to change their outlooks and practices:

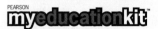

Go to the Assignments and Activities section of Chapter 1 in MyEducationKit. Open the Web activity "Award-Winning Resources for Digital Learning" to further explore this Tech Tool.

Instead of assuming the role of didactic conveyor of knowledge, the teacher can instead take the role as the visionary, or "lead learner," in addressing the curriculum. Rather than function as a gatekeeper for technology use, the teacher can instead serve as an access provider, giving students the room to use technologies both in and outside the classroom to complete learning activities. (BellSouth Foundation, 2003, p. 11)

As a teacher, your actions will either bridge or extend the digital disconnect that so many students perceive between themselves and their schools. Most students need active learning environments to do their best work in schools. Active learning can include technologies such as computers, the Web, educational software, blogs, and many other tools that make academic content easy to access and engaging to use. At the same time, students need to understand that there are good ways and poor ways to use technology. For instance, information that has been posted online is not always useful or reliable. Teaching students about technology means every teacher gets to play an exciting dual role: You teach students by using technology and you teach students how to use technology themselves. These two roles are interrelated; one without the other creates an incomplete learning experience for your students, and for you.

Learning Goals for Teachers and Students

As a teacher, you can utilize new technologies to create a **highly interactive, inquiry-based learning** environment in K–12 classrooms. *Highly interactive* means providing educational activities in which students and teachers are not just consumers of what technology offers, but are active creators, shapers, and evaluators of the information and experiences that technology presents. *Inquiry-based* means that teachers prepare, deliver, and assess lessons differently while students think critically and creatively about the learning they do and the technologies they use.

In a standard learning approach, teachers utilize websites constructed by others as parts of an instructional activity. Students visit the sites, consider the information, and report their understandings and beliefs in written papers and oral reports. In a highly interactive, inquiry-based learning model, teachers and students critically evaluate existing online materials, examining the assumptions that underlie how information is presented, and construct their own website, transforming learning by comparing and contrasting what they find available with what they create for others to read.

This change of perspective can happen in every subject field and at every grade level, as teachers and students together develop, implement, and evaluate how technology facilitates learning.

Highly interactive, inquiry-based learning connects directly to the National Educational Technology Standards for Teachers (NETS-T) and National Educational Technology Standards for Students (NETS-S). Revised in 2007 (for students) and 2008 (for teachers) by ISTE (International Society for Technology in Education), these principles define essential skills and attitudes for technology-using educators.

The transformative changes envisioned by the concept of highly interactive, inquiry-based learning and the new NETS, however, are not built in to any computer, software application, or Web-based tool. As one pioneering computer-using educator noted, "Technologies do not change schools in any sense worth talking about. Thoughtful, caring, capable people change schools, sometimes with the help of technology, sometimes not, and sometimes even despite it" (Brackett, 2000, pp. 29–30). Technologies create real change when teachers and students utilize them in exciting, participatory ways that promote active engagement, critical and creative thinking, and academic learning.

Student learning is the end goal of teaching. Everything that happens in schools from kindergarten to high school is directed toward increasing what students know and are able to do as educated

Every teacher is now a computer-using educator, accessing technology for everything from lesson planning to academic recordkeeping to ongoing professional learning.

individuals. In today's high-technology information society, learning involves more than the traditional skills of reading, writing, and mathematics. Knowledge—notably in the fields of science, engineering, and medicine—is changing so rapidly that today's facts and assumptions are quickly out of date (Popp, 2007). In a world of exponential technological change, students must become creative, innovative, flexible thinkers who can quickly adapt to changing events while connecting and collaborating with other students and teachers. The future, predicted in the New Commission on the Skills of the American Workforce (2006, p. 7), will be a place where

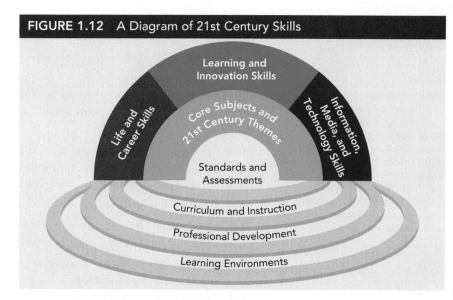

FIGURE 1.12   A Diagram of 21st Century Skills

Source: Reprinted with permission of the Partnership for 21st Century Skills (www.21stcenturyskills.org).

mathematical reasoning will be no less important than math facts, in which line workers who cannot contribute to the design of products they are fabricating may be as obsolete as the last model of that product, in which auto mechanics will have to figure out what to do when the many computers in the cars they are working on do not function as they were designed to function, in which software engineers who are also musicians and artists will have the edge over those who are not, in which it will pay architects to know something about nanotechnology, and small businesspeople who build custom yachts and fishing boats will be able to survive only if they quickly learn a lot about the scientific foundation of carbon fiber composites.

To prepare students for the future, schools must emphasize new skills that include the ability to think critically and make informed judgments, solve complex problems, think creatively, communicate and collaborate with others, use information in innovative ways, and take charge of one's personal and civic life. Such **21st century skills** (Figure 1.12) represent the knowledge, competencies, and understandings that students will need to succeed in our highly technological, information-based society (Dede, 2008; Partnership for 21st Century Skills, 2008) and parallel directly with the revised NETS-T and NETS-S.

Moving forward, this book is organized around learning goals for teachers and students that reflect knowledge and understandings that you and your students will need to succeed as technology-using learners in schools. Each learning goal is designed to focus attention on ideas and information that you need to know in order to create successful learning for students.

CHAPTER SUMMARY

FOCUS QUESTION 1: How do new technologies create new opportunities for teaching and learning?

- Educational technologies offer exciting, engaging, and effective alternatives to traditional instructional methods.
- Computer technologies can be used in ways that promote high levels of interaction and engagement among teachers and students.
- Web 2.0 tools are a new generation of technologies that can be used to create highly interactive, inquiry-based learning experiences at all grade levels.

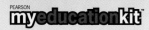
FOCUS QUESTION 2: What six key issues should a teacher consider when looking to integrate technology?

- You need to explore your interest in and experience with technology and your openness to change.

- Examine your motivations for using technology in teaching, your responses to student disaffection and disengagement with school, and your plans to include or infuse technology into your work as a teacher.

- Many future teachers know how to operate computers, search the Internet, create PowerPoint presentations, and communicate electronically, but are less sure how to use technology to transform teaching and learning in schools.

- Analyze factors and barriers that are blocking you from using technology in teaching.

- Key barriers include limited access to technology resulting from the existence of the digital divide, digital inequality, and the participation gap.

- Consider the technologies you plan to use in teaching and the extent to which you will involve students in using technology for learning.

- There are different patterns of technology use among teachers in schools. Critics of technology use in education believe it has been oversold in schools while advocates see it as a way to unleash student learning.

- Explore the different instructional methods you can use in your classroom and how these choices reflect your overall educational philosophy as a teacher. A key element of your educational philosophy is how you incorporate the National Educational Technology Standards for Teachers (NETS-T) and National Educational Technology Standards for Students (NETS-S) from the International Society for Technology in Education (ISTE) in your work as an educator.

- Examine your knowledge of and views on the technologies that students are using in and out of school. Teachers need strategies for overcoming a "digital disconnect" existing between tech-savvy youngsters and many of their teachers.

FOCUS QUESTION 3: What constitutes a highly interactive, inquiry-based learning environment?

- A technology-using educator—an "e-teacher"—is someone who confidently integrates computers and other digital and electronic resources into teaching and learning in K–12 schools.

- The learning goals of this book reflect the knowledge, competencies, and understandings that teachers and students need to succeed as technology users in schools.

KEY TERMS

Administrative/professional activities
Computer
Computer-based technologies
Digital continuum
Digital disconnect
Digital divide
Digital immigrants
Digital natives
Electronic childhood
Generation M
Highly interactive, inquiry-based learning

Information and communication
   technologies (ICTs)
Instructional practices
Noncomputer-based technologies
Rogers innovation curve
Student-centered teaching
Teacher-centered teaching
Teaching philosophy
Technology
21st-century skills
Web 2.0

1. PERSONAL EXPERIENCES WITH TECHNOLOGY

Selfe and Hawisher's (2004) interviews with individuals of different age groups indicate that early learning experiences play a role in shaping someone's personal understandings about technology. To find out more, interview another teacher candidate or a teacher in your school about that person's initial experiences with technology. Write a concise first-person narrative using the words of the person you interviewed. The following questions can help you with your interview:

- When you were growing up, when did you start using a computer regularly?
- What were the technological literacies of your parents, grandparents, and siblings?
- How do your background experiences with technology coincide with K–12 students who are younger than you? How do they differ?
- How might the technology experiences of your students affect their use of technology as learners?

2. TECHNOLOGY IN YOUR WORK AS A TEACHER

Take a tour of a school, such as one where you might be student teaching or doing a school-based practicum, and make a list of the technologies available to teachers and students.

- Which of those technologies do you feel competent using in teaching?
- Which technologies do you need to learn more about before you can use them in the classroom with students?

Now make a list of other technologies you are considering using in your professional work as a teacher, including those that you would use inside the classroom to deliver instruction and those you would use outside the classroom to support your curriculum planning and student recordkeeping.

- Which of those technologies do you feel competent using as a teacher?
- Which technologies do you need to learn more about before you can use them to support your teaching?

3. TECHNOLOGY LEARNING AUTOBIOGRAPHIES

Write a short autobiographical sketch of how you became a computer user, including experiences in school, at home, and with friends and peers. Note your experiences in elementary school, high school, college, and as an adult. As you write, consider how personal experiences may inform how one views technology and its role in schools.

4. INVESTIGATING THE DIGITAL DISCONNECT

When asked about the amount of technology use in his classes, a sixth-grader replied: "Math (3 percent), science (18 percent), social studies (1 percent), English (21 percent), Spanish (2 percent), and associated arts [a technology applications class] (70 percent)." Ask a group of students to determine the percentage of the time technology is used by teachers in their academic classes. What do your students report? What recommendations do they have for their teachers about using technology as a teaching and learning tool?

2 Transforming Learning with Unique, Powerful Technology

When I went to school . . . you went to lectures, you learned things by someone telling you. It's what I call the push model: teachers just push the information into you. Students don't do that now. They grew up on the Internet, on videogames—they look at and do what they want to do. They go on the web and click something. This is the pull model: students pull what they want. So we have to change the way we teach to suit those kids, because that's the way they're brought up. The old ways don't work as well.

—Mark Yim, University of Pennsylvania School of Engineering and Applied Science, quoted in the *Pennsylvania Gazette* (Popp, 2007)

CHAPTER LEARNING GOAL	CONNECTING to the NETS	NEW TECHNOLOGIES
Teaching and Learning Using Technology Exploring ways technology can transform teaching and learning in schools	**NETS-T** 1 Facilitate and Inspire Student Learning and Creativity **NETS-S** 1 Creativity and Innovation	• Visual learning resources • Information resources • Engagement and collaboration resources • Feedback resources • Creativity resources

CHAPTER OVERVIEW

Chapter 2 discusses how technology makes possible unique, powerful, and transformative learning through visual learning, information research and retrieval, collaborative activities, rapid feedback, and imaginative and creative self-expression. The chapter also offers an overview of contemporary theories about learning, including the different approaches of behaviorists, cognitive scientists, and constructivists.

This chapter connects directly to NETS-T Standard 1, Part a, which calls for educational experiences that "promote, support, and model creative and innovative thinking and inventiveness." It also encompasses NETS-T Standard 1, Part d, where teachers "model collaborative knowledge construction by engaging in learning with students, colleagues, and others in face-to-face and virtual environments." By using technology, teachers create opportunities for students to generate new ideas, create original works, and use models to explore systems and issues—the skills highlighted in NETS-S Standard 1, Parts a, b, and c.

FOCUS QUESTIONS

1. What are the implications of the latest research in the science of learning for teachers?
2. In what ways does technology promote unique, powerful, and transformative learning for students?
3. How do students use technology for learning visually?
4. How do students use technology to access and assess information?
5. How does technology create student engagement and collaboration?
6. How does technology provide feedback to support learning?
7. How can students express their creativity using technology?

A parent and a teacher were meeting for a midyear conference at school. After discussing how well the child was doing in class, the conversation turned to an issue troubling the parent. "Why are you emphasizing so much technology in your teaching?" the mother asked, clearly puzzled about the role of computers, videos, digital cameras, and calculators in the classroom curriculum. "We try to limit his use of computers and television at home. We want him to be able to figure things out for himself, not become reliant on machines." Pausing momentarily, the mother continued: "What can you teach with technology that you cannot teach just as well without it?"

The teacher explained that while not every experience with computers is automatically positive, youngsters gravitate to technology-based activities that offer a sense of independence, exploration, and dynamic learning. But, even after making these statements, she felt her explanation had been unconvincing. The parent remained firm in believing that less technology, not more, was best for her child. Recalling the conversation sometime later, the teacher shared how unprepared she was for the parent's question and how to answer it. An early adopter of technology (she had bought a computer for her classroom with her own money long before the school district put multiple machines in every room), the teacher assumed that having students use technology was unquestionably where education was headed in the future.

"What is it that you can teach with technology that you cannot teach just as well without it?" Teachers, parents, college students, university professors, technology developers, educational policymakers, and community members across the country are asking versions of this question as they consider how to use technology in teaching. In this chapter, we join the conversation by showing that computer technologies—when used creatively and thoughtfully by teachers—generate unique, powerful, and transformative learning experiences that do not happen in the same way or with the same impact when nonelectronic materials are used.

This chapter's learning goal is to explore how teachers and students can use computer technologies to transform education in schools. We begin with an overview of the latest research in the science of learning, including the theoretical perspectives of behaviorists, cognitive scientists, and constructivists. Then we look at five ways technology transforms teaching and learning for teachers and students—visual learning, accessing and assessing information, collaboration and engagement, feedback, and creativity (see Figure 2.1). These five concepts form the basis of new frameworks for schooling that can prepare students for an emerging high-technology, information-based society.

In thinking about technology's capacity to transform teaching and learning, we are guided by Nicholas Burbules and Thomas Callister, Jr.'s observation that "capacity for transformation is not intrinsic to the technology itself" (2000, p. 7). Simply adding computers to a school classroom or requiring students to use technology in their assignments will not in and of itself change education. Only as teachers and students adopt new attitudes and new behaviors do schools change in substantive and meaningful ways. Although technology

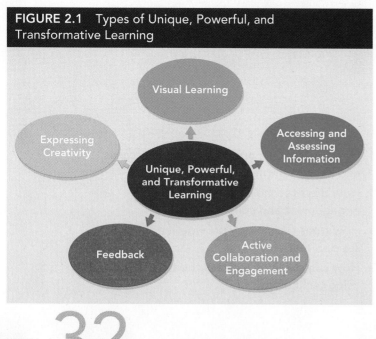

FIGURE 2.1 Types of Unique, Powerful, and Transformative Learning

alone cannot remake schools, teachers and students using technology can open new possibilities for learning across the grade levels and the curriculum.

A New Science of Learning

Nearly a decade ago, researchers from the National Academy of Sciences, the National Academy of Engineering, the Institute of Medicine, and the National Research Council issued *How People Learn: Brain, Mind, Experience, and School*. This book sought to extend the latest research about the science of learning to the issues facing teachers and schools (Donovan & Bransford, 2000). The same research team subsequently completed separate volumes on how students learn history, science, and mathematics (Donovan & Bransford, 2004a, 2004b, 2004c).

Drawing on work in social psychology, cognitive psychology, anthropology, neuroscience, and technology, the How People Learn series asserts that human learners, from the youngest infants to adults of all ages, are "goal-directed agents who actively seek information" (Donovan & Bransford, 2000, p. 10). Adopting a constructivist perspective, the editors state that "the contemporary view of learning is that people construct new knowledge and understandings based on what they already know and believe." When connections exist between the known and the new, learners are better able to contextualize new information, and, in some cases, make the intellectual leap to new understandings. Teachers, therefore, will reach more students when they associate new knowledge in what their students already know or have experienced.

In addition to the importance of connections between the known and the new, constructivism rests on several other concepts, including the idea that knowledge is constructed, not transmitted; that learning requires purpose and effort on the part of the learner; and that initial learning for students is immediate and local, rather than long-term and global (Scott, Asoki, & Leach, 2007; Scott & Mortimer, 2006).

To illustrate what we mean by constructivist teaching and learning, imagine how you might teach students that the earth revolves around the sun. Apart from simply telling them, how do you make this scientific knowledge real to students, especially because their everyday observations suggest the opposite is true? If the students look at the sky, the sun seems to be moving while we here on the earth seem to be standing still. Students view a similar phenomenon at night with the moon appearing to follow their movements riding in a car or walking outside. Bodies in the sky seem to move while the earth feels stationary.

To start the process of new knowledge building, a teacher takes her students outside early in the morning on a sunny day and asks them to trace the shadows of different-sized objects they find around the school's parking lot—signposts, a bench, a fire hydrant, as well as the tallest and shortest students in the class.

With sidewalk chalk, the students trace their shadow drawings. The class returns to the same location an hour later to repeat the shadow tracings with a different color of chalk. Again at noon and on every hour throughout the afternoon, the class traces the changing shadows, each time using another color. The multicolored tracings display each shadow's movements and changes in size and shape. Shadows shrink as noon approaches, but lengthen again as the afternoon progresses.

The students discover firsthand over 3 or 4 days that shadows are marking time by making an outdoor clock, a realization that is quite extraordinary. They have connected what they are observing (shadows have different sizes at different times of the day) with something new they had not known (the movement of either earth or the sun makes the shadows change size and move west to east in the same way day after day). Now the students are eager to pursue the mysterious question: What is causing the movement of the shadows? Answering this significant question

To learn about the processes of seasonal change, students measure their shadows at different times of day. Such active learning methods bring abstract science concepts to life through real-world experiences.

will involve the use of a mix of learning resources from online simulations to the newspaper's weather page showing day lengths changing daily, to spinning tops to simulate planets rotating in their orbits and then revolving around the sun.

The students' shadow tracings attest to the importance of active learning and metacognition. Active learning means that students are actively involved in the learning process by personally doing something, rather than passively receiving ideas and information while sitting listening to explanations, viewing video, or reading about a topic. Metacognition involves students learning how to think about their thinking (Garner & Alexander, 1989). Thinking about thinking is also known as "self-assessment" or "reflection," whereby students take charge of their learning by showing what they know and identifying what they still need to know.

In Boston University's Project Challenge, a program developed by professors Suzanne Chapin and Catherine O'Connor along with public school teacher Nancy Canavan Anderson (2003), elementary school children learn math by discussing their mathematical thinking with teachers and other adults. As students articulate their ideas, they discover essential information and possible misconceptions—in effect, they learn from their talk. While in many classrooms students learn about integers by listening to a teacher explain them, in Project Challenge "the teacher would first present students with some examples of integers—and things that weren't—and ask them to reason inductively to come up with a general definition of an integer" (McNeil, 2007, p. 38). Purposeful conversation between children and teachers, note Chapin and O'Connor, "gives students more time to hear, reflect, to think about the ideas" (McNeil, 2007, p. 38).

Active learning and metacognitive thinking have three main implications for teachers:

- Teachers must draw out and work with the preexisting understandings that their students bring with them.
- Teachers must teach some subject matter in depth, providing many examples in which the same concept is at work and providing a firm foundation of factual knowledge.
- The teaching of metacognitive skills should be integrated into the curriculum in a variety of subject areas. (Donovan & Bransford, 2000, pp. 19–21)

Three Learning Theories: Behaviorism, Cognitive Science, and Constructivism

As they use technology in teaching, educators tend to follow one of three learning theories:

- **Behaviorism** maintains that learning is a set of changes in human behavior created as a function of events in the environment. Thus, learning is a process of memorizing, demonstrating, and imitating. The teaching implication is that learners should be provided with explicit and planned stimuli. Older style computer instruction was based on this principle—typically presenting pages of text and graphics, carefully arranged, planned, and controlled by the computer, not the learner. The primary targets of such learning strategies are memory tasks and recall. The teacher, or computer, is the lecturer and source of knowledge.
- **Cognitive science** suggests that learning is also influenced by nonobservable and internal constructs, such as memory, motivation, perception, attention, and metacognitive skills. Thus, computer instruction must consider the effects of attention and perception and be based on individual learning needs and differences. Here the focus is on program design and interactions. The learner shares control of instruction with the computer. The primary targets of such learning strategies are active learning, transfer of learning, comprehension, and metacognitive skills. The teacher is the coach, facilitator, and partner.
- **Constructivism** claims that every person interprets and constructs the world in their own way. Thus, learning is a process of manipulating and interpreting the surrounding world in a unique way for each individual. In the extreme, there is no reality except as constructed by the individual. The teaching implication is to focus computer activities on learning, not teaching, stressing the actions of learners rather than those of teachers.

High Tech High

What would a school look like where teachers combine technology with a constructivist approach to learning? One answer is High Tech High (HTH) in San Diego, California. Begun in 2000 as a single charter school, High Tech High has grown to a network of five high schools, two middle schools, and one elementary school serving more than 2,500 public school students. The school's growth reflects its remarkable educational successes; every High Tech High graduate has gone on to college, most at 4-year schools.

High Tech High's educational philosophy blends new technologies with innovative approaches to teaching and learning. Responding to the issues raised by student disengagement from school and low academic achievement, High Tech High offers a rigorous, project-based learning curriculum that involves children and adolescents in every aspect of their education. Three principles of learning guide all of the curriculum and instruction, and technology is integrated seamlessly in ways that support the goals of the school (see the accompanying table).

HTH Learning Principle	Key Characteristics
Personalization	Every student has an advisor who oversees long-term goals and short-term performance.
	Every student creates personal digital portfolios to document the year's learning.
	The school supports full inclusion of students with special needs.
	Networked wireless laptops are always available for use.
Adult world connection	Students shadow adults in the community.

Adult world connection *(continued)*	Semester-long internships in local businesses and agencies are part of the curriculum experiences.
	Community service learning projects are where independent study projects begin.
	Small-group learning in technology-based labs and project areas is the norm for all students.
Common intellectual mission	No tracking or ability grouping takes place.
	All learning by students is evaluated by performance-based assessments based on learning rubrics.
	Teachers work in teams.
	All graduates go to college.

These learning principles, school founders believe, are not routinely found in most U.S. schools, yet they form the foundation for the kind of education students need for the 21st century.

Technology is a constant feature of students' everyday educational experiences at HTH. Technology acts as a tool for doing academic assignments and presentations. It is part of how the school and its students connect to the community, and it serves as a field of study of its own in terms of how technology affects society. The results include wonderful presentations and accomplishments. In 2007–2008, for example, eleventh-graders created technology-based exhibits and installations entitled "How Do Americans Respond to the Sounds They Hear?" that explored math, biology, and humanities connections they found in U.S. music.

You can learn more about High Tech High by visiting its website (http://hightechhigh.org).

Teacher-Centered and Student-Centered Approaches

The new science of learning described in the How People Learn series represents a dramatic departure from the way teaching occurs in many elementary and secondary schools. For more than 100 years, the predominant form of teaching has featured lectures by teachers, students listening passively at their desks, textbooks, worksheets, and assessment using multiple-choice tests and quizzes (Cuban, 1993, 2004; Wolk, 2008). Such methods are called *teacher-centered instruction* or **transmission teaching,** meaning the major focus and energy of a class comes from the teacher to the students.

By contrast, researchers from the National Academy of Sciences have articulated a student-centered approach to learning (also called a *learner-centered classroom*). The opposite of teacher-centered or transmission teaching, *student-centered teaching* means that students are actively part of all elements of a class from planning lessons to conducting experiments and engaging in discussions to participating in assessment of the learning (Doyle, 2008). Such methods, notes Northwestern Illinois University Professor Steven Wolk, build a "culture of inquiry" where teachers and students work together to investigate problems, pose solutions, and reflect what they are learning. Teachers "stop seeing themselves as curriculum *deliverers* and start seeing themselves as curriculum *creators*" (Wolk, 2008, p. 122).

Teacher-centered and student-centered methodologies are at opposite ends of a teaching and learning spectrum that has many versions and variations in between (Brooks & Brooks, 1999; Coppola, 2004; Resta & Semenov, 2002; Smith, 1998). Key assumptions that guide each approach are presented in Table 2.1.

Teacher-Centered. Teacher-centered methods convey information to students who are expected to learn it and use it. In this view, "knowledge is conceived as discrete facts commonly understood by everyone, and knowledge is fixed, something we can all point to and understand in the same way" (Coppola, 2004, p. 19). The goal of the teacher is to "instruct" in the most efficient and effective ways possible so that students will learn the information. For this reason, teacher-centered methods are also called "information processing" or "acquisition" approaches to teaching and learning (Duffy & Orrill, 2004, pp. 165–167).

In a teacher-centered model, students mainly listen to planned presentations, work through a fixed curriculum, and independently complete routine assignments in class and for homework. In a teacher-centered classroom, teachers ask 95 percent of the questions, mostly requiring short answers and factual recall by students (Hmelo-Silver, 2002). Students are expected to absorb and understand explicit concepts and to demonstrate understanding on factual and definition-based tests and quizzes.

Student-Centered. Student-centered approaches define classroom learning as extending from the active engagement of students with academic material and real-life situations. This is also the central assumption of constructivist approaches, where teachers seek to raise questions about students' taken-for-granted, unexamined beliefs and assumptions. As learners encounter and work to resolve such meaningful questions and puzzles, they incorporate new understandings into

TABLE 2.1   Contrasting Approaches to Learning

Teacher-Centered Approaches	Student-Centered Approaches
A view that learning is hard	A view that learning is a natural process
Learning happens best when content is broken down into small units of instruction	Learning happens best when content is integrated into real-world, problem-solving tasks and activities
Whole-group instruction	Whole-group, small-group, and one-on-one instruction
Seatwork by individual students	Cooperative learning and group projects
Discussions focusing on factual-recall answers	Discussions stressing many possible solutions to problems
Assessments based on worksheets, quizzes, and tests	Assessments based on students' projects, performances, and portfolios

their views and values. The goal of the teacher is to "create" situations where students can engage in active learning, minds-on problem solving, and thoughtful reflection about academic experiences. For this reason, student-centered, constructivist methods are sometimes called "inquiry-based" or "experiential."

In a student-centered, constructivist approach, students are actively involved in learning activities at every grade level, working alone and together to assemble knowledge and discover interconnections between different sets of information. The learning process more closely resembles the shadow-measuring lesson and the Project Challenge math approach where students are directly constructing new knowledge through engaging activities.

Technology's benefits to learners and teachers straddle the teaching/learning spectrum from one end to the other—highly useful to transmission approaches, inquiry approaches, and the various combinations in between. For example, technology lets teachers conduct drill-and-practice learning of concepts through computer-based learning games, review key material from lectures and readings using presentation software, and provide rich resources for reviewing the main ideas in textbook lessons using websites and other electronic resources. At the same time, technology can expand the curriculum to include the world beyond the classroom, providing ways for children and adolescents to engage with problems and develop solutions and introducing new authors to young readers and new audiences to young writers (Christensen, Johnson, & Horn, 2008).

Active Methods to Engage Students

Educators typically use four teaching methods to actively engage students in learning:

- **One-on-one tutoring** engages students by adapting teaching directly and individually to a learner's needs and knowledge. Real world examples would include training for high-risk careers (piloting airplanes, controlling a nuclear reactor) or preparing for professions in which high artistry is sought (master classes for musicians, personal coaching for athletes).

- **Learning groups** engage students in working out problems together in ways that produce high-quality explanations and performances among peers. Groups can take many forms, from pairs, trios, and foursomes to cooperative learning structures.

- **Inquiry learning** engages students by asking them to do authentic and active work by investigating relevant questions in a subject field. Students gain the analytical ability to use information in a variety of ways—not just those presented by a teacher lecture—by researching hypotheses, collecting data, formulating conclusions, and presenting their findings in oral and written formats.

- **Metacognitive thinking** engages students by showing them how to focus on their own learning methods through self-explanation and self-evaluation. As students gain a capacity to question and reflect on their own learning, they are able to improve their performances using skills and concepts they have been taught in school.

YOUR JUDGMENT MATTERS

As you read the list of teaching methods, consider the following questions:

- Which active learning methods did you find most valuable as a student and why?
- Which active learning methods do you plan to use as a teacher and why?
- Which of these active learning methods do you think are more or less widely used in schools and why?

Technology and Constructivist Approaches

Computer technology is well suited to support and promote student-centered, constructivist teaching, as shown in Table 2.2. Computer technologies support learning as a unique process for each

TABLE 2.2 Student-Centered Teaching Methods Supported by Technology

Student-Centered Teaching Methods	Description of the Method	Classroom Example	Technology Supports
One-to-one tutoring	Student and teacher enter into a dialogue where the teacher seeks to identify and clarify misconceptions, misunderstandings, or misinformation. The student works to improve academic performance by practicing skills and exploring new topics. Experienced teachers maintain a delicate balance, providing students with enough guidance to keep them from becoming too frustrated or too confused while maintaining a focused level of interest and engagement.	Students work with a teacher or older students to identify the rules for adding fractions with unlike denominators. They discuss their new knowledge with teachers and tutors. They then use that knowledge to design posters, comics, new math book illustrations, or PowerPoint slides to facilitate remembering new information.	• Interactive educational websites and software programs offer skills practice and opportunities to explore topics in more detail. • Intelligent tutoring systems model a student's learning and generate appropriate problems and hints. • Interactive multimedia interprets student answers and enables an online tutor to enter into meaningful interaction with the students.
Inquiry learning	Students are presented with "real-life" cases. Learning begins with a problem to be solved, and students investigate their own hypotheses. They define the problem, create hypotheses, gather and analyze data, and evaluate or justify solutions.	Students are presented with an environmental situation and they try to identify probable problems and solutions by identifying available evidence.	• Students engage in electronic communications with scientific experts. • Students conduct online research into environmental topics. • Computer interfaces support exchange and sharing of information among students, encouraging them to question processes, make mistakes, and monitor their own learning.
Metacognitive thinking	Practice and apprenticeship are the focus of the teaching activity. The student is engaged within a realistic environment and solves authentic problems.	Students interact with a complex piece of machinery to learn how to run or control it. An expert monitors and offers feedback to student performance.	• Computer environments replicate the complex environment or pieces of equipment. • Computer environments respond to the learner's actions, extend understanding, and help change belief structures by providing examples that confront the learner's current hypotheses.
Learning groups	Teachers work with students in teams to explain their reasoning to other students, thus facilitating self-expression and receiving feedback. Groupwork enables students to understand processes by which knowledge is generated, evaluated, and revised. Students participate with others because one individual cannot always hold all the knowledge required to solve a problem. The teacher's role as advisor is enhanced and learning is moved from teacher-centered instruction to student-centered collaborative inquiry.	Students work together to identify reasons why the dinosaurs may have become extinct; why one of Saturn's moons might sustain life; or why the lack of darkness at night may be harmful to plants, animals, and humans.	• Teams of students examine the topic(s) using a variety of computer-supported resources, including websites, software, blogs, wikis, and email. • Blogs and wikis support collaborative learning by enabling students to save plans, resources, and notes in an online storage space, open to all to use at any time. • Computers support students as they write and publish the results of their investigations.

individual by focusing directly on each student's actions, supporting each student's interest in formulating questions to investigate, and enabling each student to manipulate and interpret a learning environment. While lectures and textbook memorization succeed with only some students, new technologies have the potential to transform learning for disadvantaged and unmotivated students as well as students who are academically secure. The kinds of unique, powerful, and transformative learning that we describe next in this chapter not only renew and refresh but also expand and extend traditional activities by introducing new approaches (e.g., Internet research, simulations, multimedia, electronic communications, inquiry-based learning, and digital portfolios) to create learning activities that are otherwise impossible to implement in the classroom.

PEARSON
myeducationkit™

Go to the Assignments and Activities section of Chapter 2 in MyEducationKit and complete the video activity entitled "Learning with Tablet Computers."

Unique, Powerful, and Transformative Learning Using Technology

How do computers, the Internet, digital cameras, handheld and wireless devices, and other information technologies offer unique, powerful, and transformative learning opportunities? Each term conveys an idea of technology affecting attitudes and behaviors of teachers and students in ways that propel learning and organizational change. "Unique" declares that technology accomplishes what other nonelectronic materials cannot do—at least not in the same way with the same impacts. "Powerful" suggests that technology's impact will be substantive in nature and, potentially, long lasting in duration. "Transformative" states that technology can alter how teachers teach and students learn in ways that make school a different (and more relevant) place for education.

The five kinds of unique, powerful, and transformative learning experiences (which we will spend the rest of the chapter discussing)—visual learning, accessing and assessing information, student engagement and collaboration, feedback, and creativity—share the following characteristics:

- Each can happen in any subject area at any grade level.
- Each reflects the intent of NETS-T and NETS-S in emphasizing how technology can be used to create new teaching and learning experiences in schools.
- Each enables teachers and students to use the three essential elements of information technology (IT) fluency—"technical skills," "foundational concepts," and "intellectual capabilities."
- Each is intended as a starting point for further thinking and discussion.

Visual Learning Using Technology

Information technologies promote **visual learning.** Software programs, Internet sites, videos, graphing calculators, and devices like telescopes and microscopes provide compelling ways to present information dynamically. Using computers, one can recreate the past, view the present, or envision the future through moving images rather than static words and pictures. Technology reveals the ocean's depths, the immenseness of the solar system, and the structural systems of a human body. We can view tiny objects—bacteria, molecules, one-celled animals, and insects—or vast phenomena—weather systems, geological landforms, or planets and other extraterrestrial objects. We see things that we would not otherwise be able to see.

Free from the restrictions of only static images in books or print materials, teachers can promote new learning through *"visual modes of thought"* (West, 2004, p. 26). When viewed on a computer, short movies and animations, for example, often have the capacity to zoom in and out or rotate scenes in a circle, thus letting viewers see from multiple perspectives. Virtual reality environments and social simulations let students enter a setting and observe how it works from the inside. In some simulations, the user can affect the environment and determine the course of events. Technologies teachers can use to promote learning through visual experiences include

- Online simulations and experiments
- 3D virtual reality presentations and tours

- Real-time data displays and analysis
- Online video clips and streaming video
- Digitalized primary sources (such as photographs, documents, charts, graphs, or maps)
- Vodcasts (video podcasts)

People learn in multiple ways: by reading, listening, viewing visual displays, conducting hands-on trial-and-error experiments, or by other methods. Often someone's preferred mode of learning depends on what it is that the person wants to learn and remember. For example, a university colleague who serves as an academic advisor to students preparing to become teachers creates visual diagrams of what courses to take, when to take them, and what requirements they will fulfill. The students keep these diagrams and bring them for updating and revision in subsequent meetings. Having a visual map of 2 or 3 years of courses and field experiences makes the abstract concrete, enabling students to see where they are going in their teacher preparation program and to feel confident about how they are progressing toward graduation and licensure.

Visual Learning and Visual Literacy.   Designing ways for people to learn visually has been the educational focus of the information theorist Edward R. Tufte (1990, pp. 9, 12, 33, 35). In a classic book, *Envisioning Information,* Tufte observes that while "the world is complex, dynamic, multidimensional, the paper is static, flat." Even though we perceive the world in three-dimensional terms, information is presented to us "in the two-dimensionality of the endless flatlands of paper and video screens." To communicate information more effectively, writers and readers must find ways of "escaping flatland." As information consumers, notes Tufte, we are regularly besieged by crowded and cluttered information displays or "chartjunk" offering neither clarity nor detail. By contrast, "Standards for excellence for information design are set by *high quality maps,* with diverse bountiful detail, several layers of close reading combined with an overview, and rigorous data from engineering surveys." Photographs, diagrams, charts, graphs, drawings, musical notations, and pictures are examples of information that can be displayed poorly or powerfully depending on how they appear visually.

Learning visually with technology presents opportunities for teachers to promote **visual literacy** among their students (Myatt, 2008). Defined as the "study of visualization in all of its aspects of communication and education" (Braden, 1996, p. 491), visual literacy involves giving students the skills needed to critically read color and form and assess the many types of visual presentations they will encounter in school and society, including pictures, images, illustrations, diagrams, charts, and graphs. Like text literacy, visual literacy evolves from personal experience as well as from specific teaching about how images can be used to communicate ideas and information.

The Newberry Library (2002) in Chicago, for example, has placed a group of 18 historic maps online so that students can "examine the geography or geographical ideas of the time and place in which it was produced." The library's "Historic Maps in K–12 Classrooms" collection ranges from a 1492 map of Columbus's world to a 1978 map of metropolitan Los Angeles (available online at www.newberry.org/K12maps). The maps offer ways for students to probe the assumptions embedded in the images as they develop into critical evaluators of visual text. Many contemporary sources—from advertisements found on television or in print media to the charts and graphs located in textbooks and newspapers—provide excellent examples of visual images that can be analyzed by teachers and students.

Interactive Visualizations.   Learning visually and visual literacy involve learning about static images and interactive displays through a process of **data visualization** or the "graphical representation of information" (EDUCAUSE Learning Initiative, 2007, October). Historian David Staley

YOUR JUDGMENT
MATTERS

As you think about your personal learning preferences, consider the following questions:

- What information do you prefer to learn visually?
- What information do you prefer to learn by listening to others? By reading a book? By doing something through a process of trial and error?
- What implications do your preferences for learning have for you as a teacher?
- What implications do students' varied learning preferences have for you as a teacher?

40

(2003, p. 3) has defined visualization as "any graphic which organizes meaningful information in multi-dimensional spatial form." Prose is inherently one-dimensional. When we read a book, for example, the words on the page appear in a sequential order. By contrast, "maps, diagrams, panoramas, schematics, charts, and time-series graphs" do not merely illustrate a text, but they "connect symbols in two-and-three dimensional space" (p. 3). Visual displays are sometimes the best way to deliver information. For example, a typographical map or the periodic table of the elements chart communicates meaning more readily in visual rather than written form.

Visual displays increase instructional options for teachers and students. Every time a teacher enters a classroom, she or he must decide what academic content to teach *and* what teaching methods to use to teach it. Content and methods are directly connected, each an integral part of every lesson. As David Staley (2003, p. 22) noted: "Sometimes words are best; sometimes pictures best accomplish the task; occasionally it is sound or movement. The choice depends on the types of ideas one wants to convey."

Visual technology offers multidimensional ways of seeing the world, in every subject area and at every grade level. A high school history example is Raid on Deerfield: The Many Stories of 1704, a website developed by the Pocumtuck Valley Memorial Association in Deerfield, Massachusetts (see Figure 2.2). This site uses multiple digital technologies to provide interactive visual explorations of a famous pre–Revolutionary War event resulting from growing tensions and cultural clashes between French and English colonists and the native peoples living along the Connecticut and Deerfield Rivers in present-day western Massachusetts. Native peoples had lived in this area for 10,000 years but, with the arrival of the colonists, they saw their homelands usurped by settlers. On February 29, 1704, a party of Native Americans took 112 English men, women, and children from the settlement they had established in Deerfield and forced them to march 300 miles to Canada. Was the raid an unprovoked attack, a justifiable military action, or something else? Visitors to the site are invited to develop their own historical interpretations using online sources and visual materials.

To explore the multiple dimensions of the 1704 raid, the site uses computer graphics, sound, and interactive visual technologies to reveal the perspectives of multiple participants: English and French colonists and the Kanienkehaks (Mohawk), Wendat (Huron), and Wobanaki peoples. Using Macromedia Flash, a viewer can roll a mouse over a scene, spotlighting characters and artifacts and exposing more detailed descriptions and links. A "magic lens" feature provides clear transcriptions of primary source documents written in the unfamiliar handwriting script of colonial times. Another visual technology gives viewers close looks at artifacts and images by zooming in and out and panning around the page to see scenes from different perspectives.

The uniqueness of multimedia lies in its ability to produce a simulation of events. Dramatic representation enables the witnessing of events as if in real time. The Many Stories of 1704 site facilitates visual learning by using technology to set in motion a multidimensional historical view that neither privileges nor diminishes any cultural group. Visual resources help children see the past not as obscure events that happened long ago and far away from daily life but as compelling stories whose lessons connect directly to the building of better futures for themselves and their local and global neighbors. The past is not reduced to a struggle between two sides—Europeans and native peoples—but is revealed in its complexity and nuance. Students learn about the different groups involved in the incident and why those groups came into conflict over land and natural resources. Effective teachers can then blend the issues of the past with the issues of the present, because so many conflicts in today's world can be traced to struggles for power and control. Tech Tool 2.1 suggests other examples of visual learning resources.

FIGURE 2.2 Screenshot of Raid on Deerfield

Source: Reprinted with permission of the Pocumtuck Valley Memorial Association.

Go to the Assignments and Activities section of Chapter 2 in MyEducationKit. Open the Web activity "Visual Learning" to further explore this Tech Tool.

WEB RESOURCES FOR VISUAL LEARNING

- *The e-Skeletons Project* (http://web.austin.utexas.edu/eskeletons). Offers 2D and 3D full-color digitized versions of skeletons of human and nonhuman primates (developed at the University of Texas).

- *Molecular Workbench: An Interface to the Molecular World* (http://mw.concord.org/modeler/index .html). Offers interactive, visual simulations of molecular dynamics for classes in physics, chemistry, and biology (from the Concord Consortium).

- *Plants-in-Motion* (www.bio.indiana.edu/%7Ehangarterlab). Presents QuickTime movies of plant growth and reproduction cycles (from the Indiana University Biology Department).

- *Net Frog* (http://frog.edschool.virginia.edu). A leading interactive frog dissection program since the mid-1990s (from the Curry School of Education at the University of Virginia).

- *Physics Education Technology* (www.colorado.edu/physics/phet/web-pages/index.html). Offers interactive simulations of motion, heat, electricity, light, radiation, and other properties and forces (from the University of Colorado).

- *Rome Reborn 1.0* (www.romereborn.virginia.edu). Offers a model of Ancient Rome, digitally reproduced as it was on June 21, A.D. 320, during its preeminence as the capital of the Roman Empire; 10 years in the making, the site includes still images, video and audio clips, and text resources (from the Institute for Advanced Technology in Humanities at the University of Virginia).

- *Visual Dictionary Online* (http://visual.merriam-webster.com). A unique interactive reference tool supporting all K–12 subjects that extends the boundaries of traditional dictionaries by defining words visually and interactively (from Merriam-Webster).

- *The Whale Hunt* (http://thewhalehunt.org). Visually documents in 19 different slideshows 9 days in May 2007, when Inupiat Eskimos in Barrow, Alaska, planned for and executed their annual whale hunt.

Accessing and Assessing Information Using Technology

Information technologies give teachers and students unparalleled and unprecedented access to ideas and information—including the academic content and learning standards that make up a school's formal curriculum. At the same time, they place new demands on everyone to assess the quality of the information they find online. *Accessing information* refers to the activities of locating and acquiring information. *Assessing information* refers to processes of determining the reliability and usefulness of that information.

Technology has revolutionized how people get information. Computer search engines, electronic encyclopedias, CD-ROMs, DVDs, and other information storage and retrieval systems make it possible to explore any topic electronically. One can gain immediate access to information about the arrival of a spacecraft on the planet Mars, the hearings of a congressional committee, the newly released papers of a famous historical figure, or any newsworthy event or student-based inquiry. Teachers can use technologies such as the following to involve students in accessing and assessing information:

- WebQuests and other online research projects
- Classroom websites that involve students in design and maintenance
- Student-created Web materials

- Web materials used by students for critical reviews
- Online newspapers and news broadcasts
- Bookmarking and social bookmarking
- Google Wonder Wheel
- Digital dictionaries
- Multimedia time lines
- Information alerts

Information Literacy and Internet Literacy. Nearly immediate electronic access to vast resources of information brings with it the need for students to gain **information literacy,** "the ability to locate, evaluate and use information in an effective and appropriate manner" (Jurkowski, 2004, p. 319). Students at all grade levels must learn how to

- *recognize* when they need information,
- *locate* information from various sources,
- *evaluate* the quality, currency and usefulness of the information they find, and
- *organize and manipulate* that information for their own purposes. (Jurkowski, 2004, p. 320)

Chapters 5 and 6 provide more ideas and strategies for preparing students to be information literate users of the Internet and other electronic information sources.

Information literacy is essential for recognizing differences among information sources—that is, what is intended to be persuasive (campaign speeches and slogans or commercials), what is intended to be objective (scientific study or news broadcasts), and what is intended to be satirical (news on Comedy Central or in a humor magazine). Students who do not know how to find and evaluate information risk being overwhelmed by the sheer volume of images, text, and data they receive from multiple media, resulting in an information overload that diminishes critical thinking.

An important part of information literacy is **Internet literacy,** which means the skills required to understand information presented online in electronic formats. Internet literacy is the focus of a research project, Teaching Internet Comprehension to Adolescents (TICA), being conducted jointly by the University of Connecticut and Clemson University (available online at www.newliteracies.uconn.edu/iesproject/index.html).

TICA's lead researchers have noted that fewer than 10 percent of the study's seventh-grade participants check the accuracy of information they find online while some 80 percent do not read the results of a Google search because they are unsure how to figure out what it means (Ascione, 2006b). In a dramatic demonstration of this point, the TICA research team created a fictional website for the "Northwest tree octopus" (see Figure 2.3), a make-believe animal whose existence is threatened with extinction by logging and attacks by its natural predator, the sasquatch (Bettleheim, 2007). The site had academic text, supposed rare photos, and contact information. Seventh-graders who looked at the site believed the animal was real and when they were told it was a hoax, the students had difficulty identifying the fictitious elements of the tree octopus site.

To promote increased Internet literacy, the TICA project urges "reciprocal teaching," a technique to promote improved reading comprehension. Teachers read Web material aloud to students and talk about word meanings. The students then reread the material aloud, focusing on critically evaluating what is being said and what may be omitted from or obscured by the text.

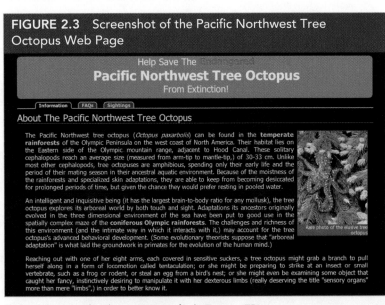

FIGURE 2.3 Screenshot of the Pacific Northwest Tree Octopus Web Page

Source: Reprinted with permission of Lyle Zapato, ZPi.

In many schools, classrooms are still organized around students sitting in rows while a teacher stands in front directing the learning. Computers and other new technologies make possible very different, more student-centered learning environments.

New Roles for Teachers and Students in Technology-Connected Classrooms. Rapid access to information through the Internet and computer databases is starting to redefine the roles of teacher and students. A more than 100-year-old model of schooling that is the standard of school structure today—the teacher as the transmitter of information; the student as passive listener receiving the information—is incontrovertibly redesigned by the potential of computer technologies to reach and teach different ages simultaneously and individually.

Historically the roles of teachers and students in U.S. classrooms have been slow to change. Viewing schools in the 1980s in his classic book, *A Place Called School,* John Goodlad (1984) found in most classrooms, most of the time, teachers talking and students passively listening, completing work-sheets, or preparing for assignments. He found this pattern across K–12 schools. Even in the youngest grades, active student participation was minimal. As a result, many children and adolescents found schools dull, boring, and seemingly purposeless. Noted Goodlad (1984, p. 241):

> From the beginning, students experience school and classroom environments that condition them in precisely opposite behaviors—seeking "right" answers, conforming, and reproducing the known. These behaviors are reinforced daily by the physical restraints of the group and classroom, by the kinds of questions teachers ask, by the nature of the seatwork exercises assigned, and by the format of tests and quizzes.

Two decades later, the patterns of teacher-centered classrooms described by Goodlad remain firmly in place in many schools, as two educational psychologists found when they compared videotapes of how mathematics is taught in eighth-grade classrooms in Japan, Germany, Australia, the Czech Republic, Hong Kong, the Netherlands, Switzerland, and the United States (Hiebert & Stigler, 2004; Stigler & Hiebert, 1999). The researchers saw a marked difference in teacher behaviors in countries where students scored consistently high on the 1999 TIMSS (Third International Mathematics and Science Study) test and teacher behaviors in the United States, where students did not score as high. They concluded that a sharp "teaching gap" holds back the achievement of U.S. students.

A computer lab changes the focuses of teaching and learning in schools. With multiple computers, students can work together actively and collaboratively with guidance from their teacher.

In the lower-scoring U.S. classrooms, teachers spent less time helping students understand underlying mathematics concepts and more time teaching the mechanics of getting the correct answer than did teachers in countries that achieved higher scores on the TIMSS test. Eighth-graders in the United States spent almost all their class time practicing skills while students in high-achieving countries looked more at the "connections and relationships embedded in the problems." U.S. teachers frequently did the mathematical work for the students at the board while the students took notes in their seats. As the researchers noted: "Compared with their international peers, 8th graders in the United States almost never got the chance (less than 1% of the time) to explore and discuss mathematical relationships while solving these problems" (Hiebert & Stigler, 2004).

Access to computers, the Internet, and other electronic information sources means a teacher is no longer the sole director of what and how students learn. In a technology-connected classroom, the teacher's role pivots from dispenser of information to manager of individual and group learning

- *The Presidential Timeline* (www.presidentialtimeline.org). Provides access to documents, photographs, audio and video recordings, and other materials from the nation's 12 presidential libraries (from the Learning Technology Center at the University of Texas at Austin).

- *The Valley of the Shadow: Two Communities in the American Civil War* (http://valley.vcdh.virginia.edu). Provides maps, letters and diaries, census and tax records, newspapers, soldiers' records, and other primary source materials from counties in Virginia and Pennsylvania from before the Civil War to the end of Reconstruction (from the Virginia Center for Digital History).

- *National Doppler Radar Sites* (http://weather.noaa.gov/radar/national.html). Offers immediate, real-time weather information for nearly every part of the continental United States, Alaska, Hawaii, Puerto Rico, and Guam; a wonderful way to introduce students to the use of real-time data to do analyses and make decisions (from the National Weather Service).

- *Fact Check* (www.factcheck.org). Uncovering bias and inaccuracy in politics and news reporting (see the accompanying screenshot) by inviting users to become their own information detectives, critically evaluating news stories, political campaign ads, press releases, policy statements, and politicians' claims (from the Annenberg Public Policy Center at the University of Pennsylvania). FactCheckED.org is specifically designed for classroom use.

- *H-BOT Historical Fact Finder* (http://chnm.gmu.edu/h-bot). Provides answers to historically based who, when, and what questions such as, "Who was Satchel Paige?" or "When did the American League begin?"

- *Cassini Equinox Mission* (http://Saturn.jpl.nasa.gov). Explores a mission to Saturn and provides information about Saturn, its moons, and the spacecraft through images and video (created by the California Institute of Technology Jet Propulsion Laboratory).

Source: Screenshot reprinted with permission of FactCheck.org. Board courtesy of SMART Technologies; copyright © 2001–2009 SMART Technologies ULC; all rights reserved.

experiences. Students need no longer be passive recipients of curriculum; they can be active researchers, analyzers, and presenters of ideas and information.

In summary, information literacy and Internet literacy are grounded in the abilities of teachers and students to play new roles in accessing and then assessing the resources they find electronically. Examples of resources for accessing and assessing information are listed in Tech Tool 2.2.

Active Engagement and Collaboration Using Technology

Information technologies make possible new patterns of active **engagement and collaboration** in classrooms. Engagement and collaboration refer to teaching and learning situations where students work together on academic activities attentively, thoughtfully, and willingly.

Technology creates multiple opportunities for engagement and collaboration. Students are drawn to the dynamism of digital environments that, in Seymour Papert's words, are "fast-paced, immensely compelling and rewarding" (1980, p. 3). In their outside-of-school lives, today's students watch television and videos, text message, use cell phones for conversation and more, surf the Internet, send emails, play video games, use remote control toys, and enjoy other forms of communication and collaboration. Teachers have ready-made opportunities to use students' technology-centered behaviors to promote learning in school. Technologies that promote active engagement and collaboration include

- Student-conducted online polls and surveys
- Collaborative digital storytelling
- Digital games for learning
- Translation software
- Online posters and website publishing
- Student-friendly programming languages and environments

Engaging students is at the heart of teaching. To motivate learning, as the philosopher John Dewey (1943) observed, teachers constantly strive to gain the "outer" and "inner" attention of students. Most of the time, however, educators focus on the outer attention (for example, requiring students to remain quietly in their seats throughout class or copy notes and assignments from the board) while neglecting the inner attention (helping students to think deeply about the topics under discussion). But inner attention is where learning happens. Noted Dewey, "This latter comes fully into being only when the child entertains results in the form of problems or questions, the solution of which he is to seek for himself . . . with growing power the child can conceive of the end as something to be found out, discovered; and can control his acts and images so as to help in the inquiry and solution. This is reflective attention proper" (1943, p. 146).

When used well, technology is a powerful motivator of student learning. For example, inquiry-based software accomplishes three learning goals simultaneously: (1) teaching a content area—math, science, reading, or history; (2) enlarging users' technological skills; and (3) engaging students' "inner attention." In this way, software fulfills Dewey's definition of deeper substantive learning for students. (See Chapter 7 for more discussion about software for teaching all K–12 curricula.)

Active Learning. **Active learning** is the name given to educational activities in which students are directly involved in the learning process. Active learning is also known as "discovery learning," "learning by doing," "inquiry-based learning," or "hands-on learning." Each of these terms suggests that students are focused on and actively engaged in writing, doing experiments, building with blocks and other materials, analyzing documents, working with other students, or using technology.

The idea that students need to experience more active learning situations in school has many supporters. Researchers Steven Zemelman, Harvey Daniels, and Arthur Hyde (2005, pp. 8–9), after reviewing important education reform reports of professional and governmental organizations from the past 30 years (including the National Council of Teachers of Mathematics, International Reading Association, and National Board for Professional Teaching Standards), contend that a "progressive consensus" exists about the changes that need to occur in classroom organization and teacher behaviors, as listed in Table 2.3.

Computer technologies, with their ability to make learning interesting, can promote higher levels of involvement and engagement among students outside of school. In an intriguing study, the national nonprofit organization Computers for Youth (CFY) found that low-income urban adolescents who regularly used computers at home reported greater levels of academic engagement at school (Tsikalas & Newkirk, 2008). That increased engagement also predicted improvements in math achievement scores for sixth- and seventh-graders. CFY recommends educators encourage family computing as a way to support academic engagement and achievement among students.

Less . . .	More . . .
Whole-class teacher-directed instruction (e.g., lecturing)	Experiential, inductive, hands-on learning
Student passivity: sitting, listening, receiving, and absorbing information	Active learning in the classroom, with all the attendant noise and movement of students doing, talking, and collaborating
Prizing and rewarding of silence in the classroom	Emphasis on higher-order thinking and learning a field's key concepts and principles
Classroom time devoted to fill-in-the-blank worksheets, dittos, workbooks, and other "seatwork"	Deep study of a smaller number of topics, so that students internalize the field's way of inquiry
Student time spent reading textbooks and basal readers	Time devoted to reading whole, original, real books and nonfiction materials
Rote memorization of facts and details	Choice for students (e.g., picking their own books, writing topics, team partners, research projects)
Stress on competition and grades in school	Cooperative, collaborative activity and developing the classroom as an interdependent community
Tracking or leveling students into "ability groups"	Heterogeneously grouped classrooms where individuals' needs are met through inherently individualized activities
Use of and reliance on standardized tests	Reliance on teachers' descriptive evaluation of student growth, including qualitative/anecdotal observations

Source: Zemelman, S., Daniels, H., & Hyde, A. (2005). *Best Practice: Today's Standards for Teaching and Learning in America's Schools.* pp. 4–6. Reprinted with permission of Heinemann.

Groupwork and Collaboration in the Classroom. In addition to promoting attentive engagement, technology creates settings where students can work together in thoughtful and productive ways. Such collaboration among classmates is called **groupwork** (students working together in pairs, trios, quartets, or other small-sized groups on an assignment or task) or **cooperative learning** (students working together, often playing different roles within in the group, including notetaker, writer, artist, researcher, teacher contact, or presenter).

In classrooms, groupwork and cooperative learning serve to minimize large- or whole-group instruction by having small groups of students doing different activities at the same time, with the teacher moving among them to facilitate and supervise the learning. "The computer is its own grown-up," one elementary school teacher told us, referring to how computers allow her to create learning centers throughout the classroom. During morning literacy time, a row of four computers direct and maintain the attention of small groups of six to eight children while she instructs reading, writing, spelling, math, or science with groups in another part of the room.

Many teachers tell us that they did not like group learning situations in elementary or secondary school, recalling how the burden of doing the work of the group seemed to fall unevenly on one or two students. Others remember the pressure that came with being asked to play unfamiliar roles in groups such as presenter, recorder, researcher, or writer. For instance, it seemed that the person who was most shy about speaking in front of the group was often designated the presenter. As a result of these unpleasant or

YOUR JUDGMENT
MATTERS

Recalling your own experiences with cooperative learning and groupwork as a student, consider the following questions:

- How successfully did your teachers use cooperative learning and groupwork as an instructional strategy?
- How do you plan to use these teaching strategies when you become a teacher?
- What steps must be taken to ensure that every student is a full participant in a groupwork or cooperative learning lesson?

- *American Memory from the Library of Congress* (http://memory.loc.gov/ammem). Makes available the library's collections under topic headings as wide-ranging as African American history, immigration and national expansion, religion, the presidency, and sports. A section entitled "Today in History" features what happened historically for every day of the year.
- *DNA from the Beginning* (www.dnaftb.org). A multimedia investigation of classical and molecular genetics as well as genetic organization and control. Each genetic concept is presented as an animation or photo gallery, as a problem to consider, or through key resources (funded by the Josiah Macy Foundation of New York to serve the medical and health profession as well as the general public).
- *Planet Tolerance* (www.tolerance.org/pt/index.html). Offers interactive multicultural storybooks and historical research and community action projects for children (from the Southern Poverty Law Center).
- *Web Scrapbook* (http://chnm.gmu.edu/tools/scrapbook). Allows individual students or classroom groups to place electronic information (images, documents, Web pages, and other materials) in an online folder and then discuss and annotate its contents (from the Center for History and New Media at George Mason University).
- *Zoomerang* (http://info.zoomerang.com). An online survey tool that teachers and students can use in their classes to poll classroom, school, or community members.
- *Poll Builder* (http://chnm.gmu.edu/tools/polls). A tool that can be included in a classroom Web page to obtain people's opinions of questions the class is posing (also developed by George Mason University's Center for History and New Media).
- *Discovering Antarctica* (www.discoveringantarctica.org.uk). Teaches historical, scientific, environmental, and zoological information through videos, maps, charts, graphs, puzzles, and activities, as well as describing what research occurs there.

Go to the Assignments and Activities section of Chapter 2 in MyEducationKit and complete the video activity entitled "Promoting Innovative Thinking and Collaboration through WebQuests."

frustrating experiences, some teachers are not eager to plan lessons in which students are engaged in group work or cooperative learning.

The importance and effectiveness of group learning activities in K–12 schools is clear. Well-organized group activities give students control and responsibility over the learning process. As sociologist Elizabeth Cohen noted: "Delegating authority in an instructional task is making students responsible for specific parts of their work; students are free to accomplish their task in the way they think best, but they are accountable to the teacher for the final product" (1994, p. 2). Groupwork does not let students do a task exclusively by themselves, but asks them to make use of the strengths that each student brings to the assignment. Groupwork promotes conceptual thinking by

> solving a word problem in arithmetic, discovering what makes a battery in a flashlight work, interpreting a passage in literature, understanding the phototropic behavior of plants, deciding what is wrong with the grammatical construction of some sentences, role-playing historical events, or learning how to plot a set of coordinates. (Cohen, 1994, p. 10)

In summary, technology facilitates a vision of education based on the idea that when students work together, they will acquire skills and exchange knowledge in ways that create and sustain lasting learning. Web resources for active engagement and collaboration are listed in Tech Tool 2.3.

Feedback Using Technology

Information technologies offer teachers and students an essential element of successful learning—rapid (often nearly instantaneous), self-correcting **feedback** about their efforts. In educational situations, *feedback* is another term for communication between a learner and an instructor. The importance of feedback lies in the presumption that students learn new ideas or skills through regular practice with supportive communication from teachers that is intended to both assess knowledge and improve performance.

Think about some new skill, talent, or activity that you have been learning recently. Perhaps it is operating a new cell phone or iPod, performing a recreational activity like golf or dancing, or learning how to record the information needed for federal and state tax forms. These activities may be self-taught, learned in a class, or acquired in an informal small-group setting. Feedback lets you know when you are proceeding in a positive direction and when you are moving off track. Feedback encourages learning from your successes as well as your mistakes.

Interactive computer software and educational websites, intelligent tutoring systems, and even simple learning machines provide rapid electronic feedback to students. Such feedback is of great importance not only in subjects like mathematics and the sciences where posing and solving problems are at the center of the curriculum, but is essential to virtually every part of school learning. The following list describes more ways that teachers can use technology for feedback.

YOUR JUDGMENT MATTERS

Thinking about different learning situations in which you have received feedback, consider the following questions:

- What kinds of feedback work best for you as a learner: praise, encouragement, criticism, or some combination of all three?
- Do you find that different types of feedback work better for you in different types of situations?

- Tutoring systems and software
- Synchronous communications (instant messaging, real-time chats)
- Asynchronous communications (email, threaded discussions, blogs)
- Student participation systems

- Tablet computers for in-class note taking, writing, and editing
- Handheld calculators
- Global positioning systems
- Interactive educational websites
- Interactive maps and galleries

Lessons from Montessori.   Immediate self-correcting feedback was a fundamental element of Maria Montessori's pioneering educational pedagogy in the early years of the 20th century and remains so today. Her designs of original educational materials (cut-out continent map puzzles that have correct sizes of land masses color keyed to a globe with the same shapes and colors; proportional-length wooden blocks that build a staircase; beads that can be threaded on strings by tens to form a cube of a thousand, and hundreds of other materials) embody three commanding features that attract the inner attention of learners:

- A point of interest that draws children to the materials
- Open-ended exploration that invites children to learn each time they use the materials
- A self-correcting feedback feature that teaches in a nonjudgmental way (Montessori, 1964)

These characteristics combine to capture a child's curiosity and desire to learn independently without the need for constant adult attention and instruction.

Similarly, computer software can deliver feedback to students in ways that are immediately useful. One example is AnimalWatch, an intelligent tutoring program designed to support mathematics learning by children in the upper elementary grades, with a particular emphasis on connecting young girls to mathematical problem solving (see Figure 2.4). Developed by researchers in computer science, psychology, and education

FIGURE 2.4   AnimalWatch

Source: Used with permission of Carole Beal, Professor of Cognitive Science, University of Arizona.

- *Wayang Outpost* (http://althea.cs.umass.edu/wayang/wayangindex.html). An intelligent tutoring project being developed at the University of Southern California and the University of Massachusetts Amherst. The system presents SAT-style geometry problems in the context of a virtual visit to a research station on the island of Borneo. Students engage in mathematical problem solving within an expansive multimedia environment that offers rapid and customized feedback designed to promote math learning and improve user self-confidence in math.

- *Blogs.* Formats for teachers and students to begin using electronic communication systems to generate online discussions about academic topics. It is estimated that a new blog is created every 7 seconds, so the popularity of this mode of communication is great. Adults and students can post ideas and information and then get electronic feedback from others who are interested in commenting on the same topics.

- *Thinkmap Visual Thesaurus* (www.visualthesaurus.com). Works as a semantic relationship tool inviting you to research word meanings and their connections to other words using an interactive mapping program. Words and their related meanings are displayed in a visual format that can be moved and changed on the screen.

- *Online interactive maps and galleries.* Provide engaging feedback for students, who can gain information visually, explore personal questions by interacting with online content, and receive immediate answers to questions. Many organizations provide interactive educational materials, including the National Weather Service (online map of weather warnings, advisories, and forecasts), the Modern Language Association (interactive maps of languages spoken in the United States), the National Endowment for the Humanities (interactive gallery of high-quality color reproductions of masterpieces of U.S. art), and the Public Broadcasting Service (interactive maps to accompany historical and science documentaries).

- *MathMovesU* (www.mathmovesu.com). A Raytheon Company site filled with interactive math experiences ranging from math fact practice to word problems for grades 3–10, with feedback and hints for helpful solving of problems.

- *American Museum of Natural History Presents Ology.* (www.amnh.org/ology). Contains 10 topics: archaeology, astronomy, biodiversity, earth, Einstein, genetics, marine biology, paleontology, water, and zoology. Each offers 10 to 30 different quizzes, games, interviews, puzzles, and activities that explore information and provide feedback in interesting ways.

at the University of Massachusetts Amherst, AnimalWatch uses adventures related to endangered species (such as right whales or giant pandas) as the context for a series of mathematical problems (such as whole number multiplication or addition of fractions) that students must solve in order to learn about more their chosen topic.

Feedback is vital to AnimalWatch's approach to computer-based learning. If students compute the correct answer to a problem, they continue on with their adventure. If an answer is wrong, the system provides encouraging hints and clues for solving the problem. If the student continues to make mistakes, the system will guide the student through the steps needed to solve the problem. The system then adjusts the level of difficulty to easier problems until the student provides enough correct answers for one type of problem to allow the system to offer more challenging puzzles.

New programming languages and environments for children are another example of computer software that provides supportive feedback. Scratch, a programming language developed by the Lifelong Kindergarten Group at the Massachusetts Institute of Technology Media Lab, features jigsaw-shaped symbols and icons instead of complex computer code. Students as young as kindergarteners can click and drag the pieces to make characters move or set in motion a series of events (Johnson, 2007, p. C5). The computer provides immediate feedback so that young designers can assess the impact of their programming decisions. Another excellent programming language software, Squeak, is an open-source problem-solving environment. (See Chapter 7 for more discussion about interactive educational software.) Web resources that provide rapid feedback are listed in Tech Tool 2.4.

Expressing Creativity Using Technology

Information technologies provide teachers and students with powerful ways to express their creativity using electronically generated words, pictures, symbols, and numbers. *Creativity* may be broadly defined as thinking and acting in ways that generate alternative approaches to people, presentations, and problems. Expressing one's ideas creatively is a highly valued talent in virtually every field from the artistic to the commercial. A 2007 report from The Conference Board, for example, found that business executives and school superintendents agree that creativity is an increasingly important, but not easy to find, talent among today's workers (Lichtenberg, Woock, & Wright, 2007).

Consider the following questions about creativity:

- How would you define creativity?
- Can only a few people in society be called truly creative?
- Do you intend to teach in ways that enable your students to be able to express themselves creatively?

Technology offers many ways to promote creativity. Word processing, drawing, design, and paint programs offer writers, artists, composers, engineers, and designers endless venues for self-expression and alternatives that support the processes of creative thinking, what has been called **information technology and creative practices** or **ITCP** (National Research Council, 2003, p. 1). The following list shows some of the ways that teachers and students can use technologies for creative self-expression.

- Writing by students using desktop or laptop computers
- Desktop publishing
- Online publishing of classroom projects
- Design tools

- Digital cameras and imaging projects
- Graphics and photo editing
- Computer animation and moviemaking
- Student-created podcasts and digital video movies

Redefining Creativity. **Creativity** is a much-prized quality in society—especially in business, entertainment, the arts, and popular culture—but is not always clearly understood in schools. Some youngsters are labeled highly creative (or talented and gifted) while many others are not. All students may have innovative ideas to contribute, but some are not asked for their ideas or opinions. Everyone seems to struggle to identify what creativity is and is not, and then how to incorporate it into learning.

Multiple intelligences researcher Howard Gardner located creativity in the actions of historically significant people such as Sigmund Freud, Albert Einstein, Pablo Picasso, Igor Stravinsky, T. S. Eliot, Martha Graham, and Mahatma Gandhi, who "solve problems, create products, or raise issues *in a domain* in a way that is initially novel but is eventually accepted in one or more cultural settings" (1994, p. 116). Social psychologist Mihaly Csikszentmihalyi (1996) contends that for an idea or contribution to be truly creative, it must pass the test of time and the judgment of many evaluators. The teenage Mozart, for example, was uniquely talented, but the society-altering impact of his compositions came over time as musical conventions changed profoundly from his influence. In this view, those who are acknowledged to be "creative" are those whose accomplishments enriched life and changed the course of history.

By contrast, most children and adolescents display their creativity in personal ways within family and school environments. Some draw, paint, or sculpt; build with blocks or clay; or explore outdoor landscapes or interior mindscapes. Others express themselves on bikes, skateboards, roller blades, or basketball courts. Still others play musical instruments, act in plays, or write stories and poetry. To be creative, children do not need to design, compose, or develop something no one has done before; they may need only to say or do things they have not thought or done before in quite the same way or style. The creative can be what is new to the individual, not new to the world.

Computers give novelists, essayists, poets, journalists, and everyday writers a qualitatively different experience from working in paper and pen. Noted one art critic:

> The computer has enabled artists to create works, and new types of work, never before possible: intricate images that could not be created by hand; sculptures formed in three-dimensional databases rather than in stone or metal; interactive installations that involve Internet participation from around the globe; and virtual worlds within which artificial life forms live and die. (Wands, 2006, p. 8)

For students in schools, computers transform the process of expressing one's ideas creatively using writing. Writing electronically features speed and flow as ideas emerge in lighted letters on a computer screen. From initial freewriting and brainstorming to final editing and publishing, writers have different ways to produce creative work. Technology profoundly affects those who are designing electronically, calculating electronically, and painting electronically. In every instance, these technology users might at first do things that seem not too different from what they can do with traditional design, calculation, or painting materials. But once images are present on the screen, amazing creative transformations are possible. From simply copying an original image, or adding details, color changes, and size modifications, to animating all of the images in a slide show or movie with added sound and text, technological tools inspire new ways to express ideas.

There is evidence that writing on computers positively affects student performance on standardized tests (Silvernail & Gritter, 2007). Since 2002, Maine has provided all seventh- and eighth-graders and their teachers with a laptop computer under a statewide one-to-one computing initiative. *One-to-one computing* means a school provides one computer for every student. A comparison of student writing scores on a statewide writing assessment for 2000 (two years before laptops) and 2005 (three years after laptops) found significant improvements among students across the state. An average scoring student in 2005, noted the authors of one study, "scored better than approximately two-thirds of all students in 2000" (Silvernail & Gritter, 2007, p. 1).

Strong gains in test scores were also found among students who used laptops as part of a writing process instructional model. (For more on writing process and technology, see Chapter 10.) An average scoring student who used computers in all phases of the writing process scored higher than 75 percent of students who did not use laptops in their school writing.

Seymour Papert's Vision of Technology Learning Environments.   An eloquent and expansive vision of how technology promotes creative self-expression can be found in the writings of MIT professor, mathematician, and artificial intelligence researcher Seymour Papert. In a series of books—*Mindstorms* (1980), *The Children's Machine* (1993), and *The Connected Family* (1996)—he set forth a sweeping vision of teaching and learning transformed by computers. According to Papert, as technology propels active engagement and creative thinking, it creates continuous opportunities for teachers to make children's thinking integral to the learning process.

Papert refers to the "child as builder" and technology as essential tools for constructing new and expansive intellectual understandings. Two key ideas, first expressed in *Mindstorms*, have been constants in his books and articles. First, "it is possible to design computers so that learning to communicate can be a natural process, more like learning French by living in France than like trying to learn it through the unnatural process of American foreign-language instruction in classrooms." Second, "learning to communicate with a computer may change the way other learning takes place" (1980, p. 6).

For Papert (1980, pp. 8–10, 179), a fundamental distinction exists between how children learn in nonformal, everyday environments such as the family or the neighborhood and how children learn in the regulated settings of schools. Outside of school, children acquire many skills—for example, learning to talk—"painlessly, successfully, and without organized instruction" through "real participation and playful imitation." However, these same qualities are not found in most schools. As typically arranged, a school classroom is "an artificial and inefficient learning environment."

To connect children to more natural ways of learning math, Papert created electronic environments where children, using computers, were free to explore and invent what happened when they used the LOGO computer language to program an electronic "Turtle" to move around a computer screen in response to a series of commands. As children move the Turtle, they are "learning how to exercise control over an exceptionally rich and sophisticated 'micro-world'" (1980, p. 12). Turtle geometry introduces concepts of shapes, sizes, angles, spaces, and places in ways that allow children to build "hierarchies of knowledge" on which understandings about the world can be firmly and permanently based. Some of these understandings are mathematical and some are broader and deal with learning about learning. Throughout, children were learning a basic foundational principle: "In order to learn something, first make sense of it" (1980, pp. 60, 63).

For Papert, LOGO learning was the foundation of a broader goal, expressed in *The Children's Machine,* where technology can "create an environment in which all children—whatever their culture, gender or personality—could learn algebra and geometry and spelling and history in ways more like the informal learning of the unschooled toddler or the exceptional child than the educational process followed in schools" (1993, p. 13). Moving forward, technology will make possible "megachange in education as far-reaching as what we have seen in medicine, but will do this through a process directly opposite to what has driven change in modern medicine. Medicine has changed by becoming more and more technical in its nature; in education, change will come by using technical means to shuck off the technical nature of school learning" (Papert, 1993, p. 56).

PEARSON myeducationkit

Go to the Assignments and Activities section of Chapter 2 of MyEducationKit and complete the video activity entitled "Learning Chemistry in a Virtual Laboratory."

New Patterns of Electronic Communication.

Technology enables teachers and students to express creativity through new patterns of communication—among people who know each other and among those who do not. Email, instant messaging, blogs, message boards, and other communication tools make possible both immediate (synchronous) and delayed (asynchronous) exchanges of ideas and information. Tablet PCs feature a real-time inking technology that in a classroom setting can enhance note taking while making possible instantaneous teacher-to-student information transfer. For instance, an instructor might add visuals and notes on a tablet computer as part of a classroom presentation. All the students in the room immediately receive those materials on their tablets for subsequent reading and review.

Electronic communication senders and receivers combine elements of face-to-face interactions with those that have been traditionally created by letters, postcards, and memos. In some cases, old issues emerge in new forms. Passing notes in class has become interacting with friends by text messaging. Teachers and administrators respond by adopting strict policies about cell phone use in school. In other cases, entirely new communication patterns may emerge, as when teachers and students engage in online discussions of topics using a blog or wiki, reading other people's ideas and responding to what others have written. (Electronic communication is explored in more depth in Chapters 8 and 9.)

In addition to its speed, informality, and access to friends, electronic communication technologies offer children and adolescents authentic occasions for speaking, reading, and writing. Some youngsters are reluctant communicators in school assignments, unable to see how writing an essay, conducting a science experiment, interpreting a primary source, or solving a math problem has relevance to their lives. Those same individuals are eager to talk, read, and write about topics personally meaningful to them. The key to learning for these students is creating environments for communication in schools where children and adults value the activities of reading, writing, and speaking. In such literacy-rich settings, notes reading researcher Yetta Goodman, "Children are involved in what they are writing about; they know why they are writing and what purposes it serves. Children see their writing as authentic experience, important to their personal lives, and they take their work seriously" (quoted in Wilde, 1996, p. 197). Web resources for creativity are listed in Tech Tool 2.5.

- *West Point Bridge Design Contest* (http://bridgecontest.usma.edu). An online design competition where middle and high school students try to create the least expensive bridge possible that will pass a simulated load test (see accompanying screenshot); users can test the viability of their creative designs on the computer (from the United States Military Academy).

- *Our Authors—Live!* (www.stonesoup.com/listen). Presents middle and high school students reading their recorded short stories aloud online, providing a dramatic publishing venue for young writers of all ages (from the magazine *Stone Soup*).

- *Poetry Writing with Jack Prelutsky* (http://teacher.scholastic.com/writewit/poetry/jack_home.htm). Offers an online writing workshop for young poets as well as audio clips of the poet reading some of his poems in dramatic, engaging ways (from Scholastic).

- *Educational Uses of Digital Storytelling* (http://digitalstorytelling.coe.uh.edu). Features strategies and examples of digital storytelling, a form of creative expression produced by combining the art of storytelling with the multimedia tools of graphics, audio, video animation, and Web publishing (from the University of Houston). See also the Center for Digital Storytelling, an organization located in Berkeley, California (www.storycenter.org/index1.html) for more examples of how to record personal stories using a variety of new technologies.

- *Poetry 180: A Poem a Day for American High Schools* (www.loc.gov/poetry/180). Poems for every day of the school year (from the Library of Congress).

- *Can I Have A Word? Creative Writing in the Classroom* (www.barbican .org.uk/canihaveaword). Invites explo-ration of four topics: the human body, changing voices, the elements, and the odyssey. Through videos where words related to the topic ap-pear, students experience the topic dramatically before writing about it in creative assignments and activities.

Source: Screenshot reprinted with permission of the U.S. Military Academy at West Point. Board courtesy of SMART Technologies; copyright © 2001–2009 SMART Technologies ULC; all rights reserved.

FOCUS QUESTION 1: What are the implications of the latest research in the science of learning for teachers?

- The latest research in the science of learning emphasizes active student engagement and a focus on metacognitive thinking to build what has been called a student-centered or knowledge production approach to teaching.

- Such research findings represent a challenge to instructional methods that feature mainly lectures and presentations by teachers to students—what can be called a teacher-centered or knowledge reproduction approach to teaching.

FOCUS QUESTION 2: In what ways does technology promote unique, powerful, and transformative learning for students?

- Computers and other information technologies, when used creatively by teachers, can redefine and dramatically change how teaching and learning is conducted in K–12 schools.

- Focusing on unique, powerful, and transformative learning experiences is a compelling way for teachers to envision using technology in teaching.

- Information technologies make possible five unique, powerful, and transformative learning experiences: visual learning, accessing and assessing information, student engagement and collaboration, feedback, and creativity.

FOCUS QUESTION 3: How do students use technology for learning visually?

- Video, multimedia presentations, software programs, Internet sites, and graphing calculators are ways to present information visually and dynamically.

- Visual literacy involves the skills needed to read and assess many types of visual presentations.

FOCUS QUESTION 4: How do students use technology to access and assess information?

- Internet sites, computer search engines, electronic encyclopedias, and CD-ROM/DVDs give teachers and students unparalleled access to information.

- Information literacy includes the ability to locate, evaluate, and use information effectively. Internet literacy involves the skills to locate, evaluate, and use online information.

FOCUS QUESTION 5: How does technology create student engagement and collaboration?

- Online surveys, digital storytelling, online publishing, discussion boards, and wikis create new patterns of engagement and collaboration for students and teachers.

- Active learning (also called inquiry-based or discovery learning) refers to the direct involvement of students in educational activities. Groupwork and cooperative learning are two highly effective ways to promote active learning in classrooms.

FOCUS QUESTION 6: How does technology provide feedback to support learning?

- Email, instant messaging, threaded discussions, blogs, student participation systems, and handheld calculators offer rapid and thought-provoking feedback to students and teachers.

- Feedback supports students' curiosity and desire to learn on their own without a constant need for teacher direction.

FOCUS QUESTION 7: How can students express their creativity using technology?

- Word processing, desktop publishing, design tools, digital cameras, digital video movies, and podcasts support expressions of creativity by students and teachers.

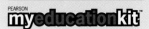

- Fostering creativity involves establishing conditions in schools where students express new ideas, create new approaches, and envision new solutions.
- Using computers for writing and electronic communication establishes new patterns of self-expression and interaction among students.

KEY TERMS

Active learning
Behaviorism
Cognitive science
Constructivism
Cooperative learning
Creativity
Data visualization
Engagement and collaboration
Feedback
Groupwork
Information literacy

Information technology and creative practices (ITCP)
Inquiry learning
Internet literacy
Learning groups
Metacognitive thinking
One-on-one tutoring
Transmission teaching
Visual learning
Visual literacy

ACTIVITIES FOR YOUR TEACHER PORTFOLIO

1. TECHNOLOGY'S IMPACT ON TEACHING

Can every part of the job of teaching be affected in positive and productive ways by computers and other information technologies? To begin answering this question, make a list of everything teachers do and see what roles computers and other information technologies might play in that work. Use the accompanying list to get started.

- Where are the clear benefits of using technology?
- Where is technology not helpful, even counterproductive, to teachers?

Work of a Teacher	Positive Role for Technology
Lesson planning	Word processing; online lesson planning templates
Student recordkeeping	Databases and spreadsheets, online grading software
Home–school communication	Email, classroom or teacher websites, blogs
Academic research	Internet resources, DVDs, WebQuests
Interactive and inquiry-based learning experiences	Educational software, educational websites, digital cameras, video
What other work do teachers do?	What other positive roles can you see?

Work of a Teacher	Negative Role for Technology
Safety and security	Surveillance and violations of privacy
Academic research	Unlimited borrowing from online sources
What other work do teachers do?	What other negative roles can you see?

2. TECHNOLOGY AND CURRICULUM FRAMEWORKS

Examine the connections and references to technology in the national curriculum frameworks published by the National Council of Teachers of English (NCTE), National Council of Teachers of Mathematics (NCTM), National Science Teachers Association (NSTA), National Council for the Social Studies (NCSS), and Association for Childhood Education International (ACEI), as well as the International Society for Technology in Education (ISTE). These curriculum frameworks are available online at the website of each of these professional organizations. Write about how you plan to meet these national expectations in your teaching.

Next, examine the connections and references to technology in your state's curriculum frameworks for English/language arts, mathematics, the sciences, history/social studies, and educational technology. State curriculum frameworks are available online at each state department of education website. Write about how you plan to meet these state and local expectations in your teaching.

3. TECHNOLOGY'S IMPACT ON PEOPLE'S LIVES

If you have access to students through an observation or practicum, ask your students how they think the lives of earlier generations may have been transformed by technology. Given the society-altering changes that have been created by computers and other new technologies, students today may assume that they are the first generation whose lives have been totally changed by technology. Ask the students to consider the historical transformations generated by earlier large-scale technological changes such as television; motion pictures; the automobile; electricity; railroads; the telegraph; the printing press; or ancient innovations such as the wheel, iron, and steel.

- What other technological developments should be added to this list?
- Write a short paper on how one of these technologies might have changed the lives of earlier people or altered their societies or have them write a brief summary of their findings.

3 Developing Lessons with Technology

In a digital world, no organization can achieve results without incorporating technology into every aspect of its everyday practices. It's time for schools to maximize the impact of technology as well.

—State Educational Technology Director's Association, International Society for Technology in Education, and Partnership for 21st Century Skills, *Maximizing the Impact: The Pivotal Role of Technology in a 21st Century Education System* (2007)

CHAPTER LEARNING GOAL

Technology-Based Lesson Planning and Assessment

Using technology tools to support how teachers develop and evaluate learning experiences for students

CONNECTING to the NETS

NETS-T

2 Design and Develop Digital-Age Learning Experiences and Assessments

NEW TECHNOLOGIES

- Web-based lesson development resources
- Electronic grading software
- Web-based K–12 testing policy information
- Online rubrics and quizzes

CHAPTER OVERVIEW

Chapter 3 discusses how teachers plan, deliver, and assess lessons that engage students and teach academic content while integrating technology into all aspects of lesson development. Two models of lesson planning, student learning objectives and understanding by design (UBD), are explained, as are the differences between test and performance assessments. Two sample lesson plans are developed step by step in the chapter so you can see ways to use technology throughout the lesson development process.

By focusing on lesson planning and lesson assessment, this chapter addresses NETS-T Standard 2, Part a, which calls for teachers to design digital-age learning experiences and assessments that promote student learning and creativity. The chapter also connects directly to NETS-T Standard 2, Part d, by providing students with multiple and varied formative and summative assessments of their academic work.

FOCUS QUESTIONS

1. What is meant by "lesson development using technology"?

2. What are the "student learning objectives" and "understanding by design" (backward design) models of lesson planning?

3. How can teachers use technology to make decisions about meeting educational standards in their lesson plans?

4. How can teachers evaluate and assess their students?

I think of the best lessons when I am cooking dinner. As I stand at the stove and listen to music and news on the radio, I get excited about what I will teach the next day. Somewhere between the cooking of the food and the beat of the music, the plans come as movies that play in the mind. It is there that I draft and redraft the way a lesson might work, who might find it interesting, how I will engage the whole class and individual students, and how I will assess what my students have learned. Planning and assessing my lessons while cooking makes me feel the most like an artist.

This vignette of a teacher designing lessons as she prepares dinner introduces this chapter's learning goal—how to make technology part of your process of developing successful lessons for your students.

Teachers rarely create a meaningful class on the spur of the moment. While there are many occasions of joyful spontaneity in teaching, teachers work from plans and they evaluate their performances. A novelist produces an overall structure for a book and then proceeds to write multiple drafts, using feedback from readers and editors to refine the characters, plot, and dramatic events. An actor reads through a script to gain a sense of the story before researching the history of the time and developing a character's personality while learning the scene-by-scene lines. Teachers produce a broad vision and structure for their curriculum before organizing lessons into a sequence of activities and evaluations for students and themselves.

Developing lessons does not require tightly scripting every interaction or rigidly adhering to a fixed plan. Effective teachers provide room for spontaneity and time to explore questions and topics that are on the minds of the students. They recognize that well-designed classes retain structure and direction and that planning allows the leeway to vary an original design and then come back to it according to the flow of the class. Without a plan (or following a poorly designed plan), students easily become distracted or disinterested, moving through activities without a clear sense of purpose or engagement.

Some teachers, especially veterans, may appear to develop lessons effortlessly. "She has her plans in her head," one student teacher observed about her cooperating teacher, who never wrote her lessons on paper, but always seemed to know exactly what to do next at any point in the school year. That teacher held broad goals in mind about what to accomplish and how to accomplish it. Years of teaching experience facilitated the freedom to begin teaching a lesson, monitor student responses, make adjustments and changes as the situation demanded, and continue making progress—all without appearing to plan the action of the day. But when asked about her procedures, the teacher explained how carefully she thought about each of the activities included in the school day as well as how closely she observed each student's progress to determine the course of the next day and the next week.

However, as a beginning teacher, you will not have the background knowledge that develops from having taught academic topics many times. You have less experience with deviating from your original plan to follow the flow of student questions or interests and then seamlessly returning to your planned activities. You are less familiar with different ways to assess student learning. As a beginner, you need plans and you need to write them down—both as a broad outline and the specifics of who is doing what with which materials. Plans and assessments are road maps charting the course and directing the learning for students and teachers.

In this chapter, we explore the advantages and the complexities of developing lessons using technology, specifically how computers, the Internet, and other digital tools support teachers in selecting academic content, planning lessons, and assessing student learning. We also contrast test assessments (also called *traditional assessments*) and performance assessments (also called *alternative* or *authentic assessments*).

Using technology in lesson development does not mean planning all your lessons on a computer or asking students to use technology during every classroom activity. It means instead to always keep in mind technology's broad potentials and to recognize the ways technology can contribute to how teachers develop lessons.

CONNECTIONS and POSSIBILITIES

Online Lesson Help

"What do I teach Monday?" is a curriculum question familiar to every teacher, whether new to the profession or experienced in the work, who faces decisions about what he or she is going to do academically with the class every day of the week and every time of the day. These lesson development decisions are part of what gives teaching its immense joy—the process of continually creating new learning experiences for students—and its intrinsic frustrations—the fact that there is more curriculum to teach than enough time to teach it.

Before computers and the Internet, teachers generally answered the "What do I teach Monday?" query by working with other teachers, consulting school curriculum guides, reading books and professional journals, and gathering materials from libraries and school resources. Today, educational websites include resources to improve teaching and extend knowledge of curricular topics. With computer-based electronic tools to aid searches for ideas and materials, teachers have easy online access to detailed and proven teaching and learning materials from educational websites whose resources for "Monday" and every other day provide ongoing lesson development for every teaching field.

Two examples of websites that offer comprehensive lesson development resources are the National History Education Clearinghouse and the National Center for Improving Student Learning and Achievement in Mathematics and Science (NCISLA). They provide lesson plans, highlight the latest research in the field, and provide collections of resources for creating lessons with a teacher's own students in mind. Each site functions as an up-to-date teacher learning and professional development resource center.

The National History Education Clearinghouse, developed by the Center for History and New Media at George Mason University and the History Education Group at Stanford University, offers "History Content" that includes website reviews, online lectures, and links to national history centers; "Best Practices" that provide exemplary teaching ideas, including multimedia

examples; "Teaching Materials" that feature a searchable database of state-by-state history standards, customizable lesson plans, and online discussion forums; and "Issues and Research" that have short updates on research and analysis in the fields of history and history education. There is a weekly quiz and an "Ask the Historian" feature where teachers and students can post their historical questions online to receive answers from noted history researchers. Reading these questions and answers offers many curriculum ideas as well.

The National Center for Improving Student Learning and Achievement in Mathematics and Science (NCISLA), a partnership of mathematics and science educators from universities in the United States and the Netherlands, features online articles and resources for teaching math and science in elementary, middle, and high schools along with links to curriculum-related resources from many educational organizations. It reports about recent research being done by university researchers and K–12 teachers on such topics as "algebraic reasoning in the elementary grades," "statistics in the middle grades," and "modeling for understanding in science education."

CONTACT INFORMATION

National History Education Clearinghouse

http://teachinghistory.org

Center for History and New Media, George Mason University
Stanford University History Education Group

National Center for Improving Student Learning and Achievement in Mathematics and Science (NCISLA)

http://ncisla.wceruw.org

University of Utrecht (the Netherlands); University of California–Los Angeles; University of Massachusetts–Dartmouth; University of Miami; Peabody College, Vanderbilt University; and University of Wisconsin–Madison

Lesson Development Using Technology

Lesson development refers to all the activities that teachers do as they create, teach, and evaluate lessons with students. Lesson development (Figure 3.1) involves a teacher's decisions about three interrelated elements of teaching lessons:

- Academic content (what to teach)
- Teaching goals, methods, and procedures (how to teach)
- Learning assessments (how to know what students have learned)

Lesson development using technology involves how teachers use electronic resources to facilitate these processes.

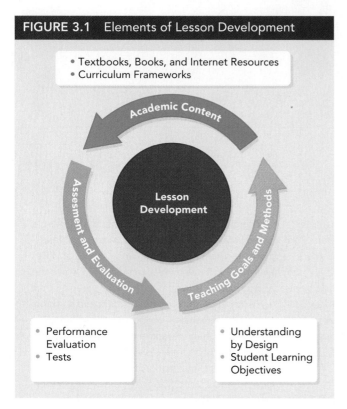

FIGURE 3.1 Elements of Lesson Development

- Textbooks, Books, and Internet Resources
- Curriculum Frameworks

Academic Content

Lesson Development

Assessment and Evaluation

Teaching Goals and Methods

- Performance Evaluation
- Tests

- Understanding by Design
- Student Learning Objectives

Academic Content (What to Teach)

Every time they teach, teachers make choices about **academic content**—the facts, concepts, ideas, skills, and understandings they intend to share with students. Clearly, school system guidelines and state and national curriculum frameworks define and in some cases mandate "what to teach." Lesson development must be connected to local curriculum frameworks, which are aligned to state and national standards. However, because no local curriculum or national standard spells out everything to teach about any given topic, classroom teachers must make choices about what will be explored or explained to students each day.

Technology plays an essential role in assisting teachers to answer the academic content or "what to teach" question. Digital content available on the Internet includes a vast collection of curriculum resources and information. Using Internet search engines, electronic databases, online encyclopedias, blogs, wikis, and other technology tools, teachers and students have access to powerful new ways to research and retrieve information. More about how to use the Internet for locating and using digital content can be found in Chapters 5 and 6.

Teaching Goals, Methods, and Procedures (How to Teach)

As they answer the "what to teach" question, teachers simultaneously decide the **teaching goals, methods, and procedures** they will use in their classes. Goals are the reason why a lesson is being taught. Methods are the instructional strategies—large groups or small groups, discussions, lectures, role-plays, simulations, case studies, inquiry-based activities, creative writing, learning and reflection journals, drill and practice exercises, online tutors, or learning games—that teachers use to convey academic content to students. Procedures are the scheduling and grouping of students by teachers during a lesson, including how much time each activity has allotted to it.

Teachers combine goals, methods, and procedures into formats for daily learning. Sometimes curriculum content dictates these processes; sometimes the goals, methods, and procedures dictate the choice of content. Either way, content, goals, methods, and procedures mutually support each other in a dynamic process of lesson development, which technology can support in a variety of ways, such as the following:

- Presentation software
- Visual thinking software
- Web-based diagram- and flowchart-making tools
- Teacher-developed websites
- Threaded discussions and email

- Podcasts, blogs, and wikis
- Interactive software
- WebQuests
- Intelligent tutoring systems
- Digital cameras and movie-making software
- Assistive technologies

These and other technology-based teaching methods are discussed in more detail throughout Part Two of this book.

Learning Assessments (Knowing What Students Have Learned)

Learning assessments occur before, during, and after teaching lessons and enable teachers to evaluate student knowledge, understanding, and performance. They can be summative (summarizing what students have learned at the end of a lesson), formative (happening as a lesson unfolds), or diagnostic (preceding a lesson as a way to measure what students already know) (McTighe & O'Connor, 2005). Assessment tools include multiple-choice and short answer tests, essays and other written tasks, oral discussions, teacher observations, class participation, and student projects, portfolios, and performances, all of which provide evidence of what students have learned and are able to do as a result of the teaching. Technology tools that support the assessment and evaluation process include

- Electronic tests and quizzes
- Digital portfolios
- Personal response systems
- Online surveys
- Online evaluation rubrics

These assessment technologies are discussed in this chapter and in Chapter 11.

Lesson Development in Action: Two Science Lessons

To guide our discussion of lesson development using technology, we use two science lessons, "Ecological Footprints" (a biology lesson for high school students) and "Rainscapes Show the Water Cycle" (a science lesson for elementary school students), as mini case studies.

Ecological Footprints: A High School Biology Lesson. "Ecological Footprints" shows students the impact that modern lifestyles, including their own, have on environmental resources. Every group of people leaves a lasting impact on the environment through natural resource consumption and waste accumulation—their "ecological footprint." As students document their own ecological footprints, they are in a position to assess the current and potential future impact of their lifestyles on the world's natural resources. The lesson challenges every student to identify ways to live on the planet without destroying it.

Rainscapes Show the Water Cycle: An Elementary School Science Lesson. "Rainscapes Show the Water Cycle" introduces students in grades 1 through 4 to the water cycle (also known as the hydrologic cycle), including the science concepts of evaporation, condensation, and precipitation, processes that are essential to life on earth, which is not possible without fresh water. By studying the water cycle, children understand how water is naturally recycled from the earth's surfaces to the atmosphere and back again, changing its characteristics from liquid to gas and back to liquid.

VOICES
from the classroom

An elementary school teacher comments on the ways technology supports her goals of higher-order thinking by students.

Technology does best in enhancing the understanding of goals. It is not the "know." The know is easy; you can read that in the book and write it. The technology gets you to that higher order of thinking; it gets you to understand that goal. It [technology] will give a visual that will get you to the "understand." For example, if you are using a video clip, you can see the significance. History classes have traditionally been taught in that know stage of memorize, test, memorize, quiz, memorize, test. It is not the way I learned history; I don't find it particularly interesting to just memorize and answer multiple-choice items.

In this lesson, small groups of children conduct water cycle observations, organized around making their own rainscapes. A rainscape is a plastic container into which a small amount of water is placed. When left alone for a short period of time, the water in the bottom of the rainscape will evaporate to the top, where it condenses, or turns back into water droplets, creating a small rainstorm that falls by simply tapping on the top of the container. Children investigate what happens when different-sized containers are placed near a window where there is lots of light or in a darkened corner, or when they are located outside on a picnic table in the direct sunlight or under a picnic table in the shade. Rainscapes, regardless of shape and location, serve as mini-environments for understanding the processes of evaporation, condensation, and precipitation.

The "Ecological Footprints" and "Rainscapes Show the Water Cycle" lessons raise important issues for teachers to consider as they design lessons that address the "what to teach," "how to teach," and "how to know what students have learned" questions. Using specific examples from the two science lessons, we show how teachers in the field have addressed these issues while including ways technology supports teaching and learning.

Approaches to Lesson Planning

Teachers' goals, methods, and procedures determine the structure of learning for whole-group, small-group, and one-on-one instruction. Organizing those three elements is *lesson planning*, and it typically follows one of two different approaches—student learning objectives or understanding by design (UBD).

Student Learning Objectives

Go to the Assignments and Activities section of Chapter 3 in MyEducationKit and complete the Web activity entitled "Planning for Instruction."

You may be familiar with **student learning objectives;** many planning, assessment, and instructional methods courses introduce this framework of lesson development. Student learning objectives are the intended or planned outcomes of your instructional activities—not the activities themselves. Objectives

1. tell *who*
2. is going to do *what*
3. *when*
4. *how much* or *how often* and
5. how it will be *measured* or *evaluated.*

Student learning objectives emphasize outcomes—specifically, what "students will be able to do" after the lesson is taught. With these learning statements in place, a teacher identifies teaching methods, writes out the lesson procedure, and states what forms of assessment will be used to measure student performance. Examples of learning objective statements for the "Ecological Footprints" and "Rainscapes" lesson plans are shown in Figure 3.2.

Planning Using Understanding by Design

Understanding by design (UBD) (also called *backward design*) is an approach to curricular development set forth in the books *Schooling by Design* and *Understanding by Design* by Grant Wiggins and Jay McTighe (1998, 2007). UBD has three main components:

- *Stage 1: Identify desired results (enduring understandings and essential questions).* To provide a frame for student exploration of a topic, the teacher identifies the lesson's **enduring understandings and essential questions.** These statements and questions are the big ideas or relevant information that students will remember long after the lesson has been taught.
- *Stage 2: Determine acceptable evidence (assessment strategies).* The teacher decides what kinds of evidence will show that students have learned the material and can articulate information and ideas about the enduring understandings and essential questions. Evidence includes papers,

FIGURE 3.2 Student Learning Objectives for Two Science Lessons

Ecological Footprints	Rainscapes
Student Learning Objectives	**Student Learning Objectives**
Students will be able to	*Students will be able to*
Calculate an ecological footprint.	Draw a diagram of the water cycle and its essential processes or act out the water cycle during a class simulation.
Connect the ecological impacts of their lifestyles with ways to reduce these impacts.	
Discuss the ecological impacts of human actions in developed and third-world societies to define the concepts of "sustainability" and "sustainable growth."	Identify evaporation, condensation, and precipitation as parts of the water cycle.
Offer insights into global ramifications of wealth and poverty through the comparison of ecological footprints of rich and poor nations.	Discuss the future consequences of changing water amounts on the earth, from lack created by drought to overabundance from melting polar ice, rising sea levels, or wildly changing weather patterns.
Are there other objectives you would add?	**Are there other objectives you would add?**

performances, or other products that students create using the new knowledge they have learned. Decisions about assessment thus precede the writing of objectives and procedures for the lesson.

- *Stage 3: Plan learning experiences and instruction (objectives and methods).* Many of the same elements found in a student learning objectives lesson plan are present in a UBD design lesson plan. The teacher chooses learning objectives, identifies teaching methods, and crafts a plan of how a lesson will be conducted.

The key ideas of the two science lesson plans, stated in terms of enduring understandings, are shown in Figure 3.3.

Using Technology in Lesson Planning

The Internet provides vast electronic resources for supporting lesson development using the student learning objectives and understanding by design approaches. Already assembled lesson plans on virtually every topic and innumerable ideas for designing engaging learning experiences

FIGURE 3.3 Enduring Understandings for Two Science Lessons

Ecological Footprints	Rainscapes
Enduring Understandings	**Enduring Understandings**
Human behaviors change our planet's ecological balance, sometimes damaging the environment in dangerous, hard-to-fix ways. For the sustainability of the planet, people must learn to live in ways that do not compromise the ability of future generations to meet their needs.	The water cycle is an essential component to life on earth. Without fresh water, life is not possible.
	Different environmental conditions—for example, temperature, ocean currents, drought, and floods—create different outcomes in the cycle.
People face choices about how much space and resources are required for humans to live the way they choose to live.	Because only 1 percent of the earth's water is available for consumption, water-wasting or water-conserving behaviors by people influence how much water will be available in the future.
There are crucial decisions about how much space and resources other species on earth require if they are to survive.	
What other enduring understandings would you add?	**What other enduring understandings would you add?**

Computer technologies change every aspect of a teacher's work, including how to plan lessons, keep records, and communicate with students, families, and colleagues.

for students are available free at educational websites such as Thinkfinity, PBS Teachers (see Tech Tool 3.1 on pages 68–69), Discovery School, and EDSITEment. Educational websites are explored in more detail in Chapter 6. Tech Tool 3.1 also includes Gliffy, a Web-based diagram- and flowchart-making tool.

Many organizations provide downloadable lesson planning templates featuring the student learning objectives and UBD models. For example, the Digital Literacy website maintained by the Media Working Group at Portland State University in Portland, Oregon, provides the following templates:

- Student Learning Objectives Lesson Plan Template at http://digitalliteracy.mwg.org/curriculum/lesson.html
- Understanding by Design Lesson Plan Template at http://digitalliteracy.mwg.org/curriculum/template.html

TrackStar—available from ALTEC (Advanced Learning Technologies in Education Consortia) at the University of Kansas Center for Research on Learning—is another portal to teacher-authored lesson plans featuring both student learning objectives and UBD models. While searching the net for resources, you can attach annotated bookmarks to various websites and access a searchable database of bookmarks authored by other teachers.

Meeting Educational Standards

As they consider "what to teach" (the academic content) for their lesson plans, many teachers list the essential ideas, key information, and important skills they want students to learn. Questions arise in choosing what to include and what to omit from the list, stemming from the reality that there is too much information in every curriculum area that students need to learn. Every teacher must make decisions about what to explore in detail, what to teach more broadly, and what to mention in passing. Age of students, time available, and accessibility of materials are some of the influences on teacher choices. But even after choosing topics that are grade-level appropriate, there will still be more information to teach than there is time to teach it.

National Curriculum Frameworks

Curriculum frameworks and learning standards guide your choices of "what to teach." Virtually every academic discipline taught in elementary and secondary schools has national, state, and local standards for teachers to follow in planning their curriculum (see Table 3.1 for a list of national curriculum standards).

The curriculum frameworks directly applicable to the "Ecological Footprints" and "Rainscapes" science lessons are the National Science Education Standards from the National Science Teachers Association and the Educational Technology Standards for Students from the International Society for Technology in Education (see Figure 3.4 on page 70). Environmental topics are also included in the framework of the National Council for the Social Studies (NCSS).

National curriculum standards narrow "what to teach," but these general frameworks leave considerable discretion about "how to teach" a topic. State and local frameworks may direct you to specific topics, but you will still have to make decisions about academic content and teaching methods. And as you make these decisions, you must consider another equally important and helpful aspect of lesson development—learning assessments.

TABLE 3.1 National Curriculum Standards for Major Academic Subjects

Teaching Field	Professional Organization	National Standards for Teachers
English	National Council of Teachers of English (NCTE)/International Reading Association (IRA)	*Standards for the English Language Arts*
Science	National Science Teachers Association (NSTA)	*National Science Education Standards*
Mathematics	National Council of Teachers of Mathematics (NCTM)	*Principles and Standards for School Mathematics*
Social Studies	National Council for the Social Studies (NCSS)	*Expectations of Excellence: Curriculum Standards for the Social Studies*
Elementary education	Association for Childhood Education International (ACEI)	*Elementary Education Standards*
Early childhood education	National Association for the Education of the Young Child (NAEYC)	*Preparing Early Childhood Professionals: NAEYC's Standards for Programs*
Foreign languages	American Council on Teaching of Foreign Languages (ACTFL)	*National Standards for Foreign Language Education*
Special education	Council for Exceptional Children (CEC)	*Programs for the Preparation of Special Education Teachers*
English as a second language education	Teachers of English to Speakers of Other Languages (TESOL)	*ESL Standards for P–12 Teacher Education Programs*
Health/physical education	American Alliance for Health, Physical Education, Recreation and Dance (AAHPERD)/ American Association for Health Education (AAHE)	*Standards for Health Education Programs* *Standards for Initial Programs in Physical Teacher Education Programs*
Reading	International Reading Association (IRA)	*Standards for Reading Professionals*
Educational computing and technology	International Society for Technology in Education (ISTE)	*National Educational Technology Standards for Teachers (NETS-T)*

 ## Assessing and Evaluating Students

As teachers plan and deliver lessons, they must simultaneously design ways to assess what students are learning. Planning, teaching, and assessing are directly connected, but they sometimes become separated when teachers think about their work in the classroom. Choosing academic content and creating engaging activities for students seems paramount when beginning a lesson or unit; assessment is left until near the lesson's completion. We see this misconception as beginning teachers submit lesson plans containing exciting, engaging instructional ideas, but limited or underdeveloped methods for assessment. Not surprisingly, new teachers are unaware or unsure of the different ways they might assess students' learning. Three factors strongly influence how teachers think about assessment:

- *Personal experiences.* Teachers tend to teach the way they were taught and assess the way they were assessed. High school teachers whose

YOUR JUDGMENT
MATTERS

As you look at the list of national frameworks in Table 3.1, consider these questions:

- Have you closely read the national standards in the area(s) you are teaching?
- What part of the standards do you find useful to you as a teacher?
- What elements of your day-to-day work as a teacher are not covered in the standards?
- As a matter of policy, should teachers use common standards established nationally or specific standards set at the state or local level?

One of the central challenges of teaching is finding new and creative ways to engage students with academic content, but trying to design learning experiences and envision different instructional approaches by oneself is very difficult. Teachers benefit immensely from online resources where they can view how other educators have organized learning experiences for students.

Thinkfinity and PBS Teachers are two widely visited lesson development sites offering academic content, instructional models, and assessment strategies. Teachers seeking answers to "What do I teach on Monday morning?" will find countless resources for curriculum and instruction in these Internet sites.

Verizon Thinkfinity

Thinkfinity, shown in the accompanying screenshot, is a gigantic storehouse of some 50,000 curriculum ideas and standards-based lesson plans, arranged by grade level and subject matter and searchable by key words. The term thinkfinity means "endless possibilities for learning and infinite intelligence," according to its primary sponsor, the Verizon Foundation.

Launched in 1997 under the name Marco Polo, Thinkfinity's partner organizations maintain subject-specific websites in the fields of English/language arts, mathematics, arts, geography, economics, history, and science that can be accessed separately or through the Thinkfinity Web portal.

Educational Organization	Website Name
National Council of Teachers of English and International Reading Association	Read/Write/Think
National Council for Teachers of Mathematics	Illuminations
National Endowment for the Humanities	EDSITEment
National Geographic Society	Xpeditions
Kennedy Center for the Performing Arts	ArtsEdge
National Council on Economic Education	EconEdLInk
Smithsonian Museum of American History	Smithsonian
American Association for the Advancement of Science	Science Netlinks

PBS Teachers

PBS Teachers is an extensive resource for educators from the Public Broadcasting Service, featuring thousands of lesson plans, professional development opportunities, videos, and blogs. There are on-demand streaming videos from selected PBS programs plus a special blog entitled "Media Infusion"

teachers lectured to them must unlearn the impulse to make lecturing their predominant mode of instruction. Similarly, teachers who took many multiple-choice tests and quizzes in elementary and secondary school often assume these tests are the best way to measure the learning of their students. Teachers do not automatically envision using portfolios, creative writing, groupwork, daily conversations, or other assessment tools with students if these techniques were not part of their own experiences as K–12 or college students.

- *Standardized testing.* A dramatic rise in **standardized testing,** accelerated by the 2001 No Child Left Behind (NCLB) law, is a major factor in all teachers' practice of assessing student learning. Standardized testing is an enormous enterprise in this country. FairTest, a testing

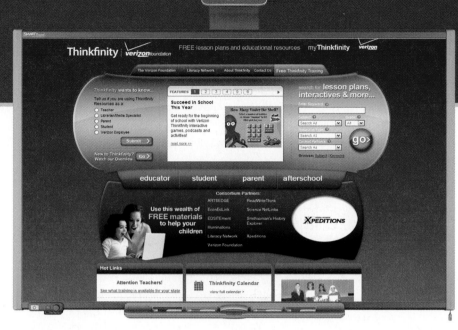

devoted to the integration of media and technology in the classroom. From this blog, teachers can learn useful strategies for infusing technology into instruction and assessment from other teachers.

Gliffy

Gliffy is a Web-based diagramming tool that teachers can use to create classroom floor plans, student seating charts, diagrams, flowcharts, and other types of visual information displays.

CONTACT INFORMATION

Verizon Thinkfinity   www.thinkfinity.org   Thinkfinity is available free of charge online.

PBS Teachers   www.pbs.org/teachers   PBS Teachers is available free of charge online.

Gliffy   www.gliffy.com   Gliffy provides basic services for free and offers enhanced features for a fee.

industry watchdog group, estimates that 100 million standardized tests are given to K–12 students in the United States every year. Children take standardized tests from kindergarten through high school, with more and more of these exams serving as **high-stakes tests,** where grade-level promotion or school graduation hinges on passing a test. Elementary school children may take 6 to 10 or more tests every year in reading, writing, mathematics, and speech and language, while middle and high school students have ongoing tests of proficiency in language arts, mathematics, science, and history. Within a climate of test score accountability, teachers can easily conclude that the only tests that matter are the ones that rank order students according to their numerical scores on local, state, and national exams.

PEARSON
myeducationkit

Go to the Assignments and Activities section of Chapter 3 in MyEducationKit. Open the Web activity "Thinkfinity" to further explore this Tech Tool.

FIGURE 3.4 National Curriculum Standards for Two Science Lessons

Ecological Footprints	Rainscapes
National Science Education Standards/Science and Technology Standard	**National Science Education Standards/Earth and Space Science Standard**
As a result of their activities in grades 5 to 8 and 9 to 12, all students should develop	As a result of their activities in grades K to 4, all students should develop
• Understandings about science and technology (including identifying a problem, proposing alternative solutions, evaluating the solution and its consequences, and communicating the problem, process, and solution)	• Understandings about changes in earth and sky
Science as Inquiry Standard	**Science as Inquiry Standard**
As a result of their activities in grades 5 to 8 and 9 to 12, all students should develop	As a result of their activities in grades K to 4, all students should develop
• Abilities necessary to do scientific inquiry	• Abilities necessary to do scientific inquiry
• Understanding about scientific inquiry	• Understanding about scientific inquiry (including the ability to plan and conduct a simple investigation)
National Educational Technology Standards for Students (NETS-S)	**National Educational Technology Standards for Students (NETS-S)**
Standard 1: Students demonstrate creative thinking, construct knowledge, and develop innovative products and processes using technology.	Standard 1: Students demonstrate creative thinking, construct knowledge, and develop innovative products and processes using technology.
Standard 4: Students use critical thinking skills to plan and conduct research, manage projects, solve problems, and make informed decisions using appropriate digital tools and resources.	Standard 4: Students use critical thinking skills to plan and conduct research, manage projects, solve problems, and make informed decisions using appropriate digital tools and resources.
What other state or local learning standards would you add?	**What other state or local learning standards would you add?**

- *Teacher tests.* Tests for teachers powerfully influence how teachers think about assessment. Most states require new teachers to pass a test before earning a teacher license. Many states use Praxis, an exam developed by the Educational Testing Service (ETS), while other states use customized teacher exams from the Evaluation Systems Group of Pearson. The goal of teacher tests is to ensure that anyone receiving a license to teach has the competencies needed to do the work, as shown by passing scores in reading, writing, and knowledge of academic content fields. New teachers might naturally assume that students must be assessed in the same way that they themselves were assessed and that passing a standardized test is the only truly valid assessment format.

No single definition precisely explains the concepts of evaluation and assessment. Educators generally define **evaluation** as what teachers do as they finish a lesson or unit to grade student performance. **Assessment,** by contrast, happens throughout a lesson or unit as a teacher constantly monitors student performance to determine who is learning easily and who may need individualized assistance, differentiated teaching methods, or alternative learning experiences.

Assessment's main goal, states one education evaluation researcher, is "reading the learner's mind or determining 'where the learner is'" (Genishi, 1997, p. 39). This is an exceedingly complex task. It is difficult for a teacher (or any adult) to determine what is going on in a student's mind, and whatever someone concludes is open to different interpretations.

Some assessment experts believe that **test assessments** (sometimes called *traditional assessments*) best determine "where the learner is" academically, showing what a student knows about a particular subject at a particular time. Test scores symbolize or "stand for what is in the minds of students" (Genishi, 1997, p. 45). In effect, the student's performance on the test is converted "into a number or quantitative statement (e.g., quality of spelling, quality of work on social studies assignment)." Such measurements are deemed "objective" because "students taking a standardized test take it under virtually the same conditions and their responses will be scored in identical ways" (Genishi, 1997, p. 37).

On the other side of the debate, experts counter that **performance assessments** (sometimes called *alternative* or *authentic assessments*) more truly demonstrate *"what learners can actually do in classrooms in the course of the day"* (Genishi, 1997, p. 43). Products, performances, publications, and presentations by students document what they know and how proficient they are in English, math, science, history, or other subjects. Such evaluations offer tangible evidence of the knowledge and skills students have learned in class. You, as a new teacher, will be expected to utilize both test and performance assessments to measure student learning. See Tech Tool 3.2 (page 72) for more information on educational testing policies.

Go to the Assignments and Activities section of Chapter 3 in MyEducationKit and complete the video activity entitled "Assessing Technology-Based Learning."

Test Assessments

To help you understand how to use assessment and evaluation more equitably for all learners, we examine test and performance assessments in more detail, including how technology supports these activities. Test assessments quantify student performance by assigning a numerical or letter grade derived from a score on a test. The basic premise is the same whether tests are local, state, or national exams given to everyone in a school district or quizzes created by individual teachers for their own students.

Norm-referenced tests compare a student's performance to other students of the same grade or age. Test takers are ranked according to how high or low they score in comparison to the norms set by the larger group. The results typically follow a bell-shaped curve with a small number at the high end, a small number at the low end, and a large number in the middle. Many of the tests given in schools are norm-referenced, including such national exams as the Iowa Comprehensive Test of Basic Skills; the Metropolitan, Stanford, and California Achievement Tests; and Tests of Academic Proficiency. An IQ test is a norm-referenced test, as are others that place student results on rank-ordered scales to determine school readiness, developmental levels, or reading or math proficiency.

Criterion-referenced tests compare a student's performance to specific objectives or standards, not to other students. Test takers are evaluated according to their own performance, and because the criterion-referenced test scores are not arranged on a bell-shaped curve, it is possible for many students to score well or poorly depending on what they know about the questions on the test. A driver's license exam is a criterion-referenced test, as are the informal quizzes or tests that teachers create to check students' recall or application of specific academic material. Figure 3.5 (page 73) presents examples of test assessments from the "Ecological Footprints" and "Rainscapes" lessons.

Using Technology: Electronic Grading Software. Many teachers use **electronic grading software** as a virtual recordkeeping system. Electronic grading software is a computer program enabling teachers to quickly calculate and record student grades on a computer. This software can be a stand-alone program for a teacher's personal use—such as Gradekeeper or Easy Grade Pro—or it can be part of a large virtual recordkeeping system purchased by a school district for all teachers to use. School- and districtwide systems manage grades, keep track of attendance, support lesson planning, manage teacher correspondence, and perform other administrative and class management functions.

The advantages of electronic grading software include its capacity to efficiently calculate and store multiple forms of student performance

YOUR JUDGMENT
MATTERS

In thinking about your role as a teacher in assessing students, consider the following questions:

- What different types of assessments have you experienced as a learner?
- Which assessment formats do you like best? Least?
- How might you use test assessments as a teacher? What information might be best assessed by a test?
- What might you use performance assessments (portfolios and other performance-based methods) to show you about student learning?
- What are the strengths and drawbacks you see in each approach?

Teachers face an ongoing challenge in keeping track of state and national policies concerning the standardized testing of students and educators. In more and more schools, test results are used to set educational policies and priorities, including the hiring of teachers. Fair Test: The National Center for Fair & Open Testing is an online resource that teachers can use to keep informed about testing policies and the wider debate in education about the usefulness of standardized tests in assessing student learning.

Fair Test is an assessment reform advocacy organization based in Massachusetts that seeks "to end misuses and flaws of standardized testing and to ensure that the evaluation of students, teachers, and schools is fair, open, valid, and educationally beneficial." The accompanying screenshot shows a page from the FairTest site dealing with K–12 testing resources for teachers.

Fair Test maintains a clearinghouse of information about testing policies at all educational levels, including testing in K–12 schools and colleges throughout the nation, disputes over test scoring errors, misuse of test scores, efforts to reform the No Child Left Behind law, impact of tests on minority test takers, gender bias in standardized tests, and other prominent testing-related issues. It provides examples of alternatives to tests, including schools that have deemphasized test scores as criteria for evaluating student learning.

CONTACT INFORMATION

Fair Test: The National Center for Fair & Open Testing www.fairtest.org
Fair Test is available free of charge online.

FIGURE 3.5 Test Assessments for Two Science Lessons

Ecological Footprints	Rainscapes
Test-Based Assessments	**Test-Based Assessments**

Exam Question

Which of the following steps will reduce the impact of the U.S. ecological footprint on the environment?

a) Recycling of paper and waste

b) Water conservation

c) Driving 55 miles an hour

d) All of the above

Quiz Question

Ecology is the scientific study of

a) interrelations between living things and the environment

b) living organisms

c) the earth's seas and oceans

d) the planet earth

Short Answer Test Question

What are the characteristics of the ecological footprints of humans living in modern industrial societies?

What other test-based assessments would you add?

Exam Question

Which of the following terms is NOT part of the water cycle?

a) Precipitation

b) Conservation

c) Evaporation

d) Condensation

Quiz Question

Which of these conditions are NOT necessary for the rainscape to work as a model for the water cycle?

a) Enclosed container

b) Plants

c) Moisture in the container

d) All of the above

Short Answer Test Question

What process occurs to make condensation at the top of the rainscape container?

What other test-based assessments would you add?

---

data from tests and quizzes, assignments, homework, participation, and other activities. Teachers can assign percentage values to different types of work (for instance, 50 percent of the student's grade is based on test scores, 25 percent on writing assignments, 15 percent on homework, and 10 percent on class participation), and the software instantly calculates the overall grade. Electronic calculation allows teachers to quickly report the performance of individuals and the entire class. Students have immediate access to their grades, and families are continually informed about a child's progress in class.

At the same time, electronic grading systems contribute to concerns about how to best assess what students know and are able to do. Not all school activities, particularly at the elementary level, translate into a numerical score equaling a grade of A, B, C, or D (Lacina, 2006). The academic performance of young learners is more nuanced than test assessments fully measure. For example, wrong answers on a test question may reveal important misconceptions for teachers to address with further instruction (Kopriva, 2008). Using test assessments to record only the right answers and enter a summary score into the virtual recordkeeping system may make teachers less inclined to look at the answers that students get wrong. In so doing, pivotal teaching moments may be lost.

As a teacher, you will likely be in a school that uses some form of virtual recordkeeping, and you may want to have your own electronic gradebook system as well. While such tools simplify the work of teachers, the success of electronic grading software depends greatly on how you use the information it provides about the progress of your students.

Instructionally Supportive Assessment. In critical response to the growing standardized test movement, some educational researchers have proposed new ways to think about the role of assessment in schools. Reviewing years of research on standardized tests, Anne Davies (2004) unequivocally concludes that "the way to improve student achievement is not to do more testing—or more drill and practice for test taking—but rather to engage students deeply in the classroom assessment process and increase the specific, descriptive feedback they receive while they are learning" (p. 1). She endorses blending three types of evidence—student work products, teacher observations of student learning, and teacher–student conversations and conferences—to produce a nuanced picture of what students know and can do with the information and skills they are learning in school.

According to UCLA professor W. James Popham (2002), the current "avalanche" of standardized tests has set in motion three undesirable consequences for students and teachers:

1. "Rampant curricular reductionism," where teachers focus only on the information and skills covered on a test.
2. "Excessive test-focused drilling," where teachers abandon a more wide-ranging curriculum in favor of activities designed to teach to the test.
3. "Outright dishonesty," where teachers adjust the test conditions so students do better or, in some instances, actually give students answers to difficult questions.

For students, the joy and purpose of learning is sapped away as they have fewer and fewer opportunities to explore topics that do not appear on the tests.

In Popham's view, we need better tests rather than no tests at all. Traditional assessments are designed to show differences among students using "comparison-focused measurement." However, what these tests mostly show is that students from higher socioeconomic backgrounds do better in school than children from low-income families. Popham campaigned for the development of tests that provide **instructionally supportive assessment** so that teachers can use the results during the school year to identify and respond to specific student learning needs.

Rethinking the use of achievement tests was also the focus of the Commission on Instructionally Supportive Assessment (2001), a prominent education reform group that urged states to make test results more explicitly useful to teachers in the field. The commission, chaired by W. James Popham, was convened by five education organizations, including the National Elementary and Secondary Principals Association, the National Middle School Association, and the National Education Association.

In the context of the commission's report, "instructionally supportive assessment" meant that educational decisions for students should not be based on the results of a single state-mandated test, although such a test can provide useful evidence of student progress and need. Instead, the commission (2001) urged states to "identify a small number of content standards, suitable for large-scale assessment, that represent the most important or enduring skills and knowledge students need to learn in school."

At the same time, and to avoid an adverse narrowing of the curriculum, states should develop "optional" assessments for content standards not included on the statewide test and support teachers in providing a "rich and deep curriculum" to students. Furthermore, the commission stressed that states must create alternative assessments (such as portfolios, performance testing, and panel reviews) for students with learning disabilities, those speaking English as a new language, and those with other special educational needs.

Other educational organizations have also developed statements about the appropriate role for test assessments. The National Council of Teachers of English (NCTE) has straightforwardly rejected a "sole reliance on standardized tests" to measure student performance, offering instead the following recommendations:

- Assessment must include multiple measures and must be manageable.
- Consumers of assessment data should be knowledgeable about the things the test data can and cannot say about learning.
- Teachers and schools should be permitted to select site-specific assessment tools from a bank of alternatives and/or to create their own. (Assessment and Testing Study Group, 2004)

To encourage the use of such practices in schools, NCTE urged, among other suggestions, that assessment be closely connected to classroom instruction, that locally developed assessments by teachers be used as part of a district's assessment system, and that students become active participants in assessing their own learning with guidance from teachers and parents.

PEARSON

Go to the Assignments and Activities section of Chapter 3 in MyEducationKit and complete the Web activity entitled "Exploring Assessment."

Effective assessment, in NCTE's view, requires that teachers integrate multiple assessment resources to produce a more complete picture of student performance. To do so means making comparisons among multiple forms of data. For example, a student who easily grasps key ideas and concepts but acts out in class, is fascinated by and focused when doing science experiments but rarely completes homework, and reads above grade level but does not prepare for tests cannot be easily categorized by any single assessment. To the extent possible, teachers and other school staff will need to combine what they know about each student and formulate strategies that will maximize learning success for every youngster.

Standards-Based Assessments. **Standards-based assessments** (or *standards-referenced testing*) are a recent variation of standardized testing. Standards-based assessment starts with national, state, or district curriculum frameworks that specify what students are expected to know and be able to do at each grade level. Tests are then used to assess the performance of students relative to those national, state, or district expectations. Test takers in a particular subject or academic skill are then grouped in terms of their scores on the standards test as "advanced," "basic," "needing improvement," or "failing."

Presently, many states are implementing mandatory standards-based tests for high school graduation, including New York, Massachusetts, California, Texas, Florida, New Jersey, Minnesota, North Carolina, Ohio, Maryland, and Washington (Center on Education Policy, 2005). In these places, statewide standards establish what high school students are supposed to know or be able to do, usually in English/language arts and mathematics, but in some cases science and history as well. The tests determine who has reached basic competency according to the standards. Such systems involve a hierarchy of tests that measure performance against state standards throughout a child's academic career.

When teachers show computer-based images and graphics on a large scale, students learn by seeing, hearing, and reading the material. Such visual learning methods sustain interest and capture the imagination of everyone in the class.

Some education reformers see standards-based testing as a way to ameliorate inconsistencies in teacher evaluations of students. They contend that there is tremendous variability among teachers in what they teach and how effectively they teach it. One youngster may have a teacher who is highly skilled in math while another child's teacher may have a much weaker base of mathematical knowledge, yet both students receive good math grades. "What does a grade really mean in such a situation?" critics ask, because there is no common measure of what each child knows or is able to do mathematically. To eliminate such variations, standards-referenced measures are used to compare every student against broad national achievement norms rather than by the teacher they had in school.

Critics of standards-referenced testing see the situation in directly opposite terms. Rather than try to remove the teacher from the process, they believe it is essential to prepare teachers to create their own assessments based on state learning standards and student performance in the classroom. It is the teacher, after all, who is the primary conductor of the curriculum. That teacher knows what was covered, how it was taught, and under what conditions the students are most likely to do their best work and demonstrate what they have learned. For these reasons, individual teachers should be creating the tests for their students—not test writers who work for testing companies far removed from the day-to-day world of the classroom.

Standards-based assessment is now a reality for college students preparing to become teachers, as we discuss in Chapter 11. Over the past decade, major professional educational organizations have issued national standards for teachers and programs that prepare teachers for licensure. Many colleges and universities, notably those accredited by NCATE (National Council for Accreditation of Teacher Education), have incorporated these national standards into their teacher preparation programs.

Performance assessments (also called *performance evaluations*) measure what someone actually does in a certain activity, assessing performance within the context of that activity. A baseball player with a .300 batting average (3 hits in every 10 at bats) is considered to be a high performer at the major league level of the sport. Skydivers who are part of a team executing complete complex aerial maneuvers together strive for a world-class level of performance based on the scores given by judges. A small business owner who successfully expands her network of coffee shops is performing above expectations in a highly competitive business field. In each of these cases—batting average, complexity of aerial formations, and profit margin—performance is measured in tangible, real-world terms.

Performance assessment in education is not the same as standards-based assessment. Tests may be involved, but these assessments regularly include educational activities other than tests. For example, a high school student in an art or design class might be evaluated on a portfolio of drawings and sketches rather than a test of artistic knowledge. In the same way, new teacher candidates in a college or university program cannot receive a teacher license without being evaluated on their performance in the classroom during student teaching. Student teachers are assessed on how well they develop and deliver curriculum, manage classrooms, communicate with students, and handle the many other responsibilities of a full-time classroom teacher.

Performance assessment is an increasingly popular concept in education, although it has many complexities. Policymakers and education leaders, for example, refer to "highly performing" or "underperforming" elementary or secondary schools, designations created by the federal No Child Left Behind (NCLB) Act. In theory, schools whose test scores and graduation rates are high or steadily improving earn the status of highly performing. By contrast, underperforming schools are those that fail to improve as measured by the test-score categories of the NCLB law.

Determining how well a school is performing depends in large part on the criteria used for assessment. In 2006, Massachusetts had the highest test scores in the nation, yet 64 percent of its schools were designated "needing improvement" according to NCLB benchmarks. The paradoxical results stemmed from a provision in the legislation that unless students with special needs show year-to-year continuous improvements on test scores (a very high bar for most schools), the school fails to meet NCLB performance expectations. State education officials responded by seeking a relaxation of federal standards. In other words, they wanted different performance evaluation criteria in determining school success.

Classroom teachers often use performance assessments to evaluate student work. Rather than give a multiple-choice test, they ask for a product, performance, or presentation as a way for students to show what they have learned. For example, to assess what students know about data analysis and statistics, a high school math teacher might ask her students to investigate the calling plans offered to individuals, small business, and large firms by major cell phone companies. Students would then prepare a written report or PowerPoint presentation featuring cost/benefit calculations that include line plots and equations detailing rate changes in cents per minute, with results for all companies covered in the report. Students find such an assignment personally relevant—cell phone rates are a topic they are intensely interested in knowing more about—and academically challenging, since they must demonstrate their knowledge and application of mathematical concepts and number operations.

Figure 3.6 presents examples of performance assessments for the "Ecological Footprints" and "Rainscapes" lessons.

Using Technology in Performance Assessment.   Technology is a powerful resource for teachers engaged in performance evaluation—both of their students and of themselves as new professionals. In Table 3.2 (page 78), the same technology tools are used by teachers to evaluate students and to prepare for evaluations by supervisors of new teachers' performance in the classroom.

Student Performance Rubrics.   As part of performance assessment, teachers use **student performance rubrics** to evaluate student work on course assignments and activities. Student

FIGURE 3.6 Performance Assessments for Two Science Lessons

Ecological Footprints	Rainscapes
Performance-Based Assessments	**Performance-Based Assessments**

Ecological Footprints

Performance-Based Assessments

Discussion Question

Which type of farming produces the largest yields that serve the most people while creating the smallest ecological footprints—organic farmers or large agribusinesses? Which type of farming should be supported by governmental policy and why?

Performance Task

Using writing, drawing, and math, describe your own ecological footprint or that of your family or neighborhood. Provide a detailed description of what resources are used and for what purposes. Make concrete proposals for reducing the wasteful use of resources.

Technology Project

Once you have assembled your ecological footprint analysis and proposals for change, create a technology-based format for communicating this information to other people. You could use PowerPoint as a way to present your findings, or you could create a website, blog, or other educational networking site devoted to ecological topics as a way to get more people involved in sustainability issues. Explain how the technology you are using provides an effective way for you to achieve your information and communication goals.

What other performance-based assessments would you add?

Rainscapes

Performance-Based Assessments

Discussion Question

Discuss how you acted like a scientist in this lesson. Why do you think scientists follow the "scientific method"?

Performance Task

Using writing and drawing, explain how a rainscape works as a model of the water cycle.

- Working in small groups, construct four rainscapes from the same materials. Place each rainscape in a different part of the room, making sure that they all receive different amounts of daylight. Put one under a box and one behind a cardboard or paper screen to shade it from windows.
- Working in the same small groups, observe the rainscapes daily, spending a few minutes at each to compare and contrast what is happening.
- Each group returns to their rainscape to record the daily details and to photograph the container through a side view.
- At the end of the week, each group shares their recorded information, highlighting any differences found in the four rainscapes.

Technology Project

Do a drawing for each stage of the water cycle. Then, using PowerPoint or the Kid Pix software program on the computer, create a slide show that shows the water cycle in action.

What other performance-based assessments would you add?

---

performance rubrics establish known-in-advance criteria to assess student performance, describe in concrete terms the differing degrees of accomplishment needed to meet those criteria, and allow students and teachers to discuss areas where best work has been done or improvement is needed (Edwards, 2001). Tech Tool 3.3 (page 79) discusses online resources for developing rubrics and quizzes.

A single assignment may have several rubrics to assess and grade different parts of the activity. For example, elementary school science students using a problem-solving model might be assessed on at least four separate performances:

- How accurately they define the problem
- How successfully they design a strategy for solving the problem
- How effectively they implement the plan
- How clearly they explain their findings and conclusions

Middle and high school students might receive similar rubrics for their science assignments, but with performance expectations that reflect more advanced work and understanding.

Teachers use rubrics so students have (1) a clear framework for how assignments will be evaluated as part of the course grading process and (2) specific activities or accomplishments to complete to achieve a certain level, score, or grade. As a new teacher candidate, you may be asked to design rubric-based assignments during your student teaching, giving you an opportunity to use this form of assessment with students.

TABLE 3.2 Roles for Technology in Performance Assessment

Technology Tools	Assessments of Students by New Teachers	Assessments of New Teachers by Supervisors
Word processing, PowerPoint, and other computer applications for preparing papers and presentations	Papers and presentations by students in classes	Papers and presentations by new teacher candidates in teacher education classes
Digital portfolios or other computer-based collections of materials	Examples of work completed by students	New teacher-made lesson plans and related curriculum materials
Video and audio tapes or podcasts	Performances by students using academic material	Field observations of teaching
Teacher-constructed websites or digital portfolios showcasing examples of best teaching practices	College admissions or job applications	In-person interviews with future employers

The key to constructing rubrics is identifying what you want students to do as part of a class activity or assignment in specific terms. For example, the statement "I want my students to write a high quality persuasive essay" sets forth a student performance goal. You must now construct a clear rubric to evaluate the essays you receive and to help students construct essays that meet your expectations. For instance, writers must complete the following steps:

- Compose an engaging introduction that captures readers' attention
- State a thesis sentence that clearly advocates a position
- Add interesting and convincing examples that support the argument
- Draft a conclusion that effectively summarizes the main idea in a new way

Stating the items to be evaluated—introduction, thesis sentence, examples, and conclusion—is only the first step. You need to explain to students what makes an introduction engaging, a thesis sentence clear, the examples convincing, and the conclusion summative. If an engaging introduction is one that uses lively language, compelling facts, or a provocative claim to focus the reader's attention on the issue being addressed, then classroom instruction must include these ideas so that the rubric corresponds to material that the students have been learning and practicing in class.

Rubrics require teachers to be relentlessly concrete in their criteria. If "A" is the highest grade on a writing assignment, then "A" specifically means a writer demonstrates critical thinking, applies concepts and ideas at an advanced level, and uses the conventions of written language appropriately. Each of those criteria can be explained in specific terms on a rubric, as follows:

- "Critical thinking" does not mean quoting what other writers have said, but using what other writers have said to formulate one's own view of a subject.
- "Applying concepts and ideas at an advanced level" means that the writer understands the complexities of a subject and can communicate about the subject from more than one point of view.
- "Using conventions of written language appropriately" means that the essay follows the standard conventions of spelling, punctuation, and grammar.

Students can then use their knowledge about how they are being assessed to inform the academic work they are doing for the teacher.

Making an assignment clear, in your own mind and in the minds of your students, is not a simple task. In our persuasive essay example, you, the rubric constructor, might choose to "drill down" into evaluation even further, for example, specifying how many new vocabulary words or how many pages the paper must contain to earn an A, B, C, or D grade. The usefulness of a rubric lies in its level of concreteness and how the criteria are explained to students. Students need to know what constitutes superior, good, poor, or unacceptable performance before they do the work.

PEARSON myeducationkit™

Go to the Tutorials section of Chapter 3 in MyEducationKit and access the practical tutorial entitled "Rubistar Tutorial." Use the tutorial to learn how to create a rubric.

For new teachers, the process of creating rubrics and designing quizzes can be very time-consuming parts of doing all phases of lesson development for the first time. Online rubric and quiz templates can be a helpful resource, allowing teachers to use a preestablished model or modify a template to fit the specific needs of their students. RubiStar and QuizStar, resources from ALTEC (Advanced Learning Technologies in Education Consortia) at the University of Kansas, are two easy-to-use Web-based templates. ALTEC also provides TrackStar, a planning tool mentioned earlier in this chapter.

 **RubiStar**

RubiStar is an online tool for creating rubrics electronically. The RubiStar system provides a set of templates that teachers can either use as written or customize to fit the parameters of a particular assignment. Rubrics are provided in six areas: Multimedia, Products, Experiments, Oral Projects, Research and Writing, and Work Skills. Two types of rating scales are available: numerical (4, 3, 2, and 1) and descriptive (excellent, good, satisfactory, and needs improvement). Each rubric area includes categories; for example, the research report rubric evaluates students on "amount of information, organization, quality of information, sources, and mechanics" (Schaapveld, 2000). Each rubric you make in RubiStar is saved to its own URL so you can access it at any time.

QuizStar

QuizStar provides software for multiple-choice, true/false, and short quiz creation with varied administrative options, including opportunities to review quiz results by class, student, and questions. Multiple data formats can be generated that are compatible with conventional data-processing programs.

CONTACT INFORMATION

4Teachers.org   www.4teachers.org   RubiStar and QuizStar are available for free. Registration is required. In addition, teachers will find a collection of other assessment and evaluation tools as well as other resources that support classroom instruction at all grade levels.

CHAPTER SUMMARY

FOCUS QUESTION 1: What is "lesson development using technology"?

- Lesson development is central to the work of every teacher.
- Lesson development is a process of creative design and decision-making that includes three elements: (1) what to teach, (2) how to teach, and (3) how to know what students have learned.
- Technology tools support all three aspects of lesson development.

FOCUS QUESTION 2: What are the "student learning objectives" and "understanding by design" (backward design) models of lesson planning?

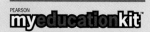
- Student learning objectives emphasize specific skills and information that students will know and be able to use. Understanding by design (UBD)—also called backward design—emphasizes enduring understandings and essential questions that students should learn.
- Successful student learning is the end goal of all lesson planning—whether the organizing schema is based on learning objectives or enduring understanding and essential questions.
- Teachers must decide whether starting with the means (learning objectives) and moving to the ends is a more useful approach than starting with the ends (enduring understandings) and moving to the means that best fit the needs of their students and school.
- Technology helps teachers plan engaging learning experiences and instructional activities through online lesson planning templates and lesson plan websites. These topics are discussed in more detail in Chapter 6.

FOCUS QUESTION 3: How can teachers use technology to make decisions about meeting educational standards in their lesson plans?

- National, state, and local curriculum frameworks help define what academic content teachers must present to students.
- The Internet is a vast source of academic content resources for teachers, who can conduct research and locate materials using Internet research. This topic is covered in more detail in Chapter 5.

FOCUS QUESTION 4: How can teachers evaluate and assess their students?

- Teachers use test and performance assessments to measure the knowledge of students before, during, and after teaching lessons.
- Technology offers multiple ways to conduct test and performance assessments, both as part of traditional measures such as tests and quizzes and in supporting performance measures such as portfolios, exhibitions, and student writing.
- Test assessment includes norm-referenced tests, which compare a student's performance to other students of the same grade or age, and criterion-referenced tests, which compare a student's performance to a set of specific objectives or standards.
- Proponents of standardized tests contend that these tests accurately measure student performance while encouraging schools to reform educational practices. Critics believe that standardized tests measure only a limited amount of student knowledge while forcing schools to deliver a narrow, teach-to-the-test curriculum.
- Standards-based assessment is used to measure student performance in terms of specific national, state, or local standards.
- Instructionally supportive assessment involves the use of multiple forms of evaluation data to provide a more complete picture of what students know and are able to do academically.
- Performance evaluation is based on assessing how students perform when they are asked to complete specific tasks or assignments.
- Rubrics provide known-in-advance performance criteria for students to use in completing school assignments, and as such, offer ways for teachers to more fairly evaluate the work of every student in a class.

KEY TERMS

Academic content
Assessment
Criterion-referenced tests
Electronic grading software
Enduring understandings and essential
  questions

Evaluation
High-stakes tests
Instructionally supportive assessment
Learning assessments
Lesson development
Norm-referenced tests

Performance assessments

Standardized testing

Standards-based assessments

Student learning objectives

Student performance rubrics

Teaching goals, methods, and procedures

Test assessments

Understanding by design (UBD)

ACTIVITIES FOR YOUR TEACHER PORTFOLIO

1. LESSON DEVELOPMENT USING STUDENT LEARNING OBJECTIVES AND BACKWARD DESIGN

After reviewing the "Ecological Footprints" and "Rainscapes Show the Water Cycle" lesson plans, choose a lesson you would like to teach and outline it using a learning objectives format and understanding by design approach.

- How do these frameworks for lesson development differ?

- How are they the same?

- What are their advantages and drawbacks?

- How might you utilize a student learning objectives or backward design model in a 3-day plan for reading groups and in a 3-week plan for science study?

- Do you prefer one format or the other for your lesson planning or does one planning framework work better with one type of lesson rather than another?

2. CURRICULUM DEVELOPMENT: THE LIFE CYCLE OF PLANTS

The life cycle of plants is a common science topic in elementary and secondary schools. Many teachers have students grow bean plants or flowers in the classroom as a way to engage directly in the study of plant biology. How might technology change the study of plants in the lower and upper grades? For example, teachers and students might visit the Plants in Motion website to see QuickTime movies, use digital or video cameras to show plant growth, utilize electronic devices to measure changes in plants, or develop a PowerPoint presentation of their research findings.

- In what other ways might technology be used in the study of plants?

- How might these uses of technology transform the teaching and learning experience?

3. HAVING STUDENTS PLAN A LESSON

Ask your students to plan a lesson for the class as a way to involve them in the processes teachers use to create stimulating learning experiences for their subject. Choose a common topic for the group—such as the planets in the solar system for grades 3 through 6—about which students are likely to have a basic working knowledge. Explain the parts of a lesson plan, and then ask students to design how they think the academic material might best be taught.

Middle and high school students will enjoy a variation of this planning process by learning about Howard Gardner's theory of multiple intelligences (1983, 2000, 2006). Again, choose a common topic that everyone knows about in general, and explain Gardner's eight intelligences (2006): linguistic, musical, logical/mathematical, spatial, bodily kinesthetic, intrapersonal, interpersonal, and naturalist.

Divide the class into groups of four to five students each and give each group two of Gardner's intelligences. Ask them to design a lesson that uses the intelligences specified to teach about the solar system or some other topic. When they have finished, discuss with the students what intelligences they believe they possess most strongly and how they think teachers could use those intelligences in the teaching of English/language arts, mathematics, science, history/social studies, and other subjects.

4

Integrating Technology and Creating Change

MYTH: Teachers need to be experts in technology in order to use it effectively in instruction.

REALITY: Research shows that effective teachers collaborate with students to understand the information landscape and think about its use. Since success with technology depends largely upon critical thinking and reflection, even teachers with relatively little technological skill can provide useful instruction.

—National Council of Teachers of English, *21st Century Literacies Policy Brief* (2007)

CHAPTER LEARNING GOAL	CONNECTING to the NETS	NEW TECHNOLOGIES
Technology Integration and Educational Change Using technology effectively as a teacher to create change in schools	**NETS-T** **5** Engage in Professional Growth and Leadership **NETS-S** **5** Digital Citizenship	• One-to-one computing • Digital pens and digital notepads • Tablet computers • Web-based technology integration resources

CHAPTER OVERVIEW

Chapter 4 discusses technology integration and educational change to help teachers infuse technology into both classroom instruction and professional work. Technology integration issues and strategies are discussed with ways for teachers to address the persistent problems of the digital divide, digital inequality, and the participation gap. Introducing concepts of "infomating" and "automating" (also called "Type I and Type II technology applications"), the chapter examines dynamics of educational change and envisions innovative uses of computers and information tools in teaching. There are also strategies for using whatever technology teachers have in classrooms to promote new directions in teaching and learning.

The chapter incorporates NETS-T Standard 5, Part b's expectation that teachers "exhibit leadership by demonstrating a vision of technology infusion" while "developing the leadership and technology skills of others."

FOCUS QUESTIONS

1. How can teachers integrate technology into their work as educators?
2. What are the key stages and pressing issues of technology integration?
3. What are "digital inequality" and the "participation gap"?
4. What instructional strategies and approaches promote technology integration while addressing the participation gap?
5. How does technology promote educational change?
6. How can teachers create change in classrooms using technology?
7. How can teachers use the technology they already have to promote successful learning?

In a talk several years ago, library scientist Joan Lippincott from the Coalition for Networked Information presented her ideas for making technology an integral part of teaching. Using the controversial 2000 presidential election as a case in point, she described how teachers could incorporate new computer-based technologies seamlessly into a high school study of that seminal event in contemporary U.S. politics, including the following activities:

- Create a PowerPoint presentation about the major party candidates, George W. Bush and Al Gore, and their positions on major issues.
- View video recordings of political speeches and debates from the campaign.
- Post and access course assignments online.
- Research political parties and electoral politics at preselected Internet sites in cooperative learning groups.
- Search online individually for additional class material.
- Share ideas and information among members of the class using email, instant messaging, or a class blog.
- Author multimedia presentations to be shown in class on key aspects of the election and its aftermath.
- Add work done in class to each student's personal e-portfolio.

Tim, a newly hired second-grade teacher, applied Lippincott's technology integration suggestions to a science terrarium study, a popular curriculum activity when winter gives way to spring in the northeast part of the country. The second-graders grow small plants inside an enclosed glass environment in the classroom as nature begins its own growing cycle outside. Tim connected technology to the terrarium study by

- Taking daily digital photographs of bean seeds sprouting on trays and biweekly digital photographs of plant growth inside the terrariums.
- Creating a short movie using the digital photos to show the growth pattern over time of the bean seeds and the terrarium plants.
- Visiting websites containing pictures and text about plants and environments.
- Recording indoor and outdoor temperatures throughout March and April (when winter becomes spring in the Northeast part of the country) with a digital thermometer to make a line graph of the daily temperatures using the Excel software program.
- Utilizing the word processing program on the school's computers for students to report information and observations in a classroom plant journal.
- Viewing Web-based movies of plant growth using a digital projector.

After reading these examples, other ways of making technologies an integral part of the study of politics or plants undoubtedly come to mind. The possibilities are varied and exciting. Websites, educational software, teacher blogs, podcasts, assistive technologies, digital portfolios, and many more of the tools that will be discussed in Part Two of this book can be used at every grade level to successfully teach students.

Strategies for successfully using technology in and out of the classroom—or *technology integration and educational change*—is the primary learning goal of this chapter. **Technology integration** refers to ways that teachers build technology into all aspects of their professional work. **Educational change** refers to innovations by teachers that create new patterns of teaching and learning in schools. Broadly speaking, technology integration and educational change together make technology a central part of education, enabling the unique, powerful, and transforming impacts of computers and other tools to be part of every student's daily experience in schools.

Technology integration and educational change do not automatically occur by including computers or other technologies in a lesson. Two elements are necessary for technology and instruction to create successful learning.

- *Teacher mindset.* Exemplary technology integration starts with a teacher mindset that asks how computers, the Internet, and other resources enable students to best meet curriculum goals and learning outcomes. Before teaching, Joan and Tim identified the key curriculum ideas each wanted to teach—the presidential election campaign or cycles of seasonal change—and then considered how technology might best promote those goals. They followed a basic guideline that "content must come before technology. In other words, technology should be thought of in terms of its effect on the teaching and learning of social studies, and should be considered for use only if it will provide an improvement in one (or both) of these areas" (National Council for the Social Studies, 2006). What is true for social studies is equally applicable to math, science, language arts, or any curriculum area.

- *Multiple pathways.* There are a wide variety of ever-increasing ways for teachers and students to use the technology in their classrooms to achieve important learning goals. Even in classrooms with limited resources, teachers can promote successful learning using technology. New teachers tend to assume that effective technology integration happens only when schools have one computer for every student. Yet, research shows that engaging and exciting instructional activities can occur using only one or two computers (Kozma, 2003). Technology integration is more about how technology is used by teachers than about the amount of technology a teacher has to use.

In many instances, integrating technology into teaching means you are acting as a change agent or an organizational innovator in your school. Technology is still an emerging force, and many schools have been slow to embrace its full potentials. Infusing technology may alter long-standing patterns for teaching and learning, and the potential consequences of those shifts may not be immediately clear. The opportunity to pioneer new approaches is part of the great excitement and creativity associated with technology in teaching, but it takes time to establish innovative practices within the culture of school organizations. As you will see, technology can either **automate** (reproduce existing practices) or **infomate** (change existing practices)—depending on how it is used by teachers (November, 2001).

Technology integration does not mean computer technologies replace nonelectric resources in every teaching situation. Thinking creatively about using technology in teaching means constantly asking, "What can teachers and students do *with* technology that cannot be done *without* it?" Every lesson can be explored to see how technology potentially transforms experiences for students because of its momentum toward creative change. In this way, you, together with your students, discover the power of computer technologies as tools for learning that belong at the center of education in K–12 schools.

Technology and the Work of a Teacher

Teachers' use of technology in teaching can be subdivided in three primary ways (see Table 4.1):

- *Inside-the-classroom teaching tools.* Teachers use technology to present academic material and create interactive learning experiences for students in the classroom.
- *Outside-the-classroom professional resources.* Teachers use technology to manage the administrative and professional demands they face in schools.
- *Inside- and outside-the-classroom learning resources for students.* Teachers ask students to utilize technology in academic learning during class time as well as outside of school.

TABLE 4.1 Educational Uses of Technology by Teachers and Students

Inside-the-Classroom Use by Teachers	Internet research PowerPoint presentations Educational software Educational websites Student participation systems Teacher-made blogs, websites, and wikis
Outside-the-Classroom Use by Teachers	Grade and attendance recordkeeping Professional correspondence Professional and personal writing Research Home–school communication Educational networking
Inside-the-Classroom and Outside-the-Classroom Use by Students	Internet research Group projects Homework assignments Creative writing Math, science, English, or history projects

To be innovative and exciting, technology integration must be meaningfully connected to lesson development and grounded in clear understandings of learning theories and curriculum goals. Otherwise, technology might be treated as an extra activity that appears too complicated and time-consuming to be useful for everyday teaching and learning.

A key to making technology a substantive part of daily teaching is to think *both* technologically and educationally. Electronic and digital tools may enable you to achieve learning goals you have for yourself and your students, as shown in the following examples.

Technology-Based Library

Technology in the form of an Internet-accessible computer gives teachers a vast collection of curriculum and instructional resources, their own **technology-based library.** Never before have teachers and their students been able to locate so much potentially useful information so easily and efficiently. No longer are teachers obligated to spend hours searching for teaching materials. There are Internet sites on every topic imaginable, along with vast databanks of lesson plans and curriculum ideas. Of course, along with useful information comes an immeasurable amount of useless and potentially harmful information. Teachers need electronic tools to (1) help them access and assess information online, (2) catalog and manage information once it is located, and (3) structure how students will use information in the classroom to promote critical thinking, creative problem solving, and inquiry thinking.

Technology-Based Textbook

Every teacher serves as a guide to what students read, from picture books and storybooks in elementary school to textbooks and other reading materials in secondary school. In addition, teachers augment their students' reading experiences with visuals shown in class: photographs, diagrams,

YOUR JUDGMENT MATTERS

As you think about using technology in your teaching, consider the following questions:

- What are specific ways that you can integrate technology into your work as a teacher inside the classroom?
- What are specific ways you can integrate technology into your work outside the classroom?
- How do these uses of technology improve classroom instruction and student learning?

maps, pictures, videos, and so on. Every teacher is now a publisher, editor, and writer, producing a classroom **technology-based textbook.** No longer bound to a single text or teacher's guide or prepackaged curriculum lessons, teachers can go online to find reading materials from every subject area: primary sources for the study of history, science simulations and visualizations, math manipulatives, and stories and poems in audio and video formats, to name a few; the list of creative possibilities goes on and on. Teachers can even author their own materials and post them on classroom websites for students to read and consider. Such expansive varieties of technology-based reading materials make it possible to teach one's subject in new ways to engage students in reading, analyzing, and authoring texts.

Technology-Based Learning Environment

Traditionally, teaching happened during a school day's class time. Teachers were limited in how they could extend learning once class was over. They could assign homework for students to practice skills, do reading assignments, and complete other learning activities that would hopefully make the next in-person class meeting more productive for everyone. But homework is often an individual activity that does little to bring students together in pursuit of learning. A **technology-based learning environment** offers new possibilities for extending the classroom beyond the school day while building a greater learning community in the school. Once class is over, teachers can post notes, discussion questions, extra readings, and assignments on a class website or wiki; students can post their work on the site as well. Online tutors and video clips provide assistance to students who need it. Discussion boards and blogs offer ways for adults and students to continue classroom discussions. Such dynamic environments make learning more interesting and engaging for students.

Technology-Based Teaching Tool

Technology can extend the time that teachers may spend with students, making it possible for teachers to individualize instruction for students who need it. As every teacher knows, some students' learning styles and needs are not well met in a typical classroom setting. Every computer equipped with high-quality software can serve as an always-ready **technology-based teaching tool** that allows teachers to do less whole-group instruction. Teachers might divide a class to have students at the computers, students working individually, and students in a learning group with the teacher, all at the same time. In a similar way, intelligent tutoring systems, speech-to-text and text-to-speech software, handwriting recognition programs, or other assistive technologies meet the needs of individual students by giving them specific tools to help them succeed. Technology gives individuals voice, confidence, and the means to show what they know. This changes how assessment is conducted as well. Students who are lagging behind in a large group may look more competent and be more engaged when experiencing both virtual teaching by machines and direct teaching by adults.

PEARSON

Go to the Assignments and Activities section of Chapter 4 in MyEducationKit and complete the video activity entitled "Tablet Computers."

Technology-Based Office

Technology gives teachers the capacity to organize and manage some or all of their professional work electronically. Whereas teachers from an earlier generation thought in terms of working at their desk, educators today increasingly think about working at their desktop. A teacher's duties can be conducted using multiple forms of information technology—from word processing, email, and blogs for correspondence and communication to grade- and recordkeeping software to manage student homework and attendance records to finance programs to record educational expenses and costs. And with a laptop computer and Internet access, teachers can carry a **technology-based office** with them from place to place.

Emerging Technologies

Do you remember when you first heard the term *Web 2.0* and began to understand its importance for technology-using teachers? The term is new, first appearing in the media as recently as 2004. It refers to interactive technologies that promote new forms of information creation and collaboration among computer users. You probably have heard about such Web 2.0 tools as blogs, wikis, social networking, folksonomies, and podcasts, but you may be far less familiar with how to integrate these emerging technologies into teaching and learning in schools.

As an educator learning about integrating technology into teaching, there are two key ideas to keep in mind about Web 2.0. First, Web 2.0 is more than just various new technological tools; it is a group of new practices among computer users. At the heart of Web 2.0 is the idea of using technology to promote greater communication and interaction among people. Such exchanges allow people to produce knowledge for themselves as opposed to having that information created solely by experts and authorities.

For example, sports fans used to get information about their favorite teams and players by reading newspapers, listening to the radio, and watching TV. Today, using blogs and wikis, those same sports fans can communicate with one another technologically by sharing information collaboratively and extending what they have learned from various media sources. They can add value to their enjoyment of sports by both reading traditional information sources (newspapers, magazines, etc.) and by accessing the new media made possible by Web 2.0 technologies. The same is true for teachers and students who can extend the teaching and learning process by getting knowledge (the goal of education) from multiple sources, both traditional (books, magazines, radio, television) and electronic (blogs, wikis, podcasts, and social networks).

Second, the pace of change in technology continues to move ever so swiftly, with new technology tools as well as newer versions of current technologies constantly arriving on the scene. Some of these technologies will last, and others will not, but as a teacher, you need ways to stay up-to-date about what is happening in the technology field. The Emerging Technologies Database and the Pew Internet & American Life Project are online resources for teachers who want to keep track of the changing world of Web 2.0 technologies.

Emerging Technologies Database

Launched in 2008, the Emerging Technologies Database is an initiative of ISTE (International Society of Technology in Education), one of the nation's leading technology education organizations. ISTE's technology education standards for teachers and students have been widely adopted by K–12 schools as well as colleges and universities that prepare teachers, and we are using them as one of the organizing features of this book.

Created by technology educators Ferdi Serim, Kathy Schrock, and the other members of ISTE's Emerging Technologies Task Force, the Emerging Technologies Database is designed to be an online collection of the best examples of teachers and students using new technologies to positively affect learning in schools. All information is being collected and distributed online. Teachers will not only be able to consult but also contribute to this database.

ISTE is drawing on Web 2.0 tools to document how educators are using Web 2.0 tools in schools. The database focuses on emerging technologies so teachers will have an ongoing and evolving collection of best practices to draw on as they integrate Web 2.0 tools in their classrooms. You can learn more about the project by visiting the ISTE website, watching a video on YouTube, and seeing emerging technology in action at the ISTE section of the virtual world, Second Life.

Pew Internet & American Life Project

A second excellent source of information about Web 2.0 technologies is the Pew Internet & American Life Project, an initiative sponsored by the Pew Research Center, a nonpartisan Washington, D.C.–based organization with funding support from the Pew Charitable Trusts.

The project provides monthly online research reports and memos dealing with the wide impact of new and emerging technologies on U.S. society. Using national telephone surveys as its primary source of research data, these reports cover such areas as "online activities and pursuits," "Internet evolution," "technology and media use," "health," "public policy," and "education." There is also a fascinating section called "Trends" that offers regularly updated information on Internet use and various online activities.

Technology Integration Stages and Issues

Integrating technology into teaching takes patience, perseverance, and willingness to involve students in learning about technology. Unlike the license you earn to become an elementary, middle, or high school teacher, there is no single group of courses and field experiences that, once completed, verify your credentials as an educator committed to using technology well. The process of gaining technological knowledge and expertise comes from applying technology-informed skills and perspectives in a classroom and then learning from those experiences. A technology-using educator can be defined as someone who

- *Makes informed choices* by both using technology wherever it increases student involvement in learning and not using it for tedious, confusing, or boring class activities. Such a teacher places student learning at the center of the curriculum and decides how best to make it happen in the fast-paced environment of a modern school. Sometimes this means using technology as a centerpiece of instruction, sometimes it means using technology as a minor part of a lesson, and sometimes it means not using technology at all.
- *Explores technology* by using it in the classroom while analyzing its role in schools and society. The interworkings of technology and its social, political, and economic implications are natural topics for classroom discussion. Students in a technology-using teacher's classroom are not just consumers of technology but creators and critics of it as well. They are aware of technology's power to improve education or to frustrate it.
- *Promotes change* at the classroom, school building, and system levels. Rather than "change for change's sake," change should be intended to make it possible for every student to reach her or his full learning potential. Technology becomes a "disruptive" force, constantly suggesting that there may be new and better ways to do things. Its presence is an invitation to rethink the way things are and the way things might be and to put into practice curriculum and instruction that builds interest in learning for all students.

Teachers teaching other teachers about technology is an effective way to make sure everyone has up-to-date knowledge about how to use the latest tools to promote learning success for students.

Inclusion and Infusion of Technology

Technology use in schools tends to follow one of two broad patterns: inclusion or infusion. **Inclusion** means that computers and other information technologies are used mainly for traditional purposes of transferring information and practicing skills. They are included, but not made a central part of the day-to-day educational experience of students. Inclusion of computers might involve scheduling every class into the computer lab weekly for 30 minutes for group instruction. Computers are part of the curriculum, but the short time period and whole-group teaching format minimizes the impact of the technology on individual learning.

Infusion, on the other hand, means that computers and other information technologies are ongoing features of teaching and learning in all academic subjects at all grade levels. They are a continuing part of the day-to-day educational experience of students. Infusion might involve equipping every classroom with multiple machines for teachers to use as a regular part of academic instruction or it could mean a single computer is designated as an integral part of daily lessons. As students regularly use computers for research, word processing, educational games, and other classroom activities, technology is infused into daily learning.

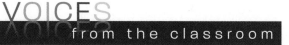

VOICES
from the classroom

An elementary school teacher explained how using different technologies became a genuine learning experience for herself and her students.

We both learned more about PowerPoint and that it is a useful tool that can be adapted to one's needs. We thought about animation and the fact that you can time it to what you need. Also, I learned how to use TaskStream [a teacher website building tool] and how easy it really is. I enjoyed making the website, and it did not take a long time. Finally, we learned how to be flexible with technology and try different methods if the first one does not work.

Decisions about including or infusing technology in teaching practices are opportunities for teachers and students to use new tools in new ways for learning. Ongoing and interesting uses of technology increase student motivation and engagement and that increases everyone's knowledge and creativity as well. Your choices about how to use technology carry great significance because they help shape larger patterns of classroom organization, student interest in learning, and technology integration in schools today.

Stages of Technology Integration

A first step in integrating technology is assessing where you are as a technology-using educator and then taking the steps needed to move to the next level (Kleiman, 2000). Marc Prensky (2005), the computer game pioneer, has characterized this process as moving from "dabbling" to "doing old things in old ways" to "doing old things in new ways" to "doing new things in new ways."

A seminal study by the Apple Classrooms of Tomorrow (ACOT) Project (1995) found teachers to be at one of five stages of technology use in their classrooms:

- *Entry.* Teachers are beginning to learn information technologies. At the **entry stage,** a teacher needs to gain specific skills in how to use computers and technologies before she or he is able to think about how to apply new knowledge to classroom situations.
- *Adoption.* Teachers "blend technology into their classroom practices without making any significant changes to those practices." At the **adoption stage,** a teacher knows enough to use technology in the classroom, but only at a basic level and only occasionally.
- *Adaptation.* Teachers fully integrate "new technologies into traditional classroom practices." At the **adaptation stage,** a teacher is using technology regularly as part of teaching.
- *Appropriation.* Teachers easily and confidently use technology both in the classroom and for their own professional work. At the **appropriation stage,** a teacher is using technology as both an inside-the-classroom and outside-the-classroom tool.
- *Invention.* Teachers start to "experiment with many instructional patterns and ways of relating to students." At the **invention stage,** a teacher is exploring new ways to creatively use technology in and out of classroom as well as adding emerging technologies to a personal repertoire of professional skills and practices.

When teachers make technology a substantive resource for learning, students benefit. K–12 students, the ACOT study found, demonstrated greater accomplishment with technology as well as improved problem-solving and collaboration skills as teachers move along the integration scale from the entry stage toward the invention stage. Significant technology use by students also contributed to a number of other positive learning developments:

- Exploring and presenting information dynamically
- Becoming more socially aware and socially confident
- Communicating effectively
- Acting as an independent self-starter
- Possessing areas of expertise and sharing knowledge spontaneously
- Working well collaboratively
- Having a positive orientation toward the future (Apple Classrooms of Tomorrow Project, 1995)

You may find your students' skills and interests increasing as you develop your skills as a technology-using educator on the ACOT scale.

Features of a Technology-Integrated Classroom

What does a technology-integrated classroom look like? Some observers define a technology-integrated classroom as a "smart classroom," equipped with a computer connected to the Internet, a video projector, a DVD player, an interactive whiteboard, digital pens, a videoconferencing

FIGURE 4.1   Key Features of a Technology-Integrated Classroom

Integration Rubric

(Top score of 5 is given for each of the following)

1. Most students are **independently choosing** the technologies appropriate to their learning objectives.

2. Students are **highly involved** with their teacher and peers **in planning** for the use of technology in a unit or lesson.

3. In group activities using technology, a **high degree of collaboration** is exhibited.

4. When using technology, **most students act ethically** and in accordance with the district acceptable use policy.

5. Most students exhibit **skill in the effective use** of available technologies at or above grade and ability levels.

6. In using technology, most students are **focused on the intended curricular objectives.**

7. Most **specific technology skills are embedded** and learned **in the context of core curriculum lesson** objectives.

8. **Problem solving and higher order thinking** is evident in most students' activities.

9. Most students **are highly engaged** in the use of technology.

10. Student use of technology is based on their **cognitive abilities and physical needs.**

11. Most technology uses represent learning activities that could **not otherwise be easily done.**

Source: Northwest Educational Technology Consortium. (2004). *Observation Protocol for Technology Integration in the Classroom (OPTIC).* Reprinted with permission of Northwest Regional Educational Laboratory.

system, and other interactive tools. In such settings, technology tools serve to empower teachers while engaging and motivating students to learn (Wong, 2008).

Other commentators define a technology-integrated classroom less in terms of tools and more in terms of what kinds of actions and behaviors result from using the tools. The Northwest Educational Technology Consortium has developed a technology integration rubric to assess how technology affects learning (NETC, 2004). Teachers and students are evaluated in the 11 areas of curriculum and instruction shown in Figure 4.1. In the figure, the key technology integration features presented in bold are activities that most students should be doing during class instructional time.

You can examine your school or classroom in terms of NETC's technology integration criteria. In addition, the online technology integration resources in Tech Tool 4.1 will help you further your skills and strategies as a technology-using educator.

Technology Integration Issues

Successful technology integration is affected by a number of issues that arise within the work of classroom teachers.

Administrative Support and Teaching Style.   Successful technology integration by teachers requires professional development training, ongoing support from school administrators, and sufficient resources to make change happen smoothly (Guskey, 2002; Watson, 2001). But a teacher's style of teaching also makes a huge impact on whether technology is integrated into classroom activities on a regular basis. In Chapter 2, we discussed teacher-centered and student-centered approaches to teaching. It can be harder for teachers with a teacher-centered approach to step aside and give over some of the control of classroom learning to students using computer technologies. For example, in one study of teachers using calculators for the first time to teach mathematics, researchers in Britain conducted interviews and found that teachers wanted more

PEARSON

myeducationkit

Go to the Assignments and Activities section of Chapter 4 in MyEducationKit and complete the video activity entitled "Steps to Successful Technology Integration."

The process of technology integration may seem especially complex to new teachers. There is so much to learn as you enter the teaching profession, from curriculum to lesson planning to student assessment to classroom management. For some, it feels as though technology integration is just too much to do with everything else to master. For new teachers facing these pressures, the following online technology integration resources can be valuable guides for how to proceed technologically.

Edutopia

Edutopia: Information and Inspiration for Innovative Teaching in K–12 Schools, a website from the George Lucas Educational Foundation, features a fine collection of technology integration resources. You can find information under the Priority Topics menu.

National Educational Technology Standards for Teachers (NETS-T)

The National Educational Technology Standards for Teachers includes two different types of resources. Its Digital Edge Learning Exchange includes video case studies of teachers who have integrated technology into classroom learning. Additionally, there are rubrics and forms for you to use to assess how effectively you are integrating technology into your own teaching.

NCTE Inbox and NCTE Inbox Blog

NCTE Inbox is a weekly email summary of important stories from the field of English/language arts, including regular updates on technology-related topics and issues. Produced by the National Council of Teachers of English, the Inbox includes hyperlinks to newspaper articles, newly-issued reports and research studies, and important policy statements from NCTE and other education organizations. Every issue includes lesson plan ideas for multiple grade levels. The NCTE Inbox Blog explores many topics of interest to technology-using teachers from any subject field.

CONTACT INFORMATION

Edutopia www.edutopia.org/adopt-and-adapt Edutopia is available for free.

National Educational Technology Standards for Teachers, 2008 (NETS-T) and **National Educational Technology Standards for Students, 2007 (NETS-S)** www.iste.org/AM/Template.cfm?Section=NETS. Available for free online from the International Society for Technology in Education (ISTE).

NCTE Inbox www.ncte.org/newsletter Free online after registering.

NCTE Inbox Blog http://ncteinbox.blogspot.com

training and more resources (Berry, Graham, Honey, & Headlam, 2007). Underlying these issues was a deep concern about how technology would change the dynamics of learning in what had been largely teacher-centered classrooms. Teachers were unsure how to organize small-group activities when they were used to large-group instruction, and some worried that students would ask them questions about the calculators they could not answer. The researchers concluded that teachers need to work together to share ideas and strategies about change rather than approach technology integration by themselves.

Unwillingness to Change Favorite Lesson Plans to Include Technology.   Many teachers have lesson plans and curriculum activities they like to do with students. Having done these activities before, they are eager to repeat them with a new class. For example, right after the school's winter vacation in February, a second-grade teacher might move from a study of different children's book authors to a unit about animals and their habitats to a community study of the town where the school is located. This is the teacher's curriculum every year. If such lessons were initially developed without involving technology, a busy teacher may lack the incentive to spend the time figuring out how to integrate computers, the Internet, or other technological resources into their teaching.

Reluctance to Use Technology When Teaching New Lesson Plans.   Disincentives to use technology occur when teachers are asked to teach material they have not taught before. If a school district realigns its curriculum to meet the requirements of state or national frameworks and assessment tests, a ninth-grade earth science teacher, for example, may be faced with teaching units on biology, chemistry, and physics as part of a redesigned integrated general science course. It takes thought and energy to organize new lesson plans and curriculum units. There are activities to design and papers or tests to assess. Infusing technology may seem like an added burden, so teachers avoid spending the extra time needed to include it.

Using Technology as a Reward or Punishment.   Many teachers, recognizing that students gravitate toward computers and other electronic devices, use technology as a reward or punishment. Youngsters who behave well or finish assignments quicker than others get to use technology as a reward. Conversely, students who misbehave or fail to get work done are denied computer time as a punishment. In these instances, students are not using technology for academic purposes; it is not central to the completion of assignments or the learning of knowledge. The potential power of technology to produce unique, powerful, and transforming learning is minimized. Moreover, reward and punishment situations create a set of destructive classroom dynamics where students come to expect (even demand) tangible rewards to complete every assignment. As social psychologist Alfie Kohn noted: "the more you reward people for doing something, the more they tend to lose interest in whatever they had to do to get the reward" (1999, p. 98). In a continual reward situation, the desire to learn loses out to an expectation that one must always be given something tangible for doing the work.

Using Technology as an Add-On to Other Activities.   Some teachers, responding to school system expectations or mandates, use technology as an add-on feature in their teaching. That is, they use technology whether it enhances or detracts from learning. In such instances, the machines deprive students of better instructional options when there is no real reason to do so. For example, students may watch movies or videos instead of researching a topic or conducting real-world investigations. Occasional video watching makes sense, particularly when students see a few segments at a time, interspersed with other activities, but using videos all the time creates a situation where the technology is replacing the opportunity for hands-on/minds-on learning by students. Another example would be using teacher-made PowerPoints to review key points at the end of a unit. While the PowerPoints may be an effective tool, those same summary points can also be generated in other ways, including student-led discussions and presentations.

Using Technology to Separate Students by Ability Groups. Some teachers have used technology to divide their students according to test scores or perceived readiness to do a certain activity. Under such arrangements, children with higher test scores are given one kind of program while the youngsters with lower scores get another kind. Separate programs seem to make sense because they appear to challenge the high achievers while not frustrating the lower achievers. But dividing a class according to perceived ability groups means that in most situations, high achievers and low achievers are rarely together for the same learning activities. This practice reinforces a sense of haves and have-nots in academic achievement. Fortunately, the multiple dimensions of technology often bring out the talents of lower achieving students in ways that other academic activities might not. Teachers tell us that students who seem underperforming in other contexts become engaged learners, sometimes classroom leaders, when using technology. By not always dividing classes according to perceived ability when using technology, teachers give students opportunities to work together and discover new aspects about each other not revealed in homogenous groupings.

The Digital Divide, Digital Inequality, and the Participation Gap

The digital divide continues to be a persistent and complex technology integration issue (Monroe, 2004). Students from low-income African American, Hispanic, and white families do not have the same level of access to computers and the Internet at school or at home as do their more affluent peers. Research shows that 80 percent of white students aged 5 to 17 use computers at home compared to 47 percent of African American and 48 percent of Hispanic students (U.S. Department of Commerce, 2008). Figure 4.2 shows the disparities in Internet access between whites and blacks and between high school educated and college educated individuals (Fox, 2005).

You will likely find that some students have markedly different experiences with technology because they have markedly different access to technology. Those with reduced access are educationally disadvantaged because they are less able to use and learn from computers and other new Web 2.0 tools. So as you plan how to integrate technology into teaching, you must decide how to enlarge the technology experiences of all your students.

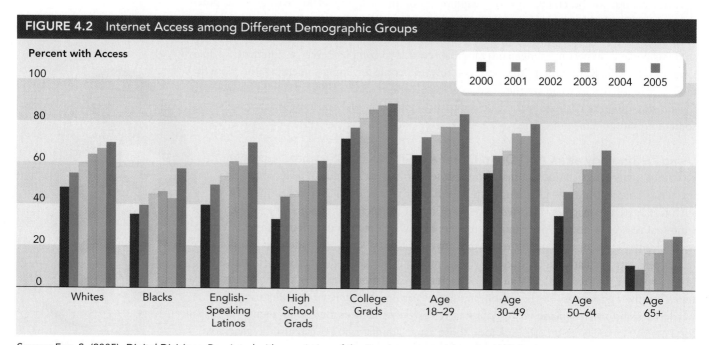

FIGURE 4.2 Internet Access among Different Demographic Groups

Source: Fox, S. (2005). *Digital Divisions.* Reprinted with permission of the Pew Internet and American Life Project.

A Digital Inequality Perspective

In discussing the digital divide, some researchers prefer to use the term **digital inequality** (Hargittai & Hinnant, 2008; Warschauer, 2003a,b). A digital inequality perspective holds that simply adding more machines to homes or schools will not, in and of itself, address differences in access to technology among different social groups. Mark Warschauer, a professor at the University of California, Irvine, has argued that it is insufficient to conclude "that the mere presence of technology leads to familiar and standard applications of technology, which in turn bring[s] about social change" (2003a, p. 44). More technology is not always the best way to solve the very problems that technology itself has helped to create.

Warschauer adopts a **social infomatics** analysis in which technology's impacts are considered within the context of larger social, economic, and political realities. Like living things and their surrounding ecosystems, "the technology and the social system continuously shape each other" (Warschauer, 2003a, p. 44). In theory, families with children who lack home computers might access the Internet and use high-quality learning software in libraries that are technologically well equipped, open nights and weekends, and located in schools or community centers, as many are in urban areas. While library use might not eliminate the digital divide, it could reduce it. In reality, if municipal budget cutting reduces library funding and hours of operation, then government policies serve to extend rather than minimize the digital separation between economic groups in the community.

Henry Jenkins, a professor at the Massachusetts Institute of Technology, has advanced the idea that lack of access to technology creates a **participation gap** between students (Jenkins et al., 2007). Jenkins sees great differences "between what students with 24/7 access can do and what students can do when their own access is through the public library or a school computer" (quoted in Long, 2008). Without ready access, students fall behind their online peers in skills and competencies with technology while also becoming bystanders in today's emerging participatory media culture. These students do not have the same experiences navigating the Internet, playing Web-based games, or engaging in online conversations, the result of which is a diminished degree of media and technology literacy.

Viewing technology in these kinds of systemic terms raises complex issues. Warschauer (2003b) and Jenkins and colleagues (2007) suggest that simply adding computers to schools may actually extend digital inequality rather than reduce it. In many schools, he notes, some students use computers for inquiry-based investigations, experiments, and research projects while other students are confined to mostly electronic worksheets with drill-and-practice exercises. Often, economically advantaged kids get to do more intellectually challenging activities, a consequence of tracking by test scores where some youngsters are seen as talented and gifted while others are defined as lacking proficiency in basic skills. If low-income and minority students are unable to use all of today's technologies as other students do, then access alone will not reduce an inequality of educational outcomes.

Integrating Technology While Addressing the Participation Gap

How can schools support the effective integration of technology into teaching while also responding to issues of the digital divide, digital inequality, and the participation gap? The strategies and approaches described in the following sections can shorten the amount of time teachers spend in large-group instruction and create highly interactive, inquiry-based learning experiences for individual students and small groups. These approaches utilize existing resources in ways that increase access to technology for every student to address the participation gap.

One-To-One Laptop Computing. **One-to-one laptop computing** means every student in a grade, school, or district has her or his own computing device to use in school (Montgomery, Wilson, & McCormick, 2005; Warschauer, 2006; Zucker, 2008). One-to-one programs are

One-to-One laptop computing is an emerging trend in schools today. Giving every student access to a computer promotes active learning and engaging exploration of academic topics.

on the rise. The Anywhere Anytime Learning Foundation of Bellevue, Washington, estimates that there are some 500,000 students in North America (the United States and Canada) involved in one-to-one laptop programs (Vascellaro, 2006). One-quarter of the nation's largest school districts have at least one grade where every student has a laptop while one in three school superintendents have indicated they are implementing one-to-one wireless computing in at least one grade level (Hayes & Greaves, 2006, 2008).

Maine has the largest laptop program, with 70,000 computers distributed to middle school students statewide (Park & Staresina, 2004). Schools in Pennsylvania, Illinois, Indiana, New Hampshire, Michigan, South Dakota, Texas, Virginia, Florida, California, and Massachusetts are also involved in one-to-one initiatives (Gillard, 2008). The city of Birmingham, Alabama, has voted to provide its 15,000 schoolchildren with one of the new XO laptops from the One Laptop One Child Foundation (eSchool News, 2008). Support for one-to-one laptop initiatives have been prompted by three interconnected developments.

- *New machines.* Computer manufacturers keep bringing new generations of powerful, low-cost, ultraportable notebook machines to the marketplace—iBooks from Apple, a host of IBM-compatible machines, and tablet PCs (see Figure 4.3). These notebook computers routinely offer considerable memory, Wi-Fi capabilities, CD-ROM players, and many other features. The Lenovo ThinkPad X41, for example, comes equipped with more than 3,000 written documents from Western civilization, including the complete works of Shakespeare, every presidential inaugural address, and numerous musical scores (Epstein, 2006, January).

- *College use.* Colleges and universities now require or strongly encourage first-year students to use a laptop computing device. Even where purchasing a laptop is not required, many courses expect students to have access to portable computing resources. The importance of every student using a computer in higher education has begun to register among public school leaders who want students to have experience with computers in elementary and secondary classrooms.

- *Research studies.* Several small-scale studies of one-to-one computing programs suggest that laptops and other information technologies can positively affect student learning—in certain ways and under certain conditions (Bebell, 2005; Lei & Zhao, 2006; Muir, Knezek, & Christensen, 2004; Russell, Bebell, & Higgins, 2003; Russell, O'Brien, Bebell, & O'Dwyer, et al., 2003a; Russell & Plati, 2001; Zucker & McGhee, 2005). Computer use has been linked to improvements in students' school attendance, homework completion, teamwork in the classroom, engagement with writing and the writing process, and motivation to learn (Zimmerman, 2007). The Michigan Freedom to Learn Project has reported gains in test scores in all subjects in one-to-one computing situations and other studies have shown increased technology proficiency among students who use their own machines. While large-scale evidence of technology's positive impacts may not be immediately apparent in these studies, examining the impact of one-to-one computers can be likened to an iceberg with a vast area unexplored beneath the surface. More research is needed to determine how one-to-one computer technology can best impact student learning in schools.

One/Two/Three Time Activities. **One/two/three time** is an instructional mode that uses technology as a central element of classroom learning. An instructional mode is a "way of structuring students' learning environment for teaching purposes" (Peelle, 2001). One/two/three time arrangements split a class of students into two or three smaller groups who rotate through a series of distinct learning experiences—one or two of which involve computers.

One/two/three time is a popular format at the elementary level, but can be used at the middle and high school levels as well. The goal is to use technology to help teachers move away from a reliance on whole-class instruction that can often leave many students detached from learning activities. For example, in teaching math, an elementary teacher might create three small-group activities through which students rotate every 20 or 25 minutes:

Activity A. Students receive direct instruction from the teacher on a concept or skill; for instance the multiplying by nines table where each of the numbers move up and down in order ($9 \times 1 = 18$, $9 \times 2 = 27$, $9 \times 3 = 36$, and so on).

Activity B. Students play a hands-on math game—for example, turning over three number cards on a Concentration-style board to get combinations that do not exceed the number 21.

Activity C. Students work together in pairs or trios at the computers on math problem-solving activities from a high-quality math software program or interactive math website.

The advantages of one/two/three time formats are readily apparent—large class sizes become more manageable and youngsters who need more individualized instruction or extra skills practice can get it from the teacher or from the machine. But in most classrooms, small-group rotation arrangements are not possible without computers. There are simply not enough adults in the school to put someone with every small group, and creating different group activities that children can do independently takes time and creativity on the part of teachers. The computer is a permanently available teacher aide, always ready to enable smaller-sized instructional groups in the classroom.

FIGURE 4.3 Screenshot of Notes Taken with a Tablet Computer

Cooperative Learning and Groupwork. Cooperative learning and groupwork formats can be found at every grade level and in every subject area (Cohen, 1994). As discussed in Chapter 2, in cooperative learning and groupwork, students work together in pairs, trios, or other configurations of small groups on projects and assignments. Instead of teaching the entire class in a large-group lecture/discussion format, the teacher is free to move around the classroom, stopping at each group to offer more specialized assistance and encouragement. After completing work in their small groups, the students then report back to the entire class, creating situations where students are teaching students—and learning the material in new ways because they are able to share it with their peers.

Computers, particularly those connected to the Internet or possessing CD-ROM encyclopedias or other information resources, are a key to the success of many cooperative learning or groupwork situations. For example, one middle school social studies teacher begins a unit on the geography and culture of the Middle East with a literature reading entitled "The Women's Baths." The class reads the story aloud, each student speaking one paragraph in a readers' theatre setting. Once the story is completed, the class is divided into different groups. One does a pictorial representation of the story, another writes a continuation of the story involving the main characters, and a third uses the Internet to research geographic information about the story's setting in modern-day Syria. Each group presents their work to the class as a culmination of the day's lesson.

In this example, computer technology was an essential ingredient of the teacher's lesson plan. The lesson could not succeed in connecting the literature reading to the geography of the region without one student group doing online research and giving a report to the rest of the class about the cultural geography of the Middle East. By including computers and the Internet as part of a cooperative learning activity, the teacher was able to seamlessly integrate technology while focusing the class on the social studies content of the lesson plan.

Electronic Textbooks.   Using computers and the Internet as electronic textbooks creates an interactive, dynamic way to integrate computer technology into the teaching of class material. This approach works either when students are in a one-to-one or two-to-one student-to-computer arrangement, or when the teacher uses an LCD projector to show the Web material on a large screen at the front of the room for everyone to see. Students can then view the content in one of two places—up front on the big screen or directly in front of them on their own computer.

Some school districts are already shifting from paper to digital textbooks and online curriculum materials. In fall 2006, close to 50 percent of K–5 students in California began learning history with "History/Social Science for California," a new series of instructional materials that combine printed text, digital materials, and active learning activities, all aligned to the state's history curriculum standards (Ascione, 2006a). The goal is to provide historically relevant activities that will engage students while reducing school system budget expenses for paper-bound textbooks. Digital learning programs for other content areas will likely follow if the program is a success.

It is not necessary to have multiple computers to make electronic textbook formats work successfully. A single computer and a digital projector can transform an otherwise routine lesson into an engaging multimedia experience. Students greatly enjoy viewing academic material on a large screen; here the overhead projector is being transformed into a more interesting tool for learning. For example, one high school history teacher uses a single computer and LCD projector to teach her students how to take multiple-choice tests. As part of the review of history units, she calls up past test questions from the state's standardized history test for the class to review as a whole group. Each question is examined closely. The class discusses all the possible answers, deciding which ones are reasonable choices and which ones include historically inaccurate information. As the students review the historical content, they also practice their multiple-choice test-taking skills.

To date, computers as electronic textbooks have been most often used in computer labs where 20 or more students have access to their own computers. As more and more computers make their way into classrooms, teachers will be able to do this type of teaching without needing to go to a computer lab.

Technology Integration and Educational Change

Even today, with computers and other devices in wide use everywhere in society, many schools remain technology-limited settings. So when you integrate technology into classroom instruction, student assignments, professional recordkeeping, or some other aspect of teaching, you will be creating educational change in your school. Such processes are complicated and do not always happen as intended. To understand the connections between technology integration and educational change we discuss five concepts important to a technology-using educator: the culture of schools, infomating and automating, Type I and Type II technology applications, computers as mindtools, and strategies for student involvement in planning for change.

Technology and the Culture of Schools

Technology's capacities to transform teaching and learning can be sidetracked or stymied by the organizational culture of schools. This is the view of change theorist Seymour Sarason as described in a series of well-known books—*The Culture of the School and the Problem of Change* (1982), *Schooling in America: Scapegoat and Salvation* (1983), *The Predictable Failure of Educational Reform: Can We Change Course Before It's Too Late?* (1993), and *Political Leadership and Educational Failure* (1998). Sarason contends that most educational change efforts—whether they involve technology or not—follow a predictable pattern that leads to their failure. As a result, "the more things change, the more they remain the same" (Sarason, 1982, p. 116).

This pattern is set in motion when policymakers and administrators propose top-down changes. Much fanfare usually accompanies these pronouncements. Expectations are raised, meetings and training workshops are held, and consultants are brought in to facilitate communication between administrators and teachers. You may recall some example of top-down districtwide changes when you were in elementary or secondary school. Perhaps your school system adopted a new reading series, revised its approach to math teaching, or rearranged the order of science topics in the curriculum. In Sarason's view, all of these initiatives were mandated by policymakers and administrators, not planned and developed by teachers at the building level.

Right from the start, teachers and other front-line staff may fail to embrace the new mandates for change—in part, because those groups have not been consulted or involved in the design of plans for change. According to Sarason, when innovative ideas, no matter how sensible or needed, are imposed from the top, they fail to alter the "behavioral and programmatic regularities of schools." In other words, ideas for change do not make their way into the culture of the school. Teachers (and students) do not see the change as something they want to make part of their normal, regular way of doing things. Lacking teacher "buy-in," the change idea stalls, loses momentum, and then fades away, only to be replaced by the next big reform idea.

To Sarason the lesson is clear: It is not a lack of new ideas that blocks change in schools. Successful change in school organizations must flow upward from teachers, students, parents, and community members, not downward from administrators or central office managers. Those most affected by a change must determine how the change will happen. Concluded Sarason, "at its root the problem of our schools is not moral, political, economic, or technical. Rather, the problem flows from the hold that custom and tradition have on our thinking" (1983, pp. 180–181).

Sarason's ideas raise a key question: If substantive change in schools can be sidetracked by administrative mandates and tradition-bound thinking, how do new or veteran teachers create the kinds of unique, powerful, and transforming technology-generated learning experiences outlined in Chapter 2?

To answer Sarason's question, we examine three educational change concepts. The terms on the left indicate that technology is being used to basically maintain existing patterns, while the terms on the right refer to situations where technology is used to create change in schools.

Maintaining Existing Patterns in Schools	Creating Change in Schools
Automate	Infomate
Type I technology applications	Type II technology applications
Learning from computers	Learning with computers

Each of these concepts illustrates that technology's impact depends on how it is used by educators. Teachers become agents of educational change when they make informed decisions about the technologies they use and the ways they use them.

Automate or Infomate

Technology educator Alan November has distinguished between people using technology to "automate" or to "infomate" everyday activities. The automate paradigm, in his view, happens when a new technology essentially recreates, usually at greater speed and sometimes with greater efficiency, existing practices. "When an organization automates," noted November (2001, p. xix), "the work remains the same, the locus of control remains the same, the time and place remain the same, and relationships remain the same. The same processes solve the same problems."

Automating also applies to individuals who incorporate a technology into everyday life. For example, a fitness runner who formerly estimated distance by driving a car around her route can automate her calculations by wearing a small pedometer on a belt or sleeve. Similarly, a teacher who used to complete student report cards using paper and pencil might automate the process and submit the same information electronically using a computer and a database program. The tools have changed, but the work and the role of the individual have not.

Infomating signifies a different process, where the technology changes an activity by fundamentally redesigning and refining it. In such cases, "there is a fundamental shift of control with infomating. Relationships change, schedules change, the use of space changes, and, most importantly, responsibility shifts to the person who is closest to solving the problem" (November, 2001, p. xxi). The fitness runner in the previous example can infomate her workouts by wearing running shoes equipped with a small electronic device that sends data in real time to her iPod. She can read the information (or hear it through ear buds) while listening to music playlists specifically customized to her pace and distance for running (Baig, 2006, May).

In our educational example, a typical report card, whether in a paper-and-pencil or electronic format, still provides an after-the-fact evaluation of a student's progress—Jane received three Bs, one C, and one D last quarter. The grades have been recorded and there is nothing Jane can do about changing them. Imagine instead a weekly electronic assessment system, emailed home to parents that would enable teachers, family members, guidance counselors, and students themselves to set goals, chart progress, note achievements, identify areas for improvement, and create instructional modifications based on immediate needs. A formerly passive evaluation procedure has become infomated by a technology-based interactive system of feedback and change.

Sometimes the same technology can be used one way to automate and another way to infomate. Consider, for example, a television remote control device. At first glance, a remote seems to *automate* the use of a TV by changing channels, programming the DVD player, and adjusting the sound electronically. Yet a remote can *infomate* as well. A viewer can use the remote to channel surf among networks and shows, avoid commercials, view programs and recordings nonlinearly, and put what one is watching on pause while performing other tasks. Used in this way, the remote makes television's largely passive experience more interactive because the viewer gets to exert greater choice and control over what she or he is watching.

Type I and Type II Technology Applications

In 2005, the editors of the journal *Computers in the Schools* devoted two double issues to "Type II" applications of computers and other technologies in educational settings. Type II is half of the Type I and Type II technology applications conceptual framework that was first proposed in *Computers in the Schools* in the mid-1980s by University of Nevada, Reno, professors Cleborne D. Maddux and D. Lamont Johnson. Type I and Type II is another way to evaluate the impact of different technologies on students and learning.

Type I technology applications represent the traditional uses of computers in schools, with a focus on direct instruction work, student recordkeeping, and information transmission from teacher to student. **Type II technology applications** represent new directions in technology use, including interactive software, communication networks, and problem-posing/problem-solving programs that foster analytical and creative thinking by students. Table 4.2 compares Type I and Type II, using direct quotes from Maddux and Johnson (2005, p. 3).

TABLE 4.2 Type I and Type II Technology Applications

Type I	Type II
"Type I usage predominates and uses computing to make traditional teaching practices easier and more efficient."	"Type II usage . . . employs computers to make available new and better ways of teaching children."
"User involvement is relatively passive, and what happens on the screen is largely predetermined by the programmer."	"The user is the most important actor in the interaction and is the primary controller of what happens on the screen."
"Rote skills are emphasized, and the computer is largely employed as an electronic flashcard machine."	"Problem solving and other thinking skills are emphasized, and the computer is employed as a tool to aid cognitive processes."

Source: Maddux & Johnson, 2005, p. 3.

Maddux and Johnson have stated that they do not want to create a dichotomy between Type I and Type II applications where the former are automatically bad and the latter are automatically good. Rather, they feel there are times when it is appropriate to use technology in traditional ways and other times it makes sense to use technology in new ways. The direction you choose to take as an educator depends on the teaching and learning situation of your school and classroom. Still, surveying more than 20 years of technology improvements, the two professors concluded that Type II applications "were then, and remain today the more scarce of the two types, and the more difficult to develop and use in an educationally advantageous way" (Maddux & Johnson, 2005, p. 3).

Computers as Mindtools

Mindtools are "computer-based tools and learning environments that have been adapted or developed to function as intellectual partners with the learner in order to engage and facilitate critical thinking and higher order learning" (Jonassen, 2000, p. 9). These computer applications have multiple functions that

- "amplify the learner's thinking by transcending the limitations of the mind"
- "engage and facilitate cognitive processing"
- serve as "critical thinking devices"
- act as "intellectual partners"
- "engage learners in representing, manipulating, and reflecting on what they know, not reproducing what someone tells them" (Jonassen, 2000, p. 10)

The mindtools approach departs dramatically from the ways computers have usually been used in education. The earliest uses of technology in schools, which still persist today, were what Jonassen calls "learning *from* computers." Computer-assisted drill-and-practice instruction, computer-based tutorials, and simple educational games are all examples of learning from computers.

A second form of technology use is "learning *about* computers," a purpose generally associated with the term **computer literacy.** As typically taught in schools, computer literacy has meant learning the names, functions, and procedures of computer hardware and software. Because today's computers are user friendly enough to operate without knowing all the parts, Jonassen sees computer literacy becoming less and less important for K–12 students and their teachers. Far more important than remembering the terms, Jonaseen argued, is understanding what kinds of activities can be performed with technology that will promote improved teaching and learning in classrooms.

PEARSON **myeducationkit**

Go to the Assignments and Activities section of Chapter 4 in MyEducationKit and complete the Web activity "Mindtools for Learning."

The third type of technology use, "learning *with* computers," is when the technology becomes a "mindtool." Jonassen (2000, p. 9) outlines five ways that students learn when computers function as mindtools:

- Computers support knowledge construction.
- Computers support explorations.
- Computers support learning by doing.
- Computers support learning by conversing.
- Computers are intellectual partners that support learning by reflecting.

This book focuses on using technologies to infomate teaching, to implement Type II technology applications, and to promote learning *with* computers. Technology by itself will not automatically promote highly interactive, inquiry-based instruction. Technologies become agents of change only when used by teachers who are aware of how computers and other tools can alter existing patterns in schools.

Involving Students in Educational Change

Reviewing the recent history of change in schools, Hofstra University professor Roberto Joseph concluded that students have been "silenced and excluded from the decision-making and educational change process" (2006, p. 35). Students are rarely consulted about what they think in a variety of areas—from school schedules to teaching approaches to homework and discipline policies.

Yet there are many important reasons why it makes sense for students to become active partners in efforts to improve schools. First, groups who are left out of a change process may resent and resist intended reforms. Giving students a real voice in reform makes it more likely that they will support the change. Second, teachers can gain valuable insights about student motivation and behavior when they listen carefully to the ideas and concerns of children and adolescents. Few teachers succeed in the classroom by constantly trying to impose rules on students. Finally, involving students in change efforts addresses key developmental needs among young people. When students find that though their voices are heard, they feel good about themselves individually, and those positive feelings contribute to more productive behavior in schools.

Building on dialogue between young people and adults, Joseph (2006, pp. 37–38) identifies eight ways for teachers to engage students in substantive change efforts in schools:

1. Conduct individual interviews with students
2. Engage students in writing exercises
3. Administer needs analysis surveys and hold open forums
4. Engage and train students to be researchers
5. Form diverse student leadership teams
6. Conduct student-run focus groups
7. Administer course evaluations
8. Engage students as educational systems designers

Students are natural allies of teachers and administrators when investigating ideas that involve technology. In surprising ways, students are technology experts, particularly if experts are defined as individuals who work with information on a daily basis, who exchange knowledge with others in the field, and who are constantly updating their skills with the newest tools in the field. All of these statements are true about students and computers. What some students lack with regard to technology is the sophistication and maturity that comes with experience and reflection about its use in teaching different individuals or communicating information in fair and accurate ways. This is where teachers must contribute guidance and wisdom to confirm that every voice matters and that the ideas of younger and older individuals can synthesize to produce ways of learning and achievement for all.

Automate or infomate? Type I or Type II technology applications? Learning *from* computers or learning *with* computers? Each of these concepts invites teachers and students to critically examine how they might use technology to change educational practices. As cases in point, consider two examples: digital pens/digital notepads and electronic class notes.

Writing with Digital Pens and Digital Notepads

A **digital pen** is a writing device that records what someone has written or spoken so it can be accessed on a computer that converts content into typed text that can be copied, edited, or emailed (Pogue, 2008). A **digital notepad** is a writing device that allows users to write and draw on regular paper and then convert those images to digital text.

In theory, digital pens and digital notepads can change how teachers manage the notes and writing applications that occupy a major portion of their work time. For example, digital notepads, when connected to a computer, function as graphics tablets, allowing teachers who have a laptop and digital projector to display real-time notes and drawings on a board for everyone to see. These notes can then be converted into a PDF file and stored on a class website. Teachers using a digital pen can make on-the-spot observations of student behaviors and then consolidate those observations later in a more permanent file. Digital pens could also be used as part of a process approach to the teaching of writing as alternative ways for students to put their ideas on paper. There are a variety of digital pen and digital note-taking technologies, including the following:

- The Digital Voice Recorder Pen is an inexpensive device (under $20) sold in Discovery Channel stores that has a 60-second audio recording function so that users can record verbal notes to themselves and play them back at a later time. The short recording time limits the usefulness of this device to short reminder notes or other brief comments.

- The ZPen from Dane Electric (less than $100) offers "any paper, any time" writing that allows you to write on whatever paper you have available (see Figure 4.4). The Mobile Digital Scribe from IoGear is another "any paper, any time" device for teachers to consider. These pens allow writers to take notes throughout the school day on conventional writing paper and later download these handwritten notes as well as emails and pictures to a personal computer for storage or further writing.

- The FLY Fusion Pentop Computer from Leapfrog will speak the words that have been written on special paper that the pen can read. Teachers and students alike can use the audio to assist them in either revising or remembering written text.

- The LiveScribe Pulse digital pen (about $175) converts writing into searchable computer files and has an audio recording function that is synchronized to your handwriting. Point the pen at one of your written notes and you can hear what was being said in the room at the time you wrote it.

In terms of the change concepts *automate* and *infomate,* all the different types of digital pens automate the process of writing by making it possible to generate printed text with great speed. However, the less expensive models do not have a powerful memory that can save large amounts of written text. The $20 pen records only your voice, not your

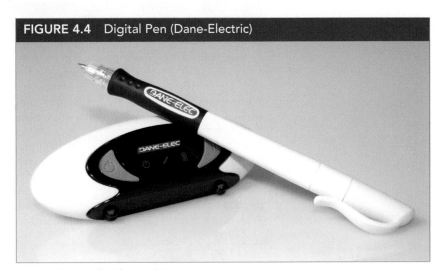

FIGURE 4.4 Digital Pen (Dane-Electric)

Source: Reprinted with permission.

Given the many different change-producing functions available on digital pens, consider the following questions:

- Which digital pen technology has the potential to change how you keep records, manage your schedule, write lesson plans, complete correspondence, or do other professional work and why?
- Which digital pen technology offers ways to support writing by your students, particularly those who lack confidence as writers, and why?
- Do you agree or disagree with the following statement: "Less expensive technologies offer fewer options for users and thus restrict any change potential while the more expensive tools create more opportunities for change."
- Do you agree or disagree with the following statement: "Any technology's potential for change will remain largely unrealized unless teachers and students explore ways to use those technologies in new and innovative ways."

writing, thus limited technological capacities of the less expensive pens restrict their potential as change-creating technologies.

However, while the most expensive digital pen seems to be the most change-producing technology, a teacher might use this technology in many different ways—some that create change and some that do not. If a teacher uses a digital pen solely as a recordkeeping device, that does little to utilize the capacity of the pen to capture words and drawings in the classroom and then store those images on a personal computer when the school day ends. On the other hand, teachers might incorporate digital pens into open-ended, creative writing situations where students are learning about genre, voice, and language by putting words on paper. The pen's speed and flexibility support students' creative expressions. In these examples, how teachers use technology either restricts or expands technology's potential to create change for learners in schools.

Consider the different technologies that you have used or are planning to use in your teaching. List these technologies in the left-hand column of Table 4.3. Then note how that technology might be used as an automating activity, and, alternatively, how it might be a used as infomating activity. To help you start, we offer three examples of our own.

There are two lessons for teachers in Table 4.3. First, a technology's design either expands or limits its impact in the classroom. Second, a technology's use either expands or limits its impact in the classroom. The capabilities of the technology and its use by a teacher and students determine how positively it will impact learning. Tablet computers are another technology whose potential teachers can exploit by using that technology in new creative and exciting ways.

Preparing Class Notes Electronically

A **tablet PC** is a portable computer with real-time inking capacity that allows users to add and save written text directly to the screen the moment it is made (see Figure 4.3 on p. 97). Given its unique technological capabilities, a tablet computer has many creative uses, including how teachers and students post and share class notes and materials.

TABLE 4.3   Using Technology to Create Change

Technology	Automate (Learning *from* Computers)	Infomate (Learning *with* Computers)
Email and instant messaging	Rapid communication between friends	Peer-to-peer and teacher-to-student homework support
Web research homework assignments	Researching content information online	Critically evaluating online information
WebQuests	Focus on specific facts or procedures; students work alone	Focus on issues and concepts; students work together
[Propose a technology example]	[Propose an automate example]	[Propose an infomate example]

Through lectures and discussions, teachers convey academic material to students who in turn are expected to take notes and then apply that information on subsequent tests, quizzes, and class projects. To assist students in taking and using notes, teachers often rely on technology. They display notes on a screen using an overhead projector, distribute typed copies of notes in class, even post notes on a class website. Here the technology has not essentially changed traditional note-taking practices—the teacher is still generating the information and the students are still recording it for later use.

Consider, by contrast, notes delivered in class using a tablet PC. A teacher might begin a lesson with key terms, concepts, or formulas on the tablet PC and display them on a large screen for everyone to see. As the class proceeds and the teacher and students begin discussing the material, new points and ideas may be added on the computer by the teacher. The original notes evolve and change, following the flow of the discussion. Students are not passive recipients of a lecture. Teacher and students are all partners in authoring the content of the class. When the class finishes, the newly revised and expanded class notes are posted electronically for everyone to access from the class website. In the process, traditional practices have been changed by how people in schools choose to use technology.

The possibilities for change are expanded even further when students have their own portable machines—a situation that is not yet a reality in most K–12 schools because of the costs involved but is the case at some colleges. Tablet PCs allow users to type using a keyboard or to write using a stylus. The machine has the capacity to recognize handwriting and convert it to typed text. In math class, students can write mathematical formulas and equations directly as presented by the teacher. There are many creative ways to combine the features of the computer and the imaginations of teachers to make educational change a reality.

Using the Technology You Have Successfully

Heather teaches high school in a low-income small town district; Sharon teaches second grade in an affluent suburban system. Their classrooms are filled with technology—large and small, fairly new or increasingly outdated, simple and complex. Each has five PC desktop computers connected to the school system's network and the Internet, an overhead projector and screen, a television and VCR on a rolling cart, a radio/CD player, small portable tape players with a microphone and rechargeable batteries, and a digital camera. These technologies have arrived in the room by different means, some purchased by the school system, some donated by colleagues after their computers were upgraded.

Visiting Heather's and Sharon's classrooms for the first time, it is amazing to see how easily they integrate different technologies into daily lessons and individual activities for students. Computers serve as always-available teacher aides, allowing Heather and Sharon to focus on small-group instruction with part of the class while other students use educational software, access electronic learning games, or do Internet research. In Sharon's room, a digital thermometer and graph-making software provide yearlong data from a study of weather and seasonal change. Heather regularly shows PBS documentaries and video clips from the Internet. Heather and Sharon seamlessly, inconspicuously integrate technology into every part of the curriculum.

For every teacher like Heather or Sharon with multiple computers and technologies, there are teachers with only a single machine in their classroom or whose access to technology is limited to occasional visits to the school's computer lab. Some curriculum ideas and instructional activities that can work well in a multiple computer classroom are often unrealistic in a classroom with a single computer. Similarly, lesson plans that involve taking students to a computer lab once or twice a week may not easily fit the needs of teachers who want to integrate technology into daily lessons without devoting an entire class period away from the classroom.

Successfully using the technology available in the classroom is an ongoing challenge for teachers. There is no single best formula for what to do, mainly because technology is not

PEARSON

Go to the Assignments and Activities section of Chapter 4 in MyEducationKit and complete the video activity entitled "Using Learning Centers."

evenly distributed among schools. As early as 2003, the average public school contained 136 instructional computers and 93 percent of teaching classrooms were connected to the Internet (National Center for Education Statistics, 2005). Despite these impressive statistics, not every classroom has a bank of up-to-date, networked, Internet-accessible computers. As a technology-using educator, you need strategies for using the available technology to its maximum learning potential.

Types of Technology-Equipped Classrooms

You can examine the availability of technology in the school where you are teaching across four dimensions, as shown in Figure 4.5. In looking at these dimensions, keep these key points in mind:

- Classrooms without computers are becoming less and less common, but there are schools where the only access to computers is in the principal's office or the school library.
- In many schools, a teacher will have a single computer, usually at her or his desk, and students can access multiple computers in the school's library or computer lab. Alternatively, the school may have a bank of portable computers on rolling carts that move from classroom to classroom. The key variables are how often lab or rolling cart computers are available to any given classroom. In some schools with high enrollments and tight schedules, students may have time in a computer lab for less than an hour a week.
- Even where there is access to computers, there may also be a question of how up-to-date the software is and whether a teacher can complement the use of computers with digital projectors, interactive whiteboards, digital cameras, and other technologies.
- Newer or recently refurbished schools often feature multiple computers in the classroom, including one for the teacher and two or more machines for students. There are a number of advantages to such arrangements. First, the presence of multiple computers in the classroom means the teacher has access for small-group use and does not have to rely on the computer

FIGURE 4.5 Four Dimensions of Technology-Equipped Classrooms

COMPUTERS	None	One	Multiple	One-to-One Computing
HARDWARE	None	Few	Many	
SOFTWARE	Few Updated	Many Updated	All Updated	
COMPUTER LAB	None	Some Access	Frequent Access	Daily Access

lab. Second, the funding that supports new or refurbished schools often means that the software is up-to-date and readily available.

- Multiple computer classrooms tend to have a host of other technologies as well. In this way, they resemble the classrooms of Heather and Sharon.

Strategies for Single and Multiple Computer Classrooms

Strategies for a single computer classroom can also be used in multiple computer classrooms, except more students will be able to access computers at the same time.

Information. Single or multiple computers in a classroom perform as always-on-call librarians and always-available tutors for individuals, pairs, or small groups. Students can access educational information all day long through Internet sites providing dictionaries, thesauri, maps, weather pages, video links, stories read aloud, math games, science demonstrations, and a variety of writing formats. For example, weather information is constantly updated online, making any weather site, or the weather page of *USA Today,* a reading comprehension activity. Similarly, news sites offer current and archived reports. Maps at Google Earth, the National Geographic website, or other sources offer up-to-date access to information and different kinds of maps. Dictionaries online can be more interactive and engaging than in texts, offering K–6 students—either native English speakers or English language learners—pictures and related information with the meanings of terms. The Little Explorers English Picture Dictionary offers translations of English words to various other languages and shows the phonetic pronunciations.

Interaction. Students can access computer and online resources where they interact with the computer for learning. Online read-alouds are one example. The children's book author Robert Munsch reads his own stories on his website in as delightful a read-aloud style as one could wish for. Poetry read-alouds and related activities are on the websites of children's authors and poets. Students can also receive interactive tutoring on computer. As an individualized tutor, math sites such as the National Library of Virtual Manipulatives have resources that are almost unlimited in scope. The science opportunities for viewing video and participating in simulations are also wondrous. Edheads is a popular site that engages all ages. For social studies photos and documents, PBS has extensive information, activities, and sources for students and teachers.

Presentation. The computer becomes a large- or small-group presentation tool when connected to a digital projector or television set. This is a very effective way to add videos, photos, maps, and other visual resources to a lesson or to summarize the learning experience after students have completed a series of individual and group activities. We discuss digital projectors and interactive whiteboards further in Chapter 9.

Rotation. The computer becomes one of three different learning experiences in the previously discussed instructional format called one/two/three time. Students are divided into groups that do learning activities at the computer, complete independent work with minimal adult supervision, or receive direct academic instruction from the teacher. The small groups rotate through these experiences either during a single day or over the course of two or three days, depending on the teaching objectives. For example, in a high school history lesson about how Europe gained world power instead of China after the mid-15th century, students analyze computer-based historical world maps in one area, complete a paper worksheet using an atlas in a second area, and discuss a reading assignment with the teacher in a third area. In one/two/three time, the computer allows teachers to work directly with smaller groups of students, an arrangement not possible when whole-group activity is the dominant mode of instruction.

PEARSON
myeducationkit™

Go to the Assignments and Activities section of Chapter 4 in MyEducationKit and complete the video activity entitled "Concept Mapping in a 1–2 Computer Classroom."

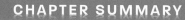
FOCUS QUESTION 1: How can teachers integrate technology into their work as educators?

- Teachers can incorporate computers and other information technologies into three major parts of their professional work: (1) classroom instruction, (2) outside-the-classroom activities, and (3) inside- and outside-the-classroom learning activities for students.

- Computers and other new technologies can function in one of five possible formats for teachers: (1) technology-based library, (2) technology-based textbook, (3) technology-based learning environment, (4) technology-based teaching tool, and (5) technology-based office.

FOCUS QUESTION 2: What are the key stages and pressing issues of technology integration?

- Technology integration is an entryway to creating unique, powerful, and transforming learning experiences for students and teachers, yet not every curriculum idea or instructional activity needs to feature computers, the Internet, or other electronic tools.

- Technology integration stages include entry, adoption, adaptation, appropriation, and invention.

- Technology integration issues include (1) unwillingness to change favorite lesson plans to include technology, (2) reluctance to use technology when teaching new lesson plans, (3) using computers as a reward or punishment for students, (4) using computers as an add-on to other activities, and (5) using computers as a way to separate students by ability groups.

FOCUS QUESTION 3: What are "digital inequality" and the "participation gap"?

- "Digital inequality" is the term used to explain how students' lack of access and use of technology is directly connected to their socioeconomic standing in society.

- The "participation gap" means that low-income and minority students have not had the same opportunities as their more affluent peers to use new technologies for learning.

FOCUS QUESTION 4: What instructional strategies and approaches promote technology integration while addressing the participation gap?

- One-to-one laptop computing initiatives provide every student with technology they can use for learning.

- One/two/three time formats use computers as a learning center or station where students do academic activities while the teacher works with other groups of students.

- Computers support cooperative learning and small-group activities by giving individual students and small groups the opportunity to work independently on academic assignments during class time or outside of school.

- Electronic textbooks provide students with learning materials they can access from any online computer.

- Dialogue among students, and between teachers and students, is a method for involving students in educational change efforts in schools.

FOCUS QUESTION 5: How does technology promote educational change?

- Change is not hard-wired into computers or any other information technology; rather it is people who influence, guide, and decide technology's impact in many everyday situations, including schools.

- The change potential of technology in schools is determined by the needs and imaginations of teachers and students and mediated by the realities of their organization goals and priorities.

- "Learning *from, about,* and *with* computers" (proposed by David Jonassen); "Type I and Type II technology applications" (proposed by Cleborne Maddux and D. Lamont Johnson); and "automate" and "infomate" (proposed by Alan November) are ways for new teachers to think about the goals they want to achieve when choosing one use of technology over another.

FOCUS QUESTION 6: How can teachers create change in classrooms using technology?

- How a technology is designed and how a technology is used will either expand or limit that technology's change impact in schools.

- Digital pens are an example of a technology that has a greater or lesser capacity to create change depending on each type's technological capabilities.

- Preparing class notes using a tablet PC is an example of how a technology can fundamentally change how teachers and students interact with academic materials.

FOCUS QUESTION 7: How can teachers use the technology they already have to promote successful learning?

- Teachers must be prepared to use the technologies they have in their schools—whether those technologies are up-to-date computers in Internet-accessible classrooms or minimally adequate machines with limited accessories and older software programs.

- Even a single computer, when connected to a digital projector, can serve as an electronic textbook and learning resource.

KEY TERMS

Adaptation stage	Mindtools
Adoption stage	One-to-one laptop computing
Appropriation stage	One/two/three time
Automate	Participation gap
Computer literacy	Social infomatics
Digital inequality	Tablet PC
Digital notepad	Technology-based learning environment
Digital pen	Technology-based library
Educational change	Technology-based office
Entry stage	Technology-based teaching tool
Inclusion	Technology-based textbook
Infomate	Technology integration
Infusion	Type I technology applications
Invention stage	Type II technology applications

1. INTEGRATING TECHNOLOGY INTO YOUR TEACHING

Choose a lesson in which you intend to use technology, and consider the following questions:

- How would you use technology if you had only one computer in the classroom; if you had several computers in the classroom; if you had a computer for every student in your classroom?

- Does the number of computers in the classroom change how you plan and deliver your lesson? Can handheld and wireless devices replace computers in your lesson plan?

- How might your lesson be done with minimal technology?

2. USING TECHNOLOGY TO ENGAGE STUDENTS

Technology integration involves two related and essential considerations—what technologies to use and what level of student engagement these technologies will create when used. Read the following situation and answer the follow-up questions.

A science teacher introduces the rock cycle to sixth-graders using a PowerPoint presentation of slides showing igneous, metamorphic, and sedimentary rocks. The students are listening, watching, taking notes, and asking questions about the presentation appearing on an overhead screen. The students, for the most part, are respectfully attentive, but not overly excited about the presentation. The following day students will have a quiz on this material. On the quiz there are only a few questions but the scores are not high.

- The teacher has included technology in his teaching, but how might he have more fully engaged the students in learning and potentially improve the quiz results?

- Might the students have responded with more enthusiasm if they had created the PowerPoint presentation and were conducting the review for the teacher instead of the other way around?

- To what extent do you think technology integration is tied to students being actively involved in the use of technology and the production of academic information?

3. AUTOMATING AND INFOMATING

Running shoes with a built-in sensor mechanism transmitting data to an iPod or personal computer is one way to substantively change a runner's exercise experience. In effect, the sensor turns running shoes into a Type II/mindtool technology application that infomates a runner's learning in unique, powerful, and transforming ways.

Consider the technologies you or your friends and families use in your everyday life—cell phones, digital cameras, automated bank machines, email, online message boards, television remote controls, or other tools. Through a class discussion or in a written reflection paper, respond to the following questions:

- How does a technology change your activity from what you did before using it?

- Do you define the technology as a mindtool?

- Can it automate or infomate your activity?

Now think about the technologies you might use in teaching—computers, word processing, PowerPoint, the Internet, handheld and wireless devices, or other tools.

- How does the technology change teaching from what a teacher might do if the technology were not present?
- Do you define the technology as a mindtool?
- Does the technology automate, infomate, or do both as a teaching or learning activity?

5 Researching and Evaluating Internet Information

I remember my mother telling me about the excitement of getting a telephone—well the Internet for me has been so much better than even that. It's a personal connector, a free long distance videophone, a post office without stamps, a worldwide library, a visual and audio window on the world, and an opportunity for self-expression.

—Anonymous Survey Respondent, quoted in *A Portrait of Early Internet Adopters* (Wells, 2008)

CHAPTER LEARNING GOAL

Internet-Based Research

Using the Internet to teach students how to access and assess online information

CONNECTING to the NETS

NETS-T

2 Design and Develop Digital Age Learning Experiences and Assessments

4 Promote and Model Digital Citizenship and Responsibility

NETS-S

3 Research and Information Fluency

5 Digital Citizenship

NEW TECHNOLOGIES

- Internet search engines
- Web evaluation tools
- Photo- and audio-sharing websites
- Electronic note-takers
- Wikipedia
- Web browser customizing tools
- Plagiarism checking software

CHAPTER OVERVIEW

Chapter 5 explores how teachers and students can critically research and evaluate the Internet as a teaching and learning environment. The chapter begins with search engines, how they work, and how to teach students to evaluate for slant, bias, and purpose of information they locate online. In this context, Wikipedia is discussed as an Internet phenomenon. Then, the chapter addresses the problem of student plagiarism when using online sources and suggests ways for teachers to address this issue.

By examining search engines, the quality of Web-based information, Wikipedia, and plagiarism, this chapter responds to the expectations in NETS-T Standard 4 and NETS-S Standard 5 that technology users model appropriate, responsible, and ethical treatment of online information, citing sources and materials when conducting research online.

The chapter concludes with our first Technology Transformation Lesson Plan, entitled "Think Globally. Act Locally! Conducting Social Studies Research on the Internet." This plan features strategies for teaching students how to use Web-based information in the analysis of societal problems and in writing and filming public service announcements about those problems.

FOCUS QUESTIONS

1. What is the meaning of information literacy for teachers and students?

2. What are search engines and how do they work?

3. What pieces of information do students need to know about Internet searching?

4. How can teachers and students thoughtfully evaluate online information resources, including the online encyclopedia Wikipedia?

5. How can teachers respond to problems of plagiarism when students use online sources?

Imagine that the world's largest library stands next to your house or apartment, steps away, as an extra wing. In your lifetime, visiting daily, you will not even begin to see, read, or hear all that it contains. In actual physical space, this place is the Library of Congress in Washington, D.C., containing some 130 million items that require approximately 530 miles of bookshelves to store. In the collection are 29 million books, 2.7 million recordings, 12 million photographs, 4.8 million maps, 5 million music items, and 58 million manuscripts, with the number of items continuously increasing.

The Library of Congress, however, is dwarfed in size by the library that every teacher or student can access with any Internet-connected computer. The vastness of the Internet is as unimaginable as the vastness of space. Consider these Internet facts from the past several years:

- The Pew Internet & American Life Project reported that on a typical day in August 2006, 26 million people in the United States (13 percent) used the Internet to get news about politics and the mid-term elections. Sixty million people said the Internet played a major role in helping them make a big decision or make their way through a major moment in their lives.

- Internet users in the United States conducted 213 million searches a day in March 2006; for the month of July 2008, Americans conducted almost 12 billion searches, according to figures provided by the website SearchEngineWatch.

- By May 2005, the search engine Google reported it was indexing over eight billion Web pages, with the number growing every day. Moreover, when pages from the so-called "Deep Web" not indexed by search engines were counted, Google estimated that the Internet has more than a trillion Web pages.

- In 2002, University of California Berkeley researchers estimated that enough new information was stored in print, film, magnetic, and optical storage media to fill 37,000 new libraries the size of the Library of Congress book collection.

This chapter's learning goal highlights how teachers and students can realize the possibilities and meet the challenges of the vast library of information known as the **Internet.** Never before have so many people been able to find so much information so readily. For students today, learning about a topic commonly means going online to access Web-based resources. However, this library of virtually endless quantity includes much material of questionable quality. There is no librarian for the Internet. Teachers and students must become their own search experts, fact-checkers, and information analysts when working online.

To do successful Internet research, states the American Library Association (ALA), everyone must know both how to *access information* (locate resources and materials on the Web) and how to *assess information* (evaluate the usefulness, accuracy, and quality of what is found among the Web's boundless resources). This capacity to access and assess information online is known as **information literacy,** defined by the ALA as the "ability to recognize when information is needed and to then have the ability to locate, evaluate, and use effectively the needed information" (Windham, 2006).

Internet research refers to the ways that teachers and students use the incredible speed and comprehensiveness of the Internet to locate resources for learning. Almost all teenagers (94 percent) use the Internet at least some of the time to do research for school (Lenhart, Arafeh, Smith, & Macgill, 2008). Locating information is only part of the process of Internet research. Before using online information, teachers must determine if it is viable and reliable—and then teach students how to do the same.

A case in point is the online encyclopedia **Wikipedia,** which offers both resources and challenges for users. The information may be more up-to-date than less frequently updated paper sources, but it may also contain bias and inaccuracies. Easy copying of information raises issues of potential plagiarism and the steps teachers and students can take to avoid it.

Information Literacy as a Learning Goal

Teachers and students need educational information. For teachers, such information enables the development of lively curriculum, updating of academic knowledge, and access to accurate answers for student questions. Whether one is a beginning teacher or a 20-year veteran, the need for current, interesting, and relevant information is constant. For students, educational information is the currency of learning. Students use this information to write papers and essays, prepare for exams, develop personal talents, and propel their quest for knowledge.

Acquiring educational information once meant (and still does) using a library, reading books and magazines, taking classes in school, and attending conferences and presentations. Today, the search for educational knowledge increasingly features the Internet—both in terms of how teachers use it professionally and how they assist students to use it academically (Hunt & Hunt, 2006; November, 2008).

Nearly all schools and almost all classrooms have access to the Internet (see Figure 5.1), although about 16 percent of schools lack high-speed Web connections (U.S. Department of Commerce, 2008).

Immediately accessible online information means teachers and students must learn new information processing skills, what the Educational Testing Service (ETS) refers to as **information and communication technology literacy (ICT literacy).** ICT literacy means the "ability to use digital information, communication tools, and networks appropriately to solve information problems in order to function in an information society" (Educational Testing Service, 2006, p. 2). Researchers at the New Literacies Research Lab at the University of Connecticut contend

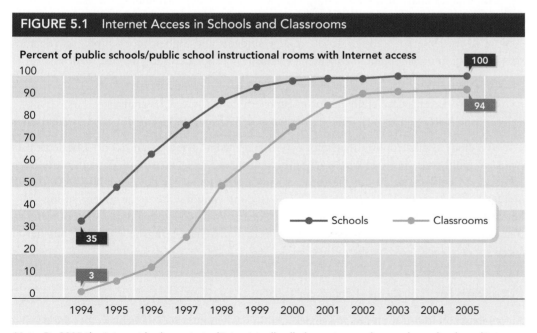

FIGURE 5.1 Internet Access in Schools and Classrooms

Percent of public schools/public school instructional rooms with Internet access

Note: By 2005 the Internet had penetrated into virtually all elementary and secondary schools and into the vast majority of classrooms. But small gaps in Internet access among classrooms continue to persist. Classrooms in secondary schools, larger schools, and schools with lower minority enrollment are slightly more likely to have access.

Source: Reprinted with permission of Education Week. Available at www.edweek.org/media/ew/tc/2008/30computer_access_tech_helpers.h27.pdf.

that online readers need many skills to complete an interrelated set of information retrieval and assessment tasks, including the following:

- Open a Web browser
- Locate a search engine
- Type a key word or phrase
- Scan the search results
- Assess the source
- Open multiple windows
- Weave answers together
- Share ideas on blogs or social network sites
- Send Web links to others
- Respond to content by posting comments (Rich, 2008)

Information literacy and *media literacy* are other terms used to signify the essential skills of locating, evaluating, and using information in a computer environment (Beach, 2007; Hollister, 2007; Windham, 2006). The National Council of Teachers of English defines media literacy as "the capacity to access, analyze, evaluate and communicate messages in a wide variety of forms" (2008a). Students learn to analyze the media they access when watching television, reading newspapers, and using the Internet as well as the media they themselves create when posting to a blog, sending electronic communications, or writing in many different genres.

Developing information and media literacy skills begins in the early grades and continues through college. According to the Information Literacy Competency Standards for Higher Education, an information-literate college student:

- Determines the nature and extent of information needed
- Accesses the needed information effectively and efficiently
- Evaluates information and its sources critically and incorporates selected information into his or her knowledge system
- Uses information effectively to accomplish a specific purpose
- Understands many of the economic, legal, and social issues surrounding the use of information ethically and legally (Association of College and Research Libraries, 2000, pp. 2–3)

Yet in an ETS pilot study of 1,400 college students and high school seniors, few demonstrated strong information and media literacy skills (Educational Testing Service, 2006):

- Only 52 percent judged the objectivity of a group of websites correctly
- Only 35 percent successfully narrowed an overly broad Internet search
- Only 12 percent constructed a presentation slide (PowerPoint) using directly relevant points

ETS study results confirm that information and media literacy is an essential basic skill in our increasingly computer- and information-driven society. As University of Wisconsin professor James Paul Gee flatly stated, "in the modern world, print literacy is not enough" (2003, p. 19). Similarly, noted two literacy researchers: "If U.S. students cannot write to the screen—if they cannot design, author, analyze, and interpret material on the Web and in other digital environments—they will have difficulty functioning effectively as literate human beings in a growing number of social spheres" (Selfe & Hawisher, 2004, p. 2).

Preparing for Work and Life in an Information Age

An emphasis on information literacy comes at a time when information technologies are driving vast changes in the nation's economic systems and social structures. In the late 1980s, the number of professional, managerial, and technical workers exceeded the number of industrial workers for the first time, marking a crucial transition from an industrial to an information society (Ehrenhalt, 1986). More than two decades later, three out of every four people in the United States provide services to the one out of four who make things on farms or in factories. Many economists and educators see literacy with technology as a key to maintaining the vitality and competitiveness of U.S. workers in a time of great change.

Preparing today's students for future roles as workers and citizens is the mission of the National Center on Education and the Economy, an economic preparedness and educational reform policy organization based in Washington, D.C. Noting the pace of technology-driven changes in a global marketplace, the Center's *New* Commission on the Skills of the American Workforce urged sweeping changes in the nation's education system (2006). Because routine work can now be done by machines or by foreign workers who earn salaries substantially less than those of U.S. workers, people in the United States must begin developing innovative new products and services to sell throughout the world. To succeed in this future economy, every U.S. student will need computer, Internet, and telecommunications expertise.

The National Council of Teachers of English (NCTE) has issued its own definition of the skills students will need in the future, called **21st-century literacies** (2007, 2008b). To live and work successfully in the new century, students need the basic competencies of reading, writing, and computation, and an array of new technology-based literacies, including proficiency with technology tools, the ability to build relationships and solve problems collaboratively, the capability to design and share information, the capacity to analyze and evaluate information from multiple sources, and the ability to handle information in ethical ways. As NCTE concluded: "These literacies—from reading online newspapers to participating in virtual classrooms—are multiple, dynamic, and malleable" (2008b).

What it means to be technologically literate also relates to an intense debate among educators and policymakers about the state of reading in today's computer-based society. Clearly, the reading habits of children and adolescents are changing. In a 2008 series on the future of reading, the *New York Times* reported that the number of 17-year-olds who read for fun every day declined from about 33 percent in 1984 to about 20 percent in 2004. The number of 17-year-olds who say they never read for fun increased from 9 to 19 percent during the same time period. Meanwhile, the average time 8- to 18-year-olds spend online every day rose to 1 hour and 46 minutes in 2004, up from 46 minutes in 1999 (Rich, 2008). Figure 5.2 shows that in every age group from 5- to 17-year-olds, children and adolescents spend more time every day reading online than reading books (Scholastic, 2008).

Is time spent online really reading? Internet critics say no, contending that reading printed books is the time-honored, proven path to intellectual and personal growth. Noted historian David McCullough: "Learning is not to be found on a printout. It is not on call at the touch of the finger. Learning is acquired mainly from books, and mostly from great books" (quoted in Rich, 2008, p. 14). Moreover, since the Web delivers high-speed information divided into small segments of text, video, sound, and pictures, that experience may actually wear away students' capacities for serious contemplation and engagement with knowledge (Carr, 2008).

Other commentators defend the Internet as a powerful and supportive reading and learning environment where youngsters learn skills of Web navigation and information synthesis that are essential for living and working in the modern world. Web surfing, social networking, and information searching, all forms of reading, collectively build intellectual frameworks that students can use for both online and print reading.

YOUR JUDGMENT MATTERS

- What are your views of reading online and its impact on today's students?
- What do you hear students saying about their online and traditional book reading habits?
- How do you plan to address the issues raised by critics and defenders of the Internet in your own teaching?

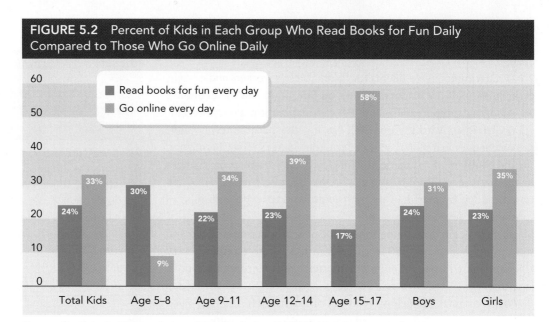

FIGURE 5.2 Percent of Kids in Each Group Who Read Books for Fun Daily Compared to Those Who Go Online Daily

Source: Reprinted with permission of Scholastic, Inc. © 2008. All rights reserved.

IT Fluency and IT FITness

IT fluency (or *information technology fluency*) has increasingly become the core goal for teachers and students who are learning about technology. Broadly defined, "fluency" means approaching a task or a topic as an expert would. A fluent person understands things from the inside, knows the interworkings, and speaks the language of the field. Fluency is already a goal for many teachers who seek to have their students learn academics from the perspective of those who perform those subjects in real-world settings. They want students to approach science like scientists, history like historians, language like writers, and so on. In a similar way, students should learn technology as it is understood and used by engineers, analysts, researchers, inventors, and other professional, managerial, and technical workers.

IT fluency in schools includes the application of computers and other technologies by teachers in all subject areas at all grade levels. The goal is **IT FITness** (Fluent with Information Technology), where students are able to "evaluate, distinguish, learn, and use new information technologies as appropriate to their own personal and professional activities" (National Research Council, 1999, pp. 2, 3). Students learn not only technical skills but also develop technology-informed mindsets and engage in real-world activities and accomplishments. For example, teachers might ask students to do multimedia projects with Web design or film production in English language arts, GPS data analysis to support mathematical problem solving, data mining to develop social science analyses, and probes to provide data for science experiments.

Connecting fluency to expertise suggests that children and adolescents will gain a high level of thinking about technology. According to Seymour Papert (1996, pp. 28, 29), "The word fluent expresses the most important aspect of the kind of knowledge children should have about technology." One develops fluency, Papert believes, not by doing exercises in books, worksheets, or multiple-choice tests, but by performing important-to-the-learner, technology-based activities in real-world settings where a person's actions have meaningful consequences. It is also learned by making mistakes, figuring things out, and constantly saying "Let me try."

Search Engines and How They Work

Conducting successful online searches, a fundamental information literacy skill, is what people do when they want to find something. An **information search** is done using paper or electronic sources and a variety of search strategies. Information searches benefit from knowing sound techniques, useful tips, and sensible shortcuts, and having good tools and a critical perspective. Knowing only how to find information is insufficient if teachers and students are to avoid becoming immersed in biased, faulty, or useless data.

Online **information research and retrieval** "is the process of searching within a document collection for a particular information need (called a query)" (Langville & Meyer, 2006, p. 1). You learned basic strategies for information research and retrieval from elementary and secondary school using the school library's card catalog to find selections of books and periodicals.

The emergence of the Internet has transformed how teachers and students research and retrieve information because in addition to its enormous size, the Web is

- "dynamic"—constantly changing,
- "self-organized"—anyone can post and link, and
- "hyperlinked"—tied together electronically (Langville & Meyer, 2006, p. 9)

The Internet has produced a new category of activity called **Web information retrieval,** where Internet users are able to seek information "within the world's largest and linked document collection." This type of searching is the opposite of traditional searches where users look for information "within smaller, more controlled, nonlinked collections" (Langville & Meyer, 2006, p. 5).

Search engines retrieve information from the Internet. A search engine is a software program that uses networks of computers to access information about a topic from its databases. What is remarkable about a search engine is its speed, propelling an Internet-connected computer instantaneously through millions of Web pages to locate topic-related websites. Anyone who has typed a keyword or phrase into a computer's search box and received tens of thousands of results knows how amazingly fast but potentially confusing online searching can be.

Broadly speaking, all search engines customize explorations of the Web using **keywords,** which are words or phrases used by search engines to locate matching Web pages. Keyword queries limit searches by focusing on specific categories, narrowing a search to specific rather than general categories. After choosing a topic of inquiry, it is useful to identify several keywords relating to the subject area before using a search engine. For example, when exploring the history of African American baseball players, you might list "Negro Leagues," "baseball history," "Jackie Robinson," "Brooklyn Dodgers," or "sports history." Any or all of these terms would be potential starting points for using a search engine. Enter a keyword or term in the search field, highlight and click on the accompanying search button, and the search engine begins. Query results in the form of active hyperlinks are displayed once the search is completed.

There are search engines available for both general and specialized searching (see Table 5.1). Each search engine allows you to restrict or expand your searching criteria and provides you with tips on modifying your searches to get the information you need. In July 2007, Google, Yahoo!, MSN, AOL, and Ask were the most widely used search engines, accounting for over 95 percent of the 7.7 billion searches conducted during that month alone (Burns, 2007).

As valuable as general-purpose search engines like Google or Ask can be in locating information, teachers and students benefit from search tools that focus more directly on academic topics, educational standards, and learning materials. In fact, it has been estimated that "less than half the searchable Web is fully searchable in Google" (University of California Berkeley Library, 2007). Educationally specialized search resources, because they focus on curriculum and school-related topics, are often more time-efficient than typing keywords into a general search engine. Table 5.1 lists a number of specialized search resources for use by teachers.

You can find more search resources in a WebQuest entitled "Specialized Search Engines and Directories" complied by Bernie Dodge at San Diego State University (2006). Tech Tool 5.1 on pages 121–122 describes two other specialized search engines, Flickr and LibriVox, which allow you to locate photo and audio resources on the Web.

YOUR JUDGMENT MATTERS

As you think about your online search experiences, consider the following questions:

- How many different search engines have you tried, either as a new teacher candidate or as a college or high school student?
- Did you prefer one search engine to another for any reason?
- If you are familiar with several different search engines, which ones do you find most useful for you as a teacher and for your students as learners?

TABLE 5.1 Specialized Search Resources for Teachers

Search Engine/Database	Specialized Use
Internet Public Library (IPL) www.ipl.org	Library of online resources housed at Drexel University and maintained by a consortium of colleges
Voice of the Shuttle (VoS) vos.ucsb.edu	Online resources for teaching the humanities housed at the University of California, Santa Barbara
Technorati www.technorati.com	Search Engine for weblogs (blogs)
Webopedia www.webopedia.com	Computer and Internet definitions
Artcyclopedia http://artcyclopedia.com	Works of art and famous artists from history and the present
Encyclopedia of Educational Technology http://coe.sdsu.edu/eet/Admin	Short multimedia articles on educational technology topics from the Department of Educational Technology at San Diego State University
California Learning Resource Network www.clrn.org/home	Software, video, and Internet learning resources for children
Library of Congress American Memory http://memory.loc.gov/ammem/browse	Primary source documents and exhibits on U.S. history
University of Texas at Austin Perry-Castaneda Library Map Collection www.lib.utexas.edu/maps/index.html	Online maps from the United States and the world
NewsLink http://newslink.org	Newspapers from around the United States and the world
Good Search www.goodsearch.com	A site that donates 50 percent of the revenue from each search (about 1 cent per search) to the charitable causes of your choice
Score (Schools of California Online Resources for Educators) www.score.k12.ca.us	Classroom and curriculum resources in math, science, history, and language arts
Search Engines 2 www.search-engines-2.com	A search engine for search engines
Wayback Machine www.archive.org/index.php	A historical archive of Web pages
Open Library www.openlibrary.org	A site whose long-term goal is to create one Web page for every book ever published
Viewzi.com www.viewzi.com/search	A visual search engine that arranges information in 10 different configurations, including photos, text, and images
VuteToo.com www.vuetoo.com/index2.htm	A content blender site that mixes multiple websites, RSS feeds, entertainment, weather, and news data into one Web page that teachers can continually monitor in a condensed mode

Taking notes to recall the information you locate using search engines is an essential skill for teachers and for students who are writing research papers or preparing poster presentations as part of school assignments. Notes summarize key ideas, concepts, and information about a topic. Using notetakers, teachers can review what others have said before formulating their own interpretations or analyses to present in class. High school students in particular are expected to take notes on readings from textbooks, online sources, and teacher lectures as a way to understand class material and prepare for exams.

Note taking is a multistep process, especially when done by hand using pen and paper or note cards. Recording quotes and citations takes time, and if the note cards are lost, the process of redoing them is doubly time consuming. In addition, sorting through many pieces of paper filled with quotes and citations is not an efficient use of time.

Electronic note taking uses computer technologies to organize and expedite note taking. Electronic note taking transfers the work of hand filing and organizing to your computer so you can concentrate on the content and meaning of your written materials.

NoteStar is an Internet-based electronic note-taking tool for teachers that can be used with elementary and secondary students as well. NoteStar can be added to a browser's toolbar, making it accessible while searching the Internet. When a student locates a Web resource to save, simply clicking on the NoteStar icon enables data-recording prompts to appear. Special functions like this make NoteStar student friendly and useful to researchers of all ages and levels of experience. NoteStar is free online at http://notestar.4teachers.org.

Another option is Office OneNote 2007, a commercial software program for either Mac or PC computers. OneNote serves as a digital notebook or multiple notebooks or binders that can house different types of data with the click of a mouse or push of a button.

Teaching Students about Internet Searching

In the 1990s, most search engines used a "crawler" search system that scanned the text of Web pages on a specific topic and then indexed or cataloged what was found in a list of sites (or "hits") ranked by how closely a Web page's content matched keyword indicators. A high ranking (one of the first sites on the search engine's list of sites) was intended to mean a site was highly relevant to the topic being searched. Not surprisingly, enterprising and/or unscrupulous advertisers and Web page creators found ways to include materials that could fool a search engine into giving their site a higher ranking. As a result, a list of top ten sites about a topic could easily contain unreliable, fraudulent, or unsuitable entries.

Google revolutionized how people conduct online searching and in so doing became the dominant search engine in the world. Stanford University students Larry Page and Sergey Brin founded Google in 1998 by ranking not only by keywords, but also by a site's popularity and how often it is cross-listed with other sites. In an interview with PBS Online, cofounder Sergey Brin described Google's page ranking as a process where computer pages interact with one another as if they were people discussing a topic of interest. Google, Brin stated, basically asks "what does one page say about another page? And what do other pages say about that one? And kind of reputation building around the whole web, translated into mathematics" (quoted in Michels, 2002).

With its acquisition of the video site YouTube, Google is one of the most visited Internet sites worldwide (Graham, 2006). Google is using its immense popularity to expand services in many directions. Google Desktop Search (desktop.google.com) provides a "photographic memory" of your computer, letting you search files by name, "search for words inside your files," and "search any Web page you've ever seen, any e-mail message you've opened and the transcript of any instant-message chat you've had" (Pogue, 2004, p. E1).

In addition, Google has entered the wireless communications market and made arrangements to add offline library resources to its databases. By typing "GOOGL" on their phone

PEARSON
myeducationkit

Go to the Assignments and Activities section of Chapter 5 in MyEducationKit and complete the Web activity entitled "Discovering Online Resources."

Pictures and sound are valuable resources for creative teaching. Students enjoy visual images and sound recordings as part of a lesson. Such materials keep students engaged and help them concentrate on the ideas a teacher is trying to get across. Moreover, pictures and sound expand the range of teaching materials beyond the teacher's voice to include multiple media in the classroom. Flickr and Librivox are two sites that enable teachers to locate photo and audio resources on the Web.

Flickr

Flickr is an online photo managing and sharing tool with a number of instructional options for teachers. You can locate, organize, and send photos that you have taken

Source: Screenshot reproduced with permission of Yahoo! Inc. © 2008 by Yahoo! Inc. YAHOO! and the YAHOO! logo are trademarks of Yahoo! Inc. Board courtesy of SMART Technologies; copyright © 2001–2009 SMART Technologies ULC; all rights reserved.

or that you locate within the site's vast online collection. This offers an almost limitless way to add visual learning resources to your curriculum. The accompanying screenshot shows the Flickr upload page.

Using Flickr, you can divide your photos into sets based on a theme you are teaching. You can be part of an online group to share photos of interest, or you can create your own group and invite others to join you. A discussion board is included for online talking as well as for picture sharing among col-

keypad, cell phone users can access local addresses and telephone numbers as well as the company's "Froogle" shopping site. These services are intended to provide a lower cost alternative to existing cell phone search services provided by Verizon, Sprint, and the Weather Channel. In December 2004, Google announced it was working with the New York Public Library and libraries at Harvard, Stanford, the University of Michigan, and the University of Oxford to make out-of-print books and related resources in those collections searchable through the Google site. Eventually millions of pages of text that are now available only on library shelves will be online worldwide.

Of special interest to teachers and students is a suite of online products called Google for Educators (www.google.com/educators). Intended as a one-stop source of academic information, curriculum ideas, and productivity tools to promote innovation in teaching, its basic tools include:

leagues. You can drag and drop photos onto a map, establishing a way for your students to explore people and places around the world. Once you have your photos in the system, you and your students can make cards, photo books, slideshows, calendars, and postage stamps.

 LibriVox

LibriVox offers free audio recordings of published books and other materials in the public domain (see the second screenshot). These materials are read aloud into digital audio files by volunteers and then made available to the general public over the Web. Note how the teachers and students can access the book in its entirety or as a chapter-a-day from iTunes.

The site's long-term goal is to make all public domain books available free in audio formats, a truly monumental project. Presently, teachers can find recordings of literature, poetry, and nonfiction materials that connect to many curriculum areas and topics.

CONTACT INFORMATION

Flickr   www.flickr.com   Flickr provides enhanced services for a fee.

LibriVox   http://librivox.org

- *Web Search.* A tutorial on how to use the Google search engine.
- *Google Earth.* A satellite imagery–based mapping project that lets users view any location on the globe in three dimensions.
- *Book Search.* A way to locate in-print, out-of-print, and public domain book titles within the search engine's database.
- *Maps.* Point-to-point directions to addresses anywhere in the United States and to many places around the globe. There is also a blog with map-related games and information.
- *Docs and Spreadsheets.* Online word processing and spreadsheet programs.
- *Blogger.* Teachers can create their own blog as well as access an easy way to share academic work, class notes, and pictures with students and colleagues online.
- *SketchUp.* A three-dimensional (3D) model-making tool.

- *Calendar.* An online calendar-building tool that enables teachers to create and access a personal schedule from any Internet-accessible computer.
- *Picasa.* A picture locating and editing tool that allows users to share pictures online.
- *Apps (Applications) for Educators.* Ways for school districts to share communication and productivity tools, including email, within an entire school community. (EDUCAUSE Learning Initiative, 2008, March)

Tech Tool 5.2 discusses how teachers can increase productivity by customizing their **Web browser** using another one of Google's tools—iGoogle. A Web browser is a computer application that enables your computer to search (or browse) the Internet, collecting information on whatever topics you request. Setting your Web browser to your own preferences retrieves information you want quickly and efficiently.

Free-Text, Keyword, and Boolean Searches

Most search engines offer three ways to search the Internet: free-text, keyword/exact match, and Boolean.

Free-Text Search. A **free-text search** (also known as *full-text search*) looks for the title, keyword, and description fields of each resource for the word or phrase you type into the search command. Free-text represents the most inclusive kind of search because it will show results that include one or more words in a phrase that was entered in the query. For example, if you type the term "presidential elections" into a free-text function, you will get a wide range of information, including a history of presidential elections, information on the controversial 2000 election, and a compilation of political cartoons and campaign information from various years.

When you are initially looking for information, free-text is a useful way to search because you will get entries covering many aspects of a topic. However, it can be time consuming to look through multiple entries. For this reason, most searchers turn to keyword/exact match or Boolean searches.

Keyword/Exact Match Search. A **keyword/exact match search** retrieves only resources that contain exactly the word or phrase you type into the text box. The word or phrase must appear either in the title, keyword, or description fields of a resource for it to be included in the results. For example, to find information only on the 2000 presidential election, you need to type those exact words into the search command—"2000 U.S. presidential election."

Boolean Search. A **Boolean search** uses the Boolean search terms AND, OR, and NOT to create more complex queries.

- "OR" is less restrictive, as it will include any and all words or phrases joined by the OR operator. (This is called an exclusive OR.)
- "AND" is more restrictive since the return must contain all words or phrases joined by the AND operator.
- "NOT" is used to exclude a certain word, such as "war AND NOT (Civil War)." This query would exclude all resources about the Civil War.

Strategies for Conducting Effective Searches with Students

Because they are so powerful, massive search engines such as Google or Yahoo! or MSN have drawbacks in teaching situations. In response to a query, a search engine will likely return thousands of potentially relevant Web page selections. For example, asking "Why do volcanoes form near oceans?" will produce returns as diverse as science sites for children to U.S. Geologic Survey links on geochemistry and satellite imagery intended for scientific specialists.

A search engine has no way of knowing who asked the question—adult or fourth-grader—so it cannot distinguish the type of site that person is looking for. Therefore, as a teacher, you must sort through masses of material to find what is relevant and age-appropriate for your class curriculum.

Turn on most computers, go to a Web browser, and what appears first is a standard page, preset by the search company. Teachers, like most busy professionals, tend to use this preset page even though it may not be the best way to meet the information management challenges you face as an educator.

iGoogle lets teachers replace the standard Google search page with one that you personally design as an educator (see the accompanying screenshot for one teacher's page). This way you open to a page that has news, weather, and other information that you want in one place. For those using Yahoo!, a product called Pipes performs similar functions.

The teacher customizing the page wanted science and weather information, so she has linked to the Discovery News and Scientific American Web pages. She wanted the date and time since she does not wear a watch. Dogs are a personal area of interest to this teacher so she also has a link to the Dog Whisperer site on her page.

You can further customize your browser by adding search engines and other data-managing software and plug-ins. Begin by choosing from a range of background themes like Walnut, which gives a wooden appearance to the desktop, or NASA Night Launch, for a more futuristic feel. Deluxe accommoda-tions include PicLens, a 3D image browser enhancer, Kodak EasyShare Gal-lery Companion, and the Greasemonkey Javascript customization tool.

CONTACT INFORMATION

iGoogle   www.google.com/ig

Pipes   www.pipes.yahoo.com

Computer technologies and Internet websites have revolutionized the processes of locating academic information. Students and teachers can discover fascinating and inspiring knowledge by doing research together.

Such sorting may take considerable time and it can be tempting to choose whatever sites appear at the top of the search engine's list. But the most popular (meaning the most often visited) sites may not be the best ones for classroom use.

Computer scientists are developing "smarter" search engines that will customize searches for educators by scanning multiple documents and summarizing what is age- and curriculum-appropriate. Until such systems are available, teachers must review and select learning-related websites, and teach students how to use the Web themselves. A number of strategies can assist your use of search engines with students.

Introduce Students to Internet Information Search Sites Designed for Students. Search engines designed for students are important sources of age-appropriate curriculum resources. When students are able to read and understand the materials they find online, they learn how to access and assess the information themselves. Table 5.2 provides a list of general and specialized Internet search tools for students. The general search sites conduct searches of all topics on the Web; the specialized search sites conduct searches within a specific information topic or category.

The Children and Technology Committee of the Association of Library Service to Children has specific criteria for evaluating whether a website communicates effectively to children, including asking whether "the purpose and content of the site is clear, the content encourages exploration and thinking, the site is easy to access, the site takes advantage of the Web's capabilities—it does more than can be done with print." You can also find strategies for using search engines, evaluating Web pages, and explaining Internet and Web jargon in *Finding Information on the Internet: A Tutorial*, a free online resource from the University of California Berkeley Library.

Inquire How Your Students Search for Information Online. Conduct an informal poll with your students about which Internet sites they use when they search for information online. Then introduce them to sites from the list in Table 5.2.

Use Visual Search Tools. Typing keywords into any search engine will produce a list of URLs for your search. Google offers alternate viewing options to the standard URL list. They are *wonder wheel* and *timeline,* different views that facilitate easy movement through the URL resources while displaying all links opened during your search. Wonder wheel transforms the list of URLs into a graphic, a circular hub with spokes that are topics from the URL list. Click on a spoke and a second search opens with a new hub and spokes. This graphic lets you move backwards and forwards without clicking navigation arrows and without losing any URL lists. Timeline creates a timeline from the earliest entries with the keyword(s) to the most recent. Clicking on the timeline itself produces other timelines of shorter periods, months, and years, with more search results to examine.

YOUR JUDGMENT
MATTERS

As you and your students compare the information presented at different sites, consider the following questions:

- Which sites attract and sustain the interest of your students?
- Which ones provide thoughtful reading rather than simply present information?
- Which ones invite interactive investigations and explorations of topics?

Ensure Safe Online Experiences for Students. To ensure safe online experiences teachers can preselect sites for students to visit. A bookmarking portal (discussed in the next chapter) confines students to only the sites you want them to view.

If preselecting sites is not possible, several companies offer software packages to restrict where children go online. Razzul from Kid Innovations is intended for families of 3- to 12-year-olds. It "permits access only to a network of websites and applications deemed safe by Kid Innovations," as well as the Yahoo! Kids Web guide (Baard, 2006).

TABLE 5.2   Internet Search Tools for Students

Site	Description
General Search Resources	
KidsClick! www.kidsclick.org	This site, created by librarians in the Ramapo Catskill (New York) Library Systems, provides a single page search system that draws from multiple databases selected by library professionals.
Ask for Kids www.askkids.com	A large search field promotes student questions instead of single word searches. Other search categories include dictionary, thesaurus, almanac, biography, science, math, and clip art.
Search 22 www.search-22.com	A single portal to 22 search engines for kids that sorts data from a wide variety of sites and combines the results into one database.
Clusty http://clusty.com	This search site scans several popular search engines for a query and then lists the results based on a comparative ranking.
Yahoo!Kids http://kids.yahoo.com	Yahoo's search website for kids features games, animals, music, jokes, and more advertisements than most sites for kids.
Quintura www.quintura.com	A visual search engine for students that features a "tag cloud" or a group of keywords in a visual display as a tool for navigating search results.
Specialized Search Resources	
FirstGov for Kids www.kids.gov	Searches and categories about governmental and non-governmental services.
NASA Kids Club www.nasa.gov/audience/forkids/kidsclub/flash/index.html	News, missions, and multimedia about NASA (National Aeronautics and Space Administration).
The Why Files: The Science behind the News http://whyfiles.org	Weekly science news stories and a Google-supported new story search feature from the Institute for Science Education and the University of Wisconsin-Madison.
U.S. Patent and Trademark Office Kids' Pages www.uspto.gov/go/kids	Games, puzzles, and information about the U.S. Patent and Trademark Office.
Time for Kids www.timeforkids.com/TFK	Searches news from around the world.
Smithsonian Education www.smithsonianeducation.org/students	The Smithsonian's collections for kids featured online.

Net Nanny and netTrekker are software programs that when installed will monitor, block, and report data-related sites visited by students. These act as filters to prevent objectionable content from being viewed at a computer, and are available for a monthly or yearly subscription fee.

The American Library Association (2007, May) has assembled a useful collection of online safety and security resources for children entitled "Especially for Young People and Their Parents." The site includes rules and suggestions for online safety and security, search resources designed for young people, and educational websites for families and teachers.

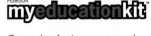

PEARSON
myeducationkit

Go to the Assignments and Activities section of Chapter 5 in MyEducationKit and complete the Web activity entitled "Teaching about Online Safety."

Evaluating Online Information

Every Internet user faces a challenge in determining the accuracy and appropriateness of online information. Quantity does not equal quality, so often an Internet searcher must sift through pages of poor or wrong information to find a few kernels of valid data.

One example of the potential difficulties of evaluating Web-based information occurred in a middle school class investigating the first Thanksgiving. Students knew from their textbook that the Pilgrims held a feast near Plymouth, Massachusetts, in 1621, but their teacher suggested that this was not the first such event in the Americas. They typed the questions "What year was the first Thanksgiving celebrated?" and "Where did the first Thanksgiving take place?" into different search engines. Plenty of information emerged about Plymouth, including invitations to visit as a tourist, but little about the question of when the first Thanksgiving actually occurred.

The teacher located informative online resources at the "Thanksgiving in American Memory" site at the Library of Congress, including a timeline of Thanksgiving feasts between Europeans and native peoples beginning in 1541 in the American southwest. From this timeline, the class learned how the holiday has evolved in U.S. history with Thanksgiving as we celebrate it becoming established as the fourth Thursday in November in 1941. The students read primary source information about how different political leaders regarded Thanksgiving. From other online resources, the class learned that native peoples celebrated harvest feasts for centuries before Europeans arrived. Much of this important historical information was not found by the students' initial online searches. It took more substantive guidance from the teacher to bring this knowledge forward for everyone in the class to learn.

Information Problems and Responses

Different kinds of information problems plague the Internet, argue researchers Nicholas C. Burbules and Thomas A. Callister, Jr., categorizing such "troublesome content" under four terms beginning with the letter *M*: "misinformation, malinformation, messed-up information, and mostly useless information" (2000, p. 96).

- **Misinformation** is information that is "false, out of date, or incomplete in a misleading way" (Burbules & Callister, 2000, p. 96). Such information is everywhere on the Internet, but sometimes hard to identify. "Disinformation" is a particular type of misinformation where "knowingly false or malicious information" is posted online, often from unknown or unidentified authors, in an attempt to discredit individuals or organizations.
- **Malinformation** is what reasonable people might consider "bad" or harmful information and includes "sexual images or material, potentially dangerous or damaging information, political views from militant fringe groups, and so on" (Burbules & Callister, 2000, p. 98).
- **Messed-up information** is information that is "poorly organized and presented" such as long lists of data without synthesis or context, Web pages marked by "gratuitous logos or other graphics that distract or clutter," or discussion boards and blogs that feature text rambling on without a clear focus or topic (Burbules & Callister, 2000, p. 100). There may be so much messed-up information about a topic that a reader is overwhelmed by the data and unable to make sense of it.
- **Mostly useless information** is information that focuses on the trivial, the mundane, the eccentric. Of course, what seems useless to one person may be vitally important to another.

Realizing the availability of "mis," "mal," "messed-up," and "mostly useless" information, note Burbules and Callister, people and organizations resort to one of the following information management and control strategies: censorship, filters, partitions, labeling, or critical reading. Each approach has important implications for teachers and students.

- **Censorship** means that material deemed offensive is banned from a school. But banning material is a notoriously slippery slope. Standards of what is inappropriate or indecent shift over time, and in a society dedicated to freedom of speech and expression, a legitimate concern exists whenever a single individual or organization has the power to decide what to censor from view. Every year the American Library Association conducts Banned Books Week to raise public consciousness about the dangers of censorship in a free society. You can learn more about this campaign at www.ala.org/bbooks.

- **Filtering software,** required in schools receiving federal funds by the Children's Internet Protection Act of 2000, attempts to block material from computers by identifying certain objectionable keywords or phrases. Schools often adopt this method of content control, much to the dismay of teachers blocked from accessing online materials (Reich, 2009, July) and many adolescents who feel that banning material from classroom and library computers conflicts with their desire to discuss issues of sexuality, race, youth culture, and academic achievement. And, from a practical sense, note Burbules and Callister (2000, p. 110), "There is no way to prevent determined youth from finding their way to 'inappropriate' material if they are motivated to do so, especially when they are pooling their skills and sharing things they find with one another."

Not all sites on the Internet contain appropriate or correct information. Adult guidance is critical as students learn to evaluate sites as legitimate sources of information.

- **Partitions,** like filtering, "restrict access only through pages (archives or 'portals' as they are sometimes called) that are themselves lists of approved sites" (Burbules & Callister, 2000, p. 110). Teachers might partition material by using a Web-based bookmarking tool (such as Portaportal or Filamentality, which are discussed in more detail in Chapter 6) to place material for student use in a restricted online space. In effect, teachers create a boundaried space within the larger Internet by limiting where students go during a particular class activity or assignment. Similarly, schools may join an Internet provider that similarly edits online content in advance. Burbules and Callister liken large-scale organizational partitions to "gated communities" that shelter homeowners from "external threats and inconveniences" (2000, p. 111). However, they wonder about the accountability of the people deciding what to allow in and what to rule out. An individual teacher or librarian is directly accountable to the community, but a large corporate provider is detached from the needs or interests of local people.

- **Labels** are classifications in a system similar to the ratings used by movie companies, telephone and satellite providers, video game makers, and other manufacturers of products and services for children. Labeling systems attempt to identify for consumers a standard of safe material for children. But such systems have been less than successful in restricting access to poor material, and they do not educate children and adolescents about what represents good material.

- **Critical reading** is a different approach that teaches children, adolescents, and adults how to read online material and decide for themselves its usefulness or appropriateness (Sutton, 2005). Burbules and Callister refer to critical reading as "hyperreading" or "giving students the tools to identify, criticize, and resist what is dangerous and undesirable on the Internet" (2000, p. 114). Many schools teach critical thinking skills and students apply those skills to assess the quality of works of literature, historical documents, science experiments, or mathematical proofs. Some schools include critical viewing skills in the curriculum so students become aware of the influences of media images on consumers and citizens. Critical reading incorporates both critical thinking and critical viewing to teach students about "selecting, evaluating, and questioning information" from the Web (Burbules & Callister, 2000, p. 82). Developing critical reading skills is a key to information literacy and is vitally important to students' understanding about how to use and contribute to online resources, such as Wikipedia, our next topic in this chapter.

Wikipedia: An Online Encyclopedia

Wikipedia is an online encyclopedia with a worldwide collection of authors. In design, Wikipedia is "an effort to create and distribute a free encyclopedia of the highest possible quality to every single person on the planet in their own language" (Wilmeth, 2005, p. 9). It is a truly massive undertaking, with more than 1.5 million entries, and hundreds of new ones added each day. By June 2006, Wikipedia had become the third most popular news and information site on the Web, trailing only CNN and Yahoo! News (Hafner, 2006).

As you examine Wikipedia and its contents, consider the following questions:

- What is your view of the idea of an encyclopedia produced, updated, and revised by everyone who wants to contribute?
- How would you explain this idea and its resources to your students?
- What entries have you found that needed revision?

In design, anyone can submit an entry to Wikipedia by adding a new listing or revising an existing one. In practice, a core staff of 1,000 volunteers evaluate each entry and decide what material gets posted online. The assumption is that high levels of accuracy and informativeness will emerge from the interchange of ideas and information generated by multiple contributors. In contrast to a voluminous bound and printed encyclopedia written by a select group of editorial board members, Wikipedia claims to make the presentation of knowledge an open and participatory process by inviting everyone online to be part of the writing.

It is possible to disagree with what has been posted on Wikipedia through its dispute resolution process. Readers who find entries that are not neutral—either factually or conceptually—can request dispute resolution through a series of steps including posting their concerns on article pages. The dispute is resolved when (1) the information in an entry is modified, (2) the information in an entry is expanded to include all competing points of view about a topic, or (3) when the person who began the dispute is unable to substantiate the claims of bias. In the last case, the entry remains as it was before the dispute began.

Many people, librarians and teachers among them, distrust Wikipedia because recognized experts do not serve as referees of the knowledge selection process. Their reservation is that without such editorial control, the trustworthiness of the database cannot be real. As a case in point, a former assistant to Attorney General Robert Kennedy in the 1960s found himself linked to both Kennedy assassinations through a false biography posted on Wikipedia for several months in 2005 (Seyele, 2005). In 2006, in response, Wikipedia began blocking certain designated entries from outside editing, including the biographies of prominent historical figures (President George W. Bush, Albert Einstein) and controversial topics (human rights in China).

Others contend that Wikipedia is a highly reliable information source. In 2005, a German magazine asked experts to compare the credibility of 66 articles on a variety of topics, and Wikipedia proved statistically more accurate than two other online encyclopedias—Brockhaus Premium 3.3 and Microsoft Encarta 3.1 (Wilmeth, 2005, p. 9). A comparison by the science journal *Nature* found that Wikipedia was only slightly less reliable than the *Encyclopedia Britannica,* a contention that the Britannica vigorously disputed ("Britannica Attacks," 2006; Giles, 2005).

Teachers in every subject area can have productive discussions with students about the merits and shortcomings of Wikipedia. Consider the following strategies for using Wikipedia with students.

Compare Wikipedia with Other Encyclopedias. Ask your students to assist you in evaluating how Wikipedia might differ from an encyclopedia. To start the activity, contrast Wikipedia with one of the other prominent online encyclopedias such as Microsoft Encarta or Encyclopedia Britannica Online. Those encyclopedias are relatively fixed bodies of information that change content only with the issuing of a new edition of the software. By comparison, Wikipedia is dynamic; its information is updated and changed all the time (unless a selection is closed by the review board).

Next, you and your students can compare Wikipedia with paper encyclopedias that have been written and edited by scholars in many fields of knowledge. By contrast, Internet readers who may or may not be experts in a field of study write and edit Wikipedia. With a paper encyclopedia, there is no way for users to disagree with the entries. Wikipedia users challenge entries by placing text under dispute.

Ask your students to add to this list of comparisons and draw conclusions about these different types of knowledge sources by contrasting paper and electronic systems in a class simulation. Choose topics that small groups of students know well (for instance, a sport, a musical form, a contemporary person, fashion design, or a notable historic event). The groups, like the experts who make printed encyclopedias, collaborate in writing and illustrating an encyclopedia entry about their topics. Everyone in the class does the same, researching and exchanging information before writing and illustrating their own group's entry.

The groups do not divulge details of their work until the day that the entries are unveiled side by side on an overhead projector for class consideration, criticism, and revision. Everyone has the

FIGURE 5.3 Web Research Guidelines for Students

1. Remain focused on your topic. Limit a search and avoid unnecessary surfing.

2. Use common sense to determine the purpose of the site. Look for potential or hidden bias. Think of the following question: Who is creating this site and why?

3. List all websites in correct form for every assignment. Websites are like books. If you use them, you must be able to document them and share with others how and where to locate the information.

4. In order to determine the reliability of a website, cross-reference your research (check the facts with another source).

5. Always check the credentials of authors whose writing appears on the Web. People publish on the Web who are not experts in a field. Always determine if the author is a reliable and credible expert.

6. Credit Web authors for their words and ideas by using proper citations. Although it is easy to copy other people's words and ideas from a computer screen, this is no different from copying directly from a book.

7. Evaluate the site and its content before downloading the information.

8. Follow teacher guidelines about the number of websites or CD encyclopedia citations allowed per assignment.

9. Keep a log of all the sites you visit for the assignment. Bookmark or highlight your favorites.

10. Share good ideas and useful information to help others with their research.

leges, or society. Despite admonitions from teachers and parents, 36 percent of high school students used the Internet to plagiarize an assignment, the Los Angeles–based Josephson Institute Center for Youth Ethics (2008) reported after surveying nearly 30,000 students in 100 schools nationwide.

Causes of Plagiarism

Three factors contribute to plagiarism in today's schools.

- *The Web.* The Internet is a vast unregulated marketplace where term papers are for sale or available free to students. The *New York Times* (McGrath, 2006) reported that one website calling itself Term Paper Relief offers college papers written to appear genuine and not plagiarized for about $10 a page. In addition, entire texts of articles and books are posted online, from which information can be easily copied.

- *High-stakes testing.* The nation's current emphasis on test results, high grades on student transcripts, and intense competition for college placement creates a context that invites plagiarism to achieve high grades.

- *Misassumptions by students.* Sometimes students venture over the line of dishonesty without realizing they have done so. For example, they locate information online and, assuming that if something is on the Internet, it must be free to use, they incorporate it in as they found it, without citing sources. At other times, when teachers ask students to write about topics experts have already explained in books and articles, youngsters may feel intimidated, realizing their content knowledge and writing style cannot match that of their online sources. They think, "I'll just turn in what I found so I will be sure to be right." Either way, the result is the same as if the student had knowingly plagiarized.

Preventing Plagiarism by Students

Teachers, not wanting to support or encourage plagiarizing, employ many different strategies to identify papers that contain uncited material, including searching the Internet themselves to find the original sources. Some schools subscribe to plagiarism checking services such as turnitin .com, ithenticate.com, or canexus.com that electronically scan student work to identify text copied directly from other sources. Turnitin reports that it receives 40,000 papers a day, and finds about 30 percent have material that makes them "less than original" (Berdik, 2005, p. B11).

Rather than focus on identifying students who have submitted plagiarized material, some educators urge teachers to address the issue before students submit their work (CCCC Caucus on Intellectual Property, 2000; DeSena, 2007). James McKenzie (1998) has identified seven ways for

YOUR JUDGMENT
MATTERS

As you read the assignment in Figure 5.4, consider the following questions:

- How has this teacher structured the assignment to make critical thinking essential and copying less likely?
- What other strategies could this teacher use to avoid plagiarism and promote original research?

teachers to combat plagiarism while teaching students important research and thinking skills:

- Distinguish levels or types of research
- Discourage "trivial pursuits"
- Emphasize essential questions
- Require and enable students to construct answers
- Focus on information storage systems
- Stress citation ethics
- Assess progress throughout the entire research process

McKenzie's suggestions emanate from the idea that the way teachers construct assignments determines how likely students are to use the Web and then plagiarize materials. If an assignment asks students only to find already established facts (for example, "Describe the climate of the Gobi Desert" or "List the characteristics of each of the planets in the solar system"), it is easier to copy verbatim information found online or in books.

But when students are asked to locate and analyze the material, there are fewer reasons to copy other people's work. For example, McKenzie recommends that instead of asking "why" something happened in the past, teachers ask students to consider "why various outcomes did not occur." The goal, he urges, is for students to "become producers of insights and ideas rather than mere consumers" of the information they locate online.

Focusing on "essential questions" is another recommended way for ending plagiarism while teaching students how to think critically and creatively. Essential questions are "investigations which might make a difference in the quality of life" or "studies which might cast light in dark corners, illuminating basic truths" (McKenzie, 1998). If teachers identify essential questions at the beginning of a curriculum unit and ask students to do research and analysis related to these topics, they will be less likely to simply repeat what others have said. In such assignments, the views, beliefs, and arguments of students matter, giving them an authentic reason to speak and write in their own words.

An Evidence Search Assignment

If the most effective way to avoid plagiarism is to give assignments that cannot be plagiarized, then what do such assignments look like in practice? Figure 5.4 presents an evidence search assignment

---

FIGURE 5.4 A Presidential Election Evidence Search Assignment

In this assignment, you will use the Internet to search information about the 2008 presidential candidates and where they stand on specific issues.

Step 1: Choose two issues from the following list to concentrate your search.

Environment	Gay marriage	Civil liberties	Health care
War on Terror	Education	Homeland security	War on drugs
Gun control	War in Iraq	Taxes	Immigration

Step 2: Find out the positions of Hillary Clinton, Barack Obama, Rudy Giuliani, John McCain, Mitt Romney, Ron Paul, or Ralph Nader on your issues. On a separate piece of paper, record your observations about each candidate based on the following criteria:

What is his or her position on the issue you are investigating?

Is this position firm or has it changed (and how) during the campaign?

What policies or programs is he or she advocating?

What evidence have you found to back up these proposals?

Step 3: Visit the official campaign website for each candidate. However, it is important that you look at a one or more of the sites listed below to get a broader view. You may also consult other sources. Please record the address of each site used in your research.

abcnews.com	thenation.com	cnn.com	democrats.org
motherjones.com	bbc.com	boston.com	rnc.org
democracynow.org	greenparty.org	nytimes.com

Step 4: Based on the information you have gathered, create a political cartoon. Choose one candidate as the focus for your cartoon. Your cartoon should portray your chosen candidate and his or her stance on at least one of the issues you have chosen to research. Need inspiration? Check out Daryl Cagle's professional cartoonist index (http://cagle.slate.msn.com).

from an eighth-grade social studies teacher whose class was studying the 2008 presidential election campaign. The goal was for students to use the Internet to locate information about candidates and their positions on issues and then produce original research that was not copied from online sources.

 TECHNOLOGY TRANSFORMATION LESSON PLAN

THINK GLOBALLY. ACT LOCALLY!
Conducting Social Studies Research on the Internet

Grade(s)	Middle School/High School
Subject(s)	History/Social Studies and English/Language Arts
Key Goal/Enduring Understanding	Social problems are issues affecting everyone in society, not just a few individuals. An effective society depends on citizens being aware of social problems and acting together in response to them.
Essential Question	How might middle and high school students identify, investigate, and respond to world social problems?

Learning Standards

National Council for the Social Studies (NCSS)—*Expectations for Excellence: Curriculum Standards for the Social Studies*

> **Theme III:** People, Places, and Environment
> **Theme X:** Civic Ideals and Practices
> **Theme XI:** Global Connections

National Council of Teachers of English (NCTE)—*Standards for the English Language Arts*

> **Standard 8:** Students use a variety of technological resources . . . to gather and synthesize information and to create and communicate knowledge.

International Society for Technology in Education (ISTE)—*NETS-S, 2007*

> **Standard 2:** *Communication and Collaboration.* Students use digital media and environments to communicate and work collaboratively, including at a distance, to support individual learning and contribute to the learning of others.
> **Standard 3:** *Research and Information Fluency.* Students use digital tools to gather, evaluate, and use information.
> **Standard 5:** *Digital Citizenship.* Students understand human, cultural, and societal issues related to technology and practice legal and ethical behavior.
> **Standard 6:** *Technology Operations and Concepts.* Students demonstrate a sound understanding of technology concepts, systems, and operations.

Learning Objectives

Student will know and be able to

- Demonstrate the value and application of essential questions to guide research about social problems.
- Apply an organized note-taking system for gathering information from diverse sources and using properly formatted bibliographic references.
- Analyze the differences among facts, opinions, and inferences in written and online sources of information.
- Use computers, video equipment, and other technology to produce informative public service announcements (PSAs) about selected issues.

Technology Uses The lesson utilizes classroom computers, the Internet as a research librarian, and video recording devices and editing software for the filming and viewing of students' public service announcements.

Minimal Technology	Infusion of Technology

Identifying
  Consult a librarian and/or card catalog
	Identifying
	  Use computer search engines and databases

Archiving
  Store information on note cards in a bibliographic file
	Archiving
	  Use computer bookmarking and electronic note-taking tools

Contacting
  Mail letters and postcards or send telephone messages
	Contacting
	  Send email

Recording
  Video recorder with tripod
  Video tape
	Recording
	  Digital video recorder with tripod
	  Mini DV tape

Editing
  Two VCRs
  Extra video tapes
  A/V cables (VCR to VCR)
  Television
	Editing
	  Digital video recorder
	  Computer
	  Windows Media Player
	  Pinnacle video editor

Viewing
  Television
  VCR
	Viewing
	  Computer
	  Windows media player
	  CD/DVD burner or computer projector

Evaluation

- Ten journal entries by students covering the research and PSA production process
- Digital archived list of governmental agencies, scientific organizations, and public interest and issue advocacy groups related to an issue of concern
- Individual and group participation in writing, performing, and recording
- Audience response sheets for each completed PSA
- Student performance rubrics completed at the level of excellent or good

LESSON PLAN DESCRIPTION

Introduction

"Think Globally. Act Locally!" uses websites and video and audio recording technology to enable students to research, write, and perform public service announcements (PSAs) about social problems that affect the local community, the nation, and the world. This lesson is intended as an activity that can be taught in middle school or high school as part of the history/social studies or language arts curriculum.

Lesson Focus

"Think Globally. Act Locally!" features active student involvement and engagement, both intellectually and technologically. By connecting large-scale global issues to local community problems, students see the immediate relevance of their investigations. By using multiple technologies (Internet, word processing, video cameras, and editing software), students are using technology through

▶

the lesson. By having opportunities to share the PSAs with wider audiences beyond the class, students see the relevance of reviewing and revising their research, writing, and performances in anticipation of viewing by community members.

Lesson Design—Minimal Technology

A minimal technology version of the lesson uses an inquiry-based approach to the investigation of social problems combined with research strategies involving library resources. Students need 10 to 12 class periods to complete the assignments.

The first step is a brainstorming activity about environmental or economic problems that have global and local significance. Students list social issues—for example, acid rain, invasive species, global warming, ozone layer depletion, pesticides and herbicides, endangered species, habitat destruction, handicap accessibility, noise pollution, air pollution, and waste/recycling. From the list of problems, each student chooses an issue and writes a persuasive paragraph explaining why she or he is interested in researching that topic.

The next step is to pose an essential question about the topic. This is the "thinking globally" stage of the lesson plan. Students must consult print resources, locate up-to-date and credible statistical information related to the topic, and document their sources in a correct bibliographic format. Students then write an answer to their essential question as well as a statement about the problem from the point of view of someone who has been affected by it, either locally or from somewhere else in the world.

After researching the topic, the students present their reports in class as part of a general discussion that summarizes the lesson and what everyone has learned about how people can address large-scale social problems, the "acting locally" stage. The teacher grades student reports, assessing the quality of research and the clarity of writing.

LESSON ACTIVITIES USING TECHNOLOGY

Computers, the Internet, and video cameras dramatically change this lesson—both how students do their research and how students present their research findings and final project.

1. *Preselect Internet Research Sites.* The Internet provides rapid access to up-to-date information sources for each of the social problems on the list brainstormed by the students. For each topic, preselect and bookmark sites so students can review policy statements, research reports, and advocacy group positions about different sides of the issues. Complex social and economic problems are debated by multiple competing interest groups seeking to convey their points of view to the public. The students begin by using preselected resources as a starting point for researching these debates. Without Internet technology, amassing and copying the breadth of resources for each topic would require an exhaustive amount of work from a teacher.

2. *Practice Web Research Skills.* To develop sound Web research skills, students are required to utilize a mix of print and electronic resources in their initial paper explaining the topic they have chosen to investigate. In citing their sources, students must demonstrate that they have done thoughtful research and not simply copied down the first entries they found after a keyword search. By the nature of the assignment, plagiarism becomes a nonissue. The students show that they were consulting diverse sources, and there is really no reason to use other people's ideas without attribution.

3. *Present Research Findings as Public Service Announcements.* At the presentation stage of the lesson, technology enables students to go beyond in-class oral reports. Listening to a lengthy series of oral presentations is a mostly passive learning experience for the other students in the class. But using computers to compose and video cameras to film PSAs changes the roles of both presenters and student audience members. Presenters must conceptualize what to say and show on tape to engage and inform their classmates. They must think in cinematic terms where words and illustrations convey meaning in convincing ways. Viewers are more likely to

▶

be an active audience when listening and responding to the PSA videos. Seeing PSAs allows these student viewers to think about issues more fully, become more interested in the topic, and offer their own ideas about how best to handle complex social problems.

4. **Design Rubrics with the Class.** With student participation, create rubrics of the qualities that interesting PSAs must include, and clearly state that no PSA is finished until all the rubric criteria meet high performance requirements. The goal here is to involve students in establishing criteria for evaluation in advance of doing the project so they will be more invested in the project and the results.

5. **Create Presentation Teams.** Teams of students with similar or comparable topics are responsible for writing, performing, and filming a short public service announcement about their topic. Class time is used for writing the PSA scripts, rehearsing the performances, and learning how to operate a video recorder or digital video recorder. Students take turns in the roles of on-air performer, camera operator, director, and video editor. Each team edits their video material just as individuals edit their writing—mindful of how best to convey their ideas to a viewing audience to make their message memorable.

6. **Film the Public Service Announcements.** Before filming the PSAs, students practice being a silent audience for the PSA performers. An eye-opening strategy is to film a short segment with members of the audience talking while other students are trying to film their ideas. When playing the film for everyone's viewing, it is obvious how noise interferes with the performance and ruins the taping. Give students time to practice using the video and audio recording equipment by assigning specific roles: director, videographer, sound technician, and on-camera performers. Rotate these roles so everyone experiences being both on camera and behind the scenes.

   The completed PSAs are shown to the class, who complete audience feedback sheets about each performance. When the lesson is completed, arrangements can then be made with the local community access station to air some of the PSAs on television.

7. **Expand the Lesson.** There are a number of ways to expand this lesson to include more time for investigation and study. If a class website or blog is a storage location for the PSAs so students in other schools can access them, the design and function of Web-based visual content becomes important. The NCTE Read, Write, Think site offers the PSA lesson plan "MyTube: Changing the World with Video Public Service Announcements" (www.readwritethink.org/lessons/lesson_view.asp?id=1069). It includes handouts that allow students to evaluate and reflect on their making of PSAs and lists Web resources for viewing other PSAs for comparison with their work.

Additionally, by asking the class to investigate the local dimensions of global social problems, the community involvement and civic engagement skills of the students can be enhanced. Students first research governmental departments and agencies responsible for reporting information about an issue of concern. After identifying online addresses of local, state, and federal agencies dealing with the issue, students send email correspondence to appropriate individuals stating their ideas and opinions. Finally, students identify other students around the country who have taken action to address social issues and communicate with them about their proposed plans for change.

ANALYSIS AND EXTENSIONS

1. Name two features you find useful about this lesson.
2. Name two areas for extension or improvement of this lesson.
3. How successfully has information technology been integrated into the lesson?
4. How might students become more involved in designing, using, and evaluating technology in the lesson?

FOCUS QUESTION 1: What is the meaning of information literacy for teachers and students?

- Instantly available information on the Internet is transforming the work of teachers, creating the need to teach students how to *access* and *assess* the resources and materials they find online.

- Teaching students how to do Internet research is a crucial element of information literacy and involves learning how to recognize and utilize high-quality electronic information.

- Information literacy and Internet research together enable students to act as critical readers and thoughtful researchers in Web-based environments.

FOCUS QUESTION 2: What are search engines and how do they work?

- Search engines, amazingly fast but not always well-understood tools, enable teachers and students to access online information by locating Web pages that have been linked to its database.

- Online information searching is also known as "Web information research and retrieval" and involves knowing how to locate and analyze information from the Internet.

- Teachers often benefit from using specialized search resources that narrow the focus of their searches to more educationally relevant materials.

- Electronic note taking offers teachers and students new ways to record and save the information they locate online.

FOCUS QUESTION 3: What pieces of information do students need to know about Internet searching?

- Google's system of ranking Web pages not only by keywords, but also by popularity and crosslisting with other sites, has propelled it to the status of world's number one search engine.

- Searching the Web involves one of three search strategies: (1) free-text, (2) keyword/exact match, or (3) Boolean.

- Search resources designed for students provide age-appropriate information and valuable Internet and information literacy learning experiences.

FOCUS QUESTION 4: How can teachers and students thoughtfully evaluate online information resources, including the online encyclopedia Wikipedia?

- Four types of information problems are found on the Web: (1) misinformation, (2) malinformation, (3) messed-up information, and (4) mostly useless information.

- Wikipedia, the online encyclopedia, provides teachers with a relevant opportunity to teach students strategies for evaluating the quality of information found on the Web.

- According to the American Library Association (ALA), high-quality online information meets five criteria: (1) accuracy, (2) authority, (3) objectivity, (4) currency, and (5) coverage.

- Paying attention to URL extensions, discussing cognitive load, using lesson plan sites selectively, and giving clear Web research guidelines are important strategies for teachers to use in teaching Internet information evaluation to students.

FOCUS QUESTION 5: How can teachers respond to problems of plagiarism when students use online sources?

- Plagiarism is the act of directly copying or misrepresenting someone else's work as one's own; students do it both intentionally and unintentionally.

- The ways that teachers structure their in-school and homework assignments can significantly reduce or even avoid situations where students plagiarize.

PEARSON
myeducationkit

To check your comprehension of the content covered in the chapter, go to the MyEducationKit for your book and complete the Study Plan for Chapter 5. Here you will be able to take a chapter quiz, receive feedback on your answers, and then access resources that will enhance your understanding of chapter content.

KEY TERMS

Boolean search
Censorship
Cognitive load
Critical reading
Electronic note taking
Filtering software
Free-text search
Information and communication technology literacy (ICT literacy)
Information literacy

Information research and retrieval
Information search
Internet
IT FITness
IT fluency
Keywords
Keyword/exact match search
Labels
Malinformation
Messed-up information

Misinformation
Mostly useless information
Partitions
Plagiarism
Search engines
21st-century literacies
URL (uniform resource locator)
Web browser
Web information retrieval
Wikipedia

ACTIVITIES FOR YOUR TEACHER PORTFOLIO

1. RESEARCHING ONLINE INFORMATION

Choose a topic that you plan to teach to students as part of your student teaching or your pre–student teaching field experiences. If you are an elementary teacher, look for topics in language arts, science, math, and history/social studies. If you are a secondary teacher, look for topics in different areas of your major academic field (for instance, U.S. literature, world literature, poetry, writing).

After choosing your topic, answer the following questions about researching online information.

- Research your topic using different search engines and by typing in different keywords. What differences do you notice between search engines, if any? How do keywords change the nature of the search process?
- Look at the kinds of information that you located through your online searching. Are there differences in the information found on sites that are .org, .com, .gov, or .net?
- Use the Web research criteria proposed in the chapter to further evaluate the quality of the information you located in your search. Which questions from our Web search guide do you find particularly useful?
- Start bookmarking the best sites from your search. What are your reasons for adding certain sites to your list of favorites?

2. STUDENTS EVALUATING WIKIPEDIA

Create an assignment for your students using the online encyclopedia Wikipedia to improve their critical reading and research skills. You might ask your students to:

- Compare and contrast how their textbook and Wikipedia discuss a topic. How are the entries different? How are they the same? Which source is more reliable and why?
- Critically evaluate the Wikipedia entry on a topic that you are studying in class. What are the strengths of the Wikipedia entry? What are its weaknesses? Would they suggest putting the Wikipedia entry under dispute? Would they suggest putting their textbook's treatment of a topic under dispute?
- Suggest ways to improve or correct an incomplete or inaccurate Wikipedia entry on a topic you are studying in class. What would they do to make the material more accurate, more inclusive, or more accessible to student readers?

3. READING AND TECHNOLOGY IN THE NEXT 10 YEARS

In a survey for its *2008 Kids & Family Reading Report,* the educational company Scholastic asked students ages 9 to 17 what reading-related technologies would be available in the next 10 years. See how your students compare to the students cited in the Scholastic report.

When reading a book online, people will be able to tag and share their favorite parts and their thoughts about the book with other people who are online.	87%
Books on the Internet will have links to different kinds of things like games, websites, and other people's opinions.	86%
When reading a book on a computer, people will be able to type notes to themselves and highlight their favorite parts of the book.	81%
People will have all their favorite books stored electronically on a computer or another electronic device.	77%
When people read for fun, they will read most books on a computer or some other kind of electronic device.	66%
Books will have secret codes and links to websites where people can join virtual worlds.	63%

GROWING AND LEADING WITH TECHNOLOGY

This activity offers an opportunity to grow as a teacher and learn to lead with technology. Begin by reviewing the Chapter 5 Learning Goal and New Technologies listed in the chart at the start of the chapter. Then read the following actual classroom scenario and consider how technologies in Chapter 5 might be integrated into the lesson. Follow-up steps to this activity can be completed at MyEducationKit.

HEATHER'S "PEOPLE OF THE CIVIL WAR" LESSON

Heather is teaching a United States history survey course to tenth-grade high school students. The course covers the major historical developments from the 1775 beginning of the American Revolution to the end of the post–Civil War Reconstruction period in 1877. Central to the course is the Civil War (1861–1865) and the themes of race, rights, and revolution that appear and reappear throughout the nation's history. The Civil War era is a major topic in the state's history curriculum framework, and the state's mandatory history achievement test for high school students includes several questions about these historical events.

Building on an approach set forth by historian Stephen B. Oates in his *Voices of the Storm* books, Heather wants her students to view the Civil War through the eyes and words of key historical figures. In designing her "People of the Civil War" lesson, Heather intends to have her class complete research reports on prominent men and women from the North and the South, including Abraham Lincoln, Jefferson Davis, Harriet Tubman, Harriet Beecher Stowe, Frederick Douglass, and Nat Turner. She wants her students to understand that these icons of history were real people with views and aspirations, not unlike people today.

Earlier in the school year, when Heather gave a historical research assignment to her class, many students struggled with the procedures and methods of locating historical information. Some copied facts directly from textbooks or Internet sites, while others did not know how to identify reliable versus biased sources. Heather decided that this assignment would not only teach her students about the people of the Civil War era, but how to locate and present information correctly and creatively using electronic sources, either using her classroom's five Internet-accessible computers or the computer lab just down the hallway from her classroom.

• Using the technologies discussed in this chapter, how would you propose that Heather integrate technology as a way to achieve her teaching goals?

PEARSON
myeducationkit

To complete the full activity, go to the Growing and Leading with Technology section in Chapter 5 in MyEducationKit and access the activity "Heather's 'People of the Civil War' Lesson."

6 Teaching with Educational Websites and Other Online Resources

The biggest most sweeping change in our relationship with the Internet may not be as much the ability to publish as it is the ability to share and connect and create with many, many others of like minds and interests.

—Will Richardson, *Blogs, Wikis, Podcasts, and Other Powerful Web Tools for the Classroom* (2006)

CHAPTER LEARNING GOAL

Digital Content and Educational Websites

Using Web-based educational materials and digital content in teaching

CONNECTING to the NETS

NETS-T

2 Design and Develop Digital Age Learning Experiences and Assessments

3 Model Digital Age Work and Learning

NETS-S

3 Research and Information Fluency

NEW TECHNOLOGIES

- Bookmarking tools
- Social bookmarking tools
- Information alerts
- WebQuests
- Virtual field trips
- Interactive maps
- Interactive videoconferencing
- Lesson plan websites
- Student-to-expert communication websites
- Real-time and recorded data websites
- Archival and primary source websites
- Skills/practice websites
- Exploration and discovery websites

CHAPTER OVERVIEW

Chapter 6 considers information management, a necessity when teachers and students utilize learning resources provided by educational websites and other online resources. The chapter introduces bookmarking, social bookmarking, and information alerts as ways to organize information that teachers need to prepare lessons aligned with local, state, and national curriculum frameworks. WebQuests and virtual field trips suggest ways to extend learning using the Web. Finally, the chapter examines six different types of educational websites that support inquiry and interactivity to fully engage students with academic content.

The chapter incorporates NETS-T Standard 3, Part d, which asks teachers and students to use digital tools to "locate, analyze, evaluate, and use information resources to support research and learning." It also supports NETS-S Standard 3's call for research and information fluency.

FOCUS QUESTIONS

1. What is information management and digital content?
2. How are information management technologies such as bookmarking, social bookmarking, and information alerts useful to teachers?
3. How do teachers organize electronic resources to address curriculum frameworks and learning standards?
4. What are WebQuests and virtual field trips?
5. What and where are different types of educational websites available to teachers on the Internet?
6. How might educational websites provide interactive and engaging learning experiences for students?

In late 2003, researchers from the School of Management and Systems at the University of California, Berkeley issued a fascinating report, *How Much Information? 2003*. The report summarized efforts to determine how much new information had been produced worldwide in the previous year. The findings included some startling statistics (Lyman & Varian, 2003, pp. 1–2, 5):

- "Print, film, magnetic, and optical storage media produced about 5 exabytes of new information in 2002. . . . [T]his is less than one-third of the new information that is communicated through electronic information flow."
- Five exabytes of information is equivalent in size to the information contained in 37,000 libraries the size of the Library of Congress's book collections.
- "The United States produces about 40% of the world's new stored information."
- "Annually, each of the inhabitants of North America consumes 11,916 sheets of paper. . . . At least half of this paper is used in printers and copiers to produce office documents."

Another team of researchers at the University of California, San Diego are continuing to catalog the growth of new information in an expanded three year How Much Information? study launched in 2008.

The *How Much Information? 2003* report spotlights this chapter's learning goal—how you and your students can successfully manage online information, digital content, and educational websites as tools for teaching and learning. **Information management** is a business term generally used to describe how organizations and systems keep track of data for making decisions and setting policies. When applied to teachers and students, information management means organizing and utilizing all the different kinds of electronic information one must handle professionally and academically.

The need for information management is not a new phenomenon. Our grandparents and great-grandparents living and working in the United States during the early and mid-20th century surely felt a need to manage the information they encountered in their daily existence. But their lives were organized around the cycles of seasonal change for those who worked on farms or the patterns of 8- to 10-hour work shifts for those employed in firms and factories. The rate and pace of change via radio, television, newspapers, and magazines was not as accelerated as in today's information-based society.

Computers, the Internet, and other technologies produce informational management demands different from those faced in the past. You may have felt that there is too much information to learn and remember among college classes, school placements, outside-of-school jobs, personal finances, recreation, and communication with friends and family.

For teachers, the need for information management—and the potentials for information overload—is severe. Teaching requires ongoing information sharing between you and your students. No new teacher walks into a classroom and teaches extemporaneously. Without having taught the material before, you will find yourself continually researching and reviewing curriculum topics, often every day. In elementary school, this means

Interactive whiteboards display images and information dynamically, involving the entire class in viewing and discussing academic ideas and concepts.

presenting multiple subject areas (language arts, math, science, and history), whereas in middle or high school, you will be teaching a specific subject field in depth.

The rapid pace of scientific and historical discoveries further complicates information management. Textbooks are quickly out-of-date, but school systems do not have money to replace them as often as needed. Many teachers tell us that they wish they had the time to create their own curriculum materials from multiple sources to compensate for the inadequacies of school-purchased materials. More and more teachers are recognizing that part of their job is to use computer technologies to create—in partnership with their students—learning materials that are rigorous, reliable, relevant, and engaging.

 ## Managing Information Electronically

Being a teacher means being a constant learner about the subjects you teach and the topics you find interesting and engaging. Gaining new knowledge to communicate to others is one of teaching's great joys. An English teacher we know is on a six-year quest to read a biography of every U.S. president from George Washington to Barack Obama. Learning about presidents and the times they lived in is a way for him to contextualize the literary efforts of men and women writers during different periods of U.S. history. Another friend, an elementary school teacher who specializes in young children's reading and writing, is constantly searching for new science information to intrigue and engage her students. She wants to show her students how adult scientists investigate questions they find interesting and puzzling, and in so doing, produce the research and writing that leads to breakthrough discoveries.

As an easily accessible source of academic information and new knowledge, the Internet is unparalleled. Such online information is known as **digital content.** Teachers can use this Web-based information to teach the school curriculum. A computer with Internet access enables a teacher to scan through any number of sites about topics of personal or professional interest, locating relevant information and enriching course material. An Internet search sets the agenda for a trip to the library or bookstore for more in-depth reading on a topic.

In addition to elucidating a teacher's own personal and professional interests, a second reason for searching the Internet is its usefulness for meeting local, state, and national curriculum frameworks. We will explain more about how teachers can use the Web to address curriculum standards later in this chapter.

Like all regular Web users, teachers seek effective ways to manage the large amounts information they find online. As one new teacher candidate remarked to us, "My Inbox is always filled and I never have the time to organize it. I need a sorter and a sifter."

Information management—the process of finding, organizing, and using information—is particularly important because few individuals can remember off the top of their heads all the facts and concepts important for a given lesson, especially in science and history, where textbooks are frequently behind the curve of the latest discoveries and developments. By necessity, teachers turn to the Web for information. With effective information management strategies, they efficiently organize information rather than being overloaded and overwhelmed.

YOUR JUDGMENT MATTERS

As you think about your own experiences for classes you are taking or teaching, consider the following questions:

- How do you manage the information you need for college classes and school teaching assignments?
- How do you keep track of the information you find from both paper and online sources?
- Why do you think the work of a teacher involves a sizable amount of time spent doing information research and management?

FIGURE 6.1 Bookmarks

- Social Impact Games...–Entertainment Goals
- Service Learning: Stu...ent in K–12 Schools
- Dropout Rates in the United States: 2005
- Reducing the Dropout Rate
- Ed games
- essential quest
- Free Icebreakers, tea...orporate icebreakers
- CampusTools HigherEd
- wfcr playlist – Google Search
- WFCR.org Quick Playlist Links
- Vygotskian Viewpoint multimedia
- InfoBridges | Google Groups

Bookmarking for Teachers

Teachers of an earlier generation used file folders, notebooks, and other types of paper organizing systems. Such systems are inefficient because they become too large, because they depend on constant refiling of material used, because new material must be continually copied and stored, and because it takes time to scan through the files to find what you need. Often an article or other resource fits in more than one category so these paper materials need to be copied more than once to allow for cross-referencing. Managing the paper flow becomes hugely time consuming.

Bookmarking tools offer teachers ways to locate information and organize it effectively using computers and the Web. Bookmarking (also called bookmarks) refers to the capacity of computers through a Web browser to remember the website addresses that you visit frequently. Using a bookmark, you can electronically catalog and subsequently access Web pages with just one simple command. Figure 6.1 shows one teacher's list of bookmarks.

Bookmarks (the term used in the Netscape Web browser) are also called **favorites** (in Internet Explorer) or **hotlists** (in Mosaic). A baseball fan might bookmark the website of her favorite team as well as sites devoted to everything from baseball scores to inside information about trades, draft choices, contract negotiations, and online leagues. The latest news about baseball is only a click away.

To understand the usefulness of bookmarking, imagine an elementary or middle school teacher in need of a lesson plan for teaching multiplication who goes to the Internet to find math resources. To begin searching, she enters the keywords "teaching multiplication" and finds the Math Cats website. While in the website she finds a blog with an entry related to the Schoolhouse Rock videos and CD-ROMs for multiplication. Reading a blogger's notes related to the subject, she finds a link that sends her directly to the Schoolhouse Rock website with the lyrics to a song she remembers from her childhood. After hearing the song she returns to the Schoolhouse Rock homepage and finds an advertisement for Sites for Teachers touting "Hundreds of Educational Websites Rated by Popularity." While there, she clicks on the School Express website because it is the top-ranked site. There she signs up for a eNewsletter that promises weekly curriculum for free.

For a moment, our teacher loses track of why she began searching the Internet in the first place. When she tries to find the original Math Cats website, her desktop is filled with so many open windows that she has a hard time locating the original page and starts over again in the search engine, trying to remember which keywords she used when she started. Becoming distracted or overwhelmed by a seemingly endless number of interesting websites is a common phenomenon not only for teachers but for students as well. Students searching for information online are easily attracted to colorful and entertaining Web pages that draw them away from their original search.

As a way to combat information distraction and overload, bookmarks serve as easy-to-find, easy-to-remember electronic signposts for teachers and students. They allow a return to important locations without spending time using a search engine. Most teachers find electronic bookmarking to be an essential organizing tool in their information management process.

For teachers, locating and bookmarking high-quality Web resources is just part of information management. The next step involves learning how to use Web resources with students while teaching. Tech Tool 6.1 highlights two tools you can use to manage bookmarked resources in your teaching.

Go to the Tutorials section of Chapter 6 in MyEducationKit and access the practical tutorial entitled "Social Bookmarking." Use the tutorial to learn to create social bookmarks.

Using Social Bookmarking

Social bookmarking expands the concept of individual bookmarking from one user/one computer to a community of users on many computers (EDUCAUSE Learning Initiative, 2005b,

TECH TOOL 6.1

USING BOOKMARKS IN YOUR TEACHING—PORTAPORTAL AND FILAMENTALITY

Sending students directly to the Web without prior guidance is generally not a good idea. Students become distracted, lost, or veer deliberately off task. There is always the possibility of visiting inappropriate sites.

To use material from the Internet successfully when teaching, many teachers preselect the Web resources they want students to visit as part of a class or homework assignment. In some cases, teachers confine students to those preselected sites as a way to minimize distractions and confusion within the classroom.

One Web-based resource preselection tool is Portaportal, a data management utility that acts as an online library of the Web pages you commonly use in your lessons. The screenshot shows how one science teacher has used her Portaportal page to link to lesson plan sites, mindtools, social bookmarking sites, and other topics she wants to share with her students.

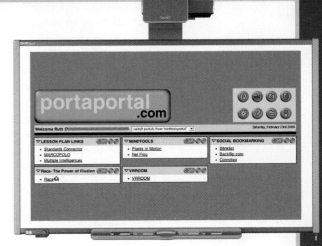

Portaportal enables teachers and students to manage Web searches by bookmarking specific websites that are accessed and organized through your Web browser. Using Portaportal, you can transport a website "favorites" page from your own personal home computer to any other computer where you might need that information.

Teachers can use this tool to focus students on websites that they have specifically chosen for their value as instructional and learning resources. For example, as part of a curriculum unit on the cultures of indigenous people of the Arctic region, a teacher might post in Portaportal a group of websites she wanted her students to tour during class time. This guided tour keeps the students on track and focused on the websites the teacher wants them to view while avoiding distractions or links related to other topics.

CONTACT INFORMATION

PortaPortal   www.portaportal.com   Free accounts are offered. Additional services are available for a fee.

Filamentality   www.kn.pacbell.com/wired/fil   Free accounts are offered. Users are required to log in at least once a year to maintain their account.

May). What was heretofore one individual's favorite sites becomes available on a public site where they can be accessed and added to by others interested in the same topics. Instead of a private library of resources seen by one person, social bookmarks create a public list that can be viewed by many readers.

Social bookmarking works as a collection of individual bookmarks. You create a bookmark or tag for an online resource you have located on a topic of interest. By posting your bookmark on a social bookmarking site, you provide other users of that site with access to your resource. In exchange, you get access to all the resources that everyone else has posted on the site. The advantages for teachers are immense. You become part of a community of users

For teachers, social bookmarking tools are astonishingly useful information management strategies. Instead of trying to locate high-quality resources by yourself, you join a community of computer-using educators who are interested in the same topics and questions. By contributing to the community as you locate useful Web resources, you benefit from the work of all the other members of the group. Look at the following tools and see how they can support your teaching.

 Delicious

Delicious is a Web-based social bookmarking tool that organizes all of your bookmarks in one place. In addition, you can sort and send these bookmarks to peers and friends.

Source: Screenshot reproduced with permission of Yahoo! Inc. © 2008 by Yahoo! Inc. Yahoo! and the Yahoo! Inc. logo are trademarks of Yahoo! Inc. Board courtesy of SMART Technologies; copyright © 2001–2009 SMART Technologies ULC; all rights reserved.

While using Delicious, you can view a Web page and capture the page by clicking on a Delicious tab in your toolbar. You can view the page later based on sorting you have created with a special tagging system. The screenshot shows a page from one teacher's Delicious account with tags displayed in a cloud format. Tag cloud terms in larger type are the ones with the most bookmarks saved to them.

Tags allow users to go back to the pages instantly using keywords. Some keywords are general—"educational technology"—and others are specific—"next week's writing." The purpose of tags is to remind you where something is and cue you to the information on any particular page.

 Backflip

Backflip is a free Web-based social bookmarking tool that keeps track of the websites you visit. When students use Backflip, they can retrace their "steps" on the Web. This feature comes in handy when students "get lost" because they have opened so many links online. In addition to being a bookmarking tool, it can serve as a Web surfing monitor that will organize and collect a history of the websites visited. By collecting all visited sites, you have a database of interesting sites to refer back to in the future. Teachers can track Web surfing trends and use the patterns to reveal opportunities for areas of study that interest students.

Connotea

Connotea, created by the publishers of the science magazine Nature, is an online reference management tool that creates and saves bibliographical information in correct citation formats on articles you

who are continually identifying their own structure of resources about key areas of the school curriculum. Such a system of resources is known as a **folksonomy** because a community of users created it rather than a panel of experts. Social bookmarking sites are described in Tech Tool 6.2.

Social bookmarking is being used by many organizations interested in finding new ways to manage and share information. For example, electronic publications such as *Educa-*

are reading. As you read an article or other online resource, Connotea, when instructed to do so, will create an entry in your reference library. You can then add your own keywords as a way to customize how you organize and search your library. Connotea can be a terrific tool for teachers who are reading and for upper-grade students who are writing research papers using bibliographic citations. Because this tool is Web-based, you can access it from any Internet-accessible computer.

Goodreads

Goodreads is designed to let you organize your favorite books online, creating shelves of titles by topic while viewing the selections of more than two million readers worldwide. Goodreads offers multifaceted resources for teachers and students. You begin by selecting books that you have read, intend to read, or want to remember, and then place them on online book shelves. You add titles to your shelves by searching through Amazon.com by author name or book title, or by entering the author and title manually. Once the book titles are entered, you can rate them (one to five stars according to criteria that you define), sort the selections (by title, author, or rating), connect with friends who share similar interests, and, if you desire, join or start a book group. Most importantly, your library is always with you, ready to be accessed for instructional activities at any computer you are using rather than being bookmarked and available solely on your personal computer.

Diigo

Diigo (pronounced DEE-go), short for Digest of Internet Information Groups and Other Stuff, allows you to bookmark sites, highlight portions of Web pages, add sticky notes that you create, tag the sites, and easily share resources. Once you embed highlights or bookmarks, your notations appear every time you open the page.

CONTACT INFORMATION

Delicious http://del.icio.us.com Free online. Users are required to register.

Backflip www.backflip.com/login.ihtml Free online. Users are required to register. Backflip does contain some advertisements.

Connotea www.connotea.org Free online. Users are required to register.

Goodreads www.goodreads.com Free online. Users are required to register.

Diigo www.diigo.com Free online. Users are required to register.

tion Week include links to social bookmarking sites. As another example, the online bookseller Barnes and Noble has created a social network–style component on its website where the most frequently searched terms are tagged and then listed for customers to browse. The larger the font size on the page, the more frequently the term has been searched by users of the website (for example, the term "Harry Potter" is in larger type than the term "national book awards").

Information Alerts and RSS Feeds

An **information alert** is an electronic notice that new information about a topic has just become available in some electronic publication format. Information alerts provide busy teachers with a convenient system of announcements about new information online.

Google Alerts, a free service for those with a Google account, is one information alert option. For information alerts using Google, you enter a keyword and the Google search engine automatically sends you an email whenever there are new results for your term. A teacher might get information alerts about a topic (planets discovered outside the solar system), a new teaching methodology (blogs and wikis), or a current educational issue (charter schools).

Google Alerts can be a time saver. Rather than searching yourself, Google Alerts does the job for you, generating five types of alerts: news (articles in newspapers and other news outlets), Web (new Internet pages), blog (new posts), group, and comprehensive. You decide how often you want to get updates and for how long. Results are based on Google's overall rating system, so the alerts you get are the most popular items.

Another source of information alerts is ProQuest, a company that started by putting dissertations and newspapers on microfilm in the 1930s and 1940s and is now one of the largest information collection and publishing services in the world, providing access to some 5.5 billion pages of materials from periodicals, newspapers, out-of-print books, dissertations, and scholarly publications. Available in many K–12 and college libraries, ProQuest offers search functions (called

---

FIGURE 6.2 Sample EdITLib Digital Library TOC Alert

Dear Robert

The latest issue of "Journal of Technology and Teacher Education" is now available on the EdITLib Digital Library.

Journal of Technology and Teacher Education Vol. 15, No. 3 (2007)

Table of Contents

Editorial: Networked Knowledge: Challenges for Teacher Education

Peter R Albion, University of Southern Queensland, Australia; Cleborne Maddux, University of Nevada, Reno, USA

Abstract: http://go.editlib.org/a/24427

Social Studies Teachers' Perspectives of Technology Integration

Yali Zhao, Georgia State University, USA

Abstract: http://go.editlib.org/a/20005

The Role of Epistemological Beliefs in Preservice Teachers' Interpretation of Video Cases of Early-Grade Literacy Instruction

Aman Yadav & Matthew Koehler, Michigan State University, USA

Abstract: http://go.editlib.org/a/20998

Digital Professional Portfolios of Preservice Teaching: An Initial Study of Score Reliability and Validity

James DiPerna, Penn State University, USA; Carol Derham, Lehigh University, USA

Abstract: http://go.editlib.org/a/21010

Small Group Collaboration in Peer-Led Electronic Discourse: An Analysis of Group Dynamics and Interactions Involving Preservice and Inservice

Chinwe Ikpeze, St. John Fisher College, USA

Abstract: http://go.editlib.org/pl21043

Source: Reprinted with permission of the Association for the Advancement of Computing in Education (AACE).

e-Library), resources dealing with current issues in society (called SIRS), and reports on different countries from a cultural and historical perspective (called CultureGrams).

The EdITLib Education and Information Technology Library provides email alerts for teachers interested in technology-related topics and issues. Sponsored by the Association for the Advancement of Computing in Education (AACE), this fee-based service will notify you whenever peer-reviewed papers and articles on topics you select are published in one of AACE's journals (see Figure 6.2). You can read paragraph-length summaries and decide whether to read the entire article. Many college or community libraries subscribe to this service, and in some cases, entire articles can be downloaded for free or for a nominal fee.

RSS feeds are another way for teachers to access the information they need for curriculum and instruction. RSS (Really Simple Syndication) is a term for Web content that is being frequently updated. News sites, blogs, political campaigns, and many other organizations use RSS feeds to make information available online. The *New York Times,* Yahoo! News: Technology, BBC News, and the *Washington Post* are widely accessed RSS feeds.

To read an RSS feed, you need an RSS feed reader or news aggregator. Google Reader is an example of a popular RSS feed reader. Once you have a feed reader, then you can locate the sites you want to read and the reader will bring continually updated content to your computer desktop, teacher website, or blog space.

 # Building Your Own Standards Connector

Virtually every state and school system now has academic curriculum frameworks for teachers and students, specifying what must be taught in each subject at each grade level. Frameworks can serve as a foundation, but not the ceiling, of the structures of learning that teachers build with their students.

Organizing Web Resources

Creating your own **standards connector** is an effective response to the demands of teaching mandated state or local curriculum frameworks. A standards connector is a collection of Web resources that facilitate teaching required topics. It is a way for you to manage information and store curriculum materials you need for the topics you must teach in your classroom.

The idea of a standards connector web comes from a project at the University of Massachusetts Amherst called VRROOM (Virtual Reference Room). Since 2002, researchers from the School of Education and the Center for Educational Software Development (CESD) have been identifying exemplary educational websites and then coding them to the Massachusetts Curriculum Frameworks (Maloy & Getis, 2002).

You can build your own standards connector web by matching Web-based academic content to the curriculum frameworks in the state or district where you are teaching. Students can assist with this collection as well; indeed, involving students in the design and maintenance of this project will make building a standards connector a powerful learning experience for everyone.

Creating your own standards connector is easy to do. You need access to the Internet, one of the data management/social bookmarking tools discussed in this chapter, and a personal or classroom website.

First, as you search online for curriculum materials, match the curriculum frameworks that you need to teach with high-quality websites that feature resources for teaching specific learning standards. Locating one or two excellent sites for each framework topic provides a starting point and you can add others later based on your own research and that of your students.

Next, bookmark your online resources using a social bookmarking tool such as Delicious to create a personal collection of Web resources that you can share with students, other teachers, and interested educators. The process is quick and creative. You record the Web address, title,

FIGURE 6.3 A History Teacher's Social Bookmarking Tags

Tags

▼ Top 10 Tags

Unitedstateshistory	**PrimarySources**
Industrialrevolution	**USII.9**
Massachusettshistory	**AfricanAmericans**
Women'shistory	**TeachingMethods**
USII.25 **CivilRightsMovement**	

▼ All Tags   66

3.11 3.12 5.31 5.7 7.11 **AfricanAmerican**
AfricanAmericans AncientHistory Cities
CivilRightsMovement CivilWar **ColdWar**
ColonialAmerica Colony
ContemporaryAmerica Education
EmmaGoldman Folksongs GildedAge
Hammurabi Immigration **Industrialrevolution**
JimCrowlaws lessonplans MarianAnderson
MartinLutherKing,Jr. MassachusettsConsti...
Massachusettshistory Music
NativeAmericans NearEast Plymouth
PrimarySource **PrimarySources**
Progressivism **Reconstruction** Religion
Segregation **Slavery** Spanish-AmericanWar
SupremeCourt **TeachingMethods**
TeachingResources Transcendentalism
Undergroundrailroad **Unitedstateshistory**
urbanization US.I.33 USG3.4 USI.29 USI.30
USI.33 USI.34 **USI.41** USI.8 USII.2
USII.25 **USII.28** **USII.29** USII.3 USII.32
USII.6 USII.8 **USII.9** **Women'shistory**
WorldHistory

and summary of each Web resource you want to save. Then "tag" the resource using a set of keywords that you select to help you remember what the resource is about. This is the creative part. You are establishing your own organizing categories for your own purposes, and that system can include the learning standards you are expected to teach students. You can search your collection of resources using these keyword tags. Figure 6.3 shows a **tag cloud** based on one history teacher's system of keywords.

The keywords in bold are the most often cited terms in this teacher's classification system, while less cited ones are in lighter font. Because this teacher is particularly interested in the history of African Americans and women, those are among the bolded terms. The teacher has also used the state learning standards as keywords. For example, "USII.25" (United States History Part II, Learning Standard 25) refers to a learning standard on the civil rights movement that is part of the state's high school history curriculum framework. Whenever this teacher needs resources for teaching that topic, she can search under either the phrase "Civil Rights Movement" or the learning standard "USII.25."

Social bookmarking is not the only way to collect and maintain information for a standards connector. Table 6.1 shows a list of resources for teaching the middle school physical science topics of the properties of matter and elements, compounds, and mixtures.

This teacher decided to list the required frameworks on one side of a Web page and Web resources on the other side. This format allowed the teacher and students to connect the Web resources directly to the learning standard being studied using the teacher's website. Either social bookmarking or listing resources on a Web page are approaches that connect online resources to the learning standards teachers are expected to teach.

TABLE 6.1   Sample Standards Connector—Physical Science: Grades 6–8

Learning Standard	Web Resources
Properties of Matter: Differentiate between weight and mass, recognizing that weight is the amount of gravitational pull on an object.	Your Weight on Other Worlds www.exploratorium.edu/ronh/weight
Properties of Matter: Differentiate between volume and mass; define density.	The Internet Plasma Physics Education Experience http://ippex.pppl.gov/interactive/matter/
Elements, Compounds, and Mixtures: Recognize that a substance (element or compound) has a melting point and a boiling point, both of which are independent of the amount of the sample.	States of Matter www.thetech.org/exhibits/online/topics/52a.html
Elements, Compounds, and Mixtures: Differentiate between physical and chemical changes through interactive simulations.	BBC K52 Bitesize Science www.bbc.co.uk/schools/k52bitesize/science/materials.shtml

Involving elementary, middle, and high school students in reviewing and selecting resources for a standards connector supports academic learning in three ways:

- It requires your students to access online material from appropriate search engines delineated by you. In the process of choosing sites, students learn to act as critical consumers of information rather than as acceptors of any sites they find or believers of whatever information they read.
- It introduces students to local, state, or national curriculum frameworks as a source of ideas and information that teachers and students have researched and reviewed together for quality, relevance, and omissions.
- It lets teachers gather resources to meet and go beyond the confines of local, state, or national curriculum frameworks. For example, a history teacher might teach a required framework by featuring the military battles and political developments of the U.S. Civil War, and then extend that framework by examining the experiences of ordinary men and women, black and white, in northern and southern communities. Similarly, English teachers can enlarge the frameworks by integrating lessons on diverse authors and genres into the study of literature, science teachers can include the latest research and new discoveries from different fields, and math teachers can add virtual simulations and online games to the study of basic number operations and functions.

WebQuests and Virtual Field Trips

"How can we make seniors want to read *Hamlet* at eight o'clock in the morning" or "How can we involve freshmen in *Romeo and Juliet* when they are preoccupied with the social aspects of high school" asked a group of English education researchers at Florida State University (Bowman, Pieters, et al., 2002, p. 88). Their answers featured using **WebQuests** as vehicles that bring alive the language, drama, comedy, and history of Shakespeare—as well as hundreds of other playwrights, poets, and authors.

WebQuests are online inquiries by students—designed and guided by teachers (Milson & Downey, 2001; Molebash & Dodge, 2003). In a WebQuest, students follow an electronic map or tour, moving from Web resource to Web resource to gather information and learn about a particular topic. In a paper environment, a student might read articles or selections from books and put the information together in a paper or a report, but in a WebQuest, the search for and the source of academic information is electronic. Students visit sites preidentified by a teacher and assess what they find. Based on their explorations and investigations, they might prepare individual or group presentations to share with their classmates. This chapter's Technology Transformation Lesson Plan, "Weather Station WebQuest," shows this method in action.

Successful WebQuests mirror the ingredients of innovative and engaging lesson plans. Teachers use a virtual environment to "give students roles, creative activities, and unique assignments designed to stretch their thinking and enhance their understanding of the text" (Bowman, Pieters, et al., 2002, p. 89). For example, any aspect of Shakespeare's life, times, and works can be the focus of a WebQuest: "Students as judges, jurors, party planners, or journalists can create plots of their own St. Crispian's Day speech for *Henry V*. They can design a Roman village for *Caesar*. They can make ball costumes for *Romeo and Juliet*" (Bowman, Pieters, et al., 2002, p. 89).

WebQuests serve as springboards for individual creativity, and in the process of doing them students learn essential Internet literacy skills of information retrieval and analysis.

Designing Successful WebQuests

Professor Bernie Dodge, along with colleagues and students in the Educational Technology Department at San Diego State University (SDSU), has organized a database of more than 2,500

PEARSON
myeducationkit

Go to the Assignments and Activities section of Chapter 6 in MyEducationKit and complete the video activity entitled "Collaborative Learning through WebQuest."

WebQuests that can be searched electronically (see Figure 6.4). In addition, they have also developed QuestGarden, an online WebQuest authoring and hosting site that assists teachers possessing little or no technological background to create their own WebQuests (available online at http://questgarden.com).

WebQuests are designed so students will explore multiple options for content learning as they complete a series of tasks. Most include the following five stages:

- *Stage setting.* Introduction by the teacher before the students begin the activity.
- *Task.* Activities students will be expected to do or create while on the quest.
- *Process.* The step-by-step instructions they will follow throughout the quest.
- *Evaluation.* How the teacher (and possibly the students themselves) will assess if the members of a class have successfully met the requirements of a quest.
- *Conclusion.* Summary of the key understandings or learning goals that were embedded in the quest.

Designing a successful WebQuest demands four considerations:

- Who are your students and what are they capable of doing successfully?
- What are the primary ideas you wish to teach?
- How will students at different skill levels productively work together?
- Is technology integrated seamlessly into the assignment?

A WebQuest is constructed using the same principles necessary for building a research project with print resources that incorporates worksheets, textbook readings, and library assignments. Such activities also must be thoughtfully designed to avoid the possibility that some students will be unable to do them.

High school teachers, for example, sometimes ask students to complete a paper text-based reading assignment requiring advanced reading skills for immediate comprehension, such as a primary source document in a history class, a technical experiment in a science class, or a fiction story in English class. Sending students who may not have strong reading skills to a source that features densely packed text sets up a learning situation where only some can successfully complete the assignment. Those who lack the reading skills to do the work may quickly become disengaged from the assignment.

The same problem arises online as well. Many websites require advanced reading levels and some students are unable to navigate through a complex site design to locate the salient ideas that the teacher is seeking. Here is where the activity's design becomes crucial to its success. Many paper assignments and WebQuests feature a cooperative learning model in which different students do different tasks. A student who is not an accomplished reader may be a talented artist who can put the information that is located in books or websites into an interesting visual summary for the other students to see. Another student may be an excellent oral communicator who can present information in class clearly and concisely. Giving different roles to different students as members of a paper assignment or WebQuest team provides teachers with a way to use everyone's strengths for everyone's learning.

Technology offers teachers an additional resource that paper activities do not. Given their speed, computers allow access to information much more rapidly than browsing through books or finding resources in a library. Speed of access and the assistance of online text reading programs allows everyone—more and less proficient readers alike—to spend more time on the analysis of information. A WebQuest is about finding information that connects to academic content students are learning, and then doing something with that information.

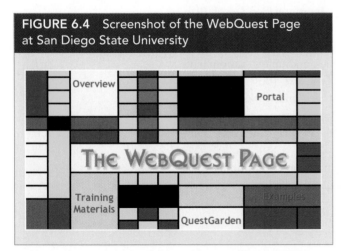

FIGURE 6.4 Screenshot of the WebQuest Page at San Diego State University

Source: Reprinted with permission of San Diego State University. Available at http://webquest.org.

With WebQuests, students can research topics of interest and controversy by locating different viewpoints involved with an issue. For example, one of the towns in our area recently had a special vote to decide whether to designate an undeveloped parcel of land as an ancestral Native American burial ground or to maintain commercial zoning in order to entice a big-box retail store to move to the community. The issue sharply divided the community, with advocates for and against the positions taken by Native American groups and commercial developers. A local high school teacher developed a WebQuest as a way for her students to learn about both viewpoints on the issues and discuss them with classmates before taking a class vote.

Go to the Assignments and Activities section of Chapter 6 in MyEducationKit and complete the video activity entitled "Technology-Supported WebQuest."

Taking Virtual Field Trips

Virtual field trips (also called *online field trips* or *virtual tours*) take students to places all over the world without ever leaving their school's classroom or computer lab (Platoni, 2008). The experience is gaining popularity in schools. When teachers have multiple computers and Internet access, groups of students may go on a virtual field trip while other students meet with the teacher or work independently. Even with one computer, a whole class can participate in a virtual field trip. An example of a site for a virtual field trip is presented in Tech Tool 6.3.

Because virtual field trips (and face-to-face conversation via the computer) are relatively new, research about online field trips is limited, but promising. One small study involving 400 students from two middle schools, one urban and one rural, showed that middle school students had higher reading comprehension scores after participating in online field trips developed by Maryland Public Television (eSchool News, 2005). The students who took the field trips performed better than a control group of students who experienced only traditional teaching methods.

Numerous museums, science centers, historical sites, and other educational organizations have developed online field trip programs that do not require any human-to-human interaction, so no reservation is needed. A class may visit one of the following popular destinations featuring virtual field trips anytime.

- Colonial Williamsburg
- Baseball Hall of Fame
- Smithsonian Institution
- U.S. Arizona Memorial
- Cleveland Museum of Art
- Lake Michigan Science Research Center
- Global Leap (for international field trips)

Interactive Videoconferencing

Interactive videoconferencing, as a feature of virtual field trips, changes the learning experience for students. Videoconferencing is a powerful distance learning technology that offers real-time access to people and places that students are unable to visit. Using videoconferencing achieves interactivity between your students (called the "near site") and people the class is visiting electronically (the "far site"). Successful conferences make participants at each site feel involved and invested in the experience.

Interactive videoconferencing requires two large-screen television monitors at each site with one or more cameras and a digital projection device. One monitor shows the near site; another shows the far

Interactive videoconferencing enables students to communicate with scientists, historians, writers, and other experts from all over the nation, extending the classroom far beyond the local community.

Interactive learning experiences are key to the success of online field trips. When students go to a site, they need opportunities to do more than read text or view pictures. They become engaged when they can interact with the site in different, interesting, and potentially surprising ways.

One example is The Cave of Chauvet-Pont-d'Arc, which shows some of the earliest cave paintings ever found. The site is maintained by the French government's Ministry of Culture and Communication and is part of a larger collection of "Great Archaeological Sites," including the medieval Abbey of Saint-Germain of Auxerre.

The cave paintings at Chauvet-Pont-d'Arc are a recent extraordinary discovery, and the story of their find is dramatic. On December 18, 1994, three friends noticed a current of air streaming from an opening at the end of small cave. When they returned a few days later, they "dug a passage, crawled through it, and soon found themselves at the edge of an obscure shaft." They found a huge chamber and then another. Shining their lights on the wall, they saw the first of hundreds of cave paintings and engravings. "They were here!" exclaimed one of the three, referring to early humans who inhabited the region some 31,000 years ago.

Anthropologists connect the cave drawings to the Aurignacian culture, which existed throughout Europe during that time period. The culture was characterized by innovations and diversifications in toolmaking; however, the volume of cave paintings as well as the use of shaping and perspective in the drawings was a shocking surprise. This discovery represented a monumental moment in learning about the peoples of the ancient past.

Taking a virtual tour of this subterranean world is one of the joys of this site. There is a map of the entire cave system with linking buttons. Clicking on a button takes you to that location in the cave with its dramatic drawings. Viewing these paintings from the ancient past may inspire students to produce their own drawings, paintings, or writings to post on walls, blogs, or their own "cave" for others to discover in the future. Archeology itself becomes a group learning activity. Moreover, the exploration of distant destinations made possible by visiting archaeology and anthropology websites may interest students in finding out about the history of local areas or visiting nearby museums.

CONTACT INFORMATION

The Cave of Chauvet-Pont-d'Arc   www.culture.gouv.fr/culture/arcnat/chauvet/en

site. The digital projector allows visual and printed text to be broadcast from one site to the other.

Some organizations customize presentations using a hybrid mix of computer-based resources and person-to-person interactive presentations through interactive videoconferencing. One example is "Ways West: The Peopling of Indiana," part of a well-developed videoconferencing program offered by the Connor Prairie Living History Museum in Fishers, Indiana (online at www.connerprairie.org). The program focuses on the year 1836 and the people who came to Indiana to settle—who they were, when they arrived, and the routes they took to get there.

Educational Websites as Teaching Resources

An **educational website** is a source of Internet-based digital content specifically designed with K–12 learning goals in mind. There are thousands and thousands of educational websites on the Internet, created and maintained by colleges and universities, historical and scientific organizations, museums, government agencies, nonprofit organizations, for-profit companies, and interested individuals. The best of these sites provide high-quality professional and instructional resources for teachers and engaging learning activities for students.

Interactive and engaging educational websites are valuable teaching and learning resources at every grade level. Locating these sites within the vastness of the Internet is not always easy given the amount of material available in any subject area.

Awards given to computer designers and manufacturers offer teachers a ready-made way to stay informed about the best new websites in the fields of technology and education. The Webby Awards, sponsored by the International Academy of Digital Arts and Sciences, honor outstanding work in website design and development. Webbys are given in many categories; those most relevant to teachers include education, family/parenting, politics, science, art, and social activism. You can get more information at the Webby website (www.webbyawards.com).

The American Association of School Librarians (AASL) has a yearly listing of "Best Web Sites for Teaching and Learning." They give awards in six categories: organizing and managing, content collaboration, curriculum sharing, media sharing, virtual environments, and social networking and communication. You can find the latest awards online (www.ala.org/ala/mgrps/divs/aasl/aboutaasl/bestlist/bestwebsites.cfm).

PEARSON myeducationkit

Go to the Assignments and Activities section of Chapter 6 in MyEducationKit and complete the video activity entitled "Social Learning."

CONNECTIONS and POSSIBILITIES

National Library of Virtual Manipulatives (NLVM), Utah State University

How does an exemplary educational website create multiple opportunities for teaching and learning in schools? One example is the National Library of Virtual Manipulatives (NLVM), a math education project created by mathematicians and instructional designers at Utah State University in Logan, Utah. NLVM is a collection of interactive Web-based games and tutorials to help K–12 students learn math concepts. The site is a huge resource for teachers, receiving more than 1.5 million hits per day from people around the world.

Begun in 1999 with a grant from the National Science Foundation, NLVM is a response to the ongoing U.S. national problem of student disengagement and low academic performance in math. In general, math educators agree that students become disengaged from math when they cannot understand the connections between relationships and operations. In other words, they cannot visualize how to work out the math in their heads. In classroom settings, teachers use physical objects so students can move items and see firsthand how their actions change math relationships.

Physical objects used in math teaching are called "manipulatives" because students actually manipulate or move objects with their own hands. To learn about fractions, for example, coins serve as useful manipulatives. Counting the coins, students see that 10 pennies is 100 percent of 1 dime and 5 dimes is 50 percent of 1 dollar. The concept of a fraction of the whole becomes visible through the student's own physical actions with manipulatives. In the language of constructivist approaches to learning, the student has actively created meaning for her- or himself, rather than simply having listened to teachers explain terms.

NLVM uses computers to create virtual settings where students can manipulate objects with the click of a mouse. It includes activities and games for all grade levels, connected to the major math education standards set forth by the National Council of Teachers of Math (NCTM): numbers and operations, algebra, geometry, measurement, data analysis and probability, problem solving, and reasoning and proof.

You can access the National Library of Virtual Manipulatives at http://nlvm.usu.edu. The site is fee-based. You can purchase a license for a single computer for under $50, and discounts are available to school districts that buy multiple licenses. You can also purchase a CD-ROM featuring over 100 of the library's most popular Web-based math tutorials from the software retailer MATTI Math.

Two books published by ISTE (International Society for Technology in Education) are useful as well: *101 Best Web Sites for Elementary Teachers* and *101 Best Web Sites for Secondary Teachers* (Lerman, 2005a, 2005b).

As a new teacher, it is also helpful to have a system of categories into which you can place the online academic content resources that you find as you explore the Web. One useful system is provided by the Center for Improved Engineering and Science Education at the Stevens Institute of Technology in New Jersey (2002). The center divided educational websites into four major categories to which we added two more based on our experience—lesson plan websites, student-to-expert communication websites, real-time and recorded data websites, archival and primary source websites, skills/practice websites, and student work publishing websites

This list is a starting point as you search the Web to find more examples and to add more categories. You will find many sites combining different functions—for example, providing lesson plans, archival material and real-time data, and communication with experts are all in the same location.

Lesson Plan Websites

Lesson plan websites are one of the most widely used types of educational websites. At these sites, teachers can find thousands of ideas for classroom lessons or download entire lesson plans with step-by-step methods and procedures. Many lesson plans feature links to interactive activities or additional resources and curriculum extensions. As part of classroom activities or homework assignments, students can be sent to these educational websites for substantive learning experiences. Like a super grocery or department store, lesson plan supersites are multipurpose resources for engaging and teaching adults and students alike. See Table 6.2 for a listing of popular lesson plan websites.

TABLE 6.2   Lesson Plan Websites

Website and URL	Brief Description
ReadWriteThink www.readwritethink.org	Lesson plans for all grade levels from the National Council of Teachers of English (NCTE) and the International Reading Association (IRA).
Blue Web'N www.kn.pacbell.com/wired/bluewebn	Sponsored by AT&T, this site offers an online library of more than 2,100 (and growing) Internet sites for teachers, browsable by subject, grade level, and type of resource.
MERLOT (Multimedia Educational Resource for Learning and Online Teaching) www.merlot.org	Maintained by the California State University Center for Distributed Learning, this site offers online teaching resources from around the world. While the primary focus is college teaching, many of the resources apply to the high school level as well.
EDSITEment: The Best of the Humanities on the Web http://edsitement.neh.gov	Created by the National Endowment for the Humanities, this site offers thousands of lesson plans and instructional resources in art and culture, literature and language arts, foreign language, and history and social studies.
The New York Times Learning Network www.nytimes.com/learning	Presented by the *New York Times*, this site provides lesson plans related to current news stories as well as an archive of past lessons.
Kathy Schrock's Guide for Educators http://school.discoveryeducation.com/schrockguide	Sponsored by Discovery Education, this site provides lesson plans and related teacher resources and a blog from teacher and technology administrator Kathleen Schrock.
EduHound www.eduhound.com	Presented by the *T.H.E. Journal* (Technological Horizons in Education), this site includes lesson plans for teachers as well as free online access to the journal itself.
The Futures Channel www.thefutureschannel.com	Multimedia math and science teaching resources for all grade levels, including lesson plans and short videos about the uses of math and science in real-world settings.

TABLE 6.3 Student-to-Expert Communication Websites

Website and URL	Brief Description
Ask Dr. Universe, Washington State University www.wsu.edu/DrUniverse	A resource for students and teachers to get answers to questions about earth and space sciences.
Ask an Earth Scientist, University of Hawaii www.soest.hawaii.edu/GG/ASK	An earth and space science resource for teachers and students.
Ask Dr. Math, Drexel University http://mathforum.org/dr.math	A math resource site for teachers, students, and parents.
BioKIDS: Kids' Inquiry of Diverse Species, University of Michigan www.biokids.umich.edu	In addition to providing curriculum resources, this site includes an electronic discussion board and ways for kids to create their own Web-based biodiversity maps.
Electronic Emissary, College of William and Mary http://emissary.wm.edu	A Web-based telementoring resource center designed for kindergarten through grade 12 teachers and students with Internet access who want to locate mentors and set up curriculum-based electronic exchanges.

Student-to-Expert Communication Websites

Student-to-expert communication websites feature exchanges of ideas and information between students in K–12 schools and adult experts in colleges, businesses, and other organizations (see Table 6.3). K–12 students have the opportunity to formulate authentic questions to send to experts in the field and then receive replies electronically. Telementoring and e-tutoring are other forms of online communication activities that link adults in communities with K–12 schools and students. Telementoring generally involves opportunities for students to learn about career opportunities in different fields from professionals in those fields, whereas e-tutoring focuses on specific help with homework and class projects.

Real-Time and Recorded Data Websites

Real-time and recorded data websites present information about many different types of scientific phenomena that K–12 students can access and analyze in their classrooms (see Table 6.4 on page 160). Like virtual field trips, real-time and recorded data sites provide opportunities for students to enter a setting as an involved observer, learning about science or history or another subject as if they were physically present at a remote location.

Archival and Primary Source Websites

Archival and primary source websites allow students to conduct contemporary or historical investigations by accessing primary and archival source materials from museums, libraries, and other organizations (see Table 6.5 on page 161). Some sites provide only informational materials; others offer activities that guide students in the use of the materials. These sources include not only print-based materials, but online images and photographs as well.

Skills/Practice Websites

Skills/practice websites offer subject-specific activities for students at all grade levels (see Table 6.6 on page 161). Many teachers use these sites as instructional options, assigning small groups

TABLE 6.4   Real-Time and Recorded Data Websites

Website and URL	Brief Description
WhaleNet Satellite Tagging Data Project, Wheelock College http://whale.wheelock.edu	Information about the movement of whales across the oceans.
Hands-On Universe, University of California, Berkeley www.handsonuniverse.org	Students can conduct scientific investigations using data from powerful space telescopes.
EstuaryLIVE, North Carolina National Estuarine Research Reserve Program www.estuarylive.org	Takes viewers into North Carolina's 400 miles of estuaries and the astonishing biomes of living matter produced by daily intermingling of river and sea water. Includes teacher ideas and resources, as well as links to related websites to enliven learning for students of all ages.
Coastal Ocean Observation Lab (COOL), Rutgers University http://rucool.marine.rutgers.edu	Real-time and archived satellite imagery, surface current and wave data, and COOL classroom where students can see the Atlantic Ocean from 500 miles above and 15 meters below the surface.
Bee Alert, Division of Biological Sciences, University of Montana http://beekeeper.dbs.umt.edu/bees/beecams	Online beehives equipped with cameras and flight recorders provide real-time and archival data about bee behaviors, including comparisons between flight activity and weather conditions.
NestCams, Cornell Lab of Ornithology, Cornell University http://watch.birds.cornell.edu/nestcams/home/index	Real-time and archival photos offer opportunities to study the nesting habits of birds.
Ice Stories: Dispatches from Polar Scientists, from the Exploratorium, The Museum of Science, Art, and Human Perception, San Francisco http://icestories.exploratorium.edu/dispatches	Videos, photos, and blogs from scientists engaged in research in the Arctic and Antarctica.
Real Time Data Sites, Center for Innovation and Engineering in Science Education, Stevens Institute of Technology, New Jersey www.ciese.org/realtimedatasites.html	Links to dozens of sites that provide weather, air, water, and satellite information from a variety of math and science fields.

to classroom computers while the teacher works directly with other students. Some skills/practice websites feature educational learning games, a technology we discuss in the next chapter.

Exploration and Discovery Websites

Exploration and discovery websites provide opportunities for students to engage in online explorations of topics of interest, often related to science and math (see Table 6.7 on page 162).

TABLE 6.5   Archival and Primary Source Websites

Website and URL	Brief Description
New York Public Library Digital Gallery http://digitalgallery.nypl.org/nypldigital/index.cfm	Over 500,000 digitized images from the library collections, easily searchable by keywords.
The Digital Vaults www.digitalvaults.org	1,200 documents, photographs, posters, sound recordings, moving images, and other materials from the National Archives in Washington, D.C.
The Smithsonian American Art Museum http://americanart.si.edu	Computer users can search the museum's collections for visual images of artists' work. There is also an online question-asking service entitled "Ask Joan of Art!"
NASA Multimedia Gallery, National Aeronautics and Space Administration www.nasa.gov/multimedia/index.html	Includes video, podcasts, images, and art related to space exploration and related science topics.
Washington Post Camera Works www.washingtonpost.com/wp-dyn/content/photo	Photos by topic from around the United States and the world.
A History of Women www.roadsfromsenecafalls.org	Resources for teaching women's history for K–12 teachers and students, including primary sources, biographies, lesson plans, and links to historic sites and museums.
The Gilder Lehrman Institute of American History www.gilderlehrman.org	60,000 primary source documents from U.S. history as well as podcasts by historians, lesson plans for teachers, online exhibits, and printable images for classroom use.
National History Education Clearinghouse, George Mason University http://teachinghistory.org	Online resources for history teachers, including primary source materials, lesson plans, and teaching practices from the Center for History and New Media at George Mason University and the Stanford University History Education Group.

TABLE 6.6   Skills/Practice Websites

Website and URL	Brief Description
National Library of Virtual Manipulatives http://nlvm.usu.edu	Math activities featuring short, interactive computer programs that explore mathematical concepts and operations from researchers at Utah State University.
PBS Kids www.pbskids.org	Games, songs, video clips, blog entries, and many other activities based on characters from PBS's favorite television shows for children.
AAA Math www.aaamath.com	Basic math games and activities for kindergarten to grade 8. The site also includes spelling practice and geography information.
NASA Kids' Club www.nasa.gov/audience/forkids/kidsclub/flash/index.html	Information and activities about space and science from the National Aeronautics and Space Administration. More activities and video material are available at the main NASA site in sections "For Students" and "For Educators."

TABLE 6.7   Exploration and Discovery Websites

Website and URL	Brief Description
National Geographic Kids http://kids.nationalgeographic.com	Games, videos, stories, and activities that promote understanding of geography around the world.
Waksman Challenge, Rutgers University http://wakschallenge.rutgers.edu/index.php	Teams of high school students respond to science project challenges in bioinformatics and structural biology created by scientists at Rutgers University.
Earthquakes for Kids http://earthquake.usgs.gov/learning/kids	A storehouse of information and activities on the science and history of earthquakes.
Journey North: A Global Study of Wildlife Migration and Seasonal Change www.learner.org/jnorth	Science students share their observations of spring classrooms, bird migrations, gray whales, plants, and length of daylight.
How Stuff Works 4 Kids www.west.asu.edu/achristie/hsw4kids/index.htm	Questions and answers about all kinds of topics researched and explained by elementary and secondary level students.
Exploratorium www.exploratorium.edu	Interactive exhibits of science and art for students.

Using Educational Websites Interactively

Educators and Web designers broadly agree that an excellent, high-quality educational website is up-to-date, factually accurate, and free of bias or "sales pitches" for products or philosophies. Beyond that, the site is constructed in ways that make information accessible and usable to students. Like an exemplary teacher, an excellent website teaches rather than presents information. Just as in a classroom where teaching is more than telling information to students, an excellent educational website is more than running text of information on a computer screen.

Excellent educational websites have the following features:

- *Interactivity.* There are ways for students to interact with Internet content by viewing simulations or demonstrations, conducting searches, responding to questions, analyzing data, or posting responses. These sites not only provide information; a computer user gains "something extra" from the interaction provided by the technology (Markopoulos, Read, MacFarlane, & Hoysniemi, 2008). Interacting with the computer produces results that would not be possible without the interaction.
- *Exploration.* There are opportunities to explore questions and topics on one's own by proceeding through the site in a nonlinear rather than a linear fashion. Computer users can chart their own course through the website, even following different paths each time they visit.
- *Engagement.* There are ways to engage with website material beyond a straightforward presentation of information through the use of a compelling storyline, interesting characters, a perplexing mystery, or a controversial issue or idea. A computer user is thus drawn to the online material in ways that could not happen with information presented in a text-based, noninteractive manner.

The following examples of high-quality websites allow students to engage in interactive and engaging explorations of topics in archaeology, history, and science.

Mysteries of Çatalhöyük! An Archaeological Investigation

Mysteries of Çatalhöyük! An Archaeological Investigation (see Figure 6.5) is an engaging and informative website from the Science Museum of Minnesota (available at http://smm.org/catal).

Description. The site's homepage opens dramatically: "Right now in Turkey" declares the first slide, "at a place called Çatalhöyük, people are asking questions: Is this the first city and why did people start living there? What is the meaning of these murals? What were they eating for dinner 10,000 years ago?"

Mysteries of Çatalhöyük! explores intriguing archaeological and historical questions by recording the process and results of an actual archeological dig. Located in central Turkey, Çatalhöyük is the ruins of a 9,000- to 10,000-year-old town, one of the ancient world's largest human settlements, with more than 10,000 inhabitants. It is being excavated and studied by an international team of archaeologists and anthropologists, and their findings are revolutionizing how we think about life in the ancient past. The mural paintings at Çatalhöyük are the oldest in the world on humanmade structures. The city itself was estimated to be more than 50 soccer fields in length, a remarkable development at a time when humans were thought to have lived only in small bands of hunters and gatherers. The name Çatalhöyük means "forked mound," in reference to the large earth mounds that were created as successive generations of people built and rebuilt the town. No one knows what the people who lived in Çatalhöyük called their homeland.

Classroom Activities. Mysteries of Çatalhöyük! is a learning adventure for elementary, middle, and high school students. A creative blend of pictures, diagrams, and text make every page an interesting reading experience. The site, easy to navigate without being bogged down in too much text, utilizes many interactive electronic presentation techniques. For instance, plates filled with the ingredients of Neolithic foodstuffs are linked to their names by a virtual pointer. In other parts of the site, small objects from the excavation zoom into larger view at the click of a mouse.

The most engaging are the mysteries themselves, where students and teachers see how the mounds were formed, make a Neolithic dinner ("Yum! Yum! Seed and Nuts"), figure out which seed is which, play an excavation game, go on virtual tours, or explore one of the city's clay brick homes. In another section, key archaeological findings are presented as interactive stories entitled "Çatalhöyük Comics." There are many activities for students and families to do online together, including painting a mural, making clay balls, and restoring a postcard. To add to the learning potential, a short movie highlights the work of archaeologists who dig deeply to uncover the distant past.

The Goody Parsons Educational Website

The Goody Parsons Educational Website (http://ccbit.cs.umass.edu/parsons/goodyparsons/home.html) is one of two sites developed in 2004 by the Center for Educational Software Development at the University of Massachusetts Amherst in partnership with Historic Northampton, a nonprofit historical organization located in Northampton, Massachusetts. The other is The Goody Parsons Witchcraft Case: A Journey to 17th Century Northampton.

FIGURE 6.5 Page from Mysteries of Çatalhöyük!

Source: Reprinted with permission of the Science Museum of Minnesota.

Description. These sites tell the story of the first outbreak of witchcraft cases in mid-17th-century colonial New England, a precursor to the Salem Witch Hysteria of 1692 that led to 25 people being put to death on charges of witchcraft. The sites are designed for use by middle and high school history classes as well as college courses and historical associations.

The Goody Parsons case emerged from social conflict between two families—the Parsons and the Bridgemans—which resulted in court cases in 1656, 1674, and 1679. Mary (Goody) Parsons and her husband Joseph had moved to Northampton in 1654. There they prospered, both economically and socially. Joseph Parsons, having previously made a small fortune in the fur trade, subsequently opened the first tavern in the town. The Parsons' rising good fortune coincided with a period of sustained financial hardship for the Bridgemans, who had neither as much wealth or business success. In 1656, the Parsons brought a slander suit against the Bridgemans, contending that the Bridgemans had defamed Mary with allegations of misconduct. In the later cases, the Bridgemans accused Goody Parsons of practicing witchcraft, following the deaths of two different members of the Bridgeman family in 1674 and 1679. The trials, with their accompanying primary source documents, offer a fascinating picture of the social dynamics, economic pressures, and religious beliefs of this group of European settlers during the early colonial period.

Classroom Activities. These websites are carefully constructed, telling part of the story while leaving other parts for students and teachers to discover on their own by reading and analyzing primary documents and related sources. The Goody Parsons Witchcraft Case: A Journey to 17th Century Northampton is a comprehensive historical site offering a rich archive of source materials. This site requires focused reading and analysis by students and may be less useful in a classroom situation than the Goody Parsons Educational Website, which contains the following parts:

- Overview of the historical story
- Explanations of witchcraft as a social phenomenon
- Primary source documents from the three court cases
- Interactive maps and displays
- Curriculum and lesson plans
- Resources for teachers

The site features interactive activities where students can access information and explore questions. Maps display information about how witchcraft cases, Indian settlements, wars, crops, and other factors changed over time. One can see quite vividly how European settlement proceeded north and south along the Connecticut River, displacing native people. There are photographic maps of the town of Northampton, then and now, so that students can locate where events took place in both historical and contemporary terms. Primary sources include the estate inventories from the two families for students to draw conclusions about social and economic factors that were present at the time.

Eyes on the Sky, Feet on the Ground: Hands-On Astronomy Activities for Kids

Eyes on the Sky, Feet on the Ground: Hands-On Astronomy Activities for Kids is an educational site from the Harvard/Smithsonian Center for Astrophysics at Harvard University (available at http://hea-www.harvard.edu/ECT/the_book/index.html).

Description. This site features a wide-ranging collection of space-related experiments for students and adults to do together. There are six chapters with multiple activities covering the earth's rotation, the earth's orbit, time and the calendar, maps and mapping, the solar system, and the moon.

Classroom Activities. Each activity gives students interactive learning opportunities. For instance, one part of the site explains what causes seasonal change. Many adults, including large number of college graduates, do not realize that the 23.6-degree tilt of the earth produces seasonal change. Without the tilt, the earth would rotate around the sun in a straight, upright position, giving everyone 12 hours of daylight and 12 hours of nighttime every day, everywhere on the globe. With the tilt, our region of western Massachusetts receives approximately 15 hours, 17 minutes of light at the summer solstice in June, but only 9 hours, 4 minutes of daylight six months later at the winter solstice in December.

Other activities include constructing models, an important form of imaginative play that teaches design and engineering concepts of size, shape, height, weight, cause, and effect. Model making is an opportunity to write about the mysteries and uncertainties of science research. Will the model work? How should the design be changed to achieve better results? What processes or forces are causing things to happen the way they do? Kids can keep science journals filled with data from their experiments along with their own research conclusions.

TECHNOLOGY TRANSFORMATION LESSON PLAN

WEATHER STATION WEBQUEST
Investigating Science Using Interactive Web Resources

Grade(s)	Elementary and Middle School
Subject(s)	Science/Social Studies
Key Goal/Enduring Understanding	Weather is a naturally occurring phenomenon that may appear unpredictable, but is actually a group of elements interacting on and with each other that can be studied, understood, and predicted.
Essential Question	What types of patterns do we see in weather and how can we use those patterns to make our own weather predictions?
Learning Standards	**National Science Teachers Association**—*National Science Education Standards*

Content Standard A

- Abilities necessary to do scientific inquiry
- Understanding about scientific inquiry
- Evidence consists of observations and data on which to base scientific explanations

Content Standard D

- Properties of earth materials
- Objects in the sky
- Changes in earth and sky

International Society for Technology in Education (ISTE)—*NETS-S*

Standard 4: *Critical Thinking, Problem Solving, and Decision Making.* Students use critical thinking skills to plan and conduct research, manage projects, solve problems, and make informed decisions using appropriate digital tools and resources.

Standard 5: *Digital Citizenship.* Students understand human, cultural and societal issues related to technology and practice legal and ethical behavior.

▶

Standard 6: *Technology Operations and Concepts.* Students demonstrate a sound understanding of technology concepts, systems and operations.

National Council for the Social Studies—*Curriculum and Content Area Standards*

> **Theme III:** People, Places, and Environments
> **Theme VIII:** Science, Technology, and Society

Learning Objectives

Students will know and be able to

- Recognize patterns in weather.
- Use tools that simulate weather patterns.
- Disseminate weather-related information using conventional paper-and-pencil reports and Web-based tools.
- Make predictions about future weather based on weather pattern data.

Technology Uses

Students begin by using paper and pencil, traditional tools for recording, analyzing, and publishing weather data, and then move to computer-based technologies that offer online weather data, multimedia weather simulations, digital mapping, and other information.

Minimal Technology	Infusion of Technology
Students use paper-and-pencil recording systems to simulate weather patterns and abstract weather-related concepts.	Students use Web-based charts, graphics, and other Web-based communication tools to investigate, simulate, and teach about weather patterns and weather-related concepts.
Students read textbooks and nonfiction literature that describe weather patterns and abstract weather-related concepts.	Students observe, document, and communicate weather patterns using Web-based multimedia tools.
Students create poster displays of weather data.	Students create digital displays of weather data.
Students give posterboard presentations.	Students give PowerPoint presentations.
Students perform live skits in front of the class.	Students record digital videos of class performances.
Students create weather logs, including charts, graphs, and maps.	Students create weather logs on computers with digitally made charts, graphs, and maps.

Evaluation

A teacher may assign similar projects for final evaluations since all of these may be produced by hand or on the computer.

LESSON PLAN DESCRIPTION

Introduction

WebQuests are inquiry-oriented, Web-based learning adventures organized around a central curriculum theme or topic. In a WebQuest, "some or all of the information that learners interact with comes from resources on the Internet" (Dodge, 1995). WebQuests create a "scaffolded learning structure that uses links to essential resources on the World Wide Web and an authentic task to motivate students' investigation of an open-ended question, development of individual expertise,

▶

and participation in a group process that transforms newly acquired information into a more sophisticated understanding" (March, 2003).

In this WebQuest lesson plan, students are asked to investigate how weather, a seemingly unpredictable daily event, in fact follows from understandable patterns in nature. Following an introduction, students visit a teacher-selected group of interactive Web resources where they will explore different aspects of weather phenomena. When they have finished the activities that are part of the WebQuest, students will prepare a digital presentation in a PowerPoint format or a digital video summarizing what they have learned.

Lesson Focus

"Weather Station WebQuest" capitalizes on students' interest in weather forecasting and weather reporting as it teaches the processes of scientific inquiry and investigation. This lesson, conducted in upper elementary and middle school classrooms, is part of the study of the environment, ecology, or geology.

Using interactive educational websites, "Weather Station WebQuest" connects directly to the learning goal of using the Internet as a teaching and learning environment, a key theme of Chapters 5 and 6. The academic content of this lesson plan comes from two sources: Web resources, the most modern of learning tools, and students' eyewitness observations of weather phenomena, the most ancient of learning tools. As they experience this lesson, students discover ways to use technology to access digital content for academic learning and ways to record personal observations as scientific data.

This lesson plan addresses standards put forth by the National Science Teachers Association (NSTA) as well as the International Society for Technology in Education (ISTE). From a science perspective, students learn about the processes of scientific inquiry as applied to the study of the earth and the environment. From a technology perspective, students learn to use technological tools for problem-solving activities and publishing their knowledge.

Lesson Design—Minimal Technology

A class weather study using minimal technology might utilize any or all of the following:

- Going outdoors for a series of days to experience the elements that create weather—sunshine, wind, or clouds—to record on a graph and describe in writing
- Making a picture graph of the daily weather: sun, clouds, precipitation, wind
- Reading fiction and nonfiction books about weather, including Gail Gibbons's *Weather Words and What they Mean* (1992), an encyclopedic picture book of weather words with illustrations
- Recording weather phenomena visible each day on a monthly calendar
- Reading the local weather report in the daily newspaper
- Writing a weather report for cities in the United States using the resources of *USA Today*'s weather page for daily reporting
- Installing a classroom thermometer showing the indoor/outdoor temperatures
- Buying or making weather station apparatus—thermometers, wind cups (anemometer), barometers, rain gauges—to install outside a classroom for daily observations
- Showing videos of weather phenomena
- Displaying cloud and weather pictures or posters, weather charts, and weather symbols
- Inviting a local weather reporter into the classroom to present information about how she or he does the job and answer questions posed by students
- Having students create their own illustrations of weather to decorate the classroom

The teacher prepares the WebQuest by selecting websites, designing or adapting activities, and structuring the experience so students will find it interesting and engaging. As you observe the students progressing through the activities, the WebQuest can be changed or revised to meet your goals for student learning.

1. *Search for Web Resources.* A variety of search engines and teacher sites will help you locate websites that will appeal to the range of skills of your students. Third- and fourth-graders need more visually oriented sites without large amounts of text that may be above their skill range. Alternatively, you may include more complex Web resources by pairing individuals or small groups of students with adult guides (teacher aides, parent volunteers, college tutors) who help students navigate through and interpret the material.

2. *Choose Interactive Websites.* An effective WebQuest incorporates three to five sites whose interactivity engages attention, fully focuses learning, and inspires conversations between learners. In identifying sites, focus on how the technology provides unique, powerful, and transforming learning experiences, as discussed in Chapter 2 of this book. A WebQuest does not replace hands-on learning or reading experiences at the skill level of the students. It provides what all other resources cannot—interactive virtual explorations of ideas and concepts. Students do not feel wind blowing from a computer screen, which is why they go outside on a windy day. On the other hand, to access visual images and immediate information about weather around the world, students use computer technologies.

3. *Sequence the Websites.* The process of a WebQuest consists of an arrangement of the Web resources that students visit electronically. Variation adds interest. If the first site shows film clips, the next may be interactive, and the last might be an activity on the Web to be completed by the students. Examples of suitable Web-based interactive resources include the following:

   - *Web Weather for Kids* (http://eo.ucar.edu/webweather). Here students explore how weather might affect and interrupt people's daily routines. In reading personal narratives of extraordinary events, they learn about individuals who have experienced out-of-the-ordinary weather events. *Ball of Lightning!* by Enrique (Henry) J. Coll details the experiences of a Canadian who had a ball of fire fly through his front door. Ask students who have had experiences of unusual weather to describe them orally or in writing.
   - *Interactive Weather Maker* (www.scholastic.com/kids/weather). This site teaches about the most important ingredients making the weather. Students can experiment with changing weather conditions by sliding temperature and humidity gauges up and down. While the students move the gauges, they observe how a small house and its surroundings are affected by the climate change they are creating. After using this site, students might create weather recipes for a snowstorm, windstorm, or rainstorm.
   - *The National Oceanic and Atmospheric Administration (NOAA)* (www.noaa.gov). To research your local weather, type in local telephone area codes and then study the maps by zooming in on different regions. Use the tabs across the top of the page to navigate among Geographical Forecasts, National Maps, Radar, Rivers, Air Quality, Satellite, and Climate Reports "At a Glance." The students can write weather reports for different cities or towns in your state, including local temperature, humidity, wind speed, barometer readings, dew point, and visibility.
   - *Edheads* (www.edheads.org/activities/weather). Here students predict weather changes and report weather using two interactive weather tools: the Weather-Tron and the Predict-o-Matic.
   - *Australia Broadcasting Company* (www.abc.net.au/science/photos/clouds). On this site pictures of clouds are accompanied by text explanations of how clouds form in the varying

▶

conditions of temperature and water. Having an adult to paraphrase the explanations and talk with students will facilitate the students' understanding of cloud formation.

- *Weather Wiz Kids* (www.weatherwizkids.com). This site allows students to choose from a topic list of all kinds of weather. For example, the category for clouds will add to the knowledge gained at the site above.
- *The Futures Channel* (www.thefutureschannel.com/dockets/realworld/predicting_weather). Here, a short movie clip features scientists explaining why they do the work they do and how they became interested in it as youngsters. Lesson plans for teachers accompany the movie.

4. *Choose How to Evaluate Student Performance.* Decide how to evaluate student learning from the WebQuest. You may decide to include rubrics, written work, final projects, or group work. The evaluation tools used are explained when the WebQuest is introduced.

5. *Set the Stage.* When introducing the WebQuest to your students, announce that this is an "out-of-the-ordinary" treasure hunt because the entire hunt will be in virtual space where students can access almost any kind of weather that they want. Include an introduction such as the following to build anticipation among the students for the activities they are doing to do: "You have been hired by News Station Channel 3 to be a guest meteorologist for a week. The station feels watchers need to know more about how to recognize and simulate weather patterns, predict future weather based on weather pattern data, and disseminate weather-related information using both conventional (paper and pencil) and Web-based tools."

This introduction may include a "hook" or opener that invites students to explore the technology as well. You might show a map of the interactive websites the students will visit as part of their quest, or a video montage of photographs or short video clips of severe weather and other weather phenomena. Ultimate Chase: Stock Footage and Storm Video Production Services at www.ultimatechase.com provides short streaming video clips of all types of weather. To show weather photographs, the StormScenes Stock Footage Archive (http://stormscenes.com) is also a helpful resource.

6. *Tell Students What They Need to Do.* In the introduction, you will need to clearly and concisely describe what you expect students to do on the WebQuest. Sometimes WebQuest tasks are project based or require building some sort of product or inventing something new. Often, there is a problem to be solved or an issue to be debated inside the task.

This is the time to discuss the process and display on a chart or bulletin board the procedure, grading expectations, and the expected learning outcomes of the WebQuest. Students will then understand the tasks, the process, and the evaluation procedure.

7. *Conclude and Evaluate: Preparing a Digital Presentation.* Once the students have collected information during the WebQuest, they decide on an option for sharing their learning: a PowerPoint and live interaction with the audience or a digital video. These presentations will include words, pictures, and resources that display the following:

- Weather patterns
- Weather simulations
- Weather reporting tools
- Weather predictions

ANALYSIS AND EXTENSIONS

1. Describe two features you find useful about this lesson.
2. How successfully has information technology been integrated into the lesson?
3. Explain two areas for extension or improvement of this lesson.
4. How might students be even more involved in designing, using, and evaluating technology in the lesson?

FOCUS QUESTION 1: What is information management and digital content?

- Information management is the process of organizing, storing, and administering the academic materials and curriculum resources used by teachers and students in schools.
- Digital content is academic information delivered using Internet technologies.

FOCUS QUESTION 2: How are information management technologies such as bookmarking, social bookmarking, and information alerts useful to teachers?

- Bookmarking, social bookmarking, and information alert technologies enable teachers and their students to manage information electronically.
- Bookmarking refers to saving website addresses on your computer to access them easily, rather than looking them up repeatedly.
- Social bookmarking happens when groups of interested people share their Web links electronically in a public Web space. Online tools such as Delicious, Backflip, and Connotea are useful social bookmarking tools for teachers. Bookmarking services such as Portaportal and Filamentality allow teachers to bookmark a group of sites in a secure space for use by students.
- Information alerts are electronic notices that teachers receive on their personal computers advising them that material on requested topics has become available in an online format.

FOCUS QUESTION 3: How do teachers organize electronic resources to address curriculum frameworks and learning standards?

- Teachers can locate local, state, and national curriculum standards online.
- Building a standards connector web is a way for teachers to locate and store Web-based academic material that can be used to teach about topics required by curriculum frameworks.

FOCUS QUESTION 4: What are WebQuests and virtual field trips?

- WebQuests and virtual field trips are innovative and engaging Web-based teaching methods that can be used at all grade levels.
- WebQuests are virtual journeys where students visit a group of preselected websites in order to explore academic topics by accessing online digital text, pictures, audio, and video.
- Virtual field trips allow teachers and students to visit places around the world as part of their academic studies.

FOCUS QUESTION 5: What and where are different types of educational websites available to teachers on the Internet?

- An educational website is a source of Internet-based digital content specifically designed to support the learning of K–12 curriculum.
- There are six major types of educational websites: (1) lesson plan websites, (2) student-to-expert communication websites, (3) real-time and recorded data websites, (4) archival and primary source websites, (5) skills/practice websites, and (6) exploration and discovery websites.

FOCUS QUESTION 6: How might educational websites provide interactive and engaging learning experiences for students?

- Educational websites provide opportunities for students to explore their own questions or go through a site in a nonlinear, self-directed manner.
- Educational websites allow students to engage with online material through stories, characters, mysteries, and controversial issues.

Archival and primary source websites
Bookmarking
Digital content
Educational website
Exploration and discovery websites
Favorites or hotlists
Folksonomy
Information alerts
Information management
Interactive videoconferencing

Lesson plan websites
Real-time and recorded data websites
RSS feeds
Skills/practice websites
Social bookmarking
Standards connector web
Student-to-expert communication websites
Tag cloud
Virtual field trips
WebQuests

ACTIVITIES FOR YOUR TEACHER PORTFOLIO

1. MANAGING EDUCATIONAL INFORMATION

Reflect on the different strategies you are using to manage the educational information you need to teach effectively.

- How have you been organizing educational information so far as a student and a new teacher candidate?

- How do you plan to organize teaching and educational information in the future?

- What role do you envision for technology-based information management tools in your information management system as a teacher?

2. EVALUATING INFORMATION MANAGEMENT STRATEGIES

Review the following information management strategies and identify the ones you plan to use as a teacher, and why.

- Listening to podcasts from major news publications such as the *New York Times,* the *Economist,* or NPR (National Public Radio) to stay informed about a wide range of events.

- Gathering information about specific subject fields from professional databases and online publications.

- Using a combination of both audio and print media. One teacher told us, "The best media is sorted in a way that I can scan it quickly for keywords. Then I arrange it in a way I can use it at a later date."

- Employing what management consultant Barbara Hemhill calls the "FAT" system, meaning "File, Act, or Toss," thereby leaving you only three decisions to make every time you encounter new information. One teacher we know tries to live by this system, although she admits to still spending about 25 percent of her workday organizing teaching-related information.

- Using electronic bookmarking and social bookmarking tools to manage information.

3. WEBSITE DESIGN BY STUDENTS

Conduct the following exercise with students. The goal of this activity is for students to become sophisticated users of online resources as they learn to design for the Web.

The enormous growth of e-commerce has made successful website design an area of high demand in the fields of product and business marketing. More and more consumers now go online to find out about goods and services. When those consumers decide to make purchases, increasing numbers of them use the Web as well. Consequently, businesses and other organizations must have attractive, user-friendly websites to interest and retain customers.

Ask students to design a website for their favorite commercial product, recreational pursuit, or educational subject. Challenge them to use words, symbols, numbers, images, and other elements creatively in their design.

In creating their designs, students must critically decide about the elements of every website: the splash page where users arrive first, the navigational tools that guide users around the site, the embedded information that appears as users explore a site in more depth, and the relevant links that offer additional information about a topic.

GROWING AND LEADING WITH TECHNOLOGY

This activity offers an opportunity to grow as a teacher and learn to lead with technology. Begin by reviewing the Chapter 6 Learning Goal and New Technologies listed in the chart at the start of the chapter. Then read the following actual classroom scenario and consider how the technologies discussed in Chapter 6 might be integrated into the lesson. Follow-up steps to this activity can be completed at MyEducationKit.

ADAM'S PROBABILITY LESSON

Adam is teaching probability to sixth-graders as part of his middle school's mathematics curriculum. His goal is to show students how probability, the study of how likely something is to happen, will help them distinguish between events that are "certain," "likely," "unlikely," or "impossible." As mathematician Jeffrey Rosenthal (2006, p. 5) has remarked, "Knowing the rules of probability, randomness, and uncertainty allows us to make better decisions and to understand the world around us more clearly."

Probability is the basis of games of chance, sports, weather forecasts, politics, the stock market, and countless other everyday situations. For students, probability is a tool for making wise decisions and thinking critically about public needs and governmental policies. For instance, on a personal level, it is "certain" that students will take achievement tests in school, but it is "unlikely" that those who do not study will earn high scores. More globally, it is "impossible" to travel long distances in a short amount of time without using planes, trains, and automobiles, but it is "likely" that fossil fuel–burning transportation machines will create environmental pollution. These and other examples allow students to understand the meanings of *certain, impossible, likely,* and *unlikely,* and to begin applying those concepts to their everyday choices and decisions.

Adam is teaching in a classroom with only one Internet-accessible computer, although he has access to a nearby lab with enough machines for every member of his class if the students work together in pairs. His class periods are 48 minutes in length and he teaches the same students at the same time every day. He has noticed that the students tend to lose interest and focus when he does large-group lessons that involve his demonstrating how to solve problems by writing on the classroom's whiteboard. When the students lose interest, discipline problems surface and Adam ends up spending valuable instructional time trying to regain his students' attention.

- Using the technologies discussed in this chapter, how would you propose Adam integrate technology into the teaching of probability as a way to enliven and extend his teaching methods?

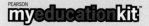

PEARSON

To complete the full activity, go to the Growing and Leading with Technology section of Chapter 6 in MyEducationKit and access the activity "Adam's Probability Lesson."

7 Problem Solving and Inquiry Learning with Software and Web Tools

Now is the time to turn the new media that children have a natural attraction to into learning tools that will build their knowledge and broaden their perspectives.

—Joan Ganz Cooney, in *D Is for Digital* (Shuler, 2007)

CHAPTER LEARNING GOAL

Inquiry Learning and Problem Solving

Using educational software and Web-based tools to promote problem solving and inquiry learning

CONNECTING to the NETS

NETS-T

2 Design and Develop Digital Age Learning Experiences and Assessments

4 Promote and Model Digital Citizenship and Responsibility

NETS-S

4 Critical Thinking, Problem Solving and Decision Making

NEW TECHNOLOGIES

- Open source software
- Composing and calculating software
- Building, inventing, and creating software
- Visual thinking and concept mapping software
- Discovery learning software
- Computer-based and Web-based educational games
- Virtual worlds
- Digital games for learning
- Intelligent tutoring systems

CHAPTER OVERVIEW

Chapter 7 overviews how educational software supports and promotes problem solving and inquiry learning for students from kindergarten to the twelfth grade. After presenting criteria for evaluating the quality of software for teaching and learning, the chapter discusses different kinds of educational software, from open source materials to commercially produced programs. The last section introduces intelligent tutoring systems as emerging instructional options for teachers, particularly in math and science education.

The chapter responds to NETS-T Standard 1, Part b where teachers "engage students in exploring real-world issues and solving authentic problems" and Standard 2, Part b where teachers "enable all students to pursue their individual curiosities." Through its focus on inquiry-based learning and problem solving, the chapter shows teachers ways to address NETS-S Standard 4.

FOCUS QUESTIONS

1. What are the standard software applications found on most computers today and what open source software alternatives are there?

2. How can teachers evaluate the different types of educational software available today?

3. How do teachers use different software programs to promote problem solving and inquiry learning?

4. How can teachers use computer games and simulations as learning resources?

5. How can teachers evaluate the effectiveness of educational software?

6. What are intelligent tutoring systems and how can students and teachers use them successfully?

Leaving an elementary school one afternoon, we poked our heads into a classroom and observed a teacher arranging the computer area of her classroom in preparation for a scheduled parent–teacher conference.

"Margaret, you think of every last detail," we remarked.

"If that were true," she replied, "I would have figured out how to give everyone the opportunity to use these computers more. I am given so much material to teach for the tests, I never have the time to find the software and games that the kids will really enjoy."

After leaving Margaret, we saw the parents, a family we knew, who were coming to the family conference. Inquiring about the family, the father promptly told us of his daughter's current fascination with her new online digital pet.

"We had been to several stores to find this creature because it is really hard to find and Rosie has in her mind that if she gets it, then she can build her online pet family. It is one of those limited-release toys that come with a special story and a registration number that is tied to an online video game."

"It is really interesting what the animals do," Rosie's father continued, "because when you buy one of them you are allowed to play a game with the animal. The animal's collar has a special ID tag that you use within the world of other special creatures. Since playing in the game, Rosie has bought a house for her pets, food, and she even has a virtual hot tub! Now if only I could get her to manage her homework and her real live pets like she manages this virtual world."

The contrast between Rosie's fascination with her computer pet and her teacher's wish to find educationally stimulating computer software introduces this chapter's learning goal of using technology to promote inquiry learning and problem-solving skills among students. Recognizing that students are drawn to the excitement and challenge of computer games and software programs, and realizing that high-quality instructional materials, available on CD-ROM or the Web, propel learning experiences at all grade levels, you as a teacher will want to find the best programs for your classroom. These choices require information and thought.

This chapter's focus is how teachers can promote inquiry learning and problem solving using educational software. These are the same methods that researchers in science, math, history, and other fields use to solve problems, and they also refer to educational activities where students ask questions, make predictions, test theories, and revise ideas based on data and evidence (National Science Teachers Association, 1996). **Problem solving** and **inquiry learning** begin with real-world situations and issues to actively engage students. In history class, students explore primary source documents—personal letters, government documents, police records, news stories, and other materials—to identify the causes of historic events. They "do" history as professional historians, reasoning about historical relationships and dynamics in addition to studying the names, dates, and places of the past (Donovan & Bransford, 2004a). Similarly, in science, math, and English classes where students undertake inquiry-based activities, they assume the roles of scientists, mathematicians, and writers (Donovan & Bransford, 2004b, 2004c). And because children and adolescents are natural inquirers, continually asking questions about every imaginable subject, problem solving and inquiry learning successfully engage students at every grade level.

Educational software (or *instructional software*) refers to computer products and Web-based tools that are designed to promote student learning in schools and homes. Most educational software is sold as brand-name products by computer software firms (Shuler, 2007).

To show how teachers can promote problem solving and inquiry learning using educational software, several types are examined, including composing and calculating software; building, inventing, and creating software; visual thinking and brainstorming software; computer games, virtual worlds, and digital games for learning; and intelligent tutoring systems.

Computers and Software

Users of computers have heard of hardware and software. **Hardware** refers to the basic machinery and circuitry of a computer. **Software** is the term for computer instructions, a collection of codes that tell a computer's hardware to perform specific functions. The two together make computer technologies work.

Computers work from instructions given to them by people; computers do what we tell them to do. For example, word processing software tells a computer to do whatever writing, editing, and publishing we request. We turn on our machine, open the word processing, database, spreadsheet, media player, photo, or email program, and start using the features provided by these different applications. We use computer software all of the time without thinking about it. For this reason, it may be helpful to review the major types and functions of computer software.

Types of Software

There are two main types of software. **System software** is responsible for the overall functioning and control of a computer. It includes the operating system, network operating system, database managers, and TP monitor. **Application software** performs specific functions in specialized ways to produce a variety of services, including word processing, databases, spreadsheets, slides and presentations, Internet browsing, email management, movie making, or DVD burning, to name a few.

Highly sophisticated application software directs the information processing work of computers. You will recognize many of these programs by their commercial names: Microsoft Word, PowerPoint, Excel, Adobe, Photoshop, Norton Antivirus, and so on. Sometimes programs are bundled together in one large computer productivity package such as Microsoft Office Home and Student 2007. Open source software applications can also perform your computer's essential information processing tasks, such as WordPress for blogging or Mozilla Firefox for web searching. Open source refers to computer code and programs that are made available free (or for minimal cost), usually over the Internet.

Standard Software Applications

Standard software applications on computers are indispensable tools. For example, we cannot imagine writing this book without the word processing speed and other functions of Microsoft Word. We are reliant on the program's features to organize, draft, revise, and print our chapters. Writers are not alone in their need for computerized tools; accountants need tax preparation software, architects need design programs, physicians need real-time data on patients, and weather forecasters need interactive models of future meteorological patterns. Name a job or activity in today's society, from auto mechanic to rocket scientist, and you will find computers and other information technologies at the center of the work.

Most likely your personal or school computer has the following standard software applications:

- **Word processing** software enables writers to enter data into a word processing document. These text-based documents have replaced those formerly produced by manual and electronic typewriters applying ink onto paper. Word processing software allows users to create digital documents that can be drafted, edited, and shared electronically.
- **Electronic databases** are data-organizing programs that allow information to be entered, parsed, and retrieved. Some teachers use electronic databases to manage their grading systems and other academic records.

- **Spreadsheets** are documents designed like paper ledgers in which you can place numerical values in horizontal and vertical columns. Because the document is digital, spreadsheet software will calculate data based on formulas that users enter into the software.
- **Web-browsing software** allows computer users to visit favorite websites or search for new information online. Popular browsers include Internet Explorer, Safari, and Firefox. We discussed Internet information research using Web-browsing software in Chapters 5 and 6.
- **Communications software** enables computer users to write or talk to other users by email, instant messaging, Internet chat, and other programs. We will discuss computer-mediated communication using different software in more detail in Chapter 8.
- **Presentation software** like PowerPoint gives computer users many creative ways to construct digital slideshows and other displays that incorporate text, sound, voice, and pictorial images. We will discuss presentations using PowerPoint in Chapter 9.
- **Antivirus software** scans a computer for malicious programs that deliberately interfere with its operation. A virus can be spread when one computer communicates with another computer, much like humans catch colds or viral infections. Antivirus software is an essential tool to protect your computer against the constant threat of these potentially dangerous programs.
- **Specialized software** allows users to do particular functions at a high degree of specialty. A teacher might build a class website using Dreamweaver, a popular Web-authoring program. In Dreamweaver, "what you see is what you get" (WYSIWYG), meaning its interface shows onscreen whatever you create as you are making it. For example, while programming the word *Welcome* to be displayed in the center of the Web page, the word will appear exactly as formatted, changing as you make alterations, and showing when finished just as it will look on your website's home page.

Open Source Software

Open source software is "open" for the public to use, copy, and recreate, usually at little or no cost. While profit-making companies develop much of the software for computers today, open source software is an alternative with proven dependability. In the open source community, individuals and organizations deliberately make the source codes available free to users and software developers with the idea that new and improved applications will emerge, thereby stimulating innovations within a wider community.

A computer user can run open source alternatives to most of the major commercial software applications. Linux, for example, is a widely used open source operating system. Table 7.1 shows several popular commercial applications and their open source alternatives. Some technology educators consider open source software to be safer to run on computers because it is more secure in terms of privacy. Firefox, for example, is often preferred in comparison to Internet Explorer, which is infamous for security vulnerability. You can learn more about open source software by visiting the website of the Open Source Initiative (www.opensource.org).

Choosing and Evaluating Educational Software

School systems often make large purchases of educational software to install on a network that serves every school in the district. Teachers will commonly find software choices that have been preselected by the district on their classroom computers. In many schools, teachers are not allowed to add their own software to the school system network, whereas in other cases, teachers may add programs only after gaining permission from a building principal or district technology administrator.

TABLE 7.1   Open Source Alternatives to Popular Commercial Software Applications

Type of Application	Commercial Product	Open Source Alternative
Operating system	Windows Mac OS X	Linux FreeBSD
Integrated applications package	Microsoft Office	OpenOffice
Web browser	Internet Explorer Safari	Mozilla Firefox
Word processing	Microsoft Word	OpenOffice Writer
Presentation graphics	Microsoft PowerPoint	OpenOffice Impress
Spreadsheet	Microsoft Excel	Xess Spreadsheet
Electronic mail	Microsoft Outlook Express Google Mail	Mozilla Thunderbird Mozilla Camino Eudora
Instant messaging	AOL Instant Messenger	Gaim Instant Messenger Jabber
Image editing	Adobe Photoshop	GIMP Image Editor

Criteria for Evaluating Educational Software

Finding and selecting quality software is a challenging task for teachers (Unger, 2007). The decision is a significant one. Some programs recreate traditional teaching practices in an electronic format. A fill-in-the-blank worksheet is a fill-in-the-blank worksheet, whether it is done electronically or on paper. By contrast, high-quality software offers wonderful opportunities to transform the learning experiences of students.

One way to identify good educational software is to recognize what constitutes poor software. Seymour Papert (inventor of the computer programming language LOGO) has identified three features of low-quality software:

- First, the program, not the child, controls the activity.
- Second, the game promotes competition, stereotyping or violence.
- Third, the software favors quick reactions over long-term thinking. (Papert, 1996, pp. 55–56)

In deciding which software to buy for learning, argues Papert (1996, p. 56), teachers need to first answer the following question: "Will the child program the computer or will the computer program the child?"

Evaluating all aspects of a computer software program is also important in order to get a full picture of what happens educationally when it is used by students. ISTE has developed an evaluation instrument that examines educational software in terms of five essential questions (see Table 7.2). Teachers can give a grade of A through F in each area. The

YOUR JUDGMENT MATTERS

Examine the desktop of a computer in the school where you are student teaching or doing teaching field experiences to see which software programs have been purchased and installed on all district computers for teacher and student use. As you view the computer desktop, consider the following questions:

- Did you find the software programs that you expected to find?
- What software programs did you find that were new to you?
- Who selects software for the school system—a single individual or a committee of teachers, administrators, parents, and students?
- Who do you think should be involved in making choices for an entire school or school system?
- If teachers are able to add their own choices to those provided by the school system, what programs would you recommend adding to the network?

TABLE 7.2 Criteria for Educational Software Evaluation

Criteria	Key Question to Ask
Teacher support	Does the software include resources for teachers?
Content	Is the content current, thorough, age-appropriate, reliable, clear, and fully referenced?
Assessment	Does assessment include pretest, posttest, recordkeeping by students and groups, and assessment guidelines?
Technical quality	Is the program easy to install and use, with high-quality sound and smooth-running video segments?
Instructional design	Does the program promote creativity, higher order thinking, collaboration, problem solving, discovery, or memorization? Does it activate curiosity, provide challenge, employ real-world connections, and allow student control?

Source: Adapted from *National Educational Technology Standards for Teachers: Preparing Teachers to Use Technology* (pp. 340–341) © 2002 ISTE® (International Society for Technology in Education), www.iste .org. All rights reserved.

PEARSON
myeducationkit™

Go to the Assignments and Activities section of Chapter 7 in MyEducationKit and complete the video activity entitled "Software for Math Instruction" and respond to the questions that accompany the video.

higher the grade, the more reliable the software program is likely to be as a teaching and learning technology.

Higher Order and Lower Order Thinking

Still another way for educators to evaluate educational software is to assess the extent to which a particular program encourages higher order thinking by students. Higher order and lower order thinking are terms associated with **Bloom's taxonomy,** a seminal educational classification tool first presented in 1956 and subsequently revised in 2001 (Anderson & Krathwohl, 2001). Bloom and his collaborators were interested in distinguishing between different forms of thinking from basic recall and interpretation of information (lower order) to comparison and evaluation of theories and perspectives (higher order). The original list of thinking levels from lowest to highest—"knowledge, comprehension, application, analysis, synthesis and evaluation"—was revised to "remembering, understanding, applying, analyzing, evaluating, and creating."

Educators are aware that different instructional approaches promote lower or higher order thinking. For example, many teachers ask students to learn vocabulary and spelling words every week. Memorizing spelling emphasizes lower order thinking whereas composing a poem or creating dialogue for a skit using those same words uses higher order thinking.

To evaluate how educationally themed video games impact the thinking skills of students, University of North Texas technology educator John Rice (2007) has designed a "Higher Order Thinking Evaluation Rubric" (see Table 7.3). Rice's rubric has 20 questions for teachers to answer about video gaming products, some of which could be used to assess other types of educational software as well. An evaluator assigns one point if a design element is present and zero points if not. To successfully promote higher order thinking, a game should earn a score of between 15 to 20 points on the rubric, meaning higher order thinking features are consistently present.

Online Software Selection Resources for Teachers

Numerous educational organizations have online resources that assist teachers in selecting software.

TABLE 7.3 Rubric for Evaluating Higher Order Thinking in Video Games

Characteristics	Yes/No (1/0)
Requires users to assume a role in the game rather than simply play.	
Offers meaningful interaction such as dialogue with NPCs (characters in the game).	
Has a storyline.	
Has a complex storyline with characters users care about.	
Offers simple puzzles.	
Has complex puzzles requiring effort to solve.	
Uses three-dimensional graphics.	
Allows multiple views or camera pans and the ability to zoom in and out.	
Allows different ways to complete the game.	
Simulates complex processes requiring adjustment of variables by users to obtain desired results (adjusting variables leads to different results).	
Allows interactions through use of avatars (an online identity adopted by the game player).	
Uses lifelike avatars.	
Requires interaction with virtual elements within the game.	
Requires knowledge of game elements beyond mouse prompts and number entry (e.g., combining elements to create new tools, understanding complex jargon).	
Requires gathering of information in order to complete.	
Requires synthesis of knowledge in order to complete or successfully engage elements in the game.	
Effectively replicates real-world environment.	
NPCs display AI (artificial intelligence) characteristics.	
NPCs display effective use of AI resulting in dynamic experiences for the user.	
Offers replay abilities with varying results.	
Total Score	

Source: "Assessing Higher Order Thinking in Video Games" by John W. Rice, *Journal of Technology and Teacher Education, 15*(1), p. 93. Copyright 2007 by the Association for the Advancement of Computing in Education (AACE). (www.aace.org) Reprinted with permission.

Educational Software Preview Guide (ESPG).   ESPG (http://ed.fnal.gov/espg) is an open access, online searchable directory of more than 1,000 software titles for use in preK–12 classrooms. It is sponsored by a consortium of nonprofit computer education organizations and published online by the Fermi National Accelerator Laboratory of the U.S. Department of Energy.

More than one expert has reviewed every title, and the online search function allows teachers to locate the program that best fits their teaching situation.

Entertainment Software Rating Board. Established in 1994, ESRB is an independent evaluation group that assesses and rates about 1,000 new pieces of software a year. Like the ratings that accompany motion pictures, ESRB symbols provide buyers with a way to determine the appropriate age level of a program, using six basic categories: EC (Early Childhood, ages 3 and up); E (Everyone, ages 6 and up); E10+ (Everyone 10 and Older, ages 10 and up); T and Older (Teen, ages 13 and up); M (Mature, ages 17 and up); and AO (Adults Only, ages 18 and up). There is also a Rating Pending designation for software that is currently under review. Ratings are available on the products themselves and online (www.esrb.org/index-js.jsp).

EvaluTech. A free online software review service for teachers sponsored by the Southern Regional Education Board, an interstate education compact serving 16 states from Maryland to Texas, the EvaluTech website offers a number of software-related services to teachers:

- Reviews of more than 10,000 software and print resources for K–12 teaching
- Links to lesson plans and Web resources
- Assessments of software products from six major e-learning companies: LeapFrog, Renaissance Learning, PLATO Learning, American Ed Corporation, Pearson Digital Learning, and Riverdeep
- Information about educational technology policy as well as online professional development for teachers
- Criteria for evaluating computer courseware, CD-ROMs, websites, online courses, videodiscs, educational Web portals, children's software, fiction and nonfiction books, and other media.

StopBadware.org. **Badware** is a type of software that fundamentally disregards a user's choice or control over how a computer will be used. Invasive software programs such as adware, spyware, and stealth dialers can enter people's computers unknowingly and disrupt normal operations by allowing pop-up ads, redirecting Web searches, working against antispyware programs, and modifying other functions to make it easier for commercial product ads and other unwanted images to appear on your screen.

StopBadware.org (www.stopbadware.org) is a software consumer watchdog organization, collaboratively run by the Berkman Center for the Internet and Society at Harvard Law School and the Internet Institute at Oxford University with corporate support from companies like Google and Sun Microsystems. (Consumer Reports WebWatch is an unpaid special advisor to the organization.) It serves as a "neighborhood watch campaign" whose goal is to identify and negate destructive, manipulative, or unscrupulous software, what the organization calls "badware."

Using Educational Software for Problem Solving and Inquiry Learning

Teachers use educational software to meet many instructional goals, including problem solving and inquiry learning (Niederhauser & Stoddart, 2001). In this section, we list types of software programs likely found in the schools that can support problem solving and inquiry learning. We include well-known programs, used effectively by teachers for years, as well as newer products offering engaging learning experiences for students. Our list is intended not to be comprehensive, but to serve as a starting point for your investigations of which software programs will energize student learning in your classroom.

Composing and Calculating Software

Microsoft Word and Excel are standard composing and calculating programs found on many computers. Because writing and mathematics are core parts of every school curriculum and every student is expected to gain increasing levels of proficiency in each area from elementary through secondary school, word processing and spreadsheet software programs serve as essential tools for teaching and learning.

A broad consensus exists that it makes sense to integrate technology directly into how students learn writing at every grade level. The Conference on College Composition and Communication (CCCC) stated in its Position Statement on Teaching, Learning, and Assessing Writing in Digital Environments that the curriculum of composition must incorporate two literacies—"a literacy of print and a literacy of screen" (2004, February). The CCCC view asserts that college students, and by extension, students in K–12 schools, need lots of hands-on use of writing technologies as well as many opportunities to critically evaluate the kinds of writing that computers make possible. This process that English educators refer to as **digital writing,** or *digital composing,* covers not only writing on a computer instead of using pen or pencil, but writing for a website, communicating by email or instant messaging, contributing to a blog or a wiki, or expressing one's ideas through another technology-based communication outlet.

Students using technology is also regarded as essential to successful math learning. In its national standards for mathematics teaching, the National Council of Teachers of Mathematics (2000, p. 3) stated: "Technology is essential in teaching and learning mathematics; it influences the mathematics that is taught and enhances student learning." NCTM believes that spreadsheets, graphing calculators, geometry visualization software that explores shapes and relationships, and interactive websites that demonstrate math concepts are all key teaching and learning resources for the math classroom. For example, the Excel spreadsheet program is widely available to teachers as part of the standard software application packages found on most school system computer networks. It can be used for many math activities. Figure 7.1 shows a spreadsheet and bar graph created using Excel for measuring how far a group of fourth- and fifth-graders can jump from a standing position.

Building, Inventing, and Creating Software

Building, inventing, and creating happen when students engage in open-ended explorations of topics and items that interest them. Such learning begins at young ages when preschoolers, kindergartners, and elementary school students play with blocks, dolls, Legos, balls, paints, and other manipulative materials. Middle and high school students have such learning experiences when they conduct science experiments, engage in investigations of historical primary sources, act in plays and skits, perform their own musical compositions or dance routines, or write creatively using genres of fiction and nonfiction. In each case, students discover knowledge by what they build, invent, and create with materials at hand and ideas in their imaginations.

Like hands-on materials, **building, inventing, and creating software** can function to provide students with environments for interactive and engaging explorations. The key to this outcome is

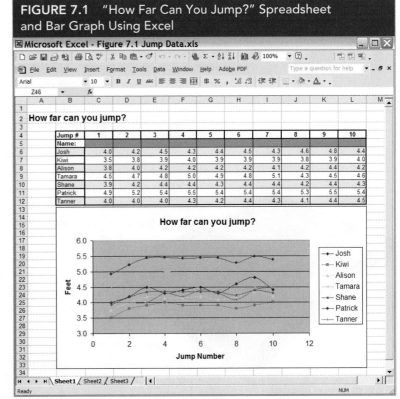

FIGURE 7.1 "How Far Can You Jump?" Spreadsheet and Bar Graph Using Excel

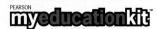

Go to the Assignments and Activities section of Chapter 7 in MyEducationKit. Select the video activity entitled "Technology Supports Second Language Learners" and complete the activity.

for students' efforts not to be determined by the software. The most effective programs are those that do not require a single right way to use them or a single right answer. Kid Pix and Google Earth are examples of building, inventing, and creating software likely to be on computers in the schools where you are teaching.

Kid Pix.   A widely used educational program for more than 20 years, Kid Pix began as a paint program and has evolved into a multimedia online art studio with an extensive collection of features. In addition to letting you draw, paint, and collage on the computer screen, you can import text and images from other files, add sound effects, resize images and other visual materials, record your voice, or build a slideshow to show viewers. Young artists and slideshow creators will use this software over and over again as they discover new ways to express their ideas creatively.

Instructionally, teachers can use Kid Pix across the curriculum to accomplish creative learning. Much of what elementary school students do on a paper worksheet can be uniquely done in Kid Pix. In math, Kid Pix invites K–6 students to make their own books and posters illustrating math facts and concepts. For example, to learn about numbers from 1 to 10 or beyond, kindergarten students can make slideshows of images they draw or print to show these numbers in entertaining displays. The stamp-creator function is a way to display addition, subtraction, multiplication, and division in action. Older students making charts and graphs, writing and illustrating word problems, or showing visual representations of fractions, decimals, and percents could use Kid Pix to publish their work in slideshows or as printed posters or cartoons. The versatility of the tools in Kid Pix for showing one's ideas to others is greater than adults can imagine until they watch students create their projects.

Google Earth.   First released as a downloadable free Web tool in 2005, Google Earth is an interactive globe inside your computer. It is composed of photographs taken by satellites and aircraft of virtually every location in the world over the past three years (updated by Google on a rolling basis). It lets users zoom down from the sky to explore landmarks, places, and points of interest and study. Google Earth 4, which became available in January 2007, has enhanced 3D modeling, time animations, large image overlays with greater details, and added layers of information (such as the Rumsey Historical Maps folder).

Teachers at every grade level can make use of the resources in Google Earth (EDUCAUSE Learning Initiative, 2006, October). Students can take virtual journeys throughout their community or across the country to visit places of current or historical interest. In an English class, for example, students could visit the places where the action in a novel occurs, providing a visual connection between the story world and the actual world. Such journeys are unique opportunities for thoughtful discussions between teachers and students. "Are you surprised that there is so much water on the land?" a teacher asked her class as they scanned the area around their school. The visual presence of lakes and rivers was an opportunity to discuss the importance of water to people's lives, a key concept in the school's environmental science curriculum.

The Google Maps function offers three settings: Map (which gives a pictorial view of roads and rivers), Satellite (which shows the same area photographically), and Hybrid (which imposes street names on the photo images). Maps invite creative searches of places all over the nation and world. The students at the Sheffield School in Turners Falls, Massachusetts, were intrigued to see how many other Sheffield schools there are in the United States and what those locations looked like from above. The students also enjoyed the "3D Warehouse" filled with three-dimensional models of real and imagined places.

Tech Tool 7.1 describes Squeak and Scratch, two more discovery learning environments for elementary and middle school students. Each uses what is called **object-oriented programming,** where computer users create a virtual object and make it do things in response to preprogrammed instructions. A student might create a ball and then program it to fall and then bounce back up over and over again. Tremendous amounts of

Teachers are always searching for open-ended Web tools that promote problem solving and inquiry learning by students. With such tools, you can readily engage students with learning, using resources that have both an instructional and cognitive function. That is, students will use the tools (instruction) in a focused and thoughtful way (cognitive). Two electronic learning environments, Squeak etoys and Scratch, provide open-ended opportunities for elementary and middle school students to explore and create on the computer.

Squeak Etoys

Squeak etoys is an open source, free, downloadable software program that supports inquiry learning and problem solving by elementary and middle school students, especially in math and science. It is an open-ended environment that can be used across grade levels and in several different academic areas. Squeak etoys is included with every computer being shipped worldwide as part of the One Laptop Per Child (OLPC) initiative.

Scratch

Scratch is an electronic toolkit that enables students to make their own games, animated stories, and interactive art. The screenshot shows a page from a game made by a middle school math student using Scratch. Developed by the Lifelong Kindergarten Group at MIT (Massachusetts Institute of Technology), this program features 2D and 3D graphics, images, text, Web pages, sound, video, and more.

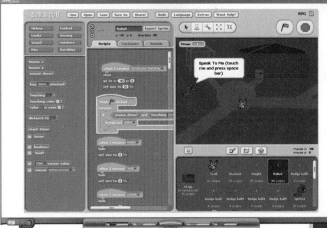

Programs like Squeak etoys and Scratch reverse the traditional educational process where students follow a teacher's directions in order to learn. Here students follow their own initiatives, learning from those activities with feedback and support from the teacher.

Board courtesy of SMART Technologies; copyright © 2001–2009 SMART Technologies ULC; all rights reserved.

CONTACT INFORMATION

Squeak etoys   www.squeak.org
Scratch   http://scratch.mit.edu

discovery learning can happen through this process. The ball's movement demonstrates the concepts of velocity and negative velocity and invites the student to discover any other ways the ball might be programmed to move.

Visual Thinking and Concept Mapping Software

Visual thinking and concept mapping software let teachers and students organize and outline their ideas visually on a computer. Kidspiration (for elementary school students), Inspiration (for high school students and adults), and InspireData (for middle and high school students) from Inspiration Software, Inc., are three highly flexible visual thinking programs. These tools include graphs, symbols, charts, voice, and other organizing devices, that are catalysts for creative self-expression by students.

How might you use Kidspiration, Inspiration, or InspireData in your own preparation as a teacher or with your students? To answer this question, consider how you personally might begin creating an original piece of writing, drawing, or representation of mathematical ideas, whether as a paper for one of your education classes, a lesson plan about a topic you have not taught before, or a report for your school principal.

The reality of original work is that it involves creating something new. When we ask students to create an original piece of writing or drawing, some report experiencing the "terror of the blank page," an overriding discomfort that may include staring at an assignment in frustration, feeling frozen intellectually, or not knowing where to start or what to write or draw.

Many teachers of writing urge students who feel blocked creatively to begin talking, writing, or drawing whatever comes to mind, without editing, as a way to stimulate their creative imagination. Expressing ideas verbally, in print, or through pictures produces a powerful momentum. Once started, new ideas often follow quickly, sometimes in smooth sequence, sometimes in a maze of thoughts, connections, and questions. Talking about ideas is very useful; then the act of committing ideas to paper provides a writer or artist or mathematician with visible and accessible raw materials that can be shaped into more coherent order through a series of edited drafts.

There are students who do not find brainstorming on paper an inspiring way to evoke ideas or solve problems. Perhaps paper is too confining and easily damaged or lost. Perhaps handwriting is too messy or time-consuming. Writing, drawing, or calculating on computers eliminates these constraints. Sometimes it is easier to create things electronically; ideas seem to appear without a sense that one had to engage in tedious, difficult work to produce results.

Kidspiration and Inspiration each have a linear writing mode, a chart- and graph-making mode, and a money counting mode as well as colorful graphics and a voice. Both can be used as a brainstorming tool and as a presentation organizer as well. Because these products promote visual learning, there are many opportunities for students to use the software to create diagrams and charts of curriculum ideas.

There are a range of other online visual thinking and brainstorming tools, either free or commercially available, and even single purpose tools can be useful, such as Persuasion Map from the National Council of Teachers of English (NCTE) on its ReadWriteThink website (www .readwritethink.org/materials/persuasion_map). Students can use Persuasion Map as an online outlining tool for composing a persuasive essay in a five-paragraph frame. A student activates the program by typing his or her name and the name of the paper. The next screen asks for a one- or two-sentence thesis statement. The following screen asks for three ideas that support the thesis statement and then for different facts that expand the ideas. With the persuasion map completed, the student has a working outline of the essay minus only the summary paragraph.

Visual thinking and brainstorming software raises questions about differences between expressing thoughts by hand (physically putting pencil to paper) and expressing thoughts on a machine using typed text accompanied by computer-made visuals and charts. Arguing that the computer is doing the work, and that this reliance on technology weakens the learning experience for the students, disregards the fact that the ease and speed of working in visual images and typed text on computers help some students. Although researchers have not decided whether a technology-based approach is inherently better than a nontechnology approach, visual thinking software offers teachers an engaging, user-friendly way for students to express and organize their ideas.

Go to the Assignments and Activities section of Chapter 7 in MyEducationKit. Select the Web activity "Uses for Inspiration and Kidspiration" and complete the activity.

Go to the Tutorial section of Chapter 7 in MyEducationKit. Select either "Inspiration" or "Kidspiration" and complete the full tutorial to learn how to use these helpful tools.

Computer Games as Learning Resources

Computer games are computer, video, and Web-based game software applications that are immensely popular among children and adolescents today. Computer games and simulations range from relatively simple programs where users simply click a mouse to select a choice or answer a question to highly interactive and dynamic multimedia experiences where users have many different ways to interact with the computer (Rieber, 2005).

Computer games, whether delivered on software, video game players, or the Web, share six basic characteristics:

- Rules
- Goals and objectives
- Outcomes and feedback
- Conflict/competition/challenge/opposition
- Interaction
- Representation or story (Prensky, 2001, pp. 118–119)

Digital Games for Learning is a rapidly expanding part of the computer technology field as educators discover the best ways to transform game playing into engaging and thoughtful learning experiences.

Computer games span a wide variety of formats, including "action games, adventure games, fighting games, knowledge games, simulation/role playing games, drill and practice games, and logical and mathematical games" (Mitchell & Savill-Smith, 2004, p. 3). In each case, whether singly or in multiuser environments, players interact with an electronic playing environment that provides some type of opposition that must be overcome. There is visual feedback on each player's actions as well as rewards for successful accomplishments.

Computer games reach into almost every home and classroom for several reasons:

- Multiple delivery systems, including computer software, CD-ROMs, video game players, and Internet sites, provide wide access to games and gaming among virtually every segment of the population. For instance, some 45 million homes have video game consoles (Federation of American Scientists, 2006, p. 10), while the number using computers and Web access for games is steadily increasing as well.
- Highly publicized connections between games and commercial products promote interest across age groups and grade levels. Beyond the actual games being played, symbols of the gaming culture appear on such commercial products as pencils, purses, notebooks, clothing, backpacks, playing cards, stuffed animals, and small figurines and logos that hide in desks and lockers while residing in the minds of kids.
- Ability to absorb children's attention through alluring storylines and characters, separate action and adventure narratives based on those characters, and stimuli and responses that become addictive make these games attractive to children. Game playing gives rise to small economies and gaming groups that become directly linked with a perception of social success for some children.

Debates about Games and Gaming

Mention games and gaming and many educators, parents, and students immediately think of **video games.** Games played on a computer or video game player are pervasive elements of youth culture today. (See Figure 7.2 for recent statistics on video game playing among children and adolescents.)

The impact of video games on the intellectual and academic development of students is a widely discussed topic in education and psychology today. Many contain violent imagery, aggressive action-oriented storylines, sexual themes, or fighting characters controlled by players to defeat opponents using sophisticated weaponry that inflicts graphic destruction on characters and

FIGURE 7.2 Video Game Playing among Children and Adolescents

- Most children and adolescents play computer and video games, although there are some gender differences in the area of video games (Walsh et al., 2005).

- Nearly nine in ten (87 percent) of 8- to 17-year-olds play video games at home—boys slightly more than girls (92 percent to 80 percent).

- M-rated games (M for mature content that can include graphic violence, sexual imagery, and profane language) are very popular with young game players.

- More than two out of three adolescents (70 percent) report playing M-rated games, with boys (86 percent) greatly exceeding girls (49 percent).

- Boys aged 8 to 14 are much heavier users of computer and video games than girls of the same age, and this difference between genders increases as boys get older. This finding is in marked contrast to the trend toward fewer gender differences in other online activities such as using the Internet for communication or for information research. In those other nongame categories, among youngsters 8 to 13, "there were no gender differences . . . in the use of the computer for chatting, visiting websites, using email, doing schoolwork, or using the computer to do a job" (Subrahmanyam, Greenfield, Kraut, & Gross, 2002, p. 9). The pattern is similar among 14- to 18-year-olds, except that boys visit many more websites than girls.

environments (for instance, Grand Theft Auto, Halo, and some massive multiplayer online role-playing games). Popular video game systems include Nintendo Wii, Xbox 360, and Playstation 3. Recent research has suggested that violent video games cause desensitization to real-life violence among game players who appear to "get used to"—that is, become "physiologically numb"—to violent and aggressive real-world behaviors (Carnagey, Anderson, & Bushman, 2007).

Table 7.4 presents a summary of contrasting views on the impacts of computer games on learning. On one side of the debate are commentators and researchers who believe that parents and teachers should severely restrict computer use by students (Alliance for Childhood, 2004; Healy, 1999; Oppenheimer, 2004). Some would totally ban young children, especially preschoolers and kindergartners, from using computers for learning or play. From this perspective, computer games are a harmful distraction from the process of developing fluent reading, writing, and thinking skills among students.

By contrast, other educators see positive educational impacts from video and computer game play (Dodge et al., 2008; Federation of American Scientists, 2006; Gee, 2003; Houssart & Sams, 2008; Prensky, 2006; Rosser et al., 2008). "The theory of learning in good video games fits well with what I believe to be the best sorts of science instruction in school," states James Gee, a professor of reading at the University of Wisconsin and a leading proponent of using games for educational purposes (2003, p. 7).

When people play games, Gee contends, "they are learning a new *literacy*," one that is grounded in learning how to "read" visual images on screens (2003, p. 13). Understanding the visual nature of experience is essential for students in schools where science textbooks often contain more images than words. Students must know how to derive meaning from such "multimodal" texts—not only in schools, but when dealing with the multiple media they encounter every day.

Gaming creates "virtual worlds for learning," state Gee and colleagues from the Games and Professional Practice Simulations (GAPPS) research group at the University of Wisconsin, Madison (Shaffer, Squire, Halverson, & Gee, 2005, pp. 105–107). Because game players take on roles in video games, they experience, at least to some extent, "the concrete realities that words and symbols describe." In other words, players develop "situated understandings." Because many kids play games in online communities

YOUR JUDGMENT MATTERS

Recalling computer, video, and Web-based games you have played, consider the following questions:

- What do you think is the effect of violence in video games on the children who play them?
- Are you familiar with games that go "against the grain" by featuring cooperation, creative thinking, and peaceful solutions to problems?
- How do you plan to include your students' interest in video games when you begin teaching?

TABLE 7.4 Contrasting Views about Computer Games and Learning

Negative Views	Positive Views
Increases aggressive and confrontational behavior	Promotes strategic and analytical thinking, problem solving, and planning skills
Decreases empathy and concern for other people	Encourages students to engage in repeated practice as a way to achieve mastery of material
Encourages sedentary behavior and less active lifestyles	Helps teenagers deal with the stress of adolescence
Emphasizes a get-the-right-answer-to-obtain-a-reward approach to learning	Promotes visual learning and visual literacy
Limits opportunities for open-ended and exploratory play with wooden blocks, paints, and countless other materials	Promotes in-the-role learning where students learn by doing what people actually do in real-world jobs and professions
What other negative viewpoints would you add to the list?	What other positive viewpoints would you add to the list?

with thousands of others, they develop "effective social practices" while trying out "new and powerful identities" as they go about acquiring "shared values." In these ways, video games foster the conditions for deep and lasting learning as players become immersed in a "community of practice."

As a new teacher, you need awareness of and information about these debates because you are inextricably part of them. Your actions as a technology-using educator will contribute to the shaping of both the terms and outcomes of these discussions.

Skills-Learning Games

There is general agreement that children and adolescents learn from playing games, although proponents and critics disagree as to whether what is learned is mainly positive or negative (Shaffer et al., 2005). Educationally themed games are an important part of the overall gaming field and have been effective in promoting middle and high school student engagement in science learning (Barnett, Yamagata-Lynch, Keating, Barab, & Hay, 2005; Cifuentes & Hsieh, 2004; Huppert, Lomask, & Lazarowitz, 2002). **Skills-learning games** use the elements of game play to involve students in learning academic material, as in the following two examples.

Math Teaching Games.   Math Blaster, Treasure MathStorm, Numbers Undercover, and Sunbuddy Math are the brand names of different educational games designed to teach mathematics by providing students practice in computational skills, addition, subtraction, multiplication, and division, as well as teaching fact families and mental math. Math learning is vitally important in the early grades. Students who do not acquire the necessary foundation of math learning in elementary school lack the skills and understandings to go on to algebra and geometry in high school. Such higher level math in high school represents the foundation for majoring in science, technology, engineering, or mathematics in college. Increasingly, an "algebra gateway" located toward the end of middle school separates the mathematical haves from the mathematical have-nots, who are disproportionately African American, Latino, and female (Katz, 2007). Education reformer Robert Moses has called math learning a "new civil right" that must be guaranteed to all persons in the United States (Moses & Cobb, 2001).

Math Blaster first appeared in 1983. Since then, several million copies have been sold, and the series now features a range of programs for children from ages 4 to 12 as well as students learning prealgebra and algebra. Math Blaster encompasses number skills practice within the structure of point-scoring games that are similar in style and play to handheld toys and video games. Therein rests its great appeal. The setting is outer space, with a full complement of aliens and obstacles that must be overcome by solving math problems involving single-digit, double-digit, or triple-digit number operations (depending on the age and skill of the game player). Accumulating points by completing math problems, the game player moves to higher levels of the game.

Teachers find many advantages to Math Blaster and similar skills-learning games that focus children's attention on attaining high point totals while practicing math skills almost without realizing they are acquiring new knowledge. There is competition, but it is competition against the game rather than against a human opponent. The games teach number operations—addition, subtraction, multiplication, and division—and counting by one, fives, and tens—skills that are strengthened when students practice them, as well as place value and its importance in addition and subtraction. One asset is how much students like playing the game.

What some educators see as the strengths of skills-learning games, others regard as weaknesses. Any competition for points as rewards is controversial because it might be understood as teaching students that the rewards of learning are extrinsic rather than intrinsic. In this view, students do not discover the joy of learning for the sake of learning because they are fixated on scoring points to win a game. Other educators see computational skill programs as merely a drill-and-practice worksheet in an interactive video format. The core of mathematical thinking—problem solving—is missing from the activities. In this view, the programs teach skills but not the intellectual frameworks for connecting and applying those skills in solving problems.

Tech Tool 7.2 offers a short summary of another type of learning game, Zoombinis Logical Journey, where students engage in mathematical problem solving within the context of a fantasy adventure game.

The "House" Series.

The "House" series is a well-known and widely used example of skills-learning games. Titles include Millie's Math House, Trudy's Time and Place House, Bailey's Book House, and Sammy's Science House. Originally developed by Edmark and now distributed by Riverdeep Interactive Learning, these programs are used by many preschool through third-grade teachers, and each is a fine home learning tool for families and children ages 4 to 8.

Sammy's Science House features five science activity areas: "Learning about Weather," "Exploring the Animals of Acorn Pond," "Playing with Pictures to Make a Movie," "Building Machines and Toys in the Workshop," and "Sorting the Pictures of Plants, Animals, and Rocks." There are several different options in each area so the program is constantly offering kids activities they have not tried before. The graphics are inviting, the information is age-appropriate, and the games retain their excitement and surprise. Even after sustained use, student interest continues.

Every choice in Sammy's Science House develops reading and math skills within the context of the program's puzzles and activities. As students play the games, they are reading blueprints in order to put pieces of objects together to build something, reading pictures to categorize animals into groups, or reading pictures to put them in sequence left to right to make science-themed movies.

Students learn science concepts and vocabulary while manipulating thermometers, wind speeds, and precipitation. The math and science concepts are easily connected through conversations with teachers; students learn about fractions while assembling parts of movies and machines, identify common attributes while categorizing animals, or discover measurement symbols while exploring cycles of weather and nature. Students practice mathematical thinking as they find patterns and solve problems. This program is not a competitive game to finish quickly in order to win points or gain a high score. The joy in this software is its wide array of interesting choices, the ease of changing activities, and the ability to pause and consider options without any penalty for doing so.

Go to the Assignments and Activities section of Chapter 7 in MyEducationKit. Open the Web activity "Digital Games for Learning" to further explore this Tech Tool.

Teachers must be creative thinkers to find interesting and engaging ways for students to develop their problem-solving skills. Problem-solving situations, by their very nature, do not always have easy-to-find answers. Students may become frustrated when they do not succeed right away. The key is for students to stay with an activity long enough to first recognize that a problem needs to be solved and then do the intellectual work needed to solve it. Problem-solving games like Zoombinis Logical Journey keep students' attention focused on both the game and the problem-solving skills that teachers want them to develop.

Zoombinis Logical Journey

Zoombinis Logical Journey is a game in the Zoombinis' series designed to teach critical thinking, problem solving, and mathematical learning to elementary school students. (Zoombinis Mountain Rescue and Zoombinis Island Odyssey are also from the same publisher, The Learning Company.)

Zoombinis are thumb-sized creatures with five different types of hair styles, eyes/eyewear, nose colors, and feet/footwear—625 different possible combinations—who have embarked on a long and difficult journey to reclaim their ancestral island home (Hancock & Osterweil, 1996). Using trial-and-error learning, data analysis, logical reasoning, and theory building, the child or children playing the game maneuver Zoombinis through a series of obstacles and puzzles that block their journey.

Multiple levels of mathematical thinking abound throughout the game, where the emphasis is less on computation and arithmetic (numbers are rarely used) and more on asking children to use their powers of observation and problem solving to make their way though the puzzles. The choices of the game player affect the outcome, but how is not known in advance. Each Zoombini has certain characteristics and children must determine how those traits affect progress in overcoming the game's obstacles. For example, only red nose Zoombinis can go across a bridge, but only blue-eyed Zoombinis can go up a cliff.

Zoombinis is not a "get the right answer and win a prize" game. Making mistakes and learning from them is central to solving every puzzle. While using trial-and-error strategies helps at the game's simplest level, the more challenging levels require more sophisticated thinking strategies such as grouping the Zoombinis by common or uncommon characteristics. The foundations for algebra are evident here as students think analytically about the distribution of traits in every band of Zoombinis and then act accordingly in the various situations. The game encourages groups of students to play and strategize together, using their collective ideas to solve the problems.

Still, Zoombinis may become largely a guess-the-right-answer game if teachers do not help students make their problem-solving strategies explicit. When students discuss with teachers, and with each other, how they are solving the puzzles and record their strategies in writing to refer back to later, it is more likely that their mental plans will be remembered and applied to other math problem-solving situations outside the context of the games. The potential of Zoombinis to explore math concepts depends less on the software itself and more on how teachers and students use it in their classrooms.

CONTACT INFORMATION

Zoombinis www.learningcompany.com/jump.jsp?itemType=CATEGORY &itemID=514 Available for purchase from the official Zoombinis' site at The Learning Company.

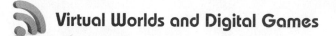

Many popular computer games are organized around **virtual worlds,** online computer-based environments where users adopt online identities (or avatars) and interact with other game players using those identities (EDUCAUSE Learning Initiative, 2006, June). Virtual worlds, however, do not always have a game structure with formal rules, specific outcomes, or defined winners and losers. Perhaps the most well-known virtual world for adults is Second Life, an online subscription game played by more than 8 million people worldwide, where players adopt an alternative persona (or avatar) through which they live and work in a 3D simulated world.

Virtual worlds for children and adolescents have emerged as a popular and profitable enterprise (Richtel & Stone, 2007). Examples of virtual worlds for children include Club Penguin (with some 4 million visitors per month), Barbie Girls, Be-Bratz, Habbo, Neopets, Nicktropolis, Webkinz, and WeeWorld (Shuler, 2007). Some organizations are developing virtual worlds that focus on specific academic topics. Sesame Workshop has created Panwapa to teach about global citizenship (see Figure 7.3) and cultural knowledge while IBM and Zula USA have launched Zula Patrol to involve students in learning about math, science, and technology (Shuler, 2007).

FIGURE 7.3 Panwapa Virtual World from Sesame Workshop

Source: Copyright © 2008 Sesame Workshop. Reprinted with permission of Sesame Workshop.

Digital Games for Learning

Digital games for learning (also known as *serious games*) are computer and Web-based games that have been designed with educational rather than entertainment goals in mind (Kafai, Hecter, Denner, & Sun, 2008; Rapaport, 2008). The term "digital games for learning" originated in 2006 when the Federation of American Scientists convened a Summit on Educational Games. Participants concluded that video game players are mastering skills that are essential for careers in a 21st-century information society—strategic thinking, interpretive analysis, problem solving, the ability to form and carry out plans, and adaptation to rapid change (Federation of American Scientists, 2006, p. 3). Moreover, game playing builds a foundation for student success in school by

- Contextual bridging (i.e., closing the gap between what is learned in theory and its use);
- High time-on-task;
- Motivation and goal orientation, even after failure;
- Providing learners with cues, hints, and partial solutions to keep them progressing through learning;
- Personalization of learning; and
- Infinite patience. (Federation of American Scientists, 2006, p. 5)

Recognizing the huge difference between games for entertainment and games for education, summit participants urged that the United States become a global leader in developing digital games for learning and pioneer the transfer of video game structures to teaching and learning in schools.

The Federation of American Scientists report further explains how going to school and playing games are vastly different experiences for most youngsters, and those differences point the way toward revolutionary change in how teaching and learning happen in K–12 education. Games are active, challenging, and demanding of focus and concentration to solve problems in innovative ways, while school is most often passive and uninspiring as students take in infor-

The River City Project

How has the development of digital games for learning, virtual worlds, and multiuser virtual environments begun to impact teaching and learning in K–12 schools? One example is The River City Project, an interactive computer simulation for middle grade science students developed by researchers at Harvard and Arizona State Universities. Since 2000, more than 8,000 middle school science and social studies teachers have used this simulation in their school curriculum.

River City is a 19th-century virtual town facing major public health crises from multiple environmentally caused illnesses. Working in an online environment, students must act as research scientists and investigators, collecting information about possible causes, forming and testing hypotheses, conducting experiments to test their ideas, and making recommendations and submitting research reports based on their findings. Their goal is to write a letter to the town's mayor explaining causes and solutions for the community's health problems.

River City functions as a multiuser virtual environment (MUVE) where teams of two to four students work as scientific investigators. MUVEs are popular computer game formats, but have not been typically used in schools to teach academic material. That situation is now changing as projects like River City show the value of these technologies for teaching and learning.

As scientific investigators in River City's MUVE, students take on the role of a digital character (or avatar) whose actions they control at their computer. The students' digital character enters River City and encounters historical artifacts and computer agents while conducting virtual experiments to try to determine what illness is sweeping through the community. At various locations throughout the town, the students receive relevant information in the form of prompts and hints. Visiting the hospital and checking the admissions records, for example, the students are told: "There are mosquitoes here now. Are there more illnesses?" (Ketelhut, 2007, p. 101).

How does participation in River City's virtual world affect student attitudes and behaviors toward learning? One study of 100 seventh-grade science students found that while some students started the project highly motivated to do inquiry-based investigations and other students were less motivated at the outset, all students increased scientific data gathering each time they visited the site. Temple University researcher Diane Jass Ketelhut (2007) concluded that a virtual learning environment like River City may help students develop positive attitudes and behaviors toward scientific inquiry in ways that traditional classroom settings do not.

You can learn more about The River City Project at http://muve.gse.harvard.edu/rivercityproject. Middle school teachers across the United States are invited to join. Short videos showing the various components of the project are available at the website.

See also the Center for Children and Technology (CCT), an initiative that began at Bank Street College in New York City in the 1980s and is now part of the Education Development Center (EDC), a nonprofit organization based in Newton, Massachusetts. CCT conducts and publishes research on how technology makes a difference in children's learning in classrooms, schools, and communities. In 2008, CCT received a $9.2 million grant to look at how game-based activities can support science and literacy instruction in schools.

mation and repeat it back on tests and papers. Today's students, familiar with action-oriented games on video screens, easily tune out teachers who are lecturing while standing at overhead projectors or writing on chalkboards. Educational games, concluded the summit's report, "might improve students' attitudes about learning even difficult subjects, including those who are not attracted to studying mathematics and science" (Federation of American Scientists, 2006, p. 17).

One example of a digital game for learning is MeCHeM: Building Better Bots through Chemistry (see Figure 7.4), a program designed by winners of the Liemandt Foundation's Hidden Agenda Game Competition, a contest where college students create games based on the concept of **stealth learning.** In stealth learning, students learn without realizing they are learning because academic information and skills are embedded within the activities of the game.

Entering the MeCHeM game, you find yourself in a vast cavernous utility garage. A robot approaches, displaying the posture of a warrior. As he stands before you, you must decide how

FIGURE 7.4 Screenshot from MeCHeM: Building Better Bots through Chemistry

Source: Copyright © 2007 The Liemandt Foundation. Reprinted with permission.

to armor him with the most robust materials that you can find. The robot's success depends on the type of armor, weapons, power generator, capacitor, and coolant you choose to make a MeCHeM strong enough to battle other MeCHeMs to the finish. Players learn the properties of chemical elements while engaging in creative problem solving.

MeCHeM uses stealth learning to foster a new approach to chemistry teaching in particular and science learning in general. In the past, while teaching complex scenarios and abstract concepts, teachers would often ask students to "imagine building a tower taller than your desk" or "imagine being a scientist and finding a way to mix these two solutions together." Now, using this interactive gaming software, students can explore "possibility landscapes." Will Wright (2004, November), author of the famous SimCity computer game, describes these landscapes as "complex, realistic simulations" where people can experience a simulation rather than simply observe.

The movement for serious games is growing. Writer and researcher Marc Prensky is one of the organizers of a website called Social Impact Games that identifies more than 500 games that promote learning, social change, and community involvement. Selected titles include Food Force (designed to educate about problems of food and starvation in the world), Outbreak at Water's Edge (dealing with responses to public health emergencies), PeaceMaker (focusing on peaceful solutions to the Israeli–Palestinian conflict), and The Mapojib Experience (teaching everyday uses of the Korean language). More digital games for learning are presented in Table 7.5.

Strategies for Using Games with Your Students

When teachers consider how to include games in their curriculum, they confront the complex issues of time and focus. Many teachers seek games to promote "time on task," but then choose games that develop only one or two specific skills (such as number operations or vocabulary words). As one teacher remarked, "If I could find another game that could teach Rachel division like this one taught her multiplication, we would both be in good shape." Problems develop by underuse or overuse of games. Some children may become bored or frustrated or otherwise lose interest in the games and stop playing. Other children will play the games repeatedly as an alternative to experiencing a teacher-directed classroom environment, but then spend so much time on the computer that they are separated from the larger classroom group for inordinate amounts of the school day.

Many schools maintain a wide selection of educational software, including games, in their libraries or resource centers.

Some skill-based games tend not to differentiate the instruction enough to target both basic skills and creative problem solving, so problem solving becomes an "add-on" as part of the narrative that keeps the game "moving." Seeking to destroy, working to recover something lost, or running to hide from danger are typical problem-solving scenarios that children encounter in skills-based educational gaming situations. However, it is unusual for both skills development and problem solving to be tied together in ways that emphasize the development of deeper thinking by students.

To reduce such problems, the following strategies can help teachers to more effectively use games and gaming in the classroom.

TABLE 7.5 Digital Games for Learning

Digital Learning Game	Description and Grade Levels
Civilization III www.civ3.com	In this popular historical simulation game, players compete to build viable societies through exploration, war, diplomacy, and the innovative application and management of new technologies (from the wheel and the alphabet to nuclear power and space-flight). **Middle and High School.**
McLarin's Adventures http://stardev.k20center.org	Developed at the University of Oklahoma, this science learning game for middle school students focuses on locating a habitable planet for use by interstellar travelers. Students create an avatar, enter a computer-animated environment, and, using tools from their virtual backpack, perform individual and group science activities such as locating an island, mapping the land, and testing the water. **Middle School.**
SimCity Societies http://simcity.ea.com	SimCity, launched in 1989, continues to be one of the most popular games world-wide. SimCity Societies allows users to create a variety of cities and cultures. Players can choose from a number of building types that can be arranged to create societies from law-abiding to lawless. Users can "Play God" by creating valleys, mountains, and other terrain; "Play Mayor" by creating a realistic city; or "Play with Your Sims" by creating, revising, and editing simulated lives. **Middle and High School.**
Making History: The Calm and The Storm www.making-history.com/hq	In this game, developed in collaboration with historian Niall Ferguson, players are in charge of nations and can create counterfactual (or alternative) histories for World War II. The game features data on some 80 countries and 800 land and sea regions. **Middle and High School.**
Quest Atlantis (QA) http://atlantis.crlt.indiana.edu	Funded by the National Science Foundation (NSF), this game combines Web-based gaming with student-engaging storylines. Players operate in a 3D multiuser virtual environment (MUVE), interacting with other students experiencing educational tasks. With 11 worlds, students can explore several villages inside the QA system, including Unity World, Culture World, Ecology World, and Healthy World. Each world features WebQuests and stories based on the world's theme. Quests reside inside each village and provide activities that students complete in combination with elements of real and game life. **High School.**
Edheads: Virtual Hip Replacement www.edheads.org/activities/hip	A step-by-step animated simulation of hip replacement surgery in which the computer user actually performs the procedure by clicking and moving the mouse. Also includes simulations for knee replacement and hip resurfacing. **Middle and High School.**
River City http://muve.gse.harvard.edu/rivercityproject	An interactive online simulation of disease transmission and the scientific method for middle school science students developed at Harvard University. **Middle School.**
Labyrinth www.educationarcade.org/labyrinth See also the game Supercharged from The Education Arcade.	An online math learning puzzle adventure game with a focus on prealgebra skills for middle school students developed by The Education Arcade, Maryland Public Television, Fablevision, Johns Hopkins University, and Marco International. Students must use math concepts to rescue a lost dog and free themselves from a mysterious labyrinth. **Middle School.**
Restaurant Empire www.enlight.com/restaurant/re_english/index.htm	Players help new chef Armand LeBoeuf to build and manage multiple restaurants in Paris, Rome, and Los Angeles. While building, decorating, and running restaurants, players seek to acquire new customers and hopefully high ratings. Challenges include hiring staff, ensuring the quality of the food, creating the interior design, choosing dishes that are popular among your customers, and serving those dishes swiftly to maximize the bottom line. **Middle and High School.**
Revolution www.educationarcade.org/node/357	An American Revolution–themed role-playing game set in 1775 in the town of colonial Williamsburg, Virginia, that has been developed by the MIT Teacher Education Program and Education Arcade. (Since the game is no longer being developed, some glitches do exist in the software.) **High School.**

Minimize the Use of Games That Teach Isolated Skills.

Many educational games target a skill like multiplication in isolation as part of a reward system. For instance, Rachel is playing a game in which she is faced with solving a multiplication fact: 2×5. In the game, if she answers correctly, her spaceship will remain intact and the alien attackers will not gain an advantage. Although Rachel can shoot her attacker by typing "10," she is not faced with making judgments about how to shoot the rocket or when to shoot the rocket. In other similar games, Rachel might be asked how and when to shoot the rocket but not asked to understand that 2×5 means *2 groups of 5*. Such games are not sophisticated enough to require Rachel to say, "I need to line the rockets up in 2 rows of 5 in order to protect them from an evil empire." Playing these isolated skill games, the child becomes more an expert at gaming than math reasoning, learning to beat the system rather than fine-tuning the skill of multiplication or understanding a math problem at a deeper level. Such software programs rarely ask children to become problem posers or question askers, instead training them to be situation reactors.

Scrutinize Games That Function Solely on Points Won or Lost.

Some educational games include role-playing scenarios that invite children on adventures where they must depend on social skills and challenges to win popularity, tokens, or empires that need to be attended to, organized, and negotiated. These games can be troublesome for teachers for two reasons. First, they often take a large amount of time and attention. Second, these games put children in situations where they feel that they must work to gain and maintain status within the gaming system. This is an added component that many psychologists find alarming, especially when children are facing challenging real-life situations. Many of these games are Web-based so children communicate with multiple anonymous players. The more players involved, the greater is the chance of a security breach, and the result could be unsafe encounters in online settings. Any Web-based game needs your approval before students play.

Discuss Games and Their Content.

For teachers there are no easy solutions to the problems of violence, aggression, and competition in computer and video games. The games themselves are soaring in popularity. Over half (54 percent) of U.S. households said they intend to buy computer or video games (Entertainment Software Association, 2004). Curtailing or even banning video games in schools is one often-suggested step, but this does little to address the wide use of gaming outside school. Kids need more guidance from adults than a statement that "this is not good for you." Child psychologists have long recommended that adults watch television with children, and then talk about what they have seen. Viewing TV shows with children and teenagers opens many opportunities for thoughtful conversations about the hidden messages and questionable values found in programs and commercials. Playing and discussing video games with students has been suggested as a useful strategy for adults who want to teach kids about games. More than half of all parents (55 percent) report that they play games with their children (Entertainment Software Association, 2004). Preview every game yourself before you use it with students to know if there is unwanted content in the game. Then you will be able to focus the attention of students on the key material you want them to learn.

Play Games Together.

Another compelling idea is to play and critique games with kids as part of school activities. Several years ago, as an assignment for one of their graduate courses, two new teacher candidates created an after-school video game club for high school students—the "Central High School Society of Gaming Critics." The club drew great interest at a city school where nearly two-thirds of the students had after-school jobs or other commitments. In this club, high school students did not just play Xbox, Playstation 2, and GameCube video games, they analyzed storylines and competitive structures. They wrote reviews of each game's quality based on game play, control, sound, graphics, and fun, and then began designing their own games. The club succeeded in meeting its founders' goal: "We wanted to unlock the creativity in all students who love gaming and drive them to be effective writers."

Inquiry Learning Using Intelligent Tutoring Systems

Intelligent tutoring systems (ITS) are powerful new software programs that promote inquiry learning by students through computer responses to student actions. As students answer questions, the computer records their responses and makes predictions about what users know and do not know. Based on these predictions, the program adjusts its presentation of problems to those a student most needs to practice. Just like a human tutor, a computer-based tutor can provide children with the structured practice they need to become better academic learners and test takers (see Figure 7.5).

Because the system is computerized, information can be gathered and presented almost instantaneously so adults and students can see how learning is progressing at any time. In an ideal case, an intelligent tutor would be similar to having one teacher for every one to three students, a sharp contrast to most classes of 20 to 30 elementary students (or 80 to 100 middle or high school students) who receive similar teaching and are expected to progress at a similar pace.

Intelligent tutoring systems have been shown to be effective in improving student learning, especially in mathematics (Arroyo, Beal, Murray, Walles, & Woolf, 2004; Arroyo, Walles, Beal, & Woolf, 2004; Beal, Walles, Arroyo, & Woolf, 2007; Koedinger, 2001; Koedinger, Anderson, Hadley, & Mark, 1997). Intelligent tutors have also positively affected the self-confidence of girls in mathematics (Arroyo, Woolf, & Beal, 2006).

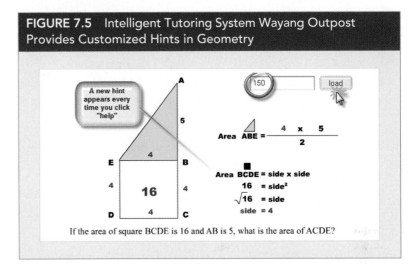

FIGURE 7.5 Intelligent Tutoring System Wayang Outpost Provides Customized Hints in Geometry

Source: Used with permission of the Department of Computer Science, University of Massachusetts Amherst.

Intelligent tutors can be constructed in a variety of formats—simulations, games, tutorials, or collaborative learning models. For example, a student might practice reading by speaking words or phrases, solve fraction problems while learning about endangered species, draw perspective lines overlaid on classic art treasures, or practice fundamental procedures for responding to cardiac arrest. Groups of learners separated in space and time may collaborate on open-ended problem solving, creative writing, or musical composition. The Web makes these systems available to any student with an Internet connection.

Compelling storylines, animated characters, and problem-solving hints are used to foster student engagement and analytical thinking. For example, in AnimalWatch, a mathematics tutor designed for upper elementary and middle school students, one expedition takes students to remote oceans to track right whales while another focuses on the rate of decline of the giant panda population in China. Learning is organized within *authentic activities and contexts* (e.g., students solve math problems to feed and save an endangered species or protect the jungle habitats from deforestation).

Not all computer-assisted tutoring systems promote inquiry learning. Many programs still deliver concepts, facts, and findings by directing students to a single correct answer. Some discipline-specific systems often serve as encyclopedic reviews rather than ways to conduct investigations of problems and cases. In such systems, the computer directs the learning, asks the questions, and evaluates the answers. By contrast, newer intelligent tutoring systems offer supportive, adaptive, and effective instruction tailored to student interests and needs by emphasizing problem solving and inquiry learning.

MAKING AND READING GRAPHS
Exploring Math Using Educational Software

Grade(s)	Elementary and Middle School
Subject(s)	Mathematics
Key Goal/Enduring Understanding	Students will understand how important information can be communicated to readers using the visual properties of different types of graphs.
Essential Question	Which kinds of graphs are best used to communicate particular types of information?

Learning Standards

National Council of Teachers of Mathematics (NCTM)—*Principles and Standards for School Mathematics*

Data Analysis and Probability
- Formulate questions that can be addressed with data and collect, organize, and display relevant data to answer them.
- Select and use appropriate statistical measures to analyze data.

International Society for Technology in Education (ISTE)—*NETS-S*

Standard 2: *Communication and Collaboration.* Students use digital media and environments to communicate and work collaboratively, including at a distance, to support individual learning and contribute to the learning of others.

Standard 4: *Critical Thinking, Problem Solving, and Decision Making.* Students use critical thinking skills to plan and conduct research, manage projects, solve problems, and make informed decisions using appropriate digital tools and resources.

Standard 6: *Technology Operations and Concepts.* Students demonstrate a sound understanding of technology concepts, systems and operations.

Learning Objectives

Students will know and be able to

- Develop thoughtful survey questions to ask other students.
- Recognize and distinguish among different types of graphs—pie graphs, bar graphs, and line graphs—and how they communicate information.
- Choose which type of graph best delivers the information collected from student survey questions.

Technology Uses

The lesson uses classroom computers and educational graph-making software as key technology tools.

▶

Minimal Technology	Infusion of Technology
Calculate survey results using tally marks or some other hand-counting system (for example, count by groups of 10s).	Calculate survey results using calculators or computers with spreadsheet software.
Display survey results using hand-drawn charts and graphs.	Display survey results using graphing software programs to create computer-generated graphs and charts.
Write summaries and reports of survey results using paper, pens, and markers.	Write summaries and reports of survey results using computers with word processing software.

Evaluation

This lesson uses multiple forms of evaluation, including the design and collection of students' own survey questions, the quality of graphs created using survey data, and the performance of students on sample graph and survey questions from state and district math exams.

LESSON PLAN DESCRIPTION

Introduction

"Making and Reading Graphs" uses students' personally designed surveys and graphs to promote information literacy and mathematical learning among elementary and middle school students. This lesson plan addresses elements of the Data Analysis and Probability Learning Standard set forth by the National Council of Teachers of Mathematics (NCTM) and uses a variety of media to Communicate Information, a standard from the International Society for Technology in Education (ISTE). In terms of the theme of Chapter 7, graph-making software demonstrates how one type of educational software supports and extends inquiry learning and problem solving by students.

Lesson Focus

Graphs convert descriptions of measures and amounts into visual symbol systems, structures that communicate information to readers in concise, easy-to-read formats with minimal text. Students at every grade level learn about graphs, the most familiar of which are pie graphs, bar graphs, line graphs, and pictographs.

Reading graphs is a part of the broad process of teaching students how to read all kinds of pictures and symbols for information. A graph is a representation of some part of social reality and representations require analysis. Given their visual nature, graphs offer a different kind of reading experience from reading written words. It is possible to know the meanings of the words that accompany a graph but still not understand what the graph is showing. Students must understand what a graph's symbols are communicating and how those symbols provide a visual rather than a textual approach to sharing information.

Lesson Design—Minimal Technology

A minimal technology version of this lesson plan features the construction of paper graphs that are published on large chart paper. Modeling survey questions that can be answered by "either/or" or "yes/no" can be used as data-gathering tools for students. Teachers might ask: "Did you eat breakfast this morning or are you waiting until snack time to eat?" "Do you have a pet?" "Did

▶

you watch television last night?" Students answer these questions by posting either their name or a symbol for their name on the poster. After this whole-group lesson students can ask their own questions and make their own graphs from the answers they receive.

LESSON ACTIVITIES USING TECHNOLOGY

1. *Model Question-Asking for Students*. Start by posing questions where students need to make personally meaningful choices among the options. "Do you want to be a millionaire?" does not encourage a meaningful choice; almost everyone automatically answers yes. By contrast, questions eliciting different viewpoints are more interesting than those generating little or no difference of opinion: "Do you want to have a job that lets you travel around the world?" or "Would you want to live on a space station circling the planet Mars for a year?" will spark conversation about personal preferences and the reasons behind them.

2. *Discuss the Content of Questions in Surveys*. Before students pose questions to investigate, discuss how the content of questions affects survey results. Begin by analyzing questions with two choices—"yes/no" or "keep/give," for instance. "Do you want to own a horse?" "If you found $100 in the street, would you give the money to someone who needs it more than you or would you keep it?" While both of these questions have two choices for an answer, one may result in more interesting conversations and more thoughtful responses.

   Then consider three-choice questions such as "yes/no/maybe" or "give/share/keep." "Would you want to own a horse if you lived on a farm?" "If you found $100, would you give the money to someone who needs it more than you, share half with someone who needs it more, or keep all of it?"

   Kindergartners and first-graders enjoy recording and asking survey questions and graphing the results. They ask simple questions at first, but as they become familiar with surveys and graphs, their questions become more sophisticated, enabling the discussion of how survey question content affects responses.

3. *Write Questions and Conduct Surveys*. Once introduced to the idea of posing questions on surveys and polls, students create, individually or in pairs, their own survey questions to ask others. They go out into the school and survey classmates and other students, collecting the data for display and analysis. Make arrangements in advance with other teachers in the school for your students to visit their classrooms to conduct their surveys, and with the office, library, and cafeteria, as well as any other staff who might be asked questions. By visiting other classes and places in the school, students have more opportunities to collect data to analyze than if they survey only classmates.

4. *Use Computer Graph-Making Software*. Once students' survey questions have been asked and the data collected, teachers and students enter the data from the surveys into a graph-making software program, such as one of the following choices:
   - *Excel*. Spreadsheet program found on many school computers, easy to use, and powerful in data-manipulating capabilities. Excel is a tool for adult computer users that upper elementary, middle and high school students can use effectively.
   - *Graphers* (Sunburst Technology) or *The Graph Club 2.0* (Tom Snyder Productions). Program that enables K–6 students to enter data and easily convert that data into four types of graphs: bar, line, pie, and pictograph.
   - *TinkerPlots* (Key Curriculum Press). Software program that is "an inquiry based software construction set of graph pieces. Students can order, stack, and separate icons to eventually build their own plots for analyzing data" (Steinke, 2005, April). Data entry is easy and since there is no menu of graphs, students must drag and click around the screen to see their graph emerge as a result of their actions. (Demonstration program of TinkerPlots is available at www.umass.edu/srri/serg/projects/tp/tpmain.html.)

▶

- *Create a Graph.* Free program from the National Center for Education Statistics, an agency of the U.S. Department of Education. This program provides colorful and visually engaging graphs that can be adjusted for size and ease of reading.

5. *Compare How Different Types of Graphs Show Information.* Graph-making software programs let students choose the type of graph they think best displays their data. In this way, students can compare and contrast how effectively information is communicated to prospective readers. They might ask, "Does a pictograph describe the survey results as successfully as a pie graph?" In some cases, a pictograph will, but in other cases, it will not.

   If students want to graph the weather for a month, graphing programs offer weather symbols to choose from to make a weather graph. Students click the sun symbol 14 times, raindrops 9 times, and clouds 7 times to generate a pictograph displaying that data. Or students might dispense with the pictures and create a bar graph of the information in colored columns.

6. *Present the Findings.* Once the graphs are completed electronically, students can present their findings to the rest of the class orally or in writing. Written presentations offer an added benefit as students learn how to express in words what the mathematical symbols are communicating visually. Graphs present information in few words because that is their function. Writing is a way for students to explain the findings as if the graph were not present. Just as the survey questions offer a way for students to learn about interrogative or question-asking sentences, short summaries of the finished graphs present a way to practice composing expository or information-sharing sentences. Describing information presented in a graph through text is a way to practice writing in different genres as well. Students may publish graphs and explanations in a letter, an announcement, a news report, or a personal journal entry.

7. *Use Graph-Making to Prepare for Standardized Math Tests.* Students are expected to be able to read and interpret graphs on state and national math achievement tests. To arrive at the correct answer, they must be able to interpret how words, numbers, and symbols fit together to communicate a point. Such interpretive skills are not intuitive. Students need considerable practice reading graphs for meaning in order to successfully answer graph questions on math tests.

ANALYSIS AND EXTENSIONS

1. Name two features you find useful about this lesson.
2. Name two areas for extension or improvement of this lesson.
3. How successfully has information technology been integrated into the lesson?
4. How might students be even more involved in designing, using, and evaluating technology in the lesson?
5. What other comments or extensions would you add?

PEARSON
myeducationkit

Go to the Technology Transformation Lesson Plan section of Chapter 7 in MyEducationKit and access the activity "Making and Reading Graphs" to practice transforming a lesson plan using technology.

CHAPTER SUMMARY

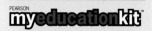
FOCUS QUESTION 1: What are the standard software applications found on most computers today and what open source software alternatives are there?

- Software refers to the codes that tell computers what functions to perform; system software controls the overall functioning of a computer while application software addresses specific functions such as word processing or communications.

- Software applications commonly used by teachers and students include word processing, electronic databases, spreadsheets, communications software, presentation software, antivirus software, and specialized programs for other specific functions.

- Open source software refers to programs that are open for anyone to use, copy, and modify.

FOCUS QUESTION 2: How can teachers evaluate the different types of educational software available today?

- Educational software commonly used by teachers and students include skills-based learning software, educational games, composing and calculating software, inquiry and discovery learning software, visual thinking and concept mapping software, simulations and virtual reality environments, and digital games for learning.

- School systems purchase software and install copies on every computer in a school or a district, thereby largely establishing what software teachers and students can use in their classrooms.

- The delivery of educational software is becoming increasingly Web-based.

FOCUS QUESTION 3: How do teachers use different types of software programs to promote problem solving and inquiry learning?

- Educational software can be used to promote skills-based learning, problem solving and inquiry learning, or many combinations of each.

- Composing and calculating software such as Microsoft Word and Excel provide extensive ways to promote learning through digital writing and computer-based mathematical computations.

- Skills-based learning software promotes the learning of basic skills such as number operations in math or vocabulary words in language arts.

- Inquiry and discovery learning software such as the "House" series, Kid Pix, and Google Earth offers students opportunities to problem solve and discover through follow-your-own-questions types of learning explorations.

- Visual thinking and concept mapping software such as Kidspiration and Inspiration provide ways for teachers and students to organize and outline their ideas on a computer.

FOCUS QUESTION 4: How can teachers use computer games and simulations as learning resources?

- Students today play computer, video, and Web-based games regularly for entertainment; boys are heavier users of video games than girls, a fact that contrasts with fewer gender differences in most other areas of technology use and online activity.

- The educational impact of gaming experiences remains intensely debated—some educators and psychologists see little value in games or gaming while other researchers envision exciting possibilities for learning when students use the intellectual skills needed in effective game playing for educational purposes.

- Digital games for learning represent a new category of educationally themed games that emphasize active learning, sustained concentration and focus, and innovative problem solving.
- Strategies for effectively using games in the classroom include minimizing those that teach isolated skills, carefully choosing games that are solely based on winning or losing points, discussing game content with students, and actually playing games with your students.

FOCUS QUESTION 5: How can teachers evaluate the effectiveness of educational software?

- High-quality educational software must be open-ended and flexible enough so that students are challenged to keep exploring the material, but not so complicated or complex that they become confused, discouraged, or bored while using the program.
- Educational software can be evaluated in terms of how it promotes higher order thinking where students engage in analysis, synthesis, and evaluation of what they are learning.

FOCUS QUESTION 6: What are intelligent tutoring systems and how can students and teachers use them successfully?

- As instructional tools, intelligent tutors present topics in a discipline, track a student's performance in achieving correct answers, and then adjust their teaching approach based on the student's learning needs.
- The use of story, characters, and feedback are the primary ways that intelligent tutors promote inquiry learning and problem solving.

KEY TERMS

Antivirus software

Application software

Badware

Bloom's taxonomy

Building, inventing, and creating software

Communications software

Computer games

Digital games for learning

Digital writing

Educational software

Electronic databases

Hardware

Inquiry learning

Intelligent tutoring systems (ITS)

Object-oriented programming

Open source software

Presentation software

Problem solving

Skills-learning games

Software

Specialized software

Spreadsheets

Stealth learning

System software

Video games

Virtual worlds

Visual thinking and concept mapping software

Web-browsing software

Word processing

ACTIVITIES FOR YOUR TEACHER PORTFOLIO

1. THE IMPACT OF VIDEO GAMES

There are two realities of students and gaming: (1) Video game play is enormously popular among children and adolescents, and (2) educators are just learning about the impacts of video games on people's psychological and sociological development. The following review shows some of the main points raised by critics and supporters of games and gaming in the classroom:

Critics

"Tech Tonic: Towards a New Literacy of Technology," a report from the Alliance for Childhood (2004) urges a go-slow approach to technology because far too many children "spend hours each day sitting in front of screens instead of playing outdoors, reading, and getting much needed physical exercise and face-to-face social interaction" (p. 1).

Failure to Connect: How Computers Affect Our Children's Minds—and What We Can Do About It, by Jane M. Healy (1999), criticizes the overuse of computers at home and the socially isolating effects of excessive computer use by children.

Supporters

What Video Games Have to Teach Us About Learning and Literacy, by James Gee (2003), offers a broad endorsement of the literacy learning power of video games.

Don't Bother Me, Mom—I'm Learning! by Marc Prensky (2006), presents a stirring, if largely one-sided defense of the positive educational impact of video games.

You can also learn more about video games from "The Video Game Revolution," a PBS video and accompanying website that provide an excellent overview of games and gaming and their place in contemporary culture (www.pbs.org/kcts/videogamerevolution).

- What are your conclusions after reviewing these materials?
- How will you use electronic games in your classroom?

2. ONLINE MATH GAMES

Investigate online math games involving graphs and charts so groups of students may learn how different types of data can be displayed visually. Upper elementary and middle school students will find challenging graph games at This is Mega Mathematics!, a website maintained by the Los Alamos National Laboratory (www.ccs3.lanl.gov/mega-math). In addition, *USA Today* publishes graphs daily on the first page of each of the paper's sections. Many of the graphs are available for teachers and students to use in the classroom (http://USAToday.com/educate/mathtoday/index.htm).

GROWING AND LEADING WITH TECHNOLOGY

This activity offers an opportunity to grow as a teacher and learn to lead with technology. Begin by reviewing the Chapter 7 Learning Goal and New Technologies listed in the chart at the start of the chapter. Then read the following actual classroom scenario and consider how technologies discussed in Chapter 7 might be integrated into the lesson. Follow-up steps to this activity can be completed at MyEducationKit.

SHARON'S TOYS, MACHINES, AND TECHNOLOGIES LESSON

Sharon teaches a unit on toys, machines, and technologies to her second-grade students as part of the state's framework for science and engineering. She is teaching in a classroom with three computers and the school has a laboratory with enough machines for all her students. Her goal is to utilize her students' interest in technology to teach them about technology— what it is, why people create it, and how it changes people's lives in ways that can be positive and problematic. She wants to show students how engineers and designers go about building new articles through a process of initial design, followed by trials, experiments, and redesigns before a finished product is achieved.

The concept of technology is at the core of Sharon's lesson idea. Technology has been defined as an innovation designed to "solve problems and extend human capabilities" (International Technology Education Association, 2000). It is a "practice, a technique, or a device for altering the experience of the world" (Solnit, 2003). In effect, technologies make accomplishing their goals easier for people.

Creating technological solutions to problems has occurred since the beginning of humankind. The wheel, stone tools, and rocks crafted into arrowheads are examples from the ancient past. The technology of written recordkeeping changed patterns of trade and communication in the Middle East, the Americas, and Asia thousands of years ago. Beginning in 1450, printing press technology transformed European society by making books and newspapers available on a scale never before imagined. Dramatic transformations in U.S. history are marked by technological advancements such as the cotton gin, use of interchangeable manufacturing parts, telegraph, telephone, electric lights, television, and most recently, information processing machines known as computers.

To begin this lesson, Sharon asks students to invent their own new technologies. She intends to use these inventions to explore the meaning and impact of technology in society.

- Using the technologies discussed in this chapter, how would you propose Sharon use them to support her students in learning about technology as they invent new toys and machines?

PEARSON
myeducationkit

To complete the full activity, go to the Growing and Leading with Technology section of Chapter 7 in MyEducationKit and access the exercise "Sharon's Toys, Machines, and Technologies Lesson."

8 Communicating and Networking with Websites, Blogs, Wikis, and More

Far from undermining libraries, the Web puts the world at students' fingertips. Letters and notes are still appropriate in many circumstances, but email, instant messaging, and electronic conferencing provide writers with an immediate and much larger audience. Educators need to tap into students' inherent interest in these methods of creating and sharing writing.

—National Commission on Writing in America's Schools and Colleges (2003)

CHAPTER LEARNING GOAL	CONNECTING to the NETS	NEW TECHNOLOGIES
Information Communication Using communication technologies to enhance learning through interactive information exchanges and networking	**NETS-T** **2** Design and Develop Digital Age Learning Experiences and Assessments **3** Model Digital Age Work and Learning **NETS-S** **2** Communication and Collaboration	• Email and instant messaging • Teacher-/student-authored websites • Teacher-/student-authored blogs • Digital image scanners • Wikis and wikitexts

CHAPTER OVERVIEW

Chapter 8 concentrates on the various ways that teachers and students can use computers and other technologies to share ideas and information in classrooms and online learning environments. The chapter begins with educational websites as an information communication medium, particularly those sites that are "home-grown" by teachers and students working together. Next we turn to email, instant messaging, threaded discussion boards, blogs, and wikis as promising ways for teachers and students to share academic information and engage in collaborative learning.

The chapter relates to NETS-T Standard 3, Part c, which notes that teachers and students should "communicate relevant information and ideas" to multiple audiences using a variety of digital tools. It also addresses NETS-S Standard 2, which calls for students to learn ways to interact and work together electronically.

FOCUS QUESTIONS

1. How can teachers use communications technologies as teaching and learning tools?

2. How can teachers use email or instant messaging to foster information exchanges with and among students?

3. How can teachers use a website or blog to improve teaching and learning?

4. How can teachers use wikis to promote collaborative learning?

A middle school student asks his teacher, "Miss B., what's this week's assignment? I really want to do a great job and get a good grade." Rather than explaining the assignment, the teacher refers to a technology tool that she has created: "Look at our class website. It has all the information you need: notes from class, links for more research, and a rubric showing how I will grade the paper. Post an entry in our class blog. It's interesting to see what everyone has to say."

Students today communicate information rapidly with cell phones and other handheld devices. Educators are developing ways to deliver academic information with these devices and use them for learning.

Using communication technologies to enhance teaching and learning is this chapter's learning goal. As our vignette shows, communicating information is an essential ingredient of education. To illustrate this point, recall the different teaching methods you have experienced as a student—lectures, discussions, cooperative learning groups, competitive tests, personal writing, interpretive essays, simulations, experiments, educational games, debates, and worksheets. All these instructional approaches—and others you may have remembered—involve communicating information from teacher to students, students to teacher, and students to students. Today, computer-based technologies are changing how the information is communicated, and therefore, how teaching happens in K–12 schools.

All of us are part of multiple communication systems. Perhaps you carry a cell phone, have an email account, use an ATM, engage in text messaging, visit online communities, use PowerPoint as part of class presentations, rely on a personal digital assistant, do online shopping, or access some other technology to share information with other people.

As a teacher, you face an array of new choices about how to integrate **communication technologies** into your instructional practices and related outside-the-classroom professional responsibilities. Communication technologies are electronic tools that use computers and the Internet to make possible the rapid exchange of information between people. Electronic communication is also known as **computer-mediated communication** and encompasses many different kinds of information exchanges between people.

There are multiple communication technologies that you might use in your teaching, including the following:

- **Email (electronic mail)** and **instant messaging (IM)** are forms of online communication that feature short electronic exchanges between individuals, such as between teachers and students or family members or between administrative and educational personnel.
- **Teacher or classroom websites** are Internet sites developed by teachers to communicate information about themselves and their classes to students, family members, and school and educational personnel.
- **Blogs** (short for **weblogs**) are publicly accessible online journals written by individuals (such as teachers) for others (such as students, families, and other educators) to read and comment on.
- **Online discussions** are electronic forums where teachers and students discuss educational topics. Online discussions are a common component of many teacher websites and blogs.
- **Wikis,** from the Hawaiian word meaning "quick" or "rapidly," are websites that teachers and students create together by reading and revising each other's ideas and comments.

In schools, different authors use each of these communication technologies to communicate with different audiences for different educational purposes (see Table 8.1). These communication technologies raise important questions for teachers:

- How might you use a classroom website, email, instant messaging, online discussion boards, blogs, or wikis with students, families, or other teachers?
- What skills and perspectives do you and your students need to learn to convey information using communication technologies?
- What combination of communication tools will create positive learning experiences for you and your students?

Answering these questions is an essential step in building your own information communication system as a teacher, a process that can be likened to customizing your cell phone or selecting components for a home entertainment system. Cell phones, for example, offer wide choices from calling plans to photo and video capabilities to Internet and email access. You choose the phone and features you need and can afford. You make similar choices when choosing a home or apartment entertainment system. You might build a system piece by piece through purchases of a television, stereo receiver, DVD player, and separate speakers to create surround-sound video and audio environments, or you may prefer having multiple functions built into one or two pieces of equipment. Just as you select the options that fit your needs and lifestyle, a teacher selects the communication components best suited to his or her teaching style and the class's needs.

TABLE 8.1 Comparisons of Communication Technologies

Type of Communication Technology	Purpose	Author	Audience	Uses by Teachers
Instant messaging (IM)	Instantaneous communication between two or more individuals	Individual	Individual	Communicating with colleagues
Email	Sending and receiving messages over the Internet	Individual	Individual or group	Communicating with students and families Communicating with other teachers
Discussion board	Exchange of ideas and information about a topic, usually moderated by an editor	Group	Group	Electronic discussions of academic material
Teacher-made website	Collection of Web pages related to a specific topic or activity	Individual	Group	Information for students and families Publishing student work
Blog	Online journal, usually maintained by one or two bloggers, featuring comments by readers	Individual	Group	Personal reflections on teaching Sharing ideas with students Professional teaching portfolio Information for students and families
Wiki	Web pages created by a collaborative group of writers and designers	Group	Group	Group projects by students Group projects among teachers

⌇ Communicating Electronically as a Teacher

Today's students are immersed in multiple electronic communication environments, regularly using email, instant messaging, blogs, or other electronic systems to talk with one another. So many of these electronic communication systems are being used in schools where administrators are instituting bans or limits on the devices during school hours. The widespread popularity of electronic communication among children and adolescents raises important questions as to how these technologies will become new catalysts for teaching and learning in and out of school.

Teacher and classroom websites, email, instant messaging, discussion boards, blogs, and wikis are the major components of any communication system you might create as a teacher. Practically speaking, it is not necessary to use them all. For example, you might choose to create a class website or blog, but not engage in email or instant messaging with your students or their families. Or you might establish an online discussion group or create a class wiki, but not use any other electronic communication options. You decide the technologies that will best meet your needs and the needs of your students.

To consider how you, as a new teacher, might use communication technologies to create engaging and productive educational activities, it is helpful to know the similarities and differences between synchronous and asynchronous electronic communication.

- **Synchronous communications** occur in real time, as with cell phone conversations or instant message exchanges. Individuals converse as if they were meeting face to face; they do not have to wait any length of time for a reply to their statements.
- **Asynchronous communications** involve a time delay, as experienced in email messages, threaded discussions, or blogs. Communicators wait for replies to their statements, although usually the time lag is dramatically shorter than for a letter or postcard sent through postal mail.

As a teacher, you already employ synchronous and asynchronous forms of communication as you convey information to your students. A classroom discussion happens synchronously when students and teachers ask and respond to questions. The comments you write on student papers are delivered asynchronously when the papers are returned after you grade them. In digital environments, the modes of delivery are different, but the ways of communicating information are similar.

Social Networking for Educators

Many people associate electronic information communication with **social networking,** a practice marked by controversy. Social networking is the process of sharing personal information and profiles online through text messaging, chatting, blogging, or viewing online communities (such as Facebook, MySpace, or Webkinz). While 96 percent of youngsters ages 9 to 17 use social networking technologies, most school districts have rules against social networking during the school day (National School Boards Association, 2007). Social networking has created unhappiness and misunderstandings between educators and students. School officials worry about inappropriate behaviors online by students as well as electronic distractions from academic activities. For their part, many students resent adult restrictions on one of their most popular forms of social and computer interaction.

At the same time, more and more teachers are engaging in **educational networking** (also called *social networking for educators*). Educational networking involves teachers using social networking technologies for educational rather than social purposes. More than 70 percent of the nation's school districts have student website programs, 50 percent engage in online collaborative projects with other districts, and 33 percent have organizational or student blogs that are used for communication and instruction (National School Boards Association,

2007). Students too value using technology for educational activities; 59 percent of students in a national survey indicated they spend time online talking about educational topics, including plans for college, career choices, jobs, and schoolwork (National School Boards Association, 2007).

Teachers can use educational networking in many productive ways:

- Teacher-to-teacher discussions about curriculum and instruction
- Book groups
- Connecting to national educational policy and reform organizations
- Exchanging information on educational research
- Group editing of projects and writing

Ning is an online service that allows users to create their own social networks, quickly and without needing any technical skills. Your network can be private (only invited people can join) or public (open to anyone). Ning reports it had 220,000 active accounts in April 2008.

Ning, with its capacity to create private networks, lets "instructors take advantage of social networking in a neutral setting" (EDUCAUSE Learning Initiative, 2008, April). Teachers can control who is part of the network and what the members of the network are talking about online. Initially, conversations can be among teachers only, for professional development purposes. Eventually, as the technology becomes more widely used, student contributions can be added to the network.

Using Electronic Communications in Your Teaching

Teachers have five major ways to use electronic communications in their inside- and outside-the-classroom professional work:

- Teaching interactively
- Sharing information
- Building learning communities
- Publishing student work
- Energizing student writing

Teaching Interactively.   An electronic communication system extends the impact of your teaching well beyond the information taught in the classroom or presented in the textbook. Teachers know time is fleeting—there is never enough of it to teach everything students need to know. At school's end each day, teachers think, "If only I could increase time teaching the material, my students would learn so much more." Trying to respond to this dilemma by developing paper-and-pencil homework for students is a large task—organizing the activities, making the copies, logging in what has been completed, and trying to individualize assignments to fit the needs of different students. Developing your own electronic communication system offers an efficient way to continue teaching your students when class or school is not in session.

Teachers can post class notes, inquiry questions, homework assignments, writing ideas, Web links for further research, suggestions for further reading, and experiments and other activities to do outside of class on a teacher or classroom website. Email, instant messaging, and discussion boards promote electronic exchanges of ideas among the members of your class. Your teaching continues electronically as students, reading and reviewing what you write and post, connect what they have been learning in school with outside-of-school activities. The process becomes interactive as students respond by submitting their own ideas, inquiries, and homework. These kinds of electronic interchanges can build and sustain momentum for learning with a generation of students accustomed to online communications.

Keeping students engaged with academics is important to your success as a teacher. Lectures and teacher-led discussions, followed by worksheets and tests, reach only some of the students some of time. A far larger majority of students learn most of what they know by trying it out for themselves in minds-on, hands-on learning situations. As psychologist Howard Gardner (1983)

PEARSON
myeducationkit™

Go to the Tutorials section of Chapter 8 in MyEducationKit and access the practical tutorial entitled "Networking."

has noted, schools mainly teach to one or two dominant learning styles, pronouncing those who do not learn well in these ways to be insufficient in their attempts to learn. The challenge for today's teachers is to expand how they teach so that more students will succeed and, enjoying this success, stay connected with academic learning. Active engagement using Web-based materials and activities puts students in the position of "doing" math, science, history, or language arts instead of listening to teachers tell them about these subjects.

Teaching online extends the ways that you can connect with your students. For example, students can review online notes or lesson plans before an exam. These materials aid in the recall of key information perhaps forgotten or missed in class. To create increased levels of student engagement, post the items used in your teaching—lesson plans, lecture notes, discussion questions, skill practice worksheets, ideas for further study, and student-written materials to reintroduce the ideas and information presented in class. Then pose thoughtful questions and interesting activities that ask students to interact with the information through individual and group discussions and presentations, both online and in class.

Sharing Information. A teacher's electronic communication system has the potential to open a 24/7 flow of information between the classroom and students' families and caregivers, as well as with other teachers and school administrators. In one national study, researchers from the Harvard University Family Research Project found that 36 percent of families used the Internet to communicate with schools, although only once or twice a year. Those families tended to have higher incomes, more education, and greater access to computers. Still, researchers found a positive connection between Internet-based family communication and higher academic achievement and expectations among twelfth-grade students (Bouffard, 2008). Just how Internet-based family–school communication helps student achievement is still not completely clear, but the researchers believe that the availability of online information may promote greater family involvement in student learning.

As a new teacher, it therefore makes sense to provide information about class assignments, grading policies, upcoming activities, homework, and other topics online in an easily updatable format. Figure 8.1 shows the material one high school chemistry teacher posted for the study of atomic structure, one of the required topics in his curriculum.

There are numerous advantages of posting information online. Rather than spending valuable in-class minutes giving assignments, students and their parents can be directed to the website to find answers to their questions. Everyone receives the information in the same way, minimizing confusion or doubt. Moreover, when families consult a teacher's website, students may be less likely to say, "I don't have any homework." Adults can locate the actual assignments and due dates online.

Other teachers and building administrators also benefit when they are able to see that information is being communicated to students and families in ways that are consistent with the mission and goals of the school. Relying solely on electronic communication, however, may disadvantage families who do not have computers or who are intimidated by school organizations. Researchers from the Harvard Family Research Project recommend that teachers establish multiple ways to communicate with families, both electronic and nonelectronic, while exploring the uses of new social networking technologies like blogs to increase family involvement (Bouffard, 2008).

FIGURE 8.1 High School Chemistry Class Website

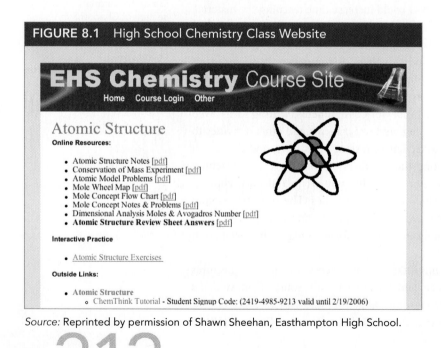

Source: Reprinted by permission of Shawn Sheehan, Easthampton High School.

Building Learning Communities.   An electronic communication system invites students to join a community of learners who are exploring topics of interest. As students read what you have posted, contribute their own ideas, and respond to what everyone else has said and done, an important collaborative activity is created. In this venue students feel part of something meaningful and relevant. Adolescents in particular are drawn to online discussions as ways to make sense of issues of self-identity and personal values. Blogs produce a similar type of collective experience by providing an electronic space for people to share ideas and interests together.

From a learning standpoint, the impact of learning communities can be quite powerful. As literacy educator Frank Smith (1998) has noted, children "learn from the company they keep." As a teacher, encourage students to be part of groups that devote themselves to serious study and academic accomplishment.

"I Wonder Questions," written and answered in online "I Wonder Journals," are immediate ways for students to explore topics of personal interest. Many topics produce interesting and extended "I Wonder" explorations, such as the following questions from second-graders: "How do snakes shed their skin?" "What is an estuary?" "Where is Madagascar?"

Rather than send students to the library or to an Internet information source to find information by themselves, teachers can post "I Wonder" questions on their website for group investigation. Younger students, with the assistance of siblings or adult family members, can research and submit what they have learned. Over time, these collective explorations will produce an impressive collection of information by everyone in your classroom.

Middle and high school students, too, have "I Wonder" questions that they would like answered. These questions are often centered on issues connected with self and peers. "What do you think?" and "What would you do?" questions open an effective format for generating online discussions among members of a learning community. Middle and high school students want to express opinions and make their voices heard on many current topics. By asking their views, and the reasons behind those views, teachers actively involve students in thinking deeply about their beliefs and why others may have different ideas.

Publishing Student Work.   A teacher's electronic communication system can be an inviting way for students to publish and display work done in the classroom or at home. Class activities and assignments take on new meaning when students realize that their work is going to be seen by more people than just the teacher. Students enjoy creating something that others are going to see, hear, or read. Every year, school science fairs, poetry readings, history projects, music and dance performances, art exhibitions, and dramatic plays generate great interest and energy from students. These students enjoy doing the work because the activity is meaningful to them and because there is an audience who is going to see the end result. Using your communication system to display the products, performances, and publications of your students generates enthusiasm and anticipation.

Classroom newspapers or newsletters that many teachers once produced using the school's copying machine have become a new experience when published online, for the following reasons:

- Production is much quicker because the material can be scanned into the computer and arranged graphically without lengthy cutting, pasting, arranging, and rearranging by hand. The results are visually appealing, particularly when students' original color choices are preserved.
- Students' work gains permanence; it is no longer confined to paper copies that get lost, ripped, or discarded before and after they are viewed by family members.
- There are opportunities to involve students in the process of creating and maintaining your news sharing system. "My class website is a work-together, everyone-learns-from-each-other concept," said one second-grade teacher who had previously spent hours after school and on weekends producing a paper newsletter for families. Her young students could not help

produce a newspaper at the copy machine, but they could go to the computer and help select which drawings, writing, and photos to post; decide in what order to present images; add their own text (either directly or through dictation to a typist); or assist other parts of the design and production process. For these students, the online newsletter became publishing that they helped to create, both the material being showcased and the electronic format being used.

Energizing Student Writing.   Establishing an electronic communication system opens multiple possibilities for students to write to you and to each other. It is an opportunity to emphasize writing at a time when the teaching of writing in schools has become, in the words of The National Commission on Writing, "the neglected 'R'" (2003, 2006). Looking at classrooms around the country, the commission painted a dismal picture of the state of writing in K–12 schools:

- Nearly all elementary school students (97 percent) spend 3 hours or less a week on writing assignments, or about 15 percent of the time they spend watching television.
- Nearly three-quarters of K–12 students "never get a writing assignment from their history or social studies teachers."
- In high schools, 4 out of 10 students "never" or "hardly ever" write a paper of three or more pages.
- By the end of high school, "most students are producing relatively immature and unsophisticated writing" while one in five young writers "produce prose with a substantial number of errors in grammar, spelling, and punctuation." (National Commission on Writing in America's Schools and Colleges, 2003, p. 20)

Despite writing's decline in schools, teenagers—and younger students—write eagerly and expressively for their own pleasure (National Commission on Writing in America's Families, Schools and Colleges, 2006). Some 85 percent of 12- to 17-year-olds send text messages, email, or post comments on social networking sites, although 60 percent of those teens do not think of their personal electronic communications as "real" writing (Lenhart, Arafeh, Smith, & Macgill, 2008). Journal writing is another favorite nonschool writing activity for many youngsters; 49 percent of girls and 47 percent of African American teens keep their own journal (Lenhart, Arafeh, Smith, & Macgill, 2008).

Ask those same students to write in school and you may observe reluctance or resistance. For many young writers, school writing assignments connote formal language, appropriate grammar, and correct spelling—conventions of writing they do not all feel confident using. By contrast, online writing seems easier to do, less restrained by adult roles and expectations. We discuss more about the issue of students writing in online environments later in this chapter.

No matter what subject you teach, you will be a teacher of writing and a teacher of communication. Every subject area requires students to write, whether it is an interpretive essay, a science report, a statement about how to solve a math problem, or a historical analysis. Similarly, every subject requires students to be able to communicate what they know and what they have learned using different forms of written expression. This may be through tests and quizzes, but also through student-created papers, presentations, portfolios, or performances in both print and electronic formats (Kist, 2004). In every case, students must learn how to clearly convey their ideas to others in words, images, symbols, and sounds.

Beyond the expectations of all the different curriculum standards, written communication is an essential skill in an information society. Writing allows students to "connect the dots in their knowledge" and is central to self-expression and civic participation (National Commission on Writing in America's Schools and Colleges, 2003, p. 14). Writing as well as verbal and artistic communication allows the communicator to express mental images of facts and information that would otherwise remain inaccessible in the mind of the individual. New synchronous and asynchronous communication technologies may be key to the successful teaching of writing in schools as they utilize habits that students want to practice—communicating textually through computers and cell phones— while offering to teachers instructional opportunities that were unavailable even 10 years ago.

Email and Instant Messaging

Email and instant messaging (IM) are examples of communication technologies that have become so widespread that while most of us simply take them for granted, teachers can use them to connect to students, colleagues, and families in new ways. Email is short for electronic mail and refers to messages sent between people using the computers and the Internet. Instant messaging (IM) or *text messaging* refers to real-time typed text interactions between people using computers or mobile devices like cell phones or personal digital assistants (Consortium for School Networking, 2007; EDUCAUSE Learning Initiative, 2005, November).

Adults use email and instant messaging for workplace communication, business networking, online shopping, family talk, and recreational pursuits. For example, more than one in four people—some 53 million Americans—use instant messaging, and the numbers are growing steadily, up 29 percent since 2000. Americans sent nearly 160 billion text messages in 2006 alone, double the number sent in 2005 (Boss, 2007).

Adolescents and children—a segment of the population where nearly four in every five individuals use the Internet—are the largest consumers of email and instant message technologies (Lenhart, Madden, & Hitlin, 2005). Table 8.2 presents recent statistics about email and instant messaging use among teenagers and young adults.

Young students are motivated by the ways that email and instant messaging enable them to communicate using the forms of talk they have with friends and peers in school corridors, neighborhood street corners, malls, and playgrounds. It allows them to use **textspeak** (see below), an abbreviated collection of symbols and letters that are used for quick communication when using cell phones or instant messaging on a computer. This is a sample email message with textspeak and Standard English translation:

Hey, Wuz ^? Nm here. U look gr8 2day Wht R U doing 2morrow?	Hi, what's up. Not much here. You look great today. What are you doing tomorrow?
Nvm. I don't care. Lol, j.k. b.r.b. ok.	Never mind. I don't care. Laugh out loud, just kidding. Be right back. Okay.
Do u know wht 4 HW? Me neither. w/e will fail 2gether.	Do you know what the homework is? Me neither. Whatever, we'll fail together.

TABLE 8.2 Email and Instant Messaging Use among Teens and Young Adults

Email	Instant Messaging
89 percent of adolescents send or read email.	62 percent of individuals ages 18 to 27 use IM.
Email is a more popular activity than visiting movie-, music-, or sports-related websites (84 percent); participating in online games (81 percent); getting news about current events (76 percent); or sending or receiving instant messages (75 percent).	21 percent use IM several times a day, and 46 percent say they use IM more often than email. Only 1 in 3 individuals ages 28 to 69 and beyond use IM.
Teenage girls (93 percent) are the most frequent users of email technology	More than half of IM users report they are doing other things—surfing the Web, watching TV, talking on the phone—"*virtually every time*" they are IMing.
	Nearly half post "away messages" while about 1 in 3 have constructed online IM profiles for others to see.
	Most IM users are communicating with 1 to 5 people. Additionally, most text messaging happens over the computer, but one in three teenagers have used a cell phone to send text messages.

Sources: Adapted from Lenhart, Madden, & Hitlin, 2005; Shiu & Lenhart, 2004.

Interestingly, instant messaging is rapidly becoming the communication system of choice for many young students, ages 12 to 17. When asked which modes of communication they use most often when communicating with friends, online teens consistently choose IM over email in a wide variety of contexts (Lenhart, Madden, & Hitlin, 2005, p. vi).

Strategies for Using Email and IM with Your Students

Email may be the more useful communication tool for teachers, having its own built-in recordkeeping system. When you email someone, you have a record of what you said, and you have a record of what is said back to you. In schools, email provides a basic accountability structure for everyone involved. Knowing that there is a record of the correspondence, students have a reason to post school-related questions and comments using appropriate and thoughtful language. Instant messaging, by contrast, is intended for informality and immediacy, and those qualities are less useful when trying to convey school information to students. Email allows you to craft a thoughtful reply, and spell check it, which is preferable to dashing off a quick response. Following are additional ideas for teachers interested in using email and instant messaging in their teaching.

Use Password-Protected Student Communication Systems to Email and IM. Teachers must implement a password-protected student communication system before using email or other Internet-based communications with students. Such systems minimize the risks associated with the Internet, such as exploitative merchandisers, scam artists, political extremists, predatory individuals, or other unsavory influences. There is also the possibility of exposure to computer viruses, spam, and various privacy infringements. Password protection restricts who can access your communications with students and your students' communications with you, thereby reducing the risk factors associated with Internet use. Many schools provide password-protected spaces for teacher/student/school communications.

Use Email and Instant Messaging to Teach about Spelling. Email and instant messages that use textspeak emphasize the "deliberate misspelling" of words (Templeton, 2004, p. 58). Rather than decry the use of nonstandard language, teachers can explore word use and spelling patterns explicitly with students. By paying attention to the "conventions of this 'underground' genre," students can become better spellers, more aware of the patterns of word sounds and the structures of word spellings (Templeton, 2004, p. 59). For more on how teachers can respond to the growth of email, instant messaging, and other new technology, see the position paper "Beliefs about Technology and the Preparation of English Teachers" on the website of the National Council of Teachers of English (NCTE).

Establish Email Connections to Libraries, Museums, and Universities. Libraries, museums, universities, and other educational organizations offer a host of email options for teachers and students. Students may ask questions on any number of academic topics and get responses from experts in that field. For example, Ask a Historian at George Mason University and Ask an Earth Scientist from the University of Hawaii (mentioned in Chapter 6) allow students to get answers to science-related questions by email. More and more educational and community organizations are providing resources to schools via email as well. One key learning goal when using email is formulating thoughtful questions based on topics in the curriculum. Remember that it may take some time for an organization to reply to a request so it is important to let your students know that not every question will get an immediate response.

Initiate Email Correspondence with Elected Officials and Other Public Policy Makers. Writing letters to elected officials or other public policy makers is a time-honored way

PEARSON

Go to the Assignments and Activities section of Chapter 8 in MyEducationKit. Complete the video activity entitled "E-mail in the Classroom" and respond to the questions that accompany the video.

for citizens to communicate with and potentially influence government policies. As students in high school civics learn, letters from everyday people can persuade legislators to change policies. In Massachusetts, a letter writing campaign by an elementary school teacher and her students is credited with helping to change a racially insensitive symbol of a pilgrim hat with an arrow through it that was used by the state's turnpike authority. Many people, including Native American groups, were offended, and legislators noted the impact of the elementary school children's letters on their decision to enact a new symbol. The turnpike's symbol today is still a pilgrim hat; however, no arrow is part of it.

Email offers a way for students to express their views to public officials. As part of social studies or English classes, students can prepare a cogent written argument advocating a change in governmental policy. Many times, emails sent to local officials receive prompt and personal replies, whereas those sent to national politicians usually receive a form letter response from a staff person. Also, change happens slowly in U.S. society on most large national issues, so students will need to be prepared for more inaction than action after they share their ideas. Still, email writing puts students in an active stance vis-à-vis the government, demonstrating that everyone's voice matters in a democratic society.

Hold Online Office Hours. Some teachers hold online office hours—regular times when they answer student questions and discuss class assignments electronically. Such arrangements function much like a telephone homework hotline, only using computer email (or in some instances, instant messaging). The day before a big exam is one popular time for such teacher–student conversations. Many students prefer to communicate using email because they do not enjoy face-to-face conversation where they lack the time to formulate thoughtful questions and considered responses.

Online communications with students has critics. Some teachers do not wish to be constantly accessible to students, preferring to draw distinct boundaries between communications in and out of school. Others worry about privacy if teachers and students are communicating in the open space of the Internet. Online office hours require careful management to ensure safety and privacy for teachers and students. Some necessary precautions include the following:

- Using password-protected sites
- Having more than one email or IM account to conduct school business in one space and personal communications in another
- Maintaining an archival record of communications

Websites and Blogs for Teachers and Students

Using free or inexpensive communications technologies, elementary and secondary teachers can produce "home-grown" websites or blogs to reach and teach students. Indeed, teacher-made sites have become part of the educational process in every subject area and at every grade level (Risinger, 2004). As one principal told a new teacher candidate from our campus during a recent job interview: "Your site was really impressive. It was a deciding factor in our wanting to hire you."

Teachers generally build one of two kinds of online sites:

- *Teacher/classroom website.* A teacher website is primarily devoted to your work as a teacher and professional educator, highlighting who you are and what you have accomplished in your educational career, but also including information about your classes and work done by your students. Such a site might additionally serve as an online digital portfolio, a topic we discuss in Chapter 11. A classroom website is primarily devoted to the activities of your classroom. It differs from the teacher website by giving more attention to work of the students than to

Go to the Assignments and Activities section of Chapter 8 in MyEducationKit. Complete the video activity entitled "Website Supports Learning" and respond to the questions that accompany the video.

FIGURE 8.2 High School History Class Website

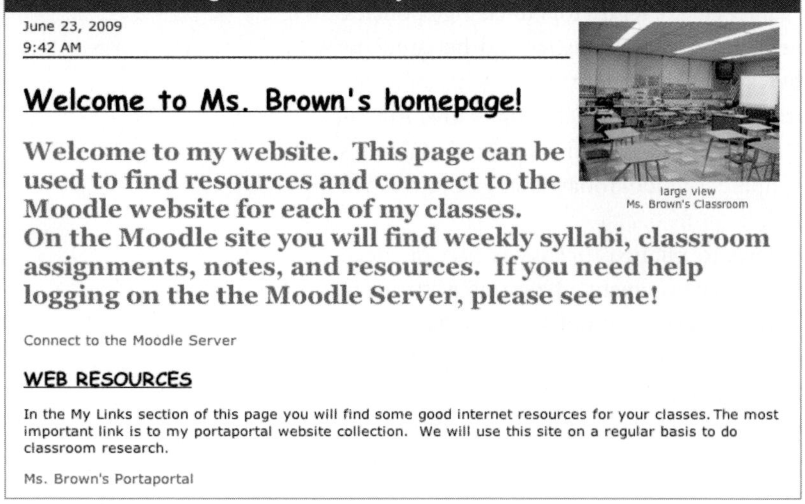

June 23, 2009
9:42 AM

Welcome to Ms. Brown's homepage!

Welcome to my website. This page can be used to find resources and connect to the Moodle website for each of my classes.
On the Moodle site you will find weekly syllabi, classroom assignments, notes, and resources. If you need help logging on the the Moodle Server, please see me!

large view
Ms. Brown's Classroom

Connect to the Moodle Server

WEB RESOURCES

In the My Links section of this page you will find some good internet resources for your classes. The most important link is to my portaportal website collection. We will use this site on a regular basis to do classroom research.

Ms. Brown's Portaportal

Source: Reprinted by permission of Kelley Brown, Easthampton High School.

work of the teacher. Figure 8.2 shows a classroom website developed by Ms. Brown, a teacher at Easthampton High School. Both teacher and classroom websites serve to engage students in academic material by giving them ways to publish their work and pursue their interests in a subject.

- *Teacher blog.* A blog (short for weblog) serves as an online journal where you post information and ideas related to your teaching (EDUCAUSE Learning Initiative, 2005, August; Penrod, 2007). It can also be a site for online interactions between you and your students or between you and other educators (Knittle, 2008; Warlick, 2005). Blogs are multipurpose instructional tools. "Students can comment on items posted. Teachers can pose questions and ask students to respond. Students can also read other students' comments" (Risinger, 2006, April, p. 130). Figure 8.3 shows a middle school teacher's blog page featuring websites related to Ancient Greece, the current topic of study, archives of past topics, a calendar, and news of interest to her students concerning the Westminster Dog Show and the new Olympic Stadium in China.

Deciding whether to create a website or blog depends on your information communication goals as a teacher. Some teachers prefer to put more emphasis on personal accomplishments through a teacher website while other educators stress the writing and research of their students through a classroom website. Blogs offer new possibilities for posting information and fostering student interaction through online discussions, as we will discuss in the next part of this chapter.

In either case, building a website or blog is an opportunity to think expansively and ambitiously about how to integrate communication technology into your teaching. To date, many teachers have used these sites as tools that provide students and families with basic information about class requirements, homework assignments, grades, and special events at school. Yet, websites and blogs can be much more than conduits of administrative information (Downes, 2004). They can be lively, interactive teaching and learning environments, particularly when students are involved in the design, construction, and maintenance of a site.

Differences between Websites and Blogs

Differences between a teacher or classroom website and a teacher blog may appear small since both usually feature postings from the teacher, class schedules, links to other sites, and a calendar of events.

One major distinction is ease of site creation and management. Blog technology is designed to offer a direct route to maintaining a constantly updated site. It offers many resources that appear whenever the blog opens: a calendar, active links

FIGURE 8.3 A Middle School Teacher's Blog Page

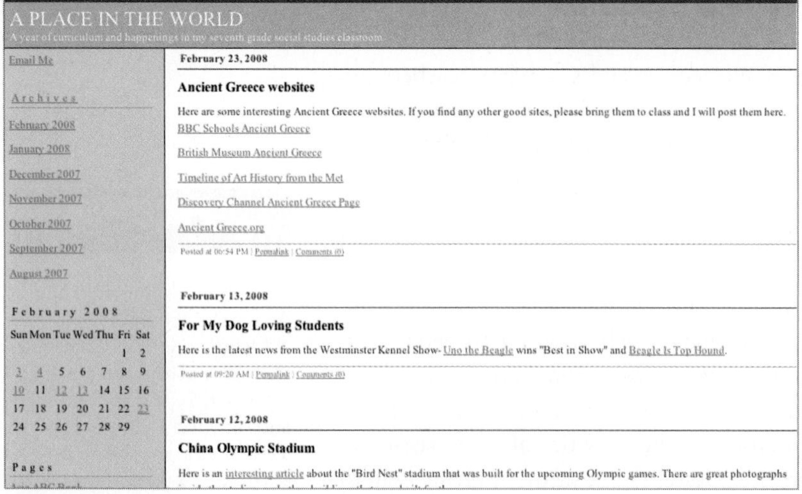

A PLACE IN THE WORLD
A year of curriculum and happenings in my seventh grade social studies classroom.

Email Me

Archives

February 2008
January 2008
December 2007
November 2007
October 2007
September 2007
August 2007

February 2008
Sun Mon Tue Wed Thu Fri Sat
1 2
3 4 5 6 7 8 9
10 11 12 13 14 15 16
17 18 19 20 21 22 23
24 25 26 27 28 29

Pages

February 23, 2008

Ancient Greece websites

Here are some interesting Ancient Greece websites. If you find any other good sites, please bring them to class and I will post them here.
BBC Schools Ancient Greece

British Museum Ancient Greece

Timeline of Art History from the Met

Discovery Channel Ancient Greece Page

Ancient Greece.org

Posted at 06:54 PM | Permalink | Comments (0)

February 13, 2008

For My Dog Loving Students

Here is the latest news from the Westminster Kennel Show- Uno the Beagle wins "Best in Show" and Beagle Is Top Hound.

Posted at 09:20 AM | Permalink | Comments (0)

February 12, 2008

China Olympic Stadium

Here is an interesting article about the "Bird Nest" stadium that was built for the upcoming Olympic games. There are great photographs

Source: Reprinted by permission of Dinah Mack, JFK Middle School.

to other websites, an archive of past blog postings, a podcasting list, a place to publish student work, and an online discussion forum.

Another difference is a blogger's ability to interject a personal voice by sharing information and opinions in an informal style. While websites can also feature a personal voice, they have tended to utilize the formal tone of a news report. Blogs, by contrast, are almost always more casual in style. Some teacher blogs sport a relaxed look with lots of links to photographs of their families or of themselves engaging in education-related activities or hobbies outside of school. Others may include top-ten lists of favorite teaching websites, interesting places to visit in the world, best books, or preferred sport teams, as well as other student-engaging information, along with commentary about work being done in school.

Tech Tool 8.1 (pages 220–221) offers three approaches to creating your own teacher website or blog: a do-it-yourself option, commercially available templates, or free online tools for creating websites or blogs.

YOUR JUDGMENT
MATTERS

As you think about the growth of blogging among middle and high school age students, consider the following questions:

- Why do you think blogging is such a popular communication activity among teenage girls?
- Why do you think blogging is considerably less popular among teenage boys?
- What do the online patterns of girls and boys suggest to you about gender roles among today's youth?
- What instructional implications do you see in the blogging behaviors of teenagers?

 ## Creating Your Own Teacher Blog

Blogging is an immensely popular online activity. Worldwide, it is estimated that "a new blog is created every second" (Berson & Berson, 2006, p. 124). In the United States, over 11 million people have authored blogs and 32 million people have read one (Pew Internet and American Life Project, 2006). Blogs are appearing in unexpected places; for example, city mayors and other elected officials from around the country are blogging with constituents as a way to promote citizen involvement in municipal government (Viser, 2008).

The teenage blogging population is growing dramatically—more than half of all youth have contributed to a blog and nearly one in five have created their own (Rainie, 2005). Blogging is very popular among teenage girls. Researchers from the Pew Internet and American Life Project found that among 12- to 17-year-old Web users, nearly one in three—35 percent of girls and 20 percent of boys—have created online journals or blogs (Lenhart, Madden, Macgill, & Smith, 2007).

Reading a personal blog is similar to opening someone's journal or diary, where the mundane facts of everyday life are paired with fascinating details, preferences, dreams, and soliloquies. Other blogs focus on particular topics and purposes, such as Paper Cuts from the *New York Times*, which discusses books and literary ideas.

K–12 teachers have many ways to tap into the blogging phenomenon:

- *Student learning.* Blogs create new forums for student learning. English teachers are using blogs to promote literacy learning through writing and the analysis of language (Huffaker, 2004). Social studies and science teachers are asking students to access news-related blogs as part of class and homework assignments. Blogs usually have definite points of view, and students can analyze the ideological perspectives of different sites on issues ranging from immigration reform to global warming.
- *Student/family communications.* Teachers can use a blog to "promote a 'transparent' classroom environment in which parents feel connected to and involved in their child's education, and teachers enhance their responsiveness to students while fostering a sense of community" (Berson & Berson, 2006, p. 125). And like other electronic communication options such as teacher websites and threaded discussion boards, blogs enlarge the classroom by creating opportunities for students to discuss ideas, share experiences, and present points of view.
- *Professional networking.* Blogs offer ways for teachers to communicate with other teachers, enabling them to stay current professionally and to receive support from colleagues concerning questions or issues in the classroom. Some teachers use microblogging tools as a way to establish connections with colleagues (Knittle, 2008). This form of blogging involves

Go to the Assignments and Activities section of Chapter 8 in MyEducationKit. Open the Web activity "Teacher Blogs and Web Building" to further explore Tech Tool 8.1.

As you think about building your own teacher website or blog, it is important to recognize that you have choices and trade-offs ranging from costly, design-your-own site software programs to less expensive preassembled commercial sites to open source resources that offer free templates to teachers and schools.

Look at the following three ways to customize your website or blog. Each option lets you create a basic information communication site and then allows you to add further features and functions such as email, online discussion boards, weblinks, or video and audio selections.

Which approach will work best for you and why?

Approach 1 (Website and Blog-Building Software)

Purchase, download to your personal computer, and learn a communication software program such as Dreamweaver or FrontPage. Such programs enable teachers to build personal websites that range in scope from the functionally basic to the elaborately sophisticated. While such programs take time to learn, the products they produce are comprehensive in scope and attractive to view. Communication software like Dreamweaver are really just design programs; you will still need more tools to take what you have designed and publish it on the Web. A teacher might put a personally designed site on a school system's server or pay for space on a public site.

Approach 2 (Commercially Available Template)

Access a commercially available website or blog builder such as TaskStream, Go Daddy, or eBlogger. These programs allow users to create many features and functions, although they do not produce either the variety or quality of graphics of the Dreamweaver or FrontPage software programs. Commercially available programs have the added feature of being password protected while offering you a ready-made publication portal for your site on the Internet. You and your students can then go online without encountering the potential dangers of communicating on the Internet where anyone can read your material.

PEARSON
myeducationkit

Go to the Tutorials section of Chapter 8 in MyEducationKit and access the practical tutorials "Blogs with Word-press" and "Blogs with Blogger." Use the tutorials to learn how to create your own online interactive site.

sending short text messages (around 140 characters) to friends or professional colleagues. Microblogging is useful because it does not take much time to establish and maintain contacts or send updates. Twitter and Plurk are two popular microblogging tools for you to consider.

There are three basic types of education-related blogs:

- "Official face" blogs serve as formal information centers for schools. Some of these organizational blogs include contributions by teachers and students.
- Single-purpose blogs address one subject area within a school, such as science or language arts.
- Active learning blogs involve students and teachers in conversations around parts of the curriculum (Harris, 2006).

As you begin to envision your own teacher blog, think of an instrument panel with multiple control buttons, typically featuring "Pages," "Archives," "Categories," "Blogroll," or "Meta." Figure 8.4 shows a blog page from a cultural diversity in education course for new teachers.

Approach 3 (Open Source Software)

Use a free online course management system (CMS) for educators such as Moodle that provides email, online discussion boards, instant messaging, and discussion forums for school districts and individual classrooms. Moodle offers numerous different administrative functions including grade record keeping and posting, selective content releases, and various filtering options. Many teachers and schools choose these systems because they are free of charge and fairly easy to use. Ease of use means that such programs may not offer some of the more advanced features found in communication software programs or commercial sites, but many teachers may not have time or need to learn more complex systems. Open source programs generally are not password protected, which may be a drawback to use in schools.

You may prefer to choose another open source option such as WordPress that you can access directly online from your home computer. Blogger is also another free blog-building option for teachers. While not an open source program, its interface is easy to navigate and it produces a professional looking site. Edmodo, a free microblogging tool, invites teachers and students to share ideas and information. Teachers can post homework assignments and invite discussion both in and out of the classroom via this easy-to-use platform.

CONTACT INFORMATION

TaskStream   https://www.taskstream.com   This is a subscription service.

Moodle   http://moodle.org   Available for free online. Users are required to register.

WordPress   http://wordpress.org/about   Available for free downloading.

Blogger   www.blogger.com/about   Available from Google.

Edmodo   www.edmodo.com/blog

Go Daddy   www.godaddy.com

The basic components of a blog include the following features:

- *Heading.* There is a heading section where you can include your name and the name of your blog ("TEAMS Tutoring Blog" in Figure 8.4).
- *Pages.* Under the Pages icon is an "About" section where you will create and update information about yourself and your site. You can add more pages as needed, and readers can post questions or comments in response to this information. For instance, you might create pages that connect users to the essential administrative information they need about your class and its assignments. Other pages could provide more abstract and conceptual connections, with

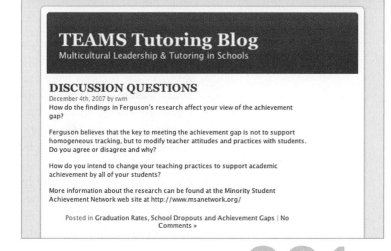

FIGURE 8.4   TEAMS Tutoring Course Blog

TEAMS Tutoring Blog
Multicultural Leadership & Tutoring in Schools

DISCUSSION QUESTIONS
December 4th, 2007 by rwm
How do the findings in Ferguson's research affect your view of the achievement gap?

Ferguson believes that the key to meeting the achievement gap is not to support homogeneous tracking, but to modify teacher attitudes and practices with students. Do you agree or disagree and why?

How do you intend to change your teaching practices to support academic achievement by all of your students?

More information about the research can be found at the Minority Student Achievement Network web site at http://www.msanetwork.org/

Posted in Graduation Rates, School Dropouts and Achievement Gaps | No Comments »

Blogs for Teachers

As blogs are becoming established in society as sources of information, how can teachers best utilize this new form of interactive communication technology? This question has many different responses. On the one hand, blogs are increasingly popular forms of communication. It has been estimated that 8 percent of the population keep a blog while 40 percent read one regularly (Windham, 2007). In this context, many observers believe that teachers need to create and read blogs in order to understand firsthand how this technology affects people's lives and patterns of communication. On the other hand, other educators worry that blogs are inappropriately displacing paper-based communication—letters, memoranda, reviews, and reports—so teachers need to teach students to communicate in traditional ways, not encourage them to rely on electronic mediums as sole sources of information.

This debate aside, teachers' use of blogs is growing not only because blogs are a convenient way to maintain a class website, but because blogs also provide new avenues for educators to communicate with one another about issues that matter to them personally and professionally. One of the great advantages of blogs is how they make possible "highly personalized discussion forums that foster communities of interest" (EDUCAUSE Learning Initiative, 2005, August). For this reason, keeping and/or reading blogs is an important new form of professional development for educators, a way to stay current in one's academic fields while also maintaining a pulse on what is happening in the profession of teaching.

Teacher Magazine (www.teachermagazine.org) is one important resource for teachers looking to find interesting and useful education-related blogs. In the Blogboard section of its website, *Teacher Magazine* hosts a variety of blogs by and for classroom educators about topics such as education reform and teaching for social change, teacher leadership, literacy learning, gifted children, the work lives of new teachers, and middle school pedagogy. This website is maintained by Editorial Projects in Education, a Bethesda, Maryland–based nonprofit organization that is also publisher of the widely read and highly respected newspaper *Education Week*.

Teacher Magazine has links to blogs from *Education Week*, including one written from widely divergent political perspectives by educators Deborah Meier and Diane Ravitch. *Education Week* has a blog detailing changes in the No Child Left Behind (NCLB) law as well as a site focusing on the learning challenges facing culturally and linguistically diverse students. *Teacher Magazine* includes other useful online resources on its website: Web Watch, providing weekly news from the Web, Trend Tracker, summarizing the latest educational research, and Classroom Technology, addressing issues about the use of technology in schools.

As a teacher, reading blogs written by other educators is part of how blogs may be useful to you professionally. Additionally, blog posts invite responses from readers. You can express your ideas in print at any of these educational blog sites. Using what is called "trackback," you can post a response to an issue on your own blog and link that comment back to the original blog where you first read about the issue (EDUCAUSE Learning Initiative, 2005, August). Referencing other bloggers in your blog widens the network of ideas being discussed, adding to the information sharing potential of the educational blogosphere.

Teacher Magazine is one of a number of organizations maintaining education-related blogs; learning.now from PBS Teachers is another, devoted to exploring the impact of the Internet on teaching and learning in schools. Look online to find other excellent blog sites where you can read and contribute to discussions about every important educational issue.

---

links to sites developed by experts and organizations in a field of study as well as connections to work done by students.

- *Archives.* The Archives icon organizes posts on the blog by month. Here you can place past information so readers have a library of material to review.
- *Categories.* The Categories icon serves as a place to organize posts into different topics or themes. In the example in Figure 8.4, categories in the TEAMS Tutoring Blog include Digital Divides and Disconnects; English Language Learning; Graduation Rates, School Dropouts, and Achievement Gaps; How Students Experience School; and so on.
- *Blogroll.* Blogroll is a place to link to other recommended sites and Web resources.
- *Meta.* This section serves as the credits section, explaining which software has been used to create the site. The TEAMS Tutoring Blog in Figure 8.4 used a template provided by Word-Press, an open source blog-building software program.

Design Decisions in Building a Teacher Blog

You have four key design decisions in building your teacher blog: content posting, reader response, audience, and authorship. Each of these decisions will help determine how effectively your teacher blog achieves your communication goals.

- *Content posting.* Content posting refers to how much and how often new content is posted on your site. Some teachers might post material at the beginning of the school year and leave it there unchanged, resulting in a basically static site. Others will change the content on a regular basis, making visiting the site a more dynamic experience for student readers. You decide how often you want to post new material on your site. Blogs make multiple postings easy to manage technologically because you can keep track of them by date and topic.

- *Reader response.* Reader response refers to the participation of student readers, from simply reading what is posted to actively responding to online material. You decide how you want to receive comments at your site. Within many blogs, comments from readers are posted for everyone to read, the idea being that students read each other's comments and make their own replies. The conversation is among the students while the teacher/blogger interjects occasionally to guide the discussion by adding comments or by reorganizing the postings. In other cases, the flow of information goes from the teacher to students and back from students to the teacher, thus limiting the amount of online conversation students have directly with each other. In either case, blogs with frequent postings encourage students to express their views whenever new material becomes available.

- *Audience.* Audience indicates who may access a site. You decide whether access is limited to a small group (for instance, the students in a course) or extended to anyone who is online (all Internet users).

- *Authorship.* Authorship explains who may create content on a site. Some sites have a single author, whereas other sites depend on multiple authors. You decide whether to be the sole author of material or to open the site to include the contributions of students. Blogs usually have multiple authors since they invite readers to add their views and comments on the topics being discussed. Multiple authorship can also take place in a wiki, a form of collaboration technology we discuss later in this chapter.

Examples of Blog Design Decisions by Teachers

When creating a blog, you must decide among the various design possibilities for content posting, reader response, audience, and authorship. Teacher A in Figure 8.5 is the single author of a site that is open to all Internet users. He changes the site regularly, but readers do not offer electronic responses to his material. If you were to plot his site on the four bars in Figure 8.5, he is at the right end of the content posting and audience bars and at the left end of the reader response and authorship bars.

Teacher B in Figure 8.5 is not the sole author of her blog site. She includes her students as creators of the site content, but she changes that content only once or twice during the school year. Access is limited by a password protection system

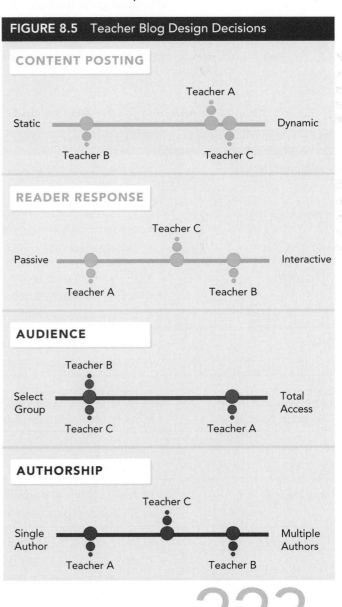

FIGURE 8.5 Teacher Blog Design Decisions

CONTENT POSTING

Static — Teacher B — Teacher A / Teacher C — Dynamic

READER RESPONSE

Passive — Teacher A — Teacher C — Teacher B — Interactive

AUDIENCE

Select Group — Teacher B / Teacher C — Teacher A — Total Access

AUTHORSHIP

Single Author — Teacher A — Teacher C — Teacher B — Multiple Authors

to the members of her classes, but she requires every student to respond to what they read online as part of how the site is used instructionally.

Teacher C constantly posts updated material on her site, usually every week. Her students read and respond electronically to questions, informational postings, and digital resources, but the audience is limited to the members of her classes. She is the primary but not exclusive author of the site. Her students are given class credit for adding material to the site.

The choices and distinctions outlined in Figure 8.5 are not absolute, and the use of blogs is being reinvented every day by users. You will join that ongoing negotiation as you decide the role of websites and blogs in your electronic communication system as a teacher. One tool that will assist you greatly in creating your blog is a **digital image scanner,** the focus of Tech Tool 8.2.

Analyzing Teacher-Made Websites and Blogs

Many school or school district websites resemble commercial sites in their presentation of organizational information that often includes a mission statement, curriculum expectations and standards by grade level, and names and backgrounds of faculty and staff as well as the schedule of academic and extracurricular events. By contrast, teacher websites and blogs are intended to catch the interest of students, inform families and colleagues about coursework and events, and, even more important, serve as an entryway to learning—anywhere, anytime. These websites are as original as the teachers who build them.

Creating a website or blog requires planning. Ideas for what inspires you and your students will emerge through analyzing what others have done. To assist you in this analysis, we present a set of criteria for evaluating teacher-made websites and blogs in Table 8.3.

TABLE 8.3   Criteria for Analyzing Teacher-Made Websites and Blogs

Parts of the Site	Key Questions
Design/aesthetics	• Is the site clear to read and navigate? • Does the structure of the site follow a logical pattern? • Does the site draw people in? • Are there pictures or other visuals? • Does the site look complete or does it appear "thrown together"?
Information	• Does information on the site relate to a class and its educational content? • Is the information easily available (directly written or downloadable)? • Is there a variety of information?
Links	• Are there links to related sources and sites? • Are there too many links without providing needed information for students?
Contact information	• Is there an easy way to contact the teacher?
Discussion options	• Are there ways to leave messages, ask questions, or discuss information and topics?
Up to date	• Is the information up to date in relation to class work and homework assignments? • Does the page contain a reference stating "last updated on . . ."?
Class logistics	• Are assignments posted? • Is a class syllabus or outline posted?
Overall impressions	• What do you like most about the site? • What do you like least about the site?

Teachers and students are writing and drawing continuously. The act of putting pencil to paper (or fingers to keyboard) is fundamental to how teaching and learning happens at every grade level. Think of what you have written or drawn in the past week: notes, exams, research papers, fiction stories, nonfiction essays, poems, scientific diagrams, mathematical calculations, historical timelines, and on and on.

All these forms of personal writing and drawing raise two important points about how you and your students use blogs, websites, wikis, and the other communication technologies discussed in this chapter:

1. Some of your writing and drawing is on computers and some is not, because there are times when it is easier to compose or calculate on paper than to use a computer word processor, drawing program, or calculator. Consequently, most of us create a variety of electronic and paper materials useful to our academic work.

2. At the same time, it is often useful to have an electronic version of writing and drawing that you have done by hand—or that someone else has published in books, magazines, and other sources. Computer access to paper materials allows teachers and students to easily store, edit, and publish what has been created.

Digital image scanners are tools that provide teachers and students with computer storage of handmade or already published writing and drawing. Think of a digital image scanner as an electronic transfer agent, photographing paper materials into a digital format to upload to a computer. The screenshot shows a student's drawing of a whale shark that has been scanned and posted to a classroom website.

Scanners are a vehicle for online publishing, making it possible to upload printed or drawn information (your own writing or drawing or that of your students) to a teacher or classroom website or blog. Scanners also allow teachers to add visual images to handouts, class notes, and learning resources that they are creating for their students.

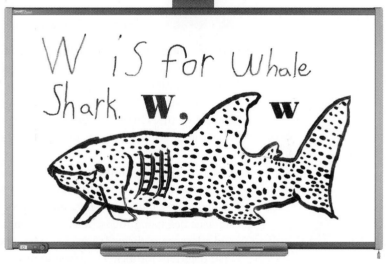

Board courtesy of SMART Technologies; copyright © 2001–2009 SMART Technologies ULC; all rights reserved.

CONTACT INFORMATION

Information about digital image scanners is available online from manufacturers such as Epson, Hewlett Packard, and Microtek.

YOUR JUDGMENT MATTERS

Using the criteria presented in Table 8.3 (p. 224) to examine the quality and effectiveness of sites created by colleagues in your school district or other educators on the Web, consider the following questions:

- How well do the sites you visited meet the evaluation criteria?
- What other criteria might be added to the list?
- How has the assessment of other sites influenced the design of your site?

In the design and development of their websites and blogs, some teachers concentrate on creating interaction rather than displaying information. Their goal is to attract students and families to use the site not solely as a source of information, but as a place where they can contribute material and extend learning outside of school.

Locally authored teacher sites generally lack the flash and style of expensive, commercially produced sites because in Web design, money makes a difference in terms of impressive graphics and ease of navigation. However, local teacher sites have a sense of authenticity and engagement that more expensive sites never match, especially when students have been involved in the site's creation and maintenance. Students feel a great sense of ownership and investment in a website or blog that they helped to author and on which their work is displayed. They want people to view the site over and over again. Students, teachers, and families will return repeatedly to even an ordinary-looking site if students helped to create it and it contains information they want to see.

Examples of locally created websites and blogs are found throughout the Internet. *Social Education,* the journal of the National Council for the Social Studies, has identified engaging Web pages created by history and social studies teachers at all grade levels (Risinger, 2004, 2006, November/December). These sites feature contributions by teachers, students, and community members. They showcase examples of student projects and publish excellent work done in class. They also contain teacher courses and assignments, summer reading and film viewing lists, important Web links such as Women's History Month and Hispanic Heritage Month sites, and current information related to events like Student Government Day.

Strategies for Incorporating Reader Response

Effective online interaction with students depends on a teacher's ability to act as a moderator—that is, carefully guiding a complex process where the emotions, beliefs, understandings, and conceptualizations of students are all in the mix. Moderating an online discussion is like trying to drive a car from the back seat. You can give guidance to the driver, but you do not have direct control of the wheel. The following suggestions can help you become a successful discussion leader in online learning situations.

Focus on Issues That Have Meaning and Relevance to Your Students. When using online discussions, student enthusiasm and interest is high at the beginning. There is excitement about the possibilities of using new forms of computer-based communication. When you find your students beginning to lose interest and enthusiasm, focus on issues and topics that have meaning and relevance to them. Ask in class what interests them about a topic and use that information to craft questions for them to address in the online setting.

Stress the Importance of Active, Thoughtful Participation. Some students are not engaged in online discussions, composing only short one or two sentence replies that are too general to advance the flow of ideas or to help the writer think about the topics under consideration. Other writers go to opposite extremes, becoming overengaged and posting judgmental and personally disparaging remarks about other students. Too little or too much participation by students requires teachers to play a crucial discussion management role. Before any online discussion begins, make it clear that you will be an active director of the communication process. This means that every student is expected to be a productive contributor to the discussion, and will be graded accordingly.

Requiring students to participate in online discussions can result in thoughtful, articulate responses, in part because students have the time to reflect on and revise their text. Online writing can promote the discovery of knowledge and new ideas through communicating with others in a meaningful dialogue.

Emphasize Rapid versus Delayed Feedback. Students need feedback—from teachers and peers—to make any learning situation feel successful, including online discussions. In theory, electronic discussions promote thoughtful conversation as students compose their own postings and read what others have written. Powerful connections are made when students are able to exchange ideas and information with other people who expresses genuine interest in reading what has been written. There is an intellectual connection—your personal ideas are being expressed and discussed—as well as the additional connection of reading what someone says in response to your statements. Finally, there is the possibility of a change in thinking as you reconsider your ideas based on the feedback you receive from others.

When feedback happens rapidly and thoughtfully, writers and readers both benefit. Writers recognize that they have an interested audience for their ideas; they are not just writing for the teacher. They also realize they have an opportunity to get valuable feedback about their ideas. Readers learn from the postings of writers and become aware of how important is it to take everyone's ideas seriously. When it is a reader's turn to write, she or he expects others will respond thoughtfully.

Establish Clear Rules for Online Conduct. In an unmoderated online discussion, it is easy for some students to try to dominate the conversation. As the discussion leader, a teacher must find ways to engage everyone and to bring forth ideas from students who are participating the least. Clear rules for online conduct, agreed on beforehand, provide a structure for online comments and responses. Rules protect individual differences that inevitably become part of every discussion and promote civility in the expression of opposing opinions. Posting the policy for responding in online discussions makes each student responsible for playing by the rules, just as in sports. One short statement might be sufficient to keep the dialogue focused on the topic: "As in face-to-face interactions in class, discussions online will refrain from judging others' views as wrong or ridiculous. Disagreeing and stating why you do so is acceptable as long as no one is disparaged through name calling or using negative labels or put downs."

Respond Directly, but Tactfully. A blunt "That's wrong!" will make it less likely that a student will respond eagerly the next time a question is asked. As a teacher, you need to affirm student comments even when those comments are not what you were expecting when you asked a question. However, affirming someone's statements does not mean always agreeing with those statements. When a student's information is incorrect or a comment is ill considered, you need to respond in ways that correct the information or rebuff a negative or discriminatory tone. For example, "Your comment made me recall a source you may find interesting. It offers more information than you have seen thus far." Or: "One's viewpoint is constructed by one's influences and life experiences. Take a look at [source or writer] and consider how your ideas conform to or disagree with this viewpoint." Offering bland affirmations—"Good job" or "Nice comment"—may cause students to dismiss your responses as insincere or disinterested. The statements "I find that interesting," "I had not thought of that," or "Thank you for mentioning it" all confirm that your attention is on what the student is saying.

Develop an Online Reading Response Form for Your Students. Teachers at the middle and high school level often ask students to post their responses to outside-of-class reading assignments on an online discussion board. Asking students to provide unfocused comments can produce statements lacking clarity, detail, or analysis. At the same time, making an online reading reaction entry too formal (in the style of a research paper with footnotes and citations) detracts from the ease and spontaneity that many students feel when posting on the Web. Figure 8.6

FIGURE 8.6 Online Reading Response Form

Name: _____

Class: _____   Date: _____

Title of the Reading: _____

1. Describe the professional and personal background of the author.

2. Consider the big themes we have been discussing in class. Select one of those themes, identify it, and write a paragraph summarizing what the reading tells you about the theme. Use at least two quotations of at least a sentence in length from the reading to explain your thoughts.

3. List several adjectives that best describe your opinion of the reading—and its usefulness for this course.

4. Assign the reading a letter grade, from A to F, with A indicating a highly favorable rating and F a failure. Comment about the criteria you used to establish the grade.

provides a template for an online reading response form. As you read it, consider how you might use this form or a variation with your students.

Wikis as a Collaborative Learning Strategy

PEARSON
myeducationkit™

Go to the Tutorials section of Chapter 8 in MyEducationKit and access the practical tutorial entitled "Wikis." Use the tutorial to learn how to create your own online interactive wiki.

A **wiki** is a website or blogspace that is collaboratively edited and maintained by a group of people (EDUCAUSE Learning Initiative, 2005, July). Wikis allow individuals or groups to edit the same Web page—"users can visit, read, re-organise and update the structure and content (text and pictures) of a Wiki as they see fit" (Augar, Raitman, & Zhou, 2004, p. 95). First appearing in the mid-1990s, wikis have grown in popularity because of the way they involve users in the process of sharing information collaboratively (Tapscott & Williams, 2006). In addition to the online encyclopedia Wikipedia (discussed in Chapter 5), there are now wikis in many wide-ranging areas including:

- WikiTravel, a worldwide travel guide
- Wictionary, a collaboratively developed dictionary
- Cookbook Wiki, a compendium of information about global cuisines
- WikiEd, a wiki for educators (developed by the Curriculum, Technology and Education Reform program at the University of Illinois at Urbana-Champaign)
- WikiHow, an effort to create the world's largest how-to manual
- WikiIndex, a wiki featuring information about wikis
- Wikibooks, a site that hosts more than 25,000 jointly created open-content books
- Curriki, a site featuring online, open source curriculum materials for K–12 teachers

In schools, wikis allow students and teachers to do the following:

- Use technology in meaningful ways in their classroom
- Collaborate with peers and colleagues
- Synthesize and explain the content they are learning through written expression and different forms of multimedia expression
- Publish their writing and other creative or scientific work
- Receive feedback about their learning both inside and outside the classroom

Letting students create and post their academic projects on school and classroom websites and wikis is a powerful way to promote active engagement and personal investment in learning.

It is true that these goals can also be achieved through the use of teacher- and student-authored websites and blogs, but wikis, because they are designed for collective writing and editing, promote high levels of collaboration and interaction among students. Certain kinds of educational projects, as we shall see in the rest of this section, lend themselves to the collaborative possibilities created by wikis.

Collaborative Learning Environments

Wikis make possible **collaborative learning environments** for teachers and students. Collaborative learning happens when students together work on different parts of a problem and discover key concepts and information for themselves. In such environments, the role of the teacher is focused on supporting peer-to-peer interaction and social learning. Collaborative learning environments encourage students to work in teams, to question processes, to make mistakes, and to monitor each other's reasoning.

Wikis have the technological capacities to model and support student-to-student collaboration. First, students need to participate with others because one individual cannot always have all the information required to build a wiki. The idea is for the group, not one or two individuals, to create a wiki. Second, wiki technology keeps track of the writing and editing process in ways that allow everyone to see what has been contributed and what has been changed.

Figure 8.7 shows a sample page from a wiki being created by high school history teachers and their students about a key topic in world history, the relationship between the religions of Islam, Judaism, and Christianity. The text highlighted in green shows a new contribution to the page while the text highlighted in red shows material that has been deleted from the text. Being able to view changes to a text while they happen helps everyone learn the material. The students can see how text can become more focused and clear as it is edited, while the teacher can keep track of which different students are adding to the text.

Collaborative learning experiences in school mirror the way information is created in society where no one individual can know enough to completely solve complex social and technological problems. Working together on a wiki becomes a way for students to understand the processes by which knowledge is generated, evaluated, and revised by groups of individuals in business, government, and many other fields (Leuf & Cunningham, 2001).

Building a Standards Wiki

Just about every teacher, as we discussed in Chapter 6, faces the challenge of teaching a standards-based curriculum, mainly because almost every school uses some set of local, state, or national curriculum frameworks to guide teaching and learning. In Chapter 6, we suggested teachers maintain a standards connector web as a way to keep track of exemplary Internet resources they can use to meet different learning standards from their curriculum framework. Teachers can also use wikis to help them address curriculum frameworks, using what we call a **standards wiki,** a collection of academic information and class notes related to specific curriculum frameworks. Teachers and students working together can create it.

Figure 8.8 shows a page from a U.S. history wikispace created by one of the authors and a group of high school history teachers and students. In this wiki, learning standards from the Massachusetts History and Social Studies Curriculum Framework are displayed on the page. Teachers and students are invited to click on a standard, read what other teachers and students have written, and add their own contributions and resources. The goal is to build a collaboratively developed and maintained collection of learning materials to use in teaching the state's mandated history standards for high school students.

FIGURE 8.7 Edited Page from a World History Wikispace

The Quran was assembled during the reign of the caliph Uthman (Muhammad did not actually write down the messages that God revealed to him). It contains both surahs (which are like chapters) and ayas (which are like verses). Normally, it is arranged in length, from the longest to the shortest, except for the opening surah. It can also be arranged chronologically, with surahs from Mecca and Medina. The Meccan surahs tend to be more poetic, filled with imagery, and generally shorter. The surahs from Medina are longer and deal more with questions of law.

C. Islam's historical relationship to Judaism and Christianity

Like the Torah, the Jewish holy book, and the Christian Bible, the Quran contains many kinds of writing, including stories, promises, warnings and instructions. There is a reason for the similarity of the Quran to Jewish and Christian holy books. Muslims, like Jews and Christians, believe in one God. They regard Adam, Noah, Abraham, and Moses as important in religious history. Muslims regard Christians and Jews as "people of the book"

D. The relationship between government and religion in Muslim societies

Islam holds that political life can only function properly within the context of Islamic law. To such believers, since God's law is universally true and beneficial to all people, any state law or action opposed to God's law would be harmful to the citizens, and displeasing to God. Many Muslims consider the Western concept of separation of Church and State to be rebellion against God's law. There is a contemporary debate in Islam whether obedience to Islamic law is ultimately compatible with the Western secular pattern, which separates religion from civic life

WHI21.JPG

Islam's historical relationship to Judaism and Christianity: A. Allah is the same God worshiped in Christianity & Judaism B. All 3 religions believe in a day of judgment, heaven and hell. C. Christians & Jews are recognized as "people of the book," because each religion had

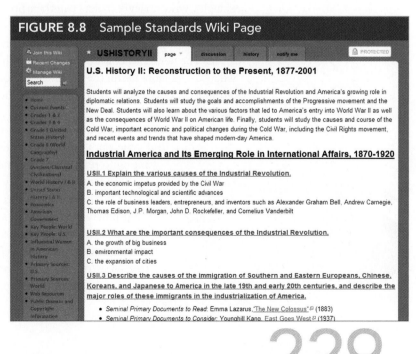

FIGURE 8.8 Sample Standards Wiki Page

USHISTORYII — page — discussion — history — notify me — PROTECTED

Join this Wiki
Recent Changes
Manage Wiki
Search

- Home
- Current Events
- Grades 1 & 2
- Grades 3 & 4
- Grade 5 (United States History)
- Grade 6 (World Geography)
- Grade 7 (Ancient/Classical Civilizations)
- World History I & II
- United States History I & II
- Economics
- American Government
- Key People: World
- Key People: U.S.
- Influential Women in American History
- Primary Sources: U.S.
- Primary Sources: World
- Web Resources
- Public Domain and Copyright Information

U.S. History II: Reconstruction to the Present, 1877-2001

Students will analyze the causes and consequences of the Industrial Revolution and America's growing role in diplomatic relations. Students will study the goals and accomplishments of the Progressive movement and the New Deal. Students will also learn about the various factors that led to America's entry into World War II as well as the consequences of World War II on American life. Finally, students will study the causes and course of the Cold War, important economic and political changes during the Cold War, including the Civil Rights movement, and recent events and trends that have shaped modern-day America.

Industrial America and Its Emerging Role in International Affairs, 1870-1920

USII.1 Explain the various causes of the Industrial Revolution.
A. the economic impetus provided by the Civil War
B. important technological and scientific advances
C. the role of business leaders, entrepreneurs, and inventors such as Alexander Graham Bell, Andrew Carnegie, Thomas Edison, J.P. Morgan, John D. Rockefeller, and Cornelius Vanderbilt

USII.2 What are the important consequences of the Industrial Revolution.
A. the growth of big business
B. environmental impact
C. the expansion of cities

USII.3 Describe the causes of the immigration of Southern and Eastern Europeans, Chinese, Koreans, and Japanese to America in the late 19th and early 20th centuries, and describe the major roles of these immigrants in the industrialization of America.

- Seminal Primary Documents to Read: Emma Lazarus, "The New Colossus" (1883)
- Seminal Primary Documents to Consider: Younghill Kang, East Goes West (1937)

Other examples of possible wiki projects include the following:

- Science Fair and National History Day projects
- Student-developed texts and open-content source books
- Literature circles and book discussion groups
- Teacher-to-teacher projects and information exchanges

Creating a Wikitext

Wikis can be used in K–12 classrooms whenever students or teachers are involved in collaborative and group projects. In so doing, they fundamentally shift the nature of the learning experience. Instead of students just reading the textbook, they can become involved in creating the textbook for their class by constructing an online educational **wikitext.** You can think of an educational wikitext as a collection of electronic resources that have been created together by teachers and students (Fontaine, 2008).

The idea of a wikitext is a promising new instructional model. Students are put in decision-making roles, becoming "not only readers and writers, but also editors and collaborators" (Richardson, 2006, p. 5). There is a heightened sense of engagement as students participate in collaboratively building wiki pages. Moreover, students come to see curriculum content as meaningful topics rather than simply information that must be learned for a test (Leuf & Cunningham, 2001, p. 16).

One model for using a wikitext comes from a foundations course for future teachers at Old Dominion University (Allen et al., 2008; Xiao, Baker, O'Shea, & Allen, 2007). Professor Dwight Allen and his graduate teaching assistants selected 77 topics typically found in foundations of education textbooks for inclusion in a student-written wikitext (provisions were made for student-generated topics to be included as well). Each student was asked to write a thousand-word essay on one topic, citing at least five references, including both scholarly and popular sources. A "sidebar" was required for each entry, reflecting how traditional textbooks approach the topic. Students also created five multiple-choice questions and one essay question to accompany their wikitext entry. Members of the class then rated each of the entries and the most highly rated ones were posted on the class wikispace.

Elementary, middle, or high school teachers can do their own versions of a wikitext development process, as one secondary school teacher noted: "I take six new terms . . . and create a page in the wiki for each term. I give the students a template and say, 'This is a structure of what I want you to find. Find examples, write reviews.' Then I pair them up, and they complete the wiki forms in groups" (Standen, 2006).

A wikitext approach places students in new roles as content creators, not simply content receivers. The new teacher candidates in Dwight Allen's college course reported that many felt their "wikitext was more useful for them because of its structure—specifically, the wikitext was broken into short, 1,000 word articles rather than the lengthy chapters characteristic of many traditional texts" (Xiao et al., 2007, p. 23).

K–12 students can use a wikitext to review important academic content without having to reread large amounts of information. Plus there is the added incentive for students of wanting to read what they and their classmates have written online. Professor Allen's students reported they spent more time interacting with the wikitext than with traditional textbooks in other classes. The collaborative writing and editing inherent in wikis seems to engage students in reading academic material in personal and critical ways.

Creating your own wiki is fast and easy. A number of companies provide free wikis on the Web. These services include a basic site (with some advertisements), but include the option to upgrade features and eliminate ads for a small yearly fee.

- PBworks (PB for peanut butter) provides descriptive videos on its website that make it easy to learn how to create a wiki. Available online at http://pbworks.com/academic.wiki
- Wikispaces has an ongoing program to provide 250,000 free wikis to K–12 teachers throughout the United States. Available online at www.wikispaces.com/site/for/teachers
- TiddlyWiki is a free open source tool that teachers and students can use for short writing activities such as book reports, research journals, or class notes. Available online at www.tiddlywiki.com

Strategies for Using Wikis with Your Students

Effective wiki projects depend on a teacher's ability to establish and maintain collaboration among students. The following suggestions can help you do wikis with your students:

- *Group processes.* Teachers can organize wiki projects in two basic formats: (1) a group of students (usually three to five in number) can contribute to a single project—for example, a science research project on a common topic, or (2) individual students can do their own individual projects for others to read and respond to—for example, a review of different time periods in a history class. Each format has advantages and drawbacks. Working together, students can support and extend each other's learning, but some group members may not contribute equally to the common goal. When everyone is responsible for a project, it is clear who has done the required work, but the element of collaboration is minimized. You can choose the format that works best in your classroom or use both at different times.

- *Nature of the wikitext.* Teachers must decide whether to have students create a new wikitext every time they teach a course or ask students from one class to work with the wiki material that other students have previously created. Either approach works well, depending on the situation. In many cases, history projects, research reports, and science experiments lend themselves to new wikis each year, as students discover new information and take material in new directions. By contrast, when teachers ask students to work with a set body of material such as a required curriculum framework, then it may make more sense to create a wiki that students will add to and improve year after year as the course is taught.

- *Inappropriate or plagiarized material.* Teachers may find that students post inappropriate or plagiarized material on a class wiki, either purposely or unknowingly. In addition to having clear rules about what to post, teachers do need to be careful editors of online content. It is possible to set the preferences of a wiki so that only the teacher has final control over what material is made public and what is not. It is also possible to lock certain pages so that only the teacher/editor can change them. Such features of wiki technology allow teachers to carefully monitor what is posted online while also teaching students about the importance of clear, accurate, and fair materials.

- *Grades for students.* Writing for a wiki represents a new and different form of academic work for many teachers and students. As such, it may be different from grading with the typical criteria for class assignments. There is no right or wrong answer as with a multiple-choice test. Students need a clear definition of what is expected of them beforehand so they recognize what they must do to receive a passing grade. The accompanying wiki project grade form outlines the specific areas that one teacher expected her students to cover in developing postings for an informational wiki on community health issues covered in a high school science class. Groups of students were expected to both create a wiki page entry and present their findings to the class in an oral presentation. You can certainly modify this form to fit your classroom and subject area.

WIKI PROJECT EVALUATION FORM

Components of Your Wiki Assignment	Criteria for Evaluation
Group Participants	Basic Contributions of Each Member
Introduction to Wiki Page	General Information
	Issues Clearly Identified
Resources Provided	Accurate
	Empirical Articles and Data
Clarity of Information	On Wiki
	In Class
Citations	APA Format
Summary of Findings	Summary Given
Written Presentation	Quality of Presentation
Oral Presentation	Quality of Presentation

 TECHNOLOGY TRANSFORMATION LESSON PLAN

BLOGGING THE NEWS FROM ROOM 145
Reading and Writing Using Web Communication Tools

Grade(s)

Elementary and middle school

Subject(s)

English/language arts

Key Goal/Enduring Understanding

News is what's happening now. People share news by broadcasting it on television or radio or publishing it in print newspapers, on the Internet, or through other media. Without these sources, news would travel slowly through face-to-face communications. For more than 200 years, newspapers served as formats for delivering the news to mass audiences. Today, Internet technologies such as blogs provide personal ways to share news with interested readers and viewers.

Essential Question

How can a classroom blog publish news about student learning and school activities to audiences of families, students, and teachers?

Learning Standards

National Council of Teachers of English (NCTE)—*Standards for the English Language Arts*

> **Standard 4:** Students adjust their use of spoken, written, and visual language to communicate effectively with a variety of audiences and for different purposes.

International Society for Technology in Education (ISTE)—*NETS-S, 2007*

> **Standard 1:** *Creativity and Innovation.* Students demonstrate creative thinking, construct knowledge, and develop innovative products and processes using technology.

> **Standard 2:** *Communication and Collaboration.* Students use digital media and environments to communicate and work collaboratively, including at a distance, to support individual learning and contribute to the learning of others.

> **Standard 6:** *Technology Operations and Concepts.* Students demonstrate a sound understanding of technology concepts, systems and operations.

▶

Learning Objectives   Students will know and be able to

- Write short news reports about academic learning activities to regularly post on a classroom blog.
- Compose captions, photos, graphs, and drawings to post on a classroom blog.
- Download photos from digital cameras, insert video clips, and scan text and drawings into a classroom blog.
- Write in different genres for a classroom blog, including factual news reports, entertainment reviews, announcements, comics, opinion pieces, and advertisements.

Technology Uses   The lesson uses computers, word processing software, scanners, and a class blog as key technology tools.

Minimal Technology	Infusion of Technology
Students read and view media such as newspapers and television to find examples of news reporting.	Students read and view media such as websites and blogs to find examples of news reporting.
Students write news reports using paper-and-pencil technologies.	Students write news reports using computers with word processing software.
Students share classroom news through a paper-based newspaper. Families read the classroom newspaper but typically do not respond to what they read.	Students share classroom news through a Web-based blog. Families read the classroom newspaper and use the interactive capabilities of a blog to respond to what they read.

Evaluation   This lesson uses multiple forms of evaluation, including rubrics based on English/language arts standards for different writing genres and technology standards for Web-based publication.

LESSON PLAN DESCRIPTION

Introduction

"Blogging the News from Room 145" uses computers, word processing software, scanners, and a class blog for students to share their academic and creative news with an audience of family members, other students, and teachers. The lesson demonstrates the differences between the old media of newspapers and television and the new media of websites and blogs.

Lesson Focus

This lesson plan addresses two realities of classroom teaching. First, students are newsmakers. Every day, they are learning and doing something new—writing, drawing, calculating, observing, and concluding thoughts about topics they are studying in math, science, history, and language arts. Yet in many schools the news about day-to-day student learning is rarely shared with anyone other than the classroom teacher. Family members, other students and teachers, and even students themselves fail to note the compelling learning experiences that are happening all the time in school. They take for granted what is truly extraordinary, the changes occurring in themselves.

Second, many teachers write a weekly classroom newsletter summarizing the learning activities of students. These newsletters are typically paper documents shared with families, school administrators, other teachers, and the students themselves. Less commonly, teacher-written classroom

▶

newsletters are posted on a classroom or teacher website. Rarely are students directly involved in the process of writing and designing these classroom newsletters for various audiences.

In this lesson plan, as a way to learn about news writing, Internet communication technologies, and the role of an audience in the writing process, students are directly involved in creating, designing, posting, and publishing the academic learning news from their classroom. Unlike a school newspaper that is written and copied on paper and distributed by hand, a classroom news blog provides an easily updatable, regularly evolving electronic record of what is happening academically in a classroom.

Additionally, a classroom news blog invites readers—family members as well as other teachers and students—to write back to student bloggers, just as newspapers invite readers to "talk back" to the paper by emailing reporters, columnists, and editors. A class news blog gives readers the opportunity to comment on and participate in students' learning experiences, while giving students the experience of an on-the-Web, interactive exchange with readers.

Lesson Design—Minimal Technology

A minimal technology version of this lesson plan features a classroom newspaper that is assembled and copied by teachers for distribution to students and their families. Alternatively, students assist teachers in creating the newspaper by copying and collating the final publication. In either case, such newspapers are paper documents composed of writing and drawing by students along with a letter to families written by the teacher.

Another version of a minimal technology lesson plan is organized around a daily classroom meeting time where teacher and students share the news with each other. Students write and draw their news reports using paper and pencil, and then read and show their work at the class meeting. Teachers may archive these reports so students can read them later in the school year. However, since it is not easy to organize and save student papers day after day, in many cases, the student news reports are unavailable after a week or so.

A paper classroom newspaper can be an especially labor-intensive activity for teachers, who must do much of the work of newspaper production, including layout, copying, and distribution. Even a daily classroom news meeting takes considerable planning by teachers in order to fit such a meeting into the regular schedule of curriculum time and related school activities.

LESSON ACTIVITIES USING TECHNOLOGY

1. ***Decide on Categories for Your News Blog.*** To begin this lesson plan using technology, it is important to decide with your students what categories you will have on your classroom blog. Categories, like the table of contents in a book, organize material into easily identifiable areas. Readers can consult the categories as a way to navigate around the site and locate material they want to read or view.

2. ***Use a Newspaper as a Model.*** Because a classroom blog is a collaborative activity, ask your students what kind of categories they want to create for their website. Younger students may not know how to make that decision. One idea to guide them is to use a local or national newspaper as a model for how those publications create different sections for readers. Most newspapers have feature stories, an entertainment section, sports pages, an editorial page, a place for letters to the editor and opinion columns, comics, product advertisements, help wanted listings, and other categories. A classroom blog might feature a version of such categories and then invite students to write material for each section.

3. ***Use Academic Curriculum Topics in Your Blog.*** Formatting by major academic curriculum areas and topics is a second way for students and teachers to choose categories for a classroom

▶

blog. An elementary school class might have sections on its blog for mathematics, science, history, and language arts as well as special features that the students decide to include. A middle or high school class might organize its blog by major subtopics in one curriculum area; for example, a class on U.S. government could have separate blog areas for its major areas of study—the president, Congress, the Supreme Court, political parties, and electoral politics.

4. *Give Roles to Students.* Giving students individually meaningful roles in writing and producing is part of the successful publishing of your news blog. Rotate the students through each of the roles on a reporting team so that everyone has an opportunity to experience each function. As the blog develops over time with the addition of new topics, students can choose different roles.

5. *Organize Curriculum Teams.* To begin, you might establish separate teams for each curriculum area—math reporters, science reporters, history reporters, and language arts reporters. Team members then have separate roles within the team, such as writers, editors, designers, and scanners. Ideally, all the students will serve on more than one curriculum area team during the year. Collectively, the team decides what material they want to post on their blog. The writers are then responsible for creating the initial draft of each posting, while the editors and designers ensure that the post is clearly and artistically done. The scanners have the responsibility of using computers to post the final copy on the blog.

6. *Encourage Talking Back to Your News Blog.* Once material has been posted on your classroom news blog, you have the potential for more exciting learning to happen when readers (particularly members of student families) respond in writing to what they have read. When readers "talk back" to your blog, students get important feedback about their work and they can respond to the responses as well. Such exchanges between student writers and outside-of-the-school readers expand the way blogs can be used instructionally by teachers. Getting readers to respond takes some advance planning by teachers. You want to avoid a situation where readers state, "Nice job!" or "Good work!" Such comments, while seemingly pleasant to read, offer no substantive feedback to students and establish no basis for further communication between student writers and blog readers.

7. *Review Key Steps in Talking Back.* There are two key steps that you can take to promote successful talking back to your classroom news blog.

   • Encourage families, other teachers, and students in other classrooms to write back with substantive observations and meaningful comments about what the students have posted.

   • Encourage student writers to create posts that invite comments from readers. A science news report might include questions to readers about the topic or a math report might feature instructions to readers about how to solve particular kinds of problems. The idea is to give readers a reason to respond to student writers.

8. *Teach about Old and New Media.* News, by definition, is information that is shared with people who want to know it. People read newspapers, watch television, listen to radio, and scan the Internet to learn about what is happening in their community, nation, and world. News reporters are writers who record the news in words and pictures and share it through multiple forms of media. Sociologists reference the terms *old media* and *new media*. Old media refers to traditional sources of information such as newspapers, magazines, and television. New media refers to Internet-based sources of information such as websites, blogs, wikis, streaming video, and more. A classroom blog teaches students about the differences between old and new media. Clearly, news that is presented on the Internet via websites, blogs, and other new technologies is a markedly different experience for readers than reading newspapers, watching television, or listening to the radio.

▶

ANALYSIS AND EXTENSIONS

1. Name two features you find useful about this lesson.
2. Name two areas for extension or improvement of this lesson.
3. How successfully has information technology been integrated into the lesson?
4. How might students be even more involved in designing, using, and evaluating technology in the lesson?

CHAPTER SUMMARY

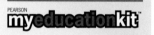
FOCUS QUESTION 1: How can teachers use communications technologies as teaching and learning tools?

- Communication technologies provide ways for teachers to connect with their students, promote meaningful learning, and extend academics beyond the confines of regular school time.

- Every teacher has choices to make when creating the type of computer-mediated communication system they intend to use professionally.

- Synchronous communications happen in real time (as in an instant messaging conversation) whereas asynchronous communications include an interruption or delay between responses (as in an email correspondence or an electronic response to a blog posting).

- Teachers have five reasons to use electronic communications: (1) teaching strategies, (2) information sharing, (3) community building, (4) publishing student work, and (5) energizing student writing.

FOCUS QUESTION 2: How can teachers use email or instant messaging to foster information exchanges with and among students?

- Children and adolescents are the largest users of email and instant messaging (IM) technologies.

- Many teachers use email as a way to communicate with students, families, and professional colleagues.

- Fewer teachers use instant messaging because the kind of informal language found in IM can be misunderstood or misused.

FOCUS QUESTION 3: How can teachers use a website or blog to improve teaching and learning?

- Websites and blogs are emerging as one of the most important ways for teachers to communicate with students, families, and colleagues.

- There are three basic types of education-related blogs: (1) "official face" blogs, (2) single-purpose blogs, and (3) active learning blogs.

- Teachers have three options for creating their own website or blog: (1) a do-it-yourself option, (2) a commercially available option, or (3) an open source option.

FOCUS QUESTION 4: How can teachers use wikis to promote collaborative learning?

- Wikis are Web pages that are created and maintained by multiple computer users.

- In schools, wikis enable collaborative learning environments where teachers and students work together to investigate topics and share information.

- A wikitext is a book or booklet that teachers and students create together as part of a class study of a topic.

KEY TERMS

Asynchronous communications
Blogs (weblogs)
Collaborative learning environments
Computer-mediated communication
Communication technologies
Digital image scanner
Educational networking
Email (electronic mail)
Instant messaging (IM)

Microblogging
Online discussions
Social networking
Standards wiki
Synchronous communications
Teacher or classroom websites
Textspeak
Wikis
Wikitext

ACTIVITIES FOR YOUR TEACHER PORTFOLIO

1. ORGANIZING CLASSES FOR ACTIVE LEARNING

John Goodlad's classic study of American education, *A Place Called School,* published in the mid-1980s, concluded that at every grade level, from the youngest elementary grade to the senior year of high school, students spend large amounts of their classroom time passively listening to teacher lectures and explanations (1984, p. 107). Teacher lecturing accounts for 18 percent of the time in early elementary grades, 20 percent in upper elementary grades, 22 percent in junior high/middle school, and 25 percent of the time in high school. Discussions between teachers and students, by contrast, amount to only 5 percent of the time at all levels while simulations and role-plays occur less than 1 percent of the time.

- How do you think teachers can design classes that rely less on lecturing and more on active learning by students?

- What teaching methods do you think will foster greater student engagement and why?

- What do you view as the strengths and drawbacks of discussions, role-plays, and small-group work using multimedia technology?

2. ONLINE READING REACTION ASSIGNMENTS FOR STUDENTS

Answer the questions about the following online reading reaction assignment. Each was given by teachers in an upper elementary school or middle/high school setting in science or history where reading outside sources is a key part of the learning experience for students.

Assignment 1. Read an article from the class reading list and respond to its main ideas or key themes with an online posting.

- What potential advantages and drawbacks do you see with this assignment?
- Do you think that students are likely to invest time and energy on this assignment? Why? Why not?

Assignment 2. Write a draft of a news report, letter to the editor, or a review of an article from the class reading list. Post it online so three other students can respond to your ideas. Revise the paper based on the comments you receive before submitting it to the instructor. In addition, read and respond to two entries by class members you have not given feedback to within the past month.

- What potential advantages and drawbacks do you see with this assignment?
- Do you think that students are likely to invest time and energy on this assignment? Why? Why not?

3. ANALYZING INSTANT MESSAGING AND MICROBLOGGING

Instant messaging (IM) and microblogging enjoy enormous popularity among adolescents today. Answer the following questions, and consider how you think adolescents would respond.

- What kind of technology are IM and microblogging? Usually called communication technology because of their capacity to connect people electronically, are they also educational technology?
- Explain how IM and microblogging serve as information technology when teachers and students use them in instruction and academic discussions.
- How are IM and microblogging like or unlike the printing press, telephone, television, or other important historical communications revolutions?
- How does language online differ from Standard English writing or speaking?

GROWING AND LEADING WITH TECHNOLOGY

This activity offers an opportunity to grow as a teacher and learn to lead with technology. Begin by reviewing the Chapter 8 Learning Goal and New Technologies listed in the chart at the start of the chapter. Then read the following actual classroom scenario and consider how technologies discussed in Chapter 8 might be integrated into the lesson. Follow-up steps to this activity can be completed on MyEducationKit.

MICHELLE'S BOOK REPORT LESSON

Michelle assigns monthly book reports to every member of her fourth-grade class. The students read a book, write a summary of the book's story and themes, and read their written report aloud to their classmates as part of Book Report Day, the last school day of the month. Michelle varies the genres and types of books from month to month so the students read fiction and nonfiction throughout the year. As the months pass, the students become unexcited by the assignment, showing less enthusiasm for book reading and writing the report while being distracted and disinterested during the read-alouds.

For Michelle, the book report activity integrates the communication skills of reading, writing, and speaking as set forth in the school's English/language arts curriculum. To create interest in and commitment to the reports, she lets students choose their books from a list

she has prepared along with the school's librarian. By asking everyone to read their reports in class, Michelle hopes to entice students to read more books. While the student reports are often read in a monotone and can be difficult to hear, Michelle sees them as ways for students to practice their oral communication skills.

- Using the technologies discussed in this chapter, how would you propose Michelle integrate technology into her monthly book report activity in ways that promote student interest and engagement while still practicing the skills of reading, writing, and speaking?

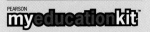

9 Creating and Sharing Information with Multimedia Technologies

Cameras are in nearly every phone. Tools for recording and editing audio and video are getting cheaper and more ubiquitous. Collaborative sites make it easy to post and share files. Network access is getting faster for more and more people. All this means that more people can make and distribute their own multimedia work.

—Tony Sindelar & Fred Zinn, *Emerging Technologies for Teaching,* June 2007

CHAPTER LEARNING GOAL

Multimedia Presentations

- Using presentation tools and multimedia technologies with students

CONNECTING to the NETS

NETS-T

2 Design and Develop Digital Age Learning Experiences and Assessments

3 Model Digital Age Work and Learning

NETS-S

2 Communication and Collaboration

NEW TECHNOLOGIES

- PowerPoint presentation software
- Multimedia projectors
- Interactive whiteboards
- Videos and DVDs
- Video sharing websites
- Webcasts
- Digital storytelling and digital art making
- Digital cameras
- Digital video recorders
- Digital video editing software
- iPods
- Podcasts and vodcasts

CHAPTER OVERVIEW

Chapter 9 moves the focus of attention from information communication in the previous chapter to information presentation using PowerPoint presentation software, videos and DVDs, digital cameras, movie-making software, and podcasts/vodcasts as tools for immersing students in creating and sharing information communication through multimedia tools.

The chapter builds on the NETS-T Standard 2, Part a, a mandate for teachers to create learning experiences "that incorporate digital tools and resources that promote student learning and creativity" and NETS-T Standard 3, which calls for teachers to collaborate with students and others to support success and innovation in school. It also addresses NETS-S Standard 2, which calls for students to learn ways to interact and work together electronically.

FOCUS QUESTIONS

1. What is multimedia technology and how can teachers use it to effectively create and share visual information dynamically in their teaching?

2. How can teachers create PowerPoint presentations for maximum teaching potential and learning impact?

3. How can teachers use video resources in their teaching?

4. How can teachers and students make their own classroom movies using digital video cameras and movie-making software?

5. How can teachers integrate podcasts and vodcasts into their teaching?

"Lights, Camera, History!" announced a class of fifth-grade history moviemakers. Using a digital video camera and their own talents as writers and performers, they began making mini-movies about topics from the school's required American history curriculum, including the indigenous peoples of the Americas, Christopher Columbus's voyages, the emergence of the slave trade, the Boston Tea Party, Paul Revere's ride, and the writing of the Constitution.

This history video project started when a teacher in a local school asked her students to write and perform historical skits as a way to enliven the study of early American history. We added a suggestion that the students make video movies of their performances. The teacher and students agreed, and soon everyone was engaged in an exciting new learning experience with writing, social studies, and film.

For their first mini-movie, the students created scenes about Christopher Columbus (his birth, his initial appearance before the king and queen of Spain, sailing across the Atlantic to the New World, landfall in the Caribbean, encounters with indigenous peoples, and his triumphant and rich return to Spain).

In groups, the students wrote narration for each scene, incorporating historical facts with their own creative interpretations of events. They made costumes and props, rehearsed their lines, and staged their skits, all before turning on the camera to record the final performance. Once the skits had been filmed, the class unanimously voted to view their productions during lunch. Connecting a digital camera to a digital projector displayed the videos on a large screen in the classroom.

Producing history videos was a classwide collaborative effort. Rather than students passively watching while adults filmed the skits, everyone had a meaningful role to play: a scene setter introduced each skit to the camera, a stage manager announced quiet on the set, a camera operator recorded the action, the teacher or a student coached the volume of the actors' voices, a technician ensured that the power cords remained connected to the electrical outlet, a stage crew moved materials between scenes, and the actors played the parts and improvised when lines were forgotten. The teacher supervised those students who knew how to operate a digital camera, and those students in turn explained the steps and tutored their peers who had not used a digital video camera before. Everyone who wanted to film had the opportunity to do so.

Without reminders to do so, the students took seriously their roles as sincere performers and respectful audience members. "Quiet on the set" meant just that. Roles were practiced earnestly and performed well. The students were eager and willing to try other types of writing for filming as well, such as commercials for historically themed products and places. There were outtakes and additions to their videos. After the school year ended, the teacher told us that making mini-movies had not only helped the students learn about American history, but promoted a spirit of positive participation and cooperative teamwork that lasted long after the history skits were completed.

Incorporating multimedia in the classroom can motivate student interest in subjects and encourage young people to develop their own skills with using various technology.

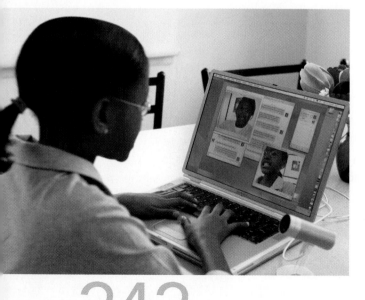

The opening vignette introduces this chapter's learning goal—how teachers and students can use multimedia technologies to create and present educational information. Teaching in schools involves a continual two-way process of information creation and presentation in which teachers provide information to students through lectures, discussions, and interactive instructional methods. Students provide information to teachers through verbal responses, personal writing, group projects, and many other forms of interactions. Multimedia technologies offer ways to convey this information creatively, catching the attention of listeners and viewers to make new material understood and vividly remembered.

Multimedia means "the presentation of material using both words and pictures" (Mayer, 2001, p. 2). "Words" refers to spoken and printed text while "pictures" includes photos, graphs, charts, illustrations, video material, and other visual images. Multimedia technologies include those tools that use words and pictures and those that integrate sound, voice, video, and animation.

Multimedia Technologies in Classrooms Today

Multimedia means combining multiple media—text, data, voice, picture, and video—in a single application or technology to establish a high-quality interaction between the user and the program. Multimedia in education occurs when multiple media supports teaching and learning in classrooms (Mayer, 2001; Moreno & Valdez, 2005). Familiar common examples include Power-Point presentations that combine words, pictures, and sounds; academically based CD-ROMs, DVDs, and video tapes; television programs, podcasts, and vodcasts downloadable to your computer, cell phone, or iPod; and concert performances combining video, light shows, and music with large screen simulcasts.

Multimedia in education rests on the assumption that student learning will be enhanced if more than one mode of learning is used in teaching situations. There are significant differences between single-mode learning and multimodal learning. Single-mode learning means that students receive information in one form; for example, a teacher talks. **Multimodal learning** happens when teachers combine spoken words with visuals or written text with audio or utilize simulations and models. Reviewing a decade of research on learning, the authors of the report "Multimodal Learning through Media" found: "Students engaged in learning that incorporates multimodal designs, on average, outperform students who learn using traditional approaches with single modes" (Metiri Group, 2008, p. 13).

Figure 9.1, taken from "Multimodal Learning through Media," shows the widely different impacts on learning gains for basic and higher-order skills within interactive and noninteractive learning situations using multiple ways to present information to students. The gains are measured against how students perform in traditional, single-mode learning situations. While noninteractive multimodal learning (boxes I and IV that include using texts with illustrations or listening to lectures with graphics) produced gains, interactive multimodal situations (box III that includes simulations, modeling, and student-to-student interactions) produced the greatest results (Metiri Group, 2008). In summary, concluded the report authors, there is an educational advantage to using multimedia, including highly interactive Web 2.0 technologies, for teaching and learning in schools.

Schools have tended to emphasize single-media, noninteractive learning. A biology teacher may show a video clip of a science event but not connect it to science-based websites or student-made movies of science events occurring in the school's backyard. An English teacher might play an audio tape or show a DVD of poets reading poetry aloud but not record students doing the same thing. When teachers incorporate multiple interactive media regularly into instruction, it

VOICES
from the classroom

A high school English teacher explained how she used video clips to engage students in the study of Arthur Miller's play, The Crucible, and its connection to the McCarthy era in American politics in the 1950s.

I launched my lesson by asking the class to generate a list of key themes in *The Crucible*. Then I introduced a video clip of a House Un-American Activities Committee hearing in 1953. I had originally considered having the students act out sections of the transcript, and I liked the idea because it would get students actively engaged with a primary source. But then I reconsidered the power of the image and, specifically, video. The students had never heard Senator [Joseph] McCarthy's voice before, or felt his presence in a courtroom. While the students watched the clip, I put three questions up on the board for them to respond to. The students were very receptive to answering these questions after the clip. Then we shifted to how *The Crucible* was an allegory of the Red Scare. I asked for volunteers to find quotes from the play that they found particularly enlightening and read them aloud to the class dramatically.

FIGURE 9.1   Impact of Multimodal Learning

The Impact of Multimodal Learning in Comparison to Traditional, Unimodal Learning

Findings Reported Separately for Basic Skills and Higher Order Skills, and by the Inclusion or Absence of Interactivity

	Basic Skills	Higher Order Skills
Interactive Multimodal Learning Includes simulations, modeling, and real world experiences; typically includes collaboration with peers, but could be an individual interacting with resource	**II.** Percentile* increase for average student +9	**III.** Percentile** increase for average student +32
Noninteractive Multimodal Learning Includes using text with illustrations, watching and listening to animations, listening to lectures with graphics on devices such as whiteboards, etc.; typically involves individualized learning, or whole-group work that includes listening, observing, or reading, but little to no interaction	**I.** Percentile* increase for average student +21	**IV.** Percentile** increase for average student +20

Average Student

*Percentile Ranking on Retention of Basic Skills

**Percentile Ranking on Higher Order or Transfer Skills

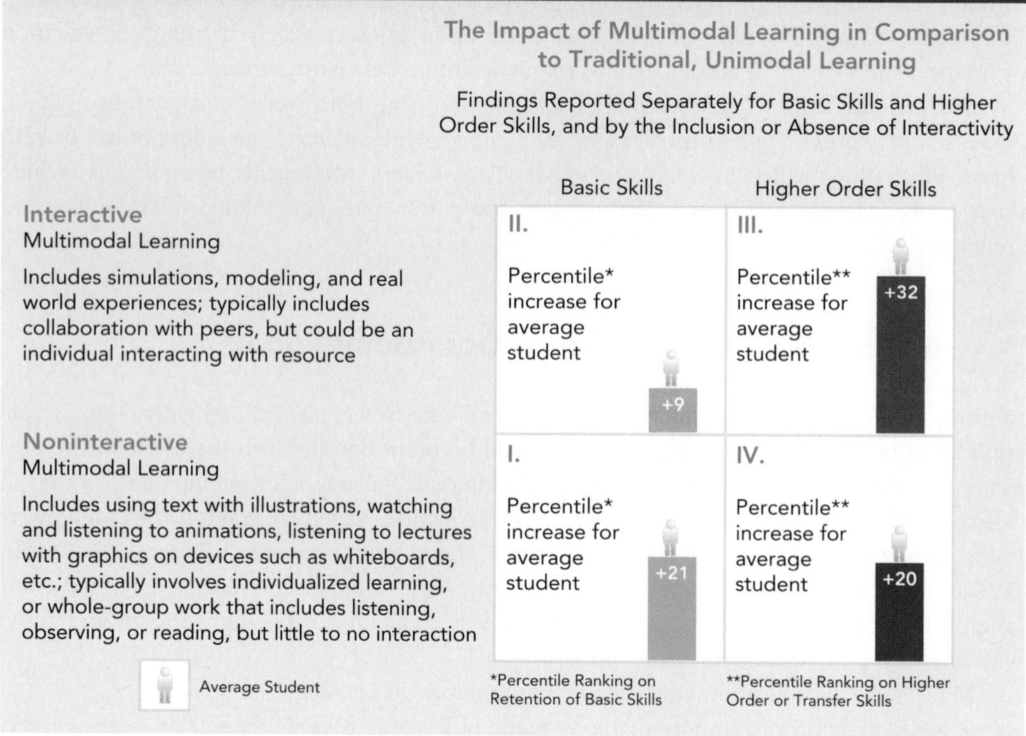

Source: Courtesy of Charles Fadel, Cisco Systems.

changes how students experience learning in schools. Ideally, by presenting educational material in words, pictures, sound, and animation, teachers can take "advantage of the full capacity of humans for processing information" (Mayer, 2001, p. 4).

A Multimedia Classroom

To help understand the potential of multimedia technologies, examine their impact on teaching and learning in a classroom. Table 9.1 lists the educational or instructional technologies found in two classrooms: an older, noncomputer technology classroom and a newer, computer technology classroom.

The noncomputer technology classroom reflects how classrooms looked technologically before the computer revolution—and how some classrooms still look today. The technologies were functional, but limited in the amount of multimedia content they could deliver. Imagine how a teacher might present the concept of the water cycle (see Figure 9.2) in a noncomputer technology classroom.

To illustrate the interconnected processes of precipitation, evaporation, and condensation, a teacher might display a poster or draw on a chalkboard, whiteboard, or overhead projector while discussing the cycle with the class. Even though these displays involve multiple media—the teacher's voice and the visual image—the presentation is relatively static. Visual images about the water cycle change only as the teacher changes them. And once materials are erased from the board, the teacher and the students cannot easily return to them for further discussion and review. Even using a VCR to watch a science program about the water cycle on the television is a largely one-way experience where students are viewing material that someone else has produced for them to see.

By contrast, in the computer technology classroom, the opportunities for multimedia learning about the water cycle are dramatically changed. Multiple forms of media can combine text, voice, images, and sound. Students could view a PowerPoint presentation on the scientific processes

TABLE 9.1 Instructional Technologies in Two Classrooms

Noncomputer technology classroom	• Chalkboard or whiteboard
	• Photocopies of material from print sources (books, magazines, etc.)
	• Overhead projector and screen
	• 35mm slide projector
	• Television with a VCR
	• Handheld microphone
Computer technology classroom	• Interactive whiteboard
	• Computers with Internet access
	• Educational software with multimedia applications (PowerPoint, MovieMaker, etc.)
	• Digital projector and screen
	• Digital cameras or camcorders
	• Digital voice recorders
	• Surround sound amplification system

featuring text, image, and animation. The teacher could use a digital projector to show an interactive Internet website to the whole class on a large screen or students could use computers in the classroom to read and respond to online resources individually or in small groups. Students' experiments with the water cycle, such as those in the rainscapes lesson plan presented in Chapter 3, could be filmed with digital cameras and the resulting photos or short movies shown to the entire class.

These ideas, and many others made possible by computer technology, extend from the use of multimedia presentations to support teaching and learning. In the rest of this chapter, we look at specific multimedia technologies to see how they extend teaching choices in new and exciting directions.

Using PowerPoint in Your Teaching

PowerPoint, a multimedia presentation software package, is a standard feature on many of today's computers. Millions of copies are in circulation, and the tool is widely used in schools. For teachers, who must continually present information to students in ways that will engage and inspire, knowing the strengths and weaknesses of PowerPoint is essential. It should be noted that PowerPoint is not the only presentation software program, just the most common. Open Office Impress, Keynote, and Corel Presentations produce high-quality presentations as well.

At its most basic level, PowerPoint computerizes presentations that were previously done with lighted transparencies on an

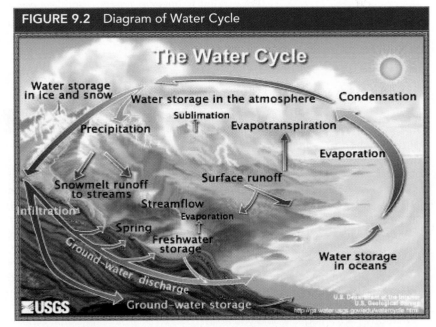

FIGURE 9.2 Diagram of Water Cycle

Source: U.S. Geologic Survey (http://ga.water.usgs.gov/edu/watercycle.html).

overhead projector or picture slides rotating through a slide projector. By loading text, data, and images into PowerPoint, teachers produce slides for visual information displays featuring colorful graphics, pop-up or slide-in windows, and many other attention-getting techniques. Moving beyond the basics, teachers can transform still photographs and scanned images into movie-like viewing experiences by adding narration features and text.

Digital projectors and interactive whiteboards, two technology tools that support PowerPoint's visual learning capabilities, are described in Tech Tool 9.1 (pp. 248–249). A **digital projector** (also known as a "multimedia projector" or simply a "projector") is a device that projects images from a computer to a large screen or other external viewing surface. An **interactive whiteboard** is a touch-sensitive wallboard that displays computer images on the board's surface. Unlike a chalkboard, teachers and students do not actually write on the whiteboard; rather they use fingers or other tools to press on the board's surface, causing the computer to project an image of the "writing" onto the board. Whiteboards are sometimes paired with student participation or audience response systems, a new technology discussed in Chapter 11.

PowerPoint's features are useful for teachers at every grade level, although there are some disadvantages to be considered (see Table 9.2). With PowerPoint, you can make slideshows of academic material and include text, pictures, charts, graphs, audio, video, and animations (Lewis, 2008). Live Web links can be inserted into presentations. You can create a basic presentation, and then shorten or lengthen it to fit the time available by masking some of the slides so they do not show or unmasking them so they do. To help remember what to say during a presentation, you can write notes on your slides that are visible only on your computer. Slides can be printed as a handout or put on a class website where students can view them whenever they want.

Students, too, enjoy using presentation software as part of school assignments. The Speak Up 2006 national survey of more than 230,000 K–12 students found that creating presentations and movies on the computer was a favorite school work activity, along with Internet research and playing educational games (Project Tomorrow, 2006).

Tufte's Critique of PowerPoint

PowerPoint has detractors as well as admirers. In a short pamphlet, *The Cognitive Style of Power-Point,* information theorist Edward R. Tufte (2003, p. 3) argued that the "ready-made designs" or templates that come with this software "usually weaken verbal and spatial reasoning, and almost always corrupt statistical analysis." In terms particularly relevant to teachers, Tufte argued that PowerPoint is *"presenter-oriented,"* and *"not content-oriented, not audience-oriented"* (2003, p. 4). Successful teaching involves skillfully weaving interactive, engaging approaches to presentation with substantive academic content that matches the needs and interests of students.

TABLE 9.2   Advantages and Disadvantages of PowerPoint

Advantages	Disadvantages
Provides short summaries of key points in a lecture or reading assignment.	Cannot take the place of more in-depth discussions and analysis.
Gives a visual dimension to class presentations.	Some students may "tune out" during a PowerPoint presentation.
Easy to use and available on most school computers.	Teachers need to spend time entering the material before showing it.
Text can be combined with pictures, charts, graphs, and other images in interesting and entertaining ways.	Computer screens may contain so much information that students become distracted from main ideas.
What other advantages would you add?	*What other disadvantages would you add?*

In Tufte's (2003, p. 26) view, the standard features of PowerPoint software create a "distinctive, definite, well-enforced, and widely-practiced cognitive style that is contrary to serious thinking." For example, an over-reliance on bullet points reduces key ideas to simple phrases. Most slides contain no more than 40 words, about "8 seconds of silent reading material." The narrative or flow of a presentation is broken into small fragments and invariably delivered in a hierarchical speaker-to-audience format similar to the way large bureaucratic organizations communicate information.

Colorful decorations, what Tufte calls "Phluff," signal a form of information presentation akin to a commercial sales pitch rather than a thoughtful discussion and analysis. Likening PowerPoint to a dangerous prescription drug, Tufte concludes that the system's side effects include "making us stupid, degrading the quality and credibility of our communications, turning us into bores, wasting our colleagues' time" (Tufte, 2003, p. 24).

Tufte (2003, p. 24) offers three main suggestions for improving the quality of electronic presentations:

- Present meaningful content that matters to your audience; "audience boredom is usually a content failure, not a decoration failure."
- "Use PowerPoint as a projector for showing low-resolution color images, graphics, and videos."
- Include paper handouts in your presentation as a way to "effectively show text, numbers, data, graphics and images."

YOUR JUDGMENT MATTERS

As you consider Tufte's critique, recall your own experiences receiving or creating PowerPoint presentations in relation to the following questions:

- Have you found PowerPoint presentations to be largely unengaging or have you consistently viewed interesting and memorable presentations?
- Has the use of PowerPoint in class promoted or interfered with teacher–student interactions?
- Do you agree or disagree with Tufte's comments about the negative effects of PowerPoint, or do you see a possible middle ground?
- What other strategies would you recommend to make PowerPoint presentations more engaging and interactive for students?

Strategies for Using PowerPoint with Your Students

Technology educators think about PowerPoint in terms of **information presentation design** (Zinn, 2007)—the arrangement of written and pictorial information so that its intended audiences can easily and clearly understand it. Information presentation design is a subset of the larger field of **graphic design,** which is the process of arranging type and images to communicate information visually.

Information presentation design informs the ways you present academic content so students remember it and ask questions about what you are teaching. Every class, every lesson plan, and every instructional activity is an occasion of information presentation design. PowerPoint, used well, communicates information memorably to students.

When using PowerPoint, it is important to ask two fundamental information presentation design questions:

- Who is my audience?
- What do I want my audience to leave knowing or remembering?

Without a focus on your students and what you want them to learn, it is easy to get lost in and spend too much time with the mechanics of the PowerPoint tool itself. It can be fun to create presentations with lots of moving and colorful images, supported by sound and video, but those devices may not always promote learning for students. To learn successfully, students need to be engaged with the material you are presenting and be able to restate the main ideas of your presentation in their own words. PowerPoint presentations succeed as a teaching tool when the visual experience is memorable, arouses students' curiosity and involvement, and promotes active discussion, writing, and reflection about the content.

Creating interactive PowerPoint presentations involves the following strategies.

Make Visual Presentations Interactive, Varied, and Memorable. Expecting students to only read slides while a teacher lectures minimizes the potential of the PowerPoint

PEARSON
myeducationkit

Go to the Assignments and Activities section of Chapter 9 in MyEducationKit and complete the video activity entitled "Multimedia Software Supports Instruction." As you watch the video and answer the accompanying questions, consider how PowerPoint can help engage students' interest.

Digital projectors and interactive whiteboards are two technology tools that expand how PowerPoint and visual learning can be used across the grade levels. Both are student-engaging types of information presentation technology. Connecting either tool to a computer or video device transforms the small screen of a single machine into a classroom theatre-like learning environment. With these machines, the experience of a PowerPoint presentation on the computer is dramatically transformed for both students (the viewers) and teachers (the presenters).

 Digital Projectors

In a classroom, a digital projector makes it possible for everyone to see in large size on a big screen what only a few people would be able to see when gathered around a desktop or laptop computer. Students not only view what is projected from the computer to the screen by the digital projector, but they use those visual images as a springboard for in-class discussion, analysis, writing, and further study (Moulton, 2007). The passivity of a teacher lecture and the singularity of students using their own computer are replaced by a highly visible public text to which anyone and everyone in the class may respond.

Some K–12 classrooms are now equipped with a digital projector mounted in the ceiling near the center of the room in front of a whiteboard or a pull-down screen and hard-wired into a teacher or classroom computer. Alternatively, a digital projector might be placed on a rolling cart with a computer to be moved in front of a screen for use. Teachers without a digital projection device achieve similar visual presentation results by connecting a computer to a large screen television and projecting the computer images onto the TV screen.

Unlike on an overhead projector, the images do not have to be static or moved by hand. Web or video resources are seen as they appear, with the projector operator controlling the speed at which images are viewed. A class can move through a website at their own pace, in a nonlinear manner, viewing still or moving images as desired. Also, unlike a film or video tape, the person running the projector may freeze the displayed image or zoom in and out, or even go to a blank screen if that is what is needed at the moment.

In high school and middle school classrooms, a digital projector serves as a useful discussion management tool. While students discuss a topic, someone takes notes on the computer, highlighting key concepts and ideas. That material is immediately transferred to the big screen for everyone to view. Students hear and read the information. The electronic summary is posted on the class website or printed in hard copy for everyone to read for review.

When choosing a digital projector, consider the type of lighting configurations you want the machine to display. Digital projectors are defined by their lumens or ability to be clear in varying degrees of ambient light. More lumens, while expensive, improve image and audience response to the machine.

tool. In the story below, a student teacher describes how he used PowerPoint to capture the attention of high school students in a lesson about the American Revolution.

A Student Teacher Uses PowerPoint

I devoted slides to the role of women and Native Americans, showing how the former served in the war and how the latter still had agency for their own actions at this point. I tried to use slides of artwork whenever possible, for example, portraits of Joseph Brant

Good quality digital projectors cost almost $1000, and replacements of projector bulbs (called projector lamps) are between $200 to $500. However, teachers have found that the digital projector's daily utility for teaching and learning is worth the expense.

Interactive Whiteboards

An interactive whiteboard and a computer can transform classroom learning. A teacher showing a PowerPoint presentation or visiting a website can add notes or symbols directly to the screen while teaching, in effect modifying and expanding the lecture as it happens while making the comments and ideas of the students a genuine part of class content. At the end of class, the annotated pages can be saved to the teacher's computer and then distributed to the students via a class or school website. For example, as they read aloud the original text of the Declaration of Independence, one high school history teacher asked students to translate unfamiliar words and concepts into modern-day language. The students then came to the front of the room and added their translations directly on the whiteboard screen. Changing the text in such a visual manner to have for future reference enlarged everyone's understanding of the Declaration as one of the nation's founding documents.

Teachers who use interactive whiteboards find themselves amazed by the possibilities. One high school English teacher noted: "Suddenly, I possessed the means to take the tools of my teaching—class discussion, essay writing, and literature—and launch them into a different dimension, a different space" (Rochette, 2007, p. 44). She could now prepare background material on the novels she was teaching, save it for later use, import digital images to add to her PowerPoint presentations, and teach students how to engage in close reading of literary text. In class, she began highlighting and annotating passages on the screen, filling the electronic pages with underlines, arrows, circles, and other visual indicators that identified key ideas, important quotations, memorable imagery, and parts of speech.

Viewing the material displayed on the interactive whiteboards, students could then draft their own analyses of the literature, a shift from asking students to write on their own without the benefit of visual summaries of class discussion and collective notes. The quality of student writing improved, becoming more thoughtful and detailed. Next, she started using the whiteboard as a way to discuss photographs, paintings, and other visual sources, generating even more ways to "appeal to the visual and digital intelligences of students" (Rochette, 2007, p. 45). You can find more information about using interactive whiteboards in the classroom from the Resource Materials and Technology Center for the Deaf and Hard of Hearing (www.fsdb.k12.fl.us/rmc/tutorials/whiteboards.html).

of the Mohawks, Margaret Gage, and others. I spent considerable time on *Washington Crossing the Delaware*, trying to get students to see that these familiar images have agendas to push.

I asked, "How many of you go boating in the summer in a rowboat or canoe?" Some hands raised.

"Do you spend a lot of time standing like this?"

No? "Would all that ice in the water make you more likely to sit down?"

Then, "Why do you think the artist used these poses?"

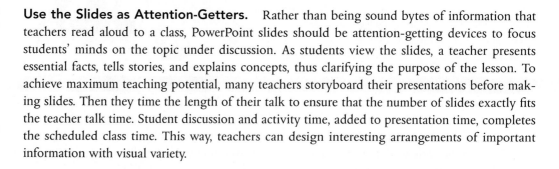

The student teacher wanted to reveal little-known historical information to his students. This was accomplished by projecting compelling images in a large, easy-to-see format that could not be ignored. Each slide was chosen to stimulate critical thinking and thoughtful discussion.

Use Visual Text To Generate Class Discussion. Students respond actively to visual images that convey academic content. A history teacher might show primary sources while the class is discussing the interpretation of past events (Maxwell, 2007). Alternatively, for a lesson on the writing of the Constitution, portraits of Thomas Jefferson, James Madison, and other key Federalists and Anti-Federalists bring faces to the historical facts that reveal clues about the socioeconomic status, education, and professions of the Founders. Similarly, the visual results of science experiments or mathematical problems gain immediacy and promote discussion when seen in large format on a big screen.

Promote Visual Analysis of Discussion Topics. Historian Marla Miller provides a wonderful example of this idea as she presents the history of women and work in colonial American society. First she displays a portrait of a Puritan woman and child from the mid-1660s and asks students to react to what they see. Then she reveals what the Worcester (Massachusetts) Art Museum discovered after its computer analysis of the painting—the portrait was altered between 1671 and 1674. Original elements that suggest a more middle class lifestyle (expensive black fabric, a book suggesting leisure time) had been painted over to present a more austere appearance in keeping with Puritan beliefs of the proper way to live a religious life. For students, seeing the two different portraits (one covering the other) and discussing the possible motivations for the revisions is an exercise in historical analysis that would not be as easily achieved nor as interestingly displayed without overlapping visual images.

Display Questions or Comments for Short Writing Assignments. Seeing a writing topic in large print on a screen focuses attention on the task at hand. Teachers in high school and college use short writing prompts as a way for students to respond succinctly, yet thoughtfully, to material presented in class. One effective example is the "50-Word Sentence." Students write 50 words crafted into one sentence to communicate the main idea of a lesson. Students and teachers like the open-ended and individualized activity, as it is not time consuming for students to compose or for teachers to read. Reading 50-word sentences is far more time efficient than reading and responding to longer essays, and displaying 50-word sentences in PowerPoint makes an efficient, engaging way to publish student writing.

Go to the Tutorials section of Chapter 9 in MyEducationKit and access the practical tutorial entitled "PowerPoint for MAC, Basics."

Use the Slides as Attention-Getters. Rather than being sound bytes of information that teachers read aloud to a class, PowerPoint slides should be attention-getting devices to focus students' minds on the topic under discussion. As students view the slides, a teacher presents essential facts, tells stories, and explains concepts, thus clarifying the purpose of the lesson. To achieve maximum teaching potential, many teachers storyboard their presentations before making slides. Then they time the length of their talk to ensure that the number of slides exactly fits the teacher talk time. Student discussion and activity time, added to presentation time, completes the scheduled class time. This way, teachers can design interesting arrangements of important information with visual variety.

Develop Your Own PowerPoint Learning Games. Homemade PowerPoint Games is a website developed by the WWILD Team (World Wide Interactive Learning Design) in the Department of Educational Psychology and Instructional Technology at the University of Georgia (http://it.coe.uga.edu/wwild/pptgames/index.html). The site's goal is to provide teachers with a collection of PowerPoint-based templates so they and their students can construct learning games for the classroom. The site declares itself to be a "constructivist alternative to WebQuests" because every game requires teachers and students to adapt the online materials to their specific classroom learning goals (Rieber, n.d.). Many preassembled online WebQuests ask students to simply follow the directions to arrive at a predetermined result. By contrast, a homemade PowerPoint game is more interactive and constructivist when students add their own questions, modifying the rules of play to fit their circumstances. Teachers and students are encouraged to submit their own home-grown games to the site, which also has useful information about using PowerPoint in teaching.

Video in the Classroom

Video is a popular and effective multimedia teaching tool at all grade levels for a number of reasons:

- *Availability in schools.* Most schools have television monitors and video players readily accessible, either in classrooms or stored on rolling carts. With equipment available, videos are used regularly for classroom instruction because they offer useful ways to present information multimodally while redirecting the focus of instruction from teacher to television for part of the class time.
- *Students are interested.* Students have been raised in a culture where television is a constant presence. Young people watch TV an average of three hours a day, and the average increases to nearly four hours a day when videos and other prerecorded media are included in the statistics (Rideout, Roberts, & Foehr, 2005, p. 26). Student response to video images is different from their response to printed text or teacher talk. In many cases, the visual images students view on screen is the material they remember most vividly and long-lastingly.
- *Abundance of resources.* There is a wealth of high-quality video material available in libraries and schools. Teachers can quickly and easily show a video related to almost any curriculum topic. Many schools have invested in a library of video resources and local libraries, museums, and educational organizations also have collections of materials for teachers to borrow.
- *Unique learning experiences.* It is impossible to recreate in classrooms the visual learning experiences offered by high-quality video programs. For instance, an English teacher reading *A Midsummer Night's Dream* or *Macbeth* can combine a read-aloud of the actual text of Shakespeare's plays with video segments from famous performances and adaptations. The same scene can be viewed from more than one play or movie to see how different actors and directors interpret the material. In science, basic processes can be revealed playfully by Bill Nye or more seriously by "Nova," but each approach is memorable in its own way.

As a free or inexpensive alternative to videotapes and DVDs in the classroom, more and more schools use video resources that are streamed on the Web. **Streaming video** is the simultaneous transfer of video, voice, and data from one computer to another. Streamed material is received in real time and can be played by software applications such as Windows Media Player or QuickTime Player. Science and social studies teachers, for example, can find more than 1,400 free video clips on natural environments in the United States at the streaming video site American Field Guide from PBS (www .pbs.org/americanfieldguide). Wonderful and informative streaming educational video materials are available to schools for free or on a subscription basis through a number of sources, with the offerings growing constantly. Tech Tool 9.2 describes additional excellent film, video, and streaming video materials for classroom use.

Film, video, and streaming video materials are important instructional resources for teachers at every grade level. Students respond positively to the visual learning inherent in high-quality video resources. For teachers, the challenge is locating excellent, age-appropriate visual resources in different subject areas. Resources for the Classroom from PBS Teachers, the National Teacher Training Institute, TeacherTube, and The Futures Channel are excellent resources for your classroom.

Resources for the Classroom—PBS Teachers

Resources for the Classroom from PBS Teachers provides up-to-date listings of the television programs being shown daily and weekly at your local public broadcasting station, including programs especially for students. There are times and summaries of programs and the schedules for PBS stations in other parts of the country as well. Teachers can also sign up for an electronic newsletter that provides more detailed information about different programs, including those that have teaching and student resource materials.

PBS-produced programs, given their excellent quality, offer wonderful teaching resources at any grade level. Information is current and presented in visually engaging formats. Many special programs have accompanying websites as well that provide lesson plans, interactive timelines, additional resource materials, and other features that will enhance video viewing in the classroom.

TV for Teachers is part of a larger site called PBS TeacherSource (www.pbs.org/teachersource) that features more than 3,000 lesson plans from all subject areas and grade levels, information on K–12 technology research, media literacy strategies, and a blog on how technology and Internet culture affect teaching and learning in schools.

The National Teacher Training Institute (NTTI)

The National Teacher Training Institute (NTTI) is a video resource for teachers featuring lesson plans written by teachers. Funded by Cisco Systems and the GE Foundation, NTTI was begun in 1989 by PBS Channel 13 in New York City as a way "to help teachers use video as a meaningful tool in the classroom." The site includes a database of hundreds of media-rich lesson plans and provides practical strategies for integrating video in teaching.

 TeacherTube/Teachers.tv

TeacherTube, launched in March 2007 as an educational version of the popular YouTube video site, provides free online space for sharing instructionally and educationally themed videos made by teachers and students. Teachers.tv is the British version of the same idea. Videos of the day are displayed on TeacherTube's main page (see the screenshot) and teachers and students can search by topics as well.

The site's categories are educator friendly, featuring "Most Recent," "Most Discussed," and "Top Rated" videos. The TeacherTube New Page notifies users of promising video clips that have been recently added to the site.

The Futures Channel

The Futures Channel is an online collection of short video movie clips related to jobs, careers, and future opportunities in the areas of mathematics, science, technology, and engineering. Many of the clips show students how math and science knowledge is used every day by people working in fields as diverse as design, theatre, marketing, and research.

In addition to the multimedia content, the site includes an impressive collection of lesson plans and related teaching resources. Virtually every resource is an entry to engaging and stimulating curriculum. For example, imagine you want to teach polygons to fourth-grade math students. There is a movie clip on polygons at The Futures Channel that you can use as the opener or launch for your lesson. Next students might move around the classroom visiting a series of polygon stations where they cut different shapes out of paper. Once 20 or more shapes have been cut, the students can then assemble them into their own personalized polygon product. Finally, the class might make its own Futures Channel–style video movie about their project. The end result is a clear understanding of polygons by your students.

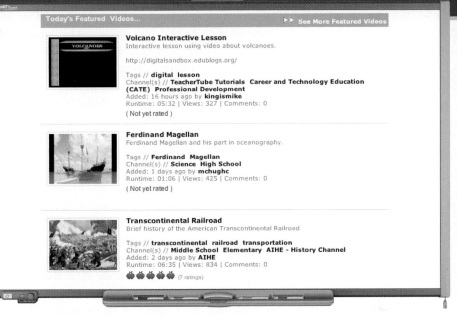

Source: Screenshot reprinted with permission of TeacherTube, LLC (www.teachertube.com). Board courtesy of SMART Technologies; copyright © 2001–2009 SMART Technologies ULC; all rights reserved.

 Annenberg Media Learner.Org

Annenberg's media website provides access to streaming video educational materials in math, science, history, literature, the arts, and foreign languages.

CONTACT INFORMATION

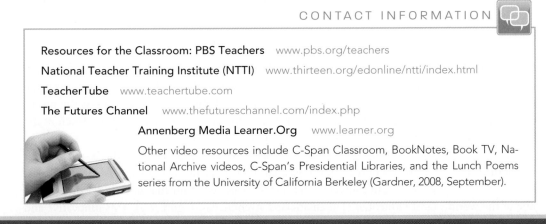

Resources for the Classroom: PBS Teachers   www.pbs.org/teachers

National Teacher Training Institute (NTTI)   www.thirteen.org/edonline/ntti/index.html

TeacherTube   www.teachertube.com

The Futures Channel   www.thefutureschannel.com/index.php

Annenberg Media Learner.Org   www.learner.org

Other video resources include C-Span Classroom, BookNotes, Book TV, National Archive videos, C-Span's Presidential Libraries, and the Lunch Poems series from the University of California Berkeley (Gardner, 2008, September).

Strategies for Using Videos and DVDs with Your Students

For effective ways to enliven and extend the video viewing experience for students, consider the following:

- *Use the pause and rewind buttons often.* Pausing a video or DVD or rewinding to review segments engages students in lively discussions about what they are viewing, making the experience interactive. Inserting these conversational opportunities ensures that students contribute their own ideas, observations, and interpretations to the discussion. Although frequent pausing or rewinding requires more class time, student discussion, questioning, reflection, and note taking greatly increase.
- *Ask students to write responses.* Students' taking notes or writing reactions while a video is playing requires attentive viewing. Inspired by the idea of an interactive notebook, students may respond using written text, hand-drawn pictures, or other symbols. The teacher reads the comments and replies, extending the interactive nature of the writing. By pairing different modes of learning—viewing and composing—teachers enhance student involvement.
- *Minimize the time video is shown in the classroom.* Showing brief segments of a video rather than viewing a program for an entire class period facilitates interactive viewing by students. Television watching, even when the program content is high quality, can be a largely passive educational experience. Students sit and stare at a screen without formal opportunities to interact with the moving pictures. The inherent passivity invites students to tune out mentally, losing focus on the key academic ideas the teacher is trying to convey. Alternatively, when teachers show one or two scenes or sections of a video, it is easier to promote discussion and analysis because the attention of the students is focused on the important academic material in the lesson.
- *Turn off the sound or the picture.* Eliminating sound or picture changes the video experience dramatically. The National Teacher Training Institute (NTTI) suggests that teachers disable the original sound track and record their own voiceover for the pictures, keyed to the students in the classroom. Another option is to turn off the visual display so that students must respond imaginatively to the narration, creating pictures in their minds of what is happening on the darkened screen. While these are uncommon ways to use videos, soundless or pictureless formats provide incentive for students to question and discuss the topic.

Strategies for using video resources are also available in *Lesson Plans for Creating Media-Rich Classrooms,* a book from the National Council of Teachers of English (Christel & Sullivan, 2007). An accompanying CD includes sample handouts, media files, and other teacher resources.

Using Webcasts in the Classroom

The term **webcast** blends the word *web* with *broadcast* to describe streaming media broadcasts of audio and video over the Internet. A high-speed Internet connection allows for speedy data transfer as the videos are streamed into your computer instead of being downloaded and saved on a hard drive.

To consider how a webcast might be used in teaching, imagine finding a document written so long ago that the text on its pages must be read with a special decoder because the document is so ancient that its words have become a mystery. You and your students are being given the chance to be some of the first people to learn what is written on the pages, to witness the meaning uncovered as the words are decoded. You have a front row seat at a computer to watch as the book is scanned by X-rays to reveal what cannot be read with the human eye.

The computer picture switches location to a scientist who explains how the X-ray scanner is working. This scientist is a host for a webcast entitled "Ancient Writings Revealed: A Webcast of Archimedes" (www.exploratorium.edu/archimedes/webcast.html) that unveils a lost book of one of the world's most influential mathematicians, Archimedes (Figure 9.3). This innovative and informative presentation allowed viewers to address the experts by writing comments or asking questions, similar to a face-to-face classroom experience. Two other excellent educational webcast sites offer outstanding programs.

- *The Library of Congress Webcasts* (www.loc.gov/today/cyberlc). The library provides a Top Ten list of frequently viewed webcasts. Most are similar to watching televised speeches by experts so they might be better suited to middle or high school students.
- *EDUCAUSE Live!* (http://net.educause.edu/live). Interactive Web seminars about important information technology topics in higher education allow guests to virtually attend through "online audio and video/image presentation technology" that gives participants the tools to interact with the host presenters.

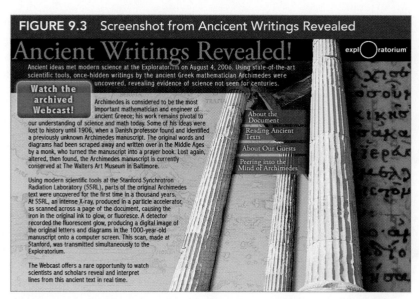

FIGURE 9.3 Screenshot from Ancient Writings Revealed

Source: Copyright Exploratium, www.exploratium.edu. Reprinted with permission of Exploratorium.

 ## Photo Taking and Movie Making by Students

Digital cameras are small but powerful tools capable of taking still photographs and video images that can be downloaded to a computer for printing, editing, and viewing. With digital cameras, teachers and students at every grade level have a vast range of visual learning options available to them through the manipulation of pictures.

There are four important reasons for a teacher to become a photographer and videographer and for students to become involved in taking pictures and making movies in school.

Go to the Tutorials section of Chapter 9 in MyEducationKit and access the practical tutorial entitled "Photoshop.com."

- *Students' experiences.* In their daily lives, students are immersed in media from the pictures they take themselves to the videos and movies they watch on television, in the movie theatre, or on the Internet. The great popularity of the YouTube video site is evidence of just how extensively the process of creating and viewing visual images interests youth today. As we have observed many times in this book, teachers who incorporate the interests of students fully engage them in academic learning.
- *Documenting learning.* Classroom learning activities are best captured with still photos and moving pictures. Photos or videos provide a unique form of remembering. Without photographic records, memories fade, leaving teachers and students recalling and revisiting what has happened through oral conversation and written records. With photographs and videos, it is possible to revisit a learning activity in an immediate sensory fashion. Students and teachers can see and, with video, hear what happened, refreshing memories and building new learning while reflecting on their past experiences.
- *Active learning.* Students enjoy photo taking and movie making because they allow active involvement in four learning processes:

  - Filming—using cameras to create still or moving pictures
  - Acting—being filmed by cameras as part of learning activities
  - Editing—crafting what has been filmed into interesting visual presentations
  - Viewing—seeing what has been produced

- *Information creation.* The process of taking photos and making movies allows students to become the creators of visual content, skills that are important to life in the 21st century. With the wide availability of digital cameras, there is no reason for students to be passive consumers of visual technologies. For a century people have been taking pictures, making movies, and

distributing their creative efforts to viewers. Today's camera technology enables students to do the same in the classroom, and in so doing, learn not only academic subject matter but also digital camera technology, itself educationally valuable.

Digital Still and Video Cameras

The new generation of digital media technologies invites students and teachers to be editors and publishers of educational and creative materials. Digital media includes multiple mediums for the exploration, investigation, and manipulation of information, including photo taking and movie making in every subject area and at every grade level. With photography and cinematography built into computer desktops, there are unique and powerful learning opportunities just waiting to be tried.

Digital cameras replace older-style cameras with simple-to-use, instant view photography. Some models record sound and video as well. With digital cameras, if you do not like a shot, delete it and take the picture again. The photographer

Students enliven and extend the study of science and social studies by filming real-world events with digital cameras and then editing their tapes to produce informative reports and videos.

decides which pictures to save. After downloading your shots into a photo editing program, changing the sizes of the photos; adding words or including speech bubbles; making slide shows; utilizing the "Ken Burns effect"; cropping; and overlapping are easy. With these cameras, everyone can be an accomplished picture taker.

Many schools have digital cameras available for teachers to use, either in classrooms or as part of the building's audio/visual or computer center. Some teachers purchase their own cameras so they are ready to record interesting events inside or outside of school to show their students. There are four types of digital cameras, categorized below in relation to picture resolution and price:

- The basic digital camera, known as a **point-and-shoot camera,** usually has a fixed lens with a few options for manually controlling the focus.
- A very inexpensive alternative to the basic digital camera is a **digital single-use camera** (also known as a disposable digital camera). Although limited to one use, the photos can still be downloaded to your computer for editing and publishing. Some disposable cameras also shoot short video clips.
- For the professional photo taker who wants to be able to manipulate some of the finer artistic details, "prosumer" cameras known as **shoot-to-print cameras** have high-end technical features that produce publication quality photos.
- **Single lens reflex (SLR) design cameras** provide maximum performance. Possessing the greatest range of available features, these high-priced devices allow the photographer to see through the viewfinder the exact image that the camera will capture. This feature is important to people who want to be able to manipulate the image in great detail before the photo is taken.

Digital video cameras are versatile, easy-to-use machines that download directly to a computer to view or edit videos. They record video and audio images at the same time. **Pocket video cameras** are handheld devices that can record up to an hour of video and audio, which can then be downloaded to a computer or uploaded to a video-sharing website through an attached USB port.

Teachers and students can use any of these still or video cameras to record school plays, talent events, morning classroom news shows, or student presentations. Digital cameras are also used as a prime documenter of events such as end-of-year celebrations, unit projects, and student research reports. It is entertaining for students to watch what is recorded, especially if they are featured in the film.

Digital Stills

Teachers and students can inexpensively photograph virtually any instructional activity from every subject area. As cameras become even more multifunctional, still photographs in combination with short video clips can be imported into PowerPoint slides or any form of digital publishing using computers and digital projectors. Some ideas for using digital still photography in a classroom include classroom bulletin boards, student posterboard presentations, class newspapers, computer screensaver photos, website or blog posts, parts of PowerPoint presentations, or pictures of science experiments, art, or class constructions.

Literacy learning in the elementary grades is one curriculum area that especially benefits from the use of still photographs. Photos are child-attracting materials that students will view and review if they and their friends are featured. As a teacher, you and your students can photograph your class reading, writing, or engaging in math and science activities and publish the photos as a book, postcards, poster illustrations, computer screensavers, or photo slideshows. Alphabet books and concept books are two classroom projects where digital still photographs promote literacy learning among 4- to 7-year-old students or third- through seventh-graders.

Alphabet Books.   **Alphabet books** are student-made books designed to teach spelling patterns, letter sounds, vocabulary words, and reading skills. Using a digital camera, alphabet books can be illustrated with photos of students. The simplest alphabet book features photos of students holding objects they have chosen that illuminate letter sounds. Monique's Eiffel **T**ower (Tt), Yehrin's **o**cean liner (Oo), and Ava's **g**lobe (Gg) are actual pages from a kindergarten alphabet book. The students chose 3D objects in the classroom, posed with them, and the pictures were printed on a computer to make a class book and then displayed on the wall as a classroom alphabet. Individual students created their own books using photographs and hand-drawn illustrations. A page from one student's alphabet book is shown in Figure 9.4.

FIGURE 9.4   Page from a Student's Alphabet Book

Each alphabet photograph displays the standard spelling of students' names with a possessive apostrophe and an item (a noun), making the letter–sound connections visible. This simple approach teaches four written language conventions:

- Letter–sound associations
- The term *noun*
- The possessive apostrophe
- Spelling of children's names

These language concepts, discussed repeatedly throughout the process of taking and displaying the digital photographs, become memorable to young students because they and their friends are the stars of the photographs. In addition, these digital photographs can be displayed as screensavers on classroom computers that continuously loop through 26 photos. Children see themselves and pause to read the screen as they walk past the computer or sit down to view the screensaver slideshow.

With the publication of this first alphabet of nouns and proper nouns, the process of producing language concept alphabets is launched. When ready, you as the teacher can repeat the process to make a verb alphabet with photographs of individuals, pairs, or groups doing things: building, jumping, washing, viewing. Verb alphabets make simple sentences with punctuation—for example, "Joshua sings." This is a sentence with a proper noun and a verb as well as punctuation, what you might call stop signs for the reader—a period, exclamation point, or question mark.

Go to the Assignments and Activities section of Chapter 9 in MyEducationKit and complete the video activity entitled "Using Digital Cameras to Support Content Learning." As you watch the video and answer the accompanying questions, note how digital photography is used in math.

In these photographs, proper names appear in color, verbs appear in black ink, and the punctuation is black, too. Punctuation can be child chosen as a way to help them practice recognizing the role of each punctuation mark. When a child decides how the sentence will be read aloud—as a declarative sentence, an exclamatory sentence, or an interrogative sentence—the appropriate stop sign is affixed. Even in kindergarten children are able to choose how they want their sentences to be read, distinguishing between an interrogative with a question mark, a declarative with a period, or an exclamatory with an exclamation point.

Teachers might vary the alphabet every two months, making new ones that feature adjectives or adverbs, or recreating nouns and verbs so the experience can be repeated for new learning practice. Photographs are the means of capturing and sustaining students' interest. Regularly writing and photographing alphabets is a fresh, creative way to study language conventions or new vocabulary in science, math, history, foreign language, or English with students in kindergarten through grade 7. Technology tools invite children to learn about language and technology simultaneously as they take photos, download them to a computer, add text, print the copies, and frame them for display on a bulletin board or bind them into a book.

Concept Books.   **Concept books** for beginning readers and English language learners offer another opportunity for teachers to use digital photography to promote literacy learning. Many concept books feature photographs that teach a single category or idea such as shapes, sizes, colors, numbers, fractions, opposites, patterns, words, letters, or continents. Classroom-made versions of concept books can be easily produced through the collaboration of teachers and students.

We worked with kindergartners to make their own version of Jan and Stan Berenstain's amusing concept book for beginning readers, *Inside, Outside, Upside Down* (1997). After reading the book aloud to small groups, each group posed for digital photographs to illustrate their text. Using a huge plastic tub large enough for four students to sit inside, we snapped photos of them inside, outside, underneath, and beside the tub. Holding it over their heads, with legs and feet protruding under it, the photos were printed upside down to illustrate the words.

Staging the photographs reinforced the meaning of the concepts for the students, particularly those learning English as a new language. The enjoyment of popping into and climbing out of the tub, holding it over their heads, and standing beside it making funny faces made the memories fun to recall. Such student-made books, printed and bound, can be viewed side by side with The Berenstain Bears original for comparing and contrasting the illustrations and reading the print in both texts.

Bookstores and libraries are filled with concept books that you can refer to as you and your students create your own using digital photographs. Tana Hoban's children's books illustrate a huge range of concepts and are among the best examples to inspire using digital cameras for literacy learning. For more than 30 years, Hoban's inventive, eye-pleasing photographs have illustrated her concept books for beginning readers, including titles such as *White on Black; I Read Signs; Shapes, Shapes, Shapes; Let's Count; Construction Zone;* and many others. The photographs facilitate reading the pictures and understanding the concepts.

Tech Tool 9.3 offers more resources for using **digital storytelling** and **digital art making** in the classroom.

Digital Videos

Inviting students to make digital videos in school is an exciting teaching approach. The lure of doing one's own acting, filming, and editing is immense for all ages, as evidenced by the popularity of television shows like "America's Funniest Videos" and the Internet site YouTube. Many of your students will have used cameras at home. We know families who give their children inexpensive camcorders to capture daily moments and important milestones. One child's video topics included "Skateboarding," "Jokes," and "Friends." The skateboarding video shows the child's attempts at mastering different jumps with special effects added, music in the background, and close-ups of the skateboard from every conceivable angle. From a curriculum standpoint, making digital videos

Go to the Assignments and Activities section of Chapter 9 in MyEducationKit and complete the Web activity entitled "Digital Storytelling." As you complete the activity, consider how you might incorporate digital storytelling into your instruction.

Go to the Assignments and Activities section of Chapter 9 in MyEducationKit. Open the Web activity "Multimedia Storytelling" to further explore this Tech Tool.

Digital Storytelling

The Center for Digital Storytelling in Berkeley, California, is devoted to supporting individuals and organizations using digital media to tell personal stories. Its slogan is "Listen Deeply/Tell Stories." "Digital storytelling" refers to ways that written text, audio, and video imagery can be combined to make unique story presentations (Alexander & Levine, 2008, November/December; EDUCAUSE Learning Initiative, 2007, January). Digital storytelling connects directly to the history/social studies and language arts curriculum. In history, students can assemble oral histories, personal memories, and life stories from people throughout the school and the community. In language arts, digital storytelling offers ways to teach about personal narrative, biography, and autobiography, as well as fiction writing.

You can locate more storytelling resources at the Educational Uses of Digital Storytelling site maintained by the College of Education at the University of Houston. The site features a useful introduction, examples, tools, evaluation criteria, and links to many resources.

Digital Art Making

The National Gallery of Art has an amazing interactive site for young artists entitled NGA Kids: The Art Zone (see the accompanying screenshot). Young artists can use different projects with color, texture, and scale features to create a unique piece of art.

"Create a Sculpture" on the Art Interactive website from the Smithsonian's Hirshhorn Museum and Sculpture Garden invites Internet users to create digital sculptures online. An assembled sculpture can then be put in a gallery setting and moved around to any location the artist decides is best for viewing the work.

Source: The NGAKids Jungle interactive was programmed by Al Jarnow of Protozone, Inc., and designed in collaboration with the National Gallery of Art. © 2008 National Gallery of Art, Washington. All rights reserved. Board courtesy of SMART Technologies; copyright © 2001–2009 SMART Technologies ULC; all rights reserved.

CONTACT INFORMATION

Digital Storytelling   www.coe.uh.edu/digital-storytelling   Maintained by the College of Education at the University of Houston.

Digital Art   http://hirshhorn.si.edu/education/interactive.html   Free online.

NGA Kids: The Art Zone   www.nga.gov/kids/zone/zone.htm   Free online.

TABLE 9.3 Digital Video Project Ideas

Subject Area	Digital Video Project Ideas
Science	• Classroom science experiments • Science news reports • Discussions among students about recent science discoveries and current controversies
History	• Oral history interviews • Public service announcements • Mock trials of famous court cases and historical persons • Reenactments of historical events • Debates among students representing different political groups
Math	• Building projects using wooden blocks, Legos, and other materials • Measurement activities using manipulatives • Counting games with objects
Language arts	• Students reading poetry aloud • Performances of adult or student-written plays • Commercials that reveal propaganda or other persuasive language techniques • Presentation of student-written music and dance

with your class is a way to produce enthusiasm for academic learning in every subject area. Table 9.3 presents digital video project ideas in science, history, math, and language arts.

Through video, students can realize change because they are able to view it with their eyes. Natural or human-made change processes that would otherwise only be personal memories, written words, or just abstract ideas when presented through a lecture or read in a book are rendered vividly real to video viewers. This is particularly true in the subjects of math and science.

Without video technology, a math class determining the distance students can long jump would measure distances using rulers or tape measures and record them in graphs, charts, or in written descriptions of personal observations. Students might photograph stills but these do not capture movement. With video cameras, those same students might record long jumping by filming an entire jump from beginning to end. They could view the film to see different jumping techniques as well as overall distances and share their results in a short movie that dynamically reveals successful long jumps in action. In this example, digital video not only supports and expands the math learning process but also shows students how to use real-world results to formulate research-based conclusions and explanations.

In science class, seasonal change offers a venue for using digital video to engage students in collecting data and formulating conclusions based on their research. The school year in most communities begins as summer becomes fall and ends as spring becomes summer. Weather patterns, animal migrations, agricultural activities, and many other aspects of daily life change seasonally, often unnoticed unless teachers and students actively explore and record what is changing. Using video cameras, students in every grade level can record all sorts of natural phenomena, from changing shadow lengths at different times of the year (a function of the 23.6 degree tilt of the Earth as it rotates on its axis) to the effects of different seasons on plants, animals, and people. The camera shots can compare and contrast both subtle and dramatic changes in nature for viewing again and again.

Video movies can document smaller-scale science investigations such as projects where students construct ramps and chutes using wooden blocks from which to propel marbles or toy cars

PEARSON
myeducationkit™

Go to the Assignments and Activities section of Chapter 9 in MyEducationKit and complete the Web activity entitled "Video Production." As you watch the video and answer the accompanying questions, note how the teacher prepares his students and sets up his lesson.

on speedy journeys across the classroom. These types of experiments can be filmed in real time and viewed repeatedly by students who want to review the experiment. Unlike photographs, videos capture the motion of the experiments, making the action real for the students.

Digital Video Editing Software

As interesting as filming with a video camera is for students, it is the use of **digital video editing software** that shifts their recorded material from the ordinary to the extraordinary. Video editing software lets teachers and students edit their video footage on the computer, deleting unwanted material and adding transitions, songs, sound effects, titles, text, voiceovers, and other special effects. iMovie for Macintosh computers and MovieMaker for PCs are widely used video editing software programs. Like sculpting clay, video editing software enables creative shaping or manipulating of video images as students sculpt the raw material of film into different kinds of finished products.

A unique feature of the software is its capacity to produce the filming style known as the "Ken Burns effect," a term given to the use of still photographs in a movie format, a hallmark of Burns's PBS series, "The Civil War" and "Baseball." Students can zoom in on and out of a photograph, pan across, and fade it from view as part of a transition to the next scene. The use of voiceovers with the photos and interviews with individuals added into the film between photos are creative features of this style of filmmaking that attract students. They can record narration to accompany their film footage, add short interviews with students, and edit these into the filming of a science experiment, a math activity, a history simulation, a geography bee, or any event where learning is occurring.

Successful video making and video editing requires students to storyboard their digital videos. **Storyboarding** is the process that writers and videographers use to outline their video stories scene by scene. The Kids' Vid website (http://kidsvid.altec.org) from the High Plains Regional Technology in Education Consortium invites students to consider the elements that professional moviemakers must consider, including placement of the actors, lighting, camera shots, audio elements, and transitions between scenes. The Kids' Vid site includes easy-to-use drag-and-drop storyboarding software for customizing characters and backdrops.

Strategies for Using Cameras with Your Students

The following strategies aid teachers' and students' use of cameras in the classroom.

- *Use cameras regularly.* Instead of utilizing digital video cameras to capture extraordinary events, make them tools for filming everyday events in the classroom. Everyone wishing to participate will use the cameras confidently with regular practice. The archive of footage that accrues will enable students to design many short films documenting daily learning that can be published in different ways for family nights and class viewing.

- *Record events while they are unfolding.* Film a math game or a science experiment in action. These snippets of filmed action allow teachers to create a broad picture of classroom activity over a day or a week, giving importance to the work that students are doing.

- *Use video as a way to generate, edit, and publish student writing.* One elementary school teacher from our program used iMovie software with her students as a way to publish their written stories. The idea arose when she realized that her students were composing stories with scant detail that lacked the key dramatic elements of characters, storyline, setting, and tension. She encouraged them to perform their stories with some members acting and the

Go to the Tutorials section of Chapter 9 in MyEducationKit and complete the tutorial entitled "iMovie" or "Moviemaker" to learn the basic skills in video editing.

Successful editing of student-made videos is a collaborative process in which everyone's participation produces a better result.

rest of the class as the audience. As some students performed, others filmed with her video camera. Once all stories were filmed, she showed their film to everyone. Then she showed a film clip where the story included interesting characters and setting as well as a point of tension that had to be resolved within the storyline. The children saw the differences between both films and were able to revise their original stories to include more excitement and suspense. The making of the video changed the story writing experience for the students. As they watched their performances, they could imagine how the characters might look, sound, and interact differently. The characters became three-dimensional as their stories changed and included greater detail and dramatic elements.

- *Create a video production and editing area in your classroom.* By mounting a video camera on a tripod, you can make a digital video recording studio in a corner of your classroom. Affix the legs of the tripod to the floor with duct tape to ensure stability. Adding icon stickers that correspond to the key buttons of record, play, and preview allow student videographers to work independently with the equipment.

Podcasts and Vodcasts as Tools for Teaching

Podcast, a term that comes from the words *iPod* and *broadcast,* is an audio recording distributed online and accessed on computers or portable media players using free software such as iTunes or Bloglines (EDUCAUSE Learning Initiative, 2005, June). The software needed to download a podcast is known as a **podcatcher.** Increasingly, some of these recordings include video as well as audio, giving rise to an extension of podcasting known as a **vodcast.**

Mention podcasts or vodcasts and most people think of an **iPod,** the immensely popular portable media player created by Apple that is a common way to listen to podcasts and vodcasts. There are over 100 million iPod devices in use worldwide. For most of your students, iPods are devices for listening to and viewing music, videos, photo slideshows, or favorite television programs in the palm of their hand. But for educators, iPods are an emerging teaching and learning technology. In what was a pioneering step at the time, Duke University gave iPods to 1,600 first-year students in 2004. The purpose was academic, not recreational, and the impact was a great success. Students began using their iPods to listen to course lectures outside of class, to record information during class and in the field, and to review material for exams (Belanger, 2005). But podcasts and vodcasts can be accessed and played on any Internet-accessible computer, making access easily within the reach of classroom teachers.

Educational podcasts are everywhere on the Web. Major news organizations including PBS (Public Broadcasting Service) and the *New York Times* provide podcasts of key stories and current events. Members of Congress, political candidates, and special interest organizations regularly post speeches and policy statements. Book authors, scientists, and leading experts discuss their latest research and creative work. The American Chemical Society offers cutting-edge science discovery podcasts for young listeners entitled "Bytesize Science" (see Figure 9.5). There are many ways to find educationally relevant podcasts.

- Browse all the categories at the Apple iTunes Store.
- Power search iTunes by keyword, author, or title.
- Search Apple's iTunesU using the terms education and podcasts (www.apple.com/education/itunesu).
- Go to a specific educational, news, or science organization site and find out what podcasts they are offering for download.
- The Education Podcast Network (www.epnweb.org) maintains an extensive inventory of podcast programming for teachers.
- Go to Podcast Alley (www.podcastalley.com) and consult its comprehensive podcast directory. This site does contain advertisements. Other directories include Podcast Pickle and Podcast Ready.

Using podcasts and vodcasts in K–12 classrooms allows for creative experimentation and innovation by teachers (Rozema, 2007). Some teachers create an audio summary of the main points of a curriculum unit, post their comments online, and encourage students to listen to them before a test. This is also a way for students who are absent to hear the main ideas that were introduced and discussed in class. Other teachers choose to extend the time they have with students by offering extra material via self-made podcasts. Audio book reports are an engaging way to involve students in thoughtfully responding to literature. Podcasts from the National Council of Teachers of English offer more ideas about connecting reading and podcasts: "Chatting About Books: Recommendations for Young Readers" and "Text Messages: Recommendations for Teen Readers" (Gardner, 2008, July).

Recording a teacher lecture or class discussion for podcasting can be a very useful learning activity (see Tech Tool 9.4 for information on how to create your own podcast). When students know that they can listen to a lecture or discussion at a later time, they become engaged in different ways during class time. There may be less frantic note taking and more attentive listening because students are not worried about missing a key point. Teachers, too, can listen to their oral presentations with a goal of recognizing how they might improve their explanations of material, identifying possible points of confusion and discovering ways to express themselves more dynamically.

Students too can generate podcast content easily and creatively. Writing assignments, "such as an essay or a fictional diary, can provide the foundation for a podcast" (Bull, Hammond, & Grimes, 2007, p. 187). Community events, special projects, and creative activities can all be recorded as news items with interviews and published through podcasting. And students of all ages enjoy the process of writing, recording, editing, and posting material on the Web so podcasting can be done in elementary, middle, and high school classrooms.

There are two more important advantages to teacher- and student-made podcasts:

- Teachers can easily record lectures, review sessions, and class discussions for students to hear outside of class. Compared to digital video, it is easier to record voice than to film a lecture or class discussion. With video, someone must handle the camera and monitor the audio recording of voices as well. By contrast, recording audio involves merely turning on a **digital voice recorder** and then conducting the class.
- Students may perform in a more relaxed and thoughtful manner when recording a podcast than when performing for a camera. With a camera, there is a tendency for some students to overact in an effort to have fun and get laughs. In such cases, a silliness factor may override more serious academic ideas. Speaking into a microphone instead of a camera can help to confine students to the activity at hand and keep them concentrating on your major educational goals.

These advantages may not outweigh one major drawback of podcasts when compared to digital video. Video is visual and many students are engaged more directly by what they can see and hear than what they can only hear. As a new teacher, you will need to decide whether video or audio best fits a particular learning situation. You may find that using a combination of video and podcasts with your students during the school year is a way to reach learners in new and exciting ways.

FIGURE 9.5 Screenshot of Bytesize Science Podcasts

Source: Courtesy of the American Chemical Society.

PEARSON
myeducationkit

Go to the Tutorials section of Chapter 9 in MyEducation-Kit and access the practical tutorial entitled "Creating a Podcast."

The iPod portable digital music player has become a common technology among today's college students. When asked what technologies students planned to bring with them to their first semester at the University of California, Berkeley, 88 percent answered an iPod, trailing only a cell phone and a personal laptop computer, items favored by 98 and 96 percent of incoming students (University of California Berkeley, 2007).

The iPod's great popularity opens exciting possibilities for teaching and learning in schools. First, iPods support anywhere/anytime learning. Teachers and students can access a wealth of audio and video educational resources and listen to them whenever they choose. Second, the portability of iPods lets students take course content anywhere. Third, teachers and students can record their own podcasts and then use their personal iPods to listen to their productions.

Creating your own podcasts offers at least three educational benefits:

1. Students can listen to their teacher (and other students) discuss important academic material as a way to review and remember what has been presented in class. Content review is particularly important at the middle and high school levels where teachers are expected to present and students are expected to learn large amounts of academic material. Students can also review material at their own pace, which is a great support for learners with hearing or other disabilities.
2. Teachers can listen to themselves (and their students) as a way to reflect on and improve how information and discussions are presented orally in class.
3. Students and teachers can develop exciting learning projects together, such as assembling oral history interviews into a podcast-based report, reading the texts of books aloud to produce a collection of audio books, building an audio tour of student-assembled exhibits, and creating personal portfolios of learning by recording students at the beginning, middle, and end of a school year.

Producing a successful podcast requires three essential tools: (1) voice recording microphone or digital voice recorder, (2) audio recording software, and (3) site for posting and distributing podcasts.

Voice Recording Microphone or Digital Voice Recorder

Teachers and students need a way to record their voices and store the material, for which there are a number of options:

- Computer with a built-in microphone
- Microphone connected to a computer or voice recording device
- Digital voice recorder with a wireless microphone
- Digital video camera
- Clip-on microphone attached to an iPod

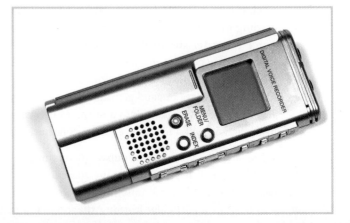

The choice for voice recording depends on the situation. Recording oneself requires only a microphone. Recording in a classroom is different because the goal is to capture teacher and student voices. In classrooms, a digital voice recorder may be the most appropriate tool for its versatility in singular or group situations. Digital voice recorders range in price from under $50 to over $250 (see the photo for a voice recorder). ITalkPro, a stereo microphone from Griffin, is less than four inches long, clips easily to an iPod, and provides clear sound recording for just over $50.

Audio Recording Software

Once you have completed your recording, you must edit the audio to eliminate unwanted or distracting material. For this step, use audio recording and editing software such as GarageBand (for Mac computers) or Audacity (an open source application for both Mac and PC machines). These programs import your voice recordings into MP3 files that can be sent out over the Internet.

Site for Posting and Distributing Podcasts

Once a podcast has been recorded and edited, distributing it to listeners requires that the material be posted online where the public can access it. Online publishing allows students, teachers, families, and others to enjoy what has been created in the classroom.

1. Listing your podcast on iTunes is one publishing option. Anyone can then subscribe and listen to your material from this site.
2. PodOmatic is a free and easy-to-use podcast posting site with audio and video sharing capabilities. You can take advantage of customizable podcast pages designed to help you give your podcast page the look and feel you want. It even has an audience statistics feature to keep track of who has tuned in during the past few days and weeks.
3. You may also be able to post podcasts on the Internet server of your school system or a nearby college or university so people can access them through the school's website.
4. Putting podcasts on your own website or blog gives you still another way to distribute material online.
5. You can play podcasts in the classroom using iMainGo from Apple, a small, lightweight, battery-powered portable speaker case that is just right for playing podcasts to small groups. An iPod fits inside the device and two high output stereo speakers project quality sound that can heard by everyone in a room. The basic unit measures 5.7 by 3.8 by 2.4 inches, weighs only nine ounces, and the sturdy case provides solid protection in case the iPod is bumped or dropped.

CONTACT INFORMATION

iPods and iTunes www.apple.com/itunes Available from Apple.

Digital voice recorder Available from manufacturers including Olympus and Sony.

Audacity http://audacity.sourceforge.net Free download.

Garageband www.apple.com/ilife/garageband Available for purchase from Apple.

iMainGo www.imaingo.com Available for purchase from Portable Sound Laboratories.

THE SHORTEST MOTION PICTURE YOU CAN MAKE IN WORDS
Writing Poetry Using Digital Cameras

Grade(s)	Grades 2 to 8
Subject(s)	Language Arts and Science
Key Goal/Enduring Understanding	Just as a microscope in a laboratory enables scientists to see small things in great detail, short poems let poets describe common moments in imaginative, expressive language.
Essential Question	How can written words and digital video combine to create short poems about occurrences in everyday life?

Learning Standards

National Council of Teachers of English/International Reading Association— *Standards for the English Language Arts*

> **Standard 4:** Students adjust their use of spoken, written and visual language (e.g., conventions, style, vocabulary) to communicate effectively with a variety of audiences and for different purposes.
>
> **Standard 12:** Students use spoken, written and visual language to accomplish their own purposes (e.g., for learning, enjoyment, persuasion, and the exchange of information).

International Society for Technology in Education (ISTE)— *NETS-S*

> **Standard 1:** *Creativity and Innovation.* Students demonstrate creative thinking, construct knowledge, and develop innovative products and processes using technology.
>
> **Standard 2:** *Communication and Collaboration.* Students use digital media and environments to communicate and work collaboratively, including at a distance, to support individual learning and contribute to the learning of others.
>
> **Standard 6:** *Technology Operations and Concepts.* Students demonstrate a sound understanding of technology concepts, systems and operations.

Learning Objectives

Student will know and be able to

- Use elements of haiku poetry to create their short poems.
- Use video recorders to capture actions in ordinary activities that can provide ideas for the poems.
- Use computers, video equipment, and other technology to publish short poems in Power-Point slideshows.

Technology Uses

The lesson features digital cameras or digital video cameras and video recording devices, with computers and editing software, to inspire students to compose and publish short poems.

▶

Minimal Technology	Infusion of Technology
Take photographs of scenes in the natural world or around the school using disposable or digital cameras.	Take photographs of scenes in the natural world or around the school using digital camcorders
Display developed photos so students can write poems from visual images.	Display digital photos or video clips using computers, Windows Media Player, and digital editing software.
Publish student poems on posterboard or classroom bulletin boards.	Publish student poems combined with video clips using computers, Windows Media Player, CD/DVD burner, or computer projector.

Evaluation

- Rubrics to record student use of technology in the activity
- Rubrics to record elements of descriptive and imaginative language in student poems

LESSON PLAN DESCRIPTION

Introduction

"The Shortest Motion Picture You Can Make in Words" lesson plan utilizes digital cameras or digital video cameras (or camera phones with video capabilities) and movie-making software to inspire the writing of short poems. The lesson can be taught throughout the elementary and middle school grade levels as part of the English/language arts or science curriculum.

Short poems employ imaginative language to describe scenes or events from daily life in few words. The goal of the poems is to convey the action and meaning of an event to readers who were not present to see it firsthand by activating a vivid motion picture in the readers' or listeners' imaginations.

Lesson Focus

This lesson fulfills two curricular goals:

- Students will explore and compose short poems.
- Students will practice closely observing and creatively describing, skills important to science study and to analyzing how words convey mental images.

Short poems are akin to the genre of haiku poetry where poems are carefully crafted word pictures. Haiku composed in classical structure is three lines of verse totaling 17 syllables (5 syllables in the first line, 7 syllables in the second, 5 syllables in the third). As important as the three-line 17-syllable structure is how a poet includes three elements—nature as a theme, a vivid description of one specific event using "only *now* words," and a sense of "the emotions the poet feels" while writing the poem (Esbensen, 1995, p. 62). In formulating Haiku, a poet "uses only as many words as can be easily spoken in one breath" to focus the reader's imagination "on one small happening in the busy world around us" (Merrill & Solbert, 1969, p. 7).

Composing short poems spoken in the length of one breath acquaints students with the original intent of haiku's form without constraining them to the 5-7-5 syllable count in a three-line structure. Writers can attend to how words help readers respond esthetically and artistically to descriptions of scenes in nature.

Scientists pay close attention to detail in their professional work, producing clear and accurate observations as they test hypotheses and produce research. As part of a science study, short poems

▶

267

are a creative way for students to practice close observation skills while recording in descriptive imaginative language events in the natural world.

Lesson Design—Minimal Technology

A minimal technology version of the lesson begins with a read-aloud of short poems. Students close their eyes as they listen to the words, imagining the "shortest motion picture you can make in words." Motion pictures communicate through the visual imagery of moving pictures; short poems communicate through the visual imagery of imaginative language.

After hearing selections of short poems, students and teacher discuss the scope of language choice poets utilize to convey images. A list of precise verbs, interesting adjectives, and words that catch readers' attention emerges from this conversation, helping young writers to think about scenes in nature they might describe poetically. Then students compose their poems about an event they want to capture in words or about something they have seen in their science study.

Students have memories of events they have witnessed in nature or they have cameras to capture outdoor photographs of topics to write about. Filmed with disposable or digital cameras by a teacher or groups of students, photographs inspire descriptions of what occurs in one moment on film in as few words as fill one breath.

Short poetry writing using minimal technology requires a camera for the photographs, paper, markers, crayons, scissors, and glue, as well as magazine illustrations and photographs for students wanting to incorporate them into their unique illustration designs.

LESSON ACTIVITIES USING TECHNOLOGY

Writing short poems using technology entails a different introduction because these pictures will move. We refer to these poems as short pictures in motion.

1. **Finding Nouns.** Introducing the short picture in motion lesson begins with defining and identifying nouns. Students gaze around them, indoors and out, naming persons, places, or things while the teacher lists the nouns on chart paper. When everyone has identified two or three nouns the teacher stops listing and focuses the discussion onto another idea—that words called *nouns* are like statues, unable to move by themselves.

2. **Reading and Making Flipbooks.** Next the teacher shows a collection of flipbooks. Flipbooks put nouns—pictures of something or someone—into motion as the viewer flips the pages. In flipbooks the nouns move as if animated. At a simple level, a flipbook is a technology that puts static images in motion.

    A make-your-own flip cartoon is a very simple way for students to animate drawings. On two sheets of identically sized paper, students draw pictures of the same item or scene—a cloud moving in front of the sun, a ball bouncing, a person jumping, a bird flapping its wings—making one slightly different from the other to show movement. When finished, lay one drawing on a table and tape the top edge to the table. Put the second drawing exactly over the first and tape its top edge to the table. Now one paper covers the other and both are securely taped at the top edge. Quickly lifting and lowering the top picture by its bottom right edge makes a moving image of the two drawings. Or roll the top drawing, from the bottom edge, around a pencil. Rapidly rolling the pencil toward the top of the drawing and back down toward the bottom, as if the top paper were a mini-window blind going up and down over the bottom drawing, makes a moving image.

    Examples of this type of cartoon animation can be found on the website of Dav Pilkey (children's book author and illustrator of the series The Adventures of Captain Underpants, The Adventures of Super Diaper Baby, and Ricky Ricotta's Mighty Robot). Dav Pilkey refers to these animated cartoons as Flip-O-Rama Action Scenes. Students can also create their own animations on his website (www.pilkey.com).

3. *Adding Verbs.* Having successfully created visual movement with two paper cartoons, the students discuss which words put language in motion. Verbs produce the power to create movement in written language. They are the electricity and the engines that put nouns in motion. Hearing this explanation, students dictate a list of verbs that the teacher records to combine with the list of nouns.

Pairing the lists, the simple sentences produce laughter: "shoes gallop," "horses cry," "books sleep." The humor from mixing the words suggests poetic possibilities of other combinations—"kids running," "shadows moving," "buses leaving," or "rain falling."

4. *Creating Action.* Short poems must convey a sense of action. Demonstrate this idea with a technology-like toy from the mid-1860s known as a "zoetrope"—a machine similar in size and shape to a hatbox without its top whose sides have see-through slits all the way around it so people can peer inside. A strip of paper with 8 to 12 sequential drawings of one scene, each slightly different to show motion, is affixed inside around the drum in a circle, underneath the slits, pictures facing toward the center. Someone gives the drum a twirl, rotating it on its base. As kids peek through the slits, they see the pictures moving, making a short movie in front of their eyes. Students then draw their own picture strips for the zoetrope and try them out.

The zoetrope can serve as a metaphor for the concepts and ideas necessary to begin composing a "shortest motion picture in words." The picture strips inside the zoetrope are put in motion by hand power. Poets aim to put visual images in motion through word power.

5. *Taking a Poetry Hike.* A "poetry hike" is an outdoor activity where teachers and students walk together as a multisensory way to inspire poetry writing. Going outdoors presents an endless panorama of nature in motion that young writers can describe in haiku-like short poems. Children and adults can hike across the schoolyard, through the neighborhood, in the countryside, or up and down city streets in search of inspiration. Even from inside a school building, looking through windows and doorways, students are observing the world outside. If it is not easy to go outside, activity inside the school provides a fine alternative set of observations.

6. *Using Digital Cameras.* Digital video cameras or video camera phones enable young poets to film short motion pictures themselves. Where photographs and drawings capture moments frozen in time (as in a portrait, a landscape, or a still life drawing) and require words from the viewer's imagination to create a sense of motion, on a poetry hike, small motion pictures are happening all the time right before one's eyes. Motion and movement is everywhere, depending on how the students observe.

For example, walking down a city sidewalk on a clear spring day, students can view the scene through a wide-angle lens—clouds racing across the sky, cars and trucks rolling down the avenue, merchants and shoppers exchanging goods. Or they can look at the same scene from a smaller, more microscopic perspective—ants scurrying in and out of a anthill, worms squirming inside the ground, leaf buds opening on the ends of branches, birds flying back and forth to nests. The possibilities for moments to record on video are everywhere.

Consider limiting each student to 15 to 30 seconds of camera time, so a choice of what to film is finite and important. The teacher and children might decide together what to record to ensure that motion and movement are clearly happening. A beautiful vista or an imposing stationary object, while interesting visually, are not moving so they are harder for youngsters to write about in a short poem format.

Ask the students to stand quietly as a group before filming to experience the physical feel of 15 seconds elapsing. This will acquaint everyone with the knowledge that this is not a long time. Explain that it is half the amount of time of a typical television commercial or about the same length of time as video segments on the television program "America's Funniest Home Videos."

7. *Writing the Poems.* After returning to the classroom, in conversation with the students, contrast the differences between filming and composing. Poetry hike videos have motion but no words. A viewer must provide words from her or his imagination to accompany the film. Short poems that students will write have words but no moving visual images. A poet's word choices provide the illusion of pictures in motion to the readers' imagination.

Video enables young poets to revisit and reenter scenes that they are writing about poetically. Before composing, everyone views the filmed scenes so they know which they want to write about. After viewing and before writing, the class discusses possibilities for poets' language choices and how parts of speech make a moving picture in words.

After composing their poems, young writers view the video again to see if their poem conveys the images they see. The poems serve as a narration of the video just as the video serves as the inspiration for the poems.

Note that the filming and writing processes will happen differently with a digital camera that takes photographs instead of video. A digital photograph remains a still image—a moment frozen in time—until the words of a child's poem put the picture into motion. Teachers who use photographs may want to open the short poem writing project with Ann Atwood's book, *Haiku-Vision in Poetry and Photography* (1977).

An alternative to a single digital photo are the four photographs shot simultaneously by an inexpensive novelty called Quad-Cam, a camera that takes four exposures in one second on a single print. Because the exposure time is short, a Quad-Cam must capture a scene that has movement and motion; otherwise, there will be no real difference between each of the four pictures. But when the four pictures show motion, the effect is moving picture–like for a viewer.

8. *Publishing the Poems.* Teachers have numerous publishing options for children's short motion picture poems. The poems can be published in a PowerPoint presentation for class viewing or posted on a class website for students and families to view and read. Electronic publishing invites the poets to record their poems in their own voices. Similar to books on tape, these are poems on audio.

A more elaborate publishing idea is inspired by "Moving Pictures: American Art and Early Film, 1880–1910," an exhibit showcasing early U.S. filmmaking mounted at the Williams College Museum of Art (Mathews, 2005). In the exhibit, some of the first motion pictures made in the United States in the late 19th and early 20th centuries were shown on flat screen televisions beside artistic renditions of the same New York City scenes. An artist's depiction of an elevated railway in Brooklyn and an industrial waterfront in New York Harbor were placed beside motion pictures of the same places. The elevated railway was filmed from the engine car of a moving train. The New York Harbor was filmed from a boat motoring around the harbor. A huge painting of Niagara Falls hung silently next to a movie of the water roaring and rushing, mesmerizing in its power. The juxtaposition of still image and moving picture created a uniquely memorable visual experience.

ANALYSIS AND EXTENSIONS

1. Name two features you find useful about this lesson.
2. Name two areas for extension or improvement of this lesson.
3. How has information technology been integrated into the lesson successfully?
4. How might students be more involved in designing, using, and evaluating technology in the lesson?

PEARSON
myeducationkit

Go to the Technology Transformation Lesson Plan section in Chapter 9 in MyEducationKit and access the activity "The Shortest Motion Picture You Can Make in Words" to practice transforming a lesson plan using technology.

FOCUS QUESTION 1: What is multimedia technology and how can teachers use it to effectively create and share visual information dynamically in their teaching?

- Multimedia (or multimodal) learning happens when multiple media (text, data, voice, picture, and video) are used to communicate information.

- Schools have largely emphasized single media, noninteractive modes of learning.

- A multimedia classroom integrates multiple technologies for teaching and learning.

FOCUS QUESTION 2: How can teachers create PowerPoint presentations for maximum teaching potential and learning impact?

- Multimedia technologies offer ways for teachers to incorporate dynamic information presentation experiences into classroom teaching and learning.

- PowerPoint, one of the most widely used computer applications in the world, is a way for teachers and students to present information in visually engaging ways.

- The use of PowerPoint has been criticized for oversimplifying complex material and creating uninteresting presentations.

- Using PowerPoint effectively requires teachers to pay attention to two information presentation design principles, the first being to stress active participation rather than passive viewing by students, and the second to inquire who the audience is and what the audience should leave knowing or remembering.

FOCUS QUESTION 3: How can teachers use video resources in their teaching?

- Videos and DVDs are widely used teaching tools that, when well made, convey important information in academically interesting, visually engaging ways.

- Video viewing can be a passive experience unless teachers create opportunities for students to interact with and respond to onscreen material.

- Successful strategies for using videos and DVDs in interactive ways include using the pause and rewind buttons, asking students to write responses to what they have seen, recognizing that briefer video segments carry a large impact, and varying the viewing experience by occasionally turning off the sound or the picture.

FOCUS QUESTION 4: How can teachers and students make their own classroom movies using digital video cameras and movie-making software?

- Students become directly involved in information creation and presentation by using digital video cameras and other devices in classroom projects and homework activities.

- Photo taking and movie making using digital video cameras promote engagement with learning by involving students in filming, acting, and editing. In each of these ways, teachers focus the attention of students on the essential academic information being conveyed.

- Digital photography and digital video present exciting ways for students at all grade levels to learn academic content by making their own picture books and digital videos.

- Instructional uses of digital photography and digital cameras include utilizing cameras regularly, recording classroom events while they are unfolding, using video to generate student writing, and creating a production area in your classroom.

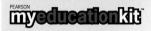

PEARSON
myeducationkit

To check your comprehension of the content covered in the chapter, go to the MyEducationKit for your book and complete the Study Plan for Chapter 9. Here you will be able to take a chapter quiz, receive feedback on your answers, and then access resources that will enhance your understanding of chapter content.

271

FOCUS QUESTION 5: How can teachers integrate podcasts and vodcasts into their teaching?

- Podcasts are online audio recordings that can be accessed by computers or portable media players (an iPod). Vodcasts are podcasts that include video and audio.

- Teachers and students can easily find podcasts and vodcasts on virtually any educational topic.

- When teachers and students produce their own podcasts and vodcasts, they make new opportunities to learn academic material outside of the classroom by hearing or viewing lectures, discussions, demonstrations, and summaries.

KEY TERMS

Alphabet books	Multimedia
Concept books	Multimodal learning
Digital art making	Pocket video cameras
Digital cameras	Podcast
Digital projectors	Podcatcher
Digital single-use camera	Point-and-shoot cameras
Digital storytelling	PowerPoint
Digital video cameras	Shoot-to-print cameras
Digital video editing software	Single lens reflex (SLR) design cameras
Digital voice recorders	Storyboarding
Graphic design	Streaming video
Information presentation design	Vodcast
Interactive whiteboards	Webcast
iPod	

ACTIVITIES FOR YOUR TEACHER PORTFOLIO

1. ELECTRONIC CHILDHOOD AND GENERATION M

The presence of television, computers, the Internet, video games, and other screen media in the lives of children and adolescents has given rise to two new terms: "electronic childhood" and "generation M" (Rideout, Vandewater, & Wartella, 2003; Rideout, Roberts, & Foehr, 2005). An electronic childhood refers to the fact that children at ages as early as six months now interact regularly with a variety of technologies and media, creating a new category of experience whose psychological and sociological impacts are still being documented. The "M" in "generation M" means either "media" or "millennials" and refers to the generation born between 1980 and 2000.

As a teacher entering classrooms filled with students who have grown up using media and multimedia technologies, answer the following questions:

- How are you going to organize your instructional strategies to capture and maintain the attention of this media generation?

- How do you select the best media to promote education rather than entertainment?

2. VIDEO MAKING AND PODCASTING

Emerging technologies like video movie making and podcasting require an investment of time to learn, but they offer exciting ways to share ideas and perspectives with others. Teachers and students do not have to be experienced filmmakers or podcasters to begin using the technologies creatively.

What do you see as the major advantages of video movie making and podcasting for students at the elementary, middle, and high school levels?

3. TECHNOLOGY-BASED PRESENTATION STRATEGIES

You are attending a faculty meeting where your colleagues are describing and explaining the work in their classes that excites them the most. Some bring projects that their students have completed. Some describe unique learning activities they have done in their classes. Still others talk about classroom projects without sharing example materials. Interestingly, these are the same presentation models that students in K–12 schools regularly use when asked to present their assignments in class. After a while, those listening lose interest. How might these largely "no-tech" presentations be made more engaging and illustrative by using technologies such as PowerPoint, podcasts, video images, or other multimedia tools?

GROWING AND LEADING WITH TECHNOLOGY

This activity offers an opportunity to grow as a teacher and to lead with technology. Begin by reviewing the Chapter 9 Learning Goal and Featured Technologies listed in the chart at the start of the chapter. Then read the following actual classroom scenario and consider how technologies discussed in Chapter 9 might be integrated into the lesson. Follow-up steps to this activity can be completed at MyEducationKit.

YVONNE'S POETRY LESSON

Yvonne will be teaching a series of classes on poetry reading and writing to fourth-graders. Three instructional goals guide her planning. First, she wants students to read and hear different types of poetry, including rhyming poems, acrostic poems, and concrete or picture poetry. Second, she wants students to write poetry as a creative way to connect reading and writing. Third, she wants students to learn and remember the meanings of poetry vocabulary words (*genre, stanza, verse,* and *rhyme*) that appear on the state's English/language arts assessment test.

Yvonne has 90-minute blocks of language arts instruction each day, and she has five days for that poetry unit. She is teaching in a classroom that has one computer with Internet access, a digital projector, a printer, and a portable television set. She has access to a nearby computer lab with computers for every member of her class that have an up-to-date collection of software programs, including word processing.

The class includes students with special educational needs as well as regular education students, and Yvonne knows from previous assignments that she has a wide range of learning styles and preferences in the class, including some students who are easily distracted by or bored with whole-group instruction.

- Using the technologies discussed in this chapter, how would you propose that Yvonne integrate technology into her poetry lesson plan in ways that will support learning success and enjoyment for all her students?

10 Promoting Success for All Students through Technology

Teachers should fashion teaching and learning so that all students have the chance to learn and to demonstrate what they have learned—not just those who happen to be gifted with words and numbers.

—Howard Gardner, "Can Technology Exploit Our Many Ways of Knowing?" (2000)

CHAPTER LEARNING GOAL

Differentiated Instruction for All Students

Using assistive technologies to differentiate instruction and promote learning success for all students

CONNECTING to the NETS

NETS-T

2 Design and Develop Digital Age Learning Experiences and Assessments

4 Promote and Model Digital Citizenship and Responsibility

NETS-S

5 Digital Citizenship

NEW TECHNOLOGIES

- UDL resources for teachers
- Assistive technologies
- Electronic spellers and dictionaries
- Handheld and online calculators
- Text reading software
- Speech recognition software
- Interactive digital storybooks

CHAPTER OVERVIEW

Chapter 10 examines how computer technologies expand opportunities for teachers to meet the learning needs of all students, and regular or special education classrooms. Technologies developed for special needs learners can be very useful for other students, because they make possible teaching activities that respond to a range of learning styles and preferences. We discuss differentiated instruction (DI) and universal design for learning (UDL) as approaches for teachers. Next we review a range of assistive digital tools that support successful learning for all students, including handheld spellers, electronic calculators, speech-to-text software, text-to-speech software, and interactive storybooks. The chapter concludes with ideas for integrating technology into the teaching of writing.

Through its focus on differentiated instruction and success for all students, the chapter reflects NETS-T Standard 4, Part b, which urges teachers to "address the diverse needs of all learners by using learner-centered strategies" that include equitable access to digital tools. It also supports the NETS-S Standard 5 in urging positive attitudes toward technology to support "collaboration, learning and productivity."

FOCUS QUESTIONS

1. What are differentiated instruction (DI) and universal design for learning (UDL)?

2. How can teachers use technology to create universally designed classrooms?

3. How does assistive technology support efforts by teachers to reach all learners?

4. How is technology used in a writing process fit for young writers to promote learning success for all students?

Dan, a college student enrolled in a science teacher education program, is taking a course entitled "The Work of the Middle and High School Teacher." One of the readings for the course is *Teachers, Their World, and Their Work* by Ann Lieberman and Lynne Miller (1984). Published a quarter century ago, this book contends that the organizational lives of teachers (their world) influence how they teach their students and make sense of their job (their work).

For Dan, the book presented an astonishingly different perspective about what teachers do in their jobs. Dan had always thought of teaching in personal terms. He enjoyed learning science and he thought he would enjoy teaching science to younger students. Now, he was confronting the reality that teaching is a complex, demanding job built on an overarching dilemma—teachers must try to meet the learning needs of every individual student while teaching in large-group situations.

Yet as Lieberman and Miller point out, one-on-one teaching is not the same as one-on-15, or one-on-20, or one-on-30 teaching. While every student could conceivably benefit from individualized responses by teachers, the realities of teaching large groups in classrooms block many educators from being able to respond to the needs and concerns of individuals. Striving to keep the entire class moving ahead, a teacher may leave the learning needs of some individuals unmet. This tension between the individual and the group is present every day in every classroom. It is a fundamental reality of the work of the elementary, middle, and high school teacher.

In a paper he wrote at the end of his college class, Dan commented that he now saw teaching in new terms, realizing that his next goal for himself as a teacher must be to find ways to reach and support all his students, both as individual learners and as members of classroom groups and communities.

This chapter's learning goal—how technology supports learning success for all students—is an effort to respond to the individual-versus-group dilemma described in Lieberman and Miller's book. As Dan realized, such dilemmas are deeply entrenched in schools for two main reasons. First, there are never enough hours for teachers to do everything they want to do educationally for every student. Teachers must make difficult choices about which students to help and for how long before moving on to the next student or the next topic in the curriculum. Second, teachers at every grade level have classes filled with such a wide range of student learning needs that no single teaching method or approach will deliver educational success for everyone, as suggested by the following learning differences:

- Those who require a teacher's presence and fixed routines while others prefer flexible situations where they can work independently on their own interests some of the time.
- Those who prefer listening to instructions and watching demonstrations before trying a new activity because of worries about making a mistake and appearing foolish in front of their peers. Other students would rather try a new activity first and learn from their mistakes. Less concerned about what others think of their efforts, they gravitate toward the spotlight provided by individual or group presentations.
- Those who learn by reading words and expressing their own ideas in written language as opposed to others who require visual images and auditory cues to understand and remember new concepts. Depending on the topic of study and personal levels of motivation, everyone prefers different combinations of reading, writing, and speaking to effectively learn something new.

Teachers respond to these situations differently. For some, trying to balance the needs of individual students with those of the larger classroom group is part of what imbues teaching with creativity, excitement, and constant challenge. These teachers find it immensely satisfying to design a class, incorporate different techniques and activities to reach different learners, and watch that class work well. For others, it is deeply frustrating to be unable to reach some students because their learning needs are so varied from others in the class. Teachers report feeling ineffective in trying to teach to the middle range of students because there is no real middle group, only many separate individuals who will respond more or less favorably to whatever a teacher is doing instructionally at the time.

PEARSON
myeducationkit™

Go to the Assignments and Activities section of Chapter 10 in MyEducationKit and complete the video activity entitled "Differentiating Instruction." As you watch the video and answer the accompanying questions, note how this school defines and incorporates inclusion.

Differentiated Instruction and Universal Design for Learning

Differentiated instruction (DI) and universal design for learning (UDL) are frameworks for teachers to use in adjusting their curriculum and instruction away from a one-size-fits-all model toward approaches that address the needs of different students within the same class.

DI and UDL are often associated with instructional changes designed to meet the needs of students with special educational needs, gifted and talented learners, or English language learners (see Figure 10.1). But many teachers have found that every student benefits when classroom activities are differentiated to address multiple learning needs and preferences.

Differentiated Instruction

Differentiated instruction (DI) is an instructional approach that gives students "multiple options for taking in information and making sense of ideas" (Hall, 2007). It means that teachers create different educational experiences as a way to meet the specific needs of students (Gregory & Chapman, 2007; Smith & Throne, 2007; Tomlinson, 2003). Learning experiences are designed to achieve maximum interest and challenge as teachers acknowledge and plan for the presence of differences among the students they are teaching (DeCourcy, Fairchild, & Follett, 2007).

For example, a differentiated math unit on probability opens with a series of student-acted skits to introduce the concept. By engaging the whole class in an opening that is thought-provoking yet humorous, where brains and bodies are active simultaneously, the beginning of the unit is constructed and shared by everyone. Following the skits, students are assigned to groups to learn similar curriculum about probability in differentiated ways.

Designing activities to teach to the learning styles of different students is the key to successful differentiated instruction. For example, a probability lesson can include the following activities:

- *Group A.* Individual students are on the computer using a program that flips coins to tally the numbers of heads and tails resulting from 100 flips.
- *Group B.* Pairs of students take turns tossing dice and recording the results from each roll, charting the outcomes from 100 tosses.
- *Group C.* Students devise new skits to perform, based on experiences that they encounter in their daily lives—for example, the probability of getting a desired lunch choice if only two choices are available and one of them is meatloaf (or fish stew or baloney sandwiches).
- *Group D.* Students work with the teacher doing practice exercises in a math book.

To conclude the math learning time, each group of students reports the result of their work to the class. Then the small groups of students choose how to record what they have learned, either alone or in their small groups, in words or drawings, by writing or typing or voice recording on the computer. In the space of one class period, multiple learning styles are addressed using different instructional methods.

FIGURE 10.1 An Overview of Students in K–12 Schools in the United States

Children or Youth with Disabilities (U.S. Department of Education, 2008; Hehir, 2006, p. 7)

- About 9 percent of the nation's 55 million students receive special education services under the provisions of the Individuals with Disabilities Education Act.

- Just over 90 percent of students with special needs face one of four learning challenges:
  - Learning disabilities
  - Speech and language disorders
  - ADHD (attention deficit/hyperactivity disorder)
  - Behavioral and intellectual disabilities

- Less than 1 percent of the total school-age population experience "blindness, deafness, and significant physical disability."

- 80 percent of children with learning disabilities have difficulties with reading, writing, and spelling, although aptitude tests often reveal that they have the intellectual capabilities to be successful readers and writers.

Gifted and Talented Students (U.S. Department of Education, 2005)

- About 6.7 percent of the 55 million students in the nation's public schools are considered gifted and talented learners.

- Figures for gifted and talented numbers vary nationally; in some states, 10 or 11 percent of the students are considered gifted while in others only 1 or 2 percent are so identified.

English Language Learners

- About 20 percent of the nation's 55 million students (about 10.8 million youngsters) are bilingual/English language learners who speak a language other than English at home (U.S. Department of Education, 2008).

- Spanish is the language most frequently spoken at home among those who speak a language other than English, accounting for 37 percent of 5- to 9-year-olds and 24 percent of 10- to 17-year-olds in 2004; 5 percent of those bilingual speakers, or 2.8 million children and adolescents, speak English with difficulty (U.S. Department of Education, 2006).

- In schools, the number of children speaking English with difficulty increased 114 percent between 1979 and 2004 (U.S. Department of Education, 2006, p. 34). California's entire population growth in the 1990s consisted of language minority speakers, who rose by 40 percent while English speakers declined by 1 percent (UC Linguistic Minority Research Newsletter, 2001).

Student learning differences, noted differentiated instruction advocate Carol Ann Tomlinson (2003, pp. 3–4), arise in four areas:

- *Readiness.* How students' prior experiences have prepared them to learn academic material
- *Interest.* How curious or committed students are to learning what school is teaching
- *Learning profile.* How students learn best in formal and informal situations
- *Affect.* How students regard themselves as learners, and how students regard the school as a place where people learn

The challenge for teachers is finding the time, resources, and tools necessary to differentiate instruction in ways that will engage the multiple learning styles and preferences of students. It is true that some students come to school with individual education plans (IEPs) that specify the adaptations, modifications, and supports that teachers must provide as part of daily classroom instruction. But not every student has an IEP designating how to maximize learning for that individual. Some students not labeled as special needs, English language learners, or gifted and talented are at risk of "falling between the cracks" of the educational system because although they may need different approaches, there is no plan in place to provide different learning experiences on a regular basis.

Still a teacher cannot design an individualized curriculum for every student every day. Often students will have to do the same activities, even if those activities might not be what is optimal for them in terms of learning style and approach. For example, a teacher introduces a new science topic using a large-group format even though she knows that some of her students have difficulty focusing in such situations. Next, she varies the delivery of the material, using spoken words, visual images, and hands-on materials as ways to reach individual students. Finally, she shortens the length of time the students spend working together on projects to keep the class moving without anyone losing attention or focus. Each of these steps differentiates the learning, but none of these steps by themselves will provide what every student needs to succeed.

Universal Design for Learning

Universal design, a concept from the field of architecture, is at the center of new approaches to how schools can serve all students well. In building design and construction, universal design involves the installation of such features as "ramps, accessible toilets, fire alarm systems with lights" (Hehir, 2005, p. 88). A curb cut is an example of universal design in architecture. It allows wheelchairs to move from sidewalk to curb, pedestrians to move more freely, and delivery persons to move large loads smoothly from the curbside to the sidewalk.

Universal design for learning (UDL) is the application of universal design principles to educational settings. UDL applies recent advances in the understanding of how the brain processes information to the design of curriculum that can accommodate broad student needs (Rose & Meyer, 2002, 2006). The Center for Applied Special Technology (CAST) has defined UDL in the following terms:

- *Multiple means of representation,* to give learners various ways of acquiring information and knowledge,
- *Multiple means of expression,* to provide learners alternatives for demonstrating what they know,
- *Multiple means of engagement,* to tap into learners' interests, offer appropriate challenges, and increase motivation. (Center for Applied Special Technology, 2006)

The purpose of universal design in schools is "full participation and access for students with disabilities while providing individualized options for all" (Hehir, 2005, p. 99). The intent is to create teaching and learning situations that serve the needs of the widest range of students without diminishing or reducing opportunities for anyone. As such, universal design "provides a blueprint for creating flexible goals, methods, materials, and assessments that meet the needs of diverse learners" (Rose, Meyer, & Hitchcock, 2005, p. 3).

By making instructional goals, strategies, and materials highly flexible, UDL lowers potential barriers to learning while increasing learning opportunities for all students. As such, the "same innovations that provide disabled individuals with everyday access to information or places also enhance the experiences of those who do not have disabilities per se but may have unrecognized situational needs, challenges, or preferences that enable them to benefit from universally designed solutions" (Rose, Meyer, & Hitchcock, 2005, p. 3). For example, a teacher might use PowerPoint to display vocabulary words and definitions on a screen in front of the room so a hearing impaired child can read the information while the class discusses the terms. Although not the teacher's

PEARSON
myeducationkit

Go to the Assignments and Activities section of Chapter 10 in MyEducationKit and complete the video activity entitled "Universal Design." As you watch the video and answer the accompanying questions, note how universal design evolved.

Computers offer multiple ways for teachers to meet the needs of individual learners. Some students learn more easily when they can proceed at their own pace and receive helpful feedback from computer software.

original intent, many regular education students may demonstrate better recall because they too can read as well as hear the material in class.

Roles for Technology

"Minimizing the impact of disability and *maximizing the opportunity* to participate in the world" is the key to adapting teaching strategies and classroom environments to fit the needs of all learners, asserts Thomas Hehir (2006, p. 8), former director of the U.S. Department of Education's Special Education Programs. Hehir wants educators to emphasize **accommodations,** where students with special educational needs have different ways to access the regular education curriculum. He wants to avoid what he calls **modification,** where students receive educational experiences less substantive than those received by regular education students.

For example, modification would occur if a learning disabled student was "required to do fewer math problems for homework because he reads slowly." By doing fewer problems than his regular education peers, the child's academic experience is lessened. Instead, that student would benefit from an accommodation that included receiving "a taped version of the assignment and expecting him to do what any other child does" (Hehir, 2006, p. 7).

Computer technology allows for never-before-possible implementations of universal design in schools. For example, schools have always been print-bound institutions, and prior to computers, it was not easy to modify or manipulate printed text so struggling readers could understand it more easily. Digital media makes print materials "malleable: they can be transformed, marked, linked, networked, and customized for each individual learner" (Meyer & Rose, 2005, pp. 17–18). Print-bound content can be displayed in different ways—on screens, through movies and animations, or with speech, sound, and pictures. Materials can be hyperlinked to other sources of information and processed at a pace and in a mode that suits each particular learner. Barriers to student learning are thus significantly and fundamentally reduced.

Classroom Learning with Technology

Every teacher is an instructional designer, deciding everything from how seating is arranged to what instructional activities will be conducted. For teachers concerned about universal design and learning success, no aspect of the classroom environment is too small or insignificant to address because even little items may make the difference between a student paying attention or drifting away from the focus of the class. For this reason, teachers must constantly design and redesign both classroom setting and curriculum content to meet the needs of students.

There are two main routes for designing your classroom using technology: changing the classroom learning environment or changing how the curriculum is delivered.

In the first instance, the classroom's physical structure is changed to fit the needs of all learners. In the second, academic curriculum is presented so students with multiple learning needs can readily access key ideas and concepts.

To begin thinking about designing your classroom, imagine ways to differentiate your teaching. You can use a range of low-tech, mid-tech, and high-tech tools, as described below:

- *Low tech* refers to changes that are made easily, inexpensively, and without applying digital or electronic materials.
- *Mid tech* involves substantive shifts in organization and delivery of curriculum that may include the use of electronic materials.

PEARSON
myeducationkit

Go to the Assignments and Activities section of Chapter 10 in MyEducationKit and complete the video activity entitled "Software for Diverse Learners." As you watch the video and answer the accompanying questions, note the efforts one state is making to incorporate technology into teaching for all students.

Meeting the Needs of Individual Learners

Because students learn at their own rates and in their own ways, how do teachers meet the needs of every individual learner in their classes? Answering this question can be hugely complex. Given the inevitable mix of learning styles and personal preferences found in any classroom group, teachers are constantly choosing between slowing the pace of instruction to help individuals learn a concept or review specific operations and keeping the curriculum moving forward for the larger classroom group. Such choices are always complicated: When too much time is spent on individual needs, progress for a larger group of students is slowed. When the larger group pushes steadily ahead, some individuals may lag behind, missing the information they need to understand the material.

While no formula or guideline fits every situation, teachers benefit when they have research-proven information on which to base their instructional decisions. One source is the Access Center, an online resource maintained by the American Institutes of Research, a nonprofit organization located in Washington, D.C. Initially funded as a national technical assistance center by the U.S. Department of Education, the Access Center's mission is supporting learning for students with disabilities within the general curriculum.

Although the Access Center's federal funding has ended, its website has been continued, and the site contains an extensive collection of resources for teachers on such topics as coteaching, computer-assisted instruction, differentiated instruction, direct instruction, English language learning, reading, writing, math, science, graphic organizers, and middle school education. Clicking on a category brings you to different types of resources, including "Briefs" (short research-based discussions of a topic), "Presentations," and "Professional Development Modules." There are also links to a searchable national database of state and district resources.

Ideas, information, and model lessons addressing "differentiated instruction" and "universal design" are also available from the Teaching Every Student (TES) website maintained by CAST (Center for Applied Special Technology), a nonprofit organization located in Wakefield, Massachusetts. CAST is a leading proponent of universal design for learning (UDL). In this website, CAST seeks to provide an interactive online learning environment for understanding ways to implement UDL in the classroom. Among its resources are the following:

- *UDL Lesson Builder* (http://lessonbuilder.cast.org). Lets teachers explore model lesson plans and then build and edit their own plans according to UDL principles.

- *UDL Book Builder* (http://bookbuilder.cast.org). Lets teachers explore children's books for teaching reading and then build their own accessible early reading resources.
- *UDL Editions.* Uses digital media with animated coaches to provide different levels of language and conceptual learning support to students reading such classic literature as the Gettysburg Address, Shakespeare's "Sonnet XVIII," and Jack London's *The Call of the Wild.*
- *Strategy Tutor.* An online tool with short video demonstrations designed to support students who are doing Internet research.

The TES site includes model UDL lessons at the elementary, middle, and high school levels. These lessons contrast a traditional or nondifferentiated approach with a UDL approach. Teachers can also register for their own free space on the TES site where you can store your work, organize Web links, and share information and feedback with other teachers. Explore both the Access Center and TES to help you make choices about how to organize your teaching in ways that improve learning for all students.

AccessIT (the National Center on Accessible Information Technology in Education) at the University of Washington features a searchable database of questions and answers about the uses of electronic and information technology at all educational levels.

CONTACT INFORMATION

Access Center
www.k8accesscenter.org/index.php

The Center for Applied Special Technology (CAST)
www.cast.org/teachingeverystudent

Teaching Every Student website is available free.

The National Center on Accessible Information Technology in Education
www.washington.edu/accessit

AccessIT is available free.

- *High tech* introduces changes associated with the integration of computers and other specialized information technologies in the classroom.

Tables 10.1 and 10.2 offer ways to differentiate essential elements in the classroom at the low-tech, mid-tech, and high-tech levels.

 ## Using Assistive Technology to Reach All Learners

Technological convergence describes the combining of multiple features and functions into one digital tool while content flows across multiple media platforms (Jenkins, 2006). Televisions

TABLE 10.1   Classroom Organization Tools

Technology Tool	Low Tech	Mid Tech	High Tech
Chairs and desks	Provide desks and chairs with adjustable heights for different-sized students. For small-sized students who slip out of their chairs easily, use gripping shelf paper to cover the seat.	Provide specially designed seat cushions or "positioning aids" for students who need them.	Provide alternative seating, such as ball chairs.
Whiteboards, chalkboards, chart paper	Write in colors that are visible to individuals who may be colorblind. Avoid light colors. Offer a hard copy of what is on the board for students who find copying from the board a challenge.	Use audio recordings made by classmates of the notes from the board or chart paper. Students can access these audio recordings and listen to the notes or directions via headphones.	Use an interactive whiteboard that offers a printout of notes and directions from the board and allows the font to be enlarged.
Pencils, paper, scissors	Provide a variety of different writing tools, markers, pencils, and crayons, in assorted sizes and different types of pencil grippers. Provide writing paper with different-sized lines and spacing; provide correction fluid or correction paper. Provide left- and right-handed scissors with padding and different finger placement accommodations.	Provide word processing software with spell checking and grammar correction tools that are developmentally appropriate. Provide different textured papers with raised lines that can be seen and felt by the writer; provide portable classroom spellers and small portable write-on and wipe-off boards.	Provide a Tablet PC with a writing stylus and writing software that translates handwritten words into typed text. Provide speech-to-text software that records student voices as text documents.
Reading materials	Provide book highlighting tape, Post-It notes, multiple copies of big books.	Provide books or CDs recorded by the teacher or students and interactive picture dictionaries.	Provide talking books made from classroom books, interactive books, word-by-word highlighting software, text-to-speech software.
Writing	Use audio recordings that can be transcribed into words, dictionaries, thesauri, and magnification tools.	Use magnification software.	Use word prediction software, speech-to-text software, enhanced keyboards.

TABLE 10.2   Classroom Teaching Methods

Delivery Method	Low Tech	Mid Tech	High Tech
Teacher lectures.	Teacher uses large charts for ease of viewing information and a child-sized sound machine to amplify voices for ease of hearing information.	Teacher uses PowerPoint to project information onto a screen. Teacher also uses a classroom amplifier to project voices throughout the entire room.	Teacher uses a personal response system or other computer network to create an interactive lecture format with the students.
Teacher demonstrates.	Teacher uses manipulative materials and provides written directions to accompany oral directions.	Teacher offers digital simulations of manipulative materials to provide a different kind of view or practice.	Teacher offers a simulation of an idea, concept, or phenomenon that cannot be replicated in the classroom without technology.
Student manipulates hands-on materials to solve problems.	Student uses physical materials for experimentation.	Student uses a digital simulation of the same experiment manipulating variables in a virtual environment.	Student accesses digital tools and materials that are not available for hands-on use in the classroom as part of the experiment.
Student works independently.	Student works independently at a desk or table.	Student works independently at a desk or table on a computer using data specifically designed for or chosen based on learning needs.	Student works independently accessing feedback from a teacher about individual work in process.
Students work in groups with a teacher.	Students work alone or share a computer and each assumes a different role in researching, testing, or documenting a hypothesis.	Students work in pairs or small groups using collaborative software while researching, testing, or documenting a hypothesis.	Students work collaboratively utilizing multiple digital feedback mechanisms to publish their research to a wider community.
Students teach each other in peer teaching activities.	Students work together to solve problems.	Students work in small groups developing or experiencing WebQuests.	Students, assigned different roles in the process, work as small-group teams developing or experiencing WebQuests.

connected to other devices in home entertainment centers, Internet navigating equipment, and video game playing consoles are examples of convergence, as are cellular telephones that make calls, take photographs, record and play video, send email messages, and surf the Net. These are all multifaceted machines in streamlined packages performing multiple functions. Broadband cable provides convergence through music downloads, streaming video, automatic bill paying, and real-time instant messenger chats. In retail stores, convergence occurs in cash registers that manage sales and inventory simultaneously while offering a digital pen for customer signatures on purchase agreements.

Technological convergence has evolved quite differently in K–12 schools than in business. For a century the chalkboard was the means by which teachers demonstrated examples, listed procedures, and articulated concepts, while pencils and paper were the tools for written communications. In recent years, Post-It notes have served students and teachers as affordable bookmarks or reminders. Most teachers, however, while relying on these low-tech methods, have not considered the multiple ways they can access the capabilities of computers and other information technologies to reach all learners. In short, they have not begun to utilize the powers of convergence.

In this section of the chapter, we apply the concept of technological convergence to the ways information technologies enable teachers to differentiate instruction and pursue universal design through use of **assistive technologies.** Broadly defined, assistive technologies "modify the interface between student and material so that the material becomes more accessible" (Hitchcock, Meyer, Rose, & Jackson, 2005, p. 49). These technologies seek to maximize learning while minimizing barriers to educational success.

Assistive technologies make it possible for individuals with hearing, sight, mobility, or cognitive challenges to translate text and understand spoken words and data with the aid of a supportive tool. Assistive technologies come in multiple forms, including hardware, software, and adaptive devices such as a handheld magnifier or a specialized keyboard for typing.

The following ideas are important for teachers to consider when using assistive technologies in the classroom:

- *Assistive technology by itself does not always provide positive learning supports for students.* As members of CAST (Center for Applied Special Technology) observed, a book on tape can help develop a child's reading skills and it can reinforce the learning of key concepts, but it can also be overused as an instructional activity. The child can become so reliant on the tape to pronounce unknown words that the technology "impedes learning and eliminates healthy challenge when it is used during a reading lesson" (Hitchcock, Meyer, Rose, & Jackson, 2005, p. 52). The use of technology must be complemented by the active involvement of teachers and other caring adults or the impact of technology use may be counterproductive.
- *While commonly used to support students with disabilities, assistive technologies create extraordinary learning opportunities for all students.* This is where the idea of technological convergence connects to assistive technology. A single tool can produce multiple results; it is not a stand-alone device that a teacher uses only for a specific task with one or two students. As examples, text-to-speech software allows Web pages to be read aloud, calculators speak numbers as well as perform calculations, and computers convert cursive writing or spoken words into printed text. In these and many other ways, assistive technologies facilitate learning activities for all students at all grade levels.
- *When used creatively by teachers, many electronic and computer-based tools can serve as assistive technologies.* Indeed, students with diverse learning needs can use tools and technologies not commonly called assistive to support learning.

The pages that follow showcase examples of electronic or computer-based assistive technologies for classroom use. Our suggestions do not exhaust the list of available resources, but serve as models of using technology to reach all learners. We discuss each tool's primary functions and offer suggestions for instructional uses.

Electronic Spellers and Dictionaries

An **electronic speller and dictionary** is a tool for learners of all ages. Beginning readers can find correct spellings, listen to words spoken aloud, and check the accuracy of their spelling without adult help. By plugging headphones into the machine, students with hearing impairments can see and hear words they may not be able to sound out phonetically. With headphones all students can use the machine without creating sounds others might hear. Middle and high school students can use these machines to support their writing and check their spelling.

Franklin Electronic Publishers, located in Burlington, New Jersey, is a leading manufacturer of handheld electronic dictionaries, encyclopedias, personal organizers, language translators, test preparation devices, and e-books (www .franklin.com). The Speaking Homework Wiz is a 7-ounce, battery-powered

FIGURE 10.2 Speaking Homework Wiz from Franklin Learning Resources

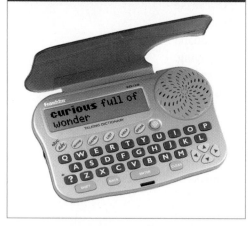

Source: Courtesy of Franklin Electronic Publishers.

device containing a 46,000-word dictionary and spell checker with word pronunciation and recognition features (see Figure 10.2). But this product is more than a portable spelling checker and dictionary. You will discover that it builds concentration and fun into how students learn word meanings and spellings.

The machine invites use and supports learning. Type in a word and the machine's voice speaks aloud a succinct, understandable definition of the term. *Computer,* for example, is "an electronic machine with games and information" while *onomatopoeia* is "when a word imitates a sound, like 'hiss.'" *Utopia* is an "impossibly wonderful place." Students can stop the machine from reading the definition by clicking on another word such as *impossibly* or *wonderful* to hear and learn the meaning of those terms, too. Clicking on a word in a definition is called "Jumping to a Word."

When typing a name, favorite word, or short phrase into the machine, students choose to view it in cursive or manuscript. It appears on the screen, one letter at a time, then the machine pronounces it. Young students in particular enjoy seeing their names as well as the names of their friends, pets, and family members appear on the screen. They exhibit intense concentration, drawn to the process of typing in the letters, watching the machine print them in cursive or manuscript letters, and listening to the automated voice.

The machine's spell checking feature is a resource for students who find spelling an unhappy or frustrating experience. The spell checker accepts words that are spelled incorrectly, offers a list of possible standard spellings, and says each one aloud for easy identification of the correct word. Instead of stopping as they write first drafts to find unfamiliar words, students can write words as they think they are spelled and check their spelling afterward with the machine. This tool enables writing to proceed as a process—writers put ideas on paper while in the flow of written self-expression, then revise the ideas to improve reader understanding, and finally edit the piece by spelling words conventionally while including appropriate punctuation.

The machine lets children create an 80-item list of their own words, including terms not already in its electronic dictionary, as in the following list of one kindergartner's favorite words.

Robin's Favorite Words List

bad hairday	cheerleader
pony	blob
one billion	infinity
ballerinas	bamboo sticks

Creating a list of "My Words" invites a focus on words students find interesting, intriguing, and worth remembering. Franklin makes other handheld electronic resources for middle or high school students, or for teachers at any grade level who want a professional reference tool. The Ultimate Reference Suite contains the 11th edition of Merriam-Webster's Collegiate Dictionary along with a thesaurus, an encyclopedia, and a collection of great documents of American history. The "Merriam-Webster Dictionary and Thesaurus" machine features 300,000 word definitions and 500,000 synonyms and antonyms. Another dictionary model offers six languages: Spanish, Portuguese, Italian, French, German, and English.

YOUR JUDGMENT MATTERS

Thinking about your own experiences with writing and spelling, consider the following questions:

- Would you encourage the use of handheld spellers by students in your classroom when writing? Taking exams? Creating posters and other visual displays?
- How might handheld electronic spellers and dictionaries support students' learning in school and at home?

Handheld Calculators

A **calculator** is a handheld device that performs mathematical operations and computations. Calculators are small computers that perform specific data operations, have electronic circuitry,

The CC16 Extra-Large Calculator from Kikkerland is an attention-engaging tool for exploring the four mathematical operations—adding, subtracting, multiplying, and dividing—and other concepts with elementary school students. The 7" by 11" tablet weighs only a few ounces, so it is surprisingly lightweight.

The major advantage of this machine is its large size. At a time when electronic products are being made smaller and smaller, here is calculator that is deliberately larger than many others. Its oversized easy-to-read number and function keys are inviting to touch and arouse curiosity. The large keys and number displays not only support visual learning for sight-impaired students, but also for everyone else in a class. Students are more interested in this product than a smaller one because of its different size and its style.

As a teaching tool, extra large calculators (see the accompanying photo) have many uses. First, they may inspire a discussion about the word *calculate* meaning "to pebble." The first calculator was a collection of small stones used by ancient humans to count their transactions by matching one-to-one amounts. One stone might represent one piece of cloth, one basket of foodstuffs, or one seed.

The Indo-Arabic numbers used throughout the world today (1, 2, 3, 4, . . .) are abstract symbols invented so people need not be physically present to match and record amounts. Number symbols combined with a counting concept of "place value" could serve the same purpose as a pile of pebbles much more flexibly. Place value means that where a number appears in a group determines its worth; 12 and 21 look similar but they do not mean the same amount. Place value is an essential idea to learn and one that a calculator helps explain. Try demonstrating the idea of place value to students using pebbles or marbles or other small objects. Count and divide quantities of these items and then show the operations using the electronic calculator.

and possess a limited memory function. You are likely to find the following four types of calculators in schools:

- *Basic calculator.* The most common type of calculator, this machine does limited number operations and has a minimal memory function.
- *Scientific calculator.* Used by research scientists, these machines are capable of performing more complex operations and possess more memory.
- *Graphing calculator.* Used in math teaching and for scientific/engineering purposes, these machines have larger screens for displaying graphs, advanced memory capabilities, are programmable, and can handle more complex formulas.
- *Other.* This category includes machines that perform specialized functions.

You can learn more about calculators in Tech Tool 10.1.

Calculators are fascinating instruments for students of all ages. One fourth-grader who carries her calculator to school every day whether she needs it or not states that she feels more prepared to learn when she has the calculator in her school bag. She marvels at how calculators do what human brains do, but more quickly and accurately.

Calculating with objects to manipulate becomes easy and familiar to students when practiced frequently. What is unfamiliar is how the same calculation that students demonstrate with objects ("There are 3 kids and 6 cookies: How many cookies does each child receive?") looks when written in numerals and text as "6 divided by 3." The calculator connects written equations with what students can do by hand using physical objects.

Math learning with calculators is improved by featuring real-life problems that have authentic meaning to young mathematicians. "How many more days until my next birthday?" "How many books can I purchase with $20 if each book costs $3.95?" "How many slices of pizza will there be at my party if three pizzas are cut into eighths?" As students calculate personally meaningful math problems, they engage in the practice needed to become better-skilled mathematicians.

Middle and high school students will enjoy visiting Jim Martindale's Calculators On-Line Center featuring links to more than 22,000 calculation programs, many with online simulations and teaching modules. You can calculate the speed of a dinosaur, daily sun and moon data, the storage capacities of an iPod, the distances between geographic locations, the physics of baseball, wind chill factors, and much more. See the accompanying screenshot of a Warp Factor Calculator based on the "Star Trek" television series.

Warp Factor Calculator

for the **Star Trek** universe

by Stephen R. Schmitt

Select version:
- ◉ Classic Star Trek
- ○ The Next Generation

Please enter Warp factor:

Now enter light years to your destination:

[Calculate]

Velocity:
_____ x C (Speed of Light)

Then, from Earth it takes: ◉ Years ○ Days
_____ to reach Alpha Centauri (4.3 Light Years)
_____ to traverse Milky Way galaxy (100,000 Light Years)
_____ to reach the Andromeda galaxy (2,000,000 Light Years)
_____ to reach your destination

[Clear]

CONTACT INFORMATION

Jim Martindale's Calculators On-Line Center www.martindalecenter.com/Calculators.html

---

Calculators are a topic of sharp debate among educators. Researchers have found that calculators support students' mathematical learning, specifically in terms of solving problems, exploring patterns, doing number operations, and working with real-world data (Ellington, 2003; Wenglinsky, 2005). Students with learning disabilities, who have short-term memory deficits and who lack confidence with number operations, may particularly benefit from calculators, allowing them to perform addition, subtraction, multiplication, and division more easily so they can pay more attention to the mathematical concepts that underlie these procedures (Center for Implementing Technology in Education, 2007).

At the same time, cautions the National Mathematics Advisory Panel (2008), calculator use should not substitute for students learning basic math facts and operations. Some educators believe students should not be allowed to use calculators in any classroom setting. The National Council of Teachers of Mathematics (2005) recommends a balanced instructional approach where students are taught to do paper-and-pencil calculations,

YOUR JUDGMENT
MATTERS

As you think about these contrasting views, consider the following questions:

- What have been your personal experiences using calculators?
- Have you found calculators to be helpful, even indispensable for completing assignments?
- How would you make calculators one of many tools in your classroom?

use mental math strategies, and electronically figure with calculators. Read more on calculator use in K–12 schools at the Research section of the Center for Implementing Technology in Education (CITEd) website (www.cited.org/index.aspx).

Speech Recognition Software

Speech recognition software translates a person's spoken words into written text on a computer screen. Also known as *speech-to-text software* or *voice recognition software*, these resources are often used by individuals with fine motor disabilities that prevent their writing by hand in cursive or typing on a keyboard. But some individuals prefer speech recognition software because they would rather speak than write or type their ideas. The technology is growing in use and represents a billion dollar a year industry (Atoji, 2007). The most well-known program is Dragon Naturally Speaking from Nuance Communications.

Speech recognition programs require users to "train the system" to recognize one or more primary voices by speaking various common phrases into the computer's microphone. The process for training the software has improved dramatically. What 15 years ago required hours of training time is now accomplished in a few minutes as the speaker reads a single paragraph into the computer. Reading to the computer teaches the software to recognize an individual's speech patterns and tonal nuances. Once the training is completed, the software will transcribe what you speak into word documents, which can then be edited using the cutting, pasting, and other editorial features and options found in word processing software programs.

For students who have been unwilling or unsuccessful writers, speech recognition software offers a new way to record their thoughts that then become their writing. It allows teachers to "capture" students' everyday stories and conversations on paper. We tell young writers that "good conversations make good stories and good poems," and this software demonstrates that idea in real time. Imagine the facial expression of a student wearing a microphone with a headset who starts speaking into the computer for the first time. Simply watching the computer screen fill with words he or she speaks can be astonishing for a reluctant writer.

Even with advancements in the technology, the process of transferring spoken words to written text requires revising and editing by student and teacher. The following example offers a sample of what a child's story might look like when first using speech recognition software. Although the child's story will need extensive editing to phrase it in Standard English, the story has at least been preserved electronically for further revision rather than lost completely if no technology had been used.

Child's Story Dictation Using Speech Recognition Software

Hello hello is this on hey is is writing what I say marco marco hello I am marco hello computer hey how does this work ms b look at the computer it is writing what I say write a story ok yesterday yesterday I went into the cafeteria and saw the principal working behind the counter the lunch counter and he said eat your vegetables they are very good for you so I took some peaches and he said that they are not vegetable that hey are fruit yut I said and took them and ate them and he came bye later and said here tie some carrots so I took them and tried them and they are good

After the dictation is complete, we read the child's text aloud to the student. The child might protest that we are not reading what he said, noting, "It's not right like that!" We then reread the text with the student to figure out why the software printed the story as it did. In the process of discussion, another more conventional version of the story emerges.

An author's misuse of a word or the software's misinterpretation of what a speaker has said will also confuse the meaning of the text. We know one young boy who continually says "yeah" for "yes." When the software printed "yeah" on the page, the student's speech pattern was visible because he could see "yeah" instead of "yes." This realization prompted him to change the text by saying "yes" so that the computer would transcribe the word he wanted on the page. The software served as a nonjudgmental proofreader, showing in print exactly what was said, giving instant feedback as a prompt for revising the text so it read the way the boy wanted it to read.

Text Reading Software

Text reading software, also known as text-to-speech software, lets computer users hear written text read aloud by the computer. These software programs are available in many versions, from simple text speech readers with few options to customized reading packages that offer selections of voices by gender or with different cadences. Some software lets users choose the pace of words read aloud per minute. Others highlight the text as the computerized voice reads it aloud. For some learners, this highlighting feature simulates an adult physically pointing to the individual words and letters in the text.

Go to the Assignments and Activities section of Chapter 10 in MyEducationKit. Open the Web activity "Multimedia e-Books as a Universal Design for Learning Approach."

There are different types of text-to-speech software available for teachers and students.

- **Screen reading software** acts as a translator of the visual page. While scanning the computer screen, the software reads the text and notifies the user of the frames and boundaries that are located on the screen. Screen reading software is often bundled with features that allow the user to understand the whereabouts and actions of the mouse, which, acting as a virtual tour guide, describes the hardware and software interactions.

    - JAWS is a highly regarded screen reader for Windows machines, available in 17 languages including English, Spanish, French, German, Portuguese, and Italian.
    - ReadPlease has a free-of-charge limited function reader and a more powerful commercial version.
    - Narrator is a limited built-in reader that is part of Windows 2000 and Windows XP software.
    - Emacspeak is a free, open source alternative.

- **Optical character recognition and reading software** enables text to be read and translated into multiple modes. Kurzweil 1000 and 3000 are the leading commercial programs. Optical character recognition (OCR) allows text from a printed book to be scanned into the software and then appear on the screen. For example, a favorite childhood book can be scanned and transferred into a readable document by the software. Optical character recognition technology converts a conventional text into a "living book," and, even more surprisingly, adds new dimensions of flexible use. Readers can parse a text into multiple interactive versions that can be selected and highlighted, thus creating a personalized, customized version of the original document. Often older literature is overlooked because it has lost shelf appeal. This software moves the words out of the book and into the ears and minds of children and teachers who might normally ignore what initially seems to be an outdated text.

- **Word prediction software** acts as a spelling and writing coach for young writers. The software predicts what the writer may be intending to write next, and offers multiple options as the writer types. For example, type the letter *s* and the program displays words from a list of frequently typed words beginning with *s*. Like speech recognition software, word prediction programs learn individual word usage habits. After typing the word *good, morning* may appear because many writers type "Good Morning" in their emails. Or after the word *happy, birthday* may pop up as a choice to enter into the text. Some versions of this software will speak the word that is typed to facilitate confirmation of the chosen word.

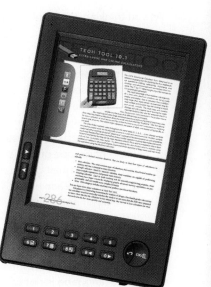

Interactive Electronic Storybooks

Interactive electronic storybooks (also called CD-ROM storybooks, e-books, or digital talking books for children) are a unique learning resource for young readers—regardless of whether a child has an identified reading problem or is developing reading skills without difficulties. Many schools, particularly at the elementary level, have invested in these resources. *Just Grandma and Me* by Mercer Meyer, *Sheila Rae, the Brave* by Kevin Henkes, and *The New Kid on the Block* by Jack Prelutsky are well-known titles from a discontinued series of interactive electronic books for children known as Living Books. Although out of production, these titles are still widely available.

An interactive electronic storybook presents literature for children on the computer. By combining the words and pictures of a book with the multimedia sound effects, graphic animations, and user interactions found in video games or other computer-based learning experiences, the text from the page becomes interactive on the computer. Children hear a story read aloud as they watch it unfold on the computer screen and interact with the characters and the scenes by clicking a mouse.

Interactive electronic storybooks are commonly presented on CD-ROM, but increasingly, these materials are available on the Web as well. Although this is changing, website storybooks tend not to be as sophisticated as software storybooks (Wepner & Cotter, 2002). Many websites offer static graphics where students simply view pictures while reading or listening to the story. Other sites offer more dynamic graphics where students interact with the story using "screen hotspots" that allow readers to go further into a scene in the story by clicking their mouse on a particular person or a specific object. Words, animations, sound effects, and other activities are "hidden" under these hotspots. Hotspot locations are not readily apparent so every page becomes a mystery for young readers to explore as they click on different items to see what will occur.

Many interactive storybooks offer multiple reading experience options as well. A story can be read aloud from beginning to end as when an adult reads a story aloud to children. Or the story can be read page by page with the machine highlighting words or phrases and pronouncing them when the reader marks the word with a mouse. In some instances, word definitions or spellings pop up when children click on a word. Many programs include "read-to-me" and "let-me-play" options. In the first instance, the story is read aloud from beginning to end; in the second, readers explore the animations and sound effects on each page before proceeding to the next page.

There is a wide range of story-like material online that could be considered interactive storybooks. Sites such as Sesame Street Stories and StoryPlace offer animated graphics that support reading skill development for young students. Commercial sites offer computer games for students that feature screen reading as central components of game play. Fiction and nonfiction stories about multicultural topics and social justice issues can be found at Planet Tolerance (at the Teaching Tolerance website at www.teachingtolerance.org) of the Southern Poverty Law Center.

YOUR JUDGMENT MATTERS

As you think about these differing viewpoints, consider the following questions:

- What have been your experiences with interactive electronic books, either reading them yourself or reading them with children?
- What do you consider their best use in a teaching/learning setting?
- How might you use these resources with different groups of students—as independent activities, as small-group tutoring activities, as small-group teaching activities, or as whole-class experiences where you discuss specific topics such as vocabulary, character, or story structure?
- How might interactive electronic books serve as learning resources for students whose home language is not English?

Advantages and Disadvantages of Storybooks. Educators have differing views about the usefulness of electronic storybooks for young readers. Advocates see interactive storybooks as open-ended classroom resources. A student can use the book individually, or with an adult tutor, to practice word recognition and decoding strategies or to think about and compose responses to story comprehension questions posed by a teacher. Groups of two or three children can read or hear the story at the same time. Connecting a computer to a television screen or video projector enables a whole class to experience these books in a theatre-like setting.

Other educators, concerned about students becoming overly dependent on computers, wonder if the interactive features of electronic storybooks may distract students from the process of reading by decoding written words (Cuban, 2001; Healy, 1999; Trushell & Maitland, 2005).

Table 10.3 presents an overview of advantages and disadvantages of electronic storybooks prepared by researchers from the University of Arkansas and Southwest Missouri State University (Lefever-Davis & Pearman, 2005). These researchers specifically explored the impact of CD-ROM storybooks on the reading activities of 6- and 7-year-olds that

TABLE 10.3 Advantages and Disadvantages of Interactive Storybooks for Young Readers

Potential Advantages	Potential Disadvantages
Engages children in the mood and setting of the story	Promotes passivity on the part of young readers
Supports the learning of new vocabulary	Produces a dependency on the computer for figuring out how to pronounce unfamiliar words
Allows children to self-select assistance	Creates potential distractions that take readers' attention away from the story
Uses animation to strengthen reading comprehension	Invites boredom because of lengthy interactive features or repetition
What other advantages would you add based on your experience with electronic storybooks?	*What other disadvantages would you add based on your experience with electronic storybooks?*

Source: Based on Lefever-Davis & Pearman, 2005, pp. 447–448.

had had little prior experience with books on computers. Reviewing the evidence, they found five points of interest to teachers.

- *Visual elements create an engaging mood.* Interactive storybooks create the mood of a story or a poem in ways that appeal to children. The visual and interactive elements can be especially compelling, drawing the young reader to the text in ways that a book cannot. As poet Jack Prelutsky reads his poem "When Tilly Ate the Chili" on *The New Kid on the Block* CD-ROM, Tilly's onscreen reactions to the hot and spicy food are hilariously rendered. Fire spews from her mouth, steam rises from her ears, and screams flow forth from her mouth. This is poetry performed in ways that draw children to hearing, reciting, reading, and rereading the poems over and over again.

- *Reading comprehension skills can be improved.* Reading comprehension skills are a focal point of many electronic books. A word or phrase that is used in the story can be seen in animated action on the screen, as when the wolf huffs, puffs, and blows the house down. The "pairing of graphics and audio not only enhances the context but also helps set the mood the author is trying to establish" (Lefever-Davis & Pearman, 2005, p. 447). In addition, these interactive storybooks highlight and pronounce words on the screen, allowing children to acquire new vocabulary by connecting spoken words with onscreen images that act out the meanings of the words.

- *Game play may override reading processes.* Children may become so engrossed in viewing the story, discovering hotspots, or playing embedded games that the computer overwhelms the imaginative elements of the story reading experience. A child who reads a paper-bound book, even one with pictures on every page, recreates the story in his or her imagination, supplying the dialogue and action while adding personal interpretations about what is happening to the characters. In an electronic storybook, the child may enter a "spectator space" where the computer does the imaginative "work" for the young reader (Lefever-Davis & Pearman, 2005, p. 450). The child uses her imagination less, allowing the computer to dictate the pace and direction of the story. Under these conditions, the electronic format shortchanges the reading experience.

- *Cued animations and sound effects (CASE) hinder understanding.* Two British social scientists found that **cued animation and sound effects (CASE)** in storybooks actually reduced children's ability to recall a story when compared with children who did not have access to these same interactive features (Trushell & Maitland, 2005, pp. 63–64). To overcome these problems, the researchers urged teachers to use interactive storybooks in conjunction with nonelectronic interactions where adults and children can more freely discuss and ask questions about a story, reread key sections, and engage in other activities that will enhance the overall reading experience.

- *Children may overrely on the computer.* Some students may develop overreliance on the machine to pronounce unknown words. Rather than trying to decode or predict a word, students let the computer say it aloud. Decoding practice is eliminated since young readers do not need to make the effort to consider what a word might be and how it is pronounced. Teachers can overcome these difficulties by ensuring that students have quality time with adult reading coaches who discuss what children have seen electronically, support vocabulary development, and converse about individual interests. All these valuable ingredients of reading for meaning depend on human, not just technology, interactions.

Criteria for Evaluating Storybooks. Teachers should examine interactive electronic storybooks carefully and use them selectively. Israeli educators Adina Shamir and Ofra Korat (2006, pp. 535–539) offer six criteria for evaluating these materials for classroom use:

- *Age-appropriateness.* The content should "arouse a child's reading motivation and curiosity." The story should match the interest level of the young reader, being neither too simple nor too complex.
- *Child control.* Users should be able to "navigate the sequence of events rather than merely responding to software-generated activities." The child should be able to make decisions about how to experience the story, which is not the case when the storybook has only a read-aloud mode or an alternative "let the reader play" function where children explore pages for hotspots of hidden information and activity.
- *Clear instructions.* Commands should be "simple, precise, and accompanied by graphic presentations as often as possible."
- *Independence.* Children should be able to learn how to use the program easily without lots of instructions and can proceed to "explore situations and objects for which they lack the perquisite skills or physical or cognitive abilities."
- *Process orientation.* The child should be able to engage in exploration and discovery learning and should see real-world relationships "vividly portrayed" in the games that are integrated into the story or the different kinds of "activations" (things that move or characters who talk) that occur at the click of a mouse.
- *Technical features.* High-quality sound, graphics, animation, and other interactive functions should enrich "the story's meaning and [make] the narrative more vivid."

Using these criteria, you can examine interactive storybook choices to find which ones you think will most likely promote reading development and independent learning by your students.

Technology and a "Writing Process Fit to Young Writers"

Writing has been called the "neglected R" in schools today (National Commission on Writing in America's Schools and Colleges, 2003). While writing is an essentially creative intellectual process, it is often taught in schools as an exercise in memorizing, editing, and manipulating of words with an emphasis on standard spelling and correct usage of conventions (National Writing Project & Nagin, 2006). Students at every grade level say they do not enjoy writing in school, often for the following reasons.

- *Pressure.* For children in kindergarten through fourth grade, the physical demands of forming letters correctly when writing in print or cursive can make writing seem intensely laborious. They may also feel pressured to spell words correctly and use punctuation, grammar, and other conventions of written language appropriately, further diminishing any sense of enjoyment from writing.
- *Lack of confidence.* Many young writers feel stymied by the terror of the blank page—a feeling of not knowing what to write—that begins in the early grades and continues on through middle and high school. It is very difficult for a child to write when she or he does not feel confident as a writer.

- *Lack of joy.* Many students fail to discover the enjoyment of and satisfaction from expressing ideas using written language. Instead, they associate writing with worksheets devoted to grammar and punctuation or with research reports about teacher-assigned topics.
- *Misdirected self-evaluation.* Some students measure their proficiency as a writer by mechanics alone, as in how they form letters, how much they know about writing conventions, or how well they spell, but usually not by their ideas or the value of what they might say. "You will not like my writing," one first grader told us at an after-school writing workshop. "It is too messy." This child equated writing with neatness, but his fine motor control skills prevented him from producing neatly arranged text on a page.
- *Lack of patience.* Other students lack the patience or calmness to write quietly. They want to be up and moving around, engaged with other students, sometimes to the distraction of the teacher and the rest of the class.
- *Ideas about being smart.* Still others connect the ease and enjoyment of writing with being smart in school. Because they do not find writing pleasant or easy to do, they conclude they are not smart, setting in motion a downward cycle of negative feelings about being a writer and a learner.

No single approach to the teaching of writing can address all of these concerns. For this reason, many teachers try to make a "fit" between the process of writing and the needs of individual students; that is, they seek the best possible combination of adult and technological supports that will promote a sense of confidence and engagement with written language for each young writer.

This match between writing and writers we call a "writing process fit to young writers," a term derived from a widely used teaching method known as "process writing." A "writing process fit to young writers" is the effort to inspire students to express their ideas creatively while learning how and when to use the conventions of written language (Edwards, Maloy, & Verock-O'Loughlin, 2003). In this approach, classroom computers, the Internet, word processing, PowerPoint software, handheld devices, and other technologies provide ongoing engaging support to children from initial brainstorming of ideas to final publishing of written work. These technologies are not frills or add-ons for writers, but ways for teachers and students to find the combination of tools that best supports each individual student as a creative writer.

Process Approaches to Writing

Process writing has been at the center of writing instruction in schools for more than 30 years (Calkins, 1986; Graves, 1991; Mermelstein, 2005). Practiced by writers of all ages, a **writing process** involves the following stages:

- *Prewriting/brainstorming.* The writer begins **prewriting/ brainstorming** by freewriting, conversing with others, listening to read-alouds, webbing ideas to connect or categorize information, or engaging in other activities that serve as a catalyst for ideas and for structuring the text.
- *Drafting.* In the **drafting** stage, the writer focuses on creating a "draft" of writing, allowing ideas to flow forth without stopping or making large changes to the text. The goal is to write whatever comes to mind and see where the ideas take the writer. While writers often talk in terms of "first draft," the process of drafting ideas may go on through many brainstorming sessions and several written copies.
- *Revising.* The writer revisits, reviews, re-visions the writing during the **revising** stage, to change it in ways that create clarity, increase interest, and support the smooth flow of ideas. An author cannot work alone in this pursuit. Through

Computers are highly motivating tools for young writers who can express and publish their ideas quickly and easily using word processing and desktop publishing software.

questions and suggestions, a teacher or other writers become involved in the process of making writing interesting to readers. Feedback from readers and listeners is then used to guide changes that produce a final draft with improved communication between the writer and the intended audience.

- *Editing.* The writer begins **editing** once a draft is revised, with the additions and deletions that clarify the meaning of the text. Editing is necessary at this point to check the actual physical structure from a reader's viewpoint. Standard punctuation and spelling make reading the writing easier, which is why these conventions exist. To ensure that editing is something young writers can do, someone knowledgeable in the rules of printed text should be the editor-in-chief, providing the expertise and support to add conventions without endless labor or confusion on the part of the writer.
- *Publishing.* The writer shares with others a complete, but not necessarily completed, text. **Publishing** may involve many different formats, from a read-aloud to a performance to a display of the writing in a public place, with the goal of making the writing available for audiences to read and to hear.

Brainstorming, drafting, revising, editing, and publishing merge together in thought and action to generate a process of writing. Writers generate ideas, compose initial versions, read and change their material, and share what they have done with readers and listeners. Throughout, the writer is not alone, but in constant conversation with other people (often teachers, but also other students) who offer new perspectives, thoughtful comments, and appreciative support. The essence of the process is the flow of ideas that dynamically connect each element to the others.

If any of the ingredients of the writing process are missing or shortchanged, then the writer and the writing suffer. Pushing young writers to write before they are ready, making them edit a text too quickly, or rushing them from first draft to publication, all create a sense of writing as a race to the finish line with the goal of getting something done as quickly as possible. Leaving the audience out of the process is also counterproductive. Writers need to have readers comment on their drafts in order to revise them and they need to receive new reader responses as the work evolves. In this way everyone becomes a writer, always working through part of the process. Otherwise writing is viewed as a singular activity that only a special few have the talent and mental resolve to do well.

Transforming Writing with Technology

Technology has been shown to have a positive impact on student writing performance (Goldberg, Russell, & Cook, 2002; Patterson, 2006; Silvernail & Gritter, 2007). With technology, teachers can support students by differentiating their responses as young writers move from initial brainstorming to completed publication of written work. Technology gives teachers more ways to "fit" the writing process to young writers, as presented in Table 10.4, where the chart shows each of the stages of the writing process, listing ways that teachers can support writing, first without technology, and then with technology integrated into every stage. Without technology, teachers have fewer options to engage and sustain writing. With technology, teachers gain flexibility in addressing the needs of individual students.

The key to a **"writing process fit to young writers"** is convincing young writers that they are writers right now. They must believe that the words and pictures in their heads are interesting and important enough to express through writing and drawing. If students believe that their ideas do matter—to themselves and to others—they will become ready writers, willing to take risks and use time to put words on paper, fingers on keyboards, voice on podcasts. They will know that they have something to say, something to revise, something to reflect on, something to write.

Inspiring and energizing young writers means individualizing the parts of the writing process as much as possible within K–12 classroom schedules and resources so students proceed at their own pace. Technology is a primary ingredient of individualizing because it expands options for teachers and students—computer-based tools maximize and differentiate support for individual writers. For example, there may

TABLE 10.4   Uses of Technology in a "Writing Process Fit to Young Writers"

Writing Process Stage	Teacher Role	Without Technology	With Technology
Prewriting/brainstorming	Teachers use openers to show children the creative possibilities of different genres and forms of writing.	Teacher openers consist of <ul><li>Read-alouds of children's literature.</li><li>Showing examples of children's writing on overhead projectors.</li><li>Playing story writing/story telling games.</li><li>Discussing genres and forms.</li></ul>	Technology openers include <ul><li>Interactive computer storybooks, CD-ROM and Web materials, or audio and videotapes.</li><li>Microphones or sound systems for read-alouds for individuals or groups.</li><li>Digital projectors to make Web and CD-ROM materials as well as children's own writing available to an entire class in a large-group setting.</li><li>Author websites with stories, interviews, and writing games.</li></ul>
Drafting	Teachers provide individualized assistance for students as they write so that young writers create a "draft" where ideas flow forth without editing of the text, from which youngsters produce multiple drafts of their writing.	Teachers support children's writing by <ul><li>Acting as a scribe.</li><li>Sharing the pencil as co-writers and co-illustrators.</li><li>Finding pleasant places for children to write.</li><li>Responding in supportive, engaging ways to questions about spelling, punctuation, and other conventions of written language.</li></ul>	Technology supports include <ul><li>Computer word processing and drawing programs for generating drafts that include written words, pictures, and drawings which can be created by students or students and teachers together.</li><li>Text-to-speech software, digital pens, tape recorders, and camcorders to generate drafts of ideas.</li><li>Brainstorming and visual thinking software.</li></ul>
Revising/editing	Teachers provide feedback to young writers about the substance and the form of their writing so they can make additions or deletions that will improve the meaning (revising) and the clarity (editing) of written text.	Teachers and young writers engage in revising or editing by using <ul><li>Paper and pencils (or pens) as well as oral conversations.</li><li>Reading written drafts in paper copy and making annotations and suggestions in writing on the text or on sticky notes.</li></ul>	Technology revising and editing include <ul><li>Email communications so teachers and young writers can respond to writing more interactively and dynamically.</li><li>Editing software such as grammar and spell checking programs.</li><li>"Track changes" editing feature on word processing programs to keep a record of changes as they are made.</li><li>Handheld spellers and dictionaries.</li></ul>
Publishing	Teachers assist young writers to "publish" their writing, making what they have written available for different audiences to read and hear.	Teachers publish and celebrate students' work by reading children's writing aloud, displaying stories and poems on bulletin boards, and assembling handmade books.	Technology publishing includes a range of possible venues beyond paper displays: <ul><li>Classroom websites</li><li>PowerPoint</li><li>Digital portfolios</li><li>Tape recorders</li><li>Movie-making software</li><li>Desktop publishing software for choices of page layouts as well as print fonts and styles to emphasize visual learning and student choice and control over how information is communicated.</li></ul>

be multiple openings to a writing activity. A teacher might read a story aloud to some members of the class to discuss how adult authors have used a particular writing genre while other students might be reading the interactive book on the computer or watching a video or CD of the book the teacher is reading. Although one teacher cannot be in three places at once, technology makes it possible for three different openers to occur simultaneously.

TECHNOLOGY TRANSFORMATION LESSON PLAN

MEASURING SHADOWS
Differentiating Science Learning Using Technology

Grade(s)	Elementary and Middle School (Grades 2 to 8)
Subject(s)	Science
Key Goal/Enduring Understanding	Shadows, a common phenomenon on a sunny day or a moonlit night, are created by sunlight striking light-blocking objects. Shadows change length, width, and shape as the movement of the earth produces variations in the angle of sunlight striking the earth's surface throughout the day. Shadows also vary in length, width, and shape at different times of the year because of seasonal changes.
Essential Question	Why do shadow lengths vary throughout the day and during different seasons of the year?

Learning Standards

National Science Teachers Association—*National Science Education Standards*

Earth and Space Science Content Standard D

All students should develop an understanding of:

- Structure of the earth system
- Changes in earth and sky

International Society for Technology in Education (ISTE)—*NETS-S*

Standard 3: *Research and Information Fluency.* Students use digital tools to gather, evaluate, and use information.
Standard 4: *Critical Thinking, Problem Solving, and Decision Making.* Students use critical thinking skills to plan and conduct research, manage projects, solve problems, and make informed decisions using appropriate digital tools and resources.
Standard 6: *Technology Operations and Concepts.* Students demonstrate a sound understanding of technology concepts, systems and operations.

National Council for the Social Studies—*Curriculum Standards for the Social Studies*

Theme III: People, Places, and Environment

Learning Objectives Students will know how and be able to

- Explain what creates shadows and why they change in length, width, and shape during the day.
- Design and conduct a shadow measurement investigation with classmates, including recording and presenting data.

▶

- Create online posters or other information displays that explain why shadows move and change every few minutes and throughout the seasons.

Technology Uses

This lesson uses a variety of computer technologies, including electronic measuring devices, digital cameras, computers with movie-making software, and a classroom website or blog.

Minimal Technology	Infusion of Technology
Students measure shadows using rulers and yardsticks.	Students measure shadows using electronic measuring devices.
Students keep track of their measurements in a paper notebook.	Students keep track of their measurements on the computer using a spreadsheet or graphing program.
Students record their observations using words and drawings in a personal notebook.	Students record their observations using digital cameras to add photos to their writing and drawing.
Students post their observations of shadows on classroom bulletin boards.	Students post their observations of shadows on a class website or blog.

Evaluation

Students will be evaluated on the creativity of their shadow investigations, including the data they have collected, the completeness of their data presentations, and the use of technology in recording and presenting information about shadows.

LESSON PLAN DESCRIPTION

Introduction

"Measuring Shadows" integrates electronic measuring devices, digital cameras, computers with movie making software, Internet resources, and a classroom website or blog into the study of shadows and seasonal change. Following the theme of this chapter, "Measuring Shadows" shows new teachers how to use technology to promote universal design for learning (UDL) and differentiated instruction (DI) to create learning success for all students.

This lesson, for grades 2 to 8 or mixed-age science clubs, is organized around the concept of inquiry learning set forth in the National Science Education Standards, specifically the science content area of "Earth and Space Sciences," including "Changes in Earth and Sky" (for students in grades K–4) and "Earth in the Solar System" (for students in grades 5–8). It also supports the International Society for Technology in Education's (ISTE) NETS-S that call for learning how to locate, evaluate, and communicate information to multiple audiences.

Lesson Focus

Shadow measurements are an engaging and challenging way for elementary and middle school students to learn about seasonal change, an often-taught science curriculum topic. Changing seasons, after all, are a part of everyone's daily life. In most communities, the school year begins as summer becomes fall and ends as spring becomes summer. Weather patterns, animal migrations, plant growth, agricultural activities, and many other parts of daily life change seasonally. The changes go unnoticed unless teachers and students study them. Massachusetts—like many states in the northern part of the country—receives 6 hours and 13 minutes more daylight at the summer solstice in June than it does at the winter solstice in December. This difference equals the length of an entire school day.

The 23.6-degree tilt of the earth in space produces seasonal change. Without this tilt, the earth's year-long revolution around the sun would occur in a straight, upright position that would produce 12 hours of daylight and 12 hours of nighttime, all year long, everywhere on the globe, as is now the case every day at or near the equator. Because the earth is a tilted planet, only twice a year everywhere in the Northern and Southern Hemispheres does the entire earth experience 12 hours of daylight and 12 hours of nighttime. The vernal and autumnal equinoxes (*equinox* means "equal night and equal day"), on the 21st or 22nd day of March and September, mark this event on the calendar. During the rest of the year the earth's tilt in its orbit gives more or lesser amounts of sunlight in different places of the year producing the cycle of seasons.

"Measuring Shadows" consists of inquiry-based science investigations that students can do throughout the school year on sunny days. These investigations include "Changing Shadow Lengths during the Day" and "Changing Shadow Lengths during Different Seasons of the Year."

Lesson Design—Minimal Technology

Shadows are fascinating phenomena to investigate with students as they learn about seasonal change. To create a shadow, two ingredients must be present—light and a solid object that does not let the light pass through it. Trees, buildings, rocks, and people are easy-to-understand examples of light-blocking solid objects.

Sunlight shining on the constantly rotating earth creates dramatic shadows to view with students. Because the earth is endlessly turning, sunlight strikes objects at different angles, depending on the time of day. As a result, all day long, shadows are moving and changing shapes as the angle of the light shifts. For this reason, shadows are longest in the morning or the afternoon when the sun appears lower in the sky and shortest at midday when the sun is directly overhead.

With a bucket of colored chalk, the class goes outdoors to a space where there is enough room to trace shadows on cement or pavement—on a parking lot, the playground, or a wide sidewalk. Pairs of students find spots away from other pairs. To begin, one student traces around the shoes of the other student to identify the exact spot they will return to for each of the shadow tracings that day.

Every hour thereafter, or three or four more times throughout the day, the class returns outdoors. Partners return to their spots to trace the shadow again in a different color of chalk each time. Whoever was traced originally continues to be the shadow maker and whoever did the tracing continues in that role. As the tracings proceed, it is obvious that all the shadows undergo similar changes. They all point in the same direction, growing or shrinking in length and width, and become remarkably different shapes from the first shadow tracing.

Inside each of the tracings, the time of the day is recorded so the idea of shadows being like hands on a clock comes into the conversation. On the following day or shortly thereafter on a sunny day, the shadow tracing experience is repeated so the partners can switch roles and the class can observe the similar results of day one's tracings and day two's tracings.

This experience, repeated on dry sunny days in different seasons, offers students the opportunity to observe similarities and differences and to feel like scientists. This is what scientists do—repeat and learn from their multiple observations and efforts.

LESSON ACTIVITIES USING TECHNOLOGY

1. ***Measure Shadows Electronically.*** Using electronic measuring devices, students can measure the shadows created by some light-blocking object (such as a tree, sign, building, or one of the students in the class) at the same location at different times of the day. The object's shadow will move its position and change its shape from morning to noon to afternoon. Digital photographs of the same location offer a way to plot the movement of the shadows through-

▶

out the day. Students' shadow measurement observations can then be posted on a classroom website or blog.

2. *Get Data from Different Seasons of the Year*. Keeping track of shadows in the same location is an activity that teachers and students can do throughout the school year. As the seasons change, students will notice changes in the length of the shadow of the same object in any given location. The shadow of a sign or tree, for example, is not as long in the spring and autumn as in the summer and fall. This is because of the sun's height in the sky early and late in the day in the summer and in the winter. Again, using measuring devices and digital photographs, the students can determine just how much shadow lengths vary throughout the year.

3. *Provide Different and Similar Roles to All Students*. From universal design for learning (UDL) and differentiated instruction (DI) perspectives, students play different roles while pursuing the same learning goals. Differentiating these roles offers choices of writing news reports, comics, or poems; creating videos; composing songs; and illustrating with painting, sculpting, or making models. As active learners, students play the same roles while participating in learning. All students trace shadows and take photographs. In partners, one stands while the other traces the shadow, and one photographs while the other suggests angles and directions of photos. On other days partners switch their roles in the activity, and then groups switch activities.

4. *Integrate Multiple Technologies to Activate Instruction*. Technology offers ways for all students to learn the science content found in the "Measuring Shadows" lesson plan. Unlike more traditional formats that emphasize whole-group instruction with limited opportunities for students to be active participants in the instructional process, technology-infused activities allow for hands-on experimentation by individual students, small-group activities, and opportunities for students to teach each other what they have learned—each proven UDL and DI strategies. As the teacher in charge, you can differentiate instruction by assigning roles and activities to your students based on their needs and preferences as learners, as in the following examples.

   - Objects and shadows need a measurement and data collection team to record length and width in feet and inches. Students with hands-on tools can be actively involved in shadow measurements while other students take digital photographs of shadow movements. These groups switch roles the next time they go out.
   - Data must be entered into the computer to produce photo slide shows and lines and graphs that illustrate differences throughout the day.
   - Student writing in science journals enables you to assess how well the students are learning the science concepts that are at the center of the lesson. Word processing and drawing programs allow students to document what they have learned using different modes of self-expression.

5. *Summarize and Publish the Findings of the Class*. Publishing the results of the shadow experiments on a class website or blog, in the words of two science educators, further differentiates instruction by "providing teachers with a user-friendly online format to reinforce strategies, introduce new topics and concepts, review important class points, and provide enrichment" (Colombo & Colombo, 2007). Publishing results online can be the responsibility of teams of student designers and editors.

ANALYSIS AND EXTENSIONS

1. Name two features you find useful about this lesson.
2. Name two areas for extension or improvement of this lesson.
3. Analyze how successfully information technology has been integrated into the lesson.
4. How might students become more involved in designing, using, and evaluating technology in the lesson?

PEARSON
myeducationkit™

Go to the Technology Transformation Lesson Plan section in Chapter 10 in MyEducationKit and access the activity "Measuring Shadows: Differentiating Science Learning" to practice transforming a lesson plan using technology.

FOCUS QUESTION 1: What are differentiated instruction (DI) and universal design for learning (UDL)?

- Every student benefits from a wide and varied range of educational experiences that can activate her or his talents and potentials as a learner.

- Teachers are crucial gatekeepers in how learning proceeds in schools and classrooms. They either move students forward with lively and demanding instruction or they separate students according to perceived needs and talents.

- Differentiated instruction (DI) and universal design for learning (UDL) involve changing institutional practices and classroom structures to promote learning success for every student.

FOCUS QUESTION 2: How can teachers use technology to create universally designed classrooms?

- Creating a universally designed classroom using technology involves changing the classroom learning environment or changing the ways curriculum is delivered.

- A teacher's technology choices for universal design can be organized in three toolkits: "low tech," "middle tech," and "high tech."

FOCUS QUESTION 3: How does assistive technology support efforts by teachers to reach all learners?

- Assistive technologies are tools that make academic material more accessible to students by minimizing barriers while maximizing opportunities for learning.

- Handheld spellers and dictionaries, speech recognition software, text reading software, and interactive electronic storybooks are all technologies that can promote learning success for many different students.

FOCUS QUESTION 4: How is technology used in a writing process fit for young writers to promote learning success for all students?

- Technology offers multiple opportunities for teachers to "fit" the writing process to the needs and interests of student writers.

- Different technologies are effective in different parts of the writing process, including prewriting/brainstorming, drafting, revising, editing, and publishing.

KEY TERMS

Accommodations	Interactive electronic storybooks
Assistive technologies	Modification
Calculator	Optical character recognition and reading software
Cued animation and sound effects (CASE)	
Differentiated instruction (DI)	Prewriting/brainstorming
Drafting	Publishing
Editing	Revising
Electronic speller and dictionary	Screen reading software

Speech recognition software
Technological convergence
Text reading software
Universal design

Universal design for learning (UDL)
Word prediction software
Writing process
"Writing process fit to young writers"

ACTIVITIES FOR YOUR TEACHER PORTFOLIO

1. A HIGH SCHOOL COMPLETION CRISIS

Nationwide, about 70 percent of all ninth-graders complete high school 4 years later. The completion rates for black, Hispanic, and Native American students are even lower: 46 percent for African American males, 52 percent for Hispanic males, and 60 percent for African American and Hispanic females (Education Week, 2007). This means that approximately 1.23 million students did not graduate with their class in 2007, part of a trend that one report characterized as a "silent epidemic" in U.S. education (Bridgeland, DiIulio, & Morison, 2006, p. 1). The crisis is deepened by the economic consequences of leaving school without a diploma. To earn a living wage in the United States, today's students need at least some college education; the median income for those with only a high school diploma or less was $12,638 in 2007.

- Why do you think the high school completion rate is not higher?

- Why do so many students leave school before graduating?

- How can you as a teacher differentiate your instruction and universally design your teaching so a majority of students are more likely to experience success and less likely to leave school?

2. GENDER ISSUES IN SPECIAL EDUCATION

Nationwide, boys comprise 51 percent of total school enrollment, but they constitute 66 percent of special education students. When special needs are identified as mainly physical (vision or hearing impairments), boys are only slightly more likely to be identified than girls. But when the learning challenges are identified as social and emotional, "boys are twice as likely to be labeled with a learning disability and more than three times as likely to be called emotionally disturbed" (Vaishnau & Dedman, 2002).

Sharp gender disparities in the labeling of special needs students exist among districts that border each other geographically, between districts that share common socioeconomic characteristics, and even between schools in the same community. "Boys make up 90 percent of the emotionally disturbed students in Kansas City, but only 55 percent in Milwaukee," noted a *Boston Globe* report (Vaishnau & Dedman, 2002), which also cited cases of significant gender differences in special education students among various districts within Massachusetts.

- Why do you think there is such a variation in special education rates among girls and boys?

- How can you as a teacher promote more successful inclusive experiences for both girls and boys in your classroom?

- What roles can technology play in promoting more equitable gender outcomes in schools?

3. DIFFERENTIATE YOUR INSTRUCTION

Ask the students in your class to differentiate the design and delivery of an upcoming lesson. Any aspect of the class is open for potential differentiation from how curriculum is delivered to how the class is conducted. For example, a science class that features teacher lectures might use Power-Point slides and Internet research instead. Or an English class that usually requires silence when students are writing might permit students to listen to music on their iPods or to use computers to draft their work.

As an added feature of the assignment, ask your students to consider how technology might promote better learning experiences. In the preceding examples, if the students want PowerPoint slides, Internet access, or iPod music, they need to explain in clear terms why these differentiations would be beneficial rather than superficial changes.

In proposing this assignment, it is important not to single out any students with disabilities by unnecessarily calling attention to their learning challenges. The goal of differentiated instruction must always be to make it possible for all students to succeed with the overall curriculum, not to create different curriculums (one more or less demanding than the others) for different students.

GROWING AND LEADING WITH TECHNOLOGY

This activity offers an opportunity to grow as a teacher and learn to lead with technology. Begin by reviewing the Chapter 10 Learning Goal and Featured Technologies listed in the chart at the start of the chapter. Then read the following actual classroom scenario and consider how technologies discussed in Chapter 10 might be integrated into the lesson. Follow-up steps to this activity can be completed at MyEducationKit.

ROBERT'S "THIS I BELIEVE" ESSAY LESSON

Robert is teaching a small class of tenth- and eleventh-graders who are preparing for the writing component of the state's English/language arts high school graduation test. These students have struggled with writing in school and some have failed the state test and need to take it for a second time.

To energize the students' enthusiasm, Robert has chosen to have them compose "This I Believe" essays. "This I Believe" essays are statements of core values and personal philosophies made popular by public broadcasting's "This I Believe" radio show, itself a revival of a 1950s radio program of the same name that was hosted by the legendary writer and journalist, Edward R. Murrow (Allison & Gediman, 2007). Robert's hope is that inviting his students to write about a topic of personal interest will reduce their reluctance toward writing and, in so doing, help them become better prepared for the state English/language arts exam.

As the students compose "This I Believe" essays, Robert plans to review skills for organizing and presenting ideas in writing, and improve those skills through multiple revisions. As a High Schools That Work (HSTW) study of some 20,000 seniors found, the process of "drafting and revising a paper that was graded" was one of the classroom practices that successfully improved the language arts skills of adolescents (Murray, 2008).

Robert's three main goals are that each student will (1) read and hear different types of "This I Believe" essays composed by well-known and ordinary Americans, including other high school students from around the country; (2) write a "This I Believe" essay expressing important personal values and ideas and share it with the other members of the class; and (3) develop greater confidence and improved skill as a creative and expressive writer who can then perform successfully on the English/language arts high school graduation exam.

Robert is also aware, given his students' past lack of success as writers in school, that he will need to differentiate his instruction in order to support each individual writer. While the broad outline of the essay-writing activity can be the same for every student, he must employ flexibility and variety in his teaching, as suggested by the "Writing Process Fit For Young Writers" segment in Chapter 10.

Robert is teaching in a classroom with multiple Internet-accessible computers and easy access to a large computer lab just down the hall. He also has a digital projector mounted in the ceiling that is connected to a teacher computer from which he can show Internet and video material to the entire class at one time. He, and many of his students, also have iPods, although the students have only used these machines as music players.

- Using the technologies discussed in this chapter, how would you propose Robert integrate technology into the "This I Believe" essay project in ways that will promote learning success for all students?

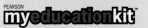

To complete the full activity, go to the Growing and Leading section of Chapter 10 in MyEducationKit and access the activity "Robert's 'This I Believe' Essay Lesson."

11 Engaging Teachers and Students in Learning and Self-Reflection

For teachers and students, assessment should have an instructional purpose, not simply an evaluative or administrative one.

—National Writing Project & Carl Nagin, *Because Writing Matters: Improving Writing in Our Schools*, 2006, pp. 76–77

CHAPTER LEARNING GOAL

Teacher and Student Self-Reflection about Learning

Using digital portfolios and other performance assessment technologies to evaluate one's own learning

CONNECTING to the NETS

NETS-T

2 Design and Develop Digital Age Learning Experiences and Assessments

5 Engage in Professional Growth and Leadership

NETS-S

3 Research and Information Fluency

NEW TECHNOLOGIES

- Digital portfolios
- Technology tools in democratic classrooms
- Online survey software
- Student participation systems and clickers

CHAPTER OVERVIEW

Chapter 11 examines how teachers and students can be active participants in evaluating and assessing their own growth as learners using technology. Teachers, as well as students enrolled in college and university teacher license programs, are engaged in dual assessments—while they are evaluating the work of their students, they, too, are being evaluated by college faculty or school personnel. The chapter explores how teachers might use performance-based portfolios, presentations, and publications for personal and student assessment. The chapter concludes with ways to use democratic classrooms, online survey software, and student participation systems to promote and increase student involvement in their own learning.

Chapter 11 connects to NETS-T for Teachers Standard 5, Part c, where teachers and students use digital tools to "evaluate and reflect on current research and professional practice." This chapter includes ideas from NETS-T Standard 2, Part b, that "students pursue their individual curiosities and become active participants in setting their own educational goals, managing their own learning, and assessing their own progress."

FOCUS QUESTIONS

1. What is performance-based assessment for teachers and for students?
2. How can teachers and students use digital portfolios as tools for learning?
3. How can students become actively involved in assessment and evaluation using technology?
4. How can teachers use student participation systems as effective assessment methods?

Midway through student teaching in tenth-grade U.S. history, Tracy learned that her cooperating teacher was retiring in December at the end of the semester. "You should apply for my position," Mrs. DuBose told Tracy. "Your work in the classroom has been truly excellent. You will be a very strong candidate."

"What do I need to do?" Tracy asked. "My chances seem slim. I am only a student teacher. I have not yet finished getting my certification. The principal hardly knows me. Will people even look at my application?"

"Finish your online teacher portfolio," her cooperating teacher replied. "That way everyone in the hiring process can see your ideas and accomplishments. Your choice of lesson plans, student work, and other materials for display will help you describe your teaching and show what you can do in the classroom as a teacher."

As she began posting her materials electronically, Tracy decided that portfolios would be valuable to use with her students. All semester, she had been puzzled by how some students refused to prepare for multiple-choice and fill-in-the-blank exams. These students seemed totally disconnected from learning, going through the motions of attending class but not putting any effort into studying or participating.

"There will be no exam when we finish our next unit," Tracy told her class the next day. "Instead, everyone will assemble a portfolio of what they have learned using class notes, research assignments, and homework papers. I want to see what you know, not just what you can remember for the test."

Initially surprised by the assignment, the students responded as Tracy had hoped. A new spirit of involvement in learning emerged. Everyone, even those she thought might complain about the amount of time and effort necessary, welcomed the opportunity to assemble a personal portfolio, and the portfolio-building process prompted valuable discussions about the importance and meaning of the academic material the class was studying. The portfolios were the glue that enabled all the students to stick with the learning process to the end.

This chapter's learning goal delves into ways technology can fully involve teachers and students in their education as participants in and assessors of learning. Tracy's professional teaching portfolio is one type of performance assessment and personal reflection; the portfolios done by her students are another. In formulating these, Tracy and her students are taking leadership roles as learners, thinking about what they have done academically and presenting it in ways that others can read and understand. Learning becomes not what happens to Tracy or to her students while sitting passively in a classroom, but a self-reflective process they are creating and shaping actively.

Portfolios, unlike standardized multiple-choice exams, employ performance-based activities (such as lesson plans, work logs, student work samples, reflective essays, and video materials) as a basis for assessing skills and accomplishments. In California, beginning in July 2008, every student in a teacher education program must pass a performance assessment before receiving a license to teach (Rothman, 2008). Connecticut, Wisconsin, and New Mexico require performance-based evaluations of newly hired teachers (Toch & Rothman, 2008).

Creating a portfolio positively affects Tracy's growth as a new teacher and her students' growth as learners in two ways. First, portfolio building involves everyone in reflectively assessing learning. As a portfolio builder weighs the merits of materials to be included in an online collection, she or he evaluates what has been learned. Self-reflection, invaluable for teachers, is an important skill to convey to students at every grade level. Being able to clearly state or demonstrate what has been learned indicates deep and lasting understanding.

PEARSON
myeducationkit™

Go to the Assignments and Activities section of Chapter 11 in MyEducationKit and complete the video activity entitled "Managing and Reporting Student Data On-line." As you watch the video and answer the accompanying questions, note how technology helps one school district track their students' progress.

Second, because Tracy and her students have constructed portfolios electronically, these provide a compelling example of how technology involves teachers and students in learning. Other technology examples might include online surveys and student participation systems with clickers.

This chapter looks at three interrelated aspects of how teachers and students can use technology to actively self-assess and reflect on learning:

- *New teacher assessment (how your supervisors will assess you).* **New teacher assessment** occurs as your performance is continually assessed and evaluated by faculty who coordinate teacher license programs and by teachers and administrators in the schools where you are teaching. Before getting your first full-time job, you will likely have to pass a state teacher license test, be observed teaching in a classroom by mentor teachers and college supervisors, and complete written summaries of what you have learned about academic subjects, teaching methods, classroom management strategies, and the ability to relate to students, families, and colleagues. Being evaluated as a new teacher also includes personal self-assessments where you ask, "Are my students learning?" and if they are not, "What can I do to change this?"

Paper-and-pencil tests are a widely used way to assess student learning, but not all students do their best work in such pressure-filled settings. Digital portfolios provide new ways for students to show what they have learned and know how to do.

- *Student assessment (how you will assess your students).* **Student assessment** is the ongoing evaluation of students, and is fundamental to the work of elementary, middle, and high school teachers. Parents, school administrators, and students themselves expect regular reports about the learning progress of every person in your class throughout the school year.
- *Student involvement in learning and assessment (how your students will participate in the assessment process).* In many schools, students are not passive recipients of teacher assessments, but active partners in learning and the evaluation of learning. **Student involvement in learning and assessment** gives students meaningful roles to play in performance assessment and is a powerful way to build their commitment to the school curriculum.

 Evaluating Teachers

Teacher evaluation is an immediate and personally relevant topic for readers of this book. Every student in a teacher license program or new teacher in the classroom gets evaluated, usually in many different ways by many different observers. Think about all the different kinds of assessments you have had or are going to have in your teacher license program, such as

- State teacher competency tests
- Tests and exams in college or university courses
- Papers, projects, and presentations for your teacher education classes
- Journals and reflection papers
- Lesson plans and other curriculum materials that you use with your students
- Field observations of your teaching by your cooperating teacher and college program supervisor
- In-person interviews with prospective future employers

YOUR JUDGMENT
MATTERS

As you think about these differing viewpoints, consider the following questions:

- As a matter of education policy, do you believe that all teacher candidates should pass a state or national competency test before receiving a license to teach?
- How might passing a test document your skills and talents as a teacher?
- As alternatives to teacher tests, how might classroom-based performance evaluation measures document your skills and talents as a teacher?

Tests for teachers lead the list, and it is a controversial policy, in part because "there is no agreed-upon definition of what competencies a beginning teacher should have" (Mitchell, Robinson, Plake, & Knowles, 2001). Teacher test proponents believe that tests ensure educator quality since everyone is held to high content and pedagogical knowledge standards (Stotsky, 2007). Opponents contend that multiple-choice questions on a test fail to capture the complexities of actual classroom situations where teachers must make rapid-paced decisions while managing learning for students in a creative and inclusive manner (Fowler, 2001; Goldhaber & Anthony, 2007; Nichols & Berliner, 2007).

From Test Assessments to Performance Evaluations

A list of evaluations includes not only tests for teachers but also performance-based assessments of good teaching as defined by a college or university program or a local school district. As discussed in Chapter 3 on performance evaluation, what you accomplish as a teacher is ascertained less through test scores and more through how you perform in the following areas:

- Do you structure your lessons to incorporate rigorous academic content and engaging teaching methods?
- Do you elicit questions from and converse fairly and consistently with boys and girls?
- Does your language convey high expectations of success for every child?
- Do you differentiate your teaching to meet the needs of individual learners?
- Do you conduct discussions well, manage class time effectively, and redirect students' attention back to academic activities if they are distracted?

These and dozens of other aspects of your skills and success as a teacher are answered daily through your performance in the classroom.

Table 11.1 shows types of performance evaluation that you might use as a teacher and that supervisors might use to assess you as a new teacher. The lists are similar because performance evaluation emphasizes work done rather than tests taken.

The assessment of teachers occurs across a spectrum of choices. At one end of the spectrum are test assessments while performance assessments occupy the other end. In between are combinations of both types of assessments designed to measure successful learning and effective teaching. This same test-to-performance evaluation spectrum that applies to how supervisors evaluate teachers also applies to how teachers evaluate students.

TABLE 11.1   Types of Performance Evaluation of Students and Teachers

Performance Evaluation of Students	Performance Evaluation of Teachers
• Student writing assignments (creative, analytical, persuasive)	• New teacher writing assignments (creative, analytical, persuasive)
• Elementary or secondary school class participation	• Teacher education course participation
• Individual and group projects	• Individual and group projects
• Homework	• Homework
• Individual presentations and performances	• Individual presentations and performances
• Open book/open note quizzes	• Open book/open note quizzes
• Student self-assessments	• New teacher self-assessments
• Teacher observations of student attitudes and behaviors	• College supervisor or cooperating teacher observations of new teacher attitudes and behaviors

Digital Portfolios as a Learning Technology

Digital portfolios offer an effective way for students and teachers alike to assess their teaching and learning accomplishments (Montgomery & Wiley, 2008). A **digital portfolio** (also known as a multimedia portfolio, electronic portfolio, e-portfolio, or webfolio) is a collection of educational materials stored in an electronic format such as a CD-ROM, website, or computer file. Broadly speaking, a digital portfolio "is a goal-driven, organized collection of artifacts that demonstrates a person's expansion of knowledge and skills over time" (Kilbane & Milman, 2003, p. 4). A digital portfolio may "contain much of the content traditional teaching portfolios include but present the materials in a digital format," and a combination of technologies can be used to present the material, "including, but not limited to, audio recordings; hypermedia programs; and database, spreadsheet, video and word processing software" (Kilbane & Milman, 2003, p. 7).

Changing from paper to digital portfolios represents a significant shift in how teachers and students communicate information about themselves and their learning. The e-portfolio becomes both a personal and a public piece of writing. A paper portfolio stored in a three-ring binder is shared only with a small number of readers to whom the author gives the material. By contrast,

CONNECTIONS and POSSIBILITIES

Teacher Education Digital Portfolios

As highly interactive Web 2.0 technologies become more prominent, how do teachers present themselves as skillful and innovative technology-using educators? This question has immediate relevance to readers who are seeking full-time teaching jobs after college or university graduation. For you, bringing more than a paper resume and a loose-leaf notebook filled with lesson plans to a teaching job interview is of the utmost importance. School hiring committees welcome evidence that you have used technology broadly and successfully with your students. A digital portfolio of teaching activities and accomplishments is an example of your skills and background experience using technology in teaching.

Our question applies equally to veteran teachers who want to use new, interactive technologies in teaching. Although you may not be in the teaching job market, you can benefit from displaying your skills and knowledge electronically. Digital portfolios let you share classroom information with students, families, and other teachers. Maintaining a professional portfolio also provides a structured way to reflect on your work, growth, and future plans as a teacher.

One example of a teacher education digital portfolio program can be found at Teachers College at Ball State University in Muncie, Indiana. Ball State has made technology one of the centerpieces of how new teachers are prepared for the classroom. Technology, the dean explains in a video posted on the school's website, is more than a set of skills, it is a "mechanism for thinking about teaching," a way for new teachers to go about "exploring uncharted territories" of teaching and learn-

ing. Visiting the school's website, you can view video in which college students describe the role of digital portfolios in their teacher education program (online at www.bsu.edu/teachers/laptops/portfolios).

Ball State integrates laptop technology into all its teacher education classes, and every student is expected to use a laptop computer. Exams and quizzes are delivered online, students submit lesson plans and other curriculum projects electronically, and professors post lecture notes and academic materials on their course websites. Teacher candidates are required to produce a digital, Web-based portfolio as part of their education program of study, informative examples of which can be found online (http://portfolio.iweb.bsu.edu).

Many other colleges and universities across the country have vibrant portfolio programs, including Johns Hopkins University's Center for Technology in Education, University of Southern California's Center for Excellence in Teaching, Seton Hall University, California State University/Los Angeles, University of Wisconsin-Madison's School of Education, University of Virginia's Curry School of Education, University of South Dakota's Technology Literacy Center, Purdue University, Connecticut College, Dartmouth College, and Valdosta State University's College of Education. Check school websites for more information about these initiatives, and look for other examples as well that will help you conceptualize the design and content of your own professional teaching portfolio.

"with digital portfolios, we ask students to hyperlink documents, form a cohesive design and navigation system, and embed images from other multimedia—all while anticipating or actually making their work public during the process" (Hicks, 2005, p. 205). These e-portfolio builders make information about themselves available to many viewers in a variety of digital formats.

Kathleen Blake Yancy of Clemson University (2004, pp. 744–746) distinguishes among three different types of digital or electronic portfolios currently in use:

- "Online assessment systems" where "students store preselected pieces of work in a commercially or institutionally designed template."
- A "print-loaded" portfolio that takes a paper text and displays it electronically.
- A "Web-sensible" portfolio that uses "text boxes, hyperlinking, visuals, audio texts and design elements" to convey a teacher's materials.

The first two portfolio types offer little that is new and do not take advantage of the transforming power of digital technology to create interactive and constantly evolving presentations of information. By contrast, according to Yancy, a "Web-sensible digital portfolio" provides portfolio builders with new kinds of spaces for creating dynamic presentations of their work. In such spaces, like museum galleries, the displays change and evolve as teachers' new understandings about themselves and their work inspire the development of new materials and activities (Yancy, 2004, p. 750).

Advantages and Disadvantages of Digital Portfolios

The advantages of electronic portfolios are multifaceted (see Table 11.2). First, as noted by technology educators Clare Kilbane and Natalie Milman (2003), electronic portfolios are accessible and portable. Information that would fill hundreds of pages when assembled and organized in a paper format are by comparison easily maintained and transported electronically. Second, electronic publication encourages new, creative expressions of one's work. Third, working with computers increases portfolio builders' technological skills and confidence. Finally, digital portfolios offer teachers connections to wider educational communities through electronic communications.

There are disadvantages as well (see Table 11.2). Digital portfolios require builders to know or learn to use computers, cameras, scanners, photo and illustrating software, and other tools. Teachers may need professional support to build a portfolio template, determine what to include in it, and decide how to describe it. The process requires energy and time, not to mention the expense of purchasing computers, software, and other equipment. In addition, not everyone in your hoped-for audience (for example, principals and superintendents involved in hiring new teachers) will view a digital portfolio or have the equipment or skills to do so. Finally, builders commonly spend more time fashioning the "look" of their portfolio than highlighting the substance of their work as a teacher as the central feature.

TABLE 11.2   Advantages and Disadvantages of Digital Portfolios

Advantages	Disadvantages
Accessibility	Knowledge and skill requirements
Portability	Professional support
Creativity	Expensive equipment
Technological self-confidence	Time and energy
Community	Need for increased viewer skills and equipment
	Presentation distracts from content

Source: Based on Kilbane & Milman, 2003, pp. 9–11.

More than a decade ago, curriculum theorist Lee Shulman (1998, pp. 34–35) foresaw five potential dangers of portfolios:

- "Lamination," where the portfolio becomes an elaborately constructed collection of materials whose appearance dominates its substance
- "Heavy lifting," where the time needed to make the portfolio distracts and discourages the portfolio maker
- "Trivialization," where unimportant materials dominate the collection
- "Perversion," where a quantitative scoring system used by evaluators minimizes the process of personal reflection, resulting in the portfolio becoming another test-like measure of performance
- "Misrepresentation," where teachers include only their best materials rather than those that truly show what happens every day in the classroom

These dangers, argued Shulman (1998, pp. 35–37), can be more than counterbalanced by the strengths of portfolios as a teacher assessment approach, including the following five major advantages:

- First, portfolios permit the tracking and documentation of longer episodes of teaching and learning than happens in supervisory observations.
- Second, portfolios encourage the reconnection between process and product.
- Third, portfolios institutionalize norms of collaboration, reflection, and discussion.
- Fourth, a portfolio can be seen as a portable residency. . . . [it] introduces structure to the field experience.
- Fifth, the portfolio shifts the agency from an observer back to the teacher intern.

Tech Tool 11.1 reviews resources for teachers who are building online digital portfolios of their professional and educational materials.

Portfolios for Teachers

Portfolios for teachers follow patterns established in other professions where writers, artists, engineers, architects, musicians, graphic designers, Web developers, and others show collections of their work to demonstrate their talents and skills to employers or customers. In some schools, student portfolios serve as an assessment alternative to standardized tests. By collecting and presenting material digitally, students demonstrate their knowledge and skills outside the test-taking mode.

Teachers design their teaching portfolios in many different and creative ways, but most collections include certain elements that document one's academics, teaching, and talents and accomplishments. The following list includes several common elements found in a teacher's e-portfolio.

Resume	Personal Talents and Accomplishments
Philosophy of Education	References
Lesson Plans or Unit Plan	Reflections
Academic Courses and Research Experiences	Video and Pictorial Segments
Teaching Experience	Resource Links

The use of **standards-based digital portfolios** has grown in teacher education in recent years. This type of portfolio "uses a database or hypertext links to clearly show the relationship between standards or goals, artifacts, and reflections" (Barrett, 2000, p. 175). The purpose is to connect teaching skills and competencies to specific professional teaching standards as a way to show that new teacher candidates are qualified to receive a license or, in the case of those who are newly hired in schools, to remain as the teacher-in-charge in the classroom. Standards can be a helpful way to organize portfolio material, but teachers may view them as a checklist of requirements to accomplish instead of an opportunity to record their competencies and reflect on their growth as an educator.

311

As with creating your own teacher website or blog (discussed in Chapter 8), your digital portfolio building choices range from premade but limited templates to do-it-yourself, more complete design programs. You can also choose among products that are free with selected design options, those that charge a modest fee and offer more ways to present your material, or specialized versions that are both more expensive and more expansive in style and scope.

 **TaskStream**

TaskStream is a popular digital archiving tool used for Web design and portfolio building (see the accompanying screenshot). TaskStream software provides users with a variety of design options including presentation portfolios, learning or work portfolios tailored to document one's learning process, and resource portfolios that can be accessed by both the world and a specified closed community. Other features include a standards manager, lesson plan and unit builders, and customizable measurement tools.

 iLife

iLife '09 is software created by Apple for Macintosh computers. After importing photo images into the latest versions of iPhoto, iMovie, iDVD, or iWeb, you can add text, titles, keywords, and sound effects to your photographs and digital video files. Combining a variety of print and digital archives, you can manipulate your portfolio with sound effects and professional quality cinematography features.

 **EduTools**

EduTools, a website sponsored by the Western Cooperative for Educational Telecommunications (WCET), provides online reviews and comparisons and consultations for teachers and schools interested in using e-learning tools, including e-portfolios. It also provides reviews of online college, advanced placement, and high school courses. EduTools (2007) has posted reviews of seven widely used

Portfolios and Reflection

Learning through personal reflection is a unique feature of portfolios, as education researcher Lee A. Montgomery (2003, p. 173) has noted:

> When employed as a tool for reflective practice, a digital teaching portfolio can enable both novice and accomplished teachers to make sense out of a myriad of professional experiences and bring into focus a clear picture of themselves as growing, changing professionals. Properly used, the digital portfolio can also be a meaningful and highly effective way to demonstrate to others the knowledge, skills, and dispositions teachers and teacher candidates have gained in the complex process of teaching.

Using a portfolio as a guide to exploring your own teaching enables you to acquire a distinguishing quality of master teachers—thinking critically and creatively about how to reach your students and meet your professional goals. Psychologically, most of us prefer to act using our taken-for-granted assumptions about everyday life. Only when extraordinary events call into question existing patterns of behavior do we take the time to examine our practices and consider

![TaskStream screenshot on a SMART Board]

TaskStream
Advancing Educational Excellence

Sample Student | My Account | Logout | Help

TaskStream

Home | Folios & Web Pages | Lessons, Units & Rubrics | Standards | Communications | **Resources** | Instant Messenger

Resources

My Work | Shared Resources | Online Storage | Pack-It-Up: Save Offline

You are using 9% (84.3 MB) of your file storage quota.

View Usage Details

My Folders ☑ Show work deleted within the last 30 days

Create New Folder

▷ **Recently Edited Items** (3 Items) — Manage Contents

▷ **Recently Deleted Items** (0 Items) — Manage Contents

▷ **My Lessons** (3 Items) — Manage Contents | Delete Folder

Assigned DRF Programs

▷ **DRF Program Work** (116 DRF Programs)

Folios & Web Pages

Go to Folios & Web Pages

▷ **Resource Folios** (8 Folios)

▷ **Presentation Folios** (16 Portfolios)

e-portfolio products: ANGEL e-Portfolio, BB e-Portfolio, e-Folio, ePortfolio.org, LiveText, Open Source Portfolio/rSmart, and TaskStream. You can consult these listings for detailed information about different portfolio delivery systems.

CONTACT INFORMATION

TaskStream   www.taskstream.com/pub

iLife   www.apple.com/ilife   Available for purchase from Apple.

EduTools   http://eportfolio.edutools.info/index.jsp?pj=1

possible new responses to people and situations. Assembling a portfolio is a structure for examining your teaching practices, identifying strengths and weaknesses, and making plans to improve or change certain aspects in the future.

Constructed without reflection, portfolios can have an almost directly opposite outcome. Rather than encouraging thinking about change, the portfolio becomes a celebratory scrapbook of the past. A lesson plan, personal essay, or curriculum project is elevated to the status of a "portfolio entry," as if the portfolio builder had decided, "Why change something already good enough to be in my portfolio?" The teacher's work is not revisited or revised. In such situations, the process of creating a portfolio actually deters rather than promotes reflection, growth, and change in teachers' minds and their work.

You, too, may face these pressures when building your own portfolio by having a tendency to post material electronically (perhaps to satisfy outside evaluators of your teaching practices) and leave it there permanently. Yet the great value of a digital portfolio is that its contents can be constantly changed to reflect your growth as a teacher and the growth of your students as learners.

Assessment should not be practiced by teachers only, but by students as well, if learning is to be successful. K–12 schools, whose mission is to prepare young people to be active and productive members of a democratic society, often minimize or negate student voice and agency—particularly when it involves making decisions about what students want to learn and how they want to learn it. Teachers who recognize the irony in this practice promote student engagement and decision-making about important matters of school operation.

But in the majority of classrooms, most of the time, students have little or no influence on curriculum topics, instructional methods, or evaluation procedures. Failure to give students a voice in educational decision-making is an opportunity lost. From a well-documented psychological standpoint, individuals are more likely to become and remain invested in activities and procedures that they have a role in creating and maintaining (Ginott, 1969; Glasser, 1998; Gordon & Burch, 1977). This is true for adult workers on the job or family members in the home, and it is true for students in schools. For students to care about rules of school conduct, they need a voice in shaping those rules (Schimmel, 1997). If a goal is that students care about the curriculum, they need input in deciding what topics to study. And if the goal is that students care about evaluation, they need substantive roles in the assessment process.

Democratic Schools and Classrooms

One leading voice for greater involvement of students in educational decision-making in schools and classrooms is the movement for **democratic schools and classrooms** (Apple & Beane, 2007; Waterman, 2006). Democratic schools and classrooms are places where students and teachers together make substantive decisions about important aspects of educational operations, from the academic curriculum to school climate and rules.

Student engagement in decisions about learning is not the same as student control of these decisions. Critics of democratic classrooms dismiss the idea by suggesting that students will make silly, ill-informed, or self-centered choices that benefit themselves, if given the opportunity to do so. They will vote to do little homework, spend lots of time socializing, and select few hard problems to solve. In this view, teachers cannot have a classroom where the students make decisions because students will choose poorly and academic standards will remain unmet.

But in democratic schools and classrooms, input and involvement require teachers and students to engage in open and frank discussions about how their classroom operates. The reality that teachers are the adults in charge is not negotiable. Teachers are responsible for delivering a curriculum and for assessing how successfully students have learned what has been taught. How learning happens and how evaluation is conducted, however, are formulated through honest dialogue, debate, and decision-making between students and teachers.

There are well-established ways to make students active partners with teachers in the organization of classroom learning, from schoolwide mission statements to everyday practices in the classroom.

Schoolwide Mission. A school might declare itself a democratic school with a mission to infuse democratic values in every aspect of the organization's culture, including the following:

- Shared decision-making among the students and staff
- A learner-centered approach in which students choose their daily activities
- Equality among staff and students
- The community as an extension of the classroom (Alternative Education Resource Organization, 2006)

Active engagement and willing participation are hallmarks of democratic classrooms where teachers and students conduct learning together.

While self-proclaimed democratic schools represent only a tiny number of the schools in the United States, many schools and teachers see themselves as teaching democratically, and they find many ways to do this within the framework of a more traditionally structured school organization. One second-grade teacher we know avoids using the teacher–student distinction whenever she can, preferring to say that in her classroom there are 20 teachers under the age of 9 and one teacher over the age of the 50. In daily routines and classroom activities, she introduces repeated opportunities for children to teach each other by sharing their reading, writing, science, math, and artwork in front of the whole class or in small groups.

Teaching Practices.   Teachers foster student engagement by establishing a balance between teacher-chosen and student-chosen activities. In creating lessons, the teacher sets the overall theme and focus for the curriculum, but students contribute to the learning process in ways such as those described by Steven Zemelman, Harvey Daniels, and Arthur Hyde from National-Louis University (2005, p. 213):

- Students select inquiry themes, books, writing topics, audiences, and so on.
- Students maintain their own records, set their own goals, and continually self-assess.
- Some themes and inquiries are built from students' own questions in a "negotiated curriculum."
- Students assume responsibility, take roles in decision-making, and help run classroom life.

Technology Use.   Teachers use technology to support multiple opportunities of student voice and involvement in the learning process. Table 11.3 lists five areas where students can play roles in the assessment process: (1) preassessments of student interest and knowledge, (2) peer editing of writing assignments, (3) self-assessments and reflections, (4) documentation of learning, and (5) participation in grading.

In each case, technology tools offer ways to promote active student involvement in processes of assessment. Next we look at two technologies that are particularly useful ways for teachers to involve students in learning and self-reflection: online surveys and student participation systems.

 ## Online Surveys for Preassessment

Preassessments occur before introducing a new lesson, topic, or unit as a way for teachers to determine what students know or can already do in order to inform subsequent plans for teaching. Pretests, writing prompts, graphic organizers, observations, questions, and surveys are widely used preassessment strategies. Preassessments are part of **prior knowledge–based learning,** the idea that when teaching new concepts, teachers need to connect their lessons to what students already know or have been taught. Prior knowledge is not immediately obvious to students; they often do not realize that they know important information about a topic. Prior knowledge needs to be

TABLE 11.3   Student Roles and Technology Tools for Assessment

Student Role in Assessment	Technology Tools
Preassessments of student interests and knowledge	Online surveys and polls
	Classroom website, discussion board, or blog
Peer editing of written assignments	Word processing for written reflections and self-evaluations
Self-assessments and reflections	
Documentation of learning	Student e-portfolios
Participation in grading	Online rubric development tools

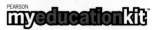

FIGURE 11.1 Screenshot of Questions from a Teacher's Online Survey

3 What strengths do you bring to the group?

4 What are your preferred areas of contribution to the group and our assignments?

- Analysis
- Creating presentations (graphics, multimedia)
- Presenting
- Research
- Strategy
- Writing

5 Do you prefer to work as a group or rotate responsibility to complete assignments?

- Work as a group on all assignments
- Rotate responsibility for all assignments among group members
- Only work as a group on major projects and rotate for rest of work
- Don't know, would like to discuss as a group

activated—brought to students' attention—through readings, discussions, and preassessment activities.

Online surveys are an effective way to activate prior knowledge and involve students in the preassessment process. An online survey is a poll that is delivered and tabulated online. Such surveys identify the skills and knowledge students have as well as the skills and knowledge they would like to learn. Students like these because they are not tests with right and wrong answers or high or low scores. Furthermore, preassessment surveys demonstrate that teachers care about what students know about a topic before a lesson begins. Finally, because students appreciate being asked about their knowledge and skills, survey preassessments create a sense of collaborative learning where students and teachers work together. Tech Tool 11.2 discusses three online survey tools that teachers can use for preassessments of student learning or to gather student opinions about important academic topics.

Online surveys are an engaging way to conduct preassessments with students while also providing teachers with useful data for documenting individual and group learning progress. See Figure 11.1 for some sample questions from a teacher's online survey.

Using a Preassessment Survey in a Community History Project

In preparation for a community history research project, a high school teacher sent the survey shown in Figure 11.2 (page 318) to her students using Zoomerang's online survey-building tool. In developing this survey, this teacher's goals were fourfold:

- To encourage student use of technology from the beginning of the community history project
- To find out the students' prior knowledge and interests
- To generate a high level of engagement with the project
- To show students her appreciation of the value and importance of their ideas about the curriculum unit they would be studying

YOUR JUDGMENT
MATTERS

As you think about this teacher's goals in using survey software with her students, consider the following questions:

- What other questions might this teacher have asked on the survey?
- How might you use an online survey for one of your teaching units?
- What other benefits for students are potentially included in online surveys (such as mathematical understanding of a graph of student responses)?

The results of the community history survey showed that almost everyone in the class was interested in researching their community's history. The survey also showed that many of the students did not have knowledge of digital media or editing while almost half had no prior experience making PowerPoint presentations. The teacher used these results to tailor her instruction to emphasize technology skill building and to ensure that everyone would explore different aspects of their town's history.

You can use surveys as preassessments in just about any curriculum area. The survey can be administered during class time in a computer lab or on the computers you have in your classroom, or it can be assigned as an outside-of-class homework assignment. Asking the students to analyze the results of the survey, and then suggest next steps, is a way to double the momentum for learning generated by the survey process. You and your students might also design a postassessment survey to track what everyone has learned since the administration of the first survey.

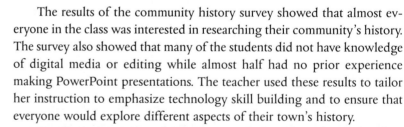

Online surveys, an engaging way to conduct preassessments with students, also provide teachers with useful data for documenting individual and group learning progress. Zoomerang, SurveyMonkey, and Poll Builder are three easy-to-use online survey building tools for teachers to conduct preassessment surveys with their students.

 **Zoomerang**

Zoomerang, like other online survey tools, provides prompts and templates based on themes that help make the purpose of the survey clearly apparent to the students taking it. Zoomerang categorizes templates by broad themes such as business, community, educational, and personal/social. It also allows you to change the design of your survey to include personalized greetings and responses. Zoomerang keeps an archive of your past surveys for reuse in their original format or as templates for recycled use.

With free basic membership, once a survey is launched, it is deployed for 10 days. If you purchase a membership you can deploy the survey for a longer period of time. Other features include a data sharing function, allowing you to make the data public, as well as deployment options that include URL links and individual computer kiosk surveys providing various routes for respondents to access your survey questions.

 **SurveyMonkey**

SurveyMonkey, like Zoomerang, is an easy-to-use online survey tool with multiple ways to formulate questions and collect information.

Poll Builder

Poll Builder from the Center for History and New Media at George Mason University allows teachers and students to conduct simple polls for free. Although this tool does have not as many options as Zoomerang or Survey-Monkey, it can be useful for quick information collection as part of a class activity.

CONTACT INFORMATION

Zoomerang   http://info.zoomerang.com   Basic surveys are offered free.

Center for History and New Media at George Mason University   http://chnm.gmu.edu/tools/polls   Poll Builder users must create an account.

SurveyMonkey   www.surveymonkey.com/Home.asp   A free basic subscription is offered to individuals for up to 10 questions and no more than 100 responses per survey.

FIGURE 11.2 Online Presurvey

Community History Research Project Survey

1. For this project you will be required to use several different technology skills. Please check the skills you feel comfortable with/have experience with:

____ PowerPoint
____ Digital Camera
____ Scanners/Scanning Pictures
____ Camcorder
____ Web Design

____ Video Editing
____ Digital Photo Editing
____ Online Research Techniques
____ Other

2. Please specify any software programs you have knowledge of.

3. What technologies, software, and/or skills would you like to learn/practice with the help of this research project?

4. What is your level of confidence in composing/writing an interview for historical research?

5. What is your level of confidence in conducting an interview for historical research?

6. What is your level of confidence in calling and setting up meetings for interviews with local residents?

7. What time period in our community's history would you be interested in researching?

____ Colonial

____ Early 19th Century (Antebellum)

____ Industrial Age

____ Early 20th Century

____ Late 20th Century to Present Day

8. Do you have preliminary ideas or interests for a topic for your historical research project?

 ## Using Student Participation Systems

Student participation systems (also known as classroom response systems or personal response systems) are handheld and wireless tools that offer interactive learning options for teachers and students (Duncan, 2005; Fies & Marshall, 2006; Garner, Shih, Rogers, & Hart, 2008). These technologies use wireless remote control devices to create real-time electronic exchanges between students and teacher (EDUCAUSE Learning Initiative, 2005a). Popular as a college-level teaching tool, more than 3,000 elementary and secondary schools nationwide also report using student participation systems, mostly at the high school level (Abrahamson, 2006).

Student participation systems are based on surveying the students as part of a lesson. Like the audience on the "Who Wants to Be a Millionaire" game show, students record individual responses to questions by pressing a button on a **clicker** device slightly smaller in size than a TV remote (see Figure 11.3). Students use this small handheld device to instantly answer questions. Depending on the particular model, students can answer multiple-choice, yes/no, true/false, ranking, numeric, and short answer questions. While the CPSPulse model in Figure 11.3 uses radio frequency technology, other models use infrared technology and have simpler answer pads for younger students. Once everyone has entered an answer, the answers of the group are instantly aggregated for everyone to see. Figure 11.4 shows how a class of 34 students answered which of eight possible factors was most important in a science problem.

Reasons for Teaching with Clickers

Student participation systems with clickers have numerous instructional advantages (Bruff, 2007; Martyn, 2007).

- *Active learning.* Rather than passively listening to the teacher, students are active participants who must express their opinions electronically. In theory, the level of student engagement is increased because individuals feel that their ideas matter.

- *Student involvement.* A "game-like" approach may encourage more students to participate than in a traditional oral discussion. Moreover, students make their selections anonymously (no one knows who has what clicker) so individuals worry less about the embarrassment of giving a wrong answer. Accordingly, students who might otherwise not participate in an oral discussion for fear of being wrong or appearing foolish have an opportunity to express their ideas in class.
- *Real-time feedback.* The teacher has immediate feedback about students' content knowledge and test performance without correcting paper-and-pencil quizzes and entering the grades.
- *Question-driven instruction.* In **question-driven instruction,** students are given a challenging question and asked individually or in small groups to consider possible answers. They enter their choice with a clicker and then participate in a whole-class discussion of student replies and the reasoning behind those replies (Beatty, Leonard, Gerace, & Dufresne, 2006). Students

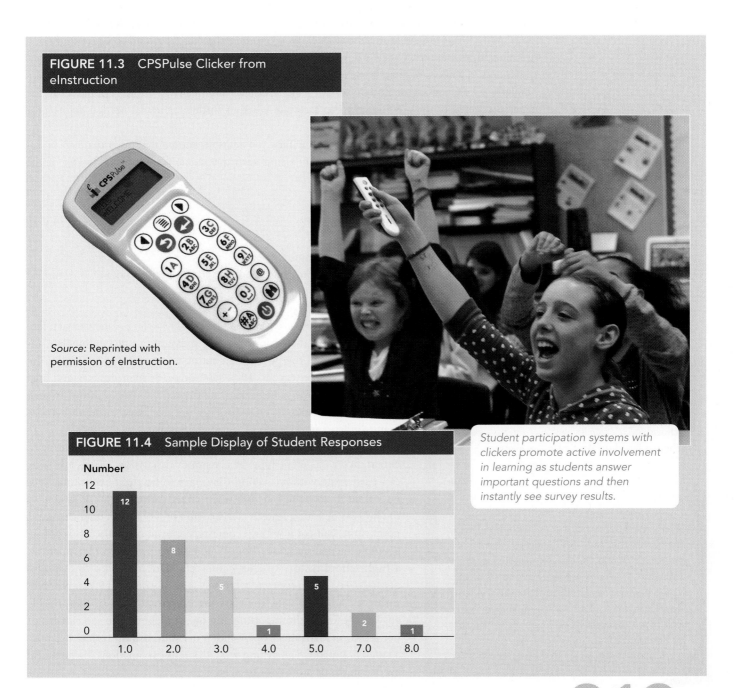

FIGURE 11.3 CPSPulse Clicker from eInstruction

Source: Reprinted with permission of eInstruction.

FIGURE 11.4 Sample Display of Student Responses

Number

Student participation systems with clickers promote active involvement in learning as students answer important questions and then instantly see survey results.

Go to the Assignments and Activities section Chapter 11 in MyEducationKit and complete the Web activity entitled "Interactive Assessment." As you complete the activity, consider the advantages of computer response systems.

thus have opportunities to think conceptually, reason critically, and practice problem-solving skills.

Student participation systems use simple radio frequency technology. The system's software lets you type questions into a computer-based question bank. When your computer is connected to a digital projector, the questions appear on a screen. Your computer is connected to the responder system's main unit, enabling the results of student voting to appear on the screen as well. When a student presses a button on the clicker or keypad, a radio receiver picks up the signal from the student's handheld and logs in the response. Once everyone has voted, the results are immediately visible. The system displays the correct answer to the question (if there is one) as well as the percentage of students in the class who chose each response.

Changing the Classroom Experience

Clickers change the classroom experience, encouraging student individuality while giving them active roles and reasons to participate in discussions (Penuel et al., 2005; Stowell & Nelson, 2007; Wit, 2003). At the high school level, an economics class might examine a case study of a firm debating whether to open a new product line or close some of its retail outlets. Using their responders, members of the class express their opinions about the firm's best course of action. Similarly, an elementary or middle school math instructor might give a short quiz based on the material covered in the previous class to ascertain whether further review is needed before proceeding to the next topic.

Every academic subject has yes/no, true/false, or multiple-choice questions that can be integrated into a student participation system. Using such questions, teachers can do any of the following:

- Design brief surveys
- Ask inquiry and opinion questions
- Give short review quizzes
- Promote discussion based on how the students vote
- Receive feedback about whether students have understood the main points of a lecture or presentation

VOICES from the classroom

A high school teacher who uses a student participation system with her students noted:

I think it [student participation system] helped them learn better together as a whole because they were trying to help each other out. Because they would say, "I think it is Answer A" and then others would say, "Yes" or "No, no, no, because choice A was in another chapter." So it caused a lot of discussion in class and even out of class. I had kids coming to me later saying, "I never would have gotten that question on the test. Now I know it so if it is on the test then I am set." Their test results went up, especially the LD [learning disability] students.

Many students are threatened by right/wrong, short answer, factual recall verbal discussions. Feeling pressured to give immediate answers, they avoid the possible embarrassment of being wrong by not responding to the teacher. They stare down at their desks, avoid raising their hands, and, when asked, simply reply, "I don't know." In such situations, academic material does not get discussed in depth because many students never express their viewpoints.

Electronic participation systems offer students the opportunity to experience a different type of classroom discussion where everyone can participate without feeling they have to be right every time. It is important that teachers include open-ended questions in the system so the process of voting leads to a discussion of key ideas rather than to "I got it right; you got it wrong" contests. For example, rather than asking a simple factual question about Columbus's voyages to the Americas, a high school history teacher could ask, "Do you think the voyages of discovery by Europeans were voyages of conquest? Yes/No/Not Entirely." After the vote, the class then discusses each of the possible answer choices without putting any one student on the spot for his or her selection. This more open-ended question-asking format becomes a launching pad for analyzing why different explanations for historical events might or might not be accurate.

Preparing for High-Stakes Tests

Participation systems offer new ways to prepare students for high-stakes academic achievement tests. Virtually every school now gives such tests, and the stakes can be very high for students, as in states where secondary students must pass a competency exam in order to graduate from high school. Invariably, achievement tests—whether in language arts, math, science, or history—include multiple-choice questions. Actual test questions from past tests can be loaded into the electronic response system and students can then practice reading, analyzing, and answering them—individually, in small groups, or as a whole class.

It is important that teachers shift the emphasis of students from quickly answering the questions to closely reading and critically analyzing both the question and the possible answer choices before choosing a response. Multiple-choice questions on achievement tests have been systematically constructed to test students' knowledge and test-taking skills. Questions usually include answers that could be right except for one or two key pieces of information. In the pressure of a test situation, students who do not look for potential "distracter" answers can miss key information easily. Most test-taking guides recommend that test takers read all the answer choices carefully and eliminate those that are not correct. For this reason, students benefit from classroom practice in "deconstructing" or "unpacking" the potential answers to test questions.

Teachers in our area are using electronic participation systems with students preparing to take the state's mandatory history test for high school graduation. They load sample questions from online test guides into the computer system. Then, after projecting a question on a large screen, they ask a member of the class to read the question with the possible answer choices aloud. Everyone votes for what he or she believes is the correct choice. The system instantly shows how the class has voted—the number of votes is shown beside each choice while a check mark indicates the correct answer.

If most of the class has identified the right answer, the class discusses how they arrived at their conclusion. If the class divides between right and wrong answers, the teacher asks the students to examine the content and phrasing of the different answer choices and how they might create confusion or misunderstanding for test takers.

These "after-the-vote" discussions are tremendously useful to the students. First, they decrease defensive feelings because it is neither apparent nor important who answered correctly and who did not. Second, classmates engage in a thoughtful discussion about question formats, vocabulary cues, and strategies for thinking critically, which enhances academic learning and test-taking performance for everyone. Elementary, middle, and high school teachers can utilize this approach for test reviews in history, science, and mathematics.

Revealing Misconceptions

Revealing and correcting student misconceptions about academic material is another important way for teachers to utilize electronic participation systems. Students regularly come to every academic class with many ill-formed ideas and misguided notions. Many science students may believe that seasonal change is caused by the distance of the earth from the sun when it is in fact the tilt of the earth as it rotates on its axis that creates winters and summers. Elementary school math students often wrongly assume that to answer "how many more" questions requires using addition rather than subtraction. Such misconceptions, and many more, result from not fully understanding the laws and rules of science, mathematics, economics, or other disciplines or not understanding the language describing the idea.

YOUR JUDGMENT MATTERS

As you recall question/answer discussions you have participated in as a student, consider the following questions:

- What kinds of questions did teachers ask (informational, opinion, open-ended, etc)?
- What were teachers hoping to accomplish instructionally by asking questions of students?
- Did teachers correctly anticipate what students would say in response to your questions? What did teachers do when they did not respond as you expected?

Go to the Assignments and Activities section of Chapter 11 in MyEducationKit and complete the video activity entitled "Audience Response Systems." As you watch the video and answer the accompanying questions, note how students respond to using a student response system in their classes.

Addressing student misconceptions is not always easy to do in class. Many students resent being challenged directly about their views, even when a teacher knows they are not thinking clearly about a problem. Teachers must walk a fine line between clarification and confrontation. Putting questions that raise potential misconceptions into a participation system and letting the class express its collective viewpoint is a less threatening way to teach students to clarify their thinking. Below is a sample misconception question for a student participation system from a high school statistics class (Lavoie, 2008).

If Apple lowers the price of iPhones, what will be the effect on revenues made from iPhones?

a) Increase
b) Decrease
c) Increase or decrease—it is hard to tell

The potential misconception inherent in this question is that the price is, in economic terms, "elastic" and that cell phone consumers purchase iPhones based only on price. The reality is that other factors may be involved. For example, if acceptable substitute phones can be found, then those will be purchased. The correct answer is c.

In class, after the students have read the question and voted their answer choices, the teacher can challenge their potential misconceptions, not by singling out any individual student, but by noting that a certain percentage of the class believes an incorrect or less likely answer to be true. The teacher can ask questions that explore this reasoning before presenting evidence to the contrary. Students, engaged but not needing to be defensive, learn new information to replace previously held ideas.

TECHNOLOGY TRANSFORMATION LESSON PLAN

ENCYCLO-ME-DIA
Documenting Student Learning Using Digital Portfolios

Grade(s)

Elementary/Middle School (Grades K to 8)

Subject(s)

Language Arts/Social Studies

Key Goal/Enduring Understanding

Learning about oneself as a unique individual, and as a contributing member of many communities (school, neighborhood, city, and country) is an essential feature of education in schools. An Encyclo-ME-dia collects the personal milestones, memorable activities, and creative work of individual students and shares the materials in ways that allow everyone to learn about each other's accomplishments and achievements as community members.

Essential Question

What personal activities and accomplishments in school could become part of an Encyclo-ME-dia and why?

Learning Standards

National Council for the Social Studies—*Curriculum Standards for the Social Studies*

> **Theme III:** People, Places, and Environment
> **Theme IV:** Individual Development and Identity
> **Theme X:** Civic Ideals and Practices

▶

International Society for Technology in Education (ISTE)—*NETS-S*

Standard 1: *Creativity and Innovation.* Students demonstrate creative thinking, construct knowledge, and develop innovative products and processes using technology.

Standard 2: *Communication and Collaboration.* Students use digital media and environments to communicate and work collaboratively, including at a distance, to support individual learning and contribute to the learning of others.

Standard 6: *Technology Operations and Concepts.* Students demonstrate a sound understanding of technology concepts, systems and operations.

Learning Objectives

Student will know and be able to

- Describe and write different genres—memories, letters, diary entries, poems, and stories.
- Make choices about what to include in the portfolio as examples of class work and personal interests.

Technology Uses

The lesson uses classroom computers, digital cameras, scanners, and editing software for the collecting and publishing of children's portfolios. There are many ways to create an Encyclo-ME-dia electronically. A teacher might create a separate folder on one of the classroom computers for each student: Dennis's Encyclo-ME-dia, Emily's Encyclo-ME-dia, and so on. Adults and students then add items into the Encyclo-ME-dia regularly throughout the school year.

Minimal Technology	Infusion of Technology
Students use markers, colored pencils, crayons, watercolor paint, glue sticks, tape and staplers, and paper of different sizes and colors to create items for their All About Me book or paper portfolio.	Students use computers with word processing and drawing programs to create items for their digital portfolio. These materials do not replace writing and drawing on paper, but add to it.
Students collect their paper-based materials.	Students use a digital camera or digital video recorder to take photos or short movies for their digital portfolio. They use software to download photos and movies to a classroom computer.
Students decide which materials to include in their collection.	After choosing materials to include, students use a scanner to import paper materials to their portfolio electronically.
Students publish their portfolio in a notebook or paper folder.	Students use a CD burner or website to publish their digital portfolio.

Evaluation

- Diversity of item types completed and included in the portfolio: films, slideshows, illustrations, and artifacts
- Range of writing genres accompanying item types in the portfolio: reports, poems, memoirs, books, essays, interviews, posters, plays, and skits

LESSON PLAN DESCRIPTION

Introduction

The "Encyclo-ME-dia" lesson plan shows elementary and middle school students how to develop a digital portfolio comprising their personal writings, drawings, illustrations, artwork, and

▶

digital photographs and movies. An Encyclo-ME-dia is an electronic collection of student-created materials that may previously have been stored in paper scrapbooks, journals, or diaries (Edwards, Maloy, & Verock-O'Loughlin, 2003).

This lesson plan directly connects to two main themes of this chapter—student involvement in performance evaluation and digital portfolios. Teachers can use the materials students put in their Encyclo-ME-dia as performance evaluation evidence of learning. Students can use those same materials to engage in self-assessment of what they have accomplished in school. As a result, teachers and students discover the powerful uses of digital portfolios as a learning technology.

Lesson Focus

While digital portfolios are generally considered tools for older students who are showcasing their learning in various subjects, younger students can also produce engaging and compelling electronic collections of their learning accomplishments. An Encyclo-ME-dia serves as a technology-based alternative to "All About Me" books or other paper portfolios in several important ways:

- *Documentation and assessment of learning.* Encyclo-ME-dia portfolios document and assess the progress of student learning. Where paper samples may become misplaced and bulky to store, scanned or photographed samples are readily available for viewing by teachers, families, and students. Classroom projects for history, science, writing, math, and creative arts are easily stored on a CD-ROM, in the computer hard drive, or on a portable data stick.

- *Creative self-expression.* Technology opens unlimited possibilities for self-expression in up-to-the-minute, attractive ways that students want to experience. An Encyclo-ME-dia uses tools to inspire writing and to enable illustrating in new ways of thinking and composing. A student who does not enjoy writing may be a wonderful photographer who captures ideas in a unique visual style to accompany poems, essays, letters, and stories. A student who does not enjoy drawing will be attracted to the design possibilities of desktop publishing. A musician will be able to compose and insert music.

- *Learning about technology.* The Encyclo-ME-dia process acquaints students with different technologies for recording and publishing personal activities and accomplishments. The International Society for Technology in Education (ISTE) Standards for Students emphasize that all students, even first- and second-graders, should use technology tools in project-based learning activities. The idea of collecting and publishing one's own work electronically teaches students of any age about technology tools, their uses, and their vast creative potential.

- *Learning about writing.* An Encyclo-ME-dia teaches writing genres of autobiographies, memoirs, and personal stories as students use portfolio building to locate themselves within the larger communities of classroom, school, neighborhood, and nation. As they use computers, cameras, scanners, and other digital tools to build an Encyclo-ME-dia, students become full-fledged authors and editors of their learning portfolio as they decide what to include and why. The list of multiple genres to record is extensive: poetry, letters, riddles and jokes, news stories—whatever students write or perform on video they can store in their digital portfolio. Comics, illustrated stories, and other material produced on paper can be scanned into an Encyclo-ME-dia.

- *Student engagement.* The process of archiving one's ideas electronically creates a powerful incentive for students to invest time and effort in their work. When students are willing to engage and are interested in a learning activity, there is an intrinsic opportunity to practice reading, writing, thinking, and all literacy skills.

Lesson Design—Minimal Technology

Paper portfolios, often called "All about Me" books, have been a staple of autobiographical writing for elementary and middle school students. These formats enable students to creatively save and

display personal writing and drawing in store-bought notebooks, storage boxes, or desk drawers. Generally, "All about Me" portfolios use minimal technology, although they often contain photocopies of student work and photographs.

Some classes begin constructing "All About Me" books and paper portfolios when the school year commences, continuing to add to the collection as the curriculum evolves. Students have the option of adding materials at any time and a teacher might assign entries as the class studies and investigates topics. Photos, drawings, paintings, maps, sketches, or timelines are illustrations. Showcasing work with classmates is easily archived in this format through photographs.

LESSON ACTIVITIES USING TECHNOLOGY

1. *Starting Encyclo-ME-dia.* The concept of a digital portfolio is new to many teachers and students. An Encyclo-ME-dia may seem time consuming and complex, but as with every new process we learn, one way to speed our understanding is to ask someone who already knows how to show us. Begin by asking your students what they know about picture taking, video technology, computer downloading, and photo and video editing. Make a list of the skills and competencies present in the classroom. Many students know more about using technology than teachers do, and they are immediately engaged by the opportunities to teach other students about computers, cameras, and other digital tools.

2. *Scale and Time Frame.* As the teacher, you decide the scale and time frame of the Encyclo-ME-dia process. You can record a single unit of study, a science project or writing genre, an entire school year of academic work, or anything in between. In February, with curriculum connected to Black History Month and Presidents Day, students might construct a portion of their Encyclo-ME-dia to examine their lives at that moment and the influences that contribute to who they are in society. Usually students do not view the present moment as extraordinary or themselves and their decisions as history making. By focusing attention on the importance of personal decisions as history-making activities, students begin to act as historians of their own lives. This is a compelling context for learning about and contrasting their own lives with those of men and women from the past.

3. *Learn Key Technologies.* Learn with your students the processes of filming still photos and movies digitally, downloading them to a computer, and then making copies to put into individuals' Encyclo-ME-dias. Review how to make slideshows, movies, greeting cards, postcards, screensavers, and almost anything else that someone might want to include in an Encyclo-ME-dia. Students who quickly and easily learn digital processes can make posters to help classmates practice the steps involved. Supervising their efforts soon requires less time from you, the teacher, as students become confident and skilled in portfolio production processes. Students will also want to teach each other and collaborate on ideas and designs for creating their Encyclo-ME-dias.

4. *Information Recording System.* Develop an information recording system that lets you easily manage the component pieces of an Encyclo-ME-dia. The archiving system will have separate computer folders for each student. A student's personal folder is then subdivided into science, math, history, writing, and art. Inside each of these sections are units of study that proceed throughout the year. For example, in science topics are segmented into particular units—rocks and soil, plants and plant growth, and seasonal change. The teacher has her own folders for each curricular area and the different genres within them, as well as for special projects throughout the school year.

5. *Assemble a Team.* Invite a team of assistants to take pictures, scan writing and drawings, download files, burn CDs, and facilitate the other jobs of an Encyclo-ME-dia. Students in the upper elementary grades can be the members of the Encyclo-ME-dia production crew for their class and for younger classes. Students from the high school along with parents, family members, or community volunteers might assist with these jobs at all grade levels.

6. *Incorporate Visual Elements and Motion Picture–Like Qualities.* Photos and short movies of students participating in learning activities are easily filmed with a digital video recorder. The camera records voice as it films, enabling students to
   - Describe what they are doing or building
   - Ask questions of the audience as they demonstrate an experiment or explain a creative idea
   - Perform in a play, skit, student-written commercial, public service announcement, puppet show, dance, read-aloud, news report, or other presentation

   Capturing moments in the lives of students has never been simpler or more attractive to do. Digital photos and movies downloaded from camera to computer are stored in folders on the computer. They are easily displayed on a television screen or digital projector via a wire connecting the camera with either a TV or computer. Seeing photos and movies of themselves on the television display is exciting for students. They like seeing themselves on a big screen.

7. *Focus on School Activities.* Encyclo-ME-dia is a timeline of activities at school where everyone has the same access to learning experiences and technology resources. When outside-of-school lives are included, then students may not be equally invested. Some students have many positive experiences—sports events, family vacations, holiday celebrations, birthdays, trips to new places—to include in an Encyclo-ME-dia whereas others are more limited in the events that can describe and display. Students may have family situations that make them less willing to share information about their lives outside of school. By keeping attention on in-school activities and accomplishments, these differences in student experiences are less relevant to this activity.

8. *Involve Students and Families.* As early as kindergarten, students and families can be actively involved in creating an Encyclo-ME-dia. On the family visiting day before the beginning of the school year, as small groups of 5-year-olds enter their new classroom, the teacher or volunteer photographer takes a digital photo of each kindergartner and adult family members. While students and adults circulate throughout the room, a volunteer takes more photos. At a point when the students are engaged in an activity without their accompanying family members, each adult records a message on the computer to accompany the family photo in a file called "Family Photos." To preserve the element of surprise, these adult voice recordings are done without the students' knowledge. The family pictures with the recorded messages become one of the first things students hear and see during their initial days in kindergarten. Then during the next few weeks in the school year, the teacher and students photograph or make videos of student writing and drawing and record messages to families to show during family–teacher conference meetings.

ANALYSIS AND EXTENSIONS

1. Name two features you find useful about this lesson.
2. Identify two areas for extending or improving this lesson.
3. How successfully has information technology been integrated into the lesson?
4. How might students be even more involved in designing, using, and evaluating technology in the lesson?

PEARSON
myeducationkit™

Go to the Technology Transformation Lesson Plan section in Chapter 11 in MyEducationKit and access the activity "Encyclo-ME-dia" to practice transforming a lesson plan using technology.

FOCUS QUESTION 1: What is performance-based assessment for teachers and for students?

- Teachers can use norm-referenced tests, criterion-referenced tests, standards-based assessments, and performance-based assessments to evaluate their students. Supervisors can use these same assessments to evaluate teachers.

- Performance evaluation bases assessment on work completed rather than tests taken, including such performance areas as student writing, individual and group projects, homework assignments, individual presentations and performances, open book exams, student self-assessments, and teacher observations.

- Performance evaluation has a dual focus for teachers—they are continually evaluating their students while their supervisors are continually evaluating them.

- Technology is a powerful tool for assessing student and teacher performance because it allows individuals to display the actual real-world learning they have experienced in the classroom.

FOCUS QUESTION 2: How can teachers and students use digital portfolios as tools for learning?

- A digital portfolio for a teacher is an individually prepared collection of work that communicates who a teacher is and what that teacher knows and is able to do in academic subjects and classroom teaching.

- A standards-based digital portfolio serves as a way for new teacher candidates to connect lesson plans, teaching evaluations, and other work done in the classroom to the specific professional teaching standards they are required to meet in order to earn a teacher license.

- The advantages of digital portfolios include easy access, ready-made portability, creative information displays, experience in developing technology skills, and the sharing of information with a wider educational community.

- The disadvantages of digital portfolios include the need for technical knowledge and skill, ongoing support, computer access, and time, as well as the possibility that style will override substance in the presentation of information.

FOCUS QUESTION 3: How can students become actively involved in assessment and evaluation using technology?

- Involving students in the process of performance evaluation builds a respectful partnership for learning in the classroom, a concept strongly supported by advocates for democratic schools and classrooms.

- Technology, including many of the tools discussed in this book, supports active roles by students in the learning assessment process.

- Online survey tools involve students in the assessment process by activating prior knowledge and offering the opportunity to help decide how material will be taught in a lesson or unit.

FOCUS QUESTION 4: How can teachers use student participation systems as effective assessment methods?

- Student participation systems use remote control devices known as clickers to allow members of a class to respond collectively to questions posed by teachers.

- Participation systems are ways to actively engage students with academic material and to conduct quick assessments of what students know or still need to learn about a topic.

- Designing interesting open-ended questions is a key to using student participation systems successfully with your students.

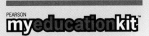

To check your comprehension of the content covered in the chapter, go to the MyEducationKit for your book and complete the Study Plan for Chapter 11. Here you will be able to take a chapter quiz, receive feedback on your answers, and then access resources that will enhance your understanding of chapter content.

Clickers

Democratic schools and classrooms

Digital portfolios

New teacher assessment

Online surveys

Preassessments

Prior knowledge–based learning

Question-driven instruction

Standards-based digital portfolios

Student assessment

Student involvement in learning and assessment

Student participation systems

ACTIVITIES FOR YOUR TEACHER PORTFOLIO

1. ALFIE KOHN'S CRITIQUE OF STANDARDIZED TESTING

In his book *The Schools Our Children Deserve,* education reformer Alfie Kohn (1999) discusses the dangers of and damages from standardized testing of K–12 students. Kohn is a longstanding critic of traditional childrearing and educational practices that he believes are unexamined in their actual outcomes.

Noting that it is "easier to measure efficiency than effectiveness," Kohn (1999, pp. 75–76) states that the process by which children learn "to understand ideas in a classroom is not always linear or quantifiable." Indeed, "once teachers and students are compelled to focus only on what lends itself to quantification, such as the number of grammatical errors in a composition or the number of state capitals memorized, the process of thinking has been severely compromised."

Kohn believes standardized tests are not "objective" because they are not neutral measures of performance. Adults write the question and inevitably insert biases of culture, language, and community. Students take the tests, and, as the pressure mounts to pass, "test anxiety" distorts the results. "The more a test is made to 'count,'" suggests Kohn, *"the less valid the scores become"* (p. 76).

Nor do the tests actually test the intellectual skills and talents of the students, concludes Kohn. Instead, the tests are "geared to a different, less sophisticated kind of knowledge" (p. 81). The tests overestimate what some students know while underestimating what others know, and never measuring important qualities of learning such as "initiative, creativity, imagination, conceptual thinking, curiosity, effort, irony, judgment, commitment, nuance, good will, ethical reflection" (p. 82).

- Based on your experiences as a taker of tests, do you mainly agree or disagree with these comments?

- After reading Kohn's ideas, what strategies would you recommend for making and using tests in schools?

2. ASSESSMENTS DEPEND ON WHAT IS BEING ASSESSED

Assessment and evaluation experts agree on this point: Teachers must know and clearly communicate what they want their assessments to measure or document. In other words, the nature of what is being assessed influences the types of assessments that are used. No "one-size-fits-all" assessment instrument exists.

The Iraq War provides a provocative example of the complexities of developing assessments. In June 2006, following allegations that U.S. soldiers may have killed unarmed civilians in one

Iraq city, the U.S. military command announced that all forces in the country would undergo "core values training." The purpose was to ensure that soldiers knew the differences in values among themselves, their enemies, and noncombatants. The military also announced that most of the 150,000 troops in the country were already operating according to high ethical standards. The announcement did not specify how the military planned to evaluate the success of the training in producing appropriate responses by soldiers.

- How should the core values knowledge and ethical standards training of soldiers in a war be assessed?

- Does it make a difference to the choice of an assessment instrument that ethical values are being assessed rather than more discrete skills such as mathematical number operations or geographical knowledge?

- How would you create a test to measure the impact of the core values training?

- What other assessment strategies might be used to determine if the training was successful?

GROWING AND LEADING WITH TECHNOLOGY

This activity offers an opportunity to grow as a teacher and learn to lead with technology. Begin by reviewing the Chapter 11 Learning Goal and Featured Technologies listed in the chart at the beginning of the chapter. Then read the following actual classroom scenario and consider how technologies discussed in Chapter 11 might be integrated into the lesson. Follow-up steps to this activity can be completed at MyEducationKit.

SUE'S MATH TEST REVIEW LESSON

Sue, a fourth-grade teacher in a rural school district, is preparing her students for the state's annual mathematics achievement test administered every May. Her students took this test for the first time as third-graders, and those scores showed some youngsters performing on or above grade level while many others were struggling to grasp basic math concepts, operations, and procedures. The state achievement test includes all the main topics in the fourth-grade math curriculum—number operations (addition, subtraction, multiplication, and division), data analysis/statistics, patterns/relations/algebra, geometry, and measurement—so Sue has taught units on each of these topics during the school year.

Given the wide number of topics on the test, Sue recognizes that her students must remember a considerable amount of information, some of which has not been discussed in class for many weeks. She wants to review math operations and problem-solving strategies in ways that will challenge her higher achieving students while not discouraging those still practicing basic math skills.

Sue's classroom has only one Internet-accessible computer, although she can sign up for the school's computer lab that has enough machines for all of her students. She does have a digital projector and a large display screen.

- Using the technologies discussed in this chapter, how would you propose Sue integrate technology into her math test review lesson in ways that will promote learning success for all her students?

329

Academic content: Ideas and information from different curriculum areas taught to students by teachers.

Accommodations: Changes to learning environments or curriculum delivery strategies to create greater access to the regular school curriculum for students with special needs.

Active learning: A form of learning that happens when students are mentally and physically engaged in the construction and evaluation of academic material.

Adaptation stage: Teachers fully integrate technology into regular classroom patterns and practices.

Administrative/professional activities: Planning, organizing, and recordkeeping that teachers do in support of the direct instruction of students.

Adoption stage: Teachers use technology without changing regular classroom patterns and practices.

Alphabet books: Student-made or student- and teacher-made books designed to teach spelling patterns, letter sounds, vocabulary words, and reading skills.

Anti-virus software: An application to scan and block programs that might interfere with the operation of a computer.

Application software: Software that directs computers to perform specific functions or applications, such as word processing or electronic communication.

Appropriation stage: Teachers use technology in all aspects of their professional work, in and outside of the classroom.

Archival and primary source website: A type of educational website that provides original historical materials for students to access and analyze.

Assessment: Ongoing evaluation of performance, such as teachers assessing student learning or educational supervisors assessing teacher effectiveness.

Assistive technologies: Tools that make academic material more accessible to students by minimizing barriers to learning.

Asynchronous communications: Information exchanges that have an interruption or time delay between responses (for example, an email exchange or a response to a blog posting).

Authentic assessment: Approach to evaluation that focuses on how students perform on projects or performance-based activities.

Automate: Technological improvements that do not fundamentally change existing practices.

Badware: Unscrupulous or deceitful software that disrupts the normal functioning of a computer by allowing spam or other unwanted programs to enter the system.

Behaviorism: Theory of learning based on the idea that students learn from repeating or reinforcing responses given by teachers; those who endorse this learning theory are called behaviorists.

Blog: Short for weblog, an online journal that people can read and respond to electronically.

Bloom's taxonomy: A hierarchical system for classifying thinking skills first proposed by psychologist Benjamin Bloom.

Bookmarking: Process of identifying and saving frequently visited Web addresses on a computer.

Boolean search: An Internet search strategy where the terms "AND," "OR," and "NOT" are used to build more complex queries.

Building, inventing, and creating software: Programs that promote open-ended opportunities for students to express themselves artistically, mathematically, or spatially.

Calculator: A small electronic device that performs mathematical operations and is often used in teaching mathematics in K–12 classrooms.

Censorship: A method used to block objectionable Internet content.

Clickers: Remote control devices used to respond to questions posed by teachers using student participation systems. *See also* Student participation systems.

Cognitive load: The presentation of information on a Web page either supports or restricts understanding and learning.

Cognitive science: The study of how learning happens through the interaction of the brain and the environment.

Collaborative learning environments: Settings where teachers and students work together to investigate curriculum topics and share academic information.

Communications software: An application that enables computer users to write or talk to other people.

Communication technologies: Systems that support computer-mediated communication; for example, email, instant messaging, blogs, or wikis.

Computer-based technologies: Technologies that are centralized in or connected to computers.

Computer games: Learning or entertainment activities featuring virtual worlds, computer-generated characters, and competition for points that determine a winning score.

Computer literacy: Learning the names, functions, and procedures of computer hardware and software.

Computer-mediated communication: Information exchanges between people using computers, the Internet, or wireless technologies. *See* Communication technologies.

Computers: Fast and powerful information-processing machines.

Concept books: Student-made or student- and teacher-made books designed to teach a single concept or idea such as shape, size, fractions, opposites, or patterns.

Concept mapping: Using words and pictures to represent relationships between concepts and ideas.

Constructivism: Theory of learning based on the idea that individuals construct meaning through their actions and reflections on those actions.

Content selection: Decisions of what academic material to teach in a class, lesson plan, or curriculum unit.

Cooperative learning: Classroom group activities where students have designated roles to perform as they work together on learning projects.

Creativity: Statements or actions by students or teachers that express something new or out of the ordinary.

Criterion-referenced tests: Tests that compare a test taker's performance to a set of specific objectives or standards.

Critical reading: Carefully analyzing Web pages to uncover their meaning.

Cued animation and sound effects (CASE): Interactive features found in electronic storybooks that may support or hinder understanding and learning.

Data visualization: Applications that allow computer users to see connections between networks and information.

Democratic schools and classrooms: Educational settings that feature active participation and collaborative decision making by students and teachers.

Differentiated instruction (DI): Approach to teaching and learning structured so students with diverse learning styles can succeed in school.

Digital art making: Students constructing their own art using computer tools and software.

Digital cameras: Cameras that record still pictures and allow users to view the image, retake shots, and store the photos taken. *See also* Digital video cameras.

Digital content: Academic resources and materials made available to teachers and students over the Internet or through other electronic means (such as CD-ROMs or disk-based software).

Digital continuum: A technology access spectrum based on socio-economic resources.

Digital disconnect: Gap in K–12 schools between tech-savvy students and less technologically confident teachers.

Digital divide: Sharp separation in computer and Internet access and use between low-income and affluent households.

Digital games for learning: New generation of games designed to maximize academic learning within the structures of online or software-based game formats.

Digital image scanners: Devices that scan handwritten or paper text and images into a digital file.

Digital immigrants: Term for today's adults who are newcomers to the world of computers, the Internet, and other information technologies. *See also* Digital natives.

Digital inequality: The idea that access to the latest computer technology varies greatly within society with low-income and non-white Americans less likely to be able to afford and use the newest tools.

Digital natives: Term for today's children and adolescents who have grown up using computers and other electronic media. *See also* Digital immigrants.

Digital notepad: Writing device that allows users to write and draw on regular paper and convert those images to digital text.

Digital pen: A writing instrument that sends someone's written text to a computer where it can be converted into printed text or emailed to others as an image file.

Digital portfolio: A collection of educational materials stored in an electronic format such as a CD-ROM, website, or computer file.

Digital projector: A digital video machine that projects computer-generated images onto a screen.

Digital single-use cameras: Cameras designed for one use only (also known as disposable cameras).

Digital storytelling: Storytelling through digital video, pictures, and words.

Digital video cameras: Digital cameras that take video images. *See also* Digital cameras.

Digital video editing software: Software that makes possible the processing, editing, and manipulating of digital video material.

Digital voice recorder: Small handheld device for recording voices and other sounds that can then be downloaded to a computer or audio sharing website.

Digital writing: Writing with computers and other electronic tools.

Drafting: Stage of the writing process where a writer creates an initial or first draft.

Editing: Stage of the writing process where a writer includes conventions of print, standard spelling, punctuation, varied sentence structure, and paragraphing to make the text easy for readers to comprehend.

Educational networking: Communication technologies that teachers and students can use to communicate electronically about educational issues and topics.

Educational software: Computer programs and Web-based tools whose purpose is to promote teaching and learning in K–12 schools.

Educational website: A source of Internet-based digital content, often designed with K–12 learning goals in mind.

Electronic childhood: Term used to describe the ubiquitous presence of computers, television, video games, movies, and other media in the lives of children and adolescents.

Electronic database: A software application that makes it possible to record and retrieve information on a computer.

Electronic grading software: A software program that allows teachers to quickly calculate and record student grades on a computer.

Electronic note taking: Using computer technologies to take notes.

Electronic speller and dictionary: Small handheld device that provides standard spellings and meanings for common English language words.

Email (electronic mail): Electronic messages sent between people using computers and the Internet.

Enduring understandings and essential questions: Big ideas and essential concepts taught to students through the "Understanding by Design" approach to lesson development.

Engagement and collaboration: Teaching and learning situations where students actively and productively work together.

Entry stage: Teachers begin learning new ways to use technology for teaching and learning.

E-portfolios: *See* Digital portfolio.

Evaluation: An approach to measuring student or teacher learning in schools.

Exploration and discovery website: A type of educational website that allows students to engage in online explorations of topics of interest.

Favorites: Bookmarks of frequently visited websites, stored on one's computer.

Feedback: Responses given to students by teachers or computers.

Filtering software: A technology used to block unwanted or objectionable websites from appearing on school computers.

Folksonomy: System for tagging and categorizing by computer users; derived from the words "folk" and "taxonomy."

Free-text search: An inclusive type of Internet information search that shows all results including one or more words in a phrase that was entered in the query.

Generation M: Term used to describe today's students who are growing up using digital technology.

Graphic design: Process of arranging words and images to communicate information visually.

Groupwork: A classroom instructional format where small groups of students work together on academic tasks.

Hardware: Basic machinery and circuitry of a computer.

Higher order thinking: Thinking skills that involve processing information and solving problems in ways that promote new meanings and understandings.

Highly interactive, inquiry-based learning: Students using technology in exciting, participatory ways promoting active engagement, critical and creative thinking, and academic learning.

High-stakes tests: Standardized tests that impose significant consequences for passing or failing scores, such as graduating from high school or gaining a teacher license.

Hotlists: *See* Favorites.

Inclusion: Placing students with special educational needs in the least restrictive educational environment possible, often in the same classroom as their regular education peers.

Infomate: A term coined by Alan November to indicate when technology is used to create new learning possibilities for students and teachers.

Information alert: An electronic notice received on a computer when new information on a topic becomes available in an electronic publication format.

Information and communication technology (ICT):   *See* Information technology.

Information and communication technology (ITC) literacy: The ability to use digital information, computer communication tools, and electronic networks to share ideas and solve problems.

Information literacy: *See* Information and communication technology (ICT) literacy.

Information management: A system for collecting, organizing, and distributing information.

Information presentation design: The design and management of digital content, often used in connection with how students and teachers display information on classroom websites or blogs.

Information research and retrieval: Ability to locate, evaluate, and use information derived from paper or electronic sources.

Information search: Process of locating information by looking through paper and electronic resources and databases.

Information technology: Term that refers to tools and devices associated with computers. *See* Computer-based technologies.

Information technology and creative practices (ITCP):   Use of computers and other technology to support creative self-expression by students and teachers.

Information technology (IT) fluency: Ability to use computers, the Internet, and other information and communication tools easily and appropriately.

Infusion: Integration of computers, the Internet, and other information technologies into the regular patterns of teaching and learning in K–12 schools.

Inquiry learning: Educational activities where students investigate questions, issues, and problems and propose answers or solutions based on personal research.

Instant messaging (IM):   Real time, typed text interactions between people using computers or mobile communication devices.

Instructionally supportive assessment: Using assessment results to guide instructional practices by teachers.

Instructional practices: Teaching methods and strategies that teachers use to convey academic material to students.

Intelligent tutoring systems (ITS):   Computer software that provides individualized coaching or teaching for students.

Interactive electronic storybooks: Digital materials that include hypertext and other interactive digital features in a story format.

Interactive videoconferencing: Real time, interactive systems that connect multiple computer users via digital video.

Interactive whiteboard: A touch sensitive whiteboard that interacts with a computer to enhance teaching and learning experiences in classrooms.

Internet: A network of billions of computing devices, people, and static documents, with ever-increasing numbers.

Internet literacy: Skills and understandings needed to be an active user and evaluator of content found on the World Wide Web.

Invention stage: Teachers use technology to create new patterns and practices for classroom learning and student involvement with computers.

iPod: Handheld music playing device made by Apple. Some models also record spoken voices.

IT FITness: Students being able to evaluate, learn about, and use new information technologies both personally and professionally.

Keyword/exact match search: Search done online that originates from keywords or phrases chosen by a computer user.

Keywords: Words or phrases used by search engines to locate matching Web pages.

Labels: Rating system of Web materials similar to others used by movie companies, telephone and satellite providers, video game makers, and manufacturers of products and services.

Learning assessments: Methods and strategies used to evaluate student knowledge and performance before, during, and after a lesson is taught.

Learning groups: *See* Groupwork.

Lesson development: All the activities that teachers do in planning, delivering, and assessing lessons with students.

Lesson plan website: A type of educational website featuring lesson plans and related teaching materials.

Lower order thinking: Thinking skills that require students to memorize or reproduce knowledge with little or no reflection or problem solving.

Malinformation: Information on the Internet that is harmful or damaging.

Messed-up information: Information on the Internet that is hard to understand or use.

Metacognitive thinking: The process of actively reflecting on one's thinking and learning, sometimes referred to as "thinking about thinking."

Microblogging: A form of blogging that involves sending short text messages, photos, or audio clips to friends or professional colleagues, often done via a cell phone or other portable communication device.

Mindtools: Learning technology that promotes problem solving and critical thinking by students and teachers; the term was coined by David Jonassen.

Misinformation: Information on the Internet that is false, out of date, or misleading.

Modification: The process of changing a teaching or learning situation to meet the needs of special education students.

Mostly useless information: Information on the Internet that is trivial and irrelevant.

Multimedia: Presentation of information using multiple media, including words, pictures, sound, and data. Also known as multimedia technologies.

Multimedia projectors: *See* Digital projectors.

Multimodal learning: Using information and images from multiple sources, such as spoken words, video, graphics, and pictures, to produce learning for students.

New teacher assessment: Process of evaluating the readiness of beginning teachers to enter the teaching field, often done by a combination of state-mandated teacher tests, school system evaluations, and college program assignments.

Noncomputer-based technologies: Technologies used in K–12 schools that do not use computers, such as overhead projectors or 35mm slides.

Norm-referenced tests: Tests that compare a test taker's performance against other test takers of the same age or grade level.

Object-oriented programming: Software that allows computer users to create an object and make it do things in response to programmed instructions.

One-on-one tutoring: *See* Tutoring.

One-to-one laptop computing: Educational settings where every student in a grade, school, or district has a computer for use in school and/or at home.

One/two/three time: A classroom grouping method where students rotate through three different activities or centers, often including

instruction by a teacher, independent work by students, and learning using computers or other technologies.

Online discussion: An electronic forum where people discuss topics of interest.

Online surveys: Internet-based surveys and polls that deliver and tabulate results electronically.

Open source software: Computer applications that are available online to anyone to use, copy, and recreate for free or minimal charge.

Optical character recognition and reading software: A type of assistive technology for users with vision impairments that enables printed text to be converted to multiple formats.

Participation gap: Students who lack 24/7 access to the latest technologies lag behind their peers technologically and educationally.

Partitions: Method used to block material from computers by identifying certain objectionable key words or phrases.

Performance assessments: Assessment of student learning accomplishments using non-standardized test measures such as presentations, projects, or class participation.

Plagiarism: Directly copying or misrepresenting someone else's work as one's own.

Pocket video cameras: Small handheld cameras that record video and audio that can then be downloaded to a computer or video-sharing website.

Podcast: Digital audio files delivered to computers by the Internet. *See also* Vodcast.

Podcatcher: Software that allows a computer user to access podcast files.

Point-and-shoot camera: Cameras, most of which have auto-focusing capabilities, which produce still photographs.

PowerPoint: Multimedia presentation software found on most computers and used to display information visually and dynamically in classrooms.

Preassessments: Activities by teachers to determine what students already know or are able to do before beginning a new lesson or curriculum topic.

Presentation software: An application that enables computer users to construct digital presentations.

Prewriting/brainstorming: Stage of the writing process where a writer generates ideas to write about and decides what formats to use in writing.

Prior knowledge–based learning: Teaching strategies that use what students already know or are able to do to facilitate learning something new.

Problem solving: Ability to apply prior knowledge and use of strategies to seek answers or solutions to a problem.

Publishing: Stage of the writing process where a writer's work is displayed for others to read and hear.

Question-driven instruction: A teaching method where teachers ask challenging questions of students to generate discussion about possible answers as well as strategies for getting those answers.

Real-time and recorded data website: A type of educational website that presents scientific data for students to access and analyze.

Revising: Stage of the writing process where a writer reworks the initial draft by adding or deleting material.

Rogers innovation curve: Theory of how people in organizations respond to innovation and change.

RSS feed: A group of Web feeds used by news organizations, blogs, and other media to provide frequently updated content.

Screen reading software: A type of assistive technology that enables computers to read printed text on a computer screen aloud.

Search engine: Computer programs that locate Web pages that have been linked to its database.

Shoot-to-print camera: Camera with advanced features that produces publication quality pictures (also known as "prosumer" cameras).

Single lens reflex design camera: High-end camera with multiple professional features including the capability of manipulating images in great detail before a picture is taken.

Skills-learning games: Software that features a drill and practice teaching methodology where students do structured activities repeatedly as a way to master basic facts and operations.

Skills/practice website: A type of educational website that provides basic learning activities for students.

Social bookmarking: An information management process where groups of interested people share their Web links electronically in an open public Web space.

Social informatics: Social science approach where technology's impacts on society are considered within the context of larger social, economic, and political realities.

Social networking: Using computers and the Internet to share personal information online.

Software: The codes that tell computers what functions to perform; often described in terms of system software and application software.

Specialized software: Applications that allow computer users to do special functions or tasks.

Speech recognition software: Software that transforms spoken words into printed text. Also known as *speech-to-text software.*

Spreadsheet: A software application that makes it possible to manipulate numbers and data on a computer.

Standardized testing: *See* High-stakes tests.

Standards-based assessments: Assessing the performance of students in terms of national, statewide, or district standards.

Standards-based digital portfolios: Electronic portfolios that explicitly link lesson plans and other educational activities done by teacher candidates to specific professional teaching standards.

Standards connector: A Web-based collection of teaching materials coded to a required curriculum framework or a group of educational standards.

Standards wiki: A wikispace focusing specifically on educational standards.

Stealth learning: Computer game activities where students learn without realizing they are learning because academic information and skills are embedded in game play.

Storyboarding: A way to organize material that combines words and pictures into a sequence of images, often used in preparing PowerPoint presentations or editing digital movies.

Streaming video: Simultaneous transfer of video, voice, and data from one computer to another to create a stream of electronic content.

Student assessment: Process of evaluating the academic performance of K–12 students, often done by a combination of standardized tests, student writing, and other teacher-created measurement tools.

Student-centered teaching: Teaching methods that organize instruction on student interests and progress. Also known as *student-centered approach.*

Student involvement in learning: Active participation of K–12 students in all aspects of their learning.

Student learning objectives: Benchmark goals for what students will know or will be able to do after instruction by teachers.

Student participation systems: Real-time electronic interactions between students and teachers using remote control devices known as clickers. Also known as *student response systems. See also* Clickers.

Student performance rubric: *See* Rubric.

Student-to-expert communication website: A type of educational website that supports exchanges of information between students and adult experts in organizations outside of school.

Synchronous communications: Information exchanges that happen in real time, as in a back-and-forth instant message conversation or discussion board.

System software: Software that controls a computer's overall hardware operation.

Tablet PC: A portable computer with real-time inking capacity that allows users to add and save writing directly to the screen.

Tag cloud: Visual display of words in social bookmarking sites. Frequently accessed sites appear in larger font sizes and colors.

Teacher-centered teaching: Teaching methods that organize instruction on teacher-decided goals and objectives. Also known as *teacher-centered approach.*

Teacher or classroom website: A website devoted to the learning activities of a school classroom.

Teaching goals, methods, and procedures: The combination of instructional strategies, interpersonal behaviors, and curriculum materials used by teachers to facilitate learning by students.

Teaching philosophy: A teacher's stated or unstated ideas and assumptions about how to teach so students will learn.

Technological convergence: Combining multiple features and functions in one digital tool.

Technology: Use of tools and materials by humans to solve problems and manage the environment.

Technology-based learning environment: Using technology to create anywhere, anytime opportunities for learning, both in and outside of school.

Technology-based library: Using technology to create and maintain a collection of resources for teaching and learning.

Technology-based office: Using technology to organize and manage the professional work of teachers.

Technology-based teaching tool: Using technology to generate new instructional opportunities for teachers and students.

Technology-based textbook: Using technology to create books and other teaching materials for students to use in class.

Technology integration: The process of making technology a central feature of teaching and learning in schools.

Test assessments: Term given to test-based evaluation practices by teachers.

Text reading software: Software that transforms printed text into spoken words. Also known as *text to speech software.*

Textspeak: Abbreviated language of letters and symbols used for quick communication in instant messaging and cell phone texting.

Transmission teaching: A view of teaching where teachers provide academic knowledge to students through instructional processes such as lectures, readings, videos, and worksheets.

Tutoring: One-on-one or one-on-small group assistance, instruction, and practice provided to students to support academic learning.

21st-century literacies: New technology-based skills for students including knowledge of technology tools, the ability to create, share, and analyze information, and the capacity to solve problems collaboratively.

21st-century skills: The knowledge, competencies, and understanding that students need to succeed in a highly technological, information-based society.

Type I Technology Applications: Activities that largely maintain existing practices.

Type II Technology Applications: Activities that innovate or challenge existing practices.

Understanding by design (UBD): Approach to lesson development where teachers formulate enduring understandings and essential questions as the basis for teaching, learning, and assessment activities with students. Also known as *backward design*.

Universal design: A term from the field of architecture for ways to adapt physical environments to provide greater access for all users.

Universal design for learning (UDL): Application of universal design principles to teaching and learning in schools through teaching methods and assessments that foster equal access to academic success for students with different learning styles and preferences.

URL (uniform resource locator): The unique address that identifies a resource on the Internet. For example, www.pearsonhighered.com is the URL for the Pearson Higher Education website.

Video games: Games played on computers or video game consoles where action is controlled by a hand-held controller or mouse and keyboard.

Virtual field trips: Online learning adventures where students are able to visit far-away places using their classroom computers.

Virtual worlds: Computer-based environments where users enter and interact as game players or through online identities.

Visual learning: Gaining knowledge through the use of pictures, drawings, video, animation, and other visual sources of information.

Visual literacy: Skills and abilities related to creating, editing, understanding, and appreciating visual images in computer and non-computer environments.

Visual thinking and concept mapping software: Software that records and extends thinking and brainstorming processes.

Vodcast: Podcasts that contain video images, delivered via the Internet. *See also* Podcast.

Web browser: A computer software application that allows computer users to systematically search the Internet for information found on Web pages.

Web-browsing software: An application that enables computer users to access websites from the Internet.

Webcast: Multimedia presentation delivered on the Internet and usually supported by streaming video.

Web information retrieval: The process of locating and analyzing information within the vast, interconnected databases of the Internet.

WebQuests: Online educational experiences where students go to one or more websites to obtain academic information or engage in other inquiry-based learning activities.

Web 2.0: Term used to describe the newer, more interactive uses of the Internet such as blogs, wikis, social networking, and other collaborative methods of information creation and exchange.

Wiki: Web pages that are created and maintained by multiple contributors; from the Hawaiian word for "rapid."

Wikipedia: An online encyclopedia, created and edited by a worldwide community of users.

Wikitext: Book or other collection of academic-related materials created by a group of Wiki users.

Word prediction software: A type of assistive technology that predicts the standard spelling of words that a writer intends to use in a typed document.

Word processing: A software application that makes it possible to create written text on a computer.

World wide web: An application found on the Internet; not a separate network but rather one of many programs that support a wide range of applications such as email, instant messaging, and online games.

Writing process: An approach to the teaching of writing where writers use the interconnected processes of brainstorming, drafting, revising, editing, and publishing.

Writing process fit to young writers: An approach to the teaching of writing with students that uses technology to expand the options young writers have at each stage of the writing process.

Abrahamson, L. A. (2006). A brief history of networked classrooms: Effects, cases, pedagogy, and implications. In D. A. Banks (Ed.), *Audience response systems in higher education: Applications and cases* (pp. 1–25). Hershey, PA: Idea Group.

Alexander, B., & Levine, A. (2008, November/December). Web 2.0 storytelling: Emergence of a new genre. *EDUCAUSE Review, 43*(6), Retrieved December 2, 2008, from http://connect.educause.edu/Library/EDUCAUSE+Review/Web20StorytellingEmergenc/47444

Allen, D. W., O'Shea, P. M., Xiao, Y., Kaufman, J., Konstantopolu, D., & Kidd, J. (2008, April). *The credibility of Wiki texts as a major component of instruction.* Paper presented at the annual meeting of the American Educational Research Association, New York.

Alliance for Childhood. (2004, September). *Tech tonic: Towards a new literacy of technology.* College Park, MD: Author.

Allison, J., & Geidman, D. (Eds.). (2007). *This I believe: The personal philosophies of remarkable men and women.* New York: Holt.

Alternative Education Resource Organization. (2006). *Democratic classrooms.* Retrieved February 17, 2007, from www.educationrevolution.org/demschool.html

American Library Association. (2007, May). *Especially for young people and their parents.* Retrieved July 14, 2009, from www.ala.org/ala/aboutala/offices/oif/foryoungpeople/youngpeopleparents/especiallyyoungpeople.cfm

Anderson, L. W., & Krathwohl, D. R. (Eds.). (2001). *A taxonomy for learning, teaching, and assessing: A revision of Bloom's Taxonomy of educational objectives.* New York: Longman.

Apple, M. W., & Beane, J. A. (2007). *Democratic schools: Lessons in powerful education* (2nd ed.). Portsmouth, NH: Heinemann.

Apple Classrooms of Tomorrow Project. (1995). *Changing the conversation about teaching, learning, and technology: A report of 10 years of ACOT research.* Cuperinto, CA: Apple.

Arroyo, I., Beal, C. R., Murray, T., Walles, R., & Woolf, B. P. (2004). Web-based intelligent multimedia tutoring for high stakes achievement tests. In J. C. Lester, R. M. Vicari, & F. Paraguaçu (Eds.), *Intelligent Tutoring Systems, 7th International Conference, ITS 2004* (pp. 468–477). Macieò, Alagoas, Brazil.

Arroyo, I., Walles, R., Beal, C. R., & Woolf, B. P. (2004). *Effects of Web-based tutoring software on students' math achievement.* Paper presented at the meeting of the American Educational Research Association, San Diego, CA.

Arroyo, I., Woolf, B., & Beal, C.R. (2006). Addressing cognitive differences and gender during problem solving. *International Journal of Technology, Instruction, Cognition and Learning, 4,* 31–63.

Ascione, L. (2006a, September 1). California schools adopt digital history program. *eSchool News Online.* Retrieved June 3, 2008, from www.eschoolnews.com/news/showStory.cfm?ArticleID=6509

Ascione, L. (2006b, September 6). Study aims to improve school literacy. *eSchool News Online.* Retrieved June 3, 2008, from www.eschoolnews.com/news/showStory.cfm?ArticleID=6578

Assessment and Testing Study Group of the NCTE Executive Committee. (2004, November). *Framing statements on assessment.* Urbana, IL: National Council of Teachers of English.

Atoji, C. (2007, November). Tired of typing? Make yourself heard. *Boston Sunday Globe,* p. D2.

Atwood, A. (1977). Haiku-vision in poetry and photography. New York: Charles Scribner's Sons.

Augar, N., Raitman, R., & Zhou, W. (2004, December). Teaching and learning online with wikis. In R. Atkinson, C. McBeath, D. Jonas-Dwyer, & R. Phillips (Eds.), *Beyond the comfort zone: Proceedings of the 21st ASCILITE Conference* (pp. 95–104). Perth, Australia. Retrieved June 4, 2008, from www.ascilite.org.au/conferences/perth04/procs/augar.html

Baard, M. (2006, July 3). Personal tech: A safe surfing experience. *The Boston Globe,* p. B8.

Baig, E. C. (2006, May 24). Apple, Nike exercise iPods to track workouts. *USA Today,* p. B1.

Barnett, M., Yamagata-Lynch, L., Keating, T., Barab, S. A., & Hay, K. E. (2005). Using virtual reality computer models to support student understanding of astronomical concepts. *Journal of Computers in Mathematics and Science Teaching, 24*(4), 333–356.

Barrett, H. C. (2000). Strategic questions: What to consider when planning for electronic portfolios. *Learning and Leading with Technology, 26*(2), 6–13.

Beach, R. (2007). *teachingmedialiteracy.com: A Web-linked guide to resources and activities.* New York: Teachers College Press.

Beal, C. R., Walles, R., Arroyo, I., & Woolf, B. P. (2007). On-line tutoring for math achievement testing: A controlled evaluation. *Journal of Interactive Online Learning, 6*(1), 43–55.

Beatty, I. D., Leonard, W. J., Gerace, W. J., & Dufresne, R. J. (2006). Question driven instruction: Teaching science (well) with an audience response system. In D. A. Banks (Ed.), *Audience response systems in higher education: Applications and cases* (pp. 96–115). Hershey, PA: Idea Group.

Bebell, D. (2005). *Technology promoting student excellence: An investigation of the first year of 1:1 computing in New Hampshire middle schools.* Chestnut Hill, MA: Boston College, e-Scholarship@BC. Retrieved April 29, 2008, from http://escholarship.bc.edu/intasc/32/

Becker, H. J. (2000, November). Findings from the teaching, learning, and computing survey: Is Larry Cuban right? *Education Policy Analysis Archives, 8*(51), 1–34.

Becker, H. J. (2001, April). *How are teachers using computers in instruction?* Paper presented at the meeting of the American Educational Research Association, Seattle, WA. Retrieved June 4, 2008, from www.crito.uci.edu/tlc/FINDINGS/special3/How_Are_Teachers_Using.pdf

Becker, H. J., & Ravitz, J. (1999). Internet use on teachers' pedagogical practices and perceptions. *Journal of Research on Computing in Education, 31*(4), 356–384.

Becker, H. J., & Ravitz, J. L. (2001). *Computer use by teachers: Are Cuban's predictions correct?* Paper presented at the meeting of the American Educational Research Association, Seattle, WA. Retrieved June 4, 2008, from www.crito.uci.edu/tlc/findings/conferences-pdf/aera_2001.pdf

Becker, H. J., Ravitz, J. L., & Wong, Y. (1999, November). *Executive summary: Teacher and teacher-directed student use of computers and software.* Retrieved June 4, 2008, from www.crito.uci.edu/TLC/findings/ComputerUse/html/body_startpage.htm

Belanger, Y. (2005, June). *Duke University iPod first year experience final evaluation report.* Durham, NC: Duke University, Center for Instructional Technology.

BellSouth Foundation. (2003). *The big difference: The growing technology gap between schools and students.* Atlanta, GA: Author.

Berdik, C. (2005, February 27). Teachers fight high-tech cheaters. *Boston Sunday Globe,* pp. B1, B11.

Berenstain, J., & Berenstain, S. (1997). *Inside, outside, upside down.* New York: Random House Books for Young Readers.

Berry, J. S., Graham, T., Honey, S., & Headlam, C. (2007). A case study of the issues arising when teachers adopt the use of a new form of technology in their teaching for the first time. *The International Journal for Technology in Mathematics Education, 14*(3), 150–160.

Berson, I. R., & Berson, M. J. (2006, April). Privileges, privacy, and protection of youth bloggers in the social studies classroom. *Social Education, 70*(3), 124–128.

Bettleheim, M. (2007, March). *Tentacled tree hugger disarms seventh graders.* Retrieved December 8, 2007, from www.inklingmagazine.com/articles/tentacled-tree-hugger-gets-legs-up-on-twelve-year-olds

Boss, C. (2007, December 10). Text messages may be classroom conduit. *The Columbus Dispatch,* p. O1A.

Bouffard, S. (2008, July). Tapping into technology: The role of the Internet in family–school communication. *Family Involvement Research Digests, Harvard Family Research Project.* Retrieved July 30, 2008, from www.hfrp.org/family-involvement/publications-resources/tapping-into-technology-the-role-of-the-internet-in-family-school-communication

Bowman, C., Pieters, B., with Hembree, S., & Mellender, T. (2002, September). Shakespeare, our contemporary: Using technology to teach the bard. *English Journal, 92*(1), 88–97.

Brackett, G. (2000). Technologies don't change schools—caring, capable people do. In D. Gordon (Ed.), *The digital classroom: How technology is changing the way we teach and learn* (pp. 29–30). Cambridge, MA: Harvard Education Letter.

Braden, R. A. (1996). Visual literacy. In D. Jonassen (Ed.), *Handbook of research for educational communications and technology* (pp. 491–520). New York: Simon & Schuster Macmillan.

Bridgeland, J. M., DiIulio, J. J., Jr., & Morison, K. B. (2006, March). *The silent epidemic: Perspectives of high school dropouts.* Washington, DC: Civic Enterprises.

Britannica attacks. (2006, March). *Nature 440,* 582.

Brooks, J. G., & Brooks, M. G. (1999). *In search of constructivist classrooms.* Washington, DC: Association for Supervision and Curriculum Development.

Bruce, B., & Hogan, M. P. (1998). The disappearance of technology: Toward an ecological model of literacy. In David Reinking et al. (Eds.), *Handbook of literacy and technology: Transformations in a post-typographic world* (pp. 269–281). Mahwah, NJ: Lawrence Erlbaum.

Bruff, D. (2007, October). Clickers: A classroom innovation. *Thriving in Academe, 25*(1), 4–8.

Bull, G., Hammond, T., & Grimes, P. (2007). Podcasting in the social studies classroom. In L. Bennett & M. Berson (Eds.), *Digital age: Technology-based K–12 lesson plans for social studies* (pp. 185–187). Washington, DC: National Council for the Social Studies.

Burbules, N. C., & Callister, T. A., Jr. (2000). *Watch IT: The risks and promises of information technologies for education.* Boulder, CO: Westview Press.

Burns, E. (2007, August 30). Top 10 search engines, July 2007. *The ClickZ Network.* Retrieved June 5, 2008, from http://searchenginewatch.com/showPage.html?page=3626903

Calkins, L. (1986). *The art of teaching writing.* Portsmouth, NH: Heinemann.

Carnagey, N. L., Anderson, C. A., & Bushman, B. J. (2007). The effect of video game violence on physiological desensitization to real-life violence. *Journal of Experimental Social Psychology, 43,* 489–496.

Carr, N. (2008, July/August). Is Google making us stoopid? *The Atlantic, 302*(1), 56–63.

Carvin, A. (2006, July 3). Wikipedia in the classroom: Consensus among educators? *PBS Teachers: learning.now.* Retrieved July 15, 2009, from www.pbs.org/teachers/learning.now/2006/07/wikipedia_in_the_classroom_con.html

Center for Applied Special Technology. (2006). *What is Universal Design for Learning?* Wakefield, MA: Author. Retrieved June 14, 2007, from www.cast.org/research/udl/index.html

Center for Evaluation & Education Policy. (2005). *What can we learn from high school students: High School Survey of Student Engagement (HSSE).* Bloomington, IN: Indiana University.

Center for Implementing Technology in Education. (2007). Beyond "getting the answer": Calculators help learning disabled students to get the answer. *LD Online.* Retrieved June 5, 2007, from www.ldonline.org/article/19274

Center for Improved Engineering & Science Education. (2002). *Exemplary collaborative projects: Higher education and K–12.* Hoboken, NJ: Stevens Institute of Technology.

Center on Education Policy. (2005, August). *High school exit exams: Basic features.* Retrieved February 11, 2007, from www.cepdc.org/highschoolexit/ExamMailers/CEPExamMailers.pdf

Chapin, S., O'Connor, C., & Anderson, N. C. (2003). *Classroom discussions: Using math talk to help students learn.* Sausalito, CA: Math Solutions.

Christel, M., & Sullivan, S. (Eds.). (2007). *Lesson plans for creating media-rich classrooms.* Urbana, IL: National Council of Teachers of English.

Christensen, C., Johnson, C. W., & Horn, M. B. (2008). *Disrupting class: How disruptive innovation will change the way the world learns.* New York: McGraw-Hill.

Cifuentes, L., & Hsieh, Y. C. J. (2004). Visualization for middle school students' engagement in science learning. *Journal of Computers in Mathematics and Science Teaching, 23*(2), 109–137.

Cohen, E. G. (1994). *Designing groupwork: Strategies for the heterogeneous classroom.* New York: Teachers College Press.

Cohen, M., Habley, M., Lam, J., Kiley, J., Jessop, S., Kim, H., & Rosen, C. (2007, October). *Children, media, and families: A benchmark.* New York: Michael Cohen Group.

Colombo, M. W., & Colombo, P. D. (2007, September). Blogging to improve instruction in differentiated science classrooms. *Phi Delta Kappan,* pp. 60–63.

Commission on Instructionally Supportive Assessment. (2001, October). *Building tests to support instruction and accountability: A guide for policymakers.* Washington, DC: Author.

Conference on College Composition and Communication (CCCC). (2004, February). *Position statement on teaching, learning, and assessing writing in digital environments.* Urbana, IL: National Council of Teachers of English.

Conference on College Composition and Communication (CCCC) Caucus on Intellectual Property. (2000, February). Use your fair use: Strategies toward action. *College Composition and Communication, 51*(3), 485–488.

Consortium for School Networking. (2007, Summer). *Instant messaging: Conversation, collaboration—and education?* Washington, DC: Consortium for School Networking.

Cooper, J., & Weaver, K. D. (2003). *Gender and computers: Understanding the digital divide.* Mahwah, NJ: Lawrence Erlbaum.

Coppola, E. M. (2004). *Powering up: Learning to teach well with technology.* New York: Teachers College Press.

Csikszentmihalyi, M. (1996). *Creativity: Flow and the psychology of discovery and invention.* New York: Harper Perennial.

Cuban, L. (1993). Computers meet classroom: Classroom wins. *Teachers College Record, 95*(2), 185–210.

Cuban, L. (2003). *Oversold and underused: Computers in the classroom* (New ed.). Cambridge, MA: Harvard University Press.

Cuban, L. (2004, Spring). What ever happened to . . . the open classroom. *EducationNext, 4*(2), Retrieved November 8, 2008, from www.hoover.org/publications/ednext/3288371.html

Davies, A. (2004, October). Transforming learning and teaching through quality classroom assessment: What does the research say? *School Talk, 10*(1), 1–3.

DeBell, D., & Russell, M. (2006, November). *Berkshire Wireless Initiative: Abstract 1, December 2005—June 2006 year 1 evaluation findings, student and teacher results.* Chestnut Hill, MA: Boston College Technology and Assessment Study Collaborative.

DeBell, M., & Chapman, C. (2006, September). *Computer and Internet use by children and adolescents, 2003* (NCES 2006–065). Washington, DC: National Center for Education Statistics.

DeCourcy, D., Fairchild, L., & Follett, R. (2007). *Teaching Romeo and Juliet: A differentiated approach.* Urbana, IL: National Council of Teachers of English.

Dede, C. (2008, June 13). *How Web 2.0 tools are transforming "learning" and "knowledge."* Presentation at the University of Massachusetts Amherst.

DeSena, L. H. (2007). *Preventing plagiarism: Tips and techniques.* Urbana, IL: National Council of Teachers of English.

Dewey, J. (1943). *The child and the curriculum and the school and society.* Chicago: University of Chicago Press.

Dodge, B. (1995). *Some thoughts about WebQuests.* Retrieved June 5, 2008, from http://edweb.sdsu.edu/courses/edtec596/about_webquests.html

Dodge, B. (2006). *Specialized search engines and directories.* Retrieved June 5, 2008, from http://webquest.sdsu.edu/searching/specialized.html

Dodge, T., Barab, S., Stuckey, B., Warren, S., Heiselt, C., & Stein, R. (2008). Children's sense of self: Learning and meaning in the digital age. *Journal of Interactive Learning Research, 19*(2), 225–249.

Dolan, T. G. (2008, October). "Must-have" technologies. *School Planning & Management, 47*(10), 44.

Donovan, M. S., & Bransford, J. D. (Eds.). (2000). *How people learn: Brain, mind, experience, and school* (Expanded ed.). Washington, DC: National Academies Press.

Donovan, M. S., & Bransford, J. D. (Eds.). (2004a). *How students learn: History in the classroom.* Washington, DC: National Academies Press.

Donovan, M. S., & Bransford, J. D. (Eds.). (2004b). *How students learn: Mathematics in the classroom.* Washington, DC: National Academies Press.

Donovan, M. S., & Bransford, J. D. (Eds.). (2004c). *How students learn: Science in the classroom.* Washington, DC: National Academies Press.

Downes, S. (2004, September/October). Educational blogging. *EDUCAUSE Review, 39*(5), 14–26.

Doyle, T. (2008, October). The learner-centered classroom. *Thriving in Academe, 26*(1), 5–7.

Duffy, T., & Orrill, C. (2004). Constructivism. In A. Kovalchick & K. Dawson (Eds.), *Education and technology: An encyclopedia* (pp. 165–172). Santa Barbara, CA: ABC-CLIO.

Duncan, D. (2005). *Clickers in the classroom.* Boston: Addison-Wesley.

Editorial Projects in Education Research Center. (2008). *Technology counts 2008: STEM: The push to improve science, technology, engineering, and mathematics.* Retrieved April 22, 2008, from www.edweek.org/go/tc08

Educational Testing Service. (2006). *2006 ICT literacy assessment preliminary findings.* Princeton, NJ: Author.

Education Week. (2007, June 12). *Diplomas count: Ready for what? Preparing students for college, careers and life after high school.* Retrieved June 5, 2008, from www.edweek.org/go/dc07

EDUCAUSE Learning Initiative. (2005a, May). *7 things you should know about clickers.* Retrieved June 5, 2008, from http://connect.educause.edu/library/abstract/7ThingsYouShouldKnow/39379

EDUCAUSE Learning Initiative. (2005b, May). *7 things you should know about social bookmarking.* Retrieved June 5, 2008, from www.educause.edu/LibraryDetailPage/666ID=ELI7001

EDUCAUSE Learning Initiative. (2005, July). *7 things you should know about wikis.* Retrieved June 5, 2008, from www.educause.edu/LibraryDetailPage/666?ID=ELI7004

EDUCAUSE Learning Initiative. (2005, August). *7 things you should know about blogs.* Retrieved June 5, 2008, from http://connect.educause.edu/library/abstract/7ThingsYouShouldKnow/39383

EDUCAUSE Learning Initiative. (2005, November). *7 things you should know about instant messaging.* Retrieved June 5, 2008, from http://connect.educause.edu/library/abstract/7ThingsYouShouldKnow/39385

EDUCAUSE Learning Initiative. (2006, June). *7 things you should know about virtual worlds.* Retrieved June 5, 2008, from http://connect.educause.edu/library/abstract/7ThingsYouShouldKnow/39392

EDUCAUSE Learning Initiative. (2006, October). *7 things you should know about Google Earth.* Retrieved June 5, 2008, from http://connect.educause.edu/library/abstract/7ThingsYouShouldKnow/39396

EDUCAUSE Learning Initiative. (2007, January). *7 things you should know about digital storytelling.* Retrieved June 5, 2008, from http://connect.educause.edu/library/abstract/7ThingsYouShouldKnow/39398

EDUCAUSE Learning Initiative. (2007, October). *7 things you should know about data visualization*. Retrieved June 5, 2008, from http://connect.educause.edu/library/abstract/7ThingsYouShouldKnow/45258

EDUCAUSE Learning Initiative. (2008, March). *7 things you should know about Google Apps*. Retrieved April 5, 2008, from http://connect.educause.edu/Library/ELI/7ThingsYouShouldKnowAbout/46436

EDUCAUSE Learning Initiative. (2008, April). *7 things you should know about Ning*. Retrieved September 16, 2008, from http://connect.educause.edu/Library/ELI/7ThingsYouShouldKnowAbout/46666

EduTools. (2007). *ePortfolio: Product list*. Retrieved June 8, 2007, from http://eportfolio.edutools.info/item_list.jsp?pj=16

Edwards, E. (2001). Assessment that drives instruction. In G. L. Taggart, S. J. Phifer, J. A. Nixon, & M. Wood (Eds.), *Rubrics: A handbook for construction and use*. Lanham, MD: Scarecrow Press.

Edwards, S. A., Maloy, R. W., & Verock-O'Loughlin, R. (2003). *Ways of writing with young kids: Teaching creativity and conventions unconventionally*. Boston: Allyn & Bacon.

Ehrenhalt, S. M. (1986, August 15). Work-force shifts in 80's. *The New York Times*, p. D2.

Ellington, A. J. (2003, November). A meta-analysis of the effects of calculators on students' achievement and attitudes in precollege mathematics classes. *Journal for Research in Mathematics Education, 34*(5), 433–463.

Entertainment Software Association. (2004). *Essential facts about the computer and video game industry: 2004 sales, demographics and usage data*. Washington, DC: Author.

Epstein, L. A. (2006, January). *Review: IBM Lenovo Thinkpad X41 Tablet PC*. Retrieved August 18, 2009, from www.tabletpc2.com/Review-IBM%20Lenovo%20ThinkPad%20X41%20Tablet20PC.htm

Esbensen, B. J. (1995). *A celebration of bees: Endless opportunities for inspiring children to write poetry*. New York: Henry Holt.

eSchool News. (2005, May 19). *Online field trips boost reading scores*. Retrieved June 7, 2008, from www.eschoolnews.com/news/showstoryts.cfm?Articleid=5671

eSchool News. (2008, April 4). Birmingham approves low-cost laptop project. Retrieved June 7, 2008, from www.eschoolnews.com/news/top-news/?i=53412

Federation of American Scientists. (2006). *Summit on educational games 2006: Harnessing the power of video games for learning*. Washington, DC: Author.

Fies, C., & Marshall, J. (2006). Classroom response systems: A review of the literature. *Journal of Science Education and Technology, 15*(1), 101–109.

Fontaine, D. (2008). Wikitexts: Learning better by writing the book. *LinuxInsider*. Retrieved June 2, 2008, from http://linuxinsider.com/story/63022.html

Fowler, C. R. (2001). What did the Massachusetts teacher tests say about American education? *Phi Delta Kappan*. Retrieved December 7, 2007, from www.pdkintl.org/kappan/k0106fow.htm

Fox, S. (2005, October 5). *Digital divisions*. Washington, DC: Pew Internet & American Life Project.

Gardner, H. (1983). *Frames of mind: The theory of multiple intelligences*. New York: Basic Books.

Gardner, H. (1994). *Creating minds: An anatomy of creativity seen through the lives of Freud, Einstein, Picasso, Stravinsky, Eliot, Graham, and Gandhi*. New York: Basic Books.

Gardner, H. (2000). Can technology exploit our many ways of knowing? In D. Gordon (Ed.), *The digital classroom: How technology is changing the way we teach and learn* (pp. 32–35). Cambridge, MA: Harvard Education Letter.

Gardner, H. (Ed.). (2006). *Multiple intelligences: New horizons*. New York: Perseus Books Group.

Gardner, T. (2008, July 22). Podcasts: The 21st century version of the radio show. *NCTE Inbox*. Retrieved July 23, 2008, from http://ncteinbox.blogspot.com

Gardner, T. (2008, September 9). Finding safe videos for the classroom. *NCTE Inbox*. Retrieved September 10, 2008, from http://ncteinbox.blogspot.com

Garner, A., Shih, M., Rogers, R., & Hart, D. (Eds.). (2008). *Personal response systems (PRS): A handbook for UMass faculty*. Amherst: University of Massachusetts Amherst. Retrieved September 19, 2008, from www.umass.edu/prs/Instructor/Research/PRS_Handbook.html

Garner, R., & Alexander, P. A. (1989). Metacognition: Answered and unanswered questions. *Educational Psychologist, 24*(2), 143–158.

Gee, J. P. (2003). *What video games have to teach us about learning and literacy*. New York: Palgrave Macmillian.

Genishi, C. (1997). Assessing against the grain: A conceptual framework for alternative assessments. In A. L. Goodwin (Ed.), *Assessment for equity and inclusion: Embracing all our children* (pp. 35–50). New York: Routledge.

Gibbons, G. (1992). *Weather words and what they mean*. New York: Holiday House.

Giles, J. (2005, December). Internet encyclopedias go head to head. *Nature, 438*, 900–901.

Gillard, C. (2008, May/June). Equity, access, and opportunity. *Harvard Education Letter, 24*(3), 1–3.

Gillard, S., Bailey, D., & Nolan, E. (2008). Ten reasons for IT educators to be early adopters of IT innovations. *Journal of Information Technology Education, 7*, 21–33.

Ginott, H. G. (1969). *Between parent and child: New solutions to old problems*. New York: Avon Books.

Glasser, W. (1998). *The quality school teacher*. New York: Harper Perennial.

Gleibermann, E. (2007, February). Teaching even 100 hours a week leaves children behind. *Phi Delta Kappan, 88*(6), 455–459.

Goldberg, A., Russell, M., & Cook, A. (2002). *Meta-analysis: Writing with computers 1992–2002*. Chestnut Hill, MA: Boston College, Technology and Assessment Collaborative.

Goldhaber, D., & Anthony, E. (2007, February). Can teacher quality be effectively assessed? National Board Certification as a signal of effective teaching. *The Review of Economics and Statistics, 89*(1), 134–150.

Goodlad, J. (1984). *A place called school*. New York: McGraw-Hill.

Gordon, T., & Burch, N. (1977). *T.E.T.: Teacher effectiveness training*. New York: David McKay.

Graves, D. (1991). *Build a literate classroom*. Portsmouth, NH: Heinemann.

Gregory, G. H., & Chapman, C. (2007). *Differentiated instructional strategies: One size doesn't fit all* (2nd ed.). Thousand Oaks, CA: Corwin Press.

Guskey, T. (2002). Professional development and teacher change. *Teachers and Teaching: Theory and Practice, 8*, 381–391.

Hafner, K. (2006, June 17). Growing Wikipedia refines its 'anyone can edit' policy. *The New York Times*. Retrieved June 5, 2008, from www.nytimes.com/2006/06/17/technology/17wiki.html

Halal, W. E. (2008). *Technology's promise: Expert knowledge on the transformation of business and society*. New York: Palgrave Macmillian.

Hall, T. (2007). *Differentiated instruction. CAST—Universal Design for Learning.* Retrieved June 5, 2008, from www.cast.org/publications/ncac/ncac_diffinstruc.html

Hammond, C., Smink, J., & Drew, S. (2007). *Dropout risk factors and exemplary programs: A technical report.* Clemson, SC: National Dropout Prevention Center/Network.

Hancock, C., & Osterweil, S. (1996, Spring). Zoombinis and the art of mathematical play. *Hands On! 19*(1). Retrieved April 30, 2008, from www.terc.edu/handson/s96/zoom.html

Hargittai, E., & Hinnant, A. (2008). Digital inequality: Differences in young adults' use of the Internet. *Communication Research 35*(5), 602–621.

Hayes, J., & Greaves, T. (2006). *America's digital schools 2006: A five-year forecast—mobilizing the curriculum.* Littleton, CO: The Greaves Group, The Hayes Connection.

Hayes, J., & Greaves, T. (2008). *America's digital schools 2008: The six trends to watch.* Littleton, CO: The Greaves Group, The Hayes Connection.

Healy, J. M. (1999). *Failure to connect: How computers affect our children's minds—and what we can do about it.* New York: Simon & Schuster.

Healy, J. M. (2004). *Your child's growing mind: Brain development and learning from birth to adolescence.* New York: Broadway.

Hehir, T. (2005). *New directions in special education: Eliminating ableism in policy and practice.* Cambridge, MA: Harvard University Press.

Hehir, T. (2006, January/February). Eliminating ableism. *Harvard Education Letter, 22*(1), pp. 8, 7.

Hicks, T. (2005, April). Beyond the "bells and whistles": Toward a visual rhetoric for teachers' digital portfolios. *English Education, 37*(3), 200–222.

Hiebert, J., & Stigler, J. W. (2004, Fall). A world of difference: Classrooms abroad provide lessons in teaching math and science. *Journal of Staff Development, 25*(4). Retrieved June 6, 2008, from www.nsdc.org/library/publications/jsd/hiebert254.cfm

Higgins, J., & Russell, M. (2003). *Teachers' beliefs about technology and instruction.* Boston: Boston College, Technology and Assessment Study Collaborative.

Hitchcock, C., Meyer, A., Rose, D. H., & Jackson, R. (2005). Equal access, participation, and progress in the general education curriculum. In D. H. Rose, A. Meyer, & C. Hitchcock (Eds.), *The universally designed classroom: Accessible curriculum and digital technologies* (pp. 37–68). Cambridge, MA: Harvard University Press.

Hmelo-Silver, C. (2002). Collaborative ways of knowing: Issues in facilitation. In G. Stahl (Ed.), *Proceedings of the conference on computer support for collaborative learning.* Mahwah, NJ: Lawrence Earlbaum.

Hollister, C. V. (2007, Spring). Having something to say. *Communications in Information Literacy, 1*(1), 1–2.

Horrigan, J. B. (2007, May). *A typology of information and communication technology users.* Washington, DC: Pew Internet & American Life Project.

Houssart, J., & Sams, C. (2008). Developing mathematical reasoning through games of strategy played against the computer. *The International Journal for Technology in Mathematics Education, 15*(2), 59–71.

Huffaker, D. (2004, June). The educated blogger: Using weblogs to promote literacy in the classroom. *First Monday, 9*(6). Retrieved April 7, 2008, from www.firstmonday.org/ISSUES/issue9_6/huffaker/index.html

Hunt, D., & Hunt, T. J. (2006, March). Research and authority in an online world: Who knows? Who decides? *English Journal, 95*(4), 89–92.

Huppert, J., Lomask, S. M., & Lazarowitz, R. (2002). Simulations in the high school: Students' cognitive stages, science process skills and academic achievement in microbiology. *International Journal of Science Education, 24*(8), 803–821.

Iding, M., & Klemm, E. B. (2005). Pre-service teachers critically evaluate scientific information on the World Wide Web: What makes information believable? *Computers in the Schools, 22*(1/2), 7–17.

International Society for Technology in Education. (2002). *National educational technology standards for teachers: Preparing teachers to use technology.* Eugene, OR: Author.

International Society for Technology in Education. (2007). *National educational technology standards for students* (2nd ed.). Eugene, OR: Author.

International Society for Technology in Education. (2008). *National educational technology standards for teachers 2008.* Retrieved July 16, 2008, from www.iste.org/Content/NavigationMenu/NETS/ForTeachers/2008Standards/NETS_for_Teachers_2008.htm

International Technology Education Association. (2000). *Standards for technological literacy: Content for the study of technology.* Reston, VA: Author.

Ito, M., Horst, H., Bittanti, M., Boyd, D., Herr-Stephenson, B., Lange, P. G., Pascoe, C. J., & Robinson, L. (2008, November). *Living and learning with new media: Summary of findings from the digital youth project.* Chicago: MacArthur Foundation.

Jackson, P. (1968). *Life in classrooms.* New York: Holt, Rinehart & Winston.

Jenkins, H. (2006). *Convergence culture: Where old and new media collide.* New York: New York University Press.

Jenkins, H., with Purvshotma, R., Clinton, K., Weigel, M., & Robison, A. J. (2007). *Confronting the challenges of participatory culture: Media education for the 21st Century.* Chicago: MacArthur Foundation.

Johnson, C. Y. (2007, May 15). With simplified code, programming becomes child's play. *The Boston Globe,* pp. A1, C5.

Jonassen, D. H. (2000). *Computers as mindtools for schools: Engaging critical thinking.* (2nd ed.). Upper Saddle River, NJ: Merrill.

Jonassen, D. H. (2005). *Modeling with technology: Mindtools for conceptual change.* (3rd ed.). Upper Saddle River, NJ: Prentice-Hall.

Joseph, R. (2006, March/April). The excluded stakeholder: In search of student voice in the systemic change process. *Educational Technology, XLVI*(2), 34–38.

Josephson Institute Center for Youth Ethics. (2008). *The ethics of American youth: 2008 summary.* Los Angeles: Author. Retrieved December 1, 2008, from http://charactercounts.org/programs/reportcard/index.html

Judson, E. (2006). How teachers integrate technology and their beliefs about learning: Is there a connection? *Journal of Technology and Teacher Education, 13*(3), 581–597.

Jurkowski, O. (2004). Information literacy. In A. Kovalchick & K. Dawson (Eds.), *Education and technology: An encyclopedia* (pp. 319–324). Santa Barbara, CA: ABC-CLIO.

Kafai, Y. B., Heeter, C., Denner, J., & Sun, J. Y. (Eds.). (2008). *Beyond Barbie and Mortal Kombat: New perspectives on gender and gaming.* Cambridge, MA: MIT Press.

Kapoun, J. (1998, July/August). Teaching undergrads WEB evaluation: A guide for library instruction. *College & Research Library News,* 522–523.

Katz, V. J. (Ed). (2007). *Algebra: Gateway to a technological future.* Washington, DC: The Mathematical Association of America.

Ketelhut, D. J. (2007). The impact of student self-efficacy on scientific inquiry skills: An exploratory investigation in River City, a multi-user virtual environment. *Journal of Science Education and Technology, 16*(1), 99–111.

Kilbane, C. R., & Milman, N. B. (2003). *The digital teaching portfolio handbook: A how-to guide for educators.* Boston: Allyn & Bacon.

Kist, W. (2004). *New literacies in action: Teaching and learning in multiple media.* New York: Teachers College Press.

Kleiman, G. M. (2000). Myths and realities about technology in K–12 schools. In D. T. Gordon (Ed.), *The digital classroom: How technology is changing the way we teach and learn* (pp. 7–15). Cambridge, MA: Harvard Education Letter.

Knittle, B. (2008, November). *All a twitter about Twitter: Micro-blogging as a professional networking tool.* Paper presented at the annual meeting of the Massachusetts Computer-Using Educators Conference, Sturbridge, Massachusetts.

Koedinger, K. R. (2001). Cognitive tutors as modeling tool and instructional model. In K. D. Forbus & P. J. Feltovich (Eds.), *Smart machines in education: The coming revolution in educational technology* (pp. 145–168). Menlo Park, CA: AAAI/MIT Press.

Koedinger, K. R., Anderson, J. R., Hadley, W. H., & Mark, M. A. (1997). Intelligent tutoring goes to school in the big city. *International Journal of Artificial Intelligence in Education, 8,* 30–43.

Kohn, A. (1999). *The schools our children deserve: Moving beyond traditional classrooms and "tougher standards."* Boston: Houghton Mifflin.

Kopriva, R. (2008, July/August). What's wrong with wrong answers? *Harvard Education Letter, 24*(4), 6–8.

Kozma, R. B. (2003). *Technology, innovation and change: A global perspective.* Washington, DC: International Society for Technology in Education.

Lacina, J. (2006, Summer). Virtual record keeping: Should teachers keep online grade books? *Childhood Education 82*(4), 252–254.

Langville, A. N., & Meyer, C. D. (2006). *Google's pagerank and beyond: The science of search engine rankings.* Princeton, NJ: Princeton University Press.

Lavoie, N. (2008). Examples of PRS questions: Example 2. In A. Garner, M. Shih, R. Rodgers, & D. Hart, *Personal response system (PRS): A handbook for UMass faculty.* Amherst, MA: Center for Educational Software Development.

Lefever-Davis, S., & Pearman, C. (2005, February). Early readers and electronic texts: CD-ROM storybook features that influence reading behaviors. *The Reading Teacher, 58*(5), 446–454.

Lei, J., & Zhao, Y. (2006). What does one-to-one computing bring to schools? In C. Crawford et al. (Eds.), *Proceedings of Society for Information Technology and Teacher Education International Conference, 2006* (pp. 1690–1694). Chesapeake, VA: AACE.

Lenhart, A., Arafeh, S., Smith, A., & Macgill, A. R. (2008, April). *Writing, technology and teens.* Washington, DC: Pew Internet & American Life Project.

Lenhart, A., Madden, M., & Hitlin, P. (2005, July 27). *Teens and technology.* Washington, DC: Pew Internet & American Life Project.

Lenhart, A., Madden, M., MacGill, A. R., & Smith, A. (2007, December). *Teens and social media.* Washington, DC: Pew Internet & American Life Project.

Lerman, J. (2005a). *101 best web sites for elementary teachers.* Washington, DC: International Society for Technology in Education.

Lerman, J. (2005b). *101 best web sites for secondary teachers.* Washington, DC: International Society for Technology in Education.

Leuf, B., & Cunningham, W. (2001). *The wiki way: Quick collaboration on the Web.* Boston: Addison-Wesley Professional.

Levin, D., & Arafeh, S. (2002, August). *The digital disconnect: The widening gap between Internet-savvy students and their schools.* Washington, DC: Pew Internet & American Life Project.

Lewis, P. (2008). *PowerPoint magic.* Washington, DC: International Society for Technology in Education.

Lichtenberg, J., Woock, C., & Wright, M. (2007). *Ready to innovate: Are educators and executives aligned on the creative readiness of the U.S. workforce?* New York: The Conference Board.

Lieberman, A., & Miller, L. (1984). *Teachers, their world, and their work: Implications for school improvement.* Alexandria, VA: Association for Supervision and Curriculum Development.

Long, C. (2008, March). Mind the gap. *NEA Today, 26*(6), 24–31.

Lyman, P., & Varian, H. R. (2000). *How much information? 2000.* Berkeley: University of California at Berkeley.

Lyman, P., & Varian H. R. (2003, October). *How much information? 2003.* Berkeley: University of California at Berkeley. Retrieved June 6, 2008, from www2.sims.berkeley.edu/research/projects/how-much-info-2003/execsum.htm#sims

Maddux, C. D., & Johnson, L. D. (2005). Information technology, Type II classroom integration, and the limited infrastructure of schools. *Computers in the Schools, 22*(3/4), 1–5.

Maloy, R. W., & Getis, V. (2002). The Standards Connector: Designing an online resource for teaching the Massachusetts history and social studies curriculum framework. *Contemporary Issues in Technology and Teacher Education* [Online serial], *2*(3). Retrieved June 6, 2008, from www.citejournal.org/vol2/iss3/socialstudies/article1.cfm

March, T. (2003). *The learning power of WebQuests.* Retrieved June 6, 2008, from http://tommarch.com/writings/wq_power.php

Markopoulos, P., Read, J., MacFarlane, S., & Hoysniemi, J. (2008). *Evaluating children's interactive products: Principles and practices for interaction designers.* Burlington, MA: Morgan Kaufmann Publishers.

Martyn, M. (2007). Clickers in the classroom: An active learning approach. *EDUCAUSE Quarterly, 30*(2). Retrieved June 8, 2008, from http://connect.educause.edu/library/abstract/ClickersintheClassro/40032

Maryland Business Roundtable for Education. (2005, March). *A progress report on technology resources in Maryland schools.* Baltimore: Maryland Business Roundtable for Education/Committee on Technology in Education.

Maryland Business Roundtable for Education. (2007). *Where do we stand in 2007?* [Online]. Retrieved July 7, 2009, from http://md.ontargetus.com/summary.asp

Mathews, N. M. (2005). *Moving pictures: American art and early film, 1880–1910.* Manchester, VT: Hudson Hills Press in association with the Williams College Museum of Art.

Maxwell, A. (2007). Ban the bullet-point! Content-based Power Point for historians. *The History Teacher, 41*(1), 39–54.

Mayer, R. E. (2001). *Multimedia learning.* New York: Cambridge University Press.

McGrath, C. (2006, September 10). At $9.95 a page, you expected poetry? *The New York Times: Week in Review.* Retrieved July 15, 2009, from www.nytimes.com/2006/09/10/weekinreview/10mcgrath.html?pagewanted=1&_r=1

McKenzie, J. (1998, May). The new plagiarism. Seven antidotes to prevent highway robbery in an electronic age. *The Educational Technology Journal, 7*(8).

McNeil, T. (2007, Spring). Exponential promise. *Bostonia*, 36–39.

McTighe, J., & O'Connor, K. (2005, November). Seven practices for effective learning. *Educational Leadership, 63*(3), 10–17.

Mermelstein, L. (2005). *Reading/writing connections in the K–2 classroom: Find the clarity and then blur the lines*. Boston: Allyn & Bacon.

Merrill, J., & Solbert, R. (Eds.). (1969). *A few flies and I: Haiku by Issa*. New York: Pantheon Books.

Metiri Group. (2008). *Multimodal learning through media: What the research says*. San Jose, CA: Cisco Systems. Retrieved October 27, 2008, from www.cisco.com/web/strategy/docs/education/Multimodal-Learning-Through-Media.pdf

Meyer, A., & Rose, D. H. (2005). The future is in the margins: The role of technology and disability in educational reform. In D. H. Rose, A. Meyer, & C. Hitchcock (Eds.), *The universally designed classroom: Accessible curriculum and digital technologies* (pp. 13–35). Cambridge, MA: Harvard University Press.

Michels, S. (2002, November 29). The search engine that could. *Online NewsHour*. Retrieved June 6, 2008, from www.pbs.org/newshour/bb/business/july-deco2/google_11–29.html

Microsoft Press Pass. (2000, September). *Research finds laptop learning yield better students and better teachers through anytime, anywhere access*. Retrieved July 6, 2009, from www.microsoft.com/presspass/press/2000/sept00/LaptopPR.mspx

Milson, A. J., & Downey, P. (2001). Webquest: Using Internet resources for cooperative inquiry. *Social Education 65*(3), 144.

Mitchell, A., & Savill-Smith, C. (2004). *The use of computer and video games for learning: A review of the literature*. London: Learning and Skills Development Agency.

Mitchell, K. J., Robinson, D. Z., Plake, B. S., & Knowles, K. T. (Eds.). (2001). *Testing teacher candidates: The role of licensure tests in improving teacher quality*. Washington, DC: National Academies Press.

Molebash, P., & Dodge, B. (2003). Kickstarting inquiry with Webquest and Web inquiry projects. *Social Education 67*(3), 158.

Monroe, B. J. (2004). *Crossing the digital divide: Race, writing and technology in the classroom*. New York: Teachers College Press.

Montessori, M. (1964). *Dr. Montessori's own handbook*. Cambridge, MA: R. Bentley.

Montgomery, B., Wilson, L., & McCormick, J. (2005). *What is a one-to-one learning environment?* Michigan Freedom to Learn. Retrieved March 13, 2008, from www.ftlwireless.org

Montgomery, K. K., & Wiley, D. A. (2008). *Building e-portfolios using PowerPoint* (2nd ed.). Thousand Oaks, CA: Sage.

Montgomery, L. A. (2003). Digital portfolios in teacher education: Blending professional standards, assessment, technology, and reflective practice. *Computers in the Schools, 20*(1/2), 171–186.

Moses, R. P., & Cobb, C. E., Jr. (2001). *Radical equations: Math literacy and civil rights*. Boston: Beacon Press.

Moulton, J. (2007). The power of the big screen: The digital projector makes instructional materials larger than life. *Edutopia*. Retrieved January, 19, 2008, from www.edutopia.org/power-big-screen

Muir, M., Knezek, G., & Christensen, R. (2004, February). *Research brief MLLSO401*. Maine Technology Learning Initiative.

Murray, R. (2008). Helping all high school students read better. *National Dropout Prevention Center/Network Newsletter, 20*(1), 5.

Myatt, L. (2008, November). The unexplored promise of visual literacy in American classrooms. *Phi Delta Kappan, 90*(3), 186–189.

National Center for Education Statistics. (2005). *Digest of education statistics: Chapter 7: Libraries and educational technology*. Washington, DC: U.S. Department of Education.

National Commission on Writing in America's Families, Schools, and Colleges. (2006, May). *Writing and school reform*. Princeton, NJ: College Entrance Examination Board.

National Commission on Writing in America's Schools and Colleges. (2003, April). *The neglected "R": The need for a writing revolution*. Princeton, NJ: College Entrance Examination Board.

National Council for the Social Studies. (1994). *Expectations for excellence: Curriculum standards for the social studies*. Washington, DC: Author.

National Council for the Social Studies. (2006). *Technology position statement and guidelines*. Retrieved July 14, 2009, from www.socialstudies.org/positions/technology

National Council of Teachers of English. (2007). *21st century literacies: A policy research brief*. Urbana, IL: Author.

National Council of Teachers of English. (2008a). *Code of best practices in fair use for media literacy education*. Urbana, IL: Author.

National Council of Teachers of English. (2008b). *The NCTE definition of 21st-century literacies*. Urbana, IL: Author.

National Council of Teachers of English & International Reading Association. (1996). *Standards for the English language Arts*. Urbana, IL, & Newark, NJ: Author.

National Council of Teachers of Mathematics. (2000). *Principles and standards for school mathematics*. Reston, VA: Author.

National Council of Teachers of Mathematics. (2005, May). *Computation, calculators, and common sense*. Reston, VA: Author.

National Education Association. (2008, May). *Access, adequacy, and equity in educational technology: Results of a survey of America's teachers and support professionals on technology in public schools and classrooms*. Washington, DC: Author.

National Endowment for the Arts. (2007, November). *To read or not to read: A question of national consequence*. Washington, DC: Office of Research & Analysis, National Endowment for the Arts.

National Mathematics Advisory Panel. (2008). *Foundations for success: The final report of the National Mathematics Advisory Panel*. Washington, DC: U.S. Department of Education.

National Research Council Committee on Information Technology and Creativity. (2003). *Beyond productivity: Information technology, innovation and creativity*. Washington, DC: National Academies Press.

National Research Council Committee on Information Technology Literacy. (1999). *Being fluent with information technology*. Washington, DC: National Academies Press.

National School Boards Association. (2007, July). *Creating & connecting: Research and guidelines on online social—and educational—networking*. Alexandria, VA: Author.

National Science Teachers Association. (1996). *National science education standards*. Arlington, VA: Author.

National Writing Project, & Nagin, C. (2006). *Because writing matters: Improving writing in our schools*. San Francisco: Jossey-Bass.

Newberry Library. (2002). *Historic maps in the K–12 classrooms*. Chicago: Author. Retrieved June 6, 2008, from www.newberry.org/k12maps/

New Commission on the Skills of the American Workforce. (2006, December). *Tough choices or tough times: Executive summary*. Washington, DC: National Center on Education and the Economy.

Nichols, S. L., & Berliner, D. C. (2007). *Collateral damage: How high-stakes testing corrupts America's schools.* Cambridge, MA: Harvard University Press.

Niederhauser, D. S., & Stoddart, T. (2001). Teachers' instructional perspectives and use of educational software. *Teaching and Teacher Education, 17,* 15–31.

Northwest Educational Technology Consortium (NETC). (2005). *Observation protocol for technology integration in the classroom (OPTIC).* Portland, OR: Northwest Regional Educational Laboratory.

November, A. (2001). *Empowering students with technology.* Glenview, IL: Skylight Professional Development.

November, A. (2008). *Web literacy for educators.* Thousand Oaks, CA: Corwin Press.

Office of the Provost. (2004). *Instructor survey on instructional technology.* Amherst: University of Massachusetts. Retrieved November 30, 2004 from www.umass.edu/resec/it/

Office of the Provost. (2007). *Classroom and instructor technology survey.* Amherst: University of Massachusetts.

O'Hara, K., & Stevens, D. (2007). *Inequality.com: Power, poverty, and the digital divide.* Oxford: OneWorld.

Oppenheimer, T. (2004). *The flickering mind: Saving education from the false promise of technology.* New York: Random House.

Papert, S. (1980). *Mindstorms: Children, computers, and powerful ideas* (2nd ed.). Cambridge, MA: Perseus Publishing.

Papert, S. (1993). *The children's machine: Rethinking school in the age of the computer.* New York: Basic Books.

Papert, S. (1996). *The connected family: Bridging the digital generation gap.* Atlanta: Longstreet Press.

Park, J., & Staresina, L. N. (2004). Tracking U.S. trends. Technology counts '04: Global links: Lessons from the world. *Education Week on the Web.* Retrieved June 6, 2008, from www.edweek.org/sreports/tc04/article.cfm?slug=35tracking.h23

Partnership for 21st Century Skills. (2008). *Framework for 21st century learning.* Retrieved July 7, 2009, from www.21stcenturyskills.org/index.php?option=com_content&task=view&id=254&Itemid=120

Patterson, N. (2006, May). Computers and writing: The research says yes! *Voices in the Middle, 13*(4), 64–68.

Peelle, H. A. (2001, Spring). Alternative modes for teaching mathematical problem solving: An overview. *The Journal of Mathematics and Science, 4*(1), 119–142.

Penrod, D. (2007). *Using blogs to enhance literacy: The next powerful step in 21st century learning.* Lanham, MD: Rowman & Littlefield.

Penuel, W. R., Crawford, V., DeBarger, A. H., Boscardin, C. K., Masyn, K., & Urdan, T. (2005). *Teaching with student response system technology: A survey of K–12 teachers.* Retrieved October 7, 2008, from http://ctl.sri.com/publications/downloads/Teaching_with_Audience_Response_Systems_Brief_Report.pdf

Percentage of public school teachers reporting significant use of computers, email, and the Internet at school, by years of teaching experience. (2001, Fall). *Connection, 17.*

Pew Internet and American Life Project. (2006). *New data on blogs and blogging.* Retrieved February 27, 2006, from www.pewinternet.org/press_release.asp?r=10

Pinkus, L. (2006, June). *Who's counted? Who's counting? Understanding high school graduation.* Washington, DC: Alliance for Excellent Education.

Platoni, K. (2008, October). Internet explorers: Virtual field trips are more than just money savers. *Edutopia.* Retrieved November 12, 2008, from www.edutopia.org/virtual-field-trips

Pogue, D. (2004, October 21). Google takes on our desktop. *The New York Times,* pp. E1, E9.

Pogue, D. (2008, July 3). Digital pens to write on any paper. *The New York Times,* pp. C1, C7.

Popham, W. J. (2002, May/June). Preparing for the coming avalanche of accountability tests. *Harvard Education Letter, 18*(1), 1–3.

Popp, T. (2007, November/December). Digital natives in tomorrow's classroom. *The Pennsylvania Gazette, 106*(2), 48–53.

Prensky, M. (2001). *Digital game-based learning.* New York: McGraw-Hill.

Prensky, M. (2001, October). Digital natives, digital immigrants. *On the Horizon, 9*(5).

Prensky, M. (2005, December). Adopt and adapt: Shaping technology for the classroom. *Edutopia.* Retrieved June 6, 2008, from www.edutopia.org/adopt-and-adapt

Prensky, M. (2006). *"Don't bother me mom—I'm learning!" How computers and video games are preparing your kids for 21st century success—and how you can help!* St. Paul, MN: Paragon House.

Prensky, M. (2007). How to teach with technology: Keeping both teachers and students comfortable in an era of exponential change. *Emerging Technologies for Learning, 2,* 40–46.

Project Tomorrow. (2006, October). *Learning in the 21st century: A national report of online learning.* Irvine, CA: Author.

Project Tomorrow. (2006). *Snapshot of selected national findings from K–12 students.* Retrieved August 10, 2009, from www.tomorrow.org/speakup/speakup_reports_archive.html

Project Tomorrow. (2008, April). *Speak up 2007 for students, teachers, parents & school leaders: Selected national findings.* Irvine, CA: Author.

Quaglia Institute for Student Aspirations. (2007). *My voice student aspirations survey: National high school (9–12) report 2006.* Portland, ME: Author.

Rainie, L. (2005, January). *The state of blogging.* Washington, DC: Pew Internet and American Life Project.

Rakes, G. C., Fields, V. S., & Cox, K. C. (2006, Summer). The influence of teachers' technology use on instructional practices. *Journal of Research on Technology in Education, 38*(4), 409–424.

Rapaport, R. (2008, August/September). Serious gaming: Computer games become potent student motivators and evaluators. *Edutopia.* Retrieved November 12, 2008, from www.edutopia.org/whats-next-2008-games-assessment

Reich, J. (2009, July 11). In schools, a firewall that works too well. *The Washington Post.* Retrieved July 16, 2009, from www.washingtonpost.com/wp-dyn/content/article/2009/07/10/AR2009071003459.html

Resta, P., & Semenov, A., with Allen, N., Anderson, J., Davis, N., Muranov, A., Thomas, L., & Uvarov, A. (2002). *Information and communication technologies in teacher education: A planning guide.* Paris: United Nations Educational, Scientific and Cultural Organization.

Rice, J. W. (2007). Assessing higher order thinking in video games. *Journal of Technology and Teacher Education, 15*(1), 87–100.

Rich, M. (2008, July 27). Literacy debate: Online, R U really reading? *The New York Times,* pp. 1, 14–15.

Richardson, W. (2006). *Blogs, wikis, podcasts, and other powerful web tools for classrooms.* Thousand Oaks, CA: Corwin Press.

Richtel, M., & Stone, B. (2007, June 5). Play sites offer safe fun—and lucrative advertising space. *International Herald-Tribune.* Retrieved December 26, 2007, from www.iht.com/articles/2007/06/05/news/dolls04.4.php?page=1

Rideout, V., Roberts, D. F., & Foehr, U. G. (2005, March). *Generation M: Media in the lives of 8–18 year-olds.* Menlo Park, CA: Henry J. Kaiser Family Foundation.

Rideout, V., Vandewater, E. A., & Wartella, E. A. (2003, Fall). *Zero to six: Electronic media in the lives of infants, toddlers and preschoolers.* Menlo Park, CA: Henry J. Kaiser Family Foundation.

Rieber, L. (n.d.). *Homemade powerpoint games: A constructivist alternative to webquests.* Retrieved August 4, 2008, from http://it.coe.uga.edu/wwild/pptgames/papers/ppt-games-paper.htm

Rieber, L. (2005). Multimedia learning in games, simulations, and microworlds. In R. E. Mayer (Ed.), *The Cambridge handbook of multimedia learning* (pp. 549–567). New York: Cambridge University Press.

Risinger, C. F. (2004, November/December). Home grown: Models of excellence in teacher-designed social studies websites. *Social Education, 68*(7), 464–466.

Risinger, C. F. (2006, April). Using blogs in the classroom: A new approach to teaching social studies with the Internet. *Social Education, 70*(3), 130–132.

Risinger, C. F. (2006, November/December). Promising practices in using the Internet to teach social studies. *Social Education, 70*(7), 409–410.

Rochette, L. C. (2007, November). What classroom technology has taught me about curriculum, teaching, and infinite possibilities. *English Journal, 97*(2), 43–48.

Rogers, E. M. (1962). *Diffusion of innovations* (1st ed.). New York: Free Press.

Rose, D. H., & Meyer, A. (2002). *Teaching every student in the digital age: Universal design for learning.* Washington, DC: Association for Supervision and Curriculum Development.

Rose, D. H., & Meyer, A. (Eds.). (2006). *A practical reader in universal design for learning.* Cambridge, MA: Harvard University Press.

Rose, D. H., Meyer, A., & Hitchcock, C. (2005). *The universally designed classroom: Accessible curriculum and digital technologies.* Cambridge, MA: Harvard University Press.

Rosenthal, J. S. (2006). *Struck by lightning: The curious world of probabilities.* Washington, DC: Joseph Henry Press.

Rosser, J. C., Lynch, P. J., Haskamp, L. A., Yalif, A., Gentile, D. A., & Giammaria, L. (2008). *Are video game players better at laparoscopic surgical tasks?* Retrieved September 20, 2008, from www.psychology.iastate.edu/~dgentile/MMVRC_Jan_20_MediaVersion.pdf

Rother, C. (2005, October). Is technology changing how you teach? *T.H.E. Journal, 33*(3), 34–36.

Rothman, R. (2008, July/August). Taking the measure of new teachers. *Harvard Educational Letter, 24*(4), 1–3.

Rozema, R. (2007). The book report, version 2.0: Podcasting on young adult novels. *English Journal, 97*(1), 31–36.

Russell, M., Bebell, D., & Higgins, J. (2003). *Laptop learning: A comparison of teaching and learning in upper elementary classrooms equipped with shared carts of laptops and permanent 1:1 laptops.* Chestnut Hill, MA: Boston College, Technology and Assessment Study Collaborative.

Russell, M., O'Brien, E., Bebell, D., & O'Dwyer, L. (2003). *Students' beliefs, access, and use of computers in school and at home.* Chestnut Hill, MA: Boston College, Technology and Assessment Study Collaborative.

Russell, M., & Plati, T. (2001, December). *Does it matter with what I write? Comparing performance on paper, computer and portable writing devices.* Chestnut Hill, MA: Boston, College, Technology and Assessment Collaborative.

Sarason, S. B. (1982). *The culture of the school and the problem of change.* (2nd ed.). Boston: Allyn & Bacon.

Sarason, S. B. (1983). *Schooling in America: Scapegoat and salvation.* New York: Free Press.

Sarason, S. B. (1993). *The predictable failure of educational reform: Can we change course before it's too late?* San Francisco: Jossey-Bass.

Sarason, S. B. (1998). *Political leadership and educational failure.* San Francisco: Jossey-Bass.

Schaapveld, E. (2000). *RubiStar: The rubric maker.* Retrieved June 6, 2008, from www.4teachers.org/techalong/erica4/

Schimmel, D. (1997, December). Traditional rule-making and the subversion of citizenship education. *Social Education, 61*(2), 70–74.

Scholastic. (2008). *2008 kids & family reading report: Reading in the 21st century/Turning the page with technology.* New York: Author.

Scott, P., Asoki, H., & Leach, J. (2007). Student conceptions and conceptual learning in science. In S. K. Abell & N. G. Lederman (Eds.), *Handbook of research on science education* (pp. 31–56). Mahwah, NJ: Lawrence Erlbaum.

Scott, P., & Mortimer, E. F. (2006). The tension between authoritative and dialogic discourse: A fundamental characteristic of meaning making interactions in high school science lessons. *Science Education, 90*(4), 605–631.

Seelye, K. O. (2005, December 4). Snared in the web of a Wikipedia liar. *The New York Times: Week in Review.* Retrieved July 15, 2009, from www.nytimes.com/2005/12/04/weekinreview/04seelye.html

Seiter, E. (2005). *The Internet playground: Children's access, entertainment, and mis-education.* London: Peter Lang.

Selfe, C. L., & Hawisher, G. E. (2004). *Literate lives in the information age: Narratives on literacy from the United States.* Mahwah, NJ: Lawrence Erlbaum.

Shaffer, D. W., Squire, K. R., Halverson, R., & Gee, J. P. (2005). Video games and the future of learning. *Phi Delta Kappan, 87*(2), 105–111.

Shamir, A., & Korat, O. (2006, March). How to select CD-ROM storybooks for young children: The teacher's role. *The Reading Teacher, 59*(6), 532–543.

Shiu, E., & Lenhart, A. (2004, September 1). *How Americans use instant messaging.* Washington, DC: Pew Internet & American Life Project.

Shuler, C. (2007, December). *D is for digital: An analysis of the children's interactive media environment with a focus on mass marketed products that promote learning.* New York: The Joan Ganz Cooney Center at Sesame Workshop.

Shulman, L. (1998). Teacher portfolios: A theoretical activity. In N. Lyons (Ed.), *With portfolio in hand: Validating the new teacher professionalism* (pp. 23–37). New York: Teachers College Press.

Silvernail, D. L., & Gritter, A. K. (2007). *Maine's middle school laptop program: Creating better writers.* Gorham: University of Southern Maine, Maine Education Policy Research Institute.

Sindelar, T., & Zinn, F. (2007, June). *Emerging technologies for teaching.* Amherst: University of Massachusetts Office of Information Technologies.

Slavin, R. E. (2005). *Educational psychology: Theory and practice* (8th ed.). Boston: Allyn & Bacon.

Smith, F. (1998). *The book of learning and forgetting.* New York: Teachers College Press.

Smith, G. E., & Throne, S. (2007). *Differentiating instruction with technology in K–5 classrooms.* Washington, DC: International Society for Technology in Education.

Snyder, L. (2003). *Fluency with information technology: Skills, concepts and capabilities* (Preliminary ed.). Boston: Addison-Wesley.

Solnit, R. (2003). *River of shadows: Eadweard Muybridge and the technological wild west.* New York: Penguin.

Solomon, G., & Schram, L. (2007). *Web 2.0: New tools, new schools.* Washington, DC: International Society for Technology in Education.

Staley, D. J. (2003). *Computers, visualization, and history: How new technologies will transform our understanding of the past.* Armonk, NY: M. E. Sharpe.

Standen, A. (2007, February 2). A glorified whiteboard: It's a Wiki-world. *Edutopia.* Retrieved August 9, 2009, from www.edutopia.org/glorified-whiteboard

State Educational Technology Directors Association, International Society for Technology in Education, & Partnership for 21st Century Skills. (2007). *Maximizing the impact: The pivotal role of technology in a 21st century education system.* Washington, DC: Author.

Steinke, T. (2005, April). TinkerPlots turns students into data analysts. *T.H.E. Journal.* Retrieved from http://thejournal.com/articles/17227

Stigler, J., & Hiebert, J. (1999). *The teaching gap: Best ideas from the world's teachers for improving education.* New York: Free Press.

Stotsky, S. (2007). *Teacher licensure tests: Their relationship to mathematics teachers' academic competence and student achievement in mathematics* (Education Working Paper). Fayetteville: University of Arkansas, Department of Education Reform.

Stowell, J. R., & Nelson, J. M. (2007). Benefits of electronic audience response systems on student participation, learning, and emotion. *Teaching of Psychology, 34*(4), 253–258.

Subrahmanyam, K., Greenfield, P. M., Kraut, R., & Gross, E. (2002). The impact of computer use on children's and adolescents' development. In S. Calvert, A. Jordon, & R. Cocking (Eds.), *Children in the digital age: Influences of electronic media on development* (pp. 3–33). Westport, CT: Praeger.

Sutton, L. (2005). *Experiences of high school students conducting term paper research using filtered Internet access.* Paper presented at the 12th National Conference and Exhibition of the American Association of School Librarians, October 6–9, Pittsburgh, Pennsylvania.

Swanson, C. B. (2008, April). *Cities in crisis: A special report on high school graduation.* Bethesda, MD: Editorial Projects in Education Research Center.

Tapscott, D., & Williams, A. D. (2006). *Wikinomics: How mass collaboration changes everything.* Portfolio.

Templeton, S. (2004, March). Spell-check this! The limitations and potential of technology for spelling. *Voices from the Middle, 11*(3), 58–59.

Toch, T., & Rothman, R. (2008). *Rush to judgment: Teacher evaluation in public education.* Washington, DC: Education Sector.

Tomlinson, C. A. (2003). *Fulfilling the promise of the differentiated classroom: Strategies and tools for responsive teaching.* Alexandria, VA: Association for Curriculum and Development.

Trushell, J., & Maitland, A. (2005). Primary pupils' recall of interactive storybooks on CD-ROM: Inconsiderate interactive features and forgetting. *British Journal of Educational Technology, 36*(1), 57–66.

Tsikalas, K., & Newkirk, C. (2008, July). Family computing and the academic engagement of low-income, urban adolescents: Findings from the Computers for Youth intervention. *Family Involvement Research Digests, Harvard Family Research Project.* Retrieved July 30, 2008, from www.hfrp.org/family-involvement/publications-resources/family-computing-and-the-academic-engagement-and-achievement-of-low-income-urban-adolescents-findings-from-the-computers-for-youth-intervention

Tufte, E. R. (1990). *Envisioning information.* Cheshire, CT: Graphics Press.

Tufte, E. R. (2003). *The cognitive style of PowerPoint.* Cheshire, CT: Graphics Press.

Unger, L. C. (2007). Software selection: Finding a needle in the haystack. In L. Bennett & M. Berson (Eds.), *Digital age: Technology-based K–12 lesson plans for social studies* (pp. 179–180). Washington, DC: National Council for the Social Studies.

United States Department of Commerce. (2002, February). *A nation online: How Americans are expanding their use of the Internet.* Washington, DC: Author.

United States Department of Commerce. (2008). *Statistical abstract of the United States: 2008.* Washington, DC: U.S. Government Printing Office.

United States Department of Education, National Center for Education Statistics. (2005). *Number and percentage of gifted and talented students in public elementary and secondary schools, by sex and state: 2000.* Retrieved June 6, 2008, from http://nces.ed.gov/programs/digest/d05/tables/dt05_053.asp

United States Department of Education, National Center for Education Statistics. (2006). *The condition of education 2006* (NCES 2006-071). Washington, DC: U.S. Government Printing Office.

United States Department of Education, National Center for Education Statistics. (2008). *The condition of education 2008* (NCES 2008-031). Washington, DC: U.S. Government Printing Office. Retrieved June 11, 2008, from http://nces.ed.gov/pubresearch/pubsinfo.asp?pubid=2008031

University of California Berkeley. (2007). *Survey of new freshman students fall 2007.* Retrieved April 23, 2008, from http://osr2.berkeley.edu/Public/STAFFWEB/DE/SONS_2007_results.htm

University of California Berkeley Library. (2007). *Finding information on the Internet: A tutorial.* Berkeley: Regents of the University of California. Retrieved December 14, 2007, from www.lib.berkeley.edu/TeachingLib/Guides/Internet/FindInfo.html

University of California Linguistic Minority Research Newsletter. (2001, Fall). Language minorities account for California's entire population growth in the 1990s. *10*(5), 1–4.

Vaishnau, A., & Dedman, B. (2002, July 8). Special ed gap stirs worry. *The Boston Globe,* A1.

Value Based Management.net. (2004). *Rogers model for the adoption and diffusion of innovations.* Retrieved November 30, 2004, from www.valuebasedmanagement.net/methods_rogers_innovation_adoption_curve.html

Vascellaro, J. E. (2006, August 31). Saying no to school laptops. *The Wall Street Journal,* D1.

Viser, M. (2008, March 9). Mayors are posting municipal musings. *The Boston Globe,* pp. B1, B5.

Waldrop, M. M. (2008, May). Science 2.0. *Scientific American,* 69–73.

Walsh, D., Gentile, D., Walsh, E., Bennett, N., Robideau, B., Walsh, M., Strickland, S., & McFadden, D. (2005, November). *Tenth annual MediaWise video game report card.* Minneapolis, MN: National Institute on

Media and the Family. Retrieved July 16, 2009, from www.mediafamily .org/research/report_vgrc_2005.shtml

Wands, B. (2006). *Art of the digital age.* New York: Thames & Hudson.

Warlick, D. F. (2005). *Classroom blogging: A teacher's guide to the blogosphere.* London: Lulu.com.

Warschauer, M. (2003). *Technology and social inclusion: Rethinking the digital divide.* Cambridge, MA: MIT Press.

Warschauer, M. (2006). *Laptops and literacy: Learning in the wireless classroom.* New York: Teachers College Press.

Waterman, S. S. (2006). *The democratic differentiated classroom.* New York: Eye on Education.

Watson, G. (2001). Models of information technology teacher professional development that engage with teachers' hearts and minds. *Journal of Information Technology for Teacher Education, 10*(1 & 2), 179–190.

Wells, A. T. (2008, February). *A portrait of early Internet adopters: Why people first went online and why they stayed.* Washington, DC: Pew Internet & American Life Project.

Wells, J., & Lewis, L. (2006). *Internet access in U.S. public schools and classrooms: 1994–2005* (NCES 2007–020). Washington, DC: U.S. Department of Education, National Center for Education Statistics.

Wenglinsky, H. (2005). *Using technology wisely: The keys to success in schools.* New York: Teachers College Press.

Wepner, S. B., & Cotter, M. (2002, February). When do computer graphics contribute to early literacy learning? *Reading Online, 5*(6). Retrieved June 7, 2008, from www.readingonline.org/newliteracies/lit_index .asp?HREF=wepner/index.html

West, T. G. (2004). *Thinking like Einstein: Returning to our visual roots with the emerging revolution in computer information visualization.* New York: Prometheus.

Westreich, J. (2000). High-tech kids: Trailblazers or guinea pigs? In D. T. Gordon (Ed.), *The digital classroom: How technology is changing the way we teach and learn* (pp. 19–29). Cambridge, MA: The Harvard Education Letter.

Wiggins, G., & McTighe, J. (1998). *Understanding by design.* Upper Saddle River, NJ: Merrill/Prentice-Hall.

Wiggins, G., & McTighe, J. (2007). *Schooling by design: Mission, action and achievement.* Alexandria, VA: Association for Supervision and Curriculum Development.

Wilde, S. (Ed.). (1996). *Notes from a kidwatcher: Selected writings of Yetta M. Goodman.* Portsmouth, NH: Heinemann.

Wilmeth, M. (2005, May 26–June 1). Wikipedia: An encyclopedia by us. *West County News,* p. 9.

Windham, C. (2006, September). *Getting past Google: Perspectives on information literacy from the millennial mind.* Boulder, CO: EDUCAUSE Learning Initiative.

Windham, C. (2007, May). *Reflecting, writing, and responding: Reasons students blog.* Boulder, CO: EDUCAUSE Learning Initiative.

Wit, E. (2003, May). Who wants to be. . . The use of a personal response system in statistics teaching. *MSOR Connections, 3*(2), 14–20.

Wolk, S. (2008, October). School as inquiry. *Phi Delta Kappan, 90*(2), 115–122.

Wong, W. (2008, October/November). The case for smart classrooms. *Community College Journal, 79*(2), 31–34.

Wright, W. (2004, November 11). Sculpting possibility space. *IT Conversations.* Retrieved July 15, 2009, from http://itc.conversationsnetwork .org/shows/detail376.html

Xiao, Y., Baker, P., O'Shea, P., & Allen, D. W. (2007, April). *Wikibook as college textbook: A case study of college students' participation in writing, editing and using a Wikibook as primary course textbook.* Paper presented at the annual meeting of the American Educational Research Association, Chicago.

Yahoo! & Carat Interactive. (2003, July). *Born to be wired! The role of new media for a digital generation: A new media landscape comes of age: Executive summary.* Retrieved June 6, 2008, from http://biz.yahoo.com/ bw/030724/245198_1.html

Yancy, K. B. (2004, June). Postmodernism, palimpsest, and portfolios: Theoretical issues in the representation of student work. *College Composition and Communication, 55*(4), 738–761.

Yazzie-Mintz, E. (2007). *Voices of students on engagement: A report on the 2006 high school survey of student engagement.* Bloomington: Center for Evaluation & Education Policy, Indiana University.

Zemelman, S., Daniels, H., & Hyde, A. (2005). *Best practice: Today's standards for teaching and learning in America's schools* (3rd ed.). Portsmouth, NH: Heinemann.

Zhao, Y., & Frank, K. (2003, Winter). Technology uses in schools: An ecological perspective. *American Educational Research Journal, 40*(4), 807–840.

Zimmerman, I. K. (2007, Summer). One to one learning for all. *Perspectives,* pp. 7–9. Wellesley: Massachusetts Association for Supervision and Curriculum Development.

Zinn, F. (2007, March). *Designing effective presentations.* Amherst: University of Massachusetts Office of Information Technologies.

Zucker, A. A. (2008). *Transforming schools with technology: How smart use of digital tools helps achieve six key education goals.* Cambridge, MA: Harvard University Press.

Zucker, A. A., & McGhee, R. (2005). *A study of one-to-one computer use in mathematics and science instruction at the secondary level in Henrico County Public Schools.* Menlo Park, CA: SRI International.

Text Credits

Pages xxviii, 30, 82, 112, 135, 142, 165–166, 174, 198, 206, 232, 240, 266, 274, 296, 304, 323: *NETS for Students: National Educational Technology Standards for Students,* Second Edition. Copyright © 2007 by ISTE (International Society for Technology in Education), www.iste.org. All rights reserved.

Pages xxviii, 30, 58, 82, 112, 142, 174, 206, 240, 274, 304: *NETS for Teachers: National Educational Technology Standards for Teachers,* Second Edition. Copyright © 2008 by ISTE (International Society for Technology in Education), www.iste.org. All rights reserved.

Pages 135, 232, 266: *Standards for the English Language Arts,* by the International Reading Association and the National Council of Teachers of English. Copyright © 1996 by the International Reading Association and the National Council of Teachers of English. Reprinted with permission. Complete set of standards can be found at www.ncte.org/standards.

Pages 135, 296, 322: *Expectations of Excellence: Curriculum Standards for Social Studies.* Copyright © 1994 by the National Council for the Social Studies. Reprinted with permission.

Pages 165, 296: Reprinted with permission from National Science Education Standards by the National Academy of Sciences. Courtesy of the National Academies Press, Washington, DC.

Page 198: *Principles and Standards for School Mathematics.* Copyright © 2000 by the National Council of Teachers of Mathematics. Reproduced with permission of National Council of Teachers of Mathematics via Copyright Clearance Center. NCTM does not endorse the content or validity of these alignments.

Photo Credits

Page xix: Courtesy of PolyVision, www.polyvision.com
Page xxiv: Shutterstock
Page 1: Konstantin Inozemtsev/iStockphoto
Page 4 (left and right): Shutterstock
Page 5, 37, 145, 210: Yuri Arcurs/Shutterstock
Pages 6, 7, 14, 25, 42, 48, 50, 60, 92, 93, 95, 100, 128, 156, 190, 191, 196, 213, 221, 230, 249, 250, 317: Copyright © Promethean, www.prometheanworld.com
Pages 7, 24, 42, 45, 48, 50, 54, 69, 72, 79, 92, 122, 125, 147, 148, 156, 185, 191, 220, 225, 248, 252, 259, 264, 286, 312, 317: Andrey Ivanov/Shutterstock
Pages 11, 17, 19, 23, 37, 40, 47, 49, 51, 67, 86, 104, 117, 119, 126, 130, 134, 145, 163, 179, 188, 219, 226, 247, 285, 290, 307, 316, 321: Pallo/Shutterstock
Pages 12, 26, 44 (bottom): Bob Daemmrich Photography
Page 23: Frank Siteman
Pages 25, 69, 72, 79, 92, 123, 125, 147, 149, 156, 185, 191, 221, 225, 253, 259, 265, 287, 313, 317: Johanna Goodyear/iStockphoto
Pages 27, 55, 79, 108, 139, 170, 202, 236, 271, 300, 327: Grafica/Shutterstock
Pages 28, 56, 80, 109, 140, 171, 203, 237, 272, 300, 327: Jaimie Duplass/Shutterstock
Pages 29, 56, 63, 81, 110, 140, 171, 178, 203, 237, 272, 301, 320, 327: Andresr/Shutterstock
Page 31: Golkin Oleg/iStockphoto
Pages 33, 242, 261: David Young-Wolff/PhotoEdit
Page 44 (top): Lindfors Photography
Pages 52, 262: Morgan Lane Photography/Shutterstock
Page 59 (main): Viktor Gmyria/iStockphoto

Pages 59 (screen image), 175 (screen image): Emrah Turudu/iStockphoto
Page 66: Patrick White/Merrill Education
Pages 75, 228: Bob Daemmrich/The Image Works
Pages 76, 132, 214: Copyright © eInstruction, www.einstruction.com.
Page 83: Katrina Brown/Shutterstock
Pages 89 (top), 208, 256, 314: Jeff Greenberg/PhotoEdit
Page 89 (bottom): Viorel Sima/Shutterstock
Page 96: Robin Nelson/PhotoEdit
Page 98: Baris Simsek/iStockphoto
Page 99: All-Turn-It ® Spinner, courtesy of AbleNet, Inc.
Page 106 (top in figure): Mircea Bezergheanu/Shutterstock
Page 106 (upper middle in figure): Gigello/Shutterstock
Page 106 (lower middle in figure): Dreamstime
Page 106 (bottom in figure): Dmitry Melnikov/Shutterstock
Page 107: Piotr Antonów/iStockphoto
Pages 113 (frames), 241 (frame): iStockphoto
Page 117: Sean Prior/Shutterstock
Page 126: Bob Daemmrich/PhotoEdit
Page 129: James Marshall/The Image Works
Pages 135, 165, 198, 230, 266, 296, 322 (laptop image): Tumanyan/Shutterstock
Pages 141, 172, 204, 238, 273, 302, 329: Timage/Shutterstock
Page 143 (keyboard and mouse): Roz Byshaka/Shutterstock
Page 144: Najlah Feanny/Corbis
Page 155: Syracuse Newspapers /D Blume/The Image Works

Page 175 (exterior): Anna Khomulo/iStockphoto
Pages 184, 311: Barbara Jablonska/Shutterstock
Page 187: Bill Aron/PhotoEdit
Page 194: Kayte M. Deioma/PhotoEdit
Page 207: RTimages/Shutterstock
Page 211: Georgy Markov/Shutterstock
Page 241 (boy): Beata Becla/Shutterstock
Page 243: Graphic Design/Shutterstock
Page 251: Lee Pettet/iStockphoto
Page 264: Alysta/Shutterstock
Page 275 (bottom left, screen bottom left): Photos courtesy of DynaVox Mayer-Johnson, Pittsburgh, PA, www.dynavoxtech.com (866-DYNAVOX)
Page 275 (top left, bottom center, bottom right; screen top left, top right, and bottom right): That's Life! Lit Series Friendship Memory Module, LITTLEmack showing interchangeable switch tops, Jelly Beamer Wireless Switch—Red *twist,* and student photos, courtesy of AbleNet, Inc.
Page 279: Ustyujanin/Shutterstock
Page 280: Ellen B. Senisi/The Image Works
Page 286: Quang Ho/Shutterstock
Page 289: Sban/Shutterstock
Page 291: Buddy Button—Hands-On, courtesy of AbleNet, Inc.
Page 293: Colin Young-Wolff /PhotoEdit
Page 294: Tango photo courtesy of DynaVox Mayer-Johnson, Pittsburgh, PA, www.dynavoxtech.com (866-DYNAVOX)
Page 305: Mike Sonnenbert/iStockphoto
Page 307: F64/Digital Vision/Getty Images
Page 319: Debbie Noda/The Modesto Bee/Newscom